Lecture Notes in Computer Science 15794

Founding Editors

Gerhard Goos
Juris Hartmanis

AF147304

The series Lecture Notes in Computer Science (LNCS), including its subseries Lecture Notes in Artificial Intelligence (LNAI) and Lecture Notes in Bioinformatics (LNBI), has established itself as a medium for the publication of new developments in computer science and information technology research, teaching, and education.

LNCS enjoys close cooperation with the computer science R & D community, the series counts many renowned academics among its volume editors and paper authors, and collaborates with prestigious societies. Its mission is to serve this international community by providing an invaluable service, mainly focused on the publication of conference and workshop proceedings and postproceedings. LNCS commenced publication in 1973.

Martin Schrepp

Editor

Design, User Experience, and Usability

14th International Conference, DUXU 2025
Held as Part of the 27th HCI International Conference, HCII 2025
Gothenburg, Sweden, June 22–27, 2025
Proceedings, Part I

 Springer

Editor
Martin Schrepp
SAP Walldorf
Walldorf, Germany

ISSN 0302-9743   ISSN 1611-3349 (electronic)
Lecture Notes in Computer Science
ISBN 978-3-031-93220-5   ISBN 978-3-031-93221-2 (eBook)
https://doi.org/10.1007/978-3-031-93221-2

Foreword

The HCI International (HCII) conference was founded in 1984 by Gavriel Salvendy (Purdue University, USA, Tsinghua University, P.R. China, and University of Central Florida, USA) and the first event of the series, "1st USA-Japan Conference on Human-Computer Interaction", was held in Honolulu, Hawaii, USA, 18–20 August. Since then, HCI International is held jointly with several Thematic Areas and Affiliated Conferences, with each one under the auspices of a distinguished international Program Board and under one management and one registration. Twenty-seven HCI International Conferences have been organized so far (every two years until 2013, and annually thereafter).

Last year, we celebrated 40 years since the establishment of the HCII conference, which has been a hub for presenting groundbreaking research and novel ideas and collaboration for people from all over the world. Over the years, this conference has served as a platform for scholars, researchers, industry experts, and students to exchange ideas, connect, and address challenges in the ever-evolving HCI field. The conference has evolved itself, adapting to new technologies and emerging trends, while staying committed to its core mission of advancing knowledge and driving change.

The 27th International Conference on Human-Computer Interaction, HCI International 2025 (HCII 2025), was held as an 'on-site' conference at the Gothia Towers Hotel and Swedish Exhibition & Congress Centre, in Gothenburg, Sweden, on June 22–27, 2025, with the additional option for 'on-line' participation. It incorporated the 21 thematic areas and affiliated conferences listed below.

A total of 7972 individuals from academia, research institutes, industry, and government agencies from 92 countries submitted contributions. 1430 papers and 355 posters (as short research papers) are included in the volumes of the proceedings published just before the start of the conference, and which are listed below. The contributions thoroughly cover the entire field of human-computer interaction, highlight the evolving role of computers in diverse contexts, and demonstrate how HCI research is shaping and improving user experiences across a wide range of domains, influencing technological progress and its effective integration into various sectors.

The HCII conference also offers the option of presenting 'Late Breaking Work', both for papers and posters, with the corresponding proceedings volumes published after the conference. Full papers are included in the 'HCII 2025 - Late Breaking Papers' volumes of the proceedings published in the Springer LNCS series, while 'Poster Extended Abstracts' are included as short research papers in the 'HCII 2025 - Late Breaking Posters' volumes published in the Springer CCIS series.

I would like to thank the Program Board Chairs and the members of the Program Boards of all thematic areas and affiliated conferences for their contribution towards the high scientific quality and overall success of the HCI International 2025 conference. Their manifold support including paper reviews (via a single-blind review process, with a minimum of two reviews per submission), session organization, and their willingness to act as goodwill ambassadors for the conference is most highly appreciated.

This conference would not have been possible without the continuous and unwavering support and advice of Gavriel Salvendy, founder, General Chair Emeritus, and Scientific Advisor. For his outstanding efforts, I would like to express my sincere appreciation to Abbas Moallem, Communications Chair and Editor of HCI International News.

June 2025   Constantine Stephanidis

HCI International 2025 Thematic Areas and Affiliated Conferences

- HCI: Human-Computer Interaction Thematic Area
- HIMI: Human Interface and the Management of Information Thematic Area
- EPCE: 22nd International Conference on Engineering Psychology and Cognitive Ergonomics
- AC: 19th International Conference on Augmented Cognition
- UAHCI: 19th International Conference on Universal Access in Human-Computer Interaction
- CCD: 17th International Conference on Cross-Cultural Design
- SCSM: 17th International Conference on Social Computing and Social Media
- VAMR: 17th International Conference on Virtual, Augmented and Mixed Reality
- DHM: 16th International Conference on Digital Human Modeling and Applications in Health, Safety, Ergonomics and Risk Management
- DUXU: 14th International Conference on Design, User Experience, and Usability
- C&C: 13th International Conference on Culture and Computing
- DAPI: 13th International Conference on Distributed, Ambient and Pervasive Interactions
- HCIBGO: 12th International Conference on HCI in Business, Government and Organizations
- LCT: 12th International Conference on Learning and Collaboration Technologies
- ITAP: 11th International Conference on Human Aspects of IT for the Aged Population
- AIS: 7th International Conference on Adaptive Instructional Systems
- HCI-CPT: 7th International Conference on HCI for Cybersecurity, Privacy and Trust
- HCI-Games: 7th International Conference on HCI in Games
- MobiTAS: 7th International Conference on HCI in Mobility, Transport and Automotive Systems
- AI-HCI: 6th International Conference on Artificial Intelligence in HCI
- MOBILE: 6th International Conference on Human-Centered Design, Operation and Evaluation of Mobile Communications

List of Conference Proceedings Volumes Appearing Before the Conference

1. LNCS 15766, Human-Computer Interaction - Part I, edited by Masaaki Kurosu and Ayako Hashizume
2. LNCS 15767, Human-Computer Interaction - Part II, edited by Masaaki Kurosu and Ayako Hashizume
3. LNCS 15768, Human-Computer Interaction - Part III, edited by Masaaki Kurosu and Ayako Hashizume
4. LNCS 15769, Human-Computer Interaction - Part IV, edited by Masaaki Kurosu and Ayako Hashizume
5. LNCS 15770, Human-Computer Interaction - Part V, edited by Masaaki Kurosu and Ayako Hashizume
6. LNCS 15771, Human-Computer Interaction - Part VI, edited by Masaaki Kurosu and Ayako Hashizume
7. LNCS 15772, Human-Computer Interaction - Part VII, edited by Masaaki Kurosu and Ayako Hashizume
8. LNCS 15773, Human Interface and the Management of Information: Part I, edited by Hirohiko Mori and Yumi Asahi
9. LNCS 15774, Human Interface and the Management of Information: Part II, edited by Hirohiko Mori and Yumi Asahi
10. LNCS 15775, Human Interface and the Management of Information: Part III, edited by Hirohiko Mori and Yumi Asahi
11. LNAI 15776, Engineering Psychology and Cognitive Ergonomics: Part I, edited by Don Harris and Wen-Chin Li
12. LNAI 15777, Engineering Psychology and Cognitive Ergonomics: Part II, edited by Don Harris and Wen-Chin Li
13. LNAI 15778, Augmented Cognition: Part I, edited by Dylan D. Schmorrow and Cali M. Fidopiastis
14. LNAI 15779, Augmented Cognition: Part II, edited by Dylan D. Schmorrow and Cali M. Fidopiastis
15. LNCS 15780, Universal Access in Human-Computer Interaction: Part I, edited by Margherita Antona and Constantine Stephanidis
16. LNCS 15781, Universal Access in Human-Computer Interaction: Part II, edited by Margherita Antona and Constantine Stephanidis
17. LNCS 15782, Cross-Cultural Design: Part I, edited by Pei-Luen Patrick Rau
18. LNCS 15783, Cross-Cultural Design: Part II, edited by Pei-Luen Patrick Rau
19. LNCS 15784, Cross-Cultural Design: Part III, edited by Pei-Luen Patrick Rau
20. LNCS 15785, Cross-Cultural Design: Part IV, edited by Pei-Luen Patrick Rau

44. LNCS 15809, Human Aspects of IT for the Aged Population: Part I, edited by Qin Gao and Jia Zhou
45. LNCS 15810, Human Aspects of IT for the Aged Population: Part II, edited by Qin Gao and Jia Zhou
46. LNCS 15811, Human Aspects of IT for the Aged Population: Part III, edited by Qin Gao and Jia Zhou
47. LNCS 15812, Adaptive Instructional System: Part I, edited by Robert A. Sottilare and Jessica Schwarz
48. LNCS 15813, Adaptive Instructional System: Part II, edited by Robert A. Sottilare and Jessica Schwarz
49. LNCS 15814, HCI for Cybersecurity, Privacy and Trust: Part I, edited by Abbas Moallem
50. LNCS 15815, HCI for Cybersecurity, Privacy and Trust: Part II, edited by Abbas Moallem
51. LNCS 15816, HCI in Games, edited by Xiaowen Fang
52. LNCS 15817, HCI in Mobility, Transport and Automotive Systems: Part I, edited by Heidi Krömker
53. LNCS 15818, HCI in Mobility, Transport and Automotive Systems: Part II, edited by Heidi Krömker
54. LNAI 15819, Artificial Intelligence in HCI: Part I, edited by Helmut Degen and Stavroula Ntoa
55. LNAI 15820, Artificial Intelligence in HCI: Part II, edited by Helmut Degen and Stavroula Ntoa
56. LNAI 15821, Artificial Intelligence in HCI: Part III, edited by Helmut Degen and Stavroula Ntoa
57. LNAI 15822, Artificial Intelligence in HCI: Part IV, edited by Helmut Degen and Stavroula Ntoa
58. LNCS 15823, Human-Centered Design, Operation and Evaluation of Mobile Communications: Part I, edited by June Wei and George Margetis
59. LNCS 15824, Human-Centered Design, Operation and Evaluation of Mobile Communications: Part II, edited by June Wei and George Margetis
60. CCIS 2522, HCI International 2025 Posters - Part I, edited by Constantine Stephanidis, Margherita Antona, Stavroula Ntoa and Gavriel Salvendy
61. CCIS 2523, HCI International 2025 Posters - Part II, edited by Constantine Stephanidis, Margherita Antona, Stavroula Ntoa and Gavriel Salvendy
62. CCIS 2524, HCI International 2025 Posters - Part III, edited by Constantine Stephanidis, Margherita Antona, Stavroula Ntoa and Gavriel Salvendy
63. CCIS 2525, HCI International 2025 Posters - Part IV, edited by Constantine Stephanidis, Margherita Antona, Stavroula Ntoa and Gavriel Salvendy
64. CCIS 2526, HCI International 2025 Posters - Part V, edited by Constantine Stephanidis, Margherita Antona, Stavroula Ntoa and Gavriel Salvendy
65. CCIS 2527, HCI International 2025 Posters - Part VI, edited by Constantine Stephanidis, Margherita Antona, Stavroula Ntoa and Gavriel Salvendy

66. CCIS 2528, HCI International 2025 Posters - Part VII, edited by Constantine Stephanidis, Margherita Antona, Stavroula Ntoa and Gavriel Salvendy
67. CCIS 2529, HCI International 2025 Posters - Part VIII, edited by Constantine Stephanidis, Margherita Antona, Stavroula Ntoa and Gavriel Salvendy

https://2025.hci.international/proceedings

Preface

The technological advancements of recent decades have profoundly impacted the way people live, communicate, and work. It is likely that this development will continue at an accelerating pace. Technologies such as virtual and augmented reality, artificial intelligence, the Internet of Things, and big data are becoming increasingly integrated into daily life, and new technologies are likely to emerge. As a result, we can expect that the rapid technological progress will induce even more significant changes in our living and working environments in the future.

This raises the importance of design, user experience, and usability (DUXU), since these qualities enable effective and efficient interaction for a broad range of individuals with a growing number of digitalized services built on an increasingly diverse range of technologies.

Design, user experience, and usability cover all aspects of the user's interaction with a product or service, how it is perceived, learned, and used. It also addresses design knowledge, methods, and practices, with a focus on deeply human-centered processes.

The rapid progress in the field of HCI makes continuous exchange between researchers from academia and industry increasingly important. The 14th Design, User Experience and Usability Conference (DUXU 2025), an affiliated conference of the HCI International conference, encouraged papers from professionals, academics, and researchers that report results and cover a broad range of research and development activities across related topics. Professionals include designers, software engineers, scientists, marketers, business leaders, and practitioners in fields such as AI, architecture, financial and wealth management, game design, graphic design, finance, healthcare, industrial design, mobility, psychology, travel, and vehicles.

The research submissions demonstrate the breadth and depth of UX-related topics, spanning from methodological advancements to practical applications across various domains. These contributions address contemporary challenges in designing and evaluating interactive systems, enhancing user engagement, and fostering inclusive experiences.

Papers discuss innovative methods for data visualization, persuasive and emotional interaction, adaptive user interfaces, and technology-enhanced learning environments. The proceedings also highlight the integration of UX principles into automotive, healthcare, education, and creative arts contexts. Furthermore, several contributions examine how digital design supports cultural transmission and enriches consumer and service experiences. Finally, considerable focus is placed on the impact of artificial intelligence (AI) in UX design and the transformative potential of emerging technologies in shaping the future of user interaction. As a whole, the works presented reflect a commitment to advancing human-centered design and improving the quality of interactions between users and digital systems.

Six volumes of the HCII 2025 proceedings are dedicated to this year's edition of the DUXU Conference, covering topics related to:

- Design, User Experience, and Usability - Part I: Information Design and Visualization; Emotional Interaction and Persuasive Design; and Interactive Systems and User Behavior
- Design, User Experience, and Usability - Part II: UX Design and Evaluation Methodologies; Inclusive Design and Accessible Experiences; and Product and Industrial Design
- Design, User Experience, and Usability - Part III: Design and the Digital Transmission of Culture; Design for Arts and Creativity; and Designing for Health and Therapeutic Experiences
- Design, User Experience, and Usability - Part IV: Consumer Experience and Service Design; Design and Evaluation of Technology-Enhanced Learning; and UX in Automotive and Transportation
- Design, User Experience, and Usability - Part V: Design Education and Professional Practice; and Human-Centered Design and Interactive Experiences
- Design, User Experience, and Usability - Part VI: AI and the Future of UX Design; and UX in AI and Emerging Technologies

The papers in these volumes were accepted for publication after a minimum of two single-blind reviews from the members of the DUXU Program Board or, in some cases, from members of the Program Boards of other affiliated conferences. I would like to thank all of them for their invaluable contribution, support, and efforts.

June 2025   Martin Schrepp

14th International Conference on Design, User Experience and Usability (DUXU 2025)

The full list with the Program Board Chairs and the members of the Program Boards of all thematic areas and affiliated conferences of HCII 2025 is available online at:

http://www.hci.international/board-members-2025.php

HCI International 2026 Conference

The 28th International Conference on Human-Computer Interaction, HCI International 2026, will be held jointly with the affiliated conferences at the Montréal Convention Centre (Palais des congrès de Montréal), in Montreal, Canada, 26–31 July 2026. It will cover a broad spectrum of themes related to Human-Computer Interaction, including theoretical issues, methods, tools, processes, and case studies in HCI design, as well as novel interaction techniques, interfaces, and applications. The proceedings will be published by Springer (part of Springer Nature) in a multi-volume set. More information will become available on the conference website: https://2026.hci.international/.

General Chair
Prof. Constantine Stephanidis
University of Crete and ICS-FORTH
Heraklion, Crete, Greece
Email: general_chair@2026.hci.international

https://2026.hci.international/

Contents – Part I

Emotional Interaction and Persuasive Design

Interactive Systems and User Behavior

Information Design and Visualization

Enhancing Public Awareness of Air Quality: Evaluating Communication Strategies and Design Prototypes Using a Design-Based Implementation Research Approach

Victoria Batz[1,3]([⊠]) [iD], Vanessa B. Liedtke[1], Petre Lameski[2] [iD], Vladimir Trajkovik[2] [iD], Steffi Hußlein[1], Christian Hansen[3] [iD], and Michael A. Herzog[1] [iD]

[1] Magdeburg-Stendal University of Applied Sciences, 39114 Magdeburg, Germany
victoria.batz@h2.de
[2] Ss. Cyril and Methodius University in Skopje, 1000 Skopje, North Macedonia
[3] Otto von Guericke University of Magdeburg, 39106 Magdeburg, Germany

Abstract. Despite the health risks associated with air pollution and the availability of data, public awareness of air quality remains limited. This paper examines communication strategies to enhance awareness in Germany and North Macedonia. Using the Design-Based Implementation Research approach, literature reviews, stakeholder interviews and surveys were conducted with 307 participants to identify knowledge gaps and effective methods.

Three citizen workshops led to the development and evaluation of five design prototypes, including an interactive installation ("Pollution Booth"), a VR application ("Visible Particulate Matter"), and a gamified learning experience ("End Game"). These prototypes addressed information accessibility, data representation, and environmentally conscious behavior. The results show that region-specific communication, interactive designs, and passive information methods in public spaces significantly improve the perception and understanding of air pollution data. Gamified approaches, such as the "End Game" prototype, were particularly effective in educating children about air pollution.

Thirty-two requirements for effective educational strategies were identified, including simplified data visualization, reduced content, and personalized information. The findings highlight the importance of local and personalized approaches, as well as methods for collective knowledge sharing, in promoting awareness and environmentally friendly behavior. Future work should further explore the long-term engagement and sustainable impact of such communication strategies.

Keywords: Air pollution · Public Awareness · Interaction Design · Science Communication · Environmental Data · Citizen Science

© The Author(s), under exclusive license to Springer Nature Switzerland AG 2025
M. Schrepp (Ed.): HCII 2025, LNCS 15794, pp. 3–25, 2025.
https://doi.org/10.1007/978-3-031-93221-2_1

1   Introduction

Outdoor air pollution is estimated to cause 4.2 million premature deaths worldwide in 2019 [30] as a result of stroke, heart disease, respiratory disease such as chronic lung diseases, asthma, and lung cancer [29]. In the same year, 90% of the world's population lived in places where the recommended air quality limits of the WHO were not met [30] and were unaware of these dangers [7,33]. However, the complex and non-transparent representation of air quality [11] is difficult to access for the general public [42], due to the scientific and technical language [35]. With the Ambient Air Quality Directives, the European Union (EU) commits to better information provision about air quality and its impacts on the public [41]. In a comparative Eurobarometer survey, Grossberndt et al. [16] found that more than half of the EU population, 59% in 2012 and 54% in 2019, were not informed about air quality problems in their country [8,9].

More people might adopt climate protection measures if they had a clearer understanding of how air pollution personally affects their health and living environment, but the impacts of air pollution are often subtle and not immediately noticeable. In addition to natural environmental factors, most air pollutants are the result of human activities, particularly in industry, heat production, agriculture, waste, and transport [31]. Even small changes in citizen transportation habits can significantly reduce their exposure to pollutants [15]. Despite the public demand for information [42], little is known about the reach and effectiveness of current information sources [14,36]. Visual representations of information can improve memory retention, facilitate decision-making, and streamline the analysis of large data sets [26]. It is also important to disseminate information across different population groups [35]. This study aims to explore design-oriented research approaches that promote interactive forms of communication to make air pollution visible, tangible, or otherwise experiential to the non-scientific public to increase awareness of the problem and encourage behavioral change or demands on decision-makers. To understand the effectiveness and user experience of the introduced communication artifacts, the following research questions are examined: (i) How well are citizens informed about the air quality in their residential areas and the impacts of airborne pollutants? (ii) Which information channels do citizens use, and what data and information are relevant to them? (iii) What impact does the use of educational technologies have on public awareness and perception of air pollution?

This paper is structured in a Related Work section, where the relevant literature and current state of research on education strategies for air pollution is introduced. Methodology describes the procedure of identifying, reviewing, developing, evaluating, and analyzing information requirements and awareness prototypes. The evaluation and results of the surveys on information needs and current information demand in the population follow. In addition, an exploratory study on the effectiveness of five different design prototypes for information dissemination is presented. The results of these investigations are then interpreted and discussed to gain insight for further developing effective communication strategies in the field of air pollution.

2   Related Work

Air quality indexes provided by the authorities are recognized as valid risk indicators, but their effectiveness in raising public awareness is limited, in part due to their technical complexity and expert-oriented presentation [35]. Residents are aware of air pollution but often lack understanding of its causes and ways to engage in solutions, often due to information overload and message fatigue. For example, in a Malaysian study, participants acknowledged air pollution but downplayed its risks unless they were personally affected [6,7].

Effective communication requires presenting air quality data in simple language with actionable advice, emphasizing health impacts and practical solutions [4]. Beaumont et al. [4] found that residents prefer plain language, historical data, and the accountability of political decision makers. Local information and positive framing resonate more with citizens, while confronting them with negative consequences can trigger cognitive dissonance. Nevertheless, emotional communication strategies prove promising effects in activating social norms and creating a sense of collective responsibility [35]. To increase awareness, air quality data can be adjusted to personal interests tailored to specific individual needs [27]. Liao et al. [22] examined the willingness of citizens (n = 347) to change behaviors using a smartphone app to avoid air pollution and found that behavioral changes are more strongly influenced by peer-to-peer interactions.

Ward et al. [19] have explored various engagement methods, including interviews, workshops, citizen science, and digital tools such as apps, sensors, AR & VR applications, and gamification [4,18,27,43]. Research highlights a growing interest in using digital tools for environmental education, such as apps, web applications, warning systems, electronic street signs, sensors, IoT devices, AR&VR, video podcasts, gamification, and data visualizations [10,18,24,40,43]. Among participatory approaches, citizen involvement in air quality monitoring is most common, often using low-cost sensors or sampling kits to measure local conditions [42]. For instance, Haddad & Nazelle [17] surveyed London participants using an app and sensors for monitoring NO and VOC levels but found no significant effect on travel behavior. Nevertheless, smart city IoT infrastructures make real-time pollution visualization more accessible, underlining the need for simple and effective government-led visualizations [36].

Smartphones are the preferred medium for accessing environmental information, with the Internet (82%) and social media (especially Instagram) as key sources [1,15]. However, information often lacks interpretation, creating barriers to understanding. Access to technology is another significant challenge [35]. Wong et al. [45] demonstrated that collaborative environments, where high school students teach older adults to use interactive pollution maps, enhance scientific understanding and foster discourse on environmental and health topics.

Artistic approaches, like Pollution Pods, use everyday experiences and concerns about air pollution to inspire political action by making the intangible tangible, the invisible visible, and by transforming the familiar into something unfamiliar. Although effective, evaluations show limited long-term behavioral effects, focusing more on evoking emotions than direct education [20,39].

The immersive nature of VR and AR enhances engagement and provides a more impactful experience compared to non-VR settings. These tools allow students to use multiple senses to perceive physical properties, creating rich sensory and emotional experiences that promote learning in environmental education and raise sustainability awareness [18]. Using an augmented reality application, Mathews et al. [24] visualize pollutants in the air, which can be viewed with mobile smart devices. The AiR application accesses the nearest air monitoring station and uses current data for particulate matter (PM10 & PM2.5), nitrogen dioxide (NO2), sulfur dioxide (SO2), carbon monoxide (CO), and ammonia (NH3). The effectiveness has not yet been tested on participants.

Existing efforts often lack detailed participant insights and focus more on engagement than knowledge transfer or regular updates. This study addresses gaps in integrating air quality information into public spaces, engagement, knowledge transfer, and sustained awareness.

3   Methodology

To investigate the research questions, we adopted the Design-Based Implementation Research (DBIR) approach, focusing on effectively communicating air quality data and raising public awareness of its health hazards. This study was conducted in four cyclical phases: preliminary research, implementation, analysis, and design refinement. The **research** phase included a snowball-method literature review [44] and stakeholder interviews with eight experts in air pollution science. Promoting environmental health literacy requires involving the public as part of the solution [13], because community engagement fosters behavioral change more effectively than individual efforts [37], such as avoiding air travel. To address this, three citizen workshops were conducted to evaluate knowledge, prioritize relevant information, and gather insights into preferred communication channels, enriched by expert input [5, 23].

Air quality has improved in Germany and other EU countries due to measures such as pollutant filters and city speed limits [3]. However, Skopje, North Macedonia, remains a global hotspot for air pollution and particulate matter [2]. An interdisciplinary team of industrial designers from Germany and computer scientists from North Macedonia [37] used insights from previous activities to develop five exploratory design prototypes. During the **implementation** phase, participants evaluated the prototypes using qualitative questionnaires and the standardized User Experience Questionnaire. The **analysis** phase examined cultural and regional differences in information reception, the findings used to refine the **design characteristics** for transparent communication.

3.1   Pre-questionnaire

The results of the online questionnaire regarding current state of knowledge about air pollution, interest, and information demand in the local population were quantitatively assessed and descriptively analyzed with SPSS software. The

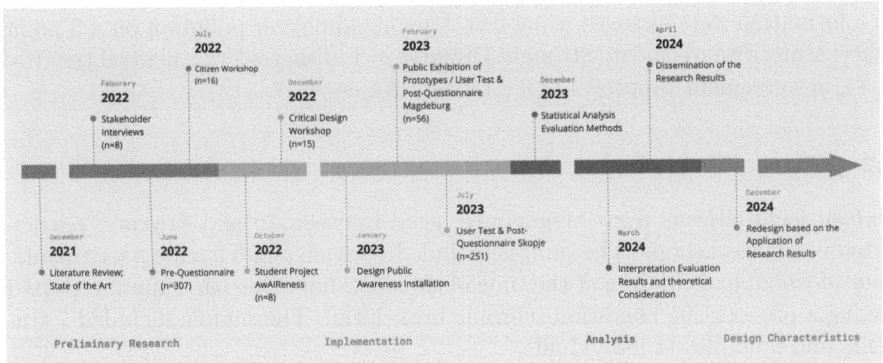

Fig. 1. Study Design according to Design-Based Implementation Research approach.

survey included 56 participants (18.2%) from Magdeburg-Stendal University of Applied Sciences and 251 participants (81.8%) from the University of Skopje. Students and academics act as "early adopters," whose opinions and experiences contribute to the development of successful and innovative dissemination strategies for different social groups [34]. The current level of knowledge and the access

Table 1. Socio-demographic data Online Questionnaire

Sociodemographic Data	N = 307
University	
Magdeburg	56
Skopje	251
Age	
18–19 years	4 (1,3%)
20–29 years	278 (90,6%)
30–39 years	20 (6,5%)
40–60 years	5 (1,6%)
Gender	
Male	153
Female	143
Diverse	11
Occupation	
Student	282
Professor / Lecturer	8
Scientific Staff	12
Administration Staff / Laboratory Engineer	4
Guest	1

to information were assessed using 6 statements about air pollution on a 5-point Likert scale: disagreement (Strongly Disagree = 1/disagree = 2), neutral (neutral = 3), or agreement (approval = 4/Strongly Agree = 5).

3.2 Citizen Workshops

Sixteen local citizens from Magdeburg, aged between 19 and 41 years, participated in the workshops. The sample included 10 male and 6 female participants, none of whom had children at the time of the workshop. One participant reported having a pre-existing condition (chronic bronchitis). The sample included 7 students and 9 employed individuals.

After a brief introduction, brainstorming sessions were conducted in small groups on key questions about air pollution. The responses were subsequently supplemented by a specialist lecture. The participants collected the results, opinions, wishes, and needs, clustering them into overarching thematic areas. Using dot voting [12], priorities for information provision were identified. A pre-test assessed demographics, societal interest, and prior knowledge of air quality sources. The post-test measured knowledge gains, increased interest, and the influence of new insights on future decisions. Qualitative questionnaires were descriptively analyzed using SPSS statistical software.

3.3 Prototypes Development and Evaluation

A team of eight industrial design students, two professors, and two researchers explored ways to communicate air quality data in public spaces through an iterative Design Science Research process [32]. This approach aimed to improve air quality awareness by presenting information interactively, creatively and artistically. The design process included the phases **Explore, Imagine, Inform, Create, and Test**.

Exploring involved an expert lecture on air quality measurement, pollutants, causes and countermeasures as well as a visit to a municipal measuring facility. Additionally, research was conducted on best practices in data visualization, speculative design, problem-solving, gamification, and interactive installations. Design methods such as brainstorming, opportunity maps, and interviews were used to generate ideas **(Imagine)**, as well as sketches, personas, and scenarios during concept development. In collaboration with the Laboratory for Eco-Informatics at Methodius University in Skopje, a seven-day design workshop **(Inform)** was held. The concepts prepared by the industrial designers were introduced to 7 computer science students from Skopje, who gave feedback. The interdisciplinary collaboration serves the exchange about the topic from different cultural as well as professional perspectives. In small groups of designers and computer scientists, the concepts are refined, and the first preliminary models are created as paper prototypes (representation of the public installation as a paper model) and video prototypes (simulation of the concept in a short film). The prototypes are used to gain feedback from citizens in Skopje. The results of

the design sprint serve to **Create** high fidelity prototypes with physical computing (sensors and microcontrollers to perform interactions with users) in a second
iteration loop. The user **Testing** determined which design approach provided the
most comprehensible knowledge transfer, intuitive access, and increased attention. The prototypes were evaluated by Magdeburg and Skopje participants (N
= 307). In Magdeburg, exhibits were displayed at a public design fair for interactive testing. In Skopje, participants assessed video prototypes, images, abstracts,
and functional descriptions. Participants in the user study were informed about
the data protection regulations and ethical aspects of their participation and
gave their consent. Effectiveness was measured using a post-questionnaire with
5 items and 2 open-ended questions. Participants rated 5 statements on a 5-point
Likert scale and the items were descriptively analyzed using SPSS.

- Item 1: I easily understood the concept and handling of the installation.
- Item 2: The installation contributes to increased awareness (in public places)
  of air pollution.
- Item 3: The conveyed information is understandable and has expanded my
  knowledge of air quality.
- Item 4: The installation is easy and intuitive.
- Item 5: The installation should be visible/usable in public places for citizens.
- Question 1: What I particularly liked about the installation ...
- Question 2: What I did not like about the installation...

The two open-ended questions provided insight into the strengths and weaknesses of the concepts and identified areas for improvement in the installations.
The free-text responses were analyzed using qualitative content analysis according to Mayring [25]. Usability was assessed using the standardized User Experience Questionnaire (UEQ), which measures UX on six scales: Attractiveness,
Perspicuity, Efficiency, Dependability, Stimulation, and Novelty [21]. Testers
rated 26 bipolar word pairs (e.g., Not understandable & Understandable) on
a 7-point Likert scale, with responses ranging from -3 (fully agree with the negative term) to +3 (fully agree with the positive term). The mean values of the
scale were compared with a benchmark dataset [38].

3.4 Awareness Prototypes

The interactive installation **Pollution Booth** is located in urban areas and
measures the current levels of particulate matter in its location. The interaction
mimics the operation of a public photo booth. Users receive a personal souvenir
photo in two versions; a regular print and a second image that depicts the particulate matter particles at the measurement location of the current hour scaled
over the faces. The confetti overlay is not just a visual effect, but also represents
various pollutants and their sources with different colors. The key terms for air
quality are explained in simple language in the back. The functional prototype
consists of a camera, printer, tablet, and computer inside the photo box, all connected via an Arduino. User interaction occurs on the tablet screen. The photo

countdown triggers the camera, which sends the photo to the computer. The current PM value is retrieved from the website of the Saxony-Anhalt air monitoring system and visualized as confetti on the photo template. The image file is then sent to the printer. The concept was selected because it can be easily installed in public spaces, buildings, or at events, and it appeals to a broad audience due to its entertaining nature.

Fig. 2. Prototypes Pollution Booth (top) & Visible Particulate Matter (bottom)

For immersion in the Virtual Reality (VR) prototype **Visible Particulate Matter** users put on a VR headset (Oculus Quest 2) and enter virtual exhibition rooms. In the foyer, players receive information on the causes and effects of air pollutants on the human body. They can choose between the cities of Skopje (North Macedonia) and Magdeburg (Germany) and select a specific day to investigate its air quality. This selection brings players to a map of the chosen city, where they can navigate across different locations. The pollutant particles float in the air. The goal is to find the place with the lowest air pollution on that day. The real-time data is sourced from the open-source platform Pulse.Eco and transferred via an API (Java Spring Boot) to the Processing software, which maps pollutant measurements to their respective locations on the map. These measurements are then displayed as virtual particles in the Unreal Engine. The VR application is particularly effective in visualizing otherwise invisible air pollutants directly in urban locations where they are present at the time.

The computer game **End Game** is mainly aimed at elementary school children and is inspired by the well-known video game Super Mario by Nintendo. Children and people with pre-existing conditions are the most affected by the health hazards of air pollution [35]. The game conveys information on behaviors to reduce risk. Instead of removing mushrooms, the avatar transforms cars into bicycles and CO2 clouds into fresh air. By jumping on the causes of air pollution, they are combated, and the air is cleaned. Players receive compact facts about the causes of air pollution. The interactive click prototype and character design were created with Adobe XD. The gamification approach lowers the inhibition threshold for engaging in the complex topic, allowing users to learn about air pollution while playing.

Fig. 3. Prototypes End Game (top), Air Where (middle) & Breathe (bottom).

The exhibit **Air Where** is a speculative design intended as a warning. The future vision transports viewers to the year 2050, where fresh air is no longer taken for granted and masks become the norm in everyday life. The speculation considers trends based on currently available research results. Air Where is not a prophecy - the narrative aims to show what could happen if the current treatment of the environment continues. A personalized device guides users as a navigation tool to fresh air zones. Upon arrival, users can remove their masks and breathe natural air without negative health effects. The speculation is conveyed in a short movie. Part of this narrative is a tangible prototype made of silicone and Scoby to best simulate the experience of skin. It is equipped with vibration motors controlled by an Arduino that navigate the user in the right direction using different vibration patterns and provide discrete distance information. This vision of the future aims to leverage the users' sense of shock to motivate them to take potential countermeasures.

The concept **Breathe** is a participatory format intended to encourage rethinking in public spaces. Artists can submit works on the theme "Clean air as a privilege." The artwork is prominently displayed on an interactive panel in urban spaces. The screen responds in real-time to the amount of harmful air pollutants in the ambient air and depicts the particles as gray "bubbles" over the artwork. When air pollution is particularly high, the pollutant particles become denser and air pollution becomes visible to passersby. Citizens can receive more information on the topic using the interactive touchscreen using the particles as buttons. For the small-scale functional prototype, the screen was divided into four vertical segments. When the battery-operated car (computer mouse) drives past the screen, the amount and color of pollutants projected onto the screen changes according to the y-value of the mouse using Visual Studio Code.

4   Results

4.1   Pre-questionnaire

The survey revealed a strong demand for accessible and comprehensible air pollution data ($M = 4.27$); however, current information provision lacks transparency ($M=4.44$). Citizens report limited knowledge and rarely seek information due to inaccessible reporting ($M = 3.01$), complex data and low self-motivation. Nevertheless, participants expressed a high willingness to adapt their behavior ($M=4.26$) if provided with clear evidence of its positive impact on air quality (see Table 2).

The t-test revealed significant differences between participants from Magdeburg (MD) and the University of Skopje (SKP) in their perception and self-reported knowledge of air pollution. The Skopje participants felt more informed ($M = 3.96$) and found information more accessible ($M = 3.76$) compared to those in Magdeburg ($M = 3.45$; $M = 2.89$). The statement "I regularly seek information about air quality in my residential area" was mostly disagreed with by Magdeburg participants ($M = 2.11$), while those in Skopje partially agreed ($M = 3.21$).

4.2   Citizen Workshops

Participants found online air quality information hard to access and understand due to technical language and data-heavy presentation. Abbreviations like AQI and PM further complicated comprehension. Although the survey indicated awareness, only 6 of 16 participants could name air quality sources or channels, and just 5 had prior engagement with the topic in Magdeburg.

The responses to four key questions about air pollution were grouped into four clusters: causes of pollution, areas of interest, information channels, and mitigation measures. The 16 participants received point stickers to prioritize

Table 2. Mean Values of Pre-Questionnaire Results

Items	N	Min	Max	M	SD
Item1 I am well-informed about air pollution (causes, effects, data collection).	307	1	5	3,87	0,958
Item 2 Information and data on air quality are easily accessible and understandable.	307	1	5	3,60	1,069
Item 3 I regularly seek information about the air quality in my residential area.	307	1	5	3,01	1,321
Item 4 I would like to know more about the current air quality and potential risks due to pollution.	307	1	5	4,27	0,947
Item 5 Air quality data need to be more accessible and easier to understand.	307	1	5	4,44	0,866
Item 6 I would adjust my behavior or habits if I knew it would contribute to improving air quality.	307	1	5	4,26	0,966

information according to their interest and relevance. A descriptive cluster analysis revealed that the participants have a broad and detailed understanding of the causes of air pollution and show interest in various topics related to air quality, pollutants, and health risks. Preventive and combative measures against air pollution are of the highest priority. Current information is often prepared for the experts, making it difficult for the general public to understand ("expert jungle"). However, participants mainly trust scientific and governmental sources that operate independently of political influence and desire traceable origins to validate its authenticity. There is increased interest in air quality information related to immediate surroundings, frequently visited locations, and the significance of threshold values for health risks.

Participants preferred passive information methods, such as air quality displays in public transport, low-cost sensors, or daily news updates, eliminating the need for active searching. The participants indicated their willingness to contribute to improving the situation. However, both urban planning and political regulations are demanded by the general public to facilitate and promote environmentally conscious actions. The expansion of measurement stations, combined with brief training on how to interpret air quality data to identify the causes and sources of locally and temporarily occurring air pollution, could increase interest and a sense of self-efficacy among the population [28].

4.3   Awareness Prototypes

Post-questionnaire. The concept and handling of the video game "End Game" were best understood (M = 4.48), while the speculative installation "Air Where" was the least understood (M=4.01), indicating that participants found it challenging to grasp its concept and purpose. The installations "Pollution Booth" (M = 4.10) and "Breathe" (M = 4.10) have the most potential to increase awareness of air pollution and be placed in public (M = 4.58; M = 4,33); whereas "End Game" (M = 3.72) contributed less to raising awareness. The "End Game" (M = 3.89) was deemed unsuitable for installation in public spaces. The most effective knowledge transfer was also produced by the "Pollution Booth" (M = 3.98), and the least informational content was found in the "Air Where" prototype (M=3.57), suggesting that it did not effectively convey educational messages about air pollution. The operation of the VR application "Visible Particulate Matter"' (M = 3.73) appeared the least intuitive to users. The usability (M=4.13) was rated highest for the "Pollution Booth."

Free-Text Responses. Based on inductive category development [25], 694 free-text responses were allocated in seven main categories by two independent researchers. The categories were considered positive aspects for responses to Question 1 and negative for free-text responses to question 2. Specifically, statements with feedback on specific functionalities or suggestions for improvement were manually selected and highlighted.

- `Attractiveness`: How much did the participants like or dislike the concept, idea and technical implementation of the prototype?
- `Interaction`: How intuitive is the operation of the prototype and how well is the method of dissemination?
- `Awareness`: Does the concept increase awareness of air pollution?
- `Knowledge Transfer`: How do participants rate the density and comprehensibility of the information?
- `Public Space`: Is the concept usable in public spaces?
- `Target Group`: Which target groups can be reached with the concept and which cannot?

The installation **Pollution Booth** showed a balanced reception, with a strong presence in both positive and negative feedback categories and received the most positive comments for its presence in public spaces. This indicates that while the concept was appealing and practical for public participation, there were challenges in its user experience. Participants suggested reducing technical terms of pollutants and providing more actionable recommendations.

The VR Application **Visible Particulate Matter** application was praised for its attractiveness and effectiveness in making invisible pollutants visible and understandable. The participants found it innovative and engaging, helping them gain a deeper understanding of air pollution. Feedback included a notable amount of negative feedback in the interaction category, suggesting issues with

Table 3. Evaluation Prototypes

Prototype	Item	N	Min	Max	M	SD
Pollution Booth	Comprehensibility	271	1	5	4,25	0,809
	Increased Awareness	271	1	5	4,10	0,903
	Knowledge Transfer	271	1	5	3,96	0,885
	Intuitive Operation	271	1	5	4,13	0,912
	Usable in Public Spaces	271	1	5	4,58	0,775
Particulate Matter	Comprehensibility	247	1	5	4,08	1,112
	Increased Awareness	247	1	5	4,06	1,040
	Knowledge Transfer	247	1	5	3,85	1,173
	Intuitive Operation	247	1	5	3,73	1,234
	Usable in Public Spaces	247	1	5	3,93	1,168
End Game	Comprehensibility	261	1	5	4,48	0,841
	Increased Awareness	261	1	5	3,72	1,145
	Knowledge Transfer	261	1	5	3,74	1,097
	Intuitive Operation	261	1	5	4,10	1,000
	Usable in Public Spaces	261	1	5	3,89	1,199
Air Where	Comprehensibility	249	1	5	4,01	1,177
	Increased Awareness	249	1	5	3,80	1,196
	Knowledge Transfer	249	1	5	3,75	1,229
	Intuitive Operation	249	1	5	3,84	1,164
	Usable in Public Spaces	249	1	5	4,03	1,130
Breathe	Comprehensibility	251	1	5	4,07	1,031
	Increased Awareness	251	1	5	4,10	0,991
	Knowledge Transfer	251	1	5	3,84	1,084
	Intuitive Operation	251	1	5	3,93	1,052
	Usable in Public Spaces	251	1	5	4,33	0,995

user engagement or usability of the interface. Criticisms included the complexity of interaction, usability issues in public places, and limited accessibility due to the cost and availability of VR headsets. The participants also noted a lack of introductory content and clear objectives.

The prototype **End Game** received the most positive mentions overall, particularly in the categories of interaction and target group. This game was highly rated for its interactive approach, ease of understanding, and effectiveness in educating children through play. It received positive comments for its gamification and user interface design. Some participants felt that the educational impact was low due to a lack of direct connection to the topic and missing data. The game was considered primarily suitable for children, with suggestions to include more concrete actions such as tree planting and waste recycling to improve its educational value.

The speculative design **Air Where** received the fewest positive and the highest number of negative mentions, especially in terms of attractiveness and suitability of public spaces. Many participants misunderstood its aim to create a deterrent effect regarding air pollution. Participants felt that it lacked immediate solutions, actionable steps, and current data. The concept was considered to be uneffective in raising awareness or encouraging behavioral changes. Some users appreciated the emotional impact and its ability to capture users' attention through a futuristic and thought-provoking scenario, acknowledging its potential to evoke a strong response and highlight the urgency of air pollution issues.

The Interactive Artwork **Breathe** received the fewest negative responses. It was praised for its direct communication, easy access, and visibility in public spaces. It effectively reminded viewers of the ongoing issue of pollution, but may also have lacked in delivering detailed information or innovative design elements.

Table 4. Number of Positive and Negative Mentions (N) in Free-Text Responses

	P. B.	P. M.	E. G.	A. W.	B.	Total
Attractiveness	45 (Pos)/ 58 (Neg)	102 (Pos)/ 16 (Neg)	66 (Pos)/ 14 (Neg)	53 (Pos)/ 33 (Neg)	63 (Pos)/ 7 (Neg)	329
Interaction	56 (Pos)/ 19 (Neg)	29 (Pos)/ 35 (Neg)	59 (Pos)/ 26 (Neg)	32 (Pos)/ 29 (Neg)	30 (Pos)/ 25 (Neg)	206
Awareness	20 (Pos)/ 6 (Neg)	27 (Pos)/ 7 (Neg)	24 (Pos)/ 5 (Neg)	23 (Pos)/ 11 (Neg)	18 (Pos)/ 9 (Neg)	112
Knowledge	24 (Pos)/ 12 (Neg)	15 (Pos)/ 9 (Neg)	33 (Pos)/ 21 (Neg)	11 (Pos)/ 14 (Neg)	10 (Pos)/ 4 (Neg)	93
Public Space	7 (Pos)/ 11 (Neg)	2 (Pos)/ 27 (Neg)	1 (Pos)/ 7 (Neg)	5 (Pos)/ 11 (Neg)	5 (Pos)/ 4 (Neg)	20
Target group	6 (Pos)/ 6 (Neg)	6 (Pos)/ 14 (Neg)	51 (Pos)/ 14 (Neg)	1 (Pos)/ 4 (Neg)	6 (Pos)/ 2 (Neg)	70
Total Pos/Neg	121 (Pos)/ 58 (Neg)	145 (Pos)/ 88 (Neg)	151 (Pos)/ 75 (Neg)	111 (Pos)/ 96 (Neg)	113 (Pos)/ 51 (Neg)	641 (Pos)/ 368 (Neg)

User Experience Questionnaire. The **Pollution Booth** prototype achieved the highest scores in the Perspicuity dimension (M=1.76), indicating that the operation of the photo booth was perceived as very intuitive and easy to learn. The lowest scores were given to the Dependability dimension (M=1.65), suggesting that the interaction was partially unexpected or hindering. Specific items such as "unpredictable - predictable" (M = 0.7) and "conventional - inventive" (M=0.7) received below average scores, indicating areas for improvement. In benchmark comparison, the dimensions Attractiveness, Perspicuity, Stimulation, and Novelty were rated "Good", indicating that the prototype is visually appealing, engaging, and creatively interesting. Efficiency and Dependability were interpreted "Above Average".

The second Prototype **Visible Particulate Matter** performed best in the Novelty dimension (M=1.69). Particularly, the item "creative - dull" (M = 2.1) stood out with an "Above Average" positive rating. The Dependability (M = 1.06) and Efficiency (M = 1.06) of the application were rated the lowest compared to the 5 prototypes, with especially low mean values for the items "unpredictable - predictable" (M = 0.2) and "complicated - easy" (M = 0.8). In the benchmark comparison, the Novelty dimension is rated "Excellent", Stimulation as "Good", Efficiency and Attractiveness "Above Average" and Perspicuity and Dependability "Below Average".

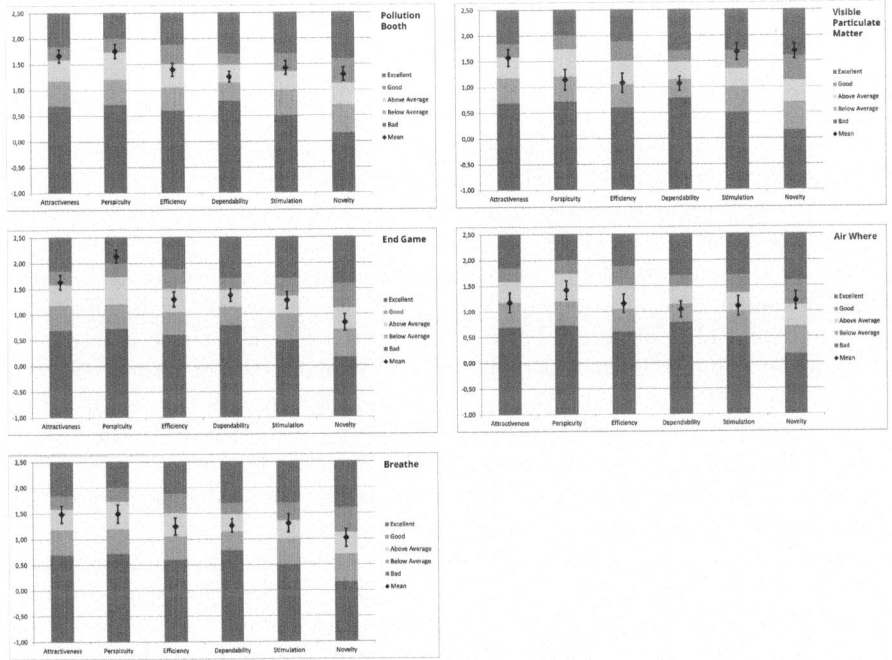

Fig. 4. Classification of the Prototypes in Benchmark Comparison.

The **End Game's** Perspicuity (M=2.14) received the highest mean value, suggesting that the game is very easy to understand and use, making it accessible to a wide audience. The Novelty (M=0.83) of the game was rated particularly low, indicating that the game may not be perceived as innovative or unique. In the benchmark comparison, Perspicuity is rated "Excellent," Attractiveness "Good," and the four other dimensions as "Above Average."

The Perspicuity of (M=1.42) of the speculative design **Air Where** was rated the highest of the 6 dimensions, indicating that the speculative design is relatively easy to understand. Dependability (M=1.04) was rated the lowest, suggesting that users experienced problems with the reliability and consistency of the interaction. However, in the benchmark comparison, the novelty dimension is rated "Good" above all others, indicating that participants found the concept creatively engaging. Perspicuity, Efficiency, and Stimulation are interpreted as "Above Average," and Attractiveness and Dependability as "Below Average."

The concept **Breathe** got the best ratings for Attractiveness (M = 1.49) and Perspicuity (M = 1.49), indicating that the installation is visually appealing and easy to understand. The low score on the dimension of novelty (M = 1.01) and a particularly poor performance on the element 'conventional - inventive' (M = 0.4) suggest the need for more innovative features. In the benchmark comparison, all seven dimensions fall in the "Above Average" range.

5   Discussion

5.1   Key Findings

Using a pre-questionnaire, we assessed (i) public knowledge and information demand regarding air quality and pollutant impacts in residential areas. Despite clear interest, current information provision is inadequate, resulting in moderate awareness and infrequent information seeking. Making air quality data more accessible and understandable has strong potential to improve public engagement. A comparison between Magdeburg and Skopje reveals local differences in perception and information behavior. Increased personal concern correlates with greater interest in local air quality and explains the increased commitment in Skopje to disseminate air quality data. Citizens feel compelled to act independently to counteract health risks in the future, whereas in Magdeburg responsibility is shifted from individuals to higher-level institutions. These findings suggest that tailored communication strategies are needed to improve air quality awareness and engagement.

(ii) Which information channels citizens use, and what data and information are relevant to them was explored conducting three citizen workshops. Indirect passive information methods, such as public displays and data at the measuring stations, are preferred. Relevant information includes causes, health impacts, and measures to combat air pollution, with a preference for local data from reliable and independent sources.

An exploratory design study investigated (iii) the impact communication strategies have in terms of raising awareness, knowledge transfer, and encouraging behavior change. Five digital prototypes were created for the interactive transfer of knowledge on air quality, which users evaluated using the standardized UEQ for usability and a questionnaire for their effectiveness. In the UEQ benchmark comparison, all five prototypes fall within a similar range in the "Good" category. The results for Attractiveness, Perspicuity, Efficiency, Dependability, Stimulation, and Novelty generally show consistent performance, with only a few extremes at the highest (full agreement) and lowest (no agreement) ends of the scale. The evaluation of the five prototypes reveals distinct strengths and limitations in communicating air quality data to the public. While some excel in interactivity, others provide visually appealing yet passive experiences. The findings suggest that no single prototype fully meets all communication requirements; instead, their respective advantages and challenges can be compared in terms of engagement, accessibility, and long-term effectiveness.

By visualizing particulate matter levels through an interactive photo experience the **Pollution Booth** makes air pollution tangible and personally relevant. However, its ability to convey in-depth knowledge is limited, as participants noted that explanations lacked clarity and contained overly technical terminology. While the installation is engaging, its effectiveness in sustaining long-term interest could be enhanced by integrating additional educational components.

The **Visible Particulate Matter** prototype leverages Virtual Reality (VR) to provide an immersive visualization of air pollution. This novel approach allows users to explore invisible pollutants in an engaging and interactive way. However, usability issues were identified, as navigation within the VR environment was challenging for some participants. Furthermore, the requirement for VR headsets limits accessibility and scalability for broader public use. A clearer introduction and simplified navigation could improve its effectiveness in educational settings.

The **End Game** effectively engages younger audiences by making environmental topics approachable through gamification. However, its effectiveness was reduced by a lack of clear connections between in-game actions and real-world air pollution effects. Additionally, the absence of real-time air quality data limited its educational depth. Providing supplementary learning materials, such as teacher guides, could further enhance its impact as an educational tool.

The **Air Where** prototype adopted a speculative design approach, using provocative future scenarios to generate awareness and public debate. This method successfully elicited strong emotional responses and stimulated reflection on environmental responsibility. However, Some participants found its message unclear and lacking present-day relevance. Enhancing its educational value could involve integrating real-world data alongside speculative elements to provide a clearer contextual framework.

The **Breathe** installation excelled in its seamless integration into public spaces, offering an intuitive and visually compelling representation of air pollution. By providing passive exposure to real-time data, it ensures continuous engagement without requiring active user input. However, the lack of interactive elements reduced its effectiveness in conveying detailed information. Participants suggested incorporating additional features, such as soundscapes or explanatory text, to enhance understanding of the visual changes in air quality representation.

A comparison of these prototypes highlights the strengths of different communication strategies. While Pollution Booth and Breathe are highly usable and effectively reach a broad audience in public spaces, Visible Particulate Matter offers an immersive experience that makes air pollution visually tangible. End

Game successfully engages younger demographics through gamification, whereas Air Where uses emotional engagement to provoke discourse. The findings suggest that a hybrid approach, combining different strategies, may be most effective. For instance, blending passive communication methods (e.g., public displays and real-time pollution indicators) with interactive tools (e.g., gamification, VR) could enhance both immediate engagement and deeper understanding.

Future developments should focus on improving accessibility, ensuring that emotional engagement is effectively linked to scientific information. The integration of real-time air quality data, simplified usability, and audience-specific adaptations could further enhance effectiveness. Regular content updates may also be necessary to maintain long-term public interest. Ultimately, the findings indicate that air pollution communication should not only be informative but also interactive, emotionally engaging, and widely accessible to ensure lasting impact.

5.2 Design Implications

Unlike previous studies, this participatory design process revealed that while users in surveys express a preference for personal smart devices, such as tablets or smartphone applications, these tools have not demonstrated a significant effect on increasing attention and knowledge acquisition. This lack of impact is attributed to the self-initiative required for individual information collection. Participants in citizen workshops highlighted a preference for collective knowledge about air pollution to collaboratively work towards a solution and ensure measures are not ignored. In addition, a shared data foundation facilitates more effective advocacy for air quality regulations with decision makers. The confrontation in urban spaces provides users with the opportunity to receive information without having to actively seek it out. The study defines 32 key design requirements across four categories, which should be taken into account by policy makers and urban planners when implementing public information systems.

Information Selection: To effectively communicate air pollution data, information must be relevant and easy to understand. Key aspects include location, ensuring that data are directly linked to the user's surroundings, and communication of health impacts, highlighting specific risks such as acute symptoms and long-term disease effects [37]. Providing practical steps that individuals can take for self-protection and clear links between actions and their impact on air quality can strengthen the educational effect. Other essential elements include historical data for trend analysis, clear identification of air pollutants and their sources, and transparent presentation of political decision-makers responsible for regulations [23].

Mediation: While the highest-rated prototype Pollution Booth does not necessarily achieve the greatest impact in terms of increasing awareness, in fact, the Air Where prototype, with its provocative speculation, demonstrates that unconventional and controversial approaches can effectively capture attention and stimulate curiosity and debate. However, for educational purposes, communication methods must go beyond artistic approaches and provide concrete and actionable information. Although emotional engagement strategies can activate social norms and collective responsibility, supplementing them with peer-to-peer interactions and clear evidence-based messaging ensures a stronger and more sustainable impact on environmental behavior [5,37]. By combining the attention-grabbing power of speculative approaches with practical, behavior-oriented communication, awareness campaigns can maximize both short-term engagement and long-term effectiveness. The attractiveness of an application is influenced by quick accessibility (e.g. structured intro tutorial), the fun factor in operation, the opportunity for active participation, the acquisition of knowledge helping to improve one's living conditions, and the curiosity to try new things. Additionally, tangible and embodied experiences, gamification elements, such as challenges and interactive storytelling, and familiar operation can improve usability and encourage users to engage with complex topics like air pollution. Citizen science initiatives can empower people with the knowledge to interpret air quality data and take action, particularly through brief training sessions that enhance self-efficacy and engagement. These educational formats should be tailored to specific target groups to maximize effectiveness. Regular updates sustain long-term engagement.

Media Channel: The study supports the use of passive communication methods, such as digital screens in public spaces, as they minimize the effort required by individuals to seek information. High-traffic areas such as transportation hubs, shopping centers, and parks are suitable locations. Educational partnerships with schools and libraries can facilitate immersive learning experiences using technologies like VR and AR. In addition, leveraging daily news channels, social networks, and mobile applications can increase reach, with the smartphone remaining the preferred device for accessing environmental information. To ensure transparency and credibility, information should come from reliable and independent sources, such as scientific or governmental institutions, free from political or economic influence.

Data Visualization: To make complex scientific data accessible to a broad audience, the installation must prioritize simple, non-technical language and avoid overwhelming users with pollutant level data. Using visual elements such as color-coded indicators, infographics, and dynamic soundscapes can make invisible pollutants tangible. Inclusive design principles, such as strong contrasts, legible fonts, audio instructions, and adjustable interfaces, ensure accessibility. The User Interface Design should have a clear, concise, and well-structured design and focus on core information. Additionally, positive framing-emphasizing solutions rather than solely highlighting negative consequences-has been shown to enhance public engagement and comprehension [37]. Finally, content reduction focusing on essential information and layering details based on user interest allows for a more effective communication approach.

5.3   Limitations

Several limitations had to be accepted in conducting the surveys in this study, which must be considered when interpreting the results. Firstly, there is an unequal distribution in sample size between Magdeburg and Skopje. Students in Skopje received extra credits as an incentive to participate in the study. Secondly, the testing in Magdeburg was conducted in person on a fixed date, while the survey in Skopje was conducted digitally and independently of time. The prototypes were available for direct use by participants in Magdeburg. Due to the large transportation effort and additional costs, only digital testing of the prototypes was possible for participants in Skopje. This may influence the subjective assessment of the communication concepts.

Furthermore, the sample does not represent a cross-section of the population. The average age is below that of the general population. Additionally, mainly university and college members were recruited for participation. These individuals tend to already have higher environmental awareness and media competence. However, studies examining the impact of demographic data on UX ratings found no significant influence on usability ratings [45]. In particular, there may already have been an interest in the topics covered for workshop participation. The workshops were conducted only in Magdeburg. Therefore, only local preferences in the prioritization of topics could be evaluated, and there was no cultural comparison.

6   Conclusion and Future Work

This study investigated the communication of air quality data to the public to raise awareness about the health hazards of air pollution. Using the Design-Based Implementation Research approach, we explored five design prototypes tested with participants from Germany and North Macedonia. Findings highlighted the population's interest in the issue but limited knowledge about air quality. Despite interest, information barriers and low motivation hinder regular engagement. The identified requirements for knowledge communication suggest that using familiar operating concepts, targeted selection and reduction of content, region-specific communication strategies with locally relevant and health-focused information, passive information methods in public spaces with minimal effort required to obtain the information, employ interactive and emotional engagement strategies and simple, illustrative presentation of information as effective tools for increasing problem awareness to promote environmentally conscious behavior. Citizen Workshops revealed a preference among participants for collective knowledge sharing, indicating a communal approach to tackling air pollution. This collective knowledge base could help in advocating for better air quality regulations.

The results demonstrated which design principles are effective in raising awareness of the issue. In addition to citizens and users, future work should also involve experts in the development process, e.g. to prioritize the identified requirements, to further develop the concepts and ideas and to evaluate the approaches from different professional perspectives. However, it remains to be determined what the optimal amount of input and the most effective communication methods are to maintain long-term attention and determine which data are of lasting interest. Enhancing the usability of the artifacts will require repeated user testing and iterative adjustments. Therefore, an implementation of designs as fully functional installations that can be used in real public environments is necessary so that they can be evaluated with different methods on site. Only after the integration of improved information channels, a subsequent survey can explore the frequency of prototype usage; whether and how often citizens inform themselves about this topic. Future research is also needed to determine the most effective locations for their placement and the specific target groups that frequently seek information versus those that do not. Since this survey focused on design of communication methods they were not targeted to measure changes in participants' actual behavior, which needs to be done in future work.

References

1. Akyol, A., Solsbach, A., Marx Gómez, J.: Entwicklung eines bedarfsgerechten umweltinformationsportals mit bürgerbeteiligung (2022)
2. Arsov, M., et al.: Multi-horizon air pollution forecasting with deep neural networks. Sensors **21**(4), 1235 (2021)
3. Bayer, T., Roloff, K., Willberg, S., Eifert, K., Maiwald, B.: Immissionsschutzbericht 2022 sachsen-anhalt. (2022)
4. Beaumont, R., Hamilton, R., Machin, N., Perks, J., Williams, I.: Social awareness of air quality information. Sci. Total Environ. **235**(1–3), 319–329 (1999)
5. Bonney, R., et al.: Citizen science: a developing tool for expanding science knowledge and scientific literacy. Bioscience **59**(11), 977–984 (2009)
6. Borbet, T.C., Gladson, L.A., Cromar, K.R.: Assessing air quality index awareness and use in Mexico city. BMC Public Health **18**, 1–10 (2018)
7. Chin, Y., De Pretto, L., Thuppil, V., Ashfold, M.J.: Public awareness and support for environmental protection-a focus on air pollution in peninsular Malaysia. PLoS ONE **14**(3), e0212206 (2019)
8. Commission E: Flash eurobarometer 360: attitudes of europeans towards air quality (2013)
9. Commission, E.: Neue eurobarometer-umfrage: Europäerinnen und europäer sind mehrheitlich der ansicht, dass die eu zusätzliche maßnahmen zur lösung von problemen bei der luftqualität vorschlagen sollte (2019)
10. Díaz, J.J., Mura, I., Franco, J.F., Akhavan-Tabatabaei, R.: aire-a web-based r application for simple, accessible and repeatable analysis of urban air quality data. Environ. Model. Softw. **138**, 104976 (2021)
11. Dietz, T., Rosa, E.A., York, R.: Environmentally efficient well-being: rethinking sustainability as the relationship between human well-being and environmental impacts. Human Ecol. Rev., 114–123 (2009)
12. Elliott, B., Moses, E.: Clean air action: Applications of citizen science to identify and address air pollution emission sources. World Resources Institute (2022)
13. Finn, S., O'Fallon, L.R.: Environmental health literacy. Springer (2018)
14. Finn, S., O'Fallon, L.: The emergence of environmental health literacy-from its roots to its future potential. Environ. Health Perspect. **125**(4), 495–501 (2017)

15. Forkan, A.R.M., Kimm, G., Morshed, A., Jayaraman, P.P., Banerjee, A., Huang, W.: Aqvision: a tool for air quality data visualisation and pollution-free route tracking for smart city. In: 2019 23rd International Conference in Information Visualization–Part II, pp. 47–51. IEEE (2019)
16. Grossberndt, S., Bartonova, A., González Ortiz, A., Castell, N., Guerreiro, C., et al.: Public awareness and efforts to improve air quality in Europe. Eionet Report-ETC/ATNI **2**, 17–30 (2020)
17. Haddad, H., de Nazelle, A.: The role of personal air pollution sensors and smartphone technology in changing travel behaviour. J. Trans. Health **11**, 230–243 (2018)
18. Hajj-Hassan, M., Chaker, R., Cederqvist, A.M.: Environmental education: a systematic review on the use of digital tools for fostering sustainability awareness. Sustainability **16**(9), 3733 (2024)
19. Kais, K., Gołaś, M., Suchocka, M.: Awareness of air pollution and ecosystem services provided by trees: the case study of Warsaw city. Sustainability **13**(19), 10611 (2021)
20. Landau, F., Toland, A.: Towards a sensory politics of the anthropocene: exploring activist-artistic approaches to politicizing air pollution. Environ. Planning C: Polit. Space **40**(3), 629–647 (2022)
21. Laugwitz, B., Held, T., Schrepp, M.: Construction and evaluation of a user experience questionnaire. In: Holzinger, A. (ed.) USAB 2008. LNCS, vol. 5298, pp. 63–76. Springer, Heidelberg (2008). https://doi.org/10.1007/978-3-540-89350-9_6
22. Liao, Y.W., Su, Z.Y., Huang, C.W., Shadiev, R.: The influence of environmental, social, and personal factors on the usage of the app environment info push. Sustainability **11**(21), 6059 (2019)
23. Mahajan, S., et al.: A citizen science approach for enhancing public understanding of air pollution. Sustain. Urban Areas **52**, 101800 (2020)
24. Mathews, N.S., Chimalakonda, S., Jain, S.: Air: an augmented reality application for visualizing air pollution. In: 2021 IEEE Visualization Conference (VIS), pp. 146–150. IEEE (2021)
25. Mayring, P., Fenzl, T.: Qualitative inhaltsanalyse. Springer (2019)
26. Myatt, G.J., Johnson, W.P.: Making sense of data iii: A practical guide to designing interactive data visualizations, vol. 3. John Wiley & Sons (2011)
27. Oltra, C., Sala, R.: Communicating the risks of urban air pollution to the public: a study of urban air pollution information services. Revista internacional de contaminación ambiental **31**(4), 361–375 (2015)
28. Oltra, C., Sala, R., Boso, À., Asensio, S.L.: Public engagement on urban air pollution: an exploratory study of two interventions. Environ. Monit. Assess. **189**(6), 1–12 (2017). https://doi.org/10.1007/s10661-017-6011-6
29. Orellano, P., Reynoso, J., Quaranta, N., Bardach, A., Ciapponi, A.: Short-term exposure to particulate matter (pm10 and pm2. 5), nitrogen dioxide (no2), and ozone (o3) and all-cause and cause-specific mortality: systematic review and meta-analysis. Environ. Inter. **142**, 105876 (2020)
30. Organization, W.H.: WHO ambient air quality database, 2022 update: status report. World Health Organization (2023)
31. Organization WH., et al: Health impact of ambient air pollution in serbia: A call to action. Tech. rep., World Health Organization. Regional Office for Europe (2019)
32. Peffers, K., Tuunanen, T., Rothenberger, M.A., Chatterjee, S.: A design science research methodology for information systems research. J. Manag. Inf. Syst. **24**(3), 45–77 (2007)

33. Pochwatko, G., et al.: Multisensory representation of air pollution in virtual reality: lessons from visual representation. In: Conference on Multimedia, Interaction, Design and Innovation, pp. 239–247. Springer (2021). https://doi.org/10.1007/978-3-031-11432-8_24

34. Raman, R., Mandal, S., Das, P., Kaur, T., Sanjanasri, J., Nedungadi, P.: University students as early adopters of chatgpt: innovation diffusion study (2023)

35. Ramírez, A.S., Ramondt, S., Van Bogart, K., Perez-Zuniga, R.: Public awareness of air pollution and health threats: challenges and opportunities for communication strategies to improve environmental health literacy. J. Health Commun. **24**(1), 75–83 (2019)

36. Ramondt, S., Zuniga, R.P., Van Bogart, B., Ramirez, A.S.: Public awareness of air pollution and health threats in the san joaquin valley: community perspectives on air quality communication. In: APHA 2016 Annual Meeting & Expo (29 Oct–2 Nov 2016). American Public Health Association (2016)

37. Riley, R., de Preux, L., Capella, P., Mejia, C., Kajikawa, Y., de Nazelle, A.: How do we effectively communicate air pollution to change public attitudes and behaviours? a review. Sustainability Sci., 1–21 (2021)

38. Schrepp, M., Thomaschewski, J., Hinderks, A.: Construction of a benchmark for the user experience questionnaire (ueq) (2017)

39. Sommer, L.K., Swim, J.K., Keller, E., Klöckner, C.A.: "pollution pods": the merging of art and psychology to engage the public in climate change. Glob. Environ. Chang. **59**, 101992 (2019)

40. Taştan, M.: An iot based air quality measurement and warning system for ambient assisted living. Avrupa Bilim ve Teknoloji Dergisi **16**, 960–968 (2019)

41. UNION P et al: Directive 2008/50/ec of the european parliament and of the council of 21 may 2008 on ambient air quality and cleaner air for europe. Official J. European Union (2008)

42. Ward, F., et al.: Engaging communities in addressing air quality: a scoping review. Environ. Health **21**(1), 89 (2022)

43. Winston, A.: Loop.ph's bmx track installation in taipei changes colour in response to air quality (2016)

44. Wohlin, C.: Guidelines for snowballing in systematic literature studies and a replication in software engineering. In: Proceedings of the 18th International Conference on Evaluation and Assessment in Software Engineering. pp. 1–10 (2014)

45. Wong, C., et al.: Visualizing Air Pollution: communication Of Environmental Health Information in a Chinese immigrant community. J. Health Commun. **24**(4), 339–358 (2019)

From Displays to Real Environments: Research and Design Guidelines for the Application of the Monk-White Illusion

Qien Gong and Lisha Duan[✉]

Guangzhou Academy of Fine Arts, Guangzhou 510006, China
1952258840@qq.com

Abstract. The Monk-White illusion is a visual illusion phenomenon that relies on colour assimilation and perceptual properties, and has gained widespread use on display-like two-dimensional planes. However, the application of the Monk-White illusion in real-world environments is relatively limited, and there is a lack of research on its application in a systematic way. The aim of this study is to explore the performance properties of the Monk-White illusion in real-world environments and the factors that influence them. This study focuses on: what factors influence the performance of the Monk-White illusion in real-world environments? How do the effects of the illusion and the perception of the number of shades of object colours differ between the display and the real environment? In this study, a qualitative research method was used to collect subjects' visual discrimination judgements on the intensity of the effect and the perception of the number of hues of the Monk-White illusion samples through field tests. It was found that factors such as frame colour (hue, lightness, purity, spacing) and object colour distribution influenced the Monk-White illusion and that the effect was stronger and the number of tones perceived was greater in the display than in the real environment. This study complements the lack of research on the application of the Monk-White illusion to real-world environments. The results of the study provide designers with design guidelines on how to effectively utilise the Monk-White illusion in real-life product applications to enhance the visual experience and interest of the product.

Keywords: Monk-White illusion · visual perception · display · realistic environment · design guidelines

1 Introduction

Visual illusion plays an important role in design. Through the clever use of visual illusion, designers can not only enhance the visual impact of the product and attract users' attention, but also improve brand recognition. Visual illusion not only optimises the user's visual experience, but also stimulates a deeper sense of interaction, thus giving the product a unique competitive advantage in the market. Therefore, the study of visual illusion not only has important theoretical value, but also provides innovative strategies and methods for actual design practice.

© The Author(s), under exclusive license to Springer Nature Switzerland AG 2025
M. Schrepp (Ed.): HCII 2025, LNCS 15794, pp. 26–42, 2025.
https://doi.org/10.1007/978-3-031-93221-2_2

Munker-White illusion is a kind of visual illusion. As shown in Fig. 1, according to the classification method of Kitaoka A, visual illusion can be divided into two categories: Shape illusion and Colour illusion, and Munker-White illusion belongs to the Colour Illusion by Assimilation [1].

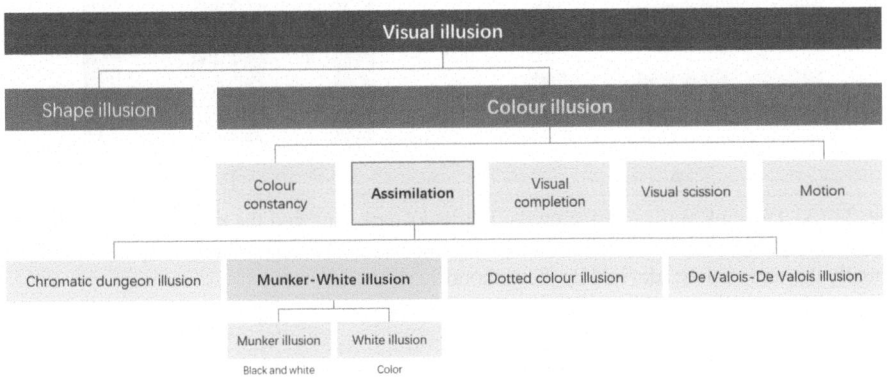

Fig. 1. This figure is a schematic of the author's output based on the classification method of Kitaoka A.

Munker-White illusion, also known as the Munker illusion or White illusion [2]. In the 1980s, psychologist White M. discovered that black and white stripes can affect the human eye's perception of colour. Another psychologist, Munker H. found that different coloured stripes can also affect the human eye's perception of colour [3]. The Munker-White illusion is specifically represented by (Fig. 2) alternating pink stripes in two different pattern areas that appear to be two colours but are actually the same colour. Because the brain can't help but bring in the surrounding colours for comprehensive consideration when judging the original colour of an object, the vertical stripes, which are exactly the same colour under the influence of different horizontal stripe colours, are perceived by the brain as different colours.

You Shiyou proposed that the composition of the Munker-White illusion requires three elements (as shown in Fig. 3), namely frame colour, object colour and background colour [4]. The frame colour is located in the top layer, which is a stripe interleaved over the object colour, and requires at least two colours; the object colour is located in the middle layer, where the colours are identical; and the background colour is located in the bottom layer, where the colours may be the same or different. For creating an illusion, the colour contrast of the frame colours is most important; the greater the difference between the frame colours, the greater the difference between the object colours [4]. Therefore, the Hue, Lightness, and Purity contrasts of the frame colours affect the Monk-White illusion effect in a display.

The Monk-White illusion has been widely used in display-like two-dimensional planes, but the specific performance in real environments and its influencing factors are still unclear, and there is a lack of research on its application in a systematic way. With the increasing demand for visual perception and design innovation, the Monk-White illusion, as an interesting visual phenomenon, should be deeply explored for

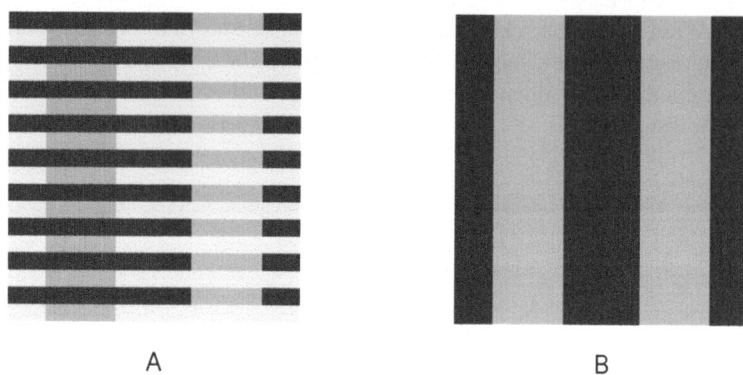

Fig. 2. (A) The pink vertical stripe on the left looks dark pink and the right is bright pink, and (B) removing the horizontal stripes of the pink vertical stripe reveals that the two pink stripes are actually the same colour (devised by the authors).

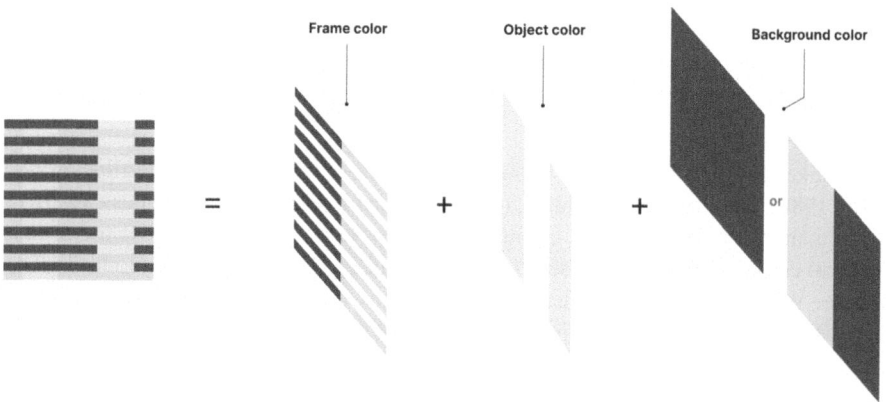

Fig. 3. This diagram is the author's schematic output based on the You Shiyou theory.

its presentation effect in real environments. Therefore, studying the performance of this illusion in the real environment has important practical reference significance and academic research value for promoting the application of the Monk-White illusion effect in product design.

2 Current Theoretical Development and Application of the Monk-White Illusion

2.1 Historical Development and Theoretical Evolution of the Monk-White Illusion

The Munker-White illusion first originated from the study of the grating illusion, a visual phenomenon first identified by Gindy in 1963 during his research on the raster illusion [5]. In 1969, Henry proposed two coloured versions of the raster illusion in a short paper, but he was apparently unaware of Gindy's early findings [6]. In 1970, Munker H. further explored the coloured versions of the raster illusion and found stronger effects than before, laying the groundwork for the formation of the Munker-White illusion [3]. It was not until 1979 that the White illusion, also known as the Munker-White illusion, was formally introduced and defined as an inexplicable lightness illusion [2].

From 1979 to 2010, most of the studies focused on the field of lightness in a more convoluted attempt to explain the mechanism of the Monk-White illusion.In 1981, White M. found that the lightness perception of grey stripes was affected by three main mechanisms: the Lightness Contrast, Lightness Assimilation and Horizontal Suppression [7].In 1995, Spehar B et al. proposed the Anchoring Theory of Lightness Perception, which argued that the White effect is not just a result of local boundary contrasts, but rather a result of the overall lightness relationship of the background stripes in conjunction with the spatial organization of the grey stripes [8]. Since then, Zaidi Q et al. [9] and Todorović D. [10] proposed the T-junctions rule, while Anderson B L. also proposed the Transparency Induced Theory [11], which also tried to explain the illusion. However, several studies between 2000 and 2005 evaluated these theories and concluded that they failed to adequately explain the new changes demonstrated by the White effect [12] [13] [14]. It is thus clear that the Wyatt illusion has become a testing ground for lightness perception theories, but so far there is still no widely agreed upon explanation [15]. It is also clear from these studies that the Monk-White illusion is closely related to lightness (also known as brightness). Although the Monk-White illusion was first discovered in the field of colour before it was extended to the field of lightness, there has been a paucity of studies on the colour version, and more on the black-and-white version.

It was not until 2021, when David Novick and A. Kitaoka extended the Monk-White illusion by presenting the confetti illusion, that the study of the Monk-White illusion in the field of colour gradually began. As shown in Fig. 4, the confetti illusion is a visual phenomenon in which a single object colour will appear in three, four or even six shades by using multiple colours in the foreground [16]. This study shows that the Monk-White illusion can cause object colours to exhibit multiple tonal variations.

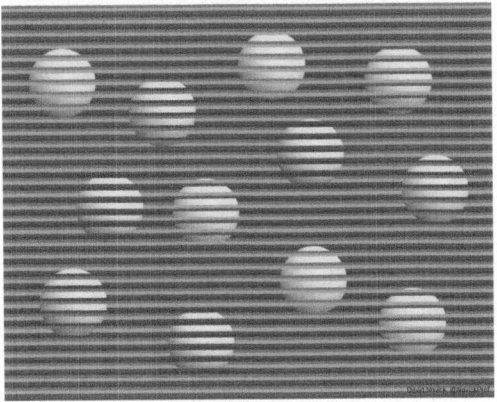

Fig. 4. Confetti illusion of four apparent colors (Image from: Novick D, Kitaoka A.: The confetti illusion. Journal of Illusion 2 (2021)).

2.2 Colour Assimilation is Used in a Number of Areas

The colour assimilation illusion, to which the Monk-White illusion belongs, has been widely used in several domains, especially in information security [17], cosmetics [18] and product sales [19] [20]. For example, Jiao, S. and Feng, J. proposed a new scheme of image steganography based on visual illusion, focusing on the use of colour assimilation illusion to subtly embed external information into an image. This method exploits the illusion mechanism of the human eye to achieve data hiding and provides an innovative solution for information security and data compression [17]. Kiritani Y et al. investigated the effect of lipstick colour on skin colour perception. It was found that lipstick colour changes the visual effect of skin tone through an assimilation effect, and red lipstick enhances the sense of redness and brightness of the face. Different lipstick shades had different effects on the perception of skin tone, and the darkness of lipstick was negatively correlated with the brightness and redness of skin tone [18].Peng M et al. investigated the application of the colour simultaneous contrast illusion in the combination of product background colours, and analysed how different combinations of background saturations affected consumer perception and decision-making for products with different attributes [19].Gegenfurtner K R. explored Gegenfurtner K R. explored how unripe green oranges can be made to appear ripe and colourful by means of an 'orange web' (shown in Fig. 5), demonstrating how colour assimilation can have an impact in everyday consumer environments [20].

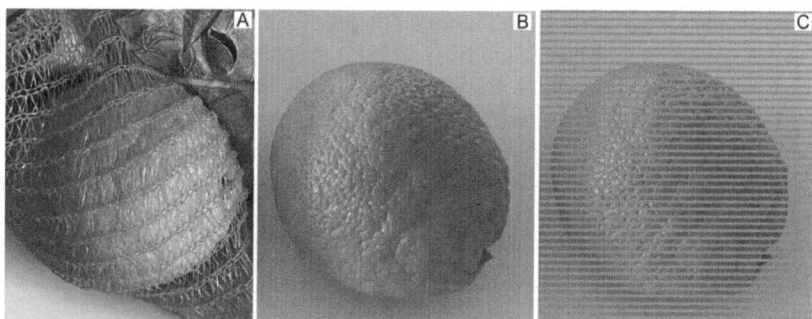

Fig. 5. Unripe green orange (A) within the orange net, (B) in isolated view, and (C) with a "Munker-net." (Image from: Gegenfurtner K R.: Perceptual ripening of oranges. i-Perception 15(4), 20416695241258748 (2024)).

In summary, the existing literature and applications mainly focus on the visual performance on the display, and there is a lack of in-depth discussion and systematic research on the application of the Monk-White illusion in the real environment. In real environments, the illusion effect may be affected by a combination of factors, especially in the transformation process from the display to the real environment, the difference between the light source colour (i.e., the light colour emitted from the screen) in the display and the surface colour (the colour reflected from the surface of the object, which is illuminated by an external light source) observed in reality may lead to a change in the illusion effect. Therefore, the following three hypotheses were proposed in this study: (1) In the real environment, the change of frame colours (hue, lightness, purity, spacing) and the way of object colour distribution have a certain influence on the illusion effect, which is shown as follows: the greater the contrast of the frame colours (hue, lightness, purity), the more pronounced is the illusion effect; the greater the spacing of the frame colours, the more the illusion effect is weakened; the illusion effect produced by regional body colour distribution is stronger than that of the stripe-like distribution; (2) the Monk-White illusion effect is stronger in the display than in the real environment; and (3) the number of hues perceived in the Monk-White illusion is greater in the display than in the real environment. In this study, a qualitative research method was used to collect subjects' visual recognition judgements of the Monk-White illusion samples in terms of intensity of effect and perception of number of hues through field tests to verify the above hypotheses.

3   Experiment

3.1   Pre-experiment Preparation

Two types of samples were used in this study: Physical Samples and Display Virtual Samples. The Physical Samples were made of wire mesh and coloured DuPont paper, while the Display Virtual Samples were created using Figama software and presented using an iPad Pro (11-inch) as the display device.

A total of 17 samples were used in the experiment, which were divided into two groups: the physical sample group and the display virtual sample group. The physical sample group contains 11 slices (Fig. 6), specifically: frame colour purity comparison (2 slices); frame colour brightness comparison (2 slices); frame colour hue comparison (2 slices); frame colour spacing comparison (2 slices); object colour distribution comparison (2 slices); 6 object colour tones (1 slice). The virtual sample group of the display screen includes 6 slices (Fig. 7), specifically: frame colour purity contrast (1 slice); frame colour brightness contrast (1 slice); frame colour hue contrast (1 slice); frame colour 3-separation spacing (1 slice); object colour zonal distribution method (1 slice); 6 object colour tones (1 slice).

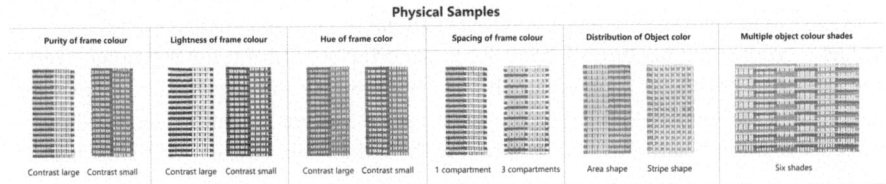

Fig. 6. 11 Physical Samples (devised by the authors).

The subjects were divided into two groups: the first group, the general group (those who had not received colour painting training, representing general users) and the professional group (those who had received colour painting training, representing designers), each group consisted of 12 people, with a male to female ratio of 1:1. All subjects

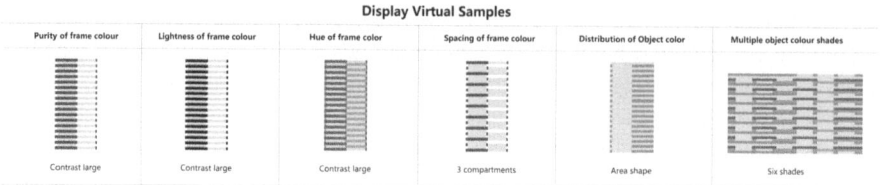

Fig. 7. 6 Display Virtual Samples (devised by the authors).

had normal or corrected-to-normal vision and were not colour blind or colour weak. The general group consisted of first-year undergraduate students (19 years old) majoring in educational technology at the College of Education and Information Technology, South China Normal University, and the professional group consisted of first-year undergraduate students (19 years old) majoring in product design at the School of Industrial Design, Guangzhou Academy of Fine Arts. The purpose of establishing the general and professional groups in this study is to take into account the fact that there is a significant difference between designers who have been professionally trained in colour and untrained general users in terms of their ability to identify and represent colours. Designers usually divide and analyse colours more finely based on their professional knowledge and experience, whereas ordinary users have a more cursory colour perception. During the design process, designers may discriminate colours based on their personal experience and expertise, whereas the average user may lack the ability to perceive colours accurately. This difference may lead to the fact that products designed by designers using the Monk-White illusion principle may not be accepted by ordinary users.

The field test was conducted at the Guangdong Province Key Lab of Innovation & Applied Research on Industry Design with a test date of 18 December 2024. To ensure the standardisation of the experiment and the reliability of the data, the sample display and observation were conducted in strict accordance with international standards, using a zero-degree light source and a 45-degree observation angle (Fig. 8). In this observation method, the light source illuminates the sample vertically and the observer observes the sample from a 45-degree angle. This setup simulates the natural light irradiation and observation angle in daily life, which can more realistically reflect the actual perception of colours. The Datacolor standard light source box used in the experiment is equipped with a D65 light source, which is a standard artificial light source that simulates daylight and has a colour temperature of 6500 K, in accordance with the international colour standards. The D65 light source can effectively eliminate the interference of external ambient light and ensure that the colour observation and identification is carried out in consistent lighting conditions, thus improving the reliability of the experimental results.

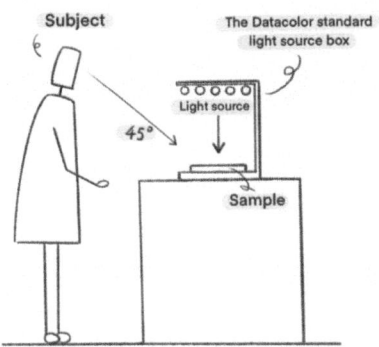

Fig. 8. Test Scene Schematic (devised by the authors).

3.2 Experiment

Before the test begins, subjects need to understand the procedure of the test. Firstly, subjects should observe the difference between the two light blue colours in the samples; next, subjects should compare the difference between the light blue colours in the two samples; finally, subjects should select the sample that they think has a greater difference (Fig. 9). This process aims to ensure that subjects can better understand the observation object and avoid bias caused by unclear task requirements, thus ensuring the reliability and comparability of experimental data.

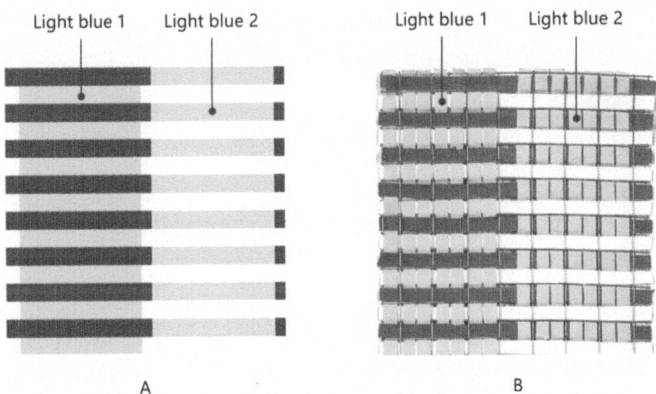

Fig. 9. (A) for a piece of display screen virtual sample Display Virtual Sample part; (B) for a piece of Physical Sample physical sample of the partial (devised by the authors).

Factors Affecting the Effect of the Monk-White Illusion.   During the test, the subject will be provided with 5 sets of physical samples (Fig. 10), each set of samples will be put into a standard light source box together for testing, and the subject will need to choose the one that he thinks is more contrasting with the light blue in each set (e.g., frame colour purity) of samples.

Physical Samples

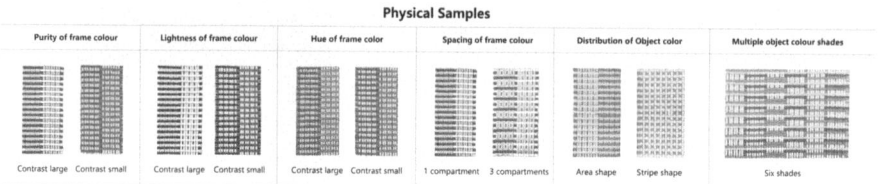

Fig. 10. Physical Samples exploring factors affecting the illusion effect (devised by the authors).

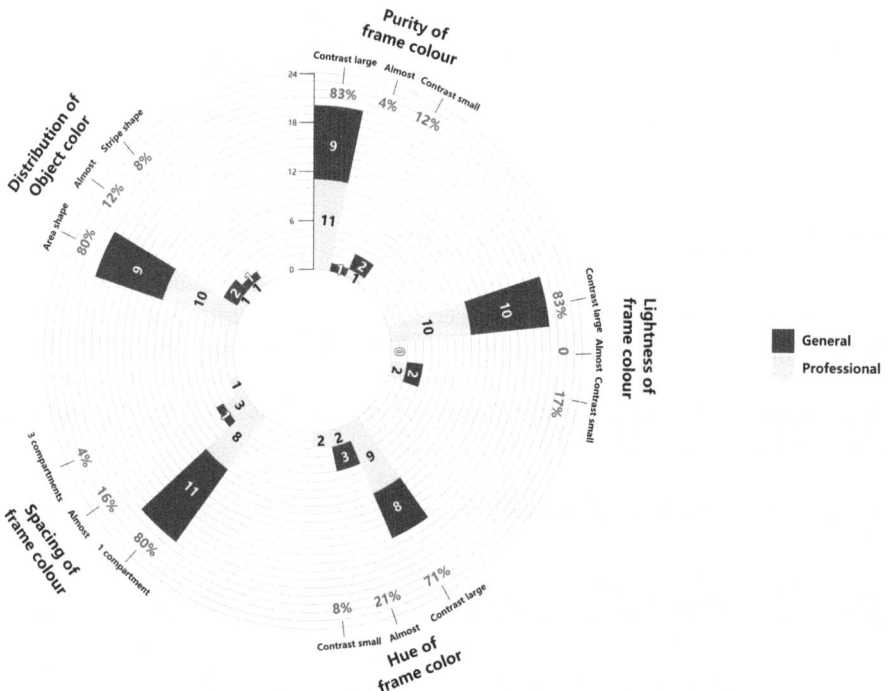

Fig. 11. Statistical chart of Physical Samples of factors affecting the illusion effect (devised by the authors).

According to Fig. 11, the statistical graph can be seen, in the physical sample group, the number of people who choose the frame colour (purity, lightness, hue) with large contrast, the frame colour spacing of 1 spacing and the object colour of regional-like distribution accounts for more than 71%, so it can be confirmed that (1) hypothesis: in the real environment, the change of the frame colour's (hue, lightness, purity, spacing) and the way of distribution of the object colour would have an effect on the illusory effect. The specific performance is as follows: the larger the contrast of the frame colour (hue, lightness, purity), the more significant the illusion effect; the larger the spacing of the frame colour, the weaker the illusion effect; and the distribution mode of the region-like body colour produces a stronger illusion effect than the stripe-like distribution mode.

The Monk-White illusion is affected by the contrast between the purity, lightness and hue of the frame colours in a realistic environment, and the greater the contrast between these three elements, the more pronounced the effect of the illusion. In this it can also be seen that the brightness and purity of the frame colour will have a greater influence on the illusionary effect than the hue. This is because the visual sensitivity of the human eye to the black and white contrast is significantly higher than the contrast between other colours, and the lightness contrast occupies an extremely important position in the colour contrast [21], while the black and white contrast is also related to the contrast between the purity of the colours [22]. Hue contrast relative to these two will appear slightly weaker, although red and green in the hue contrast stimulating eye-catching, outstanding personality, but due to the brightness of both belong to the grey category, so the effect is far less than the yellow and purple as the path of separation, contrast is strong, because in the chromatogram of the purple is the darkest, the yellow is the brightest.

In the real environment, the larger the frame colour spacing, the weaker the illusion effect. This is because the essence of the colour contrast relationship lies in the difference between different colours by means of emphasis, and when the number of colours on the surface of the colour increases, the interaction between these colours and the contrast effect will be more pronounced, which is more likely to affect the overall colour perception [23]. However, this spacing should not be too small, do not let the proportion of frame colours is larger than the object colours, or there will be a lack of primary and secondary.

The distribution of object colours also affects the presentation of the Monk-White illusion in real-world environments. By comparing the two types of distribution, area and stripe, it is found that the illusion is stronger in area than in stripe. From a visual perception point of view, area-based distribution usually involves a larger percentage of area, which makes it easier for the visual system to recognise and process this information. In contrast, the stripe-like distribution pattern, due to its dispersed nature, may make it difficult for the visual system to quickly recognise and integrate this information, thus diminishing the illusionary effect.

The data between the two groups, the general and the professional groups, were similar, and this similarity suggests that the effects of the variations of the frame colours (hue, lightness, purity, spacing) and the way in which the colours of the objects were distributed on the illusions did not depend on whether or not the subjects had been trained in colour painting. This is because the basic human colour perception mechanisms are universal, and the Monk-White illusion is essentially based on the basic responses of the visual system, which act consistently across subjects, who will respond similarly to the illusion under the same conditions regardless of whether or not they have been trained in colour painting.

Comparison of Virtual and Real Samples of Display Screen with Illusion Effect Presentation. During the test, the subject will be provided with 5 sets of samples (Fig. 12), each set of samples will be placed together in a standard light box for testing, and the subject will need to choose the one in each set that he thinks has the more pronounced difference between the two light blue colours.

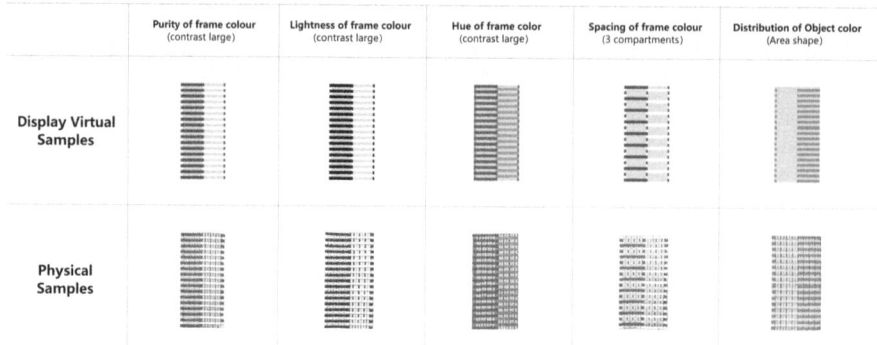

Fig. 12. Sample film exploring the difference between the illusionary effect of Display Virtual Samples and Physical Samples (devised by the authors).

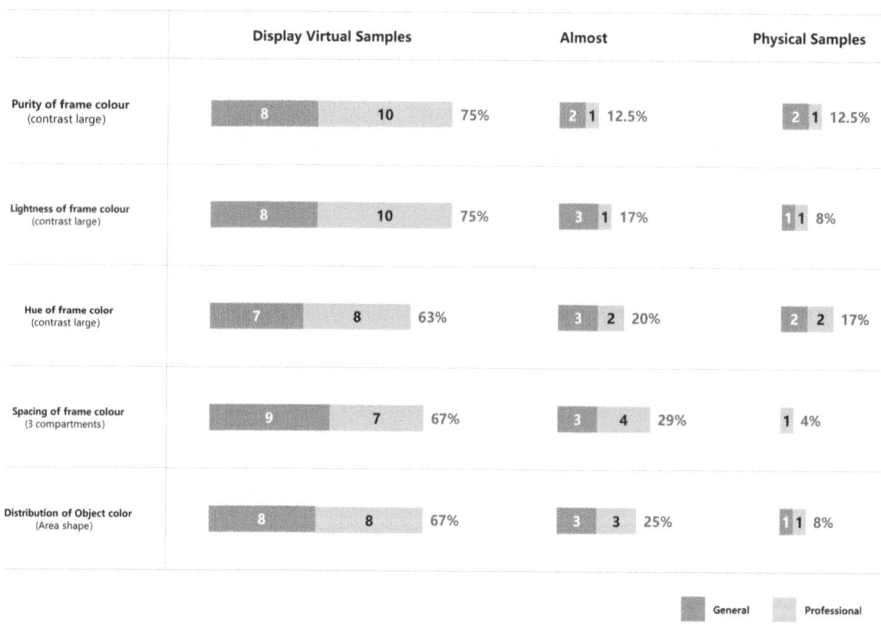

Fig. 13. Statistical Chart of Display Virtual Samples Vs Physical Samples for Illusory Effect Presentation (devised by the authors).

As can be seen from the data presented in Fig. 13 for each of the results of the comparison between the display virtual and physical samples, the number of subjects who chose the display virtual sample group were all 46%-67% more than the physical sample group. Therefore, hypothesis (2) can be confirmed: the display screen presents a stronger Monk-White illusion effect than the real environment.

This is because the principle of colour display is different between the display and the real object. The colours on the display are presented by means of self-luminescence, i.e., the display produces colours by combining the three basic colours of red (R), green (G), and blue (B), which enter directly into our eyes, and are therefore called 'additive colour method' or 'additive colour mixing' (Cuauht). '[24]. The colour of a physical object, on the other hand, is rendered by reflected light. When light hits the surface of an object, the object reflects, absorbs or transmits part of the light according to its material and surface properties, and the final reflected colour enters our eyes, a phenomenon known as 'subtractive colouring' or 'subtractive colour mixing' [24].

Displays present colours by means of a fixed RGB colour model, and the accuracy and consistency of colours can be further improved by colour correction techniques. For example, LED displays can effectively reduce colour distortion caused by ambient temperature changes or response delays through PWM dimming technology and colour correction methods (Li Zhijian, 2009) [25]. As a result, the display is more stable and consistent. On the contrary, the colour presentation of the physical samples is easily affected by environmental factors such as object surface reflectivity, light angle, etc. These variables make the colour performance of the physical samples uncertain and fluctuating, which in turn weakens the illusion. Even in a standard light source box, the physical properties of the object may still bring about subtle changes, resulting in a relatively weak illusion effect.

The data between the two groups, the general and the professional group, are also similar because the Monk-White illusion is essentially based on the basic responses of the visual system, and the production of colour contrast and visual illusions relies mainly on the brain's automatic processing of colours, lightness and contrast, and does not depend on whether or not the subjects have received training in colour painting.

Differences in the Perceived Number of Object Colour Tones between the Display and the Real Environment. During the test the subject will be provided with 2 samples (Fig. 14), each of which will be placed in a standard light box for testing, and the subject will be required to state how many colour variations he can see the light blue showing in each sample.

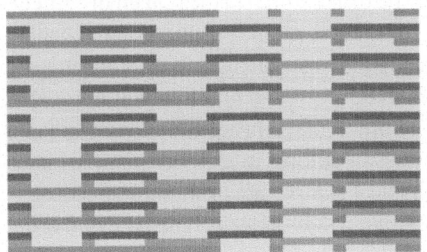   

Display Virtual Sample   **Physical Sample**

Fig. 14. Exploring the difference between Display Virtual Samples and Physical Samples in the perception of the number of shades of an object's colour in six tone number samples. (devised by the authors).

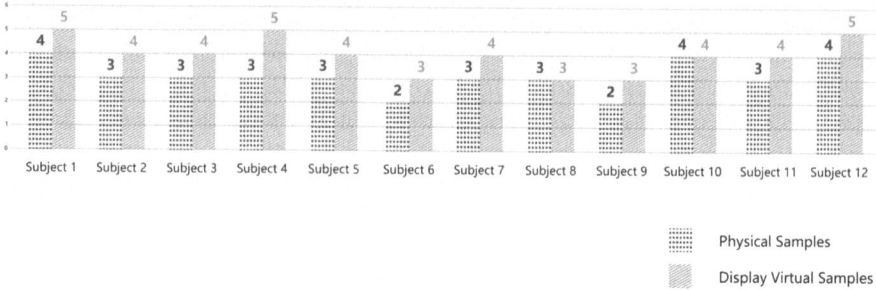

Fig. 15. Number of shades observed by subjects in the General Group (devised by the authors).

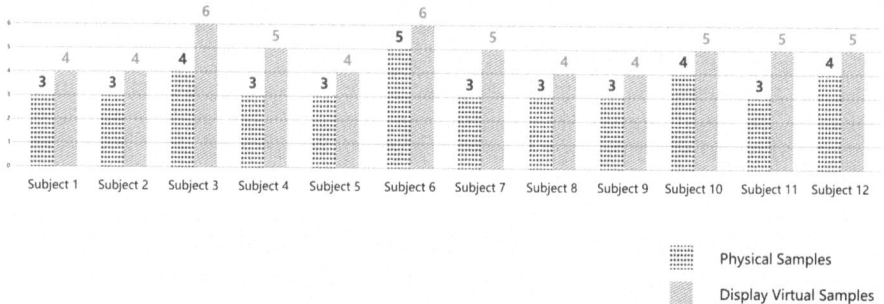

Fig. 16. Number of shades observed by subjects in the professional group (devised by the authors).

A total of 6 shades were designed for both the display and the physical samples (Fig. 15; Fig. 16), and the number of shades observed by all subjects for the physical samples did not exceed the number of shades for the display virtual samples, and 92% of the subjects observed 1 to 2 more shades in the display virtual samples than in the physical samples. Thus, hypothesis (3) can be confirmed: the number of shades of the Monk-White illusion effect is perceived more in the display than in the real environment.

The reason for this phenomenon, like the former, is related to the colour display principle of the display and the real object. The display uses an additive colour mixing model based on the three primary colours RGB (red, green and blue), which is capable of displaying a wider range of hues. At the same time, image processing algorithms on the computer may also enhance or adjust the hues, resulting in a richer range of hues seen on the screen. Whereas the colours in a physical sample are printed on, printing is a four-colour mode, CMYK, following a subtractive colour system. The RGB imaging system, which uses light, typically displays a wider range of colours than the CMYK imaging system, which uses ink. Some colour information is often lost in the RGB to CMYK conversion process. Coupled with the fact that physical samples are subject to interference from physical factors such as object surface materials and environmental reflections, the actual colour representation may suffer from problems such as dispersion and uneven illumination, which diminish the perceptibility of tonal differences. As a result, the number of Monk-White illusion object colour tones presented in the physical sample will be less than on the display.

The professional group will have better hue perception than the average user and will be able to perceive more hues. In the virtual samples on the display: subjects in the normal group could see a maximum of 5 and a minimum of 3, and subjects in the professional group could see a maximum of 6 and a minimum of 4. In the physical samples: subjects in the general group could see at most 4 kinds and at least 2 kinds, subjects in the professional group could see at most 5 kinds and at least 3 kinds. The professional group, trained in colour painting, was able to understand and apply colour theory, and through their in-depth knowledge of colour, they were able to be visually more sensitive to small variations in colour. This high sensitivity to colour differences enabled the professional group to observe more shades in the display and physical samples. In contrast, the general group lacked such professional training, and their colour perception relied mainly on intuition and daily experience, making it difficult to identify subtle differences in colour, and therefore performing less well in hue perception than the professional group, who had received training in colour painting.

4 Discussion

4.1 Monk White Illusion Design Guidelines

The purpose of this subsection is to provide designers with design guidelines for the effective use of the Monk-White illusion in real-world environments. The Monk-White illusion is a marvellous optical illusion that can produce unexpected effects and enhance the expressiveness and attractiveness of a design. In order to ensure that the illusion works optimally in real life, designers need to understand how it works and apply it flexibly to the design of their products.

Maximise the Contrast of Pulling off Frame Colours. In the Monk White illusion, the choice of frame colour and contrast design directly determine the intensity and visual impact of the illusion effect. The first thing designers need to focus on is the brightness contrast of the frame colour. The brightness difference is the key factor to produce strong illusion effect. The above research shows that lightness contrast plays a more crucial role than hue and purity in the effect of visual illusion, and designers should first ensure that the difference in lightness of frame colours is obvious. On the basis of the obvious difference in lightness, designers should further adjust the purity and hue contrast of the frame colours. The contrast of purity helps to enhance the visual impact of the illusion, and the combination of highly saturated colours can deepen the performance of the illusion. Hue contrast plays a complementary role, the choice of hue also needs to be based on the brightness to choose, such as purple and yellow contrast will be better than the contrast of red and green. Therefore, designers in the choice of frame colour, first of all to ensure that the brightness of the contrast, and then consider the purity and hue, in order to ensure that the illusion effect can be maximized presentation.

Adjusting the Appropriate Frame Colour Spacing. The spacing between the frame colours has a significant impact on the effect of the Monk White illusion. The designer needs to control the spacing of the frame colours to ensure that they are neither too dense nor too loose. If the spacing is too small, it will be difficult to distinguish between the frame colours and the object colours, so don't make the frame colours larger than the object colours. Conversely, the illusionary effect may be diminished by too much spacing between the frame colours, as the interaction and influence of the frame colours will be nullified by too much spacing. When designing, the spacing of the frame colours should be adjusted according to the contrast of the frame colours and the distribution of the object colours to ensure that they can visually produce sufficient contrasting effects to strengthen the illusionary effect.

Choose how the Object Colour is Distributed Regionally.   The way in which object colours are distributed is crucial to the performance of the Monk-White illusion. When planning the distribution of object colours, designers recommend a more concentrated, holistic distribution like zones, which makes it easier for the visual system to recognise and process the information, thus enhancing the illusion. A more dispersed distribution, such as stripes, would weaken the illusion.

There Can't be too Many Colour Variations.   There are differences in colour perception between designers and general user groups, so special consideration should be given to the colour perception ability of the target group when designing. When the design is oriented towards ordinary users, it should be noted that the Monk-White illusion presents no more than three variations of shades, preferably not more than three, other-wise there will be shades that ordinary users cannot identify, thus weakening the Monk-illusion effect.

4.2   Future Research Directions

In addition to the fact that the Monk-White illusion is affected by the changes of the frame colours (hue, lightness, purity, spacing) and the distribution of the object colours as mentioned in this study, there are other factors that affect the application of the Monk-White illusion in reality. In the process of this study, other sample films were also produced, in which it was also found that the two factors of object shape and material also have an impact on the effect of the Monk-White illusion (Fig. 17).

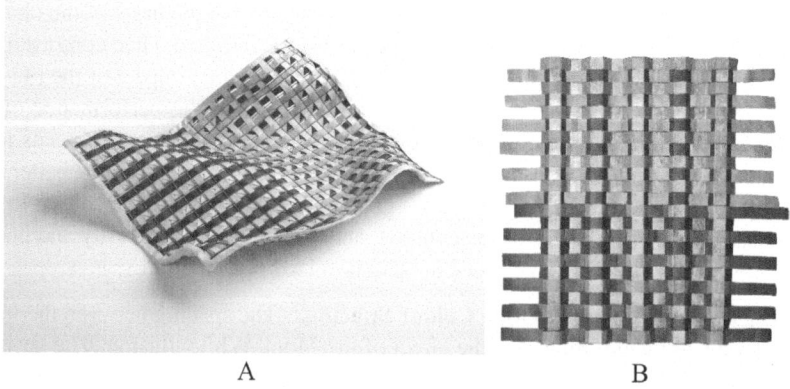

A   B

Fig. 17. (A) is sample of curved shape; (B) is sample of pearlescent material (devised by the authors).

Curved shapes present a weakened Monk-White illusion effect compared to flat shapes. Curved shapes, due to their three-dimensional curvilinear structure, cause the surface of an object to change under different viewing angles. This variation results in an uneven distribution of light and colour across the surface of the object, affecting the perception of colour contrast. Flat objects, on the other hand, are usually more consistent and are better able to maintain local contrasts in colour, thus enhancing the illusion.

The use of pearlescent DuPont paper also weakens the illusion. Pearlescent materials are often made up of tiny reflective particles (such as mica or aluminium foil) that cause a light scattering effect. This light scattering causes the surface colour to take on a 'shimmering' or 'discolouring' effect, resulting in an unstable perception of the colour. When applied to the Monk-White illusion, the contrasting perceptions of colours become blurred and the effect of the illusion is diminished.

Shape and material are also key factors that influence the use of the Monk-White illusion in reality, and therefore in-depth research can continue to be conducted on this as well. Future research could explore these two factors in further detail to understand how they affect the performance of the illusion effect. Through these further explorations, designers will be able to more accurately grasp the use of the Monk-White illusion, and thus realise the best visual effects in real life.

5   Conclusion

The aim of this study is to explore the properties and influences of the Monk-White illusion in real environments, complementing the field's application in real environments. Therefore, the main objective of this study is to analyse in depth the performance of this illusion in a realistic environment and to explore the differences between its performance and that in a display. It was found that the effect of the Monk-White illusion in real-life environments is influenced by a number of factors, including the hue, lightness and purity contrasts of the frame colours, as well as the colour spacing and the way in which the object colours are distributed. The effect of the Monk-White illusion is stronger in displays than in real environments, and the number of hues is perceived to be greater. In addition to the Monk-White illusion influences already mentioned in this study, factors such as the shape of the object and the material are also important for the application of the Monk-White illusion in reality, and are a direction for future research. This study provides an in-depth understanding of the performance characteristics of the Monk-White illusion in a realistic environment and suggests a variety of factors that influence the effect of this illusion. This provides an important basic theoretical basis for subsequent related studies and promotes the further development of the Monk-White illusion in real-life applications. Through this study, it not only supplements the insufficiency of research on the application of the Monk-White illusion in real environments, but also proposes design guidelines on how to effectively utilise the Monk-White illusion in the application of real products, which helps designers to effectively apply the illusion in real products, thus enhancing the visual effect and interestingness of the products.

References

1. Kitaoka A.: A brief classification of colour illusions. Colour: Design Creativity **5**(3), 1–9 (2010)
2. White, M.: A new effect of pattern on perceived lightness. Perception **8**(4), 413–416 (1979)
3. Munker H.: Farbige Gitter, Abbildung auf der Netzhaut und ubertragungstheoretische Beschreibung der Farbwahrnehmung. Habilitationsschrift (1970)
4. Thepaper Homepage. https://www.thepaper.cn/newsDetail_forward_22948752, Accessed 30 Nov 2024
5. Gindy, S.S.: Techniques for Subjective Colour Measurement and Their Application to Colour Contrast Phenomena. Imperial College London (1963)
6. Henry, P.S.H., Link, J.: The Shirley. Cotton Silk Man-Made Fibres Res. Assoc. (summer), 1–4 (1969)
7. White, M.: The effect of the nature of the surround on the perceived lightness of grey bars within square-wave test gratings. Perception **10**(2), 215–230 (1981)
8. Spehar, B., Gilchrist, A., Arend, L.: The critical role of relative luminance relations in White's effect and grating induction. Vision. Res. **35**(18), 2603–2614 (1995)
9. Zaidi, Q., Spehar, B., Shy, M.: Induced effects of backgrounds and foregrounds in three-dimensional configurations: the role of T-junctions. Perception **26**(4), 395–408 (1997)
10. Todorović, D.: Lightness and junctions. Perception **26**(4), 379–394 (1997)
11. Anderson, B.L.: A theory of illusory lightness and transparency in monocular and binocular images: the role of contour junctions. Perception **26**(4), 419–453 (1997)
12. Howe, P.: A Comment on Anderson and Todorovic's Explanations of White's Effect. Boston University Center for Adaptive Systems and Department of Cognitive and Neural Systems (2000)
13. Yazdanbakhsh, A., Arabzadeh, E., Babadi, B., et al.: Munker–White-like illusions without T-junctions. Perception **31**(6), 711–715 (2002)
14. Howe, P.D.L.: White's effect: Removing the junctions but preserving the strength of the illusion. Perception **34**(5), 557–564 (2005)
15. White M.: The early history of White's illusion. JAIC-J. Inter. Colour Association **5** (2010)
16. Novick D, Kitaoka A.: The confetti illusion. J. Illusion **2** (2021)
17. Jiao, S., Feng, J.: Image Steganography With Visual Illusion. Opt. Express **29**, 14282–14292 (2021)
18. Kiritani, Y., Okazaki, A., Motoyoshi, K., et al.: Color illusion on complexion by lipsticks and its impression[J]. Japanese J. Psychonomic Sci. **36**(1), 4–16 (2017)
19. Peng, M., Tong, Y., Xu, Z., et al.: How does the use of simultaneous contrast illusion on product-background color combination nudge consumer behavior? A behavioral and event-related potential study. Front. Neurosci. **16**, 942901 (2022)
20. Gegenfurtner, K.R.: Perceptual ripening of oranges. i-Perception **15**(4), 20416695241258748 (2024)
21. Zhang, X.: A brief discussion on color contrast. Chongqing Normal Univ. **01**, 63–64 (1995)
22. Zhang, J., Jin, W., Zhou, Y., et al.: Analysis of human eye color detection characteristics based on chromatics. Beijing Instit. Technol. (04), 440–443+460 (2003)
23. Ma, Q.: Color contrast relationship and its application in painting. Xianyang Normal Univ. **05**, 83–84 (2003)
24. Campos, C., Kljun, M., Sandak, J., Pucihar, K.C.: LightMeUp: Back-print Illumination Paper Display with Multi-stable Visual, Article 573, 23 pages. ACM, New York (2022)
25. Li, Z.: Research on True Color Display Technology of Full-color LED Displays. Master's Thesis, Central South University (2009)

Visualizing Peace and Transition Process Trajectories: Enhancing Decision-Making Through PeaceTech and Iterative Design

Niamh Henry[(✉)] and Tomas Vancisin

University of Edinburgh, Edinburgh, UK
{niamh.henry,tomas.vancisin}@ed.ac.uk

Abstract. Peace and transition processes are formal attempts aimed at bringing political and/or military protagonists of conflict to some sort of mutual agreement [7]. Those involved in this multifaceted area face the challenge of processing vast amounts of complex data that can greatly enhance decision-making in peace and transition processes. The Peace and Conflict Resolution Evidence Platform (PeaceRep) responds to this challenge by developing 'PeaceTech' visualization tools, with *PeaceTech* referring to innovation in the use of digital technologies to support peacebuilding [4]. We develop and design tools that leverage information/visualization design principles to enable critical interpretation and in-depth understanding of complex data. These tools are then used to support policymakers, practitioners, and researchers in making informed decisions. In this paper we describe how open-access, custom-built, and responsive PeaceTech tools critically inform decision-making, and how lessons learned can be applicable to other domains, while highlighting both current and future challenges in the area of visualization to inform peace and conflict resolution.

Keywords: PeaceTech · HCI · Information Visualization · Design

1 Introduction and Background

With growing amount of information readily available and accessible [19], pressure on decision makers to produce evidence-based policies is increasing. While visualization has emerged as a powerful tool for making sense of complex data, its application in humanities and peace and conflict resolution research presents unique challenges that stretch beyond traditional data representation - information design in this context must not only reveal patterns in data but also acknowledge the underlying real human experiences and complex social dynamics that are being represented in data form.

Visualization can transform how viewers understand complex information by triggering questions that would remain hidden in traditional close-reading techniques [22]. Grouping, structuring, categorizing, and depicting the data through visual means helps the user to quickly grasp crucial information about the

© The Author(s), under exclusive license to Springer Nature Switzerland AG 2025
M. Schrepp (Ed.): HCII 2025, LNCS 15794, pp. 43–62, 2025.
https://doi.org/10.1007/978-3-031-93221-2_3

dataset. Moreover, using Human Computer Interaction (HCI) and Information Design principles [27,28,35] to allow the user to interact with the visualization, and thus explore the data at different levels of granularity, provides an in-depth understanding of the data. All of these aspects can greatly increase the effectiveness and speed of evidence-based policy making.

Furthermore, communication of research findings regarding peace and conflict resolution through interactive visual interfaces (dashboards, maps, etc.) can be more engaging than text-based reports, and, it can prompt new discussions as well as interdisciplinary collaborations [4,24].

The Peace & Conflict Resolution Evidence Platform (PeaceRep)[1] addresses this challenge by collecting and analyzing peace agreements and local perceptions data. As an interdisciplinary team spanning political science, law, international relations, data science, and information visualization, we develop what we refer to as 'PeaceTech' tools: data-driven visual interfaces that use digital innovation to support peacebuilding practices [4]. The interactive interfaces must be accessible and timely, addressing the specific needs of policymakers and peace researchers.

This paper outlines how information design principles can be effectively applied to develop PeaceTech tools to support and enhance the decision-making process in complex peace processes. First, we discuss the theoretical foundations that inform the key methodologies used in our work. We then describe a variety interfaces we have developed, examine their impact, and highlight challenges faced both in development and by our users. Finally, we discuss how similar approaches can be leveraged across different disciplines and domains where complex data must inform critical decisions.

2 Theoretical Foundations and Design Principles

This section outlines how Information Visualization plays a role in research across disciplines, and how Information Design Principles and User-Centered Design are crucial for the effective design and development of visualization interfaces.

2.1 Information Visualization

Information visualization is directly linked to the fundamental principles of human cognition and perception. Research in cognitive psychology has established that human short-term memory has limited capacity, with the 'pictorial superiority effect' demonstrating superior recall for visual information compared to textual information [25]. Visual representations are powerful mechanisms for organizing and understanding complex data [27], taking advantage of the human visual system and its pattern recognition properties [23]. The sheer scale of this

---

[1] https://peacerep.org/ (accessed 30 January 2025).

ability can best be seen in the Zooniverse project[2] where over 2.5 million volunteers help researchers to look for patterns in their data. Information visualization takes advantage of this extraordinary visual processing capability and uses 'computer-supported, interactive, visual representations of abstract data to amplify cognition' [10]. The user of visualization can immediately see patterns in graphs, maps, charts, network diagrams, etc., and ask questions that would be time-consuming or impossible to ask by studying the same information represented in a textual or tabular form.

The impact of visualization extends across disciplines, including geography [20], biophysics [3], cultural heritage [26], library studies [8] or engineering [16]. In peace and conflict studies, visualization can help identify patterns of discrimination, understand stakeholder motivations, and track conflict evolution [4]. In peace and conflict resolution practice, visualizations can help mediators identify stakeholders' needs and interests and enhance negotiation effectiveness [4]. For policy-makers specifically, visual representations have demonstrated greater effectiveness in communicating research findings compared to traditional text-based reports [24]. However, for a visualization to be useful and effective for any type of user, it needs to adhere to Information Design Principles.

2.2 Information Design Principles

The so-called Gestalt theory [40] - a study of perception as a whole rather than just its parts - provides crucial insights for information design. Key principles such as proximity and similarity can be strategically leveraged to communicate relationships between concepts and ideas [17]. This understanding enables designers to create clear visual hierarchies while ensuring that unrelated elements remain visually distinct. The theory emphasizes the importance of contrast in distinguishing elements from their background, highlighting that visibility is fundamental to comprehension [15].

While no universal rubric guarantees design effectiveness, several fundamental principles guide the development of information systems. The principle of 'details-on-demand' allows users to access additional information selectively by preventing cognitive overload while maintaining access to deeper analysis. This approach particularly serves diverse user groups with varying information needs and expertise levels [34].

Cultural considerations significantly influence information design, especially in international contexts. While visualizations can transcend language barriers, research shows that cultural differences affect the interpretation of visual elements, color meanings, and information hierarchy [2,13,30,32]. These considerations become particularly crucial in peacebuilding contexts, where stakeholders often come from diverse cultural backgrounds [5]. For an effective design, knowing the user and tailoring features to their needs is critical - this is further outlined in the following section.

---

[2] https://www.zooniverse.org/ (accessed 30 January 2025).

2.3   User-Centered Design Approaches

An effective visualization design directly depends on multiple factors related to the end user. For example, users' visual and data literacy levels [9,14] play a crucial role, which has led to the development of approaches that support users with different literacy levels, for example, using scrollytelling [33,37]. The effectiveness of these tools also depends on their alignment with user needs and contexts. User-centered design methods ensure that tools serve their intended audiences effectively [1]. Early user testing can identify potential issues with clarity and comprehension [29], while ongoing engagement through observations, interviews, and workshops ensures continued effectiveness [28]. Petterson proposes a key principle of 'it depends' [27] which emphasizes that optimal design approaches vary based on specific contexts and user needs. This principle re-iterates the importance of understanding both the problem space and the user requirements when developing any visualization solutions.

3   Design and Development Approaches

This section outlines our approaches to data gathering, as well as our design and development process, which are guided by the theoretical foundations and design principles outlined in Sect. 2.

3.1   Data Strategy and Quality Assurance

Data Source Selection. Our data strategy prioritizes reliability, interoperability, and sustainability to support evidence-based visualization. Working primarily with our PA-X Peace Agreements Database [6], we follow FAIR principles (Findability, Accessibility, Interoperability, Reusability) [41] for both internal and external data sources. Our data selection process includes (a) validation to ensure temporal and geographic coverage; (b) evaluation of sustainable data updates via APIs or updated files; (c) source transparency through documentation and inclusion criteria; and (d) assessing potential biases or limitations in the data.

Data Processing Pipeline. The PA-X Peace Agreements Database [6] employs a four-stage pipeline to transform peace agreement documents into structured data. The process begins with translation by regional experts who ensure contextual accuracy, followed by document transcription. Expert coders then analyze the content across more than 250 thematic categories before the final database entry. Throughout each stage, specialized expertise ensures consistent and reliable data transformation, providing a robust foundation for our visualization tools.

3.2   Project Initiation and Requirements Gathering

The initiation of our PeaceTech tools occurs within specific practical constraints that shape our development approach. There are a range of gaps, priorities, stakeholders, and users to consider when developing tools that inform decisions related to peace and conflict resolution. As an academic research program, our projects are typically funded through research grants with defined deliverables/outputs within specific time frames. This creates a dual necessity: meeting rigorous academic standards while delivering practical tools for our stakeholders and intended users within strict funding cycles.

End-User Engagement. We engage with our stakeholders through (a) internal expert consultation to understand data needs and usage patterns, (b) show-and-tell sessions during inception phases to validate proposed approaches, (c) regular feedback loops with the broader research team, and (d) collaboration with Information Services (IS) for technical deployment feasibility. Through these engagements, we develop detailed user 'personas' representing our primary user groups: policy makers, peace practitioners, and academic researchers.

Each persona details relevant aspects of their (1) role and responsibilities in peace and conflict resolution, (2) primary needs, goals, and motivations for such a tool, (3) technical capabilities and limitations, (4) typical time constraints and ways of working, and (5) key pain points with existing tools and information/data access processes. We create scenarios that describe how these different personas might interact with the tool and map their user journey to identify critical interaction points.

Requirements Prioritization. Using the MoSCoW method [21], we prioritize requirements and features informed by end-user engagement, as **M**ust, **S**hould, **C**ould, or **W**on't haves to maintain project feasibility within time and resource constraints. The Must Have requirements form our minimum viable product, which undergoes iterative validation with domain experts to ensure core functionalities meet diverse stakeholder needs.

Visualization Prototyping. Whether the visual interface aims to present particular research outcomes, or, allow open-ended exploration of the data, the initial step always involves sketching and ideation. Using methods such as FDS (Five Design Sheets) [31], we identify core fields in our dataset and sketch potential visual representations of these variables. Once settled on the core visualization techniques, we focus on the interface design using tools such as Figma[3] or Miro[4]. Continuous discussions involve aspects such as the overall layout, interactivity, and functionality of the interface. To quickly examine the data for key

---

[3] https://www.figma.com/ (accessed 30 January 2025).

[4] https://miro.com/ (accessed 30 January 2025).

trends and patterns, we also use off-the-shelf visualization tools such as Tableau[5] or PowerBI[6]. These help direct the overall focus of the interface.

3.3 Development

Technical Implementation. Despite interfaces for developing custom-built visualizations 'from scratch' exist, for example, Processing[7], they require specialized Integrated Development Environments (IDE) which hampers accessibility. In order to allow our interfaces to be as accessible as possible, our custom-built visualizations are web-based. The core of our interfaces is built using the front-end component-based framework Svelte[8], which allows easy integration of core JavaScript libraries to visually depict our data. In order to achieve maximum flexibility in the customization of our visual interfaces, we use D3.js, a JavaScript library that allows binding of data to HTML elements and manipulating the entire Document Object Model[9]. As the vast majority of our data contains geospatial information, we also use Mapbox GL[10], a JavaScript library that focuses on map-based web applications. Again, at this part of the process, we discuss the layout, functionality, and usability of the interface with researchers within our interdisciplinary team, which helps to critically inform the overall design.

Evaluation and Iteration. The final stage of the design and development process involves interface testing with targeted users, ranging from informal trials with internal domain experts to formal engagements with Intergovernmental Organizations and government stakeholders. At the 2024 Conflict Research Society (CRS) conference in Edinburgh, we conducted a structured workshop with researchers, UN representatives, and policy makers to evaluate our visualization interfaces. Through hands-on demonstrations, group discussions, and questionnaires, participants provided critical feedback on functionality, accessibility, and usability, which informed both existing and in-development tools.

4   Case Studies

The outcomes of the design and development process described above are demonstrated through three visualization interfaces that support different aspects of peace process analysis and decision-making. Even though these three tools are not comprehensive of our suite of PeaceTech interfaces, they provide insights into how our iterative, user-centered methodology translates into practical tools that serve distinct user needs while maintaining core principles of accessibility

---

[5] https://www.tableau.com/en-gb.

[6] https://www.microsoft.com/en-us/power-platform/products/power-bi (accessed 30 January 2025).

[7] https://processing.org/ (accessed 30 January 2025).

[8] https://svelte.dev/ (accessed 30 January 2025).

[9] https://d3js.org/ (accessed 30 January 2025).

[10] https://docs.mapbox.com/mapbox-gl-js/guides (accessed 30 January 2025).

and analytical rigor. Each case demonstrates different aspects of our methodology approaches outlined in Sect. 3: the Messy Timeline illustrates innovative visualization of complex processes, the PA-X Tracker shows iterative platform development, and the PA-X Tracker Globe exemplifies responsive design based on user feedback.

4.1 Messy Timeline

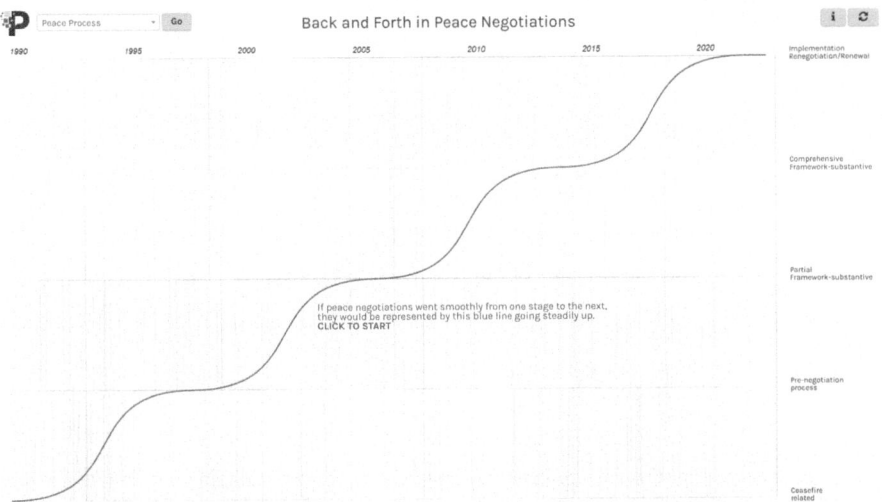

Fig. 1. Ideal trajectory of peace negotiations.

Peace and transition processes are often misunderstood as linear/upward progressions, leading practitioners and those experiencing a peace and transition process to set unrealistic expectations. The 'Messy Timeline' is a custom visualization designed to challenge these traditional assumptions by explicitly visualizing their inherent complexity. The web-based interface contrasts 'idealized' trajectories of how people assume a peace and transition process to progress over time. This is shown in Fig. 1 - a slow and direct incline from signing a ceasefire, to having talks on the negotiations and process, a comprehensive agreement to resolve substantive conflict issues, followed by implementation of these commitments. However, when we draw on the 170 peace processes in the PA-X database in this same format, the results showcase the reality of the processes: they are complex, non-linear, and 'messy' (see Fig. 2).

The interface allows users to select and study one process at a time. For example, in Fig. 3 the Philippines-Mindano process is selected, and one can see the back-and-forth nature of the peace process over time. The contrast between idealized and actual trajectories serves as a critical pedagogical tool, helping

Fig. 2. Messy and complex nature of peace negotiations in reality.

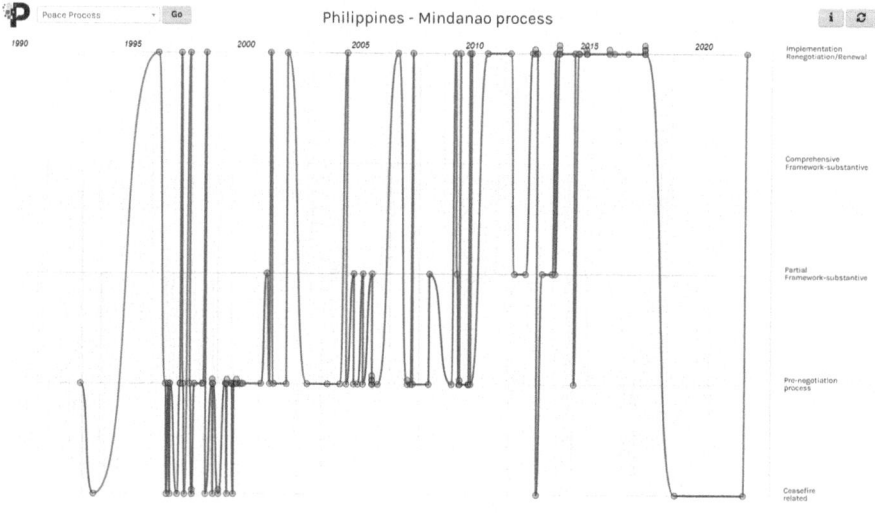

Fig. 3. Philippines-Mindanao peace process trajectory.

international mediators, donors, and practitioners develop more realistic expectations about process dynamics. User feedback, particularly from users that are experiencing a peace and transition process, indicates that the visualization provides reassurance that progress does not look the same everywhere. Complex, seemingly 'messy' process trajectories are in fact the norm.

The messy timeline has been iteratively updated and improved. It was first designed in 2019 (v4 of PA-X) and now showcases data released in 2024 (v8).

The longevity of this visualization showcases the need for reliable and stable data updates with no changes to the data model to ensure easy updates. Additionally, it showcases how open-source code and good documentation allow continuous updates and iterative improvements. The design tweaks incorporated user feedback, including (a) a button to switch between the ideal process view and the messy reality view, allowing to quickly compare and contrast the two realms, (b) responsiveness to the screen size, which expanded the usability across different devices and eliminated unnecessary blank space, and (c) a more robust peace process search, replacing the previous need to know the name of the peace process.

4.2 PA-X Tracker

The PA-X Tracker demonstrates how our iterative design process responds to complex user needs while maintaining sustainability. Development was driven by three distinct user scenarios identified through stakeholder engagement: in-country teams requiring rapid context absorption, those monitoring processes who require reliable tracking mechanisms, and researchers seeking comparative analysis capabilities.

Following our data-first approach outlined in Sect. 3, we prioritized sustainable data integration over novel visualizations. This decision reflected both user priorities and practical constraints. Through engagement with domain experts, we mapped existing data sources against criteria including update frequency, accessibility, and coverage of key peace dimensions. This systematic approach enabled us to create a sustainable platform that evolves with ongoing processes.

The platform's architecture reflects our commitment to iterative development. We chose readily available visualization tools like PowerBI, Knightlab Timeline[11], and Kumu[12]. The combination of these off-the-shelf tools provided rapid deployment to test with key users, creating an immediate feedback loop between technical implementation and user evaluation, as discussed in Sect. 3.3. These engagements showed that the off-the-shelf visualization tools were sufficient to meet their needs - their main priority was representative data from the context they worked in, depicted using simple charts with which they were familiar.

The resulting interface provides multiple entry points to peace process data to cater to our different user scenarios, from interactive timelines of formal institutional events to dashboards showing process overviews and implementation indicators across security, political, and economic dimensions. Users can contextualize a peace agreement being signed in the context, including conflict-levels surrounding agreements, and indicators to show how things are going across security, politics, economy, and humanitarian issues in the country. Additionally, we provide actor networks of parties and mediators to the agreements, to provide users with a thorough understanding of who has been involved in the

---

[11] https://timeline.knightlab.com/ (accessed 30 January 2025).
[12] https://kumu.io/ (accessed 30 January 2025).

processes historically, and use this to try and find entry points into new dialogue processes. Where possible, we also incorporate our local data collections to bridge the gap between large institutionalized datasets that record at the country level, and the reality of what is happening on the ground. See Fig. 4 for an example of the components available on a country profile.

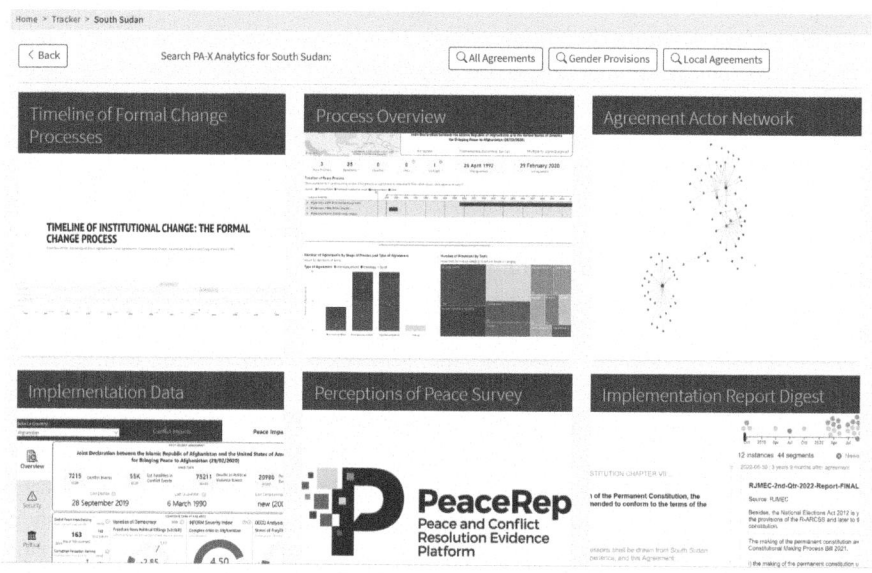

Fig. 4. South Sudan profile on the PA-X Tracker.

We have had a plethora of end-user engagements and we are continuously engaging with others to gain feedback and alternative perspectives to incorporate into the platform. This may be in the form of data to include or new features to implement. A key part of user feedback was to get access to a live global view of key data indicators that would showcase the data and provide textual summaries that update regularly. Furthermore, users indicated an interest in a quick-loading mobile-friendly interface, as they frequently need quick access to information via mobile devices in low-connectivity areas, a technically difficult task to implement due to vast amounts of underlying data. Therefore, we began developing a new PeaceTech tool that would bridge the already existing Tracker through a mobile-friendly interface outlined below.

4.3 PA-X Tracker Globe

While the PA-X Tracker provides deep analytical capabilities and easy access to a range of data indicators, users identified a need for rapid, global situational awareness. The PA-X Tracker Globe[13] provides a novel entry point into the suite

---

[13] https://peacerep.github.io/tracker_globe/ (accessed 30 January 2025).

of PeaceTech tools within the PA-X Tracker. The globe displays where formal peace agreements have been signed in the past year, alongside the number of estimated conflict-related fatalities recorded per country in the Uppsala Data Conflict Program (UCDP) Database [36].

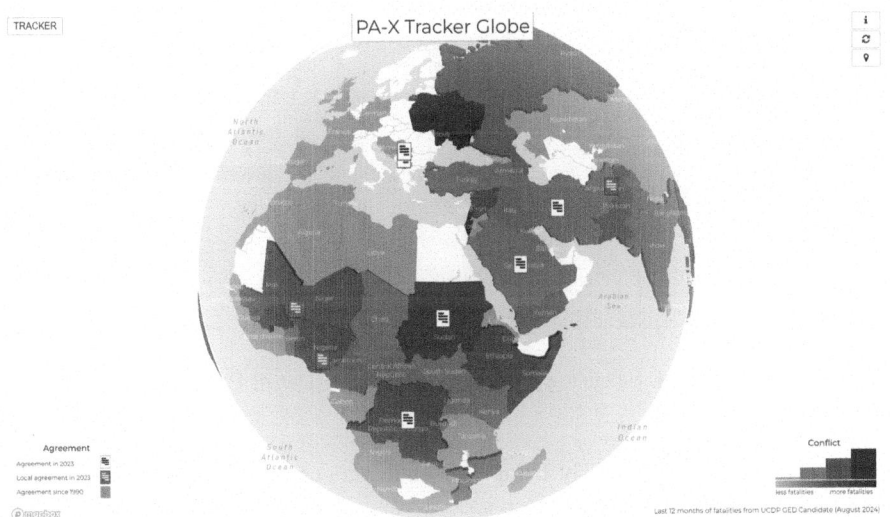

Fig. 5. PA-X Globe Tracker Overview.

The map uses a color gradient and polygon height to visually represent fatality levels. Countries with more fatalities are shaded in darker red and their corresponding country polygons protrude more. The interface allows users to obtain a current view of both conflict and peace processes on a global scale. Interacting with the visualization allows users to identify where fatality rates are high over the last 12 months, and quickly compare them across the globe. Users can select a specific country and access relevant updates on various indicators related to the peace process, including conflict levels and humanitarian issues. The platform consolidates insights from multiple data providers, offering a comprehensive overview of historical and current indicators in short text overviews that can be easily copied into reports. Users can also directly access specific PA-X Tracker components for the particular country, including timelines, actor networks, and dashboards (see Fig. 4).

The PA-X Tracker Globe is designed for a wide audience, including inter/national mediators, peacebuilding researchers, policymakers, and anyone interested in monitoring and understanding contemporary peace and transition processes. The data displayed on the map are updated monthly, ensuring that users have access to the most current information to track and monitor levels of conflict and formal peace processes. With key users in mind, the map is designed to be mobile-friendly to enable quick access to key information on any device.

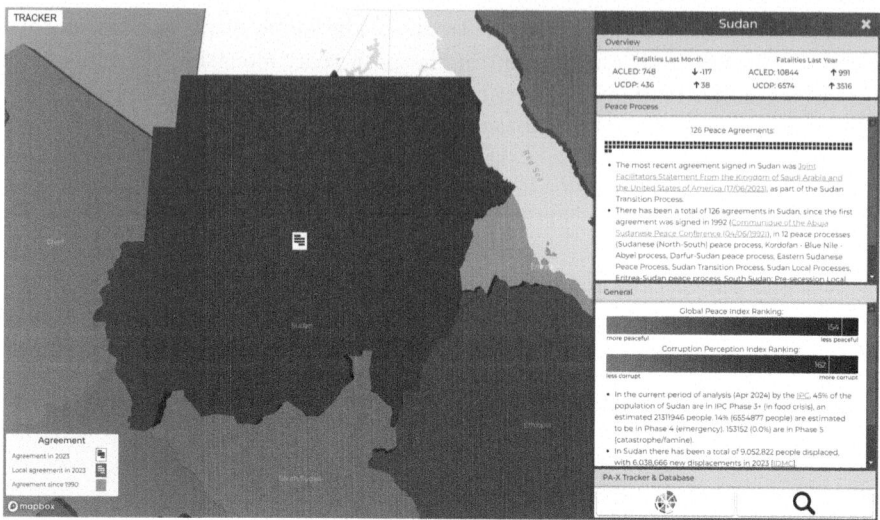

Fig. 6. Selecting a country (Sudan) + Detail Panel.

This feature came directly from user engagement and feedback from which we learned about the need to get a global view of where conflict is getting bad and where there are existing formal peace processes. Key features that directly respond to user needs are the textual summaries - although visualizations convey key trends and information better than text-based reports, details on demand is one of the core visualization principles [35] and this application provides both visual cues of key information (conflict levels and peace agreements signed) and detailed textual summaries of the data indicators. Furthermore, users who mainly work with text-based reports or those who are writing their own and want to quickly copy and paste the data summaries, can easily do so.

4.4   Integrated Support for Decision-Making

These three tools work together to support different aspects of peace process decision-making. The Messy Timeline helps stakeholders develop realistic process expectations, the PA-X Tracker provides deep analytical capabilities, and the Globe Tracker offers rapid situational awareness. Together, they demonstrate how iterative, user-centered design can create practical tools that enhance peace process understanding and decision-making.

Our experience developing these tools reveals the importance of balancing innovation with sustainability, user needs with technical constraints, and visual with textual information. The evolution from a one-off timeline visualization to an integrated global monitoring platform shows how continued user engagement shapes tool development while maintaining focus on core decision-support functions. The insights we gained from the design processes and from user engage-

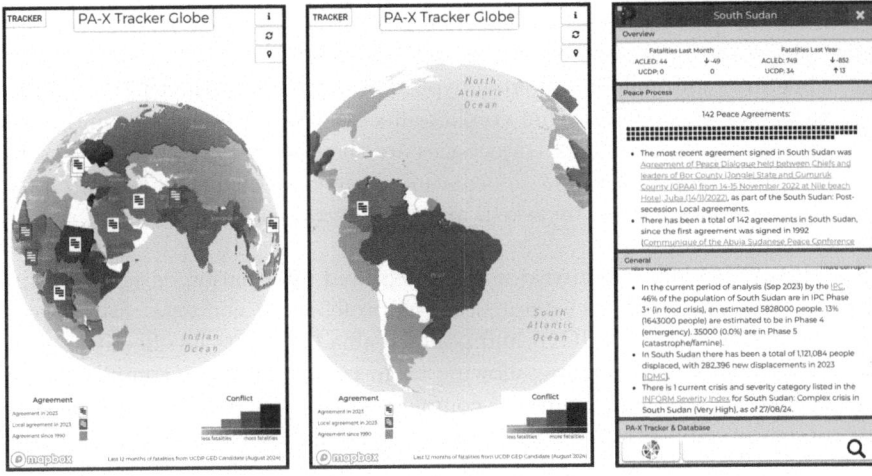

Fig. 7. PA-X Tracker Globe Mobile View.

ment have informed a range of other tools we have developed[14]. For example, 'scrollytelling' data interface[15] evolved directly from user engagement. This interface guides users through complex data gradually, combining visualizations with explanatory text to highlight key trends identified by expert researchers. By progressively introducing and explaining visualizations, the interface helps users with limited visualization experience understand complex peace process phenomena. This example demonstrates how user engagement continues to shape our approach to information design, and how our data, tools, design approaches, and research can be integrated together through visual interfaces to inform those within the field.

5   Impact, Challenges and Broader Applicability

5.1   Impact of PeaceTech Tools

The impact of our PeaceTech visualization tools demonstrates how effective information design can transform complex data into actionable insights for decision makers. Through systematic engagement with users—including peace practitioners, policy makers, and researchers—we have gathered evidence of how different visualization approaches serve their distinct information needs and decision-making contexts.

The Messy Timeline, our longest-running tool outlined in this paper, exemplifies how innovative information design can reshape understanding of complex processes. By challenging conventional linear representations, it has created 'new

---

[14] See https://pax.peaceagreements.org/visualizations/   or   https://peacerep.org/ peacetech-tools/ to explore all tools (accessed 30 January 2025).

[15] https://tvancisin.github.io/peace_scroll/ (accessed 30 January 2025).

ways of seeing' [5] as it has been effective in shifting how stakeholders concep-
tualize processes. Interestingly, the impact has differed depending on the user
type: while international donors often express concern about the lengthy nature
of peace processes, civilians from conflict-affected regions frequently find reassurance in seeing that complex trajectories are the norm rather than the exception [5]. This demonstrates how information design can challenge assumptions,
encourage new questions to be asked, and provide validation, depending on the
context.

The PA-X Tracker demonstrates how integrated information design can support rapid learning and decision-making in professional contexts. Early feedback from those working in IGOs and policy teams highlights its effectiveness in
onboarding new team members, allowing them to quickly grasp complex peace
process contexts through multiple complementary visualization approaches.
This success in supporting both overview and detailed analysis illustrates how
thoughtful information design can address varying levels of user expertise and
different decision-making needs.

With the recent launch of the PA-X Tracker Globe, we are expanding our
evaluation approach to include more diverse user perspectives, particularly from
those directly involved or affected by peace processes. This shift reflects our
commitment to developing information design solutions that not only serve professional decision-makers but also support broader societal understanding and
engagement with peace processes.

Our impact assessment methodology combines informal discussions, structured workshops (such as the workshop outlined in Sect. 3.3), and ongoing user
engagement sessions to understand how these tools support different types of
decision-making. While measuring direct societal impact remains challenging
due to the complex nature of peace processes, user feedback consistently demonstrates how effective information design can make complex data more accessible
and actionable for diverse stakeholders.

5.2   Challenges

Limitations of Off-the-Shelf Tools. Our work leverages several off-the-shelf
tools (PowerBI, Tableau, etc.) due to their accessibility through academic licens-
ing and low barriers to entry. However, they reflect broader tensions between
standardized visualization techniques and humanities methodologies. Traditional
visualizations such as line or bar charts present information definitively, without acknowledging crucial humanities aspects: data constructed-ness, people and
labor behind the visualization, uncertainties, and decisions made with the data
[12]. These aspects all influence how users interpret and engage with the visualization, and yet, they are rarely made visible to provide a more critical understanding of a visualization (see [18] for an example with uncertainty visualization). Geographic visualization tools further compound these challenges by
embedding problematic assumptions about territorial boundaries in disputed
areas. Nevertheless, in certain scenarios, when a visualization needs to be devel-

oped quickly to assess particular trends in the data, off-the-shelf tools still provide valuable insights.

Technical and Accessibility Barriers. A significant challenge for PeaceTech tools is addressing diverse user needs. Language accessibility remains a critical barrier, as most visualization tools predominantly support English and/or other dominant languages, often overlooking local and indigenous languages that are common in the areas we focus on. The development of the Yemen Timeline with its bilingual English-Arabic interface, represents one approach to addressing this limitation, but scaling such solutions across multiple languages and contexts presents ongoing challenges [5].[16] Additionally, many users in conflict-affected areas primarily access information through mobile devices with limited internet connectivity, contrasting sharply with users in Global North academic settings who often present visualizations on large immersive touchscreen devices. PeaceRep's PeaceFem project[17] exemplifies how some of these challenges can be addressed through offline-capable mobile applications available in multiple languages, but again, scaling such a solution up is currently beyond our capabilities.

Ethical Challenges in Data Representation. Varying levels of data literacy among stakeholders, from experienced researchers to local members of a conflict-affected community, necessitates thoughtful approaches to visualization design that not only presents data from different perspectives but also explains how these visualizations are to be read. One such visualization technique we use is the aforementioned scrollytelling, which highlights notable aspects in the data while also explaining what is seen.

Furthermore, working with sensitive information from conflict zones requires careful consideration of how visualization choices might impact ongoing peace processes or potentially affect vulnerable populations. For instance, the granularity of geographic data and visualization in active conflict zones must be balanced against security risks to local communities and peace-building actors. To achieve this, we always try to abide by the principle of 'Do No Harm' [11] and consider the unintended consequences the data or visualization could have.

5.3   Transferable Lessons and Broader Applicability

Information visualization has demonstrated its value across diverse disciplines, with several fields pioneering approaches that inform our work. Interactive visualization atlases, such as the World Bank's Atlas of Sustainable Development[18] and Harvard's Atlas of Economic Complexity[19], showcase how complex data

---

[16] See [5] for more information about the background of the visualization, or access it online https://pax.peaceagreements.org/visualizations/yemen-timeline/ (accessed 30 January 2025).

[17] https://peacerep.org/digital-resources/peacefem/ (accessed 30 January 2025).

[18] https://datatopics.worldbank.org/sdgatlas?lang=en (accessed 30 January 2025).

[19] https://atlas.hks.harvard.edu/ (accessed 30 January 2025).

can be made accessible through thoughtful design. In journalism, the emergence of scrollytelling techniques, exemplified by the New York Times' "Snow Fall: Avalanche at Tunnel Creek"[20], has revolutionized how complex narratives can be interactively communicated.

Building on these innovations while addressing the unique challenges of peace and conflict visualization, our approach offers valuable insights for other domains dealing with complex, sensitive data and diverse user needs. The principles outlined in our methodology (Sect. 3) – structured stakeholder engagement, robust data strategy, and iterative development – provide a framework that can be adapted across fields where decision-making involves multiple stakeholders and complex data interpretation. Our visualization approaches demonstrate potential in several domains, for example:

- **Medical Decision Support**: The Messy Timeline visualization concept could be adapted to represent patient recovery trajectories, showing how 'successful' recovery often involves setbacks and variations, much like peace processes. This could help manage expectations and provide reassurance to patients and healthcare providers alike.
- **Complex Systems Monitoring**: The PA-X Tracker's integration of multiple data sources and visualization types could serve as a model for other monitoring systems. In public health, for example, a similar approach could track disease outbreaks by combining epidemiological data, healthcare capacity indicators, and intervention timelines while providing crucial contextual information.[21]
- **Emergency Response**: The PA-X Tracker Globe's approach to rapid situational awareness which combines visual geographic indicators with accessible text summaries, could be particularly valuable in disaster response or humanitarian emergencies. Its mobile-friendly design and focus on quick comprehension of spatial data could benefit field-based decision-makers across various sectors.

These applications are particularly relevant in contexts that share key characteristics with peace processes: complex decision-making environments, sensitive data, varying levels of technical expertise among users, and the need for both rapid assessment and deep analysis. The success of our visualization approaches in the challenging context of peace and conflict studies suggests their potential value in any field where stakeholders must navigate complex, non-linear processes while maintaining awareness of broader contextual factors.

---

[20] https://www.nytimes.com/projects/2012/snow-fall/index.html#/?part=tunnel-creek (accessed 30 January 2025).

[21] See PeaceRep's Ceasefire's in a time of Covid-19 Tracker, which combines peace agreement and Covid-19 infection data: https://pax.peaceagreements.org/covid19ceasefires/ (accessed 30 January 2025).

5.4   Future Directions

Our future work focuses on addressing the challenges outlined in Sect. 5.2 through several key initiatives. Enhanced user-focused research through longitudinal studies and participatory design sessions will inform our development of visualization frameworks that better represent competing narratives while remaining culturally sensitive. To improve accessibility, we are exploring progressive web applications with offline-first architectures that function across different devices and connectivity levels. We aim to diversify our user base and data collection by increasing engagement with stakeholders in the Global South as well as with the general public, while also expanding our language offerings. Additionally, we aim to develop a provenance-driven visualization that reveals the entire data transformation process from peace agreement collection to visualization, including the human labor and expertise involved. Building on previous research [38,39], we hope this approach will promote transparency and critical understanding of peace and conflict research in the digital age. We are committed to making our methodologies reusable through our Lab[22] and GitHub repository[23], with plans to develop low-code web applications that allow users to easily adapt our visualization and data approaches.

6   Conclusion

This paper demonstrates how thoughtful information design and visualization can support complex decision-making in challenging contexts. Through our work in peace and conflict visualization, we have shown that effective information design must go beyond data presentation to address specific user needs, constraints, and cultural contexts. The success of tools like the Messy Timeline in challenging conventional assumptions, and the PA-X Tracker in supporting diverse user needs, illustrates how visualization can reshape understanding and facilitate critically informed decisions in high-stakes environments.

Our experience developing these tools highlights three key principles for information design: (1) the importance of sustained user engagement in shaping both tool functionality and visual presentation; (2) the need to balance accessibility with analytical depth; and (3) the value of combining different visualization approaches to serve diverse user needs and contexts. These insights, while developed in the context of peace and conflict studies, offer valuable lessons for information design across sectors, from healthcare to legal services, where complex data must inform critical and far-reaching decisions.

As information visualization continues to evolve, our work underscores the importance of developing tools that not only present data effectively, but also acknowledge the human processes behind data creation and use. This approach to information design, grounded in user needs and ethical considerations, offers a framework for creating visualization tools that are not just technically sophisticated but genuinely useful for decision-making in complex real-world contexts.

---

[22] https://peacerep.org/peacelab/ (accessed 30 January 2025).
[23] https://github.com/peacerep (accessed 30 January 2025).

Acknowledgements. This research is supported by the Peace and Conflict Resolution Evidence Platform (PeaceRep), building on the work of the Political Settlements Research Programme, funded by UK International Development from the UK government. However, the views expressed are those of the author and do not necessarily reflect the UK government's official policies. Any use of this work should acknowledge the author and the Peace and Conflict Resolution Evidence Platform.

Special thanks are due to the Edinburgh PeaceRep team for all their contributions that we discuss in this paper - in particular; Christine Bell, Sanja Badanjak, Benjamin Bach, Jinrui Wang, Tobias Kauer and Tim Epple for their roles in these projects.

References

1. Abras, C., Maloney-Krichmar, D., Preece, J., et al.: User-centered design. In: Bainbridge, W. (ed.) Encyclopedia of Human-Computer Interaction, vol. 374, pp. 445–456. Sage Publications, Thousand Oaks (2004)
2. Alebri, M., Rakotondravony, N., Harrison, L.: Design patterns in right-to-left visualizations: the case of arabic content. In: 2024 IEEE Visualization and Visual Analytics (VIS), pp. 251–255 (2024)
3. Anthis, N.J., Clore, G.M.: Visualizing transient dark states by NMR spectroscopy. Q. Rev. Biophys. **48**(1), 35–116 (2015)
4. Bell, C.: PeaceTech: Digital Transformation to End Wars. Springer Nature (2024)
5. Bell, C., Bach, B., Kauer, T.: Ways of seeing: peace process data-viz as a research practice. Convergence **28**(1), 150–169 (2022)
6. Bell, C., Badanjak, S.: Introducing pa-x: a new peace agreement database and dataset. J. Peace Res. **56**(3), 452–466 (2019)
7. Bell, C., et al.: PA-X Codebook, Version 8. Peace and Conflict Resolution Evidence Platform (PeaceRep). University of Edinburgh (2024)
8. Betti, A., Gerrits, D.H., Speckmann, B., Van Den Berg, H.: Glammap: visualising library metadata. In: VALA 2014 17th Biennual Conference and Exhibition, Melbourne, Australia, 3-6 February 2014, pp. 1–15 (2014)
9. Boy, J., Rensink, R.A., Bertini, E., Fekete, J.D.: A principled way of assessing visualization literacy. IEEE Trans. Visual Comput. Graph. **20**(12), 1963–1972 (2014)
10. Card, S.K., Mackinlay, J.D., Shneiderman, B.: Readings in Information Visualization: Using Vision to Think. Morgan Kaufmann Publishers (1999)
11. CDA Collaborative: The do no harm project (2024), https://www.cdacollaborative.org/cdaproject/the-do-no-harm-project/, cDA Collaborative Learning Projects
12. Drucker, J.: Humanities approaches to graphical display. Digital Humanities Q. **5**(1), 1–21 (2011)
13. Fagard, J., Dahmen, R.: The effects of reading-writing direction on the asymmetry of space perception and directional tendencies: a comparison between french and tunisian children. Laterality: Asymmetries Body, Brain Cognition **8**(1), 39–52 (2003)
14. Firat, E.E., Joshi, A., Laramee, R.S.: Interactive visualization literacy: the state-of-the-art. Inf. Vis. **21**(3), 285–310 (2022)
15. Graham, L.: Gestalt theory in interactive media design. J. Humanit. Soc. Sci. **2**(1) (2008)
16. Haber, R.B.: Visualization techniques for engineering mechanics. Comput. Syst. Eng. **1**(1), 37–50 (1990)

17. Holtzblatt, K., Wendell, J.B., Wood, S.: Rapid contextual design: a how-to guide to key techniques for user-centered design. Elsevier (2004)
18. Hullman, J.: Why authors don't visualize uncertainty. IEEE Trans. Visual Comput. Graph. **26**(1), 130–139 (2019)
19. Jackson, T.W., Farzaneh, P.: Theory-based model of factors affecting information overload. Int. J. Inf. Manage. **32**(6), 523–532 (2012)
20. Kapler, T., Wright, W.: Geotime information visualization. Inf. Vis. **4**(2), 136–146 (2005)
21. Kravchenko, T., Bogdanova, T., Shevgunov, T.: Ranking requirements using moscow methodology in practice. In: Computer Science On-line Conference, pp. 188–199. Springer (2022). https://doi.org/10.1007/978-3-031-09073-8_18
22. Moretti, F.: Distant reading, vol. 93. Verso (2013)
23. Munzner, T.: Visualization analysis and design. CRC Press (2014)
24. Nash, K., Trott, V., Allen, W.: The politics of data visualisation and policy making. Convergence **28**(1), 3–12 (2022)
25. Nelson, D.L., Reed, V.S., Walling, J.R.: Pictorial superiority effect. J. Exper. Psychol. Hum. Learn. Mem. **2**(5), 523 (1976)
26. Osaki, T., Itsubo, S., Kimura, F., Tezuka, T., Maeda, A.: Visualization of relationships among historical persons using locational information. In: Tanaka, K., Fröhlich, P., Kim, K.-S. (eds.) W2GIS 2011. LNCS, vol. 6574, pp. 230–239. Springer, Heidelberg (2011). https://doi.org/10.1007/978-3-642-19173-2_18
27. Pettersson, R.: Information design-principles and guidelines. J. Vis. Literacy **29**(2), 167–182 (2010)
28. Preece, J., Rogers, Y., Sharp, H.: Interaction Design. Inc, Beyond Human-Computer Interaction. John Wiley & Sons (2002)
29. Quispel, A., Maes, A., Schilperoord, J.: Aesthetics and clarity in information visualization: the designer's perspective. In: Arts. vol. 7, p. 72. MDPI (2018)
30. Reinecke, K., Bernstein, A.: Knowing what a user likes: a design science approach to interfaces that automatically adapt to culture. Mis Q., 427–453 (2013)
31. Roberts, J.C., Headleand, C., Ritsos, P.D.: Sketching designs using the five design-sheet methodology. IEEE Trans. Visual Comput. Graph. **22**(1), 419–428 (2016)
32. Salmerón, L., Abu Mallouh, R., Kammerer, Y.: Location of navigation menus in websites: an experimental study with Arabic users. Univ. Access Inf. Soc. **16**, 191–196 (2017)
33. Shander, B.: The past, present, and future of scrollytelling. Nightingale **15**, 2023 (2020)
34. Shneiderman, B.: The eyes have it: a task by data type taxonomy for information visualizations. In: The Craft of Information Visualization, pp. 364–371. Elsevier (2003)
35. Shneiderman, B., Plaisant, C., Cohen, M., Jacobs, S., Elmqvist, N., Diakopoulos, N.: Designing the User Interface: Strategies for Effective Human-Computer Interaction. Pearson (2016)
36. Sundberg, R., Melander, E.: Introducing the ucdp georeferenced event dataset. J. Peace Res. **50**(4), 523–532 (2013)
37. Tjärnhage, A., Söderström, U., Norberg, O., Andersson, M., Mejtoft, T.: The impact of scrollytelling on the reading experience of long-form journalism. In: Proceedings of the European Conference on Cognitive Ergonomics 2023, pp. 1–9 (2023)
38. Vancisin, T., Clarke, L., Orr, M., Hinrichs, U.: Provenance visualization: Tracing people, processes, and practices through a data-driven approach to provenance. Digital Scholarsh. Humanit. **38**(3), 1322–1339 (2023)

39. Vancisin, T., Orr, M., Hinrichs, U.: Externalizing transformations of historical documents: opportunities for provenance-driven visualization. In: 2020 IEEE 5th Workshop on Visualization for the Digital Humanities (VIS4DH), pp. 36–42 (2020)
40. Wertheimer, M.: Gestalt theory (1938)
41. Wilkinson, M.D., et al.: The fair guiding principles for scientific data management and stewardship. Sci. Data **3**(1), 1–9 (2016)

Mapping Nordic Design Policy Evolution: A Visual Analytics Approach to Governance Transitions

Wenjing Li[✉] [iD], Yan Zhang[iD], and Rui Wang[iD]

Art and Design Academy, Beijing City University, Beijing, China
l.w.j@hotmail.com

Abstract. This paper uses visual analysis to examine the evolution and governance transformation of Nordic design policy. Emerging in the middle of 1990s, Nordic design policy has progressed through three key stages, emphasizing sustainability, inclusivity, cross-sector collaboration, and policy integration. By analyzing policy documents from 1995 to 2024 and leveraging visualization tools such as Sankey diagrams and timelines, the study reveals key trends: design has shifted from being a policy goal to a foundational method for policymaking; implicit policies have gained dominance after 2015; and design has increasingly integrated into broader innovation ecosystems. These changes highlight a transition in Nordic policy design from targeted interventions to a systemic innovation framework, offering valuable insights for the development of global design policies.

Keywords: Nordic Design Policy · Governance Transitions · Visual Analytics

1 Introduction

1.1 Foundations: Emergence of Nordic Design Policy (1990s)

Within the framework of global design history, Nordic design is commonly defined as the design styles that emerged in Nordic countries, particularly Denmark, Finland, and Sweden during World War II. Scandinavian design functionalism draws inspiration from movements such as De Stijl, Futurism, the Bauhaus, and Dadaism, shaping a unique style that organically combines traditional design philosophies harmonizing with nature and modern functionalism, resulting in a clean and minimalist aesthetic. Sustainability serves as a key goal in the design process. Besides, each Nordic country values its regional characteristics and traditional craftsmanship, which are essential elements in shaping the unique identities of their designs. Throughout the years, high quality and organic modernism have become hallmarks of Nordic products in the global market.

The United Kingdom was the first country to make design a core element of its national policy. This initiative has been part of a broader effort by the British government, research institutions, and industries since the mid-19th century to promote public awareness of design and build a national identity. Design has been seen as a crucial tool for driving economic growth and addressing social issues, and British design policies became a model for many European countries to follow. As of 2015, 15 of the 28 European Member States had design included in national innovation policy (Anna Whicher 2017). Specifically, in Nordic countries, Denmark has had a design policy since 1997, including three successive strategies with *Design Denmark* in place from 2007 to 2010, and then the Danish Government published the *Vision for Danish Design 2020* in 2011 (Antonius H.& van den Broek 2012). Finland was the first country to adopt the concept of a Design Ecosystem to inform its design policy in 2013 (Ministry of Employment and the Economy, 2013). The Swedish government also mentioned how design would influence the future of architecture as early as 1997 in its action *plan Future - Architecture, Design and Design*, while the Norwegian government enacted *Norway Universally Designed by 2025* in 2008 to improve the country's infrastructure in all sectors through universal design. Iceland's national design strategy started later than the other Nordic countries, with *Design as a driver for future 2014–2018*, its first national design policy, published in 2014.

1.2 Three-Phase Evolution: Sustainability, Accessibility, and Systemic Integration

If we categorize the Nordic design policies of the past years into distinct phases, they would be as follows:

1995–2004: Continued Focus on Sustainability and Early Regional Cooperation in Design Policy. During this period, the Nordic countries began to actively craft national design policies aimed at bolstering soft power, shaping national identities, and prioritizing green design and energy efficiency, particularly in urban development. Given their geographical and climatic conditions, these nations were early adopters of sustainability-focused initiatives. For example, since the mid-1990s, the Swedish government has collaborated with the construction industry to develop strategies for eco-sustainable building, with the goal of reducing construction-related waste by 50% by 2000 (Martti Lujanen 2004).

Representing the governments of the five Nordic countries, the Nordic Council of Ministers established Nordregio in July 1997. It was formed through the consolidation of three former Nordic institutions: NordREFO (The Nordic Institute for Regional Policy Research, established in 1967), Nordplan (The Nordic Institute for Studies in Urban and Regional Planning, established in 1968), and NOGRAN (The Nordic Group for Regional Analysis, established in 1979). As a research center, Nordregio aims to integrate research resources across the Nordic region and conduct studies in areas such as green innovation, sustainable development, urban planning, socioeconomic issues, and climate change, while also promoting policy cooperation between Nordic countries.

2005–2014: Access for All. During this period, the design policies of Nordic countries shifted from advocacy to actionable plans. For example, in the area of sustainable cities and buildings, the regulations were refined to include specific rules on building materials, such as defining and restricting the content and quality of building materials, and requiring the use of building materials containing recycled resources in buildings Linda (Høibye and Henrik Sand 2018).

More importantly, Nordic design policies placed a strong emphasis on the concepts of Universal Design, Inclusive Design, and Design for All during this period. In Norway, the Ministry of Children, Equality, and Social Inclusion launched its first Action Plan (2009–2013) with the goal of achieving a universally designed Norway by 2025. The plan stated, "The Government's work is based on universal design. Universal design is an expression of the value society places on equality." (Norway universally designed by 2025). This concept was first introduced on December 3, 2001, when the European Commission, in collaboration with the European Disability Forum, made it the theme of a conference. The concept of "Design for All" was presented as an approach to making the world more accessible to people with disabilities. Additionally, during the Oslo Conference in 2012, the Nordic Council of Ministers formulated the Nordic Charter for Universal Design. In Finland, the concept of design for all is promoted through the methodology of service design. In the design policy updated by Finland's Ministry of Economic Affairs and Employment in 2013, service design was explicitly identified as a core tool for innovation in the public sector (Finnish Design Policy, 2013).

Access for All is not just about designing something, architecture, or decoration. The clarity of this concept in policy means that the focus of design policy has shifted from the design itself to a broader perspective, aiming to achieve the participation and empowerment of all people through design and provide sustainable solutions for the future.

2015–2024:Cross-departmental Collaboration and Policy Integration. There is a trend toward policy integration, where complex societal problems are addressed by higher-level institutions through policy direction and cross-disciplinary cooperation. Specific design challenges, on the other hand, are tackled by public innovation labs, which are themselves undergoing digital transformation.

The Nordic Council has developed an action plan for 2021–2024 within the framework of Vision 2030. It established an expert group made up of representatives from ministries and youth organizations in the Nordic countries, with close ties to national efforts on sustainable development. The plan states that "the Council of Ministers will implement initiatives to support and strengthen interdisciplinary work on sustainable development across all its sectors." Additionally, Denmark launched the Demand and User-Driven Innovation Policy in 2017, which involves 17 industry sectors and aims to develop a national design policy through interdisciplinary cooperation.

Moreover, public labs are undergoing digital transformation to help government departments shift from traditional management models to more digital-centric approaches. For example, the Icelandic government established the Digital Iceland Digital Innovation Lab in 2018 to assist public agencies in improving their digital services.

1.3 Summary of Nordic Design Policy

In the context of New Public Management (NPM) in the late 1990s, the capacity to design and steer policies became limited as states increasingly outsourced the delivery of public services to the private sector and civil society (Mukherjee, Coban, & Bali 2021). Nordic design policy has also exhibited several key trends:

First, design has shifted from being merely the subject of policymaking to becoming a foundational approach for policy development. Design thinking has emerged as a widely adopted practice for guiding policymaking.

Second, design policy can be seen as a blend of explicit and implicit elements. Explicit design policy refers to the formal integration of design into national policies, while implicit design policy is reflected in initiatives such as design support projects, design centers, design awards, and other promotional activities. Together, these elements form the broader design policy.

Third, design is an integral part of the innovation system. While it is considered a key area, it does not function in isolation. It is interdependent and interacts with other components. The degree to which design is understood and adopted is influenced by various related systems, meaning that design policy must be developed with careful attention to the balance and coordination between design and other elements.

2 Data and Methodology

2.1 Visualization Methods and Policy Analysis

Visual analysis presents data through graphics and charts, helping users quickly identify patterns, trends, and relationships. In policy research, time-series visualization effectively tracks policy evolution by mapping indicators like policy announcement frequency or keyword usage over years. For example, a line chart plotting design policy keywords (vertical axis) against time (horizontal axis) can visually show how terms like "sustainable design" gained prominence after 2015.

Word clouds simplify theme identification in policy documents. High-frequency words (e.g., "innovation") appear bold and large, while less common terms fade into the background, offering instant visual focus.

Network diagrams clarify policy relationships: Node-link maps use connected circles to show interactions between policymakers and stakeholders. Co-occurrence graphs reveal conceptual links by connecting words that frequently appear together, with thicker lines indicating stronger associations.

Tree diagrams organize policy hierarchies. In Nordic design frameworks, national strategies form the root, while local implementation plans branch out as sub-nodes, illustrating how broad goals translate to actionable steps.

2.2 Collection of Nordic Design Policy Texts

The primary data sources are official government websites of Nordic countries, which publish design-related policy documents, reports, and strategic plans.

Key examples include:Finland's National Research and Development Fund (SITRA), Sweden's Ministry of Culture, Denmark's Government Portal, Norway's Ministry of Trade and Industry and etc. These materials directly reflect governmental priorities in design policy.

Supplemental data came from design organizations such as: Finland's National Council for Craft and Design, Sweden's Svensk Form, Denmark's Danish Design Centre and etc. These institutions provide specialized research reports and policy analyses, offering professional insights that enhance official government data. Combined, these sources enable multi-layered analysis of Nordic design policies from both practical and academic perspectives.

Timeframe: Covered 1995–2024 to capture three decades of policy evolution.

Keyword **Search:** Used terms like "design policy," "architectural design policy," and "innovation strategy" across target websites. Keywords were translated into Nordic languages (Swedish, Danish, Icelandic, Norwegian, Finnish) to ensure comprehensive coverage.

Screening: Removed duplicates, irrelevant content (e.g., general news), and incomplete documents. Retained materials underwent detailed evaluation.

Dataset **Compilation:** Final collection includes:

- National strategies (e.g., Finland's Design 2005! Denmark's Danish *Design Policy 4th Edition*)
- Local regulations (e.g., Sweden's architectural design preservation guidelines)
- Sector-specific policies (e.g., Denmark's energy-efficient design standards, Iceland's tourism design initiatives)

Each document was cataloged with metadata: source URL, publication date, document type (policy regulation/research report/strategic plan), and design field (architecture/industrial/graphic/sustainable design). This systematic indexing streamlines data retrieval during analysis.

2.3 Categorization of Nordic Design Policies

The analysis divides Nordic design policies into three chronological periods based on publication dates: 1995–2004, 2005–2014, and 2015–2024. This temporal framework clarifies the policies' developmental phases and reveals decade-specific trends, enabling systematic tracking of their evolution. For instance, it demonstrates how these policies adapted to global shifts like economic integration, digital transformation, and the emergence of sustainable development priorities.

Beyond chronological analysis, the policies can be grouped into four thematic clusters:

- Design Education: Funding allocations, curricular standards, and talent development strategies
- Industry Support: Financial mechanisms (grants/tax incentives) and market expansion initiatives
- Sustainable Design: Environmental guidelines for resource efficiency and ecological balance
- Cultural Integration: Policies bridging traditional heritage with contemporary design practices

This thematic approach allows researchers to examine both the implementation outcomes within specific domains and the cross-sector synergies between different policy types. The dual categorization system (temporal + thematic) provides comprehensive insights into how Nordic nations have systematically cultivated their design ecosystems.

3 Visual Analysis of Nordic Design Policies

3.1 The Overall Landscape of Nordic Design Policies

Through data processing, we identified and selected 45 Nordic design policy documents. These documents were first sorted and analyzed based on their timeframes. If a document lacked a specific publication year but indicated a range (e.g., "2013–2015"), it was assigned to the starting year (2013 in this example). Next, we categorized the policies by industry, including education-related policies, industry-related policies, and policies integrating culture and design. By visualizing the data from multiple perspectives, we aimed to thoroughly understand the development patterns, key features, and connections within Nordic design policies.

For this analysis, we chose Sankey diagrams as the visualization tool. In these diagrams:

- **Nodes** represent core elements (e.g., countries, policy categories).
- **Flows** (connections between nodes) show how policies are linked to specific countries. The width of each flow corresponds to the number of policies in a category for a given country. Wider flows indicate higher policy activity, enabling viewers to instantly grasp disparities in policy focus across nations and categories.

Based on the data, the design policy development in these five countries has the following focuses: Denmark has issued the most strategic plans (seven in total), showing its determination to drive national development via design. It also focuses on Circular and Eco fields, likely emphasizing sustainable - development - related design like eco - design and circular design. Finland focuses on various design directions. With no sign of tilting towards specific fields yet, it may promote the design industry comprehensively. Iceland has issued few policies, so the focus of its design policy is unclear. Norway focuses on Innovation in two aspects and has single-focus areas in Design, Culture, and Industry. Its design policy may not only involve design but also innovation -driven development and the integration of cultural and industrial design. Sweden shows strong interest in Architecture (three instances) and equal interest in Design, Eco, and Circular (two instances each). Its design policy may center on architectural design while stressing the integration of ecology, circulation, and design for sustainable architectural design and urban planning - oriented development.

3.2 Chronological Evolution of Nordic Design Policies

When analyzing design policy timelines, we employ color-coded markers (e.g., orange for Finland, yellow for Sweden) to plot publication years along a chronological axis. Interactive tooltips display policy titles and key initiatives, enabling immediate identification of national priorities. This visualization method reveals three distinct phases in Nordic policy evolution:

- **Foundational Development (1995–2004)**: Comprising 13 policy documents, 8 explicitly reference innovation-driven development strategies. Key initiatives centered on national capacity-building efforts, exemplified by Denmark's establishment of the INDEX Award in 2003—a landmark program aligning with the global competitiveness objectives outlined in Denmark's second national design policy.

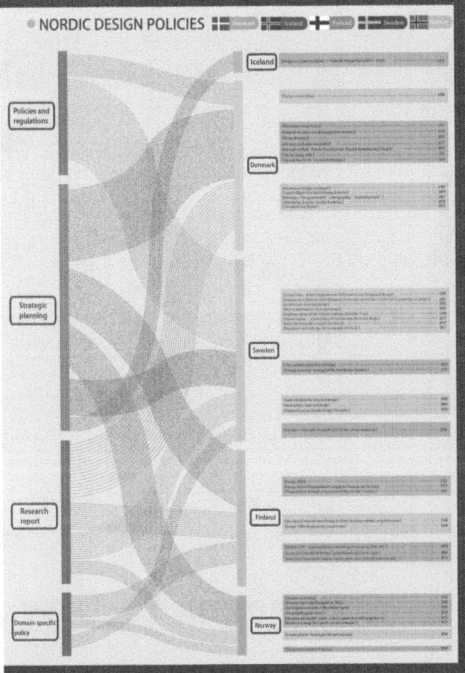

Fig. 1. Visualization of Nordic Design Policy Categories.

- **Public Service Transformation (2005–2014)**: This phase produced 14 policy instruments, with Sweden's 2009 Norwegian Innovation Policy White Paper initiative serving as a paradigm shift. The strategic focus transitioned from enhancing national influence to tackling complex public service challenges through systemic redesign frameworks.
- **Sustainable Systems (2015–2024)**: This era features differentiated circular economy roadmaps. Norway's 2021 Design-Driven Green Transition Program epitomizes the institutionalization of circular principles, simultaneously complemented by digital service transformation initiatives that synergize economic, social, and environmental priorities to advance sustainable societal transitions.

3.3   Industry Sectors Encompassed by Nordic Design Policies

Additionally, when analyzing the industries involved in the policies, we first extract the industry information from each policy and standardize it. For example, terms like "architecture" and "building" are unified to "building." We then organize the industry information into a list format, with each policy corresponding to a list of the industries it covers. We also calculate the frequency of each industry across all policies to determine the significance of the visualization elements.

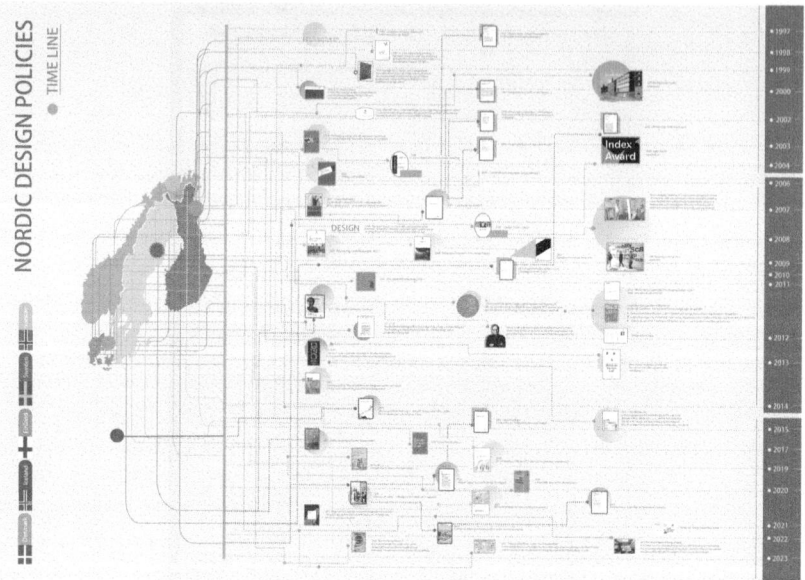

Fig. 2. Visualization of Design Policy Timeline.

Finally, we create a bar chart with industry categories on the horizontal axis, using different colored bars to represent the policy data from each country for easy differentiation. This clearly presents the characteristics of Nordic design policies in terms of industry distribution. Furthermore, we can analyze the extent of the design policies' impact on the development of different industries. For instance, the significant representation of the education sector in Finland's design policies correlates with the country's emphasis on design education and the important role of design talent in the economy.

4   Evolution of Nordic Design Policies

4.1   Design as a Pathway Basis for Policy Development

Designers are increasingly transitioning from external consultants to embedded collaborators within government structures. This shift is exemplified by Denmark's MindLab, established in 2002 as the world's first public sector innovation lab. Originally focused on service design, MindLab now tackles complex policy development and institutional reforms—tasks previously hindered by limited cross-sector understanding.

Building on this momentum, the 2013 Helsinki Design Lab (HDL) emerged from Finland's Design Capital initiative, positioning strategic design as a governance tool. HDL's 2015 Design for Government program institutionalized this approach, creating pipelines for design students to engage with policymaking while training civil servants in design methodologies.

This evolution continued with Norway's 2016 StimuLab, a joint venture between the Digitalization Agency and Design & Architecture Authority (DOGA). Their adapted

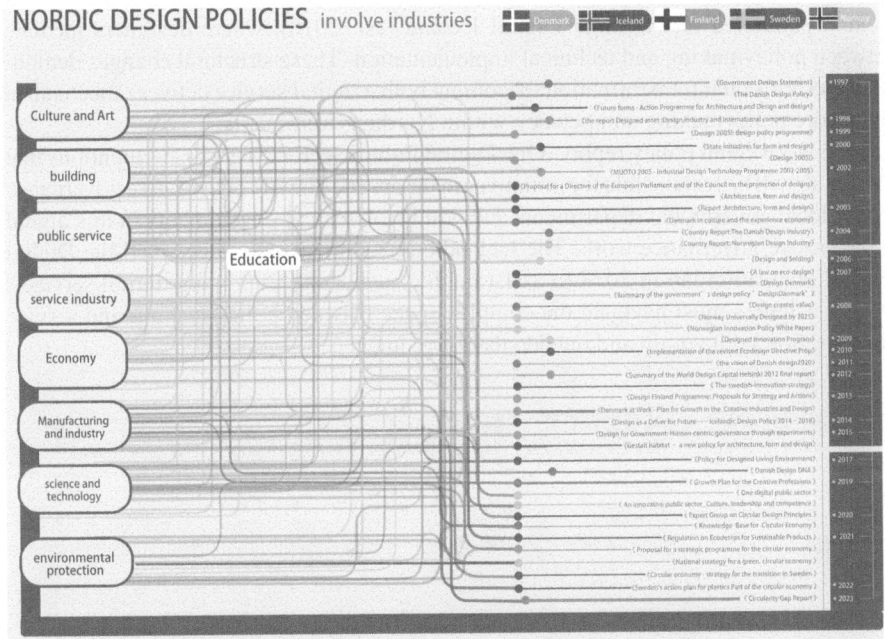

Fig. 3. Visualization of designing policies for industries.

"three-diamond model" expanded the traditional design process to address systemic public service challenges through iterative, citizen-centered prototyping.

These cases demonstrate design's transformation from a peripheral service to a core governance competency. By embedding design thinking in legislative processes and bureaucratic structures, Nordic governments are institutionalizing innovation mechanisms that bridge policymaking gaps while improving public service delivery.

4.2 Digital Transformation in the Policymaking Sector

While earlier Nordic policies emphasized digitalization for competitiveness, recent institutional shifts reveal prioritization of systemic digital governance. The 2016–2018 closures of pioneering design labs—Finland's Helsinki Design Lab and Denmark's Mind-Lab—marked a strategic pivot. Denmark replaced MindLab with the Prime Minister's Disruption Task Force, uniting industry, employment, and education ministries to overhaul civil service systems through regulatory tech frameworks and digital skills training, moving away from MindLab's human-centered design ethos.

Finland's response followed similar patterns: the Ministry of Finance's D9 digital transformation unit (2017–2018) preceded Migri Immigration Service's 2018 establishment of the permanent INLAND department, where designers now hold equal standing with policy specialists in digitizing public services. This institutionalization reflects design's evolving role from consultative input to embedded governance capacity.

Norway's *One Digital Public Sector 2019–2025* strategy formalized this transition, tasking StimuLab with implementing cross-departmental digital governance models.

Iceland paralleled this through Digital Iceland (est. 2018), where designers mediate between policymaking and technical implementation. These structural changes demonstrate design's dual transformation: becoming both a digital service delivery mechanism and a core policymaking competency within Nordic governments.

The Norwegian policy report "One Digital Public Sector 2019–2025" mentions that StimuLab will be responsible for initiatives in the area of digital collaborative governance within local government departments and will involve local governments in this digital collaborative governance work. The Icelandic government also established the Digital Iceland innovation lab in 2018 to assist public agencies in improving digital services, where designers must navigate the complex space between policy-making and service digitalization both within and outside the government.

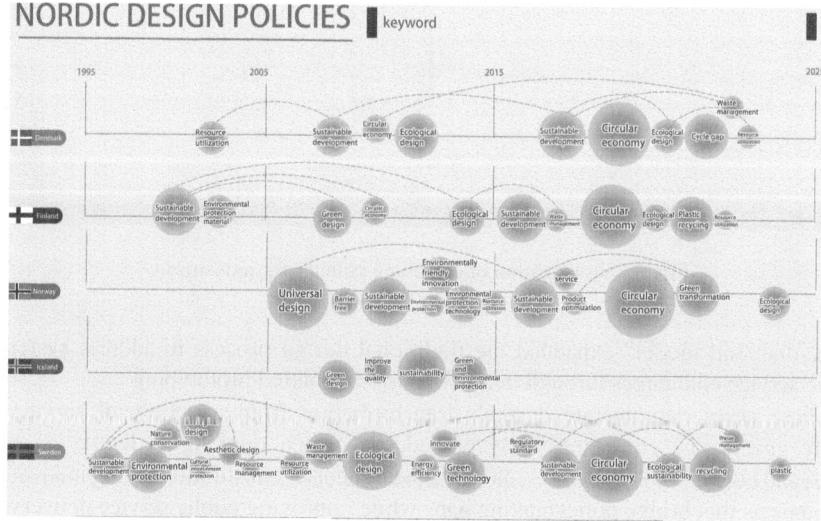

Fig. 4. Visualization of Public Innovation Lab Timeline.

4.3 Keywords Changes in Sustainability and Circular Economy Policies

Through Keyword analysis reveals a paradigm shift in Nordic sustainability approaches - from abstract economic concepts to sector-specific implementation frameworks. Early policy language emphasized economic sustainability through resource efficiency and growth stability, prioritizing industrial longevity over ecological considerations.

The emergence of "ecodesign" and "circular economy" terminology marked a critical transition. Norway's 2021 National Innovation Strategy exemplifies this operational shift, mandating full lifecycle management in battery production through standardized recycling protocols. Similarly, Denmark's textile industry transformation initiative demonstrates circular economy principles in practice, with the Danish Design Center pioneering closed-loop systems to combat fast fashion waste.

Three sectoral implementations highlight this evolution:

- **Industrial Design**: Electric vehicle infrastructure development paired with battery recycling networks
- **Fashion**: Transition to organic materials and design-for-repair methodologies
- **Healthcare**: Durable medical equipment standards and optimized treatment workflows

This lexical progression from broad sustainability rhetoric to technical specifications reflects Nordic policymakers' growing recognition of design as an implementation mechanism. The vocabulary shift mirrors institutional changes - where terms like "resource efficiency" evolved into measurable targets like "95% battery component recovery rates".

Such linguistic patterns establish design policy as both environmental safeguard and economic catalyst, providing transferable models for global sustainability governance. The Nordic experience demonstrates how policy language must evolve from aspirational concepts to operational blueprints for effective ecological transition.

5 Conclusion

Through visual analysis, we observe that Nordic design policy evolution primarily manifests in three key aspects:

Design as Policy Framework Design has transitioned from being a policy target to serving as a methodological foundation for policymaking. The application of design thinking in policy formulation has become institutionalized practice across Nordic governments.

Implicit Policy Dominance: Post-2015 policy instruments increasingly emphasize implicit design integration through support programs (e.g., Nordic Innovation Fund initiatives), design infrastructure development (national design centers), and recognition systems (INDEX Award reforms) rather than explicit regulatory mandates.

Systemic Innovation Integration: While recognized as crucial, design operates within broader innovation ecosystems. The restructuring of agencies like Denmark's Disruption Task Force demonstrates the necessity for balanced coordination between design strategies and complementary policy domains (digitalization, sustainability, education).

This tripartite evolution reflects the Nordic approach to policy design - transitioning from sector-specific interventions to systemic innovation frameworks where design acts as both catalyst and integrator.

Acknowledgments. This paper is an interim outcome of the Major Program in Arts of the National Social Science Fund of China, titled "National Design Policy Research in the Context of the Belt and Road Initiative" (Project Number: 20ZD10).

References

Whicher, A.: Design ecosystems and innovation policy in Europe. Strategic Design Res. J. **10**(2), 117–125 (2017)

Lujanen, M (ed.). Housing and Housing Policy in the Nordic Countries, vol. 7. p. 286 (2004) van den Broek, A.H.: Strategy development in the design sector: a theoretical perspective. In: Bohemia, E., Liedtka, J., Rieple, A. (eds.) Leading Innovation through Design. pp. 331–332 (2012)

Høibye, L., Sand, H.: Circular economy in the Nordic construction sector: Identification and assessment of potential policy instruments that can accelerate a transition toward a circular economy. Nordic Council of Ministers (2018)

Ragnheiður Elín Árnadóttir. Nordic Tourism Policy Analysis,Nordic Council of Ministers, (2019)

Ishani Mukherjee, M., Coban, K., Bali, A.Z.: Policy capacities and effective policy design: a review. Policy. Sci. **54**, 243–268 (2021)

Sharif, N.: Emergence and development of the National Innovation Systems concept. Res. Policy (2006)

Attention Characteristics of Dynamic Content by Visual Elements

Yusei Sakata and Wonseok Yang(⊠)

Shibaura Institute of Technology, 3-7-5, Toyosu, Koto-ku, Tokyo 135-8548, Japan
cy21267@shibaura-it.ac.jp

Abstract. Social networking services (SNS) are widely used for self-expression and marketing, with visual content playing an increasingly significant role. Features like Stories and Shorts on Instagram and YouTube effectively capture users' attention, making them powerful tools for creators. This research examines how different visual element expressions in dynamic content influence users' attention and impressions. The first experiment used a sample of YouTube shorts to verify how Visual Elements impact attention. Statements uttered during the experiment were recorded and categorized by element and assessment. The results of Experiment 1 showed that most statements related to "Text" and that "prominence" and "readability" were important for high ratings. This confirmed that Text significantly influences viewers' content evaluation and both high and low evaluations. Next, to clarify how different Text expression methods affect users' attention and impressions, we conducted Experiment 2 using a sample with reference to the WUS survey method. The results of Experiment 2 revealed that Text size, position, and color are factors that significantly affect users' attention span and impressions. We believe that these are important factors that improve visual impressions. This research highlights that Visual Elements play a crucial role in shaping user attention and perception in Short Videos. Understanding these effects allows creators to design content that quickly attracts viewers and enhances message clarity. By optimizing the visual presentation of Short Videos, creators can leave a lasting impression, improve user engagement, and effectively guide viewers toward their main content or channel.

Keywords: Short Videos · Visual Elements · Text Info

1 Introduction

Social networking services (SNS) platforms are widely used to transmit information, connect with others, and for self-expression. Although, at first the main purpose of SNS was for personal interaction More recently, companies have used them for sales promotion and marketing, thus diversifying their role [1]. SNS have evolved from Text-based information dissemination to visual content and video-based information dissemination, making it an important platform for self-expression and brand building [2]. They are attracting attention as a means of enhancing message delivery and making strong impressions on the recipients. Images and videos combine visual impact with emotional appeal,

M. Schrepp (Ed.): HCII 2025, LNCS 15794, pp. 75–90, 2025.
https://doi.org/10.1007/978-3-031-93221-2_5

increasing the speed and effectiveness of communication. Against this backdrop, SNS have allowed companies and individuals to deepen their connections with third parties.

In addition, the individual creators who use SNS are becoming more prolific and are gaining opportunities for self-expression and monetization by ever-widening audience bases. This has formed new ecosystems such as influencer marketing and the creator economy with SNS attracting attention as platforms for generating economic value. A highly notable development is the proliferation of truncated video formats such as "Short Videos" and "Stories". These videos quickly and effectively capture viewers' attention and are proliferating as a means of improving communication efficiency. By utilizing these formats, creators can now express and promote themselves without frequently posting lengthy content. In addition, Short Videos function as "gateways" that entice viewers to more detailed content in proprietary channels by strategically deepening viewer engagement [3].

The proliferation of Short Videos is also closely linked to the social networking platforms' algorithms. Short videos arrest viewers' attention instantly and are more likely to be delivered to a wide range of users through the platform's recommendation function. This makes them effective for gaining new followers and strengthening engagement with existing viewers. In sum, using Short Videos that leverage visual appeal and messaging is an important element for creators to deepen their relationship with audiences and make for more effective communication. Creator activities and marketing methods utilizing SNS will certainly continue to evolve making them a key element in the creation of new media.

2   Visual Information and User Cognitive Characteristics in Short Videos

This research investigated the impact of Short Videos on users through visual information to consider how the expressions of Visual Elements affect users' attention and impressions.

2.1   Cognitive Processes for Visual Information

Short Videos, such as on YouTube shorts and TikTok, are media that effectively employ visual information to promote user behavior from the cognitive stage to purchase decisions. This process comprises three stages: sensory, perceptual, and cognitive. In the sensory phase, dynamic elements (movement, color, and sound) input through vision and hearing activate sensory memory and attract the user's initial attention [4]. In the perceptual stage, these features are integrated, and the meaning and value of information are recognized through elements such as thumbnails and titles [5]. The cognitive stage involves concept-driven processing based on past experiences and expectations and data-driven processing based on external visual information [4]. Throughout, dynamic visuals and sounds play an important "cognitive" role leading to purchase behavior. For example, in TikTok, a short video shows the attractiveness of a product, followed by the audience using Google and YouTube to search, compare, consider, and finally purchase the product, completing the purchasing behavior flow [6]. Thus, by increasing product awareness and guiding consumer behavior to the next stage, Short Videos are powerful tools early in the marketing funnel (Fig. 1).

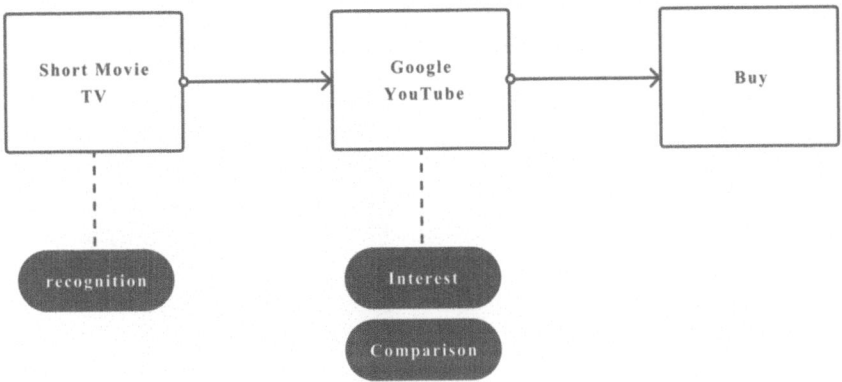

Fig. 1. Process of purchasing behavior using Short Videos.

2.2   Effects of Dynamic Elements and Visual Information

1. Visual attention

Visual attention comprises two types: bottom-up attention, which is automatically stimulated, and top-down attention, which is based on knowledge and goals. In bottom-up attention, salient features such as motion and color are likely to attract attention [7], e.g., in Itti and Koch's (2001) model, these features are integrated to form a "saliency map," which identifies the parts of visual information that need attention. Top-down attention is a mechanism that consciously focuses on specific information based on individual experiences and goals.

2. Dual coding theory

Paivio's (1986) dual encoding theory combines visual and verbal information to facilitate memory and comprehension. In this theory, linguistic information (Logogens) and nonverbal imagery (Imagens) are interrelated, which makes information transfer more efficient [8]. Educational content and advertisements combining visual motion and audio information based on this theory exemplify designs for achieving effective information transfer.

Effective use of dynamic elements can attract visual attention and, in combination with verbal information, reinforce memory and understanding. This enables the information recipient to recognize and retain the content efficiently in memory (Fig. 2).

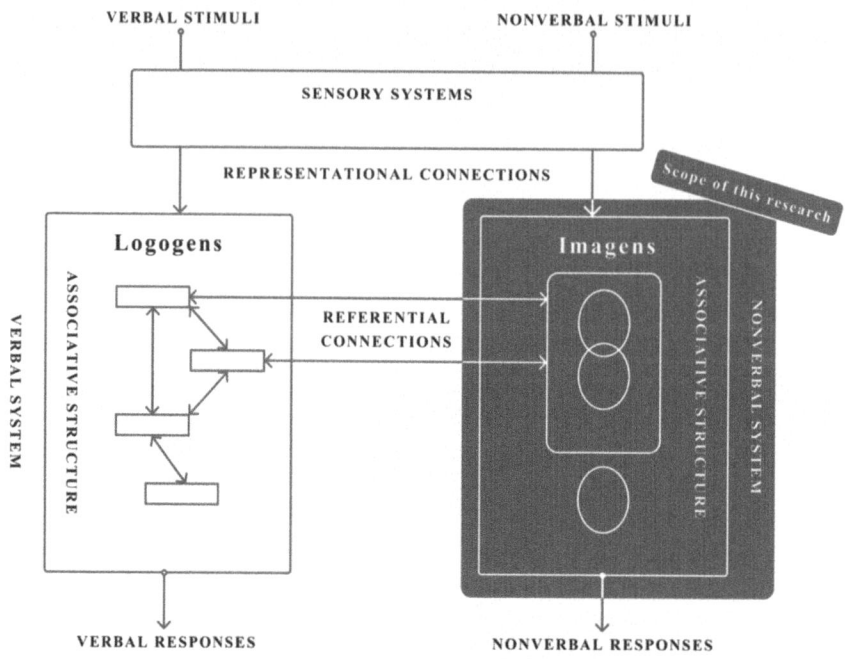

Fig. 2. Dual Coding Theoretical Model.

2.3 Impact of Short Videos on User Perception

Short Videos serve as an important window to capture users' attention, and numerous applications are evolving to take advantage of this characteristic [9, 10]. Because of their role in capturing viewers' attention quickly and guiding them to deeper content and more detailed information, they are expected to be used strategically by creators and companies. The ease and immediacy of Short Videos have enabled creators to easily express themselves and promote their presence. In the elaboration prospect model (Petty & Cacioppo, 1986), viewers may go through interest formation in the peripheral route to deep information processing in the central route [9]. Short Videos are often introductions that lead viewers to the main content [11]. For example, posting a video on YouTube Shorts and placing a link to a longer video or a related website in the description or comment section effectively leads viewers to more detailed information, which is a method based on this theory. This is particularly effective in product promotion and brand awareness, where short visual appeals serve to attract interest and then connect viewers to detailed explanations and shopping pages. Thus, Short Videos are media, which combine visual appeal and effective engagement, serving as a highly effective marketing and communication tool. This study focuses on using Short Videos to clarify how Visual Elements in dynamic content impact users' attention and impressions (Fig. 3).

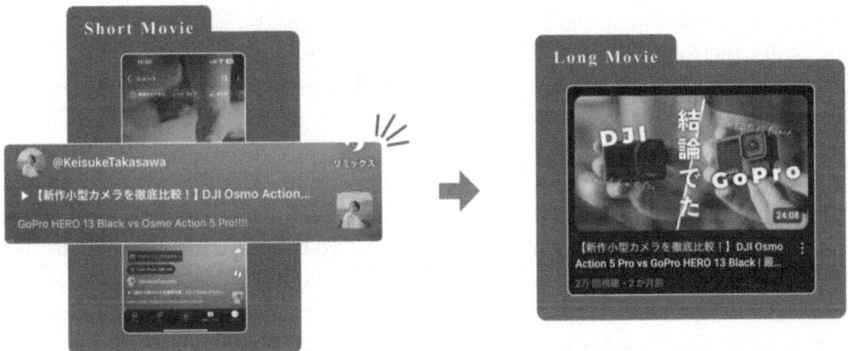

Fig. 3. Method of inducing YouTube shorts.

3 Research Method

Initially, we conducted an investigation of the impact of Visual Elements on attention in YouTube shorts, and then proceeded with an experiment focusing on Text. The main flow of the research is as follows. (see Fig. 4).

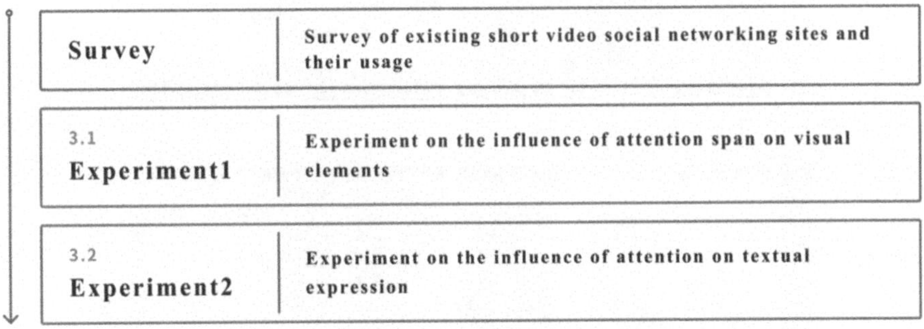

Survey	Survey of existing short video social networking sites and their usage
3.1 **Experiment1**	Experiment on the influence of attention span on visual elements
3.2 **Experiment2**	Experiment on the influence of attention on textual expression

Fig. 4. Research Process.

3.1 Investigation of the Influence of Attention Span on Visual Elements

In order to clarify the effect of differences in the way Visual Elements are expressed on the level of attention, we conducted an experiment using the thought-speech method, in which 10 subjects who had previously completed an awareness survey on short YouTube use were asked to watch three samples on their smartphones. For the purpose of validity, the samples were created by dividing them into six categories, each with an average balance, and focusing on genres unrelated to those preferred by the subjects in the awareness survey. The sample created is shown below (see Fig. 5).

During the experiment, the subjects were asked to speak mainly about Visual Elements. After the experiment, the Visual Elements were categorized (see Fig. 6), and after transcribing the statements made during the experiment, they were categorized by element and evaluation and compared.

1. Use of the thought-speech method

The think-aloud method is one of the methods used to investigate the thinking and problem-solving process, in which participants are asked to vocalize their thoughts at the same time they perform a task. Analysis based on the speech data obtained from the thought-speech method is called protocol analysis. This analysis is used to determine what thoughts resulted in a person's behavior in a particular situation [12, 13]. The use of thought-speech methods has been used extensively in user interface evaluation and other areas. This research utilized such a method to analyze the impact of the Visual Elements of a YouTube short on the user's attention span.

Fig. 5. Experimental Sample.

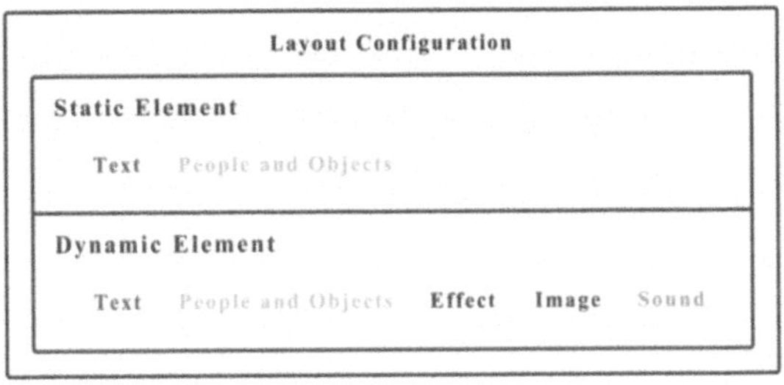

Layout Configuration

Static Element

Text   People and Objects

Dynamic Element

Text   People and Objects   Effect   Image   Sound

Fig. 6. Classification of Visual Elements.

3.2 Investigation of the Influence of Attention on Textual Expression

In order to clarify the effects of the different Text presentation methods on users' attention and impressions, eight samples were created from the orthogonal table of L8(2^3) using the design of experiment method (see Fig. 7), with the top three factors (size, position, and color) that were frequently cited in the results of the previous study as factors. A questionnaire was then administered after each sample was viewed. In the questionnaire, items suitable for evaluating the videos against the three evaluation axes of likability, ease of viewing, and image were created with reference to the WUS survey method (see Fig. 8), and the experiment was conducted on 30 subjects.

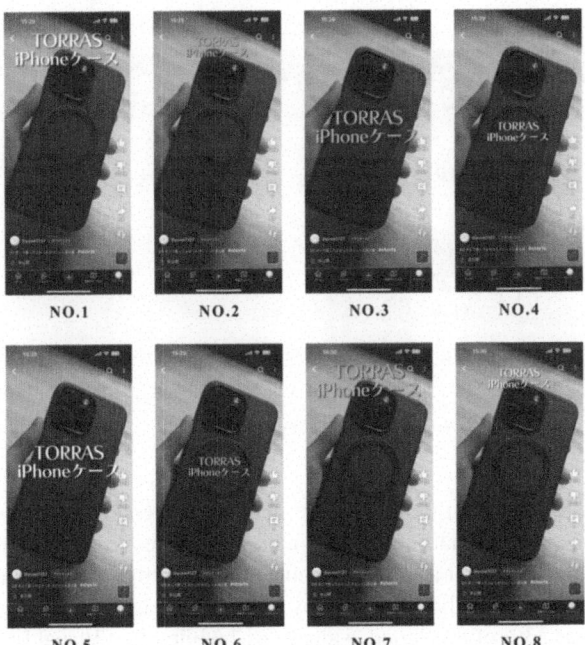

Fig. 7. Experimental Sample.

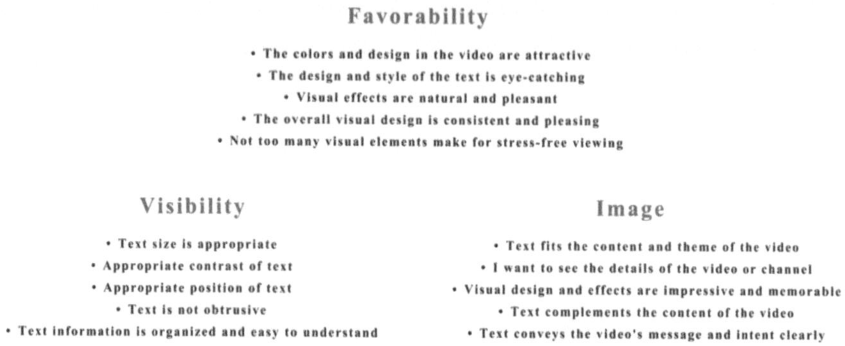

Favorability

• The colors and design in the video are attractive
• The design and style of the text is eye-catching
• Visual effects are natural and pleasant
• The overall visual design is consistent and pleasing
• Not too many visual elements make for stress-free viewing

Visibility

• Text size is appropriate
• Appropriate contrast of text
• Appropriate position of text
• Text is not obtrusive
• Text information is organized and easy to understand

Image

• Text fits the content and theme of the video
• I want to see the details of the video or channel
• Visual design and effects are impressive and memorable
• Text complements the content of the video
• Text conveys the video's message and intent clearly

Fig. 8. Investigation items of the experiment.

4 Results and Discussion

4.1 Experiment Results and Discussion on Attention Span to Visual Elements

1. Percentage of influence of Visual Elements

It was found that "Text" accounted for the highest percentage (29%) of all Visual Elements. This suggests that Text plays an important role in judging the visual impression and attractiveness of content (Fig. 9).

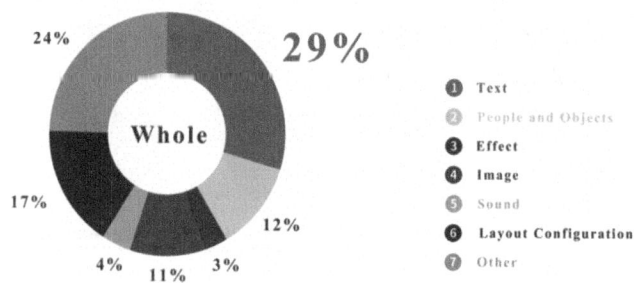

Fig. 9. Influence of Visual Elements.

2. Percentage by evaluation

While it was confirmed that there were many statements regarding Textual information, it was also found that there were many references to layout and structure. In particular, Text accounted for a large percentage (40%) of the "bad evaluation," indicating that viewers were strongly influenced by Textual information. It was also clear that Text accounted for 33% of the "good evaluations," while other Visual Elements such as people and objects (16%), effects (15%), and images (7%) were also a constant criterion for evaluation. These results indicate that while the evaluation of Visual Elements is centered on Text, multiple elements have a comprehensive impact (Fig. 10).

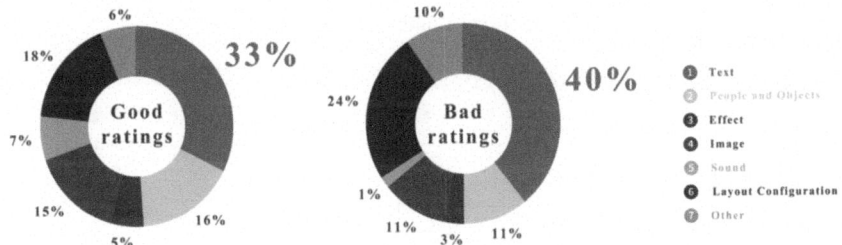

Fig. 10. Overall rating of Visual Elements.

3. Percentage by genre

While the proportion of Text was prominent in the Text-based type, accounting for 43%, the proportion of people and objects was also found to be high in the product focus and trend news types. In addition, the percentage of effects and images tends to be relatively high in the Recommendation and Trend News types. These results indicate that the weight of Visual Elements differs by genre. In particular, it can be considered that Visual Elements according to the characteristics of the genre are important when viewers evaluate videos. For example, Textual information plays a major role in the Text-driven type, which requires information to be conveyed in an easy-to-understand manner, while in the product-focused type, which conveys the attractiveness of products, people and objects showing actual objects are more important than Text. Thus, it is highly likely that the selection of Visual Elements that match the characteristics of each genre will contribute to the improvement of the viewing experience (Fig. 11).

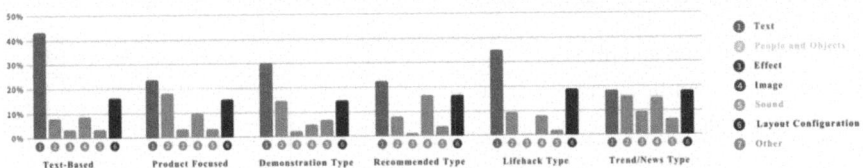

Fig. 11. Visual Elements by genre.

4. Text feature analysis

Next, among the Visual Elements, we focused on "letters" and conducted a feature analysis of letters by rating. It was found that visually, "prominence" and "high readability" were important factors affecting high evaluation. Specifically, "size: large," "position: center," "color: yes," "Text content: keywords," "effect: border," and "boldness: very thick/bold" are considered to be factors that increase visibility and attract viewers' attention. These elements are visual devices that increase visibility and give viewers a quick and clear impression in Short Videos that convey information in a short period of time. Therefore, we found that viewers were strongly influenced by Text when evaluating content, and that this was related to both good and bad evaluations (Table 1).

Table 1. Text feature analysis result.

Good ratings																	
Size		Contrast ratio		Time one appears		Position		Text Movement		Color		Text Content		Effect		Boldness	
Large	14	Average	6.38	Average	2.71	Top	5	Zoom	3	White	14	Keyword	21	Shadow	6	Very Thick	10
Medium	9					Center	17	Slide in	4	Black	3	Subtitles	4	Rim	10	Bold	5
Small	2					Bottom	1	None	18	Full Color	8			Border	1	Medium	7
						Top and Bottom	2							Background Fill	5	Thin	3
						Full screen	0							Gradient	1		
														Lines	1		

Bad ratings																	
Size		Contrast ratio		Time one appears		Position		Text Movement		Color		Text Content		Effect		Boldness	
Large	3	Average	5.12	Average	2.57	Top	6	Zoom	2	White	18	Keyword	13	Shadow	7	Very Thick	2
Medium	12					Center	10	Slide in	3	Black	2	Subtitles	9	Rim	4	Bold	2
Small	7					Bottom	4	None	17	Full Color	2			Border	1	Medium	11
						Top and Bottom	0							Background Fill	4	Thin	6
						Full screen	1							Gradient	1		
														Lines	0		

4.2 Experiment Results and Discussion on Textual Expression

1. Analysis of variance received for each size, position, and color

In order to clarify whether there is a change in the user's attention and impression depending on the size, position, and color of the Text, we conducted a bivariate analysis of the questionnaire results and colored the items with a p-value of 0.05 or less as shown below to indicate whether there is a significant difference according to the p-value value (Table 2).

Table 2. The impact of Text on users.

evaluation items	size	position	color
Colors and design are attractive	n.s.	n.s.	$p < 0.01$
Text design is eye-catching	n.s.	$p < 0.05$	n.s.
The effect is natural and pleasant	n.s.	n.s.	$p < 0.01$
The design is unified and gives a good impression	n.s.	n.s.	$p < 0.01$
Not too many elements, easy to view	n.s.	$p < 0.01$	$p < 0.01$
Appropriate text size	$p < 0.05$	n.s.	n.s.
Appropriate contrast	n.s.	n.s.	$p < 0.01$
Appropriate text position	$p < 0.05$	n.s.	n.s.
Text is not obtrusive	n.s.	$p < 0.01$	n.s.
Information is organized and easy to understand	n.s.	n.s.	n.s.
Fits the content and theme	n.s.	n.s.	$p < 0.01$
I want to see the details of the video	n.s.	n.s.	$p < 0.01$
The design is memorable	n.s.	n.s.	n.s.
It complements the content	n.s.	n.s.	$p < 0.05$
The message is easy to understand	n.s.	n.s.	$p < 0.01$

2. Comparison received by size, location, and color from the mean

Next, we produced averages for the items for which significant differences were found, and made comparisons for each factor.

1. Comparison by size

In terms of differences in impression by size, "Size: Medium" tended to be more easily perceived. This indicates that font size plays an important role in visual appropriateness and design balance. Font size of "Size: Medium" is highly visible to users, neither excessive nor insufficient, and thus is considered to provide optimal conditions for understanding and accepting information. Excessively large font sizes may create a sense of visual oppression or disrupt the overall design balance, while too small font sizes may reduce visibility and impair the efficiency of information delivery (Table 3).

Table 3. Average of size.

evaluation items	large	medium
Appropriate text size	3.67	3.97
Appropriate text position	3.19	3.60

2. Comparison by position

In terms of impressions by position, users tended to be more impressed with "Position: Center" for "Text design is eye-catching" and "Position: Top" for "Not too many elements and easy to view" and "Text is not obtrusive". This indicates that Text placement plays an important role in users' visual impression and visibility. The result that "Position: Center" was more likely to make an impression is thought to reflect the psychological characteristic that the eye naturally tends to focus on the center of the screen. Placing Text in the center makes it easier to attract visual attention and maximize the appeal of the Text design. On the other hand, the result that "Position: Top" is more likely to make an impression suggests that the top placement has the effect of organizing information and presenting important information to the viewer in an easy-to-understand manner. Based on these results, when selecting the position of Text, it is important to devise the placement according to the nature of the information to be conveyed and its visual purpose. If the goal is to "catch the eye," the center placement is effective, while if the goal is to "make it easy to view" or "not get in the way," the top placement is considered appropriate (Table 4).

3. Comparison by color

In terms of impressions by color, "Color: White" tended to make a more positive impression. This indicates that "color: white" is a color that gives a sense of visual cleanliness and unity, and gives a positive impression in many items. White tends to give users a positive impression because of its simplicity, flexibility, and characteristics that make

Table 4. Average of position.

evaluation items	top	center
Text design is eye-catching	3.53	3.88
Not too many elements, easy to view	4.06	3.60
Text is not obtrusive	4.33	3.03

it easy to harmonize with other colors and design elements. The items "attractive in hue and design," "natural and pleasant in effect," and "unified design and good impression" indicate that white plays a role in reducing visual noise and emphasizing the overall unity of the design. Color: white" was also rated highly in the items 'not too many elements, easy to view' and 'appropriate contrast,' indicating that it improves the visibility of information and allows users to receive information without stress. Furthermore, the items "fits the content and theme," "wants to see the details of the video," "complements the content," and "makes the message easy to understand" were also rated in favor of white, presumably because of its effect of enhancing other design elements and strengthening the delivery of the information and message (Table 5).

Table 5. Average of color.

evaluation items	white	full color
Colors and design are attractive	4.03	3.03
The effect is natural and pleasant	3.98	3.03
The design is unified and gives a good impression	4.31	3.21
Not too many elements, easy to view	4.17	3.49
Appropriate contrast	4.21	2.98
Fits the content and theme	4.16	3.55
I want to see the details of the video	4.08	3.74
It complements the content	3.38	3.01
The message is easy to understand	3.47	2.98

4. Comparison by sample

In the sample-by-sample comparison, the impact of the combination of size, position, and color on the user's impression was remarkable. In particular, the combination of "size: medium," "position: center," and "color: white" was highly rated in terms of visibility, unity, and design attractiveness, and is considered to be an important factor in creating a positive impression on users. On the other hand, conditions such as "Size: Large" and "Position: Top" were also effective in certain situations, and should be adjusted appropriately according to the purpose of the design. These results suggest that each element in a design does not function independently, but rather interacts with each other to form an overall impression (Fig. 12).

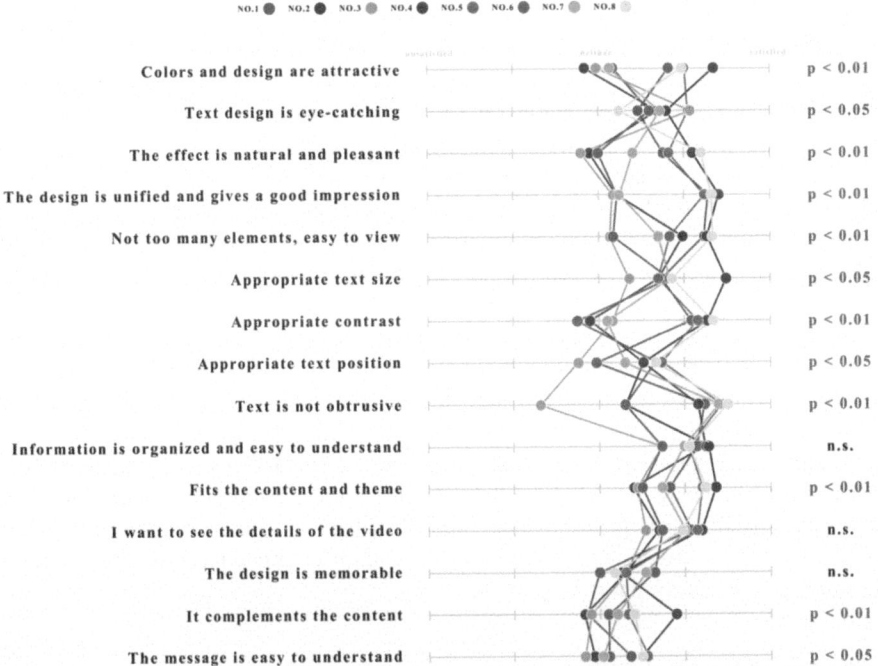

Fig. 12. Analysis of variance results "each sample".

5   Conclusion

This research attempted to clarify the effects on attention and perception of differences in the presentation of Visual Elements in Text when users view a series of Short Videos. The results of this research also established an effective method for presenting information when creating YouTube shorts.

1. Investigation of the influence of attention span on Visual Elements

An experiment was conducted using the thought-speech method, intending to clarify the effects of different ways of presenting Visual Elements on the attention potential. During the experiment, the participants were asked to verbalize mainly Visual Elements, and after transcribing the verbalizations, a comparison was made between the elements and the evaluations. The results of the experiment revealed that, overall, there were many comments on the "Text" and that "prominence" and "high readability" were particularly important factors affecting high evaluation. Thus, it was found that viewers were strongly influenced by Text when evaluating content and that this was related to both good and bad evaluations.

2. Investigation of the influence of attention on Textual expression

An experiment was conducted to clarify the effects of different Text expression methods on users' attention and impressions. The results of the experiment showed that the size, position, and color of Text are factors that significantly impact users' impressions. "Size: Medium" was highly rated for visibility and balance, and can be considered the optimal size, neither excessive nor insufficient. "Position: Center" attracts attention easily and enhances the attractiveness of the design, while "Position: Top" is excellent for organizing information and improving visibility. "Color: White" gives a sense of cleanliness, uniformity, and effectively communicates information and enhances the message. The combination of "Size: Medium," "Position: Center," and "Color: White" is optimal and important as a factor that improves the visual impression.

The results of this research are novel since they focus on the specific impact of visual factors while supporting previous researches [14–16] that showed the impact of Short Videos on users' attention and behavioral intentions on YouTube and TikTok. In addition, compared to researches that showed that Visual Elements in infographic videos contribute to impression evaluation such as "affinity" and "sophistication" [17], this unique research focuses on the short video format and clarifies how elements such as specific Text size, position, and color affect user attention and impression. It clarifies how factors such as Text size, position, and color affect the user's attention and perception. We believe that this research has allowed us to examine effective methods of presenting information in YouTube shorts.

6 Further Work

In this research, when examining how Visual Elements in Short Videos impact users' attention and impressions, we limited our investigation to "Text." We also narrowed down the Text elements to "size," "position," and "color," and clarified their impact on users' impressions. However, there are many other Visual Elements to be examined, such as font type, Text animation, and effects, and these should also be examined in future research. Furthermore, the visual impression of a short video is greatly influenced by a complex of factors other than Text, e.g., video, audio, and effects. By clarifying the impact of these factors on users' impressions and actions more comprehensive design guidelines can be constructed. In addition, since the content of a short video itself has a significant impact on user perception, an analysis must be conducted that factors in differences based on the theme of the video and the target audience. In the future, to accurately measure the effects of Visual Elements, experiments must be conducted under uniform conditions and analyzed by genre and purpose. Addressing the above issues would generate a more detailed understanding of the impact of Visual Elements on information transfer and engagement in Short Videos and support effective design techniques.

References

1. Ministry of Internal Affairs and Communications (MIC): Information and Communications White Paper, 2024, pp. 152–157. https://www.soumu.go.jp/johotsusintokei/whitepaper/ja/r06/pdf/n2170000.pdf, Accessed 6 Jan 2024
2. Kaplan, A.M., Haenlein, M.: Users of the world, unite! the challenges and opportunities of social media. Bus. Horiz. **53**(1), 59–68 (2010)
3. TikTok for Business: Making TikTok videos for high engagement: The complete guide. https://ads.tiktok.com/business/en/blog/tiktok-short-video-best-practice, Accessed 6 Jan 2024
4. Yamaoka, T., Okada, A., Tanaka, K., Mori, R., Yoshitake, R.: Basics of Design Ergonomics. MUSABI Social Management Co., Tokyo (2015)
5. Dresp-Langley, B.: Principles of perceptual grouping: Implications for image-guided surgery. Front,. Psychol. 6 (2015)
6. Galileo, Maezono, T.: The Ultimate Guide to TikTok Business: New Rules for Achieving Results in SNS Marketing from Zero Followers. Gijutsu-Hyoronsha, pp. 60–63 (2023)
7. Ward, L.M.: Attention. Scholarpedia 3(10), 1538 (2008)
8. Paivio, A.: Can α dian. J. Psychol. **45**, 255–287 (1991)
9. Petty, R.E., Cacioppo, J.T.: The elaboration likelihood model of persuasion. Adv. Exp. Soc. Psychol. **19**, 123–205 (1986)
10. Paivio, A.: Mental Representations: A Dual Coding Approach. Oxford University Press (1986)
11. Behera, R. K., Gunasekaran, A., Gupta, S., Kamboj, S., Bala, P. K.: Personalized digital marketing recommender engine. J, Retailing Consumer Serv. **53**(6) (2020)
12. Fukuda, T., Fukuda, R.: Human Engineering Guide—Methods for the Science of Sensibility. Scientist Co. (2009)
13. Kaiho, H.: Introduction to Protocol Analysis: What Can Be Read from Speech Data. Shinyo-sha, Tokyo (2004)
14. Jeong, Y.-J., Lee, N.-J., Lee, J.-H.: The effects of YouTube summary contents features and contents provider credibility on users' flow and satisfaction. J. Korea Convergence Soc. **12**(2), 35–44 (2021)
15. Liu, Y.: A study on the factors affecting continuous usage intention of short video apps: Focusing on the Chinese TikTok (Douyin) app. Master's thesis, Graduate School, Sungkyunkwan University, pp. 85–92 (2019)
16. Wang, X., Wang, N., Park, B.-J.: Influence of TikTok's short-form video features and IT affordances on consumers' purchase intentions. J. Digital Contents Soc. **25**(1), 153–163 (2024)
17. Okuno, R., Kitani, Y.: A study on the components and impression evaluation of infographic videos. Proc. Japan Soc. Design Res. **70**, 102–103 (2023)
18. Kimura, K.: The Ultimate Textbook for YouTube Video SEO for PR and Marketers. Shoeisha (n.d.)
19. Morinaka, R.: The Power of Web Videos: Practical Know-How for Maximizing ROI in Video Marketing. Shoeisha (n.d.)
20. OPT, Inc.: 100 New Rules for Instagram Marketing: Techniques to Inspire Desire with a Single Photo. Impress (n.d.)
21. Furuhashi, Y., Yang, W.: Research about usability improvement in cursor operation of 3D configurator. In: Yang, W., Furuhashi, Y. (eds.) HCII 2023. LNCS, vol. 14032, pp. 157–170. Springer, Heidelberg (2023). https://doi.org/10.1007/978-3-031-35702-2_11
22. Uwajima, Y., Yang, W.: Relation between different UI information representation methods and user cognition. In: Yang, W., Uwajima, Y. (eds.) HCII 2023. LLNCS, vol. 14032, pp. 386–397. Springer, Heidelberg (2023). https://doi.org/10.1007/978-3-031-35702-2_27

23. Owa, S., Yang, W.: On the use of verbs for micro interactions in UI. Interdisciplinary Pract. Indust. Design **144**, 198–204 (2024)
24. Muto, M., Yang, W.: The Influence of Microcopy on User Decision-Making. Interdisciplinary Pract. Indust. Design **144**, 188–197 (2024)
25. Otsuka, J., Yang, W.: Consideration of the problem of digital divide in the development of ICT. Interdisciplinary Pract. Indust. Design **144**, 205–214 (2024)
26. Umino, M., Yajima, R., Yang, W.: Design of home appliance operation sounds based on the metaphorical nature of sound. Interdisciplinary Pract. Indust. Design **144**, 157–167 (2024)

Utilization of CMF Elements as Kansei Value in UI Design

Kana Uenoyama and Wonseok Yang(⊠)

Shibaura Institute of Technology, Koto-ku, Tokyo 135-8548, Japan
cy21271@shibaura-it.ac.jp

Abstract. The diversification of digital devices has heightened the importance of usability. UI design aims to provide intuitive operation and a comfortable experience. With technological advancements, UI designs have become more complex and sophisticated, emphasizing not only usability but also visual beauty and atmosphere. In this context, a preliminary research revealed that recent UI designs prioritize Kansei values, such as enjoyment and beauty, over purely functionality-centered approaches. Therefore, this research focuses on CMF (Color, Material, Finish), a key expressive element in product design, to explore its application in UI design. This research examined both product design and UI design transitions. Initially, the role of CMF in product design was analyzed to clarify the impressions created by each CMF element. Subsequently, the CMF components in various UI design styles, including skeuomorphism, flat design, material design, and others, were assessed. Findings indicate that finish elements play a crucial role in shaping user impressions and enhancing perceived value. Specifically, finishes improve Kansei value by providing visual texture. Understanding and applying CMF to UI can enhance design consistency, convey the intended impression, and deliver an enriched experience to users. This approach is expected to contribute to recent design trends emphasizing Kansei-centered value in digital interfaces.

Keywords: UI design · CMF design · Kansei Value

1 Introduction

In recent years, the digitization of products has accelerated with the development of ICT, and interface design, including IoT products, is becoming one of the most important criteria for product selection [1]. Under these circumstances, design methods to improve the visual and tactile experiences of users are required, and Color, Material, Finish (CMF) is widely used in product design. However, in user interface (UI) design, usability (e.g. operability and functionality) is often emphasized, and research on design methods that aim to provide sensory value is limited.

Hirata et al. propose a design method that focuses on the efficiency of device operation by using formal concept analysis in a GUI design [2]. In addition, Sakamoto examines the influence of texture representation on the interface on operability and shows certain findings on the influence of visual elements on the user's sense of operation [3]. Furthermore, Zhang et al. revealed differences in the degree and efficiency of icon identification

© The Author(s), under exclusive license to Springer Nature Switzerland AG 2025
M. Schrepp (Ed.): HCII 2025, LNCS 15794, pp. 91–102, 2025.
https://doi.org/10.1007/978-3-031-93221-2_6

in skeuomorphism and flat design [4]. However, all these studies focused on usability, and the factors directly involved in users' emotional and sensory values have not been sufficiently considered.

Given this background, the efficient application of the CMF concept to UI design can appeal to user emotions and provide sensory value through visual and tactile elements. Furthermore, the application of CMF may make the experience brought about by UI design more distinctive and memorable and contribute significantly to enhancing and differentiating the overall value of the service. Based on the above background, this research aims to clarify design characteristics from the perspective of CMF through a survey on the transition of UI design. In particular, by comparing the role of CMFs in product design, we will clarify their uniqueness in UI design and explore the possibility of a new design approach that aims to improve sensory value in addition to the conventional usability-centered design approach. This is expected to broaden the scope of the application of the CMF concept in UI design.

2   The Impact of CMF Elements on Kansei

This research examines the usefulness of the CMF concept in UI design by clarifying design characteristics from the perspective of CMF through an research of UI design transitions.

2.1   Impression Formation and the Function of Kansei

As it has a broad definition, in this research, based on the work of Hsu, we define Kansei as a reaction to external sensory stimuli [5]. Because Kansei is closely related to sensation and perception [6], we first discuss the human cognitive processes. Cognitive processes are 1) "sensation," in which information from the five senses passes through the central nervous system to indicate what is felt, 2) "perception," in which things are recognized by the information received, and 3) "cognition," in which what is perceived is interpreted based on thought processes such as past experience and memory [7]. The information is then evaluated by "checking" it against individual values and cultural backgrounds, and the emotional response that occurs during this process is Kansei [8], which differs from person to person even for the same information [9]. This series of cognitive processes can be viewed as a mechanism of impression formation. (Fig. 1).

In the field of product design, the impression of an object depends on visual and tactile elements as well as individual perception and experience [10]. In particular, because humans are said to obtain more than 80% of their information from sight [11], visual elements are the most important factors in impression formation. In this research, we focused on these four items to examine external information (e.g. materials and finishes) that influences sensory value.

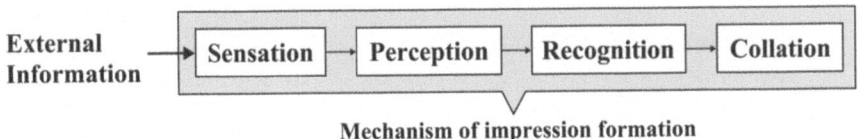

Mechanism of impression formation

Fig. 1. Mechanism of impression formation.

2.2 The Impact of CMF on Kansei Value and Its Applicability to UI

Kansei value refers to the impression or sympathy obtained from a product or service [12]. According to Nagata et al., physical factors such as color and surface quality are elements that form impressions of products [13]. One of these sensory factors in surface design is CMF, which comprises three elements. It is a design method that adds value to a product by adjusting the surface texture and tactile feeling, rather than the shape of the product. CMF is a design method that adds value to a product by adjusting its surface texture and feel, rather than its shape [14].

First, the impression brought about by color changes depends on the color difference, and a favorable impression is likely to be held toward a product that has a high degree of conformity between the color image and the desired image [15]. For example, black is considered to represent "sincerity" and "seriousness," [16, 17] and in a comparison of different brightness, black with a higher brightness gives a stronger impression [15].

Next, Material is a factor that determines the basic properties, such as the strength, weight, and durability, of a product [14]. Yamane et al. have found that elements such as "fineness of cross-section," "unevenness," and "twist" in surface shape influence the impression formation of the product and contribute to the evaluation of Kansei such as "luxury," "uniqueness," and "softness" [18].

Furthermore, Finish is an element that is closely related to the expression of the material and evokes diverse images [14]. According to Yuzawa, the impression of a product changes depending on the strength of the luster, with a strong luster giving the impression of "luxury" and a low luster giving the impression of "moist" or "bewitching" [19].

As described above, there are many studies on the impressions given by each CMF element individually, but only a few studies have examined these three elements in an integrated manner. Therefore, this research aims to comprehensively reinterpret the three elements of CMF and explore their applicability to UI design, thereby, contributing to the improvement of the product use experience.

3   Research Method

First, research of Kansei elements in product cases was conducted, followed by research of Kansei elements in UI design transitions. The main flow of the research is as follows (Fig. 2).

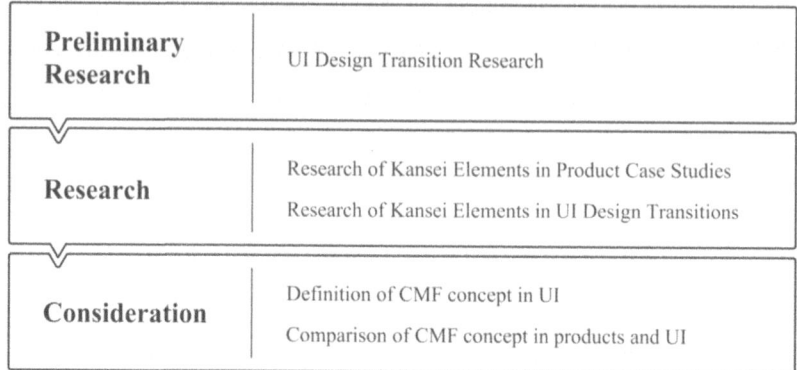

Fig. 2. Research process.

3.1 Research of Kansei Elements in Product Case Studies

Expressing texture and emotional appeal through color, material, and finish (CMF) is a critical aspect of product design. In considering the application of the CMF concept to UI design, it is important to reassess the role of CMF in product design. This research aims to clarify the roles and impressions conveyed by each CMF element in product design. As part of the research, eight products featuring prominent CMF elements were selected (Table 1). Based on case studies, these products were analyzed from a CMF perspective to organize and evaluate the impressions created by each element. The products were selected because preliminary research indicated that many CMF-applied products are lifestyle-related and demonstrate a wide variety of CMF applications.

Table 1. Eight products selected as the subjects of this research.

Sample1 : Cleaner	Sample2 : Automobile	Sample3 : PC	Sample4 : Smart Phone
Sample5 : Chair	Sample6 : Wrist Watch	Sample7 : Toaster	Sample8 : Washing Machine

3.2   Research of Kansei Elements in UI Design Transitions

In this research, to clarify the roles of each CMF element and the impressions they convey, we investigated six major design styles from the evolution of UI design: skeuomorphism, flat design, material design, neumorphism, glassmorphism, and claymorphism(Fig. 3). Based on a case research analysis, these UI designs were examined from the perspective of CMF, organizing how each element is expressed.

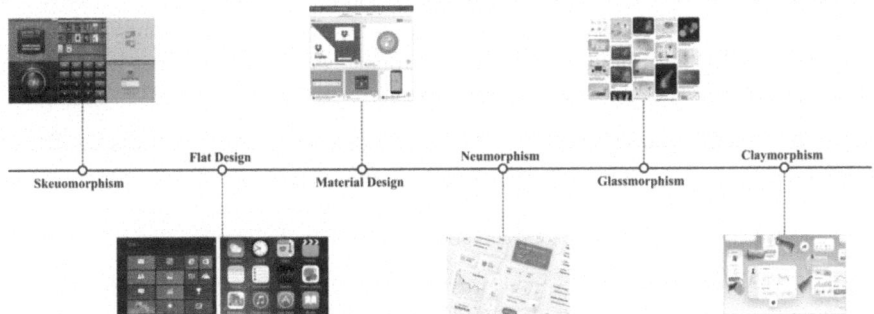

Fig. 3. History of UI design.

4   Results and Discussion

4.1   Research Results and Considerations of Kansei Elements in Product Design

Sample 1. Color uses an innovative combination of playful purple, blue, yellow, and silver to create a visual futuristic and luxurious feel. In addition, the consistent use of red for the detachable button gives the impression of intuitive and easy-to-understand functionality. Material uses lightweight and durable plastic to make the product lighter and more durable. In the case of Finish, a combination of matte and glossy finishes is used to give the overall product a sophisticated look.

Sample 2. As for Color, deep colors are used for the body to create a sense of calmness and luxury. The interior is also uniformly colored red and black, emphasizing a refined and luxurious feel, and the materials used include carbon fiber and aluminum to achieve light weight and high rigidity while expressing a sense of luxury. Finishes include metallic and pearl finishes, which reflect and refract light to create an even more luxurious sensation.

Sample 3. The color employs a subdued and calm tone, providing a gentle impression without causing visual strain. The material is lightweight yet durable magnesium alloy, achieving a balance between durability and reduced weight. The finish features a matte texture, creating a sophisticated and calming effect while offering practical benefits such as reduced visibility of fingerprints and smudges.

Sample 4. The colors used are highly saturated pink, green, and blue, which give a cute impression and motivate customers to purchase the product. The black and white colors, however, are designed to create a sense of luxury and cleanliness. With regard to Finish, the glass provides a glossy finish that is both smooth to the touch and clean. In addition, a rough finish is used on the sides to provide a tactile and comfortable feel while expressing the practical non-slip characteristics.

Sample 5. As for Color, the overall color scheme is low in brightness, creating a pop yet calm impression. The use of uniform colors throughout the chair gives the impression of a simple and sophisticated design. A lightweight yet durable plastic material is used, giving the impression of both ease of use and robustness. Finish is characterized by a modern and luxurious design with a glossy finish.

Sample 6. Bright white is used to provide a fresh and futuristic impression. Black creates an overall calm impression, whereas the highly saturated yellow gives a pop and friendly impression. The band is made of soft urethane to ensure comfort. This matte finish also has practical benefits such as reducing the risk of slipping.

Sample 7. As for Color, black and gray are used to create a sense of luxury and calmness. The white color is sophisticated and beautiful, while the chocolate color is less saturated, creating a beautiful and calm impression. It gives a friendly impression with no sense of coldness. In addition, the finish is resistant to fingerprints and scratches, thereby, ensuring practicality.

Sample 8. Sand glaze, an intermediate color between gray and beige, is used to express both sophistication and warmth simultaneously. The material used for the doors is clear glass, which provides a fresh impression. The overall matte finish provides the product with a luxurious experience. In addition, the finish is free of bumps and seams, emphasizing the impression of sophistication.

The CMF elements in the examined products were analyzed by considering the three components of Color—brightness, saturation, and hue. For Material and Finish, elements were extracted with reference to the CMF concept proposed based on the work of Tamai, and the comparative analysis results were summarized in Table 2.

Through this research, we were able to reconfirm how CMF elements are expressed in product design. The following section provides a discussion from the perspective of each CMF element.

1. Color

Color is a key element that determines the first impression of a product. For instance, highly saturated colors often create a playful and vibrant impression, whereas low-brightness colors convey a sense of calmness. Consistent use of specific colors across products can emphasize functional elements, such as operational buttons, aiding in user understanding. Furthermore, products that are closely associated with personal identity or style—such as "cars," "smartphones," and "chairs"—tend to offer a wide range of color variations and are designed with high brightness for visual appeal.

Table 2. Comparative analysis results in product.

		cleaner	Automobile	PC	Smart Phone	Chair	Wrist Watch	Toaster	Washing Machine
		Dyson	LEXUS	Fujitsu	Apple	Virta	G-SHOCK	BALMUDA	Panasonic
		Detect Slim Fluffy(SU46 FF)	LC500	LIFEBOOK U7	iphone16	Panton Chair	CBD-300-1 JF	The Toaster	LX129D
Color	Brightness	High	High	Middle	High	High	High	Middle	High
	Saturation	High	Middle	Low	High	Middle	Middle	Low	Low
	Hue	Red Purple Silver	White Gray Silver Black Red Copper Yellow Green Blue	Black Green Silver Brown	Black White Pink Green Blue	White Blue Red Brown Black Pink Green	Yellow Black White	Black White Cocoa Gray	Beige white
Material	Weight	Light	Heavy	Light	Light	Light	Light	Normal	Heavy
	Stiffness	High	High	Middle	High	High	High	High	High
	Flexibility	×	×	×	○	○	○	×	×
	Size	Normal	Large	Normal	Small	Normal	Normal	Normal	Large
	Workability	○	○	○	○	×	○	○	○
Finish	Glossy	○	○	×	○	○	×	×	○
	Matte	○	○	○	○	×	○	○	○
	Uneven	×	×	×	×	×	○	×	×
	Texture	○	○	×	○	×	○	○	×
	Reflection	○	○	×	○	×	×	○	○
	Depth	○	○	×	○	×	○	×	×

2. Material

Material influences both the physical properties of a product and the sensory experience through texture and touch. The tactile and visual qualities of materials convey the product's purpose and perceived quality. For example, metal materials evoke a sense of luxury, while wood imparts warmth and a natural feel. Household appliances such as "toasters" and "washing machines" often employ materials with high rigidity, which enhances the perception of stability and reliability.

3. Finish

Finish enhances the visual appeal of a product and plays a role in product differentiation. Glossy finishes convey a futuristic and premium look, while matte finishes create a calm and sophisticated impression. Textured finishes can improve usability by offering better grip and preventing slippage. Additionally, finish contributes to the overall design coherence, shaping impressions aligned with the product's concept. Products that emphasize luxury—such as "cars" and "smartphones"—frequently incorporate finishes that express light, reflection, and depth to heighten their visual impact.

4.2 Research Results and Considerations of Kansei Elements in UI Design

Skeuomorphism. Color expresses a realistic atmosphere using vivid colors of the same hue, saturation, and brightness as the appearance of real objects. As for Material, the warmth and reality of the bookshelf are expressed by reproducing a wood grain tone, and the texture of the metal is emphasized to give a realistic impression of being able to touch the bookshelf. In the case of Finish, a glossy finish is applied to the buttons to create a realistic three-dimensional effect, and shadows and highlights are used to make the button surfaces appear smooth and realistic. Shadows and highlights were used to provide the button surfaces with smooth, realistic textures.

Flat Design. Color is primarily used to distinguish elements on the interface and organize information, thus, facilitating the visual categorization of each function. In addition, to indicate hierarchy and importance, expressions using vivid colors for elements that are particularly emphasized are employed. However, Material and Finish were not used.

Material Design. Color plays a role in indicating the visual hierarchy, especially in expressing the prominence of important elements through the use of contrast. It also has a functional meaning, such as red for errors and green for success, to intuitively understand the situation. In addition, by expressing physical height using shadows, the importance of each element can be visually conveyed in an easy-to-understand manner. However, we found that Finish was not used.

Neumorphism. Color is characterized by the use of monochromatic and pastel tones, which provide a calm and soft impression of the entire UI. Material focuses on digitally expressing "softness" and "lightness" rather than using physical materials. In addition, shadows and light are used to reproduce a "pushed-out" or "hollowed-out" feeling, creating a realistic three-dimensional effect. This also makes it easier to distinguish elements from the background. Finish does not use actual gloss or texture but mainly uses a matte finish to give a sophisticated impression. In addition, it creates a smooth impression that blends with the background, resulting in unity and consistency.

Glassmorphism. Colors express visual depth and three-dimensionality using vivid gradations. Material adds depth to the overall UI design by mimicking the feeling of frosted glass. Finish creates a realistic sense of transparency of glass by incorporating bright gradations and hues to express the reflection and refraction of light. It also achieves a glossy finish using an illuminating effect, giving the impression of sophistication.

Claymorphism. Color expresses friendliness through the use of pastel colors and soft hues that are not too bright. The use of simple monochromes and subdued gradations in the elements gives the design a soft, three-dimensional feel, while Material gives a soft, friendly impression by digitally representing a material that resembles actual clay. Finish uses a matte finish with a low sheen to create a visually soft impression. This finish eliminates the impression of hardness, emphasizes friendliness, and maintains a sense of unity throughout the interface.

The CMF elements in UI design were analyzed as follows. For Color, the three components that define color—brightness, saturation, and hue—were considered. For Material, four key elements representing material on the UI—imitation, sense of material, shadow, and highlight—were identified. Regarding Finish, elements were extracted and organized based on CMF concepts referenced from Tamai (2023), with the comparative analysis results summarized in Table 3.

Table 3. Comparative analysis results of UI design.

		skeuomorphism	Flat Design	Material Design	Neumorphism	Glassmorphism	Claymorphism
Color	Brightness	Middle	High	Middle	High	Middle	Middle
	Saturation	Middle	High	Middle	Low	High	Low
	Hue	Natural color tones with emphasis on reality	Monochromatic / Vivid	Functional color scheme	Pastel / Soft colors	Semi-transparent / Gradation	Pastel color
Material	Imitation	○	×	×	×	×	×
	Sense of material	○	×	×	×	○	○
	Shadows	○	×	○	○	○	○
	Highlight	○	×	×	○	○	○
Finish	Glossy	○	×	×	×	○	×
	Matte	○	×	×	○	×	○
	Uneven	○	×	×	○	×	○
	Texture	○	×	×	×	○	○
	Reflection	○	×	×	×	○	×
	Depth	○	×	×	○	○	○

Through this research, we were able to confirm how CMF is expressed in UI design. The following sections provide a discussion from the perspectives of each CMF element.

1. Color

The role of color in UI design has evolved from initially replicating realism to conveying functionality and ultimately providing emotional value. Color is considered a crucial element that surpasses mere functionality by delivering sensory impressions and appealing to users' emotions. Designs such as flat design and glassmorphism showed a tendency to use high-saturation colors. Additionally, it was found that relatively newer designs like neumorphism and claymorphism tend to use low-brightness colors.

2. Material

In the early stages, material in UI design focused on replicating realism and familiarity. Over time, it has advanced to contribute to functionality and information organization. Incorporating organic textures has enabled materials to convey sensory impressions while enhancing element differentiation through depth, thereby improving visibility. Material is no longer limited to representing texture but plays a crucial role in reinforcing information hierarchy, usability, and enhancing visual and tactile experiences on the interface. In addition, skeuomorphism, glasmomorphism and claymorphism had techniques that expressed materiality; in particular, skeuomorphism imitated real materials, and all four items of imitation, materiality, shadows, and highlights were applicable.

3. Finish

The role of finish in UI design initially emphasized reproducing realism. However, it has since shifted to adapt real-world finishing elements to match the design concept of the interface, serving to create unique impressions. As a result, finish elements now play a significant role in unifying the overall aesthetic of UI design, making them essential components for both functionality and emotional engagement. Moreover, the only design to which all items were applied was skeuomorphism, as well as differences in expression, varied from design to design. In particular, few designs utilized gloss and reflections, and there was a trend toward the absence of expressions such as three-dimensionality.

4.3 Comparison of the CMF Concept in Product and UI Design

The comparison of the CMF concepts in product and UI design clarified in the previous sections is presented in Table 4. This aims to reveal the characteristics of CMF in UI design by comparing its role in product design.

Table 4. The comparison of the CMF concepts in product and UI design.

	Product	UI
Color	• Used as an element that determines the first impression of a product • Used to give users an impression of "luxury" or "beauty"	• Used to increase functionality and visibility • Used to maintain a sense of unity of the entire interface
Material	• Used to determine the physical characteristics, durability, texture, weight and feel of the product • Used as a criterion for the user to select a product	• Shadows and highlights are used to create hierarchy and convey information in an easy-to-understand manner • Used to enhance visibility and operability and visually improve the experience on the interface
Finish	• Used to determine the look and feel of a product • Used to unify and add value to the atmosphere	• Used to differentiate from other interface designs and give a different impression • Used to unify the atmosphere of the entire interface

1. Comparison by color

   In product design, color plays a crucial role in shaping the first impression of a product. Similarly, in UI design, color is used to maintain a sense of visual consistency across the interface. Thus, both in product and UI design, color serves as a key factor in impression formation. However, a notable difference lies in the role of color within UI design, where emphasis is placed on enhancing functionality and visibility. This functional aspect distinguishes the use of color in UI from that in product design.

2. Comparison by Material

   In product design, physical materials such as metal and plastic significantly influence the characteristics of the product. In contrast, UI design replicates a sense of "materiality" digitally through visual effects like shadows and highlights, utilizing these to organize information and define hierarchical structures. This difference suggests that the concept of "material" is perceived differently in product and UI design.

3. Comparison by Finish

It has been revealed that in both UI and product design, the "finish" serves as an element that unifies the overall atmosphere and provides users with a distinct impression compared to other objects. Additionally, the finish element plays a role in enhancing the added value of products. Therefore, incorporating visual finish in UI design is expected to improve the Kansei value of the design.

Based on the findings, it has become evident that the "finish" element plays a crucial role in influencing the impression and added value perceived by users in UI design. This suggests that UI design can transcend mere functionality and visibility, becoming a means to provide users with experiential value, such as freshness and enjoyment, through Kansei-driven design.

5 Conclusion

This research aims to examine the potential use of the CMF concept in UI by clarifying design characteristics from the CMF perspective through a survey of UI design transitions. Consequently, we clarified the uniqueness of CMF in UI design by comparing it with its role in product design. As a survey of the Kansei elements in the transition of UI design, we analyzed them from the perspective of CMF, organized "how each element was expressed," and defined the concept of CMF in UI based on the results.

Consequently, we were able to define Color as an element that "enhances functionality and visibility" and "maintains a sense of unity throughout the interface." Material could be defined as an element that "uses shadows and highlights to create hierarchy and convey information clearly" and "enhances visibility and usability, visually enhancing the experience on the interface." Finish could be defined as an element that "differentiates from other interface designs and gives a different impression" and "is used to unify the atmosphere of the entire interface."

Finally, a comparison of the CMF concept in both the product and UI was conducted, showing that the Finish element played an important role, especially in influencing the impression and added value given to the user.

6 Further Work

In this research, we focused on the transition of UI design, considered the impression that the sensory element provides, and clarified the CMF concept in UI through product comparison. Future issues include examining the possibility of utilizing the CMF concept in digital interface design. In particular, as products have become increasingly digitalized in recent years, UI has become an important criterion in product selection. Consequently, there is an increasing emphasis on designs that provide consistency between the product and the UI.

Therefore, it would be beneficial to incorporate the CMF concept into the digital interfaces of consumer electronic products. Subsequently, when designing a UI, it will be possible to achieve a design that provides users with sensory value while giving them an impression of the purpose by expressing it based on the design concept.

References

1. Center for Research and Development Strategy. https://www.jst.go.jp/crds/pdf/2022/WR/CRDS-FY2022-WR-10.pdf Accessed 17 Jan 2025
2. Hirata, I., Mitsuya, K., Yamaoka, T.: GUI design method using GUI Design Pattern. Proc. Japan Soc. Design Sci. **59**, 91–92 (2012)
3. Makiba, S.: Relationship between operation and texture and stereoscopic feeling of screen. In: International Conference on Biometrics and Kansei Engineering (ICBAKE), pp. 29–32. IEEE (2017)
4. Spiliotopoulos, K., Rigou, M., Sirmakessis, S.: A comparative study of skeuomorphic and flat design from a UX perspective. Multimodal Technol. Interact. **2**(2), 31 (2018)
5. Xu, S.: Empirical kansei information processing based on the intuitive judgment. In: Proceedings of the 9th International Conference on Cognitive Science, vol. 21 (2005)
6. Imai, S., Sudo, N., Hosoda, S.: A cognitive psychological study on Kansei. Psychol. Rev. **37**(1), 1–18 (1994)
7. Inoue, K.: Designing Attractive Interfaces. Industrial Research Society, Tokyo (2008)
8. Handa, M., Munechika, M.: Selection if Terms for Questionnaire of KANSEI Quality. In: Proceedings of the 26th Annual Meeting of the Japan Society for Quality Control, pp. 99–102. Japan Society for Quality Control, Tokyo (1996)
9. Ministry of Economy, Trade and Industry, Kansei Creation Initiative – Proposal of the Fourth Value Axis – Kansei☆21 Report. https://www.nopa.or.jp/copc/pdf/kansei-honbun.pdf (Accessed 17 Jan 2025)
10. Lee, M., Honda, S., Narita, Y.: Kansei evaluation for perception of objects – focus on the relationship between 3D object model and impression. In: Proceedings of the Design Engineering and System Division Conference, vol. 20, pp. 3203–3204 (2010)
11. The Illuminating Engineering Institute of Japan (ed.): Guide to Indoor Lighting. Denki Sho-in, Tkyo (1980)
12. Iguchi, S., Inoda, K., Kobayashi, S., Tanabe, S., Nagata, N., Nakamura, T.: Human Communication Engineering Series – Kansei Information Processing, Ohmsha, Tokyo (1994)
13. Nagata, N.: Kansei indexing and its application to product design. J. Instit. Electr. Inform. Commun. Eng. **102**(9), 873–880 (2019)
14. Tamai, M.: Color, material, and finish in surface design. Surface Technol. **74**(11), 549–556 (2023)
15. Shoyama, S., Urakawa, R., Kouda, M.: Influence of shirt colors of job interview suits on impression formation. J. Design Sci. **50**(6), 87–94 (2004)
16. Hayasaka, Y.: Visual Design Laboratory, The Bookshelf of Colors – Volume 2. Visual Design Laboratory, Tokyo (1991)
17. Japan Color Research Institute.: Color One Point. Japan Standards Association, Tokyo (1993)
18. Yamane, K., Kitani, Y.: Influence of the surface shape of objects on emotional experiences -from the viewpoint of tactile, Case of a seal. Proc.Japan Soc. Design Sci. **67**, 360–361 (2020)
19. Yuzawa, Y.: Color technology and color design development in paints and coatings. Surface Technol. **74**(11), 557–563 (2023)

Visualization Analysis of Literature in the *Design Issues* Journal from the Perspective of Sustainable Development

Haochen Wang[1] and Chi Zhang[2]($\boxtimes$)

[1] Beijing Normal University, Beijing 100875, China
[2] Beijing Institute of Fashion Technology, Beijing 100029, China
20180024@bift.edu.cn

Abstract. This study employs bibliometric analysis to explore the research trends and developments of *Design Issues* over the past decade, focusing on its research priorities and close connection to the topic of "social sustainability". Using tools such as CiteSpace and VOSviewer, the study generates a series of visual knowledge maps, including keyword co-occurrence networks and highly cited literature distributions, to comprehensively illustrate the journal's academic contributions over the past ten years. The findings reveal that authors of *Design Issues* have demonstrated a strong interest in the theory and practice of "social design", leveraging this focus to advance social sustainability from a design perspective. Finally, the study discusses the journal's exploration of "sustainability", particularly through the lens of "social design", examining its relevance to "social sustainability" values from both design methodology and design practice perspectives, provides unique insights and perspectives on the broader discourse of "sustainability".

Keywords: Social Sustainability · Bibliometric · Information Visualization · *Design Issues*

1 Introduction

Design *Issues* is an international academic design journal published by MIT Press, founded in 1983, and published four times a year. Focusing on the history, theory, and criticism of design, the journal has sparked numerous academic debates on design culture and related issues. It covers regular features as well as specific editions curated by guest editors, topics range from history of design, service design, and organizational design, etc. In recent years, the journal has paid special attention to the impact of social culture on design research, especially in regulating the conflicts and problems in various aspects of society, and the development of social and cultural "sustainability" has gradually become a new direction for design research.

In the current context, the concept of sustainable development has been widely accepted, yet there is a relative lack of academic research on social sustainability, one of the three dimensions of sustainable development. This phenomenon may be partly

M. Schrepp (Ed.): HCII 2025, LNCS 15794, pp. 103–114, 2025.
https://doi.org/10.1007/978-3-031-93221-2_7

attributed to the wide range of research areas, vague definitions, and complexity of measurement criteria of social sustainability, which leads to the challenge of comprehensive and precise analysis for researchers [1]. Social sustainability essentially refers to the ability of human societies to continue to develop and achieve positive progress over time. According to the concept and goals of sustainable development, the core concern of social sustainability is the "principle of equity", i.e., to ensure that everyone has equal opportunities for survival and development, centered on the fair and equitable distribution of resources between current and different generations. The existing literature dis-aggregates social sustainability into regional, urban, and community dimensions, [2] noting that it is significantly influenced by factors such as culture, customs, and geographic characteristics. Currently, many design studies are centered around the daily habits of residents and local trends of thought, aiming to support social sustainability through social research. This study focuses on relevant articles published in the journal *Design Issues* over the past decade, and through bibliometric and visual analysis methods, explores in-depth the discourses and practices of social sustainability in the field of design, to provide new research perspectives and experience sharing on the issue of social sustainability from the perspective of design.

2 Fundamental Analysis of Literature

The data of this study comes from Web of Science (WOS) database, and the time period of search is from 2013 to 2023, after sorting and screening, a total of 367 valid journal documents of the journal *Design Issues* were obtained. Then, analysis tools, CiteSpace and VOSviewer, were used to analyze the relevant data of the above literature with the help of literature analysis methods, conduct visual text analysis, and draw the knowledge map related to the literature data, so as to excavate the research dynamics and development trend of the journal *Design Issues*, and to provide data support for the subsequent research.

3 Research Context and Development Trends

3.1 Hot Word Clustering and Research Context

By utilizing the VOSviewer analysis software to process the data, a co-occurrence map of keywords can be generated. From the word frequency statistics, a total of 854 different keywords were produced. After removing invalid keywords and merging synonyms in the keyword preview, 677 keyword data points were obtained. The keyword co-occurrence network for the *Design Issues* journal from 2013 to 2023, generated from this data, is shown in Fig. 1. In the keyword co-occurrence network of Fig. 1, the size of the nodes represents the frequency of keyword appearances, and the thickness of the edges indicates the level of keyword co-occurrence frequency.

Using CiteSpace to perform cluster analysis on keywords yields the results shown in Fig. 2. There are primarily 6 knowledge clusters: Social Design, Design Education, Service Design, Design Strategy, Design as Communication, and Dialogic Interaction. By

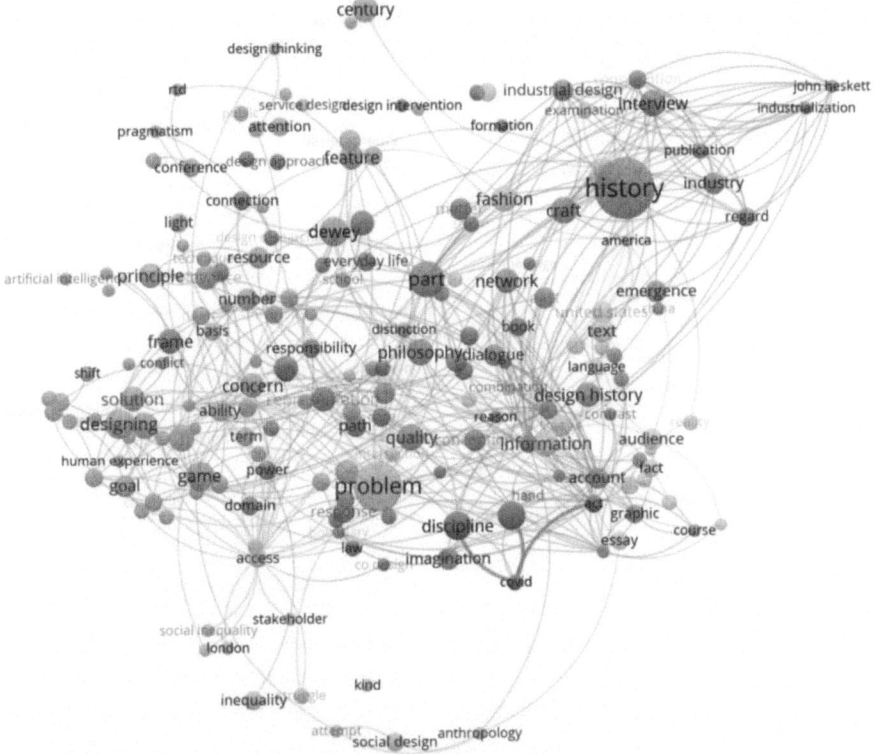

Fig. 1. Keyword Co-occurrence Network.

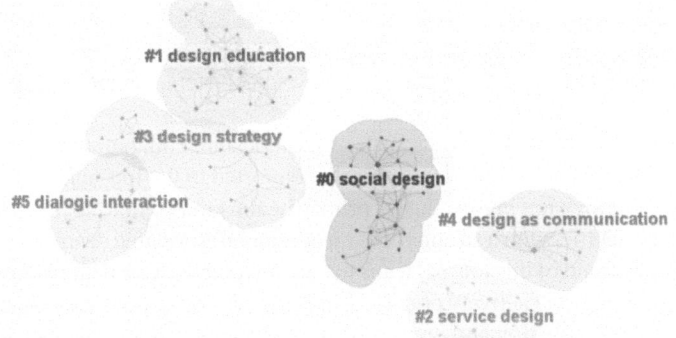

Fig. 2. Keyword Clustering.

Table 1. Keyword Clustering Organization'.

Cluster number	Cluster name	Keywords
1	Social design	social design; collaborative design; citation network; participatory art; participatory design; frame innovation; collective action; social movements
2	Design education	design education; information design; data visualizations; covid-19; design discourse; design practice; design knowledge; artificial intelligence; data-driven design; learning systems
3	Service design	service design; design philosophy; conceptual models; human-centered design; design capacities; game design; critical design; design research; service innovation
4	Design strategy	design strategy; design management; organization design; design principles; design thinking: competitive advantage; human-centered design; legal design; dialectical logic
5	Design as communication	design as communication; graphic designers; grid systems; cross-culture design; folk drawing; designer-client relationship; actor-network theory; national style; material semiotics
6	Dialogic interaction	dialogic interaction; industrial design; design history; product design; action research; design activism

categorizing and organizing the contents of these six clusters, the information presented in Table 1 can be obtained.

Among these clusters, keywords such as legal design, collaborative design, participatory design, and action research are closely connected to the top-ranked social design cluster. The design vision in this cluster primarily aims to promote social harmony and improve quality of life, with a strong focus on community-oriented design. This suggests that the research trend of this journal leans toward advocating social innovation practices initiated by designers but actively practiced and even led by the public, emphasizing high levels of social participation and engagement. In Clusters 3 and 4, hot words related to dialectical thinking and critical design highlight reflective design methodologies. This may indicate that scholars in the design field are increasingly inclined to re-examine both design and designers themselves, seeking to break away from conventional logic and pursue innovative reforms that address real-world issues.

Through the analysis of the keyword timeline generated by CiteSpace, we can observe six distinct key word clusters, each representing a series of keywords arranged sequentially along the timeline. These arrangements are based on keyword frequency, time of occurrence, and co-occurrence relationships. Notably, the "social design" cluster has demonstrated a high frequency of occurrence in academic journal articles over the past decade and continues to be a focal point, underscoring its significance in scholarly discussions. Within this cluster, keywords such as "participatory design" (2016), "collaborative design" (2018), "participatory art" (2020), and "collective action" (2022) form a chronological axis that reflects the growing academic attention to public participation and community development in design discourse. On the other hand, "design education" has emerged as another active keyword axis, with related articles focusing on modern technological themes such as artificial intelligence and data-driven design. This trend highlights the increasing integration of advanced technology into design education, aiming to enhance both the effectiveness and efficiency of design practice. This analysis not only illustrates the evolution of keywords over time but also reveals shifts in academic interests and focal points within specific research fields, offering valuable insights for further studies (Fig. 3).

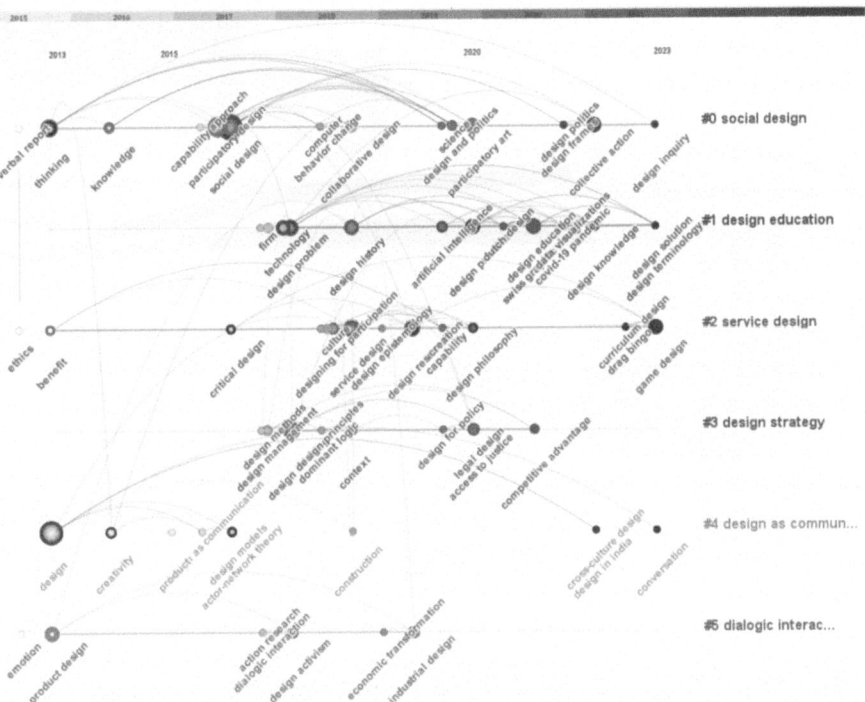

Fig. 3. Keyword Cluster Timeline.

3.2   Highly Cited Literature Clustering and Development Trends

Between 2013 and 2023, citation analysis revealed a total of 9,164 journal articles with recorded citations. By setting the minimum co-occurrence threshold to 5, 58 highly cited articles were identified. The co-occurrence network of these articles is visually represented in Fig. 4, where different colors indicate four distinct clusters. Further analysis, as shown in Table 2, reveals that these clusters correspond to four key research areas: design thinking, design value, social design, and human-centered design. Notably, the clustering themes align closely with the trends observed in keyword analysis. A comprehensive review of these findings suggests that, in recent years, research trends have increasingly emphasized innovation and public participation in social design, as well as the growing significance of critical design thinking.

In terms of design methodology, journal authors tend to favor speculative design approaches that challenge and disrupt existing systems, as well as design activism that places greater emphasis on local and regional characteristics. At the level of design practice, research increasingly supports a multi-stakeholder collaboration model led by designers, involving public participation and community co-maintenance. This model aims to enhance public awareness of design participation and unlock their creative potential. Furthermore, the focus of design has shifted from specific individuals or groups to more fluid and inclusive communities, and even to the societal level as a whole. By exploring the shared characteristics and needs of the public, researchers seek to enhance people's initiative and engagement in design activities.

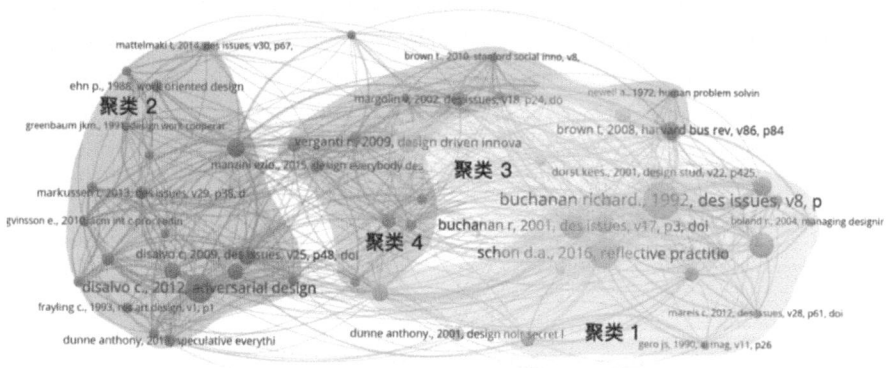

Fig. 4. Co-occurrence Network of Cited References.

4   Hot Word Trends in *Design Issues* and Social Sustainability

4.1   "Social Sustainability" Involved in the Hot Word Trends of *Design Issues*

Since 2015, the concept of "sustainability" has been widely integrated into the theoretical framework of "Big Design" and has gradually been recognized globally as a core value in design ethics. Amid the emergence of new ideas, sustainability has quietly become a

Table 2. Organization of Key Cited Reference Clusters.

Cluster number (Color)	Cluster name	Highly Cited References
1 (Green)	Design Thinking	1. *Wicked Problems in Design Thinking* 2. *The Reflective Practitioner: How Professionals Think in Action* 3. *Design Research and the New Learning*
2 (Red)	Design Values	1. *Adversarial Design* 2. *Participatory Design* 3. *Design and the Construction of Publics* 4. *Design Activism: Beautiful Strangeness for a Sustainable World*
3 (Yellow)	Social Design	1. *Design-Driven Innovation* 2. *Change by Design: How Design Thinking Transforms Organizations and Inspires innovation* 3. *Design Research and the New Learning*
4 (Blue)	Human-centered Design	1. *Wicked Problems in Design Thinking* 2. *The Reflective Practitioner: How Professionals Think in Action* 3. *A "Social Model" of Design: Issues of Practice and Research*

deep-seated and self-evident presence [3]. Using bibliometric analysis, this study reveals the evolving trends of sustainable design as a research hot word. In the research trends of *Design Issues,* a clear focus on sustainability can also be observed. Notably, the journal adopts "social design" as a starting point to explore the closely related values of "social sustainability," aiming to provide unique perspectives and insights on the topic of sustainability.

Climate change, energy conservation, and environmental protection have been global hot topics since the 21st century, making sustainable development a strategic choice for humanity's continued survival [4]. The concept of sustainable development was first thoroughly articulated by scholar Gro Harlem Brundtland in *Our Common Future* (1987), marking an academic effort to connect the development and reform of the natural environment, social environment, and economic policies. Among these, social sustainability is a key component of the sustainability concept, emphasizing social equity and harmony while ensuring the long-term well-being of citizens [5]. In past research, the topic of "social sustainability" has often been equated with social capital, social inclusion, and exclusion [6], leading researchers to focus more on addressing basic needs and underdevelopment issues while overlooking discussions in more developed regions. Similarly, urban communities also face significant social sustainability challenges. Scholar Hege Hofstad points out that a community's social sustainability is centered on preserving traditional culture, values, and customs that people wish to maintain. Therefore, it should not be measured solely by objective standards but should also consider the subjective meaning and value it holds for residents [7]. This perspective provides an entry point for design research on social sustainability—not only addressing common issues in underdeveloped areas but also considering the social sustainability challenges present in urban communities.

Scholars such as Suzanne Valiance have summarized social sustainability from a more comprehensive perspective into three levels: development sustainability, connection sustainability, and maintenance sustainability [8]. These three levels are progressive and influence each other. Development sustainability emphasizes basic human needs; connection sustainability mainly explores the relationship between humans and the ecological environment; maintenance sustainability discusses how to increase social cohesion and positive forces, providing people with a high quality of life and living environment. Based on these three levels of social sustainability, the essential components of social sustainability can be defined as: basic needs, social equity, and social capital [9]. Taking these three elements as the starting point for design can lead to a series of research and practices for developing social sustainability.

Through an in-depth analysis of articles published in this academic journal over the past decade, we find that its research focus primarily revolves around social design, human-centered design, participatory design, and critical design. These studies are largely based on residents' daily habits and local intellectual trends, exploring social issues with design concepts that emphasize meeting basic needs, promoting social justice, and enhancing social capital - key topics within social sustainability. In discussions on social sustainability, the relationships between individuals and nature, as well as between individuals and communities, represent the most fundamental and closely connected forms of interaction. Compared to addressing product or visual design challenges, designing these relationships is particularly crucial in this context, requiring designers to apply critical thinking to navigate complex social dynamics and conflicts. Additionally, regionality is a key factor influencing social sustainability. The history, geography, and culture of a region profoundly shape local lifestyles and intellectual currents. Therefore, designers must take regional factors into account when engaging in socially sustainable design. In the following discussion, this paper will examine how authors in this academic journal adopt more critical approaches to mediate complex real-world relationships and conflicts, as well as how they reassess the impact of regionality on individuals from a more experimental perspective in design practice.

4.2 Design Approaches for Developing "Social Sustainability"

In the process of exploring the development of "social sustainability", designers are required to deeply analyze and understand the fundamental contradictions within society and the complexities of its structural systems. This task spans multiple disciplines and involves intricate relationships between various groups and systems. Traditionally, design methodologies have often relied on linear reasoning. However, when addressing issues related to social sustainability, these challenges tend to be nonlinear and difficult to resolve, making conventional design approaches less effective. As a result, researchers have begun exploring more radical and critical design methods - approaches that challenge the status quo, break conventions, and seek to drive innovative social reform by questioning existing structures and norms.

In *Design Issues*, scholars tend to adopt non-traditional design strategies to overcome the limitations imposed by fixed ways of thinking, thereby fostering innovation in design at the societal level. As a result, papers published in this journal frequently reference critical design, dialectical thinking, and non-affective design as key methodologies. These approaches go beyond conventional research paradigms, delving into individual motivations and community interactions to uncover the deeper meanings embedded in everyday behaviors. For example, the journal features a practice-based study utilizing critical design thinking, titled *Domestic Reflections, Electric Reflections: Design Interventions Foregrounding Energy Mundanity in the Home* [10].This paper conducts an in-depth review of literature related to household energy use and thoroughly examines historical design interventions aimed at household energy consumption. Through this process, the authors encourage the public to reflect on their daily energy consumption habits, offering fresh perspectives for sustainable home energy design. Additionally, the paper highlights how interpersonal relationships within families and communities influence individual resource use. The authors argue that when assessing daily sustainability-related practices in home life, it may be more appropriate to adopt "critical design"—a method that challenges traditional "affirmative design." This approach emphasizes questioning the status quo and fostering reflection, ultimately driving thoughtful and innovative transformations toward sustainable household living.

The concept of critical design emerged in the mid-1990s, initially defined by Anthony Dunne and Fiona Raby. It aims to challenge restrictive assumptions and ingrained preconceptions through speculative methods, [11] thereby deeply exploring the role and significance of products in everyday life. Rooted in Dunne & Raby's concerns about technological progress and humanity's blind dependence on technology, critical design encourages the public to adopt a critical mindset rather than passively accepting the status quo. In design practice, critical design is regarded as an essential dialectical thinking approach, particularly in social contexts, where it seeks to promote the fair use of resources and urges individuals to reconsider the purpose and necessity of household energy consumption, beyond mere utility and function. This approach not only disrupts traditional ways of thinking about designed objects but also provides designers with a new perspective that critiques everyday life. At the same time, it pushes designers to reflect on the role of design itself, questioning the relationship between design, users, and broader societal issues throughout the design process.

4.3 Design Practices' Attempts at "Social Sustainability"

In the field of design practice, discussions on social sustainability emerged later compared to those on environmental sustainability. This delay can be attributed to two main factors: Social issues often become more visible only when economic development faces challenges; The complexity of social issues far exceeds the scope of traditional product, spatial, or service design. Over the past decade, we have witnessed a growing number of socially responsible designers who have moved beyond commercial design to engage in social design practices. These practices, centered on social issues, have evolved in several key ways: From one-directional initiatives led by designers to multi-directional participation involving the broader public; From problem-solving approaches targeting specific issues to strategic interventions addressing complex systemic challenges;

From single-discipline design solutions to interdisciplinary, open-ended social engagement models. By optimizing its organizational framework, design practice is increasingly fostering participation from diverse social sectors in building social sustainability. Additionally, regionally specific design initiatives, aimed at innovating social organizational structures, are becoming an integral part of the contemporary design landscape.

Authors of the *Design Issues* journal also tend to adopt multi-stakeholder collaboration models in their experimental design practices. Articles in the journal frequently discuss design activism, decolonization, and neoliberalism, emphasizing the regional and public dimensions of design research. For example, in the design activism context, the article *Design Activism in an Indonesian Village* [12] investigates various design practices in Indonesia. The authors explore how local community organizations and economic industries employ sustainable design concepts to mitigate cultural biases and environmental crises. Cases include the hidden use of bamboo materials and the decolonization of village culture. Analyzing these local initiatives through the lens of design activism, the article proposes that design activism movements should begin at the local level rather than adopting a broad, global approach from the outset.

The concept of design activism can be traced back to 1960s Finland, originating from participatory design movements of that era. It is a distinctive practice that incorporates sociological and political theories into non-governmental and non-profit activities, often with a critical perspective. Unlike traditional design practices, design activism focuses on exploring and developing innovative methods and practices that foster social connections. It leverages design thinking and imagination—whether consciously or unconsciously—to create a "counter-narrative", aiming to drive positive social, institutional, environmental, or economic change. Design activism operates by initiating radical actions in the real world as catalysts for change or by creatively utilizing traditional communication channels such as exhibitions, films, and books to shape visions of the future and directly intervene in society [13].

In the field of sustainable development, design activism is regarded as a radical form of social practice, primarily focused on promoting collaborative participation, challenging established mainstream models, and exploring new sustainable lifestyles. According to previous literature, design activism advocates for deeply exploring local knowledge from the perspective of cultural stakeholders, integrating innovative forces into communities, and actively fostering interconnections between individuals, society, and the environment to build a mutually beneficial model. In discussions on sustainability, the socio-cultural dimension plays a crucial role. Its core values lie in driving social change, strengthening shared beliefs in sustainability, and questioning and challenging mass production and consumerism's impact on daily life.

5 Conclusion

By analyzing the foundational data of *Design Issues* over the past decade, this study reveals the journal's academic trends and research focus. Through keyword analysis, social design, design practice, and service design emerge as key knowledge clusters, while highly cited literature analysis indicates that design thinking, design value, and social design are the most prominent research areas. Furthermore, the study highlights that innovative and highly participatory social design, along with critical design thinking, have become major research hot word in recent years. In terms of methodology, the journal's articles predominantly adopt radical design approaches that challenge the status quo, alongside design activism that emphasizes local and regional characteristics. In terms of design practice, studies stress a multi-stakeholder collaboration model, where designers lead, the public participates, and communities co-govern, aiming to foster public agency and creative potential. The research scope has expanded beyond specific individuals or groups to encompass more fluid and inclusive communities and broader society, emphasizing shared needs and collective engagement in design activities.

To summarise, by analyzing *Design Issues* over the past ten years, this study clearly outlines the academic evolution and research trends within social design-related fields, identifying key research hot word and methodological tendencies, while also demonstrating the journal's strong connection to social sustainability discussions. These findings not only provide valuable insights into the current state of design research but also offer a meaningful perspective on the evolving relationship between design and society.

Acknowledgement. This article is a phased achievement of The Beijing Normal University Future Design Seed Fund Project "Research on Contemporary Design Trends and the Development of Future Design Education".

References

1. de Fine Licht, K., Folland, A.: Redefining 'sustainability': a systematic approach for defining and assessing 'sustainability' and 'social sustainability' Theoria, 1–15 (2024)
2. Fei, Y.: The impact factors of social sustainability of urban communities: evidence from residential communities in Harbin, China (in Chinese). Master Thesis. Harbin Institute of Technology, Harbin (2019)
3. Chen, R., Zhang, C.: Bibliometric-based research hotspots and trends in sustainable design - an examination centered on design and culture (in Chinese). J. Nanjing Univ. Arts (Fine Arts Design) **06**, 89–94 (2023)
4. Chen, X.: Inherit regional cultures and create with the times: practices and thinking of contemporary Lingnan architectural designs (in Chinese). Contemporary Architect. **01**, 26–28 (2020)
5. Liu, Y., You, Z., Hou, Y.: The digitalization of intangible cultural heritage and public participation in small and medium-sized museums from a social sustainability perspective: a case study of the Museum of English Rural Life (in Chinese). Art Design **2**(12), 97–99 (2024)
6. Bramley, G., Power, S.: Urban form and social sustainability: the role of density and housing type. Environ. Plann. B. Plann. Des. **36**(1), 30–48 (2019)
7. Hofstad, H.: Well understood? A literature study defining and operationalising community social sustainability. Local Environ. **28**(9), 1193–1209 (2023)
8. Vallance, S., Perkins, H.C., Dixon, J.E.: What is social sustainability? A clarification of concepts. Geoforum **42**(3), 342–348 (2011)
9. Laine, M.: Defining and measuring corporate sustainability: are we there yet. Soc. Environ. Accountability J. **34**(3), 187–188 (2014)
10. McKinnon, H.: Domestic reflections, electric reflections: design interventions foregrounding energy mundanity in the home. Des. Issues **32**(4), 29–39 (2016)

11. Dunne, A., Raby, F.: Speculative everything: Design, Fiction, and Social dreaming. The MIT Press, Cambridge (2013)
12. Crosby, A.: Design activism in an Indonesian village. Des. Issues **35**(3), 50–63 (2019)
13. Shi, X., Yang, X.: Design activism's "local" strategies. J. Jiangsu Normal Univ. (Philos. Soc. Sci. Edn) **46**(6), 112–122 (2020)

From Drawings-Centered to Space-Centered: The Application of a Model-Based Spatial Database and Visualization in the Interior Design of the Palace Buildings in Yuanmingyuan

Huan Wang[1], Lin Wang[1], and Jie Hao[2](✉)

[1] Capital Normal University, Beijing 100048, China
whuan@cnu.edu.cn
[2] Beijing Institute of Fashion Technology, Beijing 100029, China
jhaohj@126.com

Abstract. Leveraging digital technology, research on traditional Chinese architecture has advanced to three-dimensional modeling. However, the architectural zhuangxiu (interior partition, encloseing and decoration) of Qing Dynasty structures is intricate and thoughtfully crafted. This study addresses the challenges in studying the 'disappeared' zhuangxiu of Yuanmingyuan's palace buildings, where scarce drawings and Qing palace records complicate spatial restoration. A certain degree of incompatibility exists between current research methodologies supported by digital technology and the complexity of Qing zhuangxiu. This study advocates a shift from 'drawings-centered' to 'space-centered' research, utilizing digital modeling and information technology to develop a model-based spatial database. This approach transcends traditional restoration modeling, enabling extended research capabilities. Three case studies from Yuanmingyuan illustrate the practical applicability of this methodology.

Keywords: Model-based spatial database · Design · Architectural zhuangxiu · Yuanmingyuan

1 Introduction

The Qing Dynasty palace gardens, epitomized by Yuanmingyuan, represent the pinnacle of traditional construction techniques. Here, emperors embraced garden residences, transforming the palace gardens into multifunctional spaces for ceremonial activities, governance, and relaxation. The architecture features grand hall-like structures of high rank and capaciousness. These edifices are embellished with intricate zhuangxiu (装修), which includes architectural elements such as doors, windows, geshan (槅扇), zhao (罩), and ceilings. Positioned between columns and beams, these elements serve to enclose, separate, and beautify spaces, defining functional areas beneath the roof, enhancing aesthetics, and shaping the building's purpose. Regarded as a distinct craft, zhuangxiu is detailed in historic texts such as 'Yingzao Fashi' (Jie Li, Song Dynasty, 《

营造法式》) and 'Gongcheng Zuofa Zeli' (Construction department of Qing Dynasty, Qing Dynasty,《工程做法则例》), where its significance is considered second only to major woodwork and tiling. From a modern design perspective, zhuangxiu is essential to the interior design of architecture [1].

The diversity of zhuangxiu types and the complexity of construction methods allow for flexible design layouts within architectural spaces. In royal architecture, zhuangxiu is typically executed in collaboration with other crafts such as sculpture, goldsmithing, silversmithing, and enamel work, resulting in exquisite materials and unpredictable spatial variations in the interior spaces of royal garden architecture. Among these, Yuanmingyuan is the apex of construction, epitomizing the spatial functions and aesthetic preferences of the Qing Dynasty royal family. It encapsulates their daily pursuits, routine activities, and leisure needs, reflecting the traditional culture of interior spaces and serving as an essential component in the study of traditional Chinese architecture.

Enabled by digital modeling technology, scholars can now preliminarily construct interior space models of buildings through the interpretation of historical archives, thus approaching a realistic and concrete representation of spatial appearance. However, when the subject of research is Yuanmingyuan, the premier royal palace garden of the Qing Dynasty, simple spatial modeling fails to accurately capture the zhuangxiu's spaces. Moreover, the evolution of interior design across multiple periods necessitates a shift in analytical approach. The fundamental expansion of these technologies represents a return to the core spatial issues of research, exploring the diverse applications of spatial models and their role as a database.

2 Background

Unlike typical palace architecture, the spatial layout of buildings in Yuanmingyuan is notably diverse. The architecture varies from five to seven kaijians (开间, a unit of minimal constructional space defined by 4 pillars) in width, to depths ranging from a single hall to three connected halls, and includes expansions of interior space through the use of baosha (抱厦, spatial units attached to the main structure) and suite halls. It has evolved from conventional rectangular layouts to include polygonal plan types such as connected halls, I-shaped halls, II-shaped halls, return-shaped halls, and bat-shaped halls (Fig. 1). These buildings facilitate a variety of spatial divisions through interior zhuangxiu, thereby achieving a flexible spatial layout that accommodates the diverse needs of various areas within a large space, such as incorporating scenic views, leisure, theater viewing, and creating intimate yet exquisite spaces for worship.

At the same time, the more than 20,000 abstract drawings of Yuanmingyuan style illustrate the original appearance of the architecture. Among these, at least 2,999 drawings of interior zhuangxiu depict the spatial layout of the halls, with 1,063 identifiable drawings from various periods, primarily from the Jiaqing era, with the most preserved from the Xianfeng, Daoguang, Guangxu, and Tongzhi periods [2] (Figs. 1). The drawings encompass various types, including floor layouts of zhuangxiu, elevation patterns of zhuangxiu, and paper models, illustrating interior space design from multiple plan and elevation angles. Notably, the drawings are primarily preserved for large halls such as Fengsanwusi Hall (奉三无私殿), Shende Hall (慎德堂), Yuanmingyuan Hall (圆明

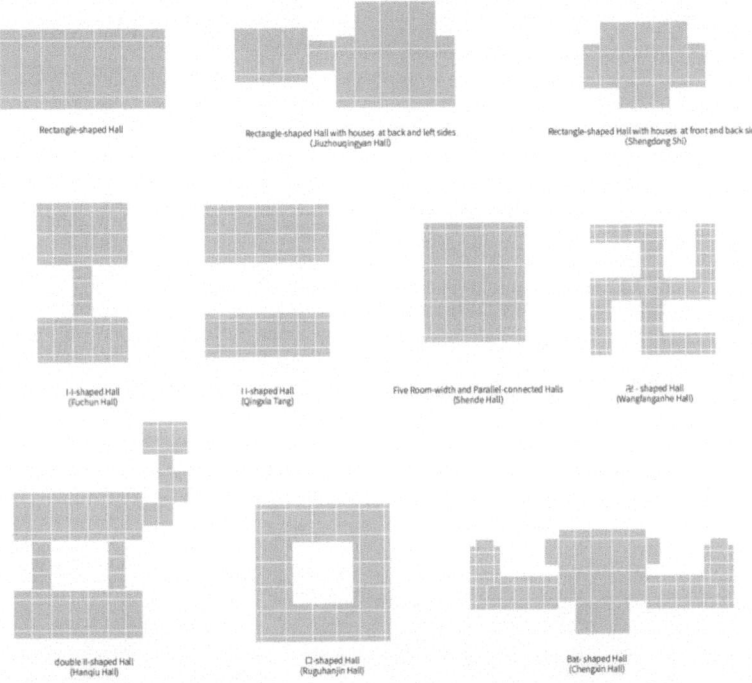

Fig. 1. Various layout forms of palaces in Yuanmingyuan.

园殿), Guanlan Hall (观 观堂), and Tiandiyijiachun Hall (天地一家春殿). Some architectural drawings include renovation schemes spanning multiple periods; for instance, Shende Hall has over a hundred drawings from the Daoguang to Tongzhi periods (Figs. 2, 3). For instance, Wanfanganhe (万方安和) has preserved Yangshi Lei's drawings and a paper model corresponding to the 'Forty Views of Yuanmingyuan' (圆明园四十景图) (Figs. 4 and 5), which clearly delineate the internal spatial layout, emphasizing the significance of architectural interior design and engineering.

Compared to other cultural heritage sites, the architectural zhuangxiu of Yuanmingyuan has largely disappeared; however, its design achievements are still evident in Qing Dynasty construction archives and drawings. Research into architectural zhuangxiu can bridge the gaps in the forms, concepts, and culture of Qing Dynasty interior space design. Nevertheless, research findings must be presented in a manner that is accessible to modern audiences to facilitate the dissemination of traditional culture.

Thus, studying the architectural zhuangxiu of Yuanmingyuan offers a distinctive approach to cultural heritage research by sorting out existing materials in various historical archives. This is followed by mutual verification and support from textual archives across different periods to reconstruct the original spatial designs. This research paradigm, traditionally centered on human cognition, is evolving to incorporate spatial modeling and

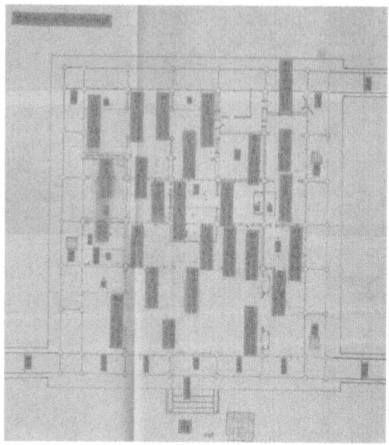 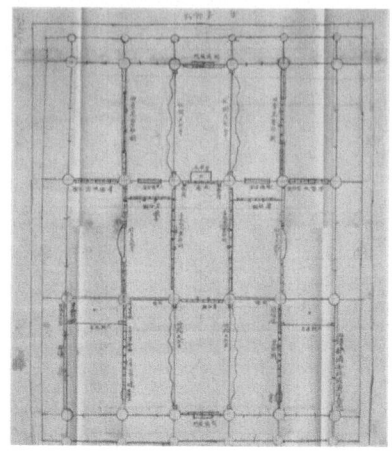

Fig. 2. No. 005–0004 Site drawing of interior eaves zhuangxiu dimensions of Shende Hall (11th year of Daoguang reign) [3].

Fig. 3. No. 060–0077 The inner zhuangxiu of Shende Hall are plainly decorated (Twelve Years of Tongzhi) [4].

Fig. 4. Forty Views of Yuanmingyuan—Wangfanganhe (Tang Dai, Shen Yuan, Leng Mei, Qing Dynasty, Year 9 of Qianlong (1744)).

Fig. 5. Paper model of Wanfanganhe (Collected by the Department of Ancient Architecture of the Palace Museum).

database construction, thereby facilitating the processing of complex historical information. This innovative approach can further inspire more visual representations and creative designs of traditional culture.

3 Related Research and Work

Since the 1990s, with the advent of computer technology in China's design field, scholars and practitioners have begun employing computer models to simulate the now-vanished architecture of Yuanmingyuan. Led by the School of Architecture at Tsinghua University, a digital research project was completed, aiming to digitally restore the main buildings of Yuanmingyuan's major scenic areas through site scanning, document interpretation, and architectural space deduction [5]. The project's outputs have primarily consisted of rendered images and animations of digital models' periods (Figs. 6, 7). In recent years, these digital models have supported exhibitions with virtual reality technology, further enhancing engagement and utilization.

Fig. 6. Digital Restoration of Shangxiatianguang [6].

Fig. 7. Yuanmingyuan ER Exhibition [7].

In terms of digital research on ancient architecture and its zhuangxiu, the Palace Museum is also expanding its research and application fields. Its achievements include a navigation system under the 'Digital Palace' concept, the Palace Museum app, and related games, enhancing the use of digital media technology in exhibitions to create immersive and interactive multidimensional exhibition experiences. These efforts are advancing the research and application of traditional Chinese architecture, reflecting contemporary endeavors to innovate and perpetuate traditional culture.

In 2006, the National Library publicized part of its construction archives and documents, including a collection of architectural style drawings of Yuanmingyuan and research on related ancient texts from these drawings' perspective, alongside an exhibition based on this material, providing new avenues for contemporary research. Since 2014, the project leader has been studying Qing Dynasty craftsmanship, and the research team began collecting, interpreting, and organizing the newly released Yuanmingyuan drawings from the National Library in 2018. The visual restoration research of Guanlan Hall's architectural zhuangxiu is complete, with presentations through digital animation videos and VR (Fig. 8). This research primarily utilizes architectural literature from Yuanmingyuan, beginning with the interpretation and analysis of types, characteristics, and design methods of the interior zhuangxiu [8]. It methodically constructs a data repository for the interior zhuangxiu of Yuanmingyuan, restoring various representative architectural zhuangxiu spaces and achieving multidimensional presentation through contemporary computer modeling and digital media technology.

Recent research indicates that the sole use of digital modeling for the study of ancient architecture's zhuangxiu is inadequate. It is essential to integrate digital information technology within the research framework to enhance the study of ancient architectural interior space design, which should cater not only to traditional design paradigms but also to future innovations.

Fig. 8. 3D model VR panorama of Guanlan Hall

4 Challenges

4.1 Difficult in Achieving Precise Restoration Models

General research on traditional Chinese architecture seeks to replicate spaces using digital technology modeling, providing a tangible and nearly accurate representation of the original designs. However, it is crucial to note that in large palace complexes like Yuanmingyuan, the interior spaces of buildings have often been modified multiple times. It remains uncertain whether finalized plans are depicted in the drawings or exceed their scope. Interior space design encompasses, on one hand, the spatial division and layout, involving the arrangement of various partition structures among indoor column grids for spatial reorganization. On the other hand, design outcomes largely depend on the scale, style, materials, and craftsmanship of the partition interfaces. These details are frequently only minimally recorded in the ground and elevation samples of style reference drawings, such as the lattice of the Bishachu, the panels of the railing cover, and the components of the Feizhao. Few elevation drawings illustrate their styles, yet the specific methodologies remain elusive. Consequently, even with the completion of spatial modeling aimed at restoration, accurately and objectively representing the original design remains challenging.

4.2 Difficult in Reflecting Multiple Periods of Design

The zhuangxiu of palace buildings in Yuanmingyuan was a focal point of imperial construction, often involving significant adjustments and discussions across multiple periods. This includes debates on the functional layout of spaces, alterations to the division of 'rooms', and changes to individual partition structures. While the overall dimensions and structure of a building may remain unchanged, multiple renovation drawings from various periods have been preserved, some still including the elevation drawings of the renovation modifications. The design process is the outcome of conflicts among various functional 'powers'. At this point, identifying the final solution becomes less crucial than exploring the design process itself, as it reflects the underlying logic of design philosophy and culture. A restoration model based solely on a single finalized solution cannot adequately address these complex design issues.

4.3 Limited Applicability

While digital modeling can indeed achieve a restoration of architectural zhuangxiu that approximates accuracy, it fails to objectively depict the overall construction. This is partly due to the 'processing design' characteristic of the interiors in Yuanmingyuan buildings and also because interior design relies on various handicraft factors such as materials, styles, and methods of each zhuangxiu. Moreover, this painstaking modeling neither accurately expresses the original design nor effectively supports research into multiple historical schemes. Traditional singular spatial modeling is in a state of limbo, caught between various functional demands without satisfying any.

Therefore, drawing from prior digital research on Yuanmingyuan's architecture, this paper responds to contemporary needs for the inheritance and innovation of construction culture. Current research should timely adjust the digital application in traditional architectural zhuangxiu studies, returning to the essence of research and advocating for the construction of a digital information repository for space.

5 Research Methods and Process

5.1 Research Methods

To determine how digital technology can assist in the design of architectural zhuangxiu for Yuanmingyuan, it is essential to revisit the most fundamental research questions: What is the ultimate research goal? What specific needs does the use of digital technology address? What are the methods and processes in researching architectural zhuangxiu? These questions must consider the context of Qing Dynasty construction, specifically restoration methods supported by the Craftsman System and construction history archives.

The most influential research group on ancient architecture in modern China, the 'Chinese Society of Architecture,' has spearheaded the study of traditional Chinese construction, based on the Craftsman System and construction archives. Mr. Zhu Qiqian, the president, emphasized 'Communication with Craftsmen' at the society's inception, focusing on 'the pursuit of substantial construction.' Later, in 1943, Liang Sicheng expanded Zhu Qiqian's concept of 'Communication with Craftsmen' into 'Structural Technology + Environmental Thought' in the preface of 'A History of Chinese Architecture'—aiming to bridge classical studies and craftsmanship. Construction archives and other literature are utilized to interpret classical studies issues, and the craftsman system addresses the content and methods of various crafts in actual construction. Thus, a logical research trajectory is established from design philosophy to construction methods, analyzing design issues by returning to the essence of architecture.

Building A Model-based Spatial Database is no longer confined to restoring a single building but involves constructing a three-dimensional, multi-layered digital information repository of interior spaces (Figs. 9). Research begins with the spatial drawings in style reference drawings, constructing a modeled space centered around a collection of various archives, documents, and drawings. First, archival information is digitized, then, 'room' serves as the spatial unit for zhuangxiu layout, with construction nodes acting as the vertical time coordinates, aligning various information such as multi-period related archives and drawings. Subsequently, the dimensions, styles, and positions of zhuangxiu's components in the interior space form a foundational database, creating a multi-layered modeled spatial database. Finally, this model database serves as a source, which can be transformed into visualized 2D diagrams, 3D animations, and comparative studies of construction across different periods. It can even inspire innovative designs in expressing design philosophy and culture.

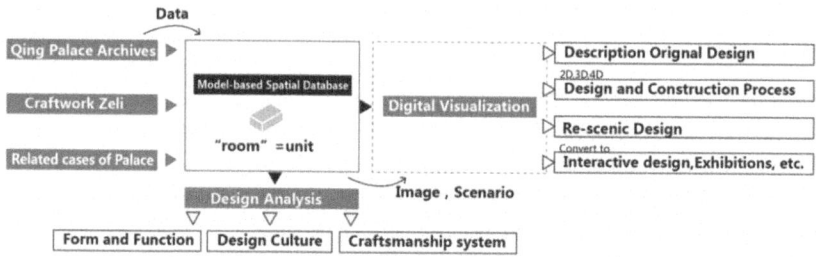

Fig. 9. Research Logic of the Model-based Spatial Information Database for Architectural Zhuangxiu of Yuanmingyuan.

5.2 Research Process

The research process of this study relies on construction literature and systems, interpreting data from zhuangxiu components to deduce the original spatial layout and construct an interior space model. This model serves as a database for zhuangxiu's components and focuses on creating diverse design expressions. These expressions include direct proposals for ancient designs through two-dimensional and three-dimensional presentations, as well as showcasing the construction process. Additionally, it features presentations in fields such as interactive design, game design, and exhibition design, aimed at contemporary promotion and dissemination (Figs. 10).

   1- Data research and spatial construction. Based on construction archives, Yangshi Lei's drawings, and other literary sources such as novels and biographies, this research involves reading and digitally converting information, focusing on large woodwork craft construction and zhuangxiu. For content not directly covered, deductions are made from construction literature with the support of woodwork handicraft systems standards, thereby obtaining:

   2- Basic data collection, processing, and modeling.

1. **For large woodwork construction, data can be organized from literature and drawings to include:** a) the spatial layout, dimensions, and form of the architecture;

b) the dimensions and construction methods of large woodwork components, thereby constructing the spatial structure and data of large woodwork construction.

2. **For zhuangxiu work, data can be organized and interpreted to include:** a) the layout and types of zhuangxiu; b) the construction methods of various zhuangxiu types, specifically the dimensions and forms of components [9]; c) the materials and styles of each zhuangxiu. This allows for the classification of data on various types of components and spatial information, facilitating the overlay analysis of construction data from different periods, aiding in accurately deducing the design-centered space.

3. **For interior space,** this research modeled the components of large woodwork construction and zhuangxiu work, establishing a spatial model with assigned values. It records specific data through the model and conducts layered divisions during the construction phase, transforming data and information from 'Craftsman System - Interior Space.'

3- Data Analysis and Research. a) This part focuses on the Craftsman System. Data on zhuangxiu's components supports quantitative analysis and research on component dimensions, materials, labor, and processing techniques, further revealing the institutional issues of Qing Dynasty zhuangxiu craftsmanship; b) Regarding interior space design, this research utilizes modeling and visualization of Yuanmingyuan's interior space to compare representative spatial designs from various periods and analyze the formal, functional, and cultural issues addressed in architectural design.

4- Design Expression. Including: a) Expressions through two-dimensional drawings, three-dimensional spatial representations, and animation based on spatial models. b) By utilizing digital media technology to present the construction process, adjustments to architectural zhuangxiu schemes of Yuanmingyuan across multiple periods, as well as the production process of the zhuangxiu, can be more intuitively expressed. Innovative multidimensional expressions can be achieved through visual reality technology, serving as a popular science interactive interface, and potentially expanding into a game.

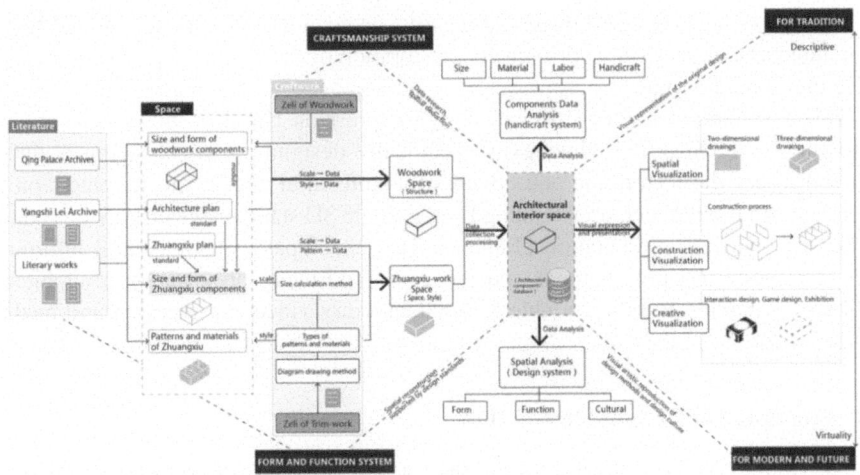

Fig. 10. Research process of Yuanmingyuan architectural zhuangxiu.

6 Case Study

Supported by the research ideas and frameworks described, the research team has completed three representative case studies on the architectural zhuangxiu and reproduction of Yuanmingyuan's palace buildings. These cases focus on interior space and construct a research path of 'Archives—Model-based Spatial Database—Research—Presentation', exemplifying the 'space-centered' approach of digital information technology in studying traditional Chinese construction as proposed in this study.

6.1 Overview of Design: Guanlan Hall

Guanlan Hall, situated in the 'Jiexiu Mountain House (接秀山房)' scenic area of Yuanmingyuan, was originally designed as a courtyard replicating the Yangzhou Jiufeng Garden. According to 'Yangjizhai Conglu', in the twenty-second year of Jiaqing (1817), the 'Jiexiu Mountain House' was completed. The interior zhuangxiu was undertaken by the salt administration of the two Huai regions, featuring elements such as rosewood window frames, multi-treasure racks, and floor covers. During this period, the Guanlan Hall, in the southern section of the scenic area, was frequently mentioned in poems by Emperor Jiaqing, becoming a significant building for leisure and residence along the banks of Fuhai. It later served as the prototype for the Shende Hall sleeping palace during the Daoguang period, reflecting the exploration of functionality and form in garden architecture [8].

From the architectural drawings of Guanlan Hall in the style of Yuanmingyuan, combined with on-site measurements of the ruins (Figs. 11 and 12), it is apparent that the interior and exterior zhuangxiu are diverse, establishing a clear distinction between primary and secondary spaces and creating a rich and varied composite space. This suggests unique ingenuity in the design of interior and exterior eaves of large garden residences during the Qing Dynasty. Although such architectural zhuangxiu are rarely seen in the remaining structures of today's palace gardens, by comprehensively utilizing style drawings, archives, and historical records, one can interpret the layout and form of architectural zhuangxiu, approximate a restoration of the original eaves pattern, and delve into spatial design.

This case employs a 'descriptive' design expression based on the virtual model restoration of architectural zhuangxiu, specifically designing and producing a video that showcases the restoration and effects of architectural zhuangxiu. It centers on a digital information model, transitioning from a single 3D static image display to a comprehensive dynamic presentation (Table 1). This encompasses architectural information, restoration research methods and processes, and the re-presentation of architectural space, making it more suitable for contemporary video consumption and media dissemination.

6.2 Processing of Design: Shende Hall

Shende Hall, located on the west road of the Jiuzhou Qingyan Scenic Area, was built in the eleventh year of the Daoguang era and served as an important daily governance and resting place for Emperors Daoguang and Xianfeng. The interior zhuangxiu from the

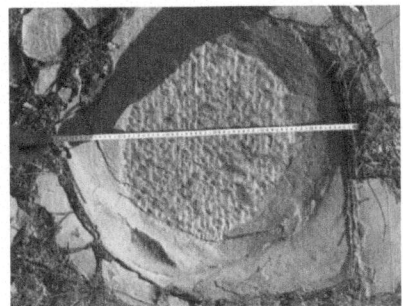

Fig. 11. Measured data of the column capital at the Guanlan Hall site.

Fig. 12. Measured data of the column capital at the Guanlan Hall site.

Daoguang period to the restoration during the Tongzhi period showcases a wide array of zhuangxiu, including Bisha cabinets, various covers, and partition walls (Figs. 13, 14). The Xianfeng period introduced unique elements such as the Pilu hat and spiral staircases, culminating in the indoor theater ' Hu Tian Xian Lai ' [10]. Shende Hall was destroyed during the Yuanmingyuan disaster and was later rebuilt as a key project during the Tongzhi restoration phase. While the architecture was modified to include a four-connected corridor, the interior spatial dimensions remained unchanged. The renovation layout method that followed marked a significant departure from previous dynasties, revealing changes in the function and style of the parallel-connected Hall.

This study focuses on the multi-period construction and its interrelations, organizing renovation drawings, construction archives, and other related activities of the Qing Palace by their respective periods and locations. Based on spatial modeling, it primarily analyzes the design evolution of the interior zhuangxiu of the large buildings in Yuanmingyuan, and quantitatively explores local spatial design issues with the support of a database (Fig. 15). This research delves deeper into the functional and cultural issues of the interior spaces of the Qing Palace.

6.3   Re-scenic of Design: Hanqiu Guan

During the Jiaqing period, significant construction occurred in Qichun Garden, with Hanqiu Guan completed in the tenth year of Jiaqing [13]. It was one of the 'Thirty Scenic Views of Qichun Garden', alongside Fuchun Hall (敷春堂), Qingxia Zhai (清夏斋), and Shengdong Shi (生冬室), each representing a theme of the four seasons. These structures are large-scaled palace buildings with non-single rectangular plans. Among them, Hanqiu Guan features the most complex layout—two large halls with seven bays each at the front and back, a central double-girder corridor with three bays, a northeast extending corridor with five bays connecting to two side halls, and three halls at the back, with the rear hall and the three back halls each connecting to a side hall to the west. Currently, the scenic area has restored parts of the architectural platforms, the Immortal's Terrace, and the surrounding mountain roads (Figs. 16, 17), but the main building, Hanqiu Guan, no longer exists [14].

Table 1. Sections of Guanlan Hall video scene settings.

Phase	Section 1	1-1 Overview	1-2 Interpretation of Yangshi Lei's drawings
Archives' description	Data description		
	Section2	2-1 Related Zeli(Yuanmingyuan Zeli)	2-2 Related Zeli(Trim-work Zeli)
Craftwork Zeli	Data processing		
Modeling database	Section3	3-1 Digital Space Model Information Library	3-2 Wookwork craft
	Data modeling	Overview of crafts	Woodwork craft
		3-3 Architectural trim-work craft(interior)	3-4 Architectural trim-work craft(outdoor)
	Database construction	3-5 Database	
Visualization	Section5	5-1 Digital visualization(interior)	5-1 Digital visualization(outdoor)

 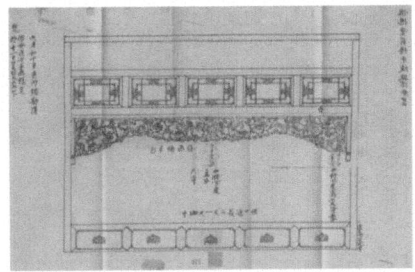

Fig. 13. No. 010–0014 The Elevation Drawing of Shende Hall [11].

Fig. 14. No. 015–0008-02 The Elevation Drawing of Feizhao at the eastern part in Shende Hall [12].

The zhuangxiu drawings of Yangshi Lei for Hanqiu Guan are relatively sparse and do not reflect the evolution of interior zhuangxiu design across multiple periods. However, numerous related architectural drawings and site plans exist, depicting the design evolution of the architectural courtyard and the island on which it is situated. These documents emphasize the relationship with the surrounding space (Figs. 16–17). This relationship significantly influences the outdoor scenery views from within and is considered in the indoor spatial layout facing outdoor landscape resources. This case holds substantial research value in the study of architectural landscape aesthetics.

In this case study, the author focuses on a design re-presentation primarily aimed at reproducing the artistic conception. This involves a detailed understanding and analysis of the architectural zhuangxiu layout of Hanqiu Guan and its relationship with the surrounding spatial configuration. Select typical surrounding architectural segments were chosen to render an animated presentation that encapsulates the spatial experience conveyed by the architecture and landscape. The significance of this case study lies in its expression of design layout and functional analysis within the realm of architectural forms, particularly in conveying the artistic conception of traditional Chinese garden design (Figs. 18, 19).

The outcome has been exhibited at the Zhengjue Temple in Yuanmingyuan from June to July 2024, as part of the works in the Beijing Cultural and Art Fund's 'Three Mountains and Five Gardens' project.

The three cases discussed all begin with organizing graphic archives related to construction activities, digitizing, and modeling this data. Based on this foundation, suitable research angles are selected for design output according to the characteristics of the zhuangxiu design activities of different large palatial structures. Accompanied by the expression of visualization, research has also been conducted on various aspects such as component scale, spatial layout, and design culture, supported by data. These cases involve the intersection of periods and design schemes. However, due to the lack of more detailed implementation information, it is impossible to accurately restore the design space of a specific historical period, nor can one simply discuss the design issues of the architectural space of Yuanmingyuan based solely on digital architectural space models.

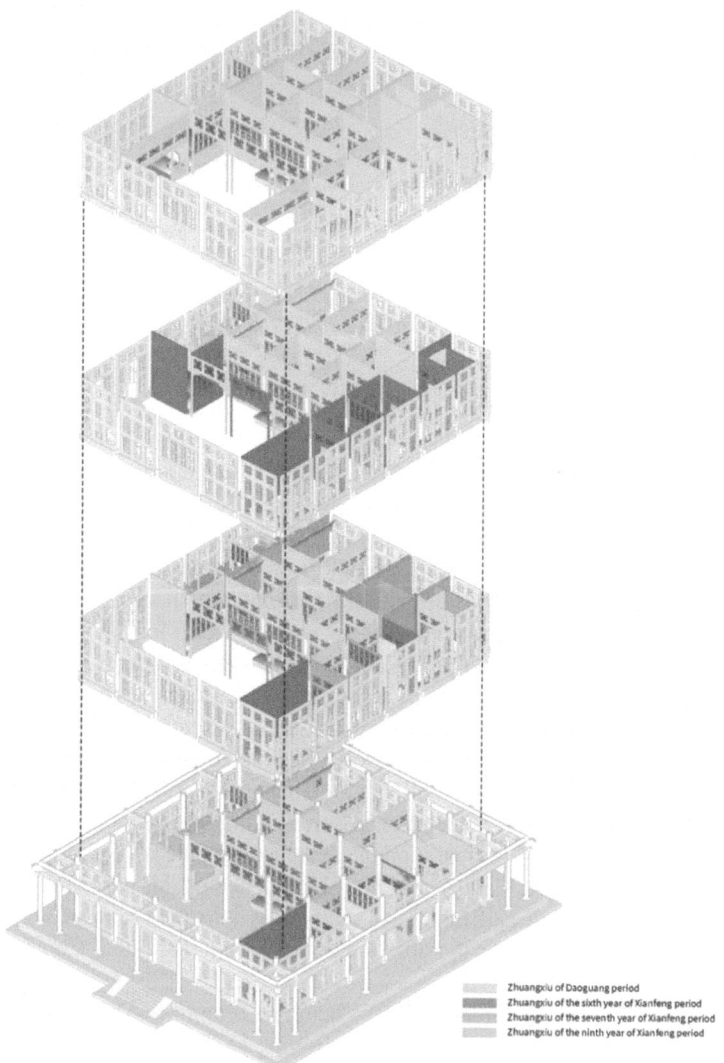

Fig. 15. The period distribution of zhuangxiu in Shende Hall.

The model-based spatial database provides a convenient and efficient working platform for such complex designs and can also generate more interesting innovative designs.

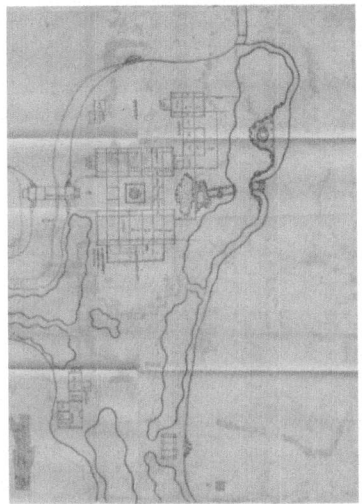

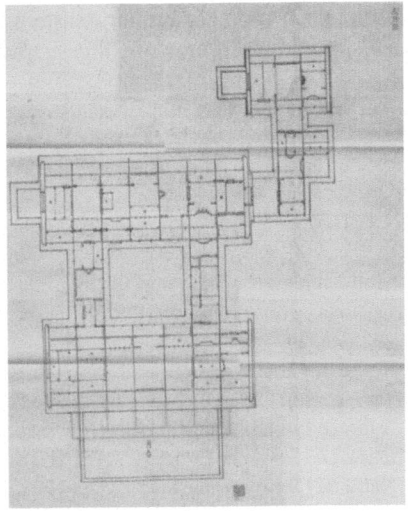

Fig. 16. No. 091–0015 Hanqiu Guan [Site accurately drawing] [15].

Fig. 17. No. 099–0002 Hanqiu Guan [Site drawing] [16].

Fig. 18. The digital innovative design of Hanqiu Guan is expressed in artistic conception1.

Fig. 19. The digital innovative design of Hanqiu Guan is expressed in artistic conception2.

7   Conclusion

In the context of the comprehensive penetration of information technology across various industries, the study of traditional Chinese architecture actively embraces technology and makes reasonable use of it. This aims to leverage information-based and visual digital technologies to allow traditional culture to be interpreted, understood, and inspire new creative vitality in contemporary contexts.

This study focuses on the interior spaces of palace buildings in Yuanmingyuan, proposing a 'Space-centered' model-based spatial database to assist in interpreting and digitizing the research on zhuangxiu practices within the traditional craftsman system, and modeling spatial models of components from multiple periods. It is hoped that this article can promote further research and contribute contemporary strength to the inheritance and innovation of Chinese traditional culture.

Acknowledgments. This study was funded by Social Science Fund of Beijing (No. 23YTC044).

References

1. Moll-Murata, C.: State and Crafts in the Qing Dynasty (1644–1911). Amsterdam University Press, Amsterdam. JSTOR (2018). https://doi.org/10.2307/j.ctv6hp2q9. Accessed 19 Jan 2025. pp.207
2. Rong, X.: Identification and Research on Yangshi Lei Archives of Interior Architectural Trimwork in Qing Dynasty, pp. 25–30. Tianjin University (2020)
3. National Library. Yangshi Lei's Drawings and Archives of in the National Library-The Sequel to the Old Summer Palace, vol. (5), p. 18. National Library Press. Beijing (2017)
4. National Library. Yangshi Lei's Drawings and Archives of in the National Library-The Sequel to the Old Summer Palace, vol. (6), p. 10 . National Library Press. Beijing (2017)
5. Guo, D., He, Y.: The Yuanming Yuan is Hidden in the Memory Heritage: Archives of Yangzhi Fang, vol. 2, p. 108. Shanghai Far East Publishing House, Shanghai (2016)
6. The Video of Jiuzhouqingyan's Restoration. https://www.mhymy.com/szfy/fysp/14948.html. Accessed 25 July 2024
7. Return to the Old Summer Palace: Digital Sensor Interactive Exhibition of the Old Summer Palace. https://www.manamana.net/activityDetail/404#!en, Accessed 11 July 2020
8. Wang, H., Zhong, J., Li, W., Clarke, C.: Study on restoration-oriented digital visualization for architectural trim-work of guanlan hall in yuanming yuan. In: Rau, PL. (eds) Cross-Cultural Design. Applications in Health, Learning, Communication, and Creativity. HCII 2020. LNCS, vol 12193, Springer, Cham (2020). https://doi.org/10.1007/978-3-030-49913-6_47
9. Wang, H., Study on architectural trimwork's size calculation for official buildings of qing dynasty: focusing on zuofa. J. Nanjing Univ. Arts (Fine Arts Design) (06), 60–65(2023)
10. Zhang. Y: Research on the Dramatic Activities of Yuanmingyuan. Shanxi Normal University, p. 89 (2019)
11. National Library. Yangshi Lei's Drawings and Archives of in the National Library-The Sequel to the Old Summer Palace, vol. (5), p. 17. National Library Press. Beijing (2017)
12. National Library. Yangshi Lei's Drawings and Archives of in the National Library-The Sequel to the Old Summer Palace, vol. (6), p. 47. National Library Press. Beijing (2017)
13. He, Y.: Analysis of the evolution of qichun garden in qing dynasty. Historical Archives **03**, 85–95 (2020)
14. He, Y.: Yuanmingyuan Imperial Poetry Anthology of the Qing Dynasty, pp. 326–336. China Encyclopedia Publishing House, Beijing (2020)
15. National Library. Yangshi Lei's Drawings and Archives of in the National Library-The Sequel to the Old Summer Palace, vol. (11), p. 24. National Library Press. Beijing (2017)
16. National Library. Yangshi Lei's Drawings and Archives of in the National Library-The Sequel to the Old Summer Palace, vol. (11), p. 25. National Library Press. Beijing (2017)

A Study on the Visualization of Parts Manufacturing Prognoses Based on Machine-Learning Algorithms for Supporting Decision-Making in CAD Modelling

Christian Wölfel[1]([⊠]) [iD], Moritz Ratzke[1] [iD], Christiane Kunath[1] [iD],
Sebastian Langula[2] [iD], Martin Erler[2] [iD], Alexander Brosius[2] [iD],
and Jens Krzywinski[1] [iD]

[1] TU Dresden, Chair of Industrial Design Engineering, Dresden, Germany
{christian.woelfel,design}@tu-dresden.de
[2] 1TU Dresden, Chair of Forming and Machining, Dresden, Germany
ff-if@mailbox.tu-dresden.de

Abstract. Design for manufacturability is considered part of the general skill set of mechanical engineers. However, the requirements in practice are significantly more complex. An approach that uses learning algorithms to set parameters and requirements for specific manufacturing processes, materials, tools, and machines related to component geometries is presented. This approach is evaluated, and forecasts are created. A user interface is being developed to integrate the approach into the working environment of design engineers. This interface is designed to equip engineers with the pertinent information necessary for informed design decisions regarding component geometry. The efficacy of this assistance system, encompassing both the system itself and its user interface, was empirically evaluated in the present study. The results indicated that the system was perceived as helpful by the study participants, and the usability of the user interface was favorably assessed.

Keywords: information visualization · AI-based support · CAD modeling

1 Introduction

Machining is one of the oldest and most productive manufacturing processes in the production of parts. In the product development process, functional or human-centered requirements and factors related to production cost and quality must be considered. Designers play a key role in this process, determining up to 85% of all subsequent costs in the early design phases (Ehrlenspiel and Meerkamm 2017). Typically, designers should consider the manufacturing requirements when designing components. From a production planning perspective, designers' self-perceptions regarding their competence

M. Schrepp (Ed.): HCII 2025, LNCS 15794, pp. 131–142, 2025.
https://doi.org/10.1007/978-3-031-93221-2_9

in parts manufacturing do not always correspond to the actual requirements of industrial production. Therefore, design proposals are rarely optimally designed for production planning.

Although design for manufacturing is taught in mechanical engineering studies and is considered part of mechanical engineers' skills profile, the requirements in practice are much more complex. Manufacturing technologies and associated processes are constantly evolving. This requires flexible planning skills and process knowledge. Linear planning gives way to an iterative approach with several alternative manufacturing processes. This expands the necessary knowledge: The focus is not only on the selection and basic consideration of a manufacturing process, but also on the design for optimal production of components in specific materials with specific tools on specific machines. This requires comprehensive knowledge of manufacturing processes and their potential and specific requirements. The growing number of processes and specific requirements further exacerbates the skills gap problem (cf. Deneka et al. 2010). The classic CAD-CAM chain no longer meets these requirements (Matta et al. 2010).

The (Pareto) optimal CNC machining of components is an approach to meet the diverse requirements in the field of tension between component geometries, manufacturing features, specific machines and tools, materials as well as production quality and costs. Meeting all these requirements often requires time-consuming NC programming by highly qualified personnel. The specialization of departments leads to ever-increasing demands on these skills (Mandolini et al. 2020). Companies and development teams need to deliver this to be competitive. However, the typical design engineer in an SME is often employed as a generalist and cannot provide them. As a result, there is a risk that the smaller batch sizes typical of SMEs will become increasingly uneconomical. The advantage of SMEs—their flexibility and cost efficiency even with small batch sizes (Zhou, Chen and Xie 2007)—is in danger of being lost due to a design that is not ready for series production and the associated increased production costs.

Tools based on artificial intelligence are currently being used in various domains to make complexity manageable and to support people in professional contexts in making decisions and achieving better results. For example, research has been conducted into how learning algorithms can improve the manufacturability of components. Such algorithms can set and evaluate parameters and requirements of specific manufacturing processes, materials, tools and machines in relation to component geometries and create forecasts. However, the information obtained by such algorithms must be made available so that designers can understand it and derive the correct design decisions - this is precisely the subject of the study presented here. For a possible assistance system, visualizations of a manufacturing planning forecast were examined as an aid for computer-aided part modelling. It should enable engineers and designers to optimize pro-duction time and quality and thus cost efficiency by providing information on manufacturing planning-relevant parameters of the current component properties, such as its geometry, during the design process.

2   User Interface of an Assistance System for Component Modeling

The integration of the approach into the designers' working environment is being facilitated by the development of a user interface. It provides designers with the relevant information to make design decisions regarding component geometry. The aim is an assistive system which.

– takes component geometry, material, machine tools and tools into account in a learning algorithm,
– creates a preliminary manufacturing plan,
– predicts costs and quality and
– establishes correlations between component geometry and resulting manufacturing characteristics.

Situation-specific recommendations for action and support measures in product development improve collaboration and efficiency and offer the following benefits:

– First-time-right
– Enables forward-looking capacity planning
– Transparency and data consistency
– Direct industrial applicability
– Can also be used by untrained personnel
– Intuitive operation

The project can make a significant contribution to countering the constantly growing pressure on staff to gain qualifications.

The requirements, parameters and consequences of component design are complex. From the designer's point of view, however, the focus is initially on function, connection points, force flows, etc. Manufacturing aspects are only a part of all requirements (Bender and Gericke 2021). For successful use, the goals, skills, experiences, mental models and conventions of the designers must be considered when designing the user interface of the assistance system (Cross 2004; Casakin and Badke-Schaub 2015; cf. e. g. EN ISO 9241, in particular parts 11, 110).

In order to make the approach usable, the information must be categorized, correlated and prioritized. The processing and presentation must be cognitively and physiologically ergonomic. In addition to the requirements of software ergonomics (see EN ISO 9241, parts 11, 110), conventions of established CAD user interfaces and mental models of the designers must also be taken into account. Furthermore, non-instrumental aspects of user interaction should be designed with equal attention, as they directly impact motivation and acceptance, ensuring the quality of the designers' work results (e. g. Thüring and Mahlke 2007).

When designing the graphical user interface (GUI) for the developed production planning analysis tool, an attempt was made to strike a balance between innovation and familiarity to ensure that users could seamlessly transition from existing CAD interfaces. An initial study was therefore conducted to determine the requirements for a supporting system and its user interface, as well as the preferences of engineers and designers for specific visualization approaches (Erler et al. 2024, Langula et al. 2024). Various CAD platforms' interfaces were analyzed to design a new interface that aims to maintain consistency with established user experiences while improving usability. Key GUI guidelines such as simplicity, human-centered design and system consistency were prioritized to enable an intuitive workflow. Accessibility was a key focus, with attention paid to contrast optimization and accessible color schemes to accommodate users with visual impairments. We followed the Web Content Accessibility Guidelines (WCAG) to ensure good readability of text and appropriate color contrast. Icons were developed to facilitate quick recognition of important and complex CAD-specific terms where possible.

The user interface consists of an independent program window, which is started via an icon from the standard CAD software and then displayed on a large monitor. The window essentially comprises two areas: an annotated three-dimensional representation of the component and an area with abstracted information (see Fig. 1). In the left-hand area, the component representation can be rotated and positioned in the usual way from CAD systems. In the right-hand area, tabs can be used to view summarized visualized analyses for production, component analysis and the predicted work plan (Fig. 2). Interactions and the selection of features are possible in both areas; every selection made takes effect in both areas.

3   Empirical Evaluation of the User Interface

3.1   Study Design

An online survey was conducted to evaluate the proposed user interface of the assistance system. The Survey was divided into three main parts: an abbreviated version of the questionnaire on the basic understanding of consequences in manufacturing from a previous project (Erler et al. 2024, Langula et al. 2024), the presentation of our proposed design of a user interface of a data-driven support system in CAD Modelling and subsequent evaluation of the proposed design, including items from the UEQ + (Schrepp & Tomaschewski, 2019; Schrepp, 2021). Questions were designed to first establish a base line in accordance with the previous study (Erler et al. 2024, Langula et al. 2024) and evaluating the plausibility of the proposed design regarding the general appearance and level of detail for different aspects of the interface. Answers were collected on 5-level and 6-level Likert Scales, or 7-level semantic differential scales in the case of the UEQ + (scales on attractiveness, perspicuity, usefulness, intuitive use, clarity). In addition, the following demographic variables were collected: professional experience, field of work and company size.

3.2   Sample

The sample consisted of N = 22 participants. All participants were required to have had previous experience with CAD modelling in metal milling. This requirement was chosen because we wanted to evaluate if experts in the field could benefit from integrating the proposed design into their work. We restricted participants to certain domains, however, as we wanted to consider as many different areas for future application of the design as possible. The participants were acquired within companies that are involved in the

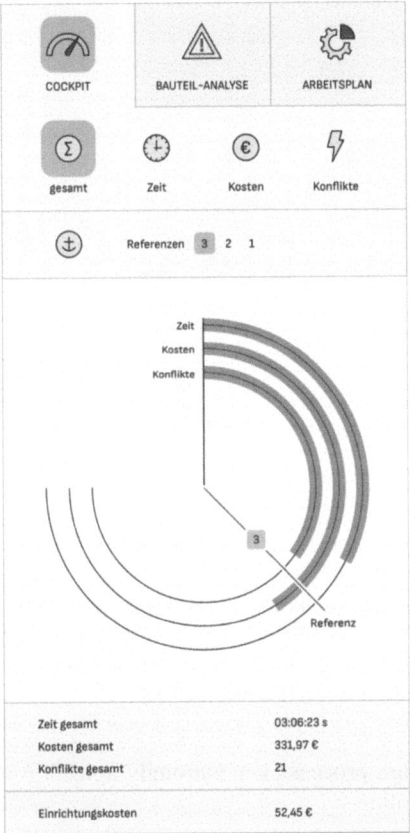

Fig. 1. The user interface provides the visualization of important manufacturability process indicators in the form of a speedometer, which is a familiar, intuitively understandable and accepted form of visualization.

project. They did not receive any additional compensation. 50% of participants worked in engineering service companies, 13.1% worked in production facilities with their own designs, and 9.1% worked in research and development. 27.3% were in the "others" category. Company sizes ranged between less than ten and several thousand employees; almost half of the participants worked in small and medium-sized companies (44,4% with ≤ 49 employees). Over two-thirds of participants had more than five years of professional experience in engineering (68.5%).

3.3 Study Program

The online survey was conducted using Sosci Survey. Participants used a device of their choice to take part. They were given background information about the project goals and partners. First, participants were asked demographic questions. They then rated the extent to which they felt that certain aspects of production were influenced by their

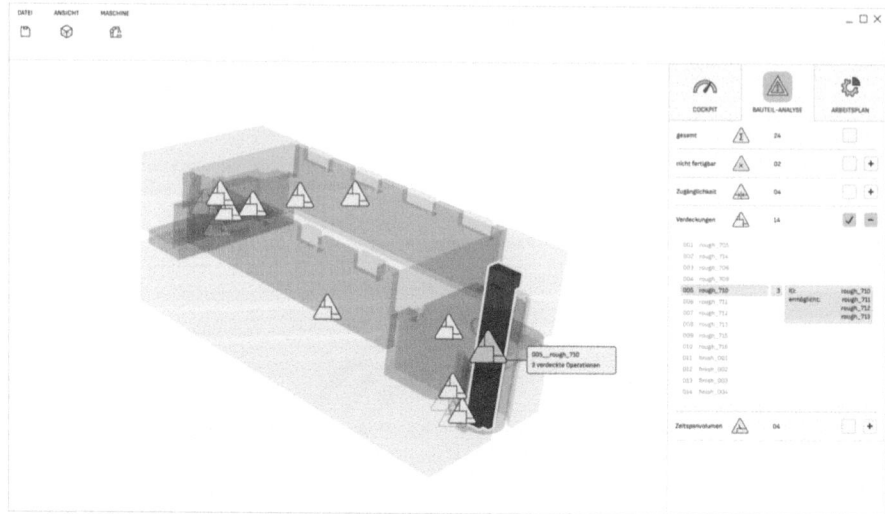

Fig. 2. Preliminary graphical user interface design of the assistance system. Specially developed icons were used to visualize essential and complex CAD-specific terms in a simple way. The right area provides information visualizations on manufacturing parameters, machining features or the machining work plan. The left area provides a three-dimensional view of the part. Machining features can be selected on either area and are then highlighted in both areas, so the user can relate the highlighted geometry (left) to the respective data (right).

decisions during the design process (1 = "strongly agree"; 6 = "strongly disagree"). The statements were as follows;

– When modeling components in CAD, I...

  – always keep an eye on production costs.
  – watch the production time always.

– I make sure that my design decisions...

  – require as few tool changes as possible.
  – require as few clamping changes as possible.
  – fit the machine tool and its limitations.

After being familiarized with the graphical user interface (Figs. 1, 2), the participants were also asked to assess the extent to which the interface presented would help them to observe these parameters during the production process.

Participants then rated the level of detail of certain aspects of the interface presented (from –2 = "too low" to + 2 = "too high"). They then answered modules of the UEQ + questionnaire (Schrepp & Tomaschewski, 2019; Schrepp 2021) in relation to the proposed design as a measure of their assessment of further dimensions of user experience and usability. In this stage of development, a working prototype of the interface was not available. Accordingly, an actual user experience or usability assessment has not been conducted. Participants were also given the opportunity to provide additional feedback on the project. The entire survey took about 20 to 30 min to complete.

3.4 Results

Understanding of Manufacturing. The statements on the understanding of manufacturing show that the participants incorporate manufacturing-related aspects into their design process to very different degrees. The range of responses for all statements except for the statement on costs extends from the minimum (1) to the maximum (6). On average, the participants tended to agree with all statements. A similar picture emerges for the assessment of the extent to which the interface would help to include certain manufacturing parameters in the design process (Table 1, Fig. 3). Here, the mean values of all five items are between "mostly agree" (2) and "rather agree" (3).

Table 1. Self-assessment on considering manufacturing parameters during CAD modeling; perceived impact of the system and its interface on considering manufacturing parameters. Higher values correspond to less agreement with the statements. (cf. Figure 3). N = 22.

	During CAD modeling I pay regard to …		The systems helps to pay regard to …	
	Mean	Std. dev.	Mean	Std. dev.
manufacturing costs	2.91	1.36	2.18	1.18
manufacturing time	3.27	1.41	2.23	1.15
tool change	3.14	1.67	2.55	1.30
clamping planning	3.18	1.47	2.90	1.26
fit	2.82	1.58	2.45	1.54

Levels of Detail of the Interface. The scales range from -2 = "too low" to $+ 2$ = "too high". For the cockpit (Fig. 1), the level of detail (mean = 0.00; SD = 0.44), the number of menu items (mean = 0.05; SD = 0.49) and the amount of information displayed simultaneously (mean = 0.05; SD = 0.49) were rated as exactly right on average (Fig. 4). For the assessments of the part manufacturability analysis (cf. Figure 2), the level of detail (mean = -0.09; SD = 0.61), the number of different symbols (mean = 0.14; SD = 0.56) and the amount of information displayed simultaneously (mean = 0.27; SD = 0.70) were also rated as exactly right on average (Fig. 5). For the evaluations of the work plan, the level of detail (mean = 0.41; SD = 0.59), the number of different symbols (mean = 0.32; SD = 0.48) and the amount of information displayed at the same time (mean = 0.36; SD = 0.49) were rated as between "just right" and "slightly too high" (Fig. 6). In all evaluations, there was only one evaluation with an extreme value at one end of the scale (-2 in production feasibility analysis: amount of information displayed simultaneously). The results indicate that most participants generally found the chosen level of detail for all evaluated aspects acceptable.

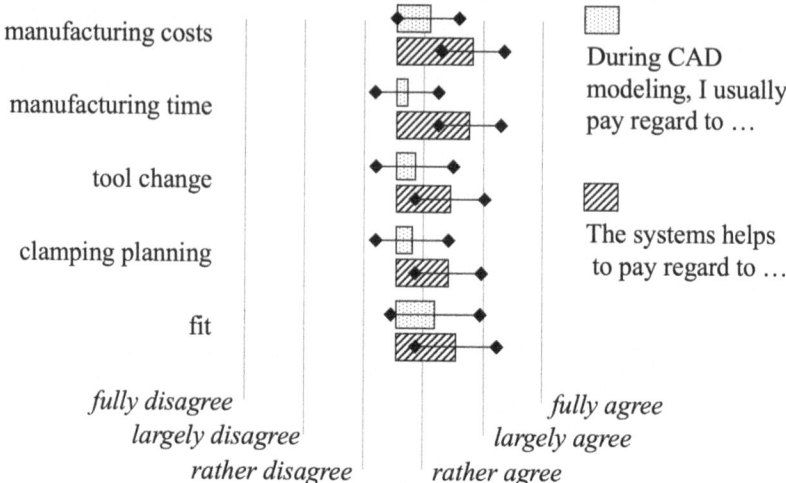

Fig. 3. Comparison of the values for self-assessed attention to manufacturing parameters during CAD modeling to the perceived influence of the assistance system on improving attention to the respective manufacturing parameters. Error bars: 95% CI. N = 22.

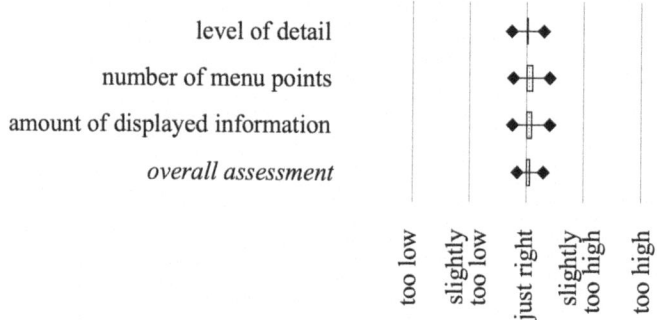

Fig. 4. Ratings of the level of detail concerning aspects of the cockpit (cf. Figure 1) N = 22; error bars = standard deviation.

Other Dimensions of Perceived User Experience and Usability. The average scale values of the UEQ + for attractiveness, perspicuity, usefulness, intuitive use and clarity have been calculated from the five items per scale of the standardized questionnaire modules. The results were all in the positive range, including their confidence intervals. This means all the scales recorded were rated positively (Table 2, Fig. 7).

Summary of the Evaluation. The participants rated the tool as helpful for becoming aware of the various manufacturing properties. This is in line with the results of a previous study that identified a need for such applications (Erler et al. 2024, Langula et al. 2024). The level of detail of the various aspects of the proposed graphical user interface was also rated on average, indicating a good match with the participants' professional requirements. In addition, the results of the UEQ + show that the proposed

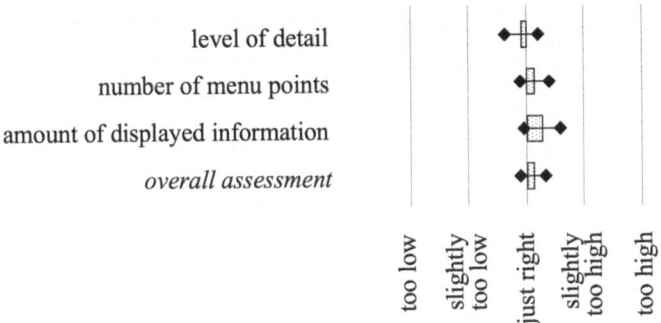

Fig. 5. Ratings of the level of detail concerning aspects of the part machinability analysis (cf. Figure 2); N = 22; error bars = standard deviation.

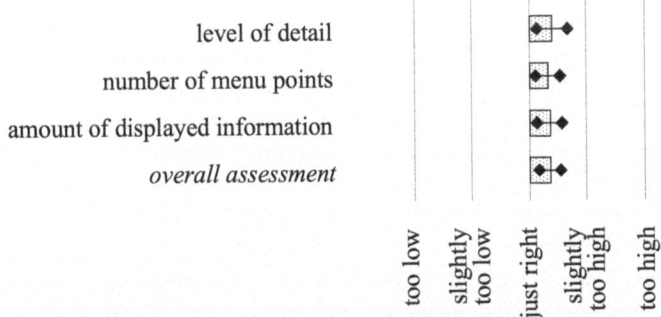

Fig. 6. Ratings of the level of detail concerning aspects of the work plan; N = 22; error bars = standard deviation.

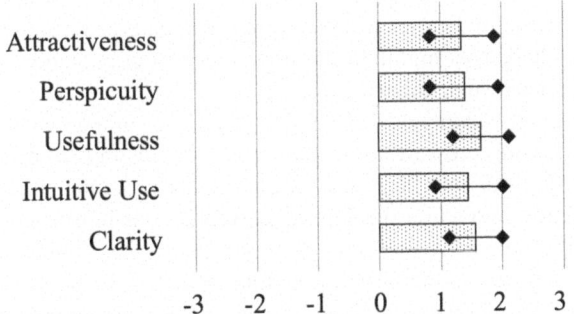

Fig. 7. Mean values of the UEQ + dimensions used. Values above 0.8 represent a positive evaluation (Schrepp & Tomaschewski, 2019; Schrepp, 2021). Error bars: 95% CI. N = 22.

user interface meets the participants' needs in terms of attractiveness, clarity, usefulness, intuitive operation and transparency.

Table 2. Mean values of the UEQ + scales used. N = 22.

Scale	Mean value	Variance	Std. dev.	Confidence interval	
Attractiveness	1.36	1.54	1.24	0.85	1.88
Perspicuity	1.41	1.81	1.34	0.85	1.97
Usefulness	1.67	1.26	1.12	1.20	2.14
Intuitive Use	1.47	1.98	1.40	0.88	2.05
Clarity	1.58	1.10	1.04	1.14	2.01

4 Discussion and Outlook

Developing a user interface specifically tailored to support design engineers can make a significant contribution to bridging the gap between component design and manufacturability. By integrating manufacturing parameters, the user interface provides real-time insights that enable designers to make informed decisions. The user interface provides a comprehensive framework that connects the designer's intent with manufacturing feasibility. By presenting actionable insights in an intuitive and accessible format, it supports a "first-time-right" design philosophy and reduces the need for iterative adjustments. In addition, the intuitive design and adherence to ergonomic principles enable a seamless user experience for both novice and experienced users, reducing the need for training. The system also improves collaboration between departments by providing a unified platform that integrates design, manufacturing and cost analysis and promotes a culture of transparency and consistency.

Although the user interface was well received, there is still room for improvement in tailoring the information density to users' understanding. Participants emphasized that certain aspects, such as the routing analysis, were too detailed. Ensuring the system's adaptability to different industries and user levels also emerged as a priority for future iterations. These challenges highlight the importance of continuous user feedback to achieve a balance between detail and clarity.

The system directly addresses the pressing challenges in the manufacturing sector, including the increasing pressure to upskill staff. By reducing the reliance on highly skilled workers, the user interface enables companies to maintain high productivity and quality standards with a less specialized workforce. Integrating real-time decision-making tools enables predictive capacity planning and ensures optimal resource allocation. In addition, the ergonomic design principles ensure sustainable user-friendliness and designer satisfaction, promoting long-term acceptance and effectiveness.

The results of this study pave the way for several future research and development directions. One promising direction is to utilize advanced predictive analytics and machine learning algorithms to refine cost and quality predictions. Another potential improvement is extending the system's applicability to non-metallic manufacturing and additive manufacturing processes, thus increasing its industrial relevance. These future developments would further cement the system's role as a critical tool in modern engineering workflows.

As a direct continuation of the study presented, a functional prototype of the assistance system has already been created, including a further development of the UI described. An empirical evaluation of this prototype regarding the intended support performance in component modeling and usability is being prepared. While the study presented here was still carried out with static mock-ups, the subsequent evaluation can also include processing work tasks using a working prototype. This will allow even more robust findings on the effectiveness of the assistance system presented.

By providing actionable recommendations and intuitive tools, it bridges the gap between design engineers and production planning, offering practical and forward-thinking solutions. The system successfully addresses key challenges in the manufacturing sector, including the need for efficient collaboration, transparency and reduced reliance on highly skilled personnel. Empirical evaluation confirms the system's ease of use and effectiveness, with participants recognizing the potential to increase design efficiency and decision-making processes. In addition, adherence to ergonomic and user-centered design principles ensures accessibility for different user groups, making the system suitable for broad industrial implementation.

References

Bender, B., Gericke, K.: Pahl/Beitz Konstruktionslehre. Springer (2020)

Casakin, H., Badke-Schaub, P.: Mental models and creativity in engineering and architectural design teams. In: Design Computing and Cognition 2014, pp. 155–171. Springer International Publishing, (2015).https://doi.org/10.1007/978-3-319-14956-1_9

Cross, N.: Expertise in design: an overview. Des. Stud. 25(5), 427–441 (2004)

Denkena, B., Lorenzen, L.-E., Charlin, F., Dengler, B.: Quo vadis Arbeitsplanung? Industrial Engineering: Fachzeitschrift des REFA-Verbandes 63, 6–11 (2010)

Ehrlenspiel, K., Meerkamm, H.: Integrierte Produktentwicklung mit Faser-Kunststoff-Verbunden. In: May, D. (ed.) Integrierte Produktentwicklung, pp. 1–28. Carl Hanser Verlag GmbH & Co. KG, München (2017)

Erler, M., Langula, S., Wölfel, C., Schneider, J., Kunath, C., Königs, M.: Data-driven support for CAD parts modelling based on automated estimated production planning–approach and user research. Proc. Design Soc. 4, 573–582 (2024)

ISO DIN EN ISO 9241–11:2018 Ergonomics of human-system interaction – Part 11: Usability: Definitions and concepts (2018)

ISO EN ISO 9241–110:2020 Ergonomics of human-system interaction – Part 110: Interaction principles (2020)

Langula, S., et al.: Interaktion mit lernenden Algorithmen zur Unterstützung fertigungsgerechter Bauteilkonstruktion. In: Paetzold-Byhain, Krzywinski, Augsten (Hg.): Entwerfen Entwickeln Erleben 2024, pp. 368–380 (2024). https://doi.org/10.25368/2024.EEE.030

Mandolini, M., Campi, F., Favi, C., Germani, M., Raffaeli, R.: A framework for analytical cost estimation of mechanical components based on manufacturing knowledge representation. Int. J. Adv. Manuf. Technol. 107, 1131–1151 (2020)

Review, A., Matta, A.K., Ranga Raju, D., Suman, K.N.S. The integration of cad/cam and rapid prototyping in product development. Materials Today: Proceedings 2, 3438–3445 (2015)

Schrepp, M.: User Experience Questionnaires: How to Use Questionnaires to Measure the User Experience of Your Products? (2021)

Schrepp, M., Thomaschewski, J.: Handbook for the modular extension of the User Experience Questionnaire. In: Mensch & Computer 2019 (2019)

Thüring, M., Mahlke, S.: Usability, aesthetics and emotions in human-technology interaction. Int. J. Psychol. **42**(4), 253–264 (2007)

Zhou, Z., Chen, D., Xie, S.: Springer Series in Advanced Manufacturing (2007).

Visualization of the Relationship-Creation Process in Online Environment

Wonseok Yang and Soya Hirano(⊠)

Shibaura Institute of Technology, Koto-ku, Tokyo 135-8548, Japan
cy21278@shibaura-it.ac.jp

Abstract. The rapid spread of social networking and the evolving online environment significantly impact traditional human relationships. As inherently social beings, humans have adapted their relationship-building processes to technological and social changes. With SNS, relationships shift from "maintenance" to "development," making conventional analyses of "state" and "outcome" insufficient to capture their complexity. This research focuses on the relationship-building process in contemporary communication environments, including SNS, and develops a methodology for analyzing its characteristics in a dynamic and quantitative manner.

Specifically, by creating an influence relationship model diagram utilizing the DEMATEL method and visualizing the causal relationships between behavioral elements, the important characteristics and factors in the human relationship formation process were clarified. The research paid particular attention to the characteristics of SNS-use in the youth segment and quantitatively evaluated the degree of influence of the behavioral elements by classifying them into "entry" and "exit" categories. The results suggest that the external factor "reputation from the public" is a key in facilitating relationship building in the online space. Furthermore, it was confirmed that online behavioral elements play a distinct role in relationship building and that their interaction with offline behavioral elements is relatively weak.

These findings help organize human relationship characteristics in modern societies and offer practical value for business relationship strategies. The findings provide an important perspective for understanding how the online environment impacts the formation and dynamics of human relationships, as well as thinking about how it can be used for the design of new Internal Communication strategies.

Keywords: Behavior Visualization · SNS · Internal Communication

1 Introduction

Humans are social beings and find it difficult to live without connections with others [1]. People have been searching for ways of relating to each other, adapting to different communication environments at different times. It can be said that they have repeatedly gone through the process of setting up the foundations for forming a common understanding, constructing a scale appropriate to the time, and restructuring it as necessary.

M. Schrepp (Ed.): HCII 2025, LNCS 15794, pp. 143–155, 2025.
https://doi.org/10.1007/978-3-031-93221-2_10

In recent years, the rapid development of social networking has facilitated the diversification of human relationships and significantly impacted corporate business strategies and marketing methods. Furthermore, the historical social and economic inflexion point of the coronavirus pandemic has enabled diverse ways of working and a reconsideration of the nature of the corporate work environment [2]. In line with this, the importance of creating an environment in which people can concentrate on their work and maximize their productivity is being emphasized more than ever before.

Against this background, new strategies that effectively support information sharing and communication are required to facilitate relationship building [3]. In particular, Internal Communication using online tools and SNSs is becoming increasingly important for achieving trust and efficiency inside and outside the organization, and understanding and utilizing these characteristics is increasingly important. Internal Communication strategies both facilitate smooth information transfer and awareness sharing within an organization and attract attention as a basis for supporting more efficient and reliable relationship building [4].

Conversely, the online environment has made it increasingly difficult to identify the characteristics of human relationships accurately. Through a research using a single interface function, Araki et al. (2016) revealed the limits of human information-processing capacity in online environments and considered its impact on SNS strategies [5]. However, almost a decade later, and the increased complexity of human relationships has become more pronounced, and existing methods have not been able to cope with this change.

Existing research has mainly visualized relationships through social network analysis (SNA) [6]. However, these focus on the "outcome" or "state" of existing relationships, and the dynamic processes of how relationships are formed, developed, and disintegrated have not been fully elucidated. In particular, as the role of SNSs in the online environment shifts from "relationship maintenance" to "relationship development," there is a growing need for new methods to visualize dynamic processes.

Furthermore, in business situations where the need for relationship building is high, it is essential to understand the characteristics of communications in the online environment as a basis for supporting intra-individual trust and task efficiency. In today's business environment, relationship building using social networking and online tools is increasingly directly linked to successful projects and smooth decision-making, and we believe that new Behavior Visualization methods in human relationships and the perspectives that can be gained from them are required to address these issues.

2   Behavioral Component Analysis of Interpersonal Cognition and Relationships

In this research, the process of interpersonal cognition was created on the basis of two models and the structuring of the process to action and its algorithms. Through this structuring, the importance of dynamic analysis in relationships is discussed in the light of contemporary SNS characteristics.

2.1   Dual-Process Models and Three-Level Models in Interpersonal Cognition

In interpersonal cognition, the basic concept of the dual-process model comprises two processes, one at the latent level and the other at the manifest level [7]. Latent-level reasoning is an unconscious and automatic process, while manifest-level reasoning occurs when cognitive resources are sufficient and accompanied by the intention to reason.

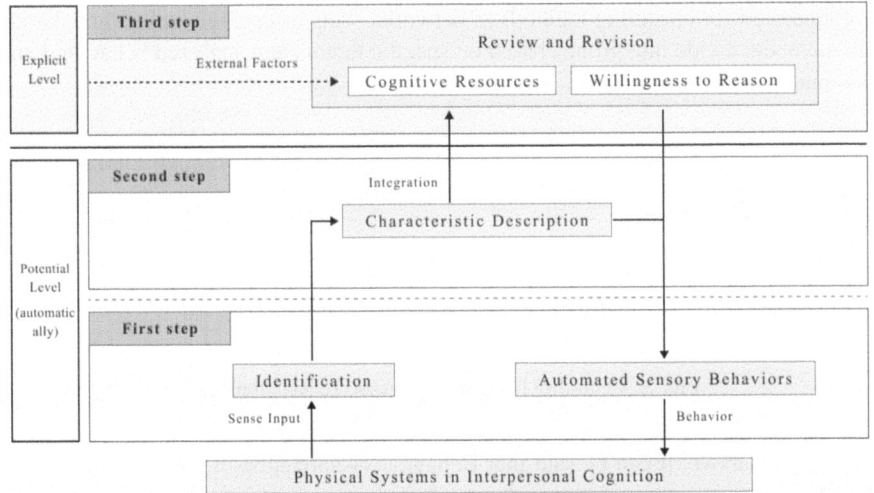

Fig. 1.   Integration Process of Dual-Process and Three-Step Models

The three-stage model proposed by Gilbert (1989) can be referred to as the normal order in these two types of processes [8]. When observing the behavior of another person, categorization helps identify which properties the behavior has (stage 1) based on the categorization, a property description helps infer the properties corresponding to the behavior (stage 2). The causes of the behavior are then examined, including the circumstances under which the behavior occurs, and if external factors are present, the characteristics inferred in the second stage are reviewed and modified (stage 3) [9]. The integrated model created from the above two models is shown in Fig. 1.

As Nakama highlights, the impact of conscious triggers on behavior change, behavior that has passed the manifest level is considered to play an important role in the subsequent relationships and continuity of behavior [10]. Particularly in the present day, when the role is shifting from "maintenance" to "development" due to the spread of SNSs, analytical methods are required to address the complexity of the amount of information and the dynamic changes in relationships. The Behavior Visualization of processes focusing on the causal relationships has the potential to extract the characteristics of increasingly opaque relationships and provide new insights into the contemporary communication environment.

2.2 Visualization of Static Elements

This concept is in contrast to the elements. One method for visualizing these static elements is social network theory. Based on graph theory, social network theory aims to visualize the structure of human relationships and is an approach that reveals the characteristics of individual nodes (individuals) and edges (relationships) through clustering and centrality analysis (Fig. 2). In particular, Zachary's work on karate clubs is widely recognized as one of the most representative studies in social network theory and laid the foundation for clustering methods in networks. This research modelled how karate club members divide into groups based on specific factors and analyzed behavioral and relational characteristics [6].

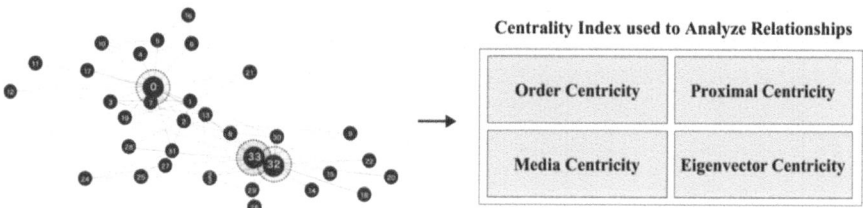

Centrality Index used to Analyze Relationships

Order Centricity	Proximal Centricity
Media Centricity	Eigenvector Centricity

Fig. 2. Centrality Index used to Analyze Relationships

From the above, it can be said that Behavior Visualization of static elements provides an effective approach for understanding the characteristics and challenges of relationships, and for analyzing and evaluating types of relationships.

2.3 Visualization of Dynamic Elements

Dynamic elements refer to concepts that focus on changes and developments in relationships, as opposed to static elements. One method for visualizing these dynamic elements is the Decision Making Trial and Evaluation Laboratory (DEMATEL) method, which is used to clarify complex intertwined problems and causal relationships between elements. The methodology is useful in that it quantitatively assesses the influence relationships between behavioral elements and 'visualizes' influential elements and their causal relationships The DEMATEL method has been used in diverse fields, such as solving regional problems and developing marketing strategies.

For example, in Murakami's (2003) research, the DEMATEL method was used to identify priorities of local issues and organize causal relationships between issues [11]. (Fig. 3) By utilizing this method, this research aims to elucidate the factors behind SNS use behavior and quantitatively assess the role of online behavioral elements and their causal relationships.

3 Research Method

First, a survey was conducted on the characteristics of SNS use in the modern era, followed by an experiment focusing on causal relationships between behavioral elements. The main flow of the research is as follows. (Fig. 4).

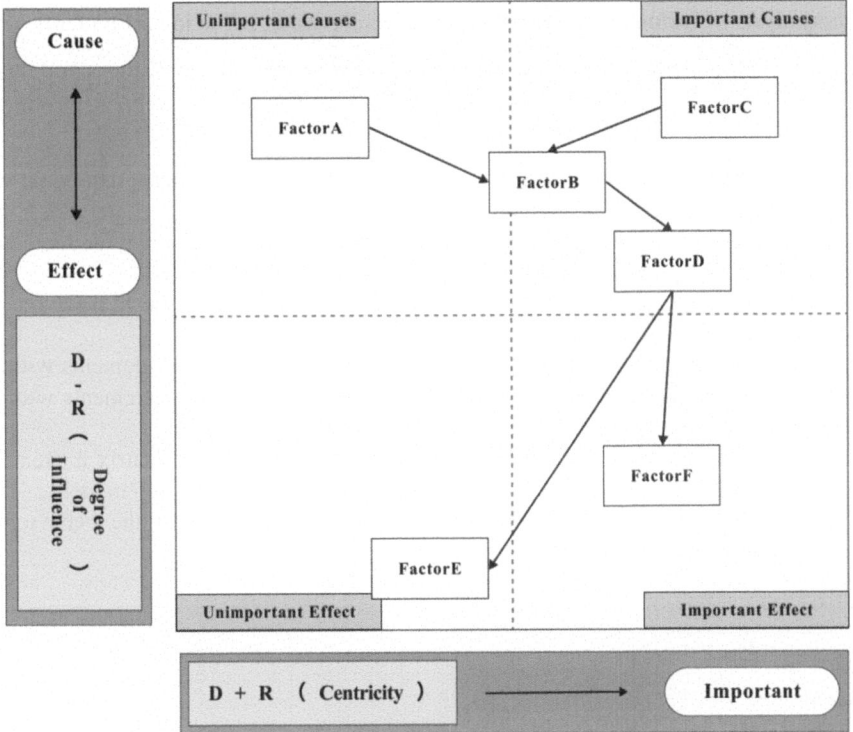

Fig. 3. How to View Influence Models in the DEMATEL Method

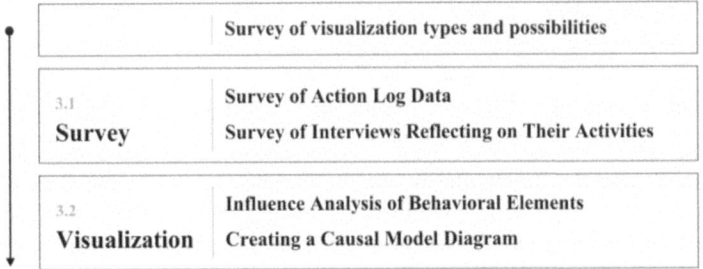

Fig. 4. Experiment Process

3.1 Observation and Analysis of Behavioral Elements in SNS Use

In order to identify the characteristics of SNS use among young people, a survey was conducted combining action log data from LINE, Instagram and Twitter (current X) and user interviews. Four university students (equal gender ratio) were selected as subjects and asked to browse SNS for 10 min without any purpose. Semi-structured interviews were conducted after the end of the session to interview them about the background to the selection of each action element and their emotional reactions to it.

3.2   Analysis of Influence Relationship Models Between Behavioral Elements

An analysis utilizing the DEMATEL method was conducted to elucidate the causal relationships between behavioral elements during SNS use. The subjects were 39 university students who use SNS on a daily basis, and the following procedure was used.

1) ask the subjects to rate the importance of all 12 behavioral elements that could be selected in the survey in 3.1 on a five-point scale
2) ask them to rate the strength of the impact of each behavioral element on the other elements on a 4-point scale
3) calculate the average D-R value (degree of influence) for each of the 12 behavior-al elements based on the evaluation data
4) based on the five-stage evaluation for each subject, the behavioral elements with a score above the average are extracted and weighted as behavioral elements with a high level of importance
5) based on the four-stage evaluation for each subject, an influence matrix is created and the DEMATEL method is used to create an influence relationship model.
6) visualize the causal relationships, considering the weighting of the behavioral elements for each subject.

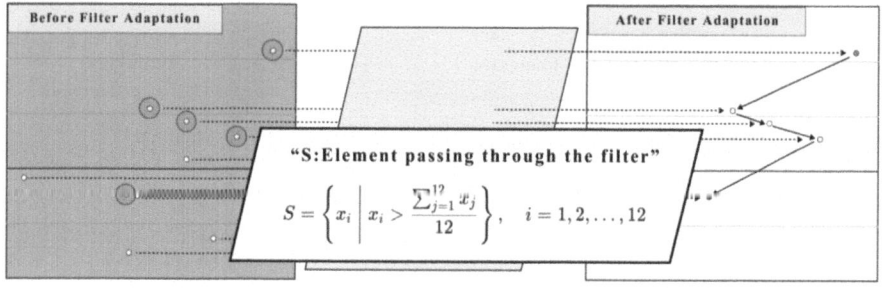

Fig. 5. Importance weighting being adapted after Impact Model Creation

When designing the survey questionnaire, the questionnaire created by Murakami was used as a reference [8], and while there are many studies dealings with the DEMA-TEL method, in this research, the weighting of importance is adapted after the influence relationship model is created. (Fig. 5) The reason for this is that, from the discussion in 3.1, no overall trend could be identified in the elements used to con-struct the relationship. Even if the DEMATEL method, which is useful for visualizing importance, was used, it was considered necessary to add a more limited perspective.

4   Results and Discussion

4.1   Presentation and Discussion of Influence in Behavioral Elements

In this research, the DEMATEL method was used to analyze the causal relationships between behavioral elements in the relationship-building process using SNSs. The results confirm that "public reputation" is the main factor facilitating relationship-building to be perceived as a relationship-building partner. The results of the influence analysis contributed to this result (Table 1).

Table 1. Top 3 Impact and Non-Impact for each channel.

	Behavioral Component	D-Y Average	Rank
Cause Element	7.Mention	0.900945	1
	8.Hashtag	0.683431	2
	2.Video Calls	0.535286	3
	9.Movie Sharing	0.422972	4
Middle Element	1.chat	0.191780	5
	5.Comment	0.109960	6
	10.Live Distribution	0.027214	7
	4.DM	-0.128019	8
	12.Talk (Off-Line)	-0.169602	9
Result Element	11.Greetings (Off-Line)	-0.602075	10
	3.SNS browsing	-0.7033049	11
	6.Reaction	-0.1238843	12

When the "entrance" element in the DEMATEL method is defined as a behavioral element in which the subject is recognized as a relationship-building partner, the causal element, i.e., the element with the highest average D-Y value, was shown to be relevant. It is conceivable that behavioral elements such as "mentions," "hashtags," and even "video calls" enjoy a high degree of public recognition in relationship-building with the subject. These elements can be said to play a particularly important role in the "trigger" part of relationship building in social networking.

Another of the considerations that could be extracted because of creating the influence relationship model diagram for all 39 samples, the "degree of evaluative involvement from the target," is also a research result that reinforces this consideration. The results of these considerations reaffirm the shift of the main axis of contemporary behavior online and can be interpreted as evidence that it is easier to attract the public's attention online than offline.

4.2 Presentation and Discussion of Influence in Behavioral Elements

The causal relationships between the behavioral elements were analyzed and an influence relationship model was developed based on the results. The analysis revealed that presently the online element plays an important role in the early stages of relationship building, particularly in the formation of "triggers." The offline element has been found to be a behavioral element in relationship building that is perceived as "evidence," where the subject is regarded as the other party in the relationship-building process. A number of online elements are diverse facilitators leading up to the major cycle A (Fig. 6) of the behavioral element as that "evidence."

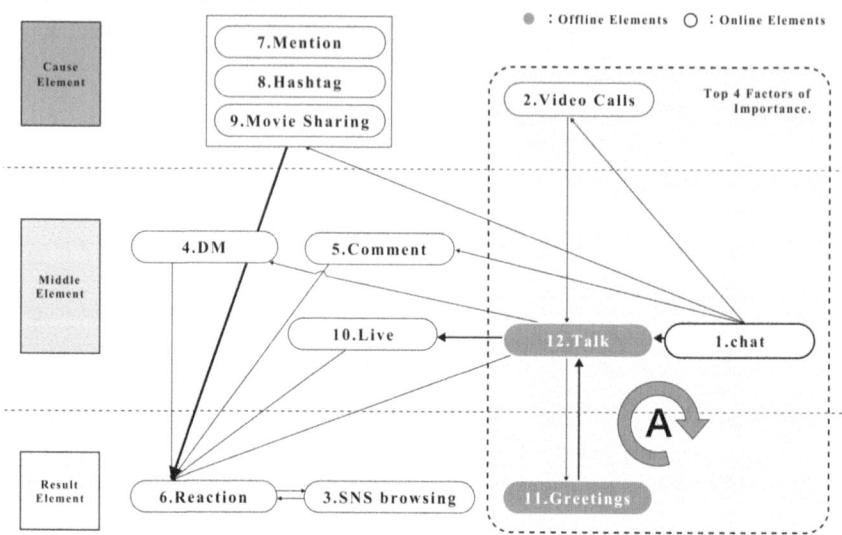

Fig. 6. Influence Relationship Model Diagram of action elements

It was also evident that the interaction between online and offline elements was weakening. The clear roles of online and offline elements before and after Cycle A, shown in Fig. 6, were confirmed (Table 2).

Table 2. Importance of Modern Relationship building factors.

Behavioral Component	Aggregate Results (Persons)					Response Rate (%)					Importance Rating points
	Extremely important.	Quite important.	important	Slightly important	Not important.	Extremely important.	Quite important.	important	Slightly important	Not important.	
1.chat	12	12	4	9	2	30.8	30.8	10.3	23.1	5.1	65
2.Video Calls	8	10	8	9	4	20.5	25.6	20.5	23.1	10.3	56
3.SNS browsing	2	2	11	12	12	5.1	5.1	28.2	30.8	30.8	31
4.DM	3	9	11	4	12	7.7	23.1	28.2	10.3	30.8	42
5.Comment	1	3	13	9	13	2.6	7.7	33.3	23.1	33.3	31
6.Reaction	0	4	9	17	19	0.0	10.3	23.1	35.9	23.1	30
7.Mention	2	8	5	14	10	5.1	20.5	12.8	30.8	25.6	36
8.Hashtag	0	0	2	12	25	0.0	0.0	5.1	30.8	64.1	10
9.Movie Sharing	4	1	8	7	19	10.3	2.6	20.5	17.9	48.7	27
10.Live Distribution	1	0	2	8	28	2.6	0.0	5.1	20.5	71.8	10
11.Greetings (Off-Line)	17	16	3	3	0	43.6	41	7.7	7.7	0.02	80
12.Talk (Off-Line)	32	4	3	0	0	82.1	10.3	7.7	0.0	0.0	94

Note 1: Values are expressed as values obtained from DEMATEL analysis multiplied by 1,000.
Note 2: The ( ) in impact and affectedness represents the maximum value of the matrix element.
Note 3: Matrix elements with the largest impact or impactedness are coloured.

Table 3. Assessment Results on interrelationships between elements.

Behavioral Component	1	2	3	4	5	6	7	8	9	10	11	12	Sum	Rank
1.chat	/	90	49	40	44	57	43	18	59	24	72	87	583	1
2.Video Calls	71	/	49	40	29	50	27	11	43	32	78	91	521	3
3.SNS browsing	31	10	/	51	44	76	12	7	14	13	25	25	308	10
4.DM	50	40	63	/	36	65	17	11	41	24	61	70	478	5
5.Comment	45	16	50	57	/	69	18	5	8	15	48	53	384	7
6.Reaction	20	6	55	38	31	/	15	5	8	11	26	32	247	11
7.Mention	46	25	72	62	55	80	/	21	16	16	41	48	482	4
8.Hashtag	34	12	45	32	34	62	28	/	10	9	28	29	323	9
9.Movie Sharing	68	24	57	56	31	49	18	7	/	11	28	48	398	6
10.Live Distribution	22	14	32	24	16	28	11	4	8	/	24	24	207	12
11.Greetings (Off-Line)	54	24	40	37	16	47	7	3	5	14	/	95	342	8
12.Talk (Off-Line)	82	59	65	66	39	67	23	11	36	28	104	/	580	2
Sum	523	320	577	503	375	650	219	103	248	197	535	602	4852	/

Note 1: The figures for each element are the sum of the ratings (on a scale of 4: 0 to 3) given by respondents on how the issues shown in the row (left) affect the issues shown in the column (top).

Note 2: Direct rating values of 97.5 or more (2.5 rating points for 39 respondents) and row and column sums of 400 (average score) or more for each element are shown in bold.

Note 3: The higher the ranking of an element, the greater its direct impact on other elements.

Table 4. Total Impact Matrices.

Behavioral Component	1	2	3	4	5	6	7	8	9	10	11	12	Impact
1.chat	268	317	361	317	257	405	179	81	230	146	398	444	3403 (444)
2.Video Calls	349	165	332	291	216	362	143	65	193	147	379	420	3064 (420)
3.SNS browsing	179	105	146	209	167	281	76	38	91	75	182	195	1744 (281)
4.DM	290	207	326	203	209	356	116	60	175	124	323	356	2745 (356)
5.Comment	240	143	265	254	123	315	101	42	103	94	260	283	2222 (315)
6.Reaction	142	85	207	169	131	137	70	30	70	63	160	179	1444 (207)
7.Mention	276	178	339	298	239	379	86	76	133	109	286	316	2715 (379)
8.Hashtag	190	112	225	187	158	270	105	28	87	70	193	207	1831 (270)
9.Movie Sharing	288	167	288	264	183	299	108	49	98	92	243	290	2369 (299)
10.Live Distribution	127	86	152	128	93	158	57	25	61	37	138	147	1210 (158)
11.Greetings (Off-Line)	251	158	242	218	145	272	82	38	99	91	185	339	2120 (339)
12.Talk (Off-Line)	380	268	375	345	243	409	144	68	191	148	433	306	3312 (433)
Non-influence	2981 (380)	1992 (317)	3258 (375)	2884 (345)	2164 (257)	3643 (409)	1268 (179)	601 (81)	1531 (230)	1196 (148)	3181 (433)	3482 (444)	/

Note 1: Values are expressed as values obtained from DEMATEL analysis multiplied by 1,000.

Note 2: The ( ) in impact and affectedness represents the maximum value of the matrix element.

Note 3: Matrix elements with the largest impact or impactedness are coloured.

In addition, it was possible to examine the basis for developing a relationship-building strategy for each channel from the analysis data used to create the influence relationship

Table 5. Basic Sheet for the Preparation of Influence Relationship Model Diagrams.

Elements with significant impact on the element concerned.		Behavioral Component	Importance		Elements with significant impact from the element concerned.
No.12 (380)	→	1.chat	65	→	No.12 (444)
No.1 (317)	→	2.Video Calls	56	→	No.12 (420)
No.12 (375)	→	3.SNS browsing	31	→	No.6 (281)
No.12 (345)	→	4.DM	42	→	No.6 (356)
No.5 (257)	→	5.Comment	31	→	No.6 (315)
No.1 (409)	→	6.Reaction	30	→	No.3 (207)
No.1 (179)	→	7.Mention	36	→	No.6 (379)
No.1 (81)	→	8.Hashtag	10	→	No.6 (270)
No.1 (230)	→	9.Movie Sharing	27	→	No.6 (299)
No.12 (148)	→	10.Live Distribution	10	→	No.6 (158)
No.12 (433)	→	11.Greetings (Off-Line)	80	→	No.12 (339)
No.1 (444)	→	12.Talk (Off-Line)	94	→	No.11 (433)

Note 1: Importance ratings of 50 and above are marked with a colour.
Note 2: Parentheses ( ) indicate the overall impact of the matrix element.

model diagram. Based on these results, the DEMATEL method can be applied to Internal Communication strategies in business situations where there is a high need for relationship building. From the above, it can be said that the DEMATEL method is effective as a new method for quantitatively visualizing complex causal relationships such as the process of building human relationships(Tables 3, 4, 5 and 6).

Table 6. Top 3 Impact and Non-Impact Levels by Element.

Element No.	Highly Influential Factor No.			Non Influential Factor No.		
	First Rank	Second Rank	Thied Rank	First Rank	Second Rank	Thied Rank
No.1	No.12 (444)	No.6 (405)	No.11 (398)	No.12 (380)	No.2 (349)	No.4 (290)
No.2	No.12 (420)	No.11 (379)	No.6 (362)	No.1 (317)	No.12 (268)	No.4 (207)
No.3	No.6 (281)	No.4 (209)	No.12 (195)	No.12 (375)	No.1 (361)	No.7 (339)
No.4	No.6 (356)	No.12 (356)	No.3 (326)	No.12 (345)	No.1 (317)	No.7 (298)
No.5	No.6 (315)	No.12 (283)	No.3 (265)	No.5 (257)	No.12 (243)	No.7 (239)
No.6	No.3 (207)	No.12 (179)	No.4 (169)	No.1 (409)	No.1 (405)	No.7 (379)
No.7	No.6 (379)	No.3 (339)	No.4 (298)	No.1 (179)	No.2 (144)	No.12 (143)
No.8	No.6 (270)	No.3 (225)	No.11 (193)	No.1 (81)	No.7 (76)	No.12 (68)
No.9	No.6 (299)	No.12 (290)	No.1 (288)	No.1 (230)	No.2 (193)	No.12 (191)
No.10	No.6 (158)	No.3 (152)	No.12 (147)	No.12 (148)	No.2 (147)	No.1 (146)
No.11	No.12 (339)	No.6 (272)	No.1 (251)	No.12 (433)	No.1 (398)	No.2 (379)
No.12	No.11 (433)	No.6 (409)	No.12 (306)	No.1 (444)	No.2 (420)	No.4 (356)

5 Conclusion

This research targeted the human relationship-building process in modern online environments, including SNSs, and aimed to elucidate the characteristics of online and offline behavior and their causal relationships by quantitatively visualizing these relationships between the behavioral elements. For this, a Behavior Visualization model integrating the dual-process model and the three-stage model is presented, and modern SNS characteristics are employed as a theoretical background. In addition, attention was paid to analyzing dynamic elements such as the relationship-building process, on which there have been few studies. The causal relationships between behavioral elements were analyzed based on the SNS usage characteristics of the youth segment.

The results of this research identified "reputation with the public" as a major factor in online behavioral elements and confirmed that the interaction between online and offline behavioral elements is weakened. The influence model diagram created using the concepts of "entrance" and "exit" showed its usefulness as a practical tool in the formulation of relationship-building strategies by providing a systematic understanding of the role of SNS behavioral elements.

Furthermore, the research confirmed that while online behavioral elements play a central role in the "trigger" part of modern relationship building, the role of offline behavioral elements must also be re-evaluated. This clarified the relative importance of behavioral elements in SNS use and considered the possibility of building integrated online and offline strategies.

Future work is required to expand the scope of Behavior Visualization in relationships and to develop methods for analyzing more complex behavioral elements. We believe that by further investigating the interactions between online and offline behavioral elements, we can advance a comprehensive understanding of relationship building in the modern era.

The results of this research provide a new perspective for understanding the characteristics of SNS use behavior and developing new relationship-building methodologies in the online environment. We also believe that in business settings, where relationship-building is of particular importance, this research will help to consider how behavioral elements that contribute to facilitating Internal Communication strategies can be utilized.

6 Further Work

The present research analyzed social networking behavior among young people and revealed the characteristics of relationship building in an online environment. However, to deepen these insights and obtain findings with wider applicability, the following issues must be resolved in future research.

1) Extending the scope of Behavior Visualization in human relationships

Against the background of significant technological development, this research visualized the process of building human relationships, focusing on online behavioral elements based on SNS. However, there are certain limitations in its scope of application. In particular, it is limited to SNSs and only considers the generalized perspective of the business case, which means that it is insufficiently adaptable to scenarios involving different communication methods and environments.

In the future, hybrid relationship-building situations, not limited to online environments, must be considered. For this, a comprehensive view of the influence of different contexts and technologies is needed to clarify the characteristics of diverse contemporary relationship-building.

Furthermore, to realize such an extended analysis, it is essential to diversify behavioral data collection methods and analysis techniques. In addition to the analysis of text data and behavior logs, using advanced technologies such as facial expression recognition and speech analysis will enable more elaborate relationship-building models to be constructed. Expanding the scope of Behavior Visualization is expected to provide a comprehensive understanding of the diverse aspects of individual behavior and relationships, and new knowledge for a deeper understanding of human relationships in contemporary society.

2) Reassessing the role of offline behavioral elements

While the results suggest that the influence of online behavioral elements is pronounced, the phenomenon of relatively weak interactions with offline behavioral elements requires further examination. Clarifying how the influence of offline behavior remains and how it complements online behavior is necessary in contemplating metrics for each future period.

We assert that addressing these issues will facilitate a more comprehensive understanding of the relationship-building process in each era and how this knowledge can be applied to actual communication strategies and relationship-building methods.

References

1. Hasegawa, M.: Human prosociality from the perspective of evolutionary psychology. Jpn. J. Cogn. Neurosci. **18**(3–4), 108–114 (2016)
2. Yamamoto, I., Ishii, K.: Economic and workstyle changes during the COVID-19 pandemic: rapid spread of telework and potential new inequalities. Trends Sci. **26**(12), 50–53 (2021)
3. Ministry of Health, Labour and Welfare. Report of the Study Group on New Work Styles for a New Era. Ministry of Health, Labour and Welfare of Japan (2023)
4. Nakajima, K., Uehara, K., Tsuru, Y.: The impact of internal communication networks on productivity: a quantitative evaluation using wearable sensors. Keizai Kenkyu (Econ. Res.) **69**(1), 18–34 (2018)
5. Araki, N., Hinagata, Y., Tadaki, S.: The Dunbar number and its origin in SNS: Data analysis and modeling. IPSJ Trans. Comput. Vis. Appl. (2016)
6. Zachary, W.W.: An information flow model for conflict and fission in small groups. J. Anthropol. Res. **33**(4) (1977)
7. Gawronski, B., Bodenhausen, G.V.: The associative-propositional evaluation model: theory, evidence, and open questions. In: Zanna, M.P. (ed.) Advances in Experimental Social Psychology, vol. 44, pp. 59–127. Academic Press, New York (2011)
8. Gilbert, D.T.: Thinking lightly about others: automatic components of the social inference process. In: Uleman, J.S., Bargh, J.A. (eds.) Unintended thought, pp. 189–211. Guilford, New York (1989)
9. Taniguchi, Y., Ikegami, T.: The influence of psychological distance on interpersonal cognition: from the perspective of construal level theory. J. Hum. Res. **69**, 99–114 (2018)
10. Nakama, R.: Exploring the significance of diversity in consciousness aiming for self-transformation: comments on Chishima's paper. J. Youth Psychol. **26**, 164–168 (2015)

11. Murakami, M.: Application of DEMATEL method in regional problem identification surveys. Hokkaido Land Improvement Design Technol. Assoc. **15**, 61–70 (2003)
12. Furuhash, Y., Yang, W.: Research about usability improvement in cursor operation of 3D configurator. In: Marcus, A., Rosenzweig, E., Soares, M.M. (eds) Design, User Experience, and Usability. HCII 2023. Lecture Notes in Computer Science (LNCS, volume 14032), pp. 157–170. Springer, Cham (2023). https://doi.org/10.1007/978-3-031-35702-2_11
13. Uwajima, Y., Yang, W.: Relation between different UI information representation methods and user cognition. Lecture Notes in Computer Science (LNCS, volume 14032), pp. 386–397. Springer, Cham (2023). https://doi.org/10.1007/978-3-031-35702-2_27
14. Owa, S., Yang, W.: On the use of verb for micro interactions in UI. Interdisc. Pract. Ind. Design **144**, 198–204 (2024)
15. Muto, M., Yang, W.: The influence of microcopy on user decision-making. Interdisc. Pract. Ind. Design **144**, 188–197 (2024)
16. Otsuka, J., Yang, W.: Consideration of the problem of digital divide in the development of ICT. Interdisc. Pract. Ind. Design **144**, 205–214 (2024)
17. Umino, M., Yajima, R., Yang, W.: Design of home appliance operation sounds based on the metaphorical nature of sound. Interdisc. Pract. Ind. Design **144**, 157–167 (2024)

Nudging with Narrative Visualization: Communicating to a Student in the MOOC Courseware

DanDan Yu[✉], XiaoShuang Zhang, and Bo Yu

Art & Design Academy, Beijing City University, Beijing, China
diane@139.com

Abstract. In the rapidly evolving landscape of online education, Massive Open Online Courses (MOOCs) offer a unique platform for learning at scale. However, the challenge remains in effectively engaging students and guiding them through the vast array of content. This paper explores the concept of nudging the use of subtle interventions to influence student behavior through narrative visualization within MOOC courseware. By integrating narrative elements with information visualizations, we aim to create a more engaging, personalized, and motivating learning experience. This approach draws on the principles of narrative visualization to design narratives information that not only convey complex information but also subtly guide students toward desired learning behaviors, such as increased engagement, timely completion of tasks, and deeper understanding of content. The paper examines the theoretical underpinnings of nudging in digital learning environments and proposes a framework for the effective use of narrative visualization in MOOCs. Case studies and examples from current MOOC platforms are analyzed to demonstrate how narrative-driven visual cues can enhance student interaction, foster a sense of progress, and improve overall learning outcomes. Ultimately, this work contributes to the growing body of research on human-centered design in educational technology, offering practical insights for course designers and educators looking to optimize student engagement and retention in online learning environments. This study contributes a better grasp of how technologies such as narrative visualization, using different visual communication strategies, can deliver more complex messaging.

Keywords: Visualization · Narrative Visualization · Storytelling · Nudging · MOOC Courseware

1 Background

By the end of 2024, China had established over 30 online course platforms, hosting more than 97,000 MOOCs, with a total of 1.39 billion enrollments [1]. MOOCs, as a form of online education, have become an essential component of higher education. Various elective courses, compulsory courses, and blended programs in universities are now delivered online. Survey data indicates that students participating in MOOC learning come from a wide range of academic disciplines, including the humanities and social sciences, science and engineering, business, and the arts. This demonstrates that MOOCs, as open learning platforms, attract students from diverse academic backgrounds, breaking down disciplinary boundaries and providing a convenient way to supplement cross-disciplinary knowledge. Consequently, MOOCs have emerged as a prominent conduit for university students, underscoring their significance in broadening access to higher education and catering to the varied learning requirements of students.

MOOCs were initially developed as educational resources for students who, due to geographical, temporal, or resource limitations, were unable to participate in face-to-face courses. This unique teaching model places significant demands on learners' initiative and self-directed learning abilities. In this learning environment, students must be self-motivated, adhere to learning by step, actively participate in course discussions, and independently complete assignments and assessments. As MOOCs increasingly become a mandatory component of university curricula, either as credit-bearing courses or essential modules, disparities in their teaching outcomes have become more pronounced. Some students may lack the persistence and self-discipline required, leading to suboptimal learning results.

To address these challenges, the design of MOOC courseware must focus more on the effectiveness of learning. The goal is to capture students' interest, stimulate their intrinsic motivation, and ensure the successful achievement of teaching objectives. This requires not only attention to course content but also innovation and diversification in course formats. Encouraging students to actively engage with the teaching material through interaction and communication fosters a stronger interest in learning and sustained participation in the course. Furthermore, the provision of personalised learning pathways empowers students to customise their learning experience according to their individual circumstances and pace, thereby optimising overall outcomes. In light of these considerations, we have adopted narrative visualisation as a design strategy for courseware, with the objective of enhancing the teaching effectiveness of MOOCs. This approach aims to stimulate students' interest and autonomy by establishing multi-layered communication and interaction channels. By leveraging these strategies, we ensure that students can fully utilise MOOC resources and achieve superior learning outcomes.

2 Research Context and Concepts

As a teaching model for resource-sharing, MOOCs have been widely adopted in Chinese universities, playing a significant role in promoting educational equity and enhancing learning efficiency. However, the development of MOOCs still faces sever-al challenges, such as inconsistent course quality and a lack of diversity in teaching models, necessitating further optimization and improvement. Aim to these issues, we conducted a survey focusing on art and design students at Beijing City University. The objective was to gain insights into the current state of MOOC learning among students in this field, providing a foundation for identifying areas of improvement in course design and delivery.

2.1 Current Situation and Problems of Teaching in MOOCs

Learning Duration Analysis. The average time that students spend per session on MOOCs exhibits a certain distribution pattern, with the majority, 61.68%, spending between one and three hours per session. However, the effective learning time remains relatively short: 39.25% of students engage effectively for only 15 to 30 min, 30.84% for 15 min or less, and a mere 3.74% for 2 h or more. This indicates that although students allocate some time to MOOC learning, their ability to sustain effective learning for extended periods is limited. It has been observed that students often engage in multitasking, playing course videos while concurrently performing other activities, driven by the time demands of the course.

This observation underscores the necessity for course chapters to be more fragmented and tailored to align with students' habits and preferences. Effective course design is imperative to capture students' interest and attention, thereby addressing this issue. Only through such measures can MOOCs enhance teaching efficiency and facilitate students in leveraging resources to achieve deeper knowledge accumulation.

Dual Challenges in Content and Format. Students face a dual challenge regarding course content and format. The most prominent issue is the dullness of course content. Survey data show that 50.47% of students find the content unengaging, significantly reducing their motivation to learn. For instance, in courses such as Modern Design History, theoretical explanations are often dry and rigid, consisting of mere listings of design genre, events, and figures. This lack of vivid case studies and in-depth analysis makes it difficult for students to immerse themselves in the material.

In terms of format, students report poor interactivity and monotonous delivery methods. Most courses rely on one-way lectures by instructors, with videos lacking interactive elements or supplementary tools such as animations to enhance understanding. Over time, this leads to scattered attention, diminished interest, and a loss of motivation. Many students enroll in courses out of curiosity or academic requirements, rather than interesting and intrinsic curiosity, and are quick to abandon their efforts when faced with challenges.

Limitations in Platform Interactivity and Resource Quality. MOOC platforms are hindered by subpar interactivity. Online discussion forums are often inactive, with students' questions receiving delayed responses. Teacher involvement is limited, and student collaboration remains superficial due to a lack of an engaging and collaborative atmosphere. In terms of resource quality, there is significant redundancy in course construction, with outdated and superficial content that fails to meet advanced learning needs. Resource updates are slow, leaving students without access to emerging knowledge or cutting-edge examples. This disconnect between course material and real-world developments lowers students' sense of achievement and prevents them from staying aligned with the latest trends in their disciplines.

Addressing these issues requires innovative course design, improved platform interactivity, and timely updates to course resources. By tackling these challenges, MOOCs can better meet students' learning needs, foster engagement, and achieve deeper learning outcomes.

2.2   Analysis MOOC Interaction and Teaching Methods

Based on survey on existing MOOCs and research into previous studies by related scholars, the interaction levels between students and MOOCs can be categorized from low to high as operational interaction, informational interaction, and conceptual interaction (1). Specifically, these interactions include interface clicks, forums and discussion boards, instant messaging tools, peer reviews and mutual assistance, social media and web tools, as well as emails and announcement platforms. These methods of interaction primarily revolve around courseware, providing students with tools to understand knowledge points effectively. However, the dissemination and presentation of knowledge largely mimic traditional classroom teaching methods, with courses divided into units and chapters. Each chapter consists of resources such as lecture videos, teaching materials, and exercises. Compared to traditional classrooms, MOOCs often lack real-time feedback, eye contact, and interpersonal interaction, leading to a deficiency sense of participation. Although MOOC platforms offer communication tools, these tools mainly focus on facilitating knowledge comprehension and mastery through human-to-human interaction.

Digital platforms, however, have inherent characteristics and advantages that differ from traditional classrooms. Unlike the one-way output typical in traditional teaching, digital platforms allow for interactive information exchange between humans and machines. Digital education platforms have the potential to break away from conventional modes of information transmission, enabling users to select and organize knowledge points based on their unique characteristics and needs. This empowers students to construct personalized knowledge frameworks tailored to their interests and learning objectives. Despite these potential advantages, current MOOC teaching methods have not fully leveraged the strengths of digital platforms. Instead, they perpetuate traditional teaching approaches while weakening the benefits of face-to-face instruction. By failing to embrace the interactive and adaptive capabilities of digital platforms, MOOCs risk limiting their potential to provide innovative and engaging learning experiences.

To truly harness the power of digital platforms, MOOCs must move beyond replicating traditional classroom methods. By integrating adaptive, interactive, and user-centered features, MOOCs can enhance the learning experience, foster deeper engagement, and unlock the full potential of digital education.

2.3   Methods and Cases of Narrative Visualization

Hullman & Diakoplous define narrative information visualizations as "a style of visualization that often explores the interplay between aspects of both explorative and communicative visualization [2]. Narrative information visualization is a method of presenting information using the logic and structure of storytelling. By employing narrative techniques, this approach facilitates the understanding and communication of complex information, enabling individuals to grasp the underlying stories behind data and information, and it evokes resonance and reflection. In essence and by definition, Information visualization is interactive and exploratory. They typically rely on a combination of persuasive, rhetorical techniques to convey an intended story to users as well as exploratory, dialectic strategies aimed at providing the user with control over the insights she gains from interaction [2]. Narrative visualization leverages visual elements such as animations, timelines, arrows, and illustrations to present the development, changes, and relationships within information. This approach enables users to gain a deeper understanding of the context and details of the underlying story. Additionally, narrative visualization fosters user engagement by allowing interaction, enabling individuals to participate actively in the communication process and create personalized information pathways. Common interactive features in narrative visualization include navigation, filtering, search, zooming, and timeline controls. These tools not only enhance the user's ability to explore and analyze information but also contribute to a more dynamic and immersive learning experience [3].

Narrative visualization has been widely applied in various fields, leveraging the combination of data visualization and storytelling to enhance the communication of complex information.

In journalism, narrative visualization helps journalists and editors convey intricate information more effectively. A notable example is the data visualization project "Migration to Distant Lands" by Caixin Data News Center, which used line graphs, animations, and videos to illustrate the volume and flow of global migrations across different regions. Users could simulate the Earth's rotation by swiping the screen and switch between data for different time periods and content on a single map. This approach not only enhanced the readability of the information but also increased the interactivity and appeal of the project (see Fig. 1).

In the medical field, narrative visualization is utilized to simplify the presentation of complex medical data and processes. By doing so, it helps doctors and patients better understand medical conditions and treatment plans [4].

In cultural studies, narrative visualization is employed to deeply analyze the intricate plot structures and character relationship networks in classic literary works, offering fresh insights and interpretations.

In education, narrative visualization supports students in understanding and memorizing complex concepts. For instance, animations and interactive charts can vividly illustrate the process of cell division in biology, while historical events can be presented as data-driven stories to trace their chronological development. This approach not only enhances learning efficiency but also sparks students' interest in the subject matter.

By enabling dynamic, interactive, and engaging presentations, narrative visualization has demonstrated its potential to enrich communication and understanding across diverse domains.

In summary, narrative information visualization demonstrates the following advantages in information communication:

1. Enhanced Comprehension and Retention

Narrative information visualization constructs the logical relationships between data and information through storytelling, enabling users to understand and remember data more easily.

2. Encouragement of Exploration

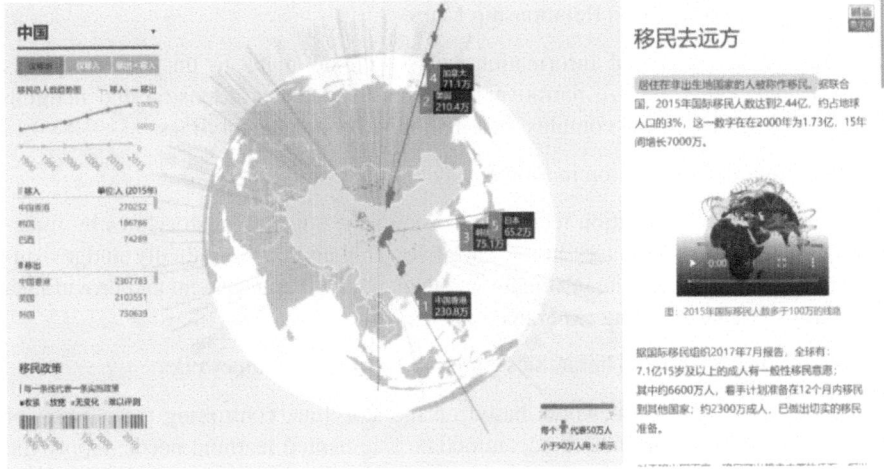

Fig. 1. The Narrative Visualization Case in the Field of Communication: "Migration to Distant Lands" [5].

The interactive features of narrative information visualization allow users to explore data from different perspectives and paths based on their interests. This enables each user to uncover unique insights.

3. Increased Engagement and Appeal

By integrating storytelling, narrative information visualization captures users' attention and interest, making the information more compelling and engaging.

4. Emotional and Cultural Connection

Narrative information visualization conveys the emotional and cultural significance behind the data by incorporating the emotional and cultural aspects of stories. This enhances users' emotional resonance with the information.

3 Narrative Visualization in MOOCs

In education, stories support knowledge transfer and retention by storing narrative chunks in memory as separate pieces that can be retrieved as a coherent whole (Black & Bower, 1979) [4]. To address the current stagnation in MOOC courseware caused by the uniformity of information dissemination, the method of narrative visualization can be applied to courseware design. Narrative visualization, characterized by coherence, interactivity, readability, and exploratory features, enriches the learning experience, engages students in instructional activities, and stimulates their initiative and participation. By leveraging storytelling, students can connect knowledge points within course content, build knowledge frameworks, and better achieve course objectives. The following methods outline how narrative visualization can nudge knowledge information in MOOC courseware design:

1. Establishing Information Relationship Maps

Reorganize fragmented information into relational maps to uncover storylines between data points. Utilize narrative structures to create plot tension and nudging students through exploring complex information via coherent storylines.

2. Introducing Personification in Stories

Incorporate personification techniques to immerse students in storylines by imagining themselves as characters in the narrative. This approach gradually nudges students to delve deeper into the information, enhancing their engagement and providing a potentially enriched learning experience.

3. Constructing Narrative Hierarchies Through Interaction Frameworks

Design interactive frameworks based on the storyline, controlling the amount of information delivered at once to accommodate fragmented learning needs. Apply the three primary visualization structures proposed by Segel and Heer in narrative visualization: the Martini Glass visualization structure, Interactive slideshows, and Drill-downs [3].

4. Enhancing the Visual Appeal of Narratives

Combine data, visuals, and narratives to make dull information more vivid. Utilize videos and animations to enhance expressiveness, making information more intuitive and comprehensible. Visualizations can nudge students to grasp knowledge from perspectives such as hierarchical, progressive, parallel, comparative, causal, and inductive relationships.

5. Encouraging Participation Through Interactive Design

Integrate interactive elements to draw users into the storyline, enabling nonlinear storytelling, customization, varying levels of detail, and explanations [3]. By capturing users' attention and sparking curiosity, interactive design assists students in exploring additional information.

By incorporating narrative visualization into MOOC courseware design, abstract concepts and scattered knowledge points can be transformed into tangible graphics and images. Storyline nudging aids students in better understanding and remembering the material, while interactive information design provides personalized information acquisition pathways. Personalized learning empowers students with diverse interests, attention spans, and needs to take control of their learning (West, 2012) [4].

4   Case: Narrative Visualization Design for Learning Nudging in the Arts and Crafts Movement MOOC Courseware

The History of Modern Design course is a mandatory subject for art and design students at Beijing City University, with approximately 700 students enrolled each year. The course currently employs a blended teaching approach, with the first and last classes conducted face-to-face by the instructor. The first class focuses on providing an overview of design history, organizing key content along a timeline, and highlighting important topics for study. The final class serves as a session for summarizing, discussing, and addressing questions about the course content. Between these two sessions, students are required to engage in online learning through pre-recorded videos and resources provided on the MOOC platform.

Over several years of teaching practice, it has been observed that students' autonomous online learning outcomes are often suboptimal. Many students struggle to focus on the instructional videos during their self-study time. Although the course content on the MOOC platform is organized into sections based on knowledge points, students still face difficulties in constructing a complete knowledge framework. The MOOC learning experience is often likened to an audiobook, placing high demands on students' autonomy. Given the diversity among students in terms of learning habits, abilities, and interests, we have redesigned the MOOC courseware for History of Modern Design using narrative visualization methods to nudge students toward better self-directed learning. This paper will illustrate this approach using the chapter on the Arts and Crafts Movement as a case study.

4.1 Establishing a Storyline

The course team analyzed the key figures of the Arts and Crafts Movement, their main ideas, and representative works, creating a knowledge graph built from various knowledge points (see Fig. 2). Since the movement represents a reflection on social phenomena, the team crafted a storyline featuring two central figures of the movement, set against a backdrop of vibrant ideological exchanges. In this story, students are no longer passive observers but active participants. They engage in cross-temporal conversations with historical figures, experiencing an intellectual feast. Through communicate with story figures, students explore the origins of the Arts and Crafts Movement and empathize with the profound concerns these pioneers expressed about the aesthetic deficiencies caused by industrialization and mechanized production. Stu-dents gain insights into their advocacy for craftsmanship, rejection of excessive ornamentation, and pursuit of natural harmony and beauty. Moreover, students witness how the movement inspired successive generations of artists and designers, shaping modern design principles and ideologies (see Fig. 8).

4.2 Establishing Information Hierarchies

For the Arts and Crafts Movement chapter, we adopted a hybrid approach combining the Martini Glass visualization structure and the Interactive Slideshow. At the top level, students select a key figure to begin their journey (see Figs. 3 and 4). The overarching narrative framework introduces the origins, core ideas, representative works, dissemination, and subsequent influence of the movement, connecting various knowledge points through interaction (see Figs. 5 and 6).

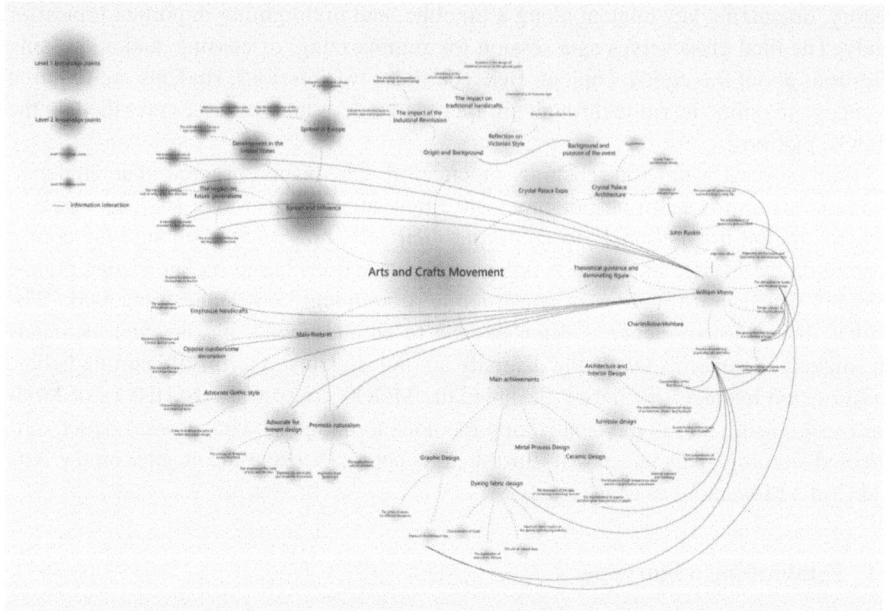

Fig. 2. The Knowledge Map of the Arts and Crafts Movement.

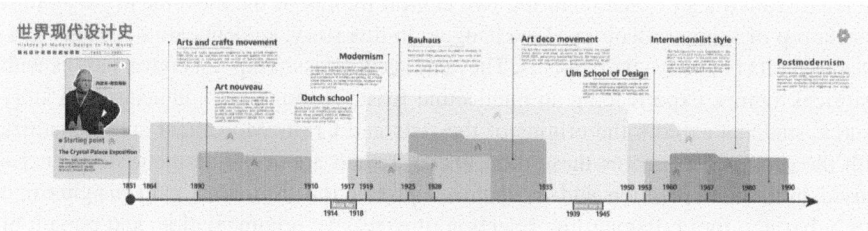

Fig. 3. Timeline of Modern Design History.

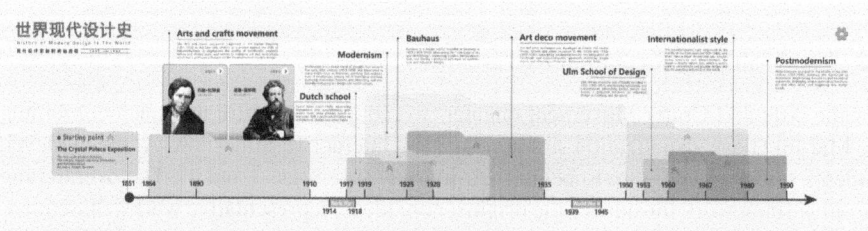

Fig. 4. Students can select relevant knowledge points based on their learning progress.

Fig. 5. The story officially begins. Students can engage in dialogue and choose the direction of the storyline.

Fig. 6. Students can choose the discussion topics with the story protagonist.

4.3 Narrative Progression and Learning Nudging

The story unfolds through a series of engaging interactions between students and historical figures, guiding students in exploring knowledge points as if embarking on a journey through time. At the beginning of the story, a thoughtful and approachable central figure appears, playing the role of both nudging and key to unlocking the unknown. Under their guidance, students choose different narrative branches (see Figs. 5 and 6), each leading to a new world filled with discoveries and surprises.

For instance, students might choose to enter the "Collection Room," where various representative works from the period paintings, furniture, and writings are displayed. Each artifact embodies the intellectual sparks of the time. Students can observe, analyze, and deeply understand the underlying ideas (see Figs. 7 and 8). They can also engage in real-time discussions with AI-powered tools or participate in peer discussions (see Figs. 8 and 10). These figures were the pioneers of reform during that time, each possessing unique insights and profound analyses of the phenomenon of industrial mass production. Students can listen to their eloquent narratives, feeling the passion and wisdom conveyed in their words. This enables students to gain a more comprehensive understanding of the social background, ideological trends, and cultural landscape of that era (see Figs. 9, 10 and 11).

Fig. 7. William Morris's Collection Gallery.

Throughout this narrative, students continually explore and learn, constructing their own knowledge frameworks. The central figure remains a reliable companion and mentor, providing guidance, answering questions, and supporting students in their discovery journey.

Fig. 8. William Morris Introducing His Works.

Fig. 9. Students Can Choose Which Master's Insights to Listen To.

4.4 Visualizing Nudging Information

According to Segel and Heer (2010), seven genres are commonly used in narrative visualization, including Slideshow, Data Comics, Annotated Charts, Magazine Style, and Flow Chart [3]. For important knowledge points, information visualization methods are employed to present abstract, complex data, processes, elements, and changes in a vivid and comprehensible manner. For example, on the course homepage, a timeline spanning

Fig. 10. John Ruskin Expressing His Views.

Fig. 11. Joseph Paxton Introducing His Works.

modern history connects various figures, events, movements, and organizations, clearly illustrating the sequence and development of significant historical events. This provides students with a macro framework and basic understanding of modern design history (see Fig. 3).

For topics such as the Crystal Palace and the 1851 Great Exhibition in London, students can access visualized information about the structure, dimensions, site, and designer of the building. They can also learn about the exhibits, booths, and influence of the exhibition through interactive charts (see Fig. 12). This allows students to grasp the grandeur of the event and its profound impact on subsequent design.

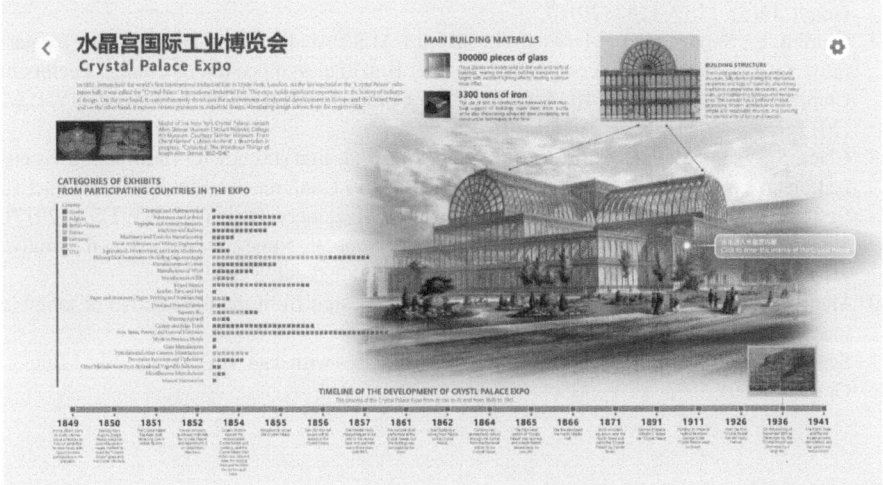

Fig. 12. Crystal Palace Information Visualization Diagram.

5   Conclusion

In this paper, an approach to nudging communication to students in the MOOC Courseware for arts and design students is set out, using the narrative visualization strategy. A five-aspect analysis of different level communication strategies is provided, including an examination of the information framework, storyline, anthropomorphism, visualization elements, and interaction. The overarching aim of the MOOC courseware design strategy is to encourage students to become interested, active, and relaxed in mastering the course content and constructing their own knowledge frame-work. The course has been meticulously designed to proactively engage students in the acquisition of knowledge by stimulating their cognitive and communicative abilities.

References

1. Upgrading catechism to help digital transformation of higher education. http://paper.jyb.cn/zgjyb/html/2024-12/20/content_144741_18108291.htm. Accessed 20 Dec 2024
2. Boy, J., Detienne, F., Fekete, J.-D.: Storytelling in information visualizations: does it engage users to explore data?. In: Proceedings of the 33rd Annual ACM Conference on Human Factors in Computing Systems, pp. 1449–1458. Association for Computing Machinery, New York, NY, USA (2015)
3. Borges, M., Correa, C.M., Silveira, M.S.: Fundamental elements and characteristics for telling stories using data. J Interact. Syst. **13**(1), 77–86 (2022)

4. Baldwin, S., Ching, Y.-H.: Interactive storytelling: opportunities for online course design. TechTrends **61**(2), 179–186 (2017)
5. SOHU.com. https://learning.sohu.com/a/587923790_120113933. Accessed 23 Jan 2025
6. Segel, E., Heer, J.: Narrative visualization: telling stories with data. IEEE Trans. Vis. Comput. Graph. **16**(6), 1139–1148 (2010)
7. Ghidini, E., Santos, C.Q., Manssour, I., Silveira, M.S.: Analyzing design strategies for narrative visualization. In: Proceedings of the XVI Brazilian Symposium on Human Factors in Computing Systems, pp. 1–10. Association for Computing Machinery, New York, NY, USA (2017)
8. Claes, S., Vande Moere, A.: the impact of a narrative design strategy for information visualization on a public display. In: Proceedings of the 2017 Conference on Designing Interactive Systems, pp. 833–838. Association for Computing Machinery, New York, NY, USA (2017)
9. Santana, B., Campos, R., Amorim, E., Jorge, A., Silvano, P., Nunes, S.: A survey on narrative extraction from textual data. Artif. Intell. Rev. **56**(8), 8393–8435 (2023)
10. Meng, L., Yingqing, X.: Research on information design from the perspective of tangible interactive narratives. Art Design **09**, 24–28 (2021)
11. Segel, E., Heer, J.: Narrative visualization: telling stories with data. IEEE Trans. Vis. Comput. Graph. (2010)

Emotional Interaction and Persuasive Design

The Influence of Emotional Elements on UI Cognition Through Interaction

Shunsuke Owa, Rie Suzuki[(⊠)], and Wonseok Yang[(⊠)]

Shibaura Institute of Technology, 3-7-5, Toyosu, Koto-ku, Tokyo 135-8548, Japan
cy20206@shibaura-it.ac.jp

Abstract. With the proliferation of digital devices, interaction in UI is becoming more important for e-commerce sites and portal sites because of the large volume of information and the difficulty of judging content designed with complex IA structures. However, it is considered difficult to provide impressive experiences for users and elicit emotional empathy with interactions that lack cognitive characteristics. Therefore, it is necessary to provide detailed visual and sensory information about feedback and current status in response to actions, and effective use of Micro-interactions can promote a Call to Action and a sense of familiarity with the service. This research focuses on interactions that incorporate Emotional elements and examines their novelty and emotional impact. We believe that the use of "human facial expressions" as a medium for conveying emotions, using physical states and thoughts as metaphors, and anthropomorphizing the UI as if it has emotions, will make it interesting and make people feel attached to the UI. In this research, we aimed to create a denser experience through interactions that utilize Emotional elements, and proceeded as follows. First, we conducted an impression evaluation experiment to clarify how the overall impression of the screen is affected by adding anthropomorphism to the interaction. Next, we conducted a sketching experiment to clarify the factors that influence the user's pleasant impression.

Keywords: Micro-interaction · Emotional elements · Call to Action · UI

1 Introduction

The main purpose of UI design is to design the appearance and arrangement of buttons, menus, icons, etc. on websites and applications so that users find products and services "easy" and "comfortable" to use [1]. However, since many users have become familiar with existing UI interaction methods with the spread of digital devices [2], it has become difficult to create a strong impression on users by simply providing functional interactions. In particular, e-commerce sites and portal sites have a large amount of information, and services designed with complex IA structures make it difficult for users to determine their intended actions, so interaction in the UI becomes important [3]. However, it is difficult to provide memorable and impressive experiences and elicit emotional empathy from users with conventional interactions centered on visual elements. Therefore, it is

© The Author(s), under exclusive license to Springer Nature Switzerland AG 2025
M. Schrepp (Ed.): HCII 2025, LNCS 15794, pp. 173–184, 2025.
https://doi.org/10.1007/978-3-031-93221-2_12

considered necessary to promote behavioral ventilation and increase user recognition by devising and using micro concepts. Micro-interaction is defined by Dan Saffer as the smallest unit of interaction that performs only one task based on a single scenario [4]. When using a website or app, users perform numerous detailed and simple tasks that they are not even aware of, and each of these moments can lead to a better experience by devising small interactions between the user and the service. In other words, it is necessary to visually and sensitively convey feedback and current status in detail to users in response to their actions. Depending on the timing and direction of the use of Micro-interactions, it is also possible to make users feel more familiar with the service.

This research focuses on interactions that incorporate Emotional elements, examines their novelty and emotional impact, and aims to construct a design method that provides users with impressive and emotional value. For the medium to convey emotions, we utilized "human facial expressions" that can convey physical states, thoughts, etc. as metaphors, and thought that by personifying the interaction in the user's experience as if the UI had emotions, it would be possible to make the user feel amused and attached to the UI [5].

2 Literature Review

2.1 Role of Interaction in UI Design

In a software market in which functionality has become generalized and mature, devising a User Interface (UI) design can improve the competitiveness and quality of the user experience [6]. A UI design requires a focus on interaction, which serves as the foundation for shaping the user experience and encompasses aspects such as operability, ease of learning, emotional connection, cultural adaptability, and other aspects that can be encompassed by interaction [7, 8]. Good interactions not only add value to the user but are also crucial factors in the success of a product or service. In addition, interactions can alert users to new options and information through feedback, exploratory manipulation, and visual cues. This awareness plays an important role in deepening the user's understanding and increasing satisfaction and engagement with the product or service [9].

2.2 Emotional Influences on Cognition and Behavior

Emotions have been shown to be highly influential on everyday cognitive behavior. In particular, emotions have a strong effect on judgment and decision-making orientation [10], resulting in a significant influence on decision-making strategies and satisfaction, as shown in Fig. 1 [11]. Therefore, the appropriate use of emotions to promote behavioral ventilation is expected to improve the quality of decisions and actions. Designers can promote positive user emotions by incorporating staging elements, such as gimmicks and fun, to elicit enjoyment and interest in the operation. Such an approach is effective in interface design for enriching the user experience and encouraging active involvement in the task [6]. A good product cannot be created based on usability alone; it must have a beautiful design that appeals to emotions [12].

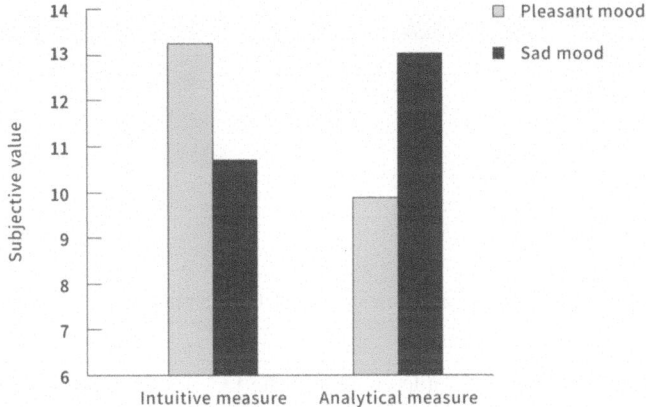

Fig. 1. Mood and Decision-Making Strategies

2.3   The Importance of Emotion in Interaction

Interaction should be more than simply a means of movement and attention; it should evoke feelings of "friendliness" and "enjoyment" in the user and encourage emotional change throughout the entire service [12]. Such emotional value is the key to enriching the user's experience when using a service and providing a higher level of satisfaction [13]. By utilizing appropriately designed interactions, users can feel more familiar with the service and experience "enjoyment" and "comfort" in the process of using it. Consequently, these emotional effects are considered to be the factors that improve the overall experience value of a service [6]. Furthermore, changes in emotions may motivate users to use a service, leading to long-term use.

3   Experimental Evaluation of Impressions of UI Samples Using Emotions

3.1   Experimental Preparation

In this research, we selected an apparel e-commerce (EC) site that is mainly used by 20-somethings who intuitively interact with Emotional elements [14]. The purchase flow of the apparel EC site was then organized in light of the AISAS model and the action phases were selected [15]. As shown in Fig. 2, the product search/category selection phase fits into search and the action phase fits into the action process. These two action phases were selected because they were considered particularly important in stimulating a Call to Action between the search phase of product search/category selection and the action phases of add to cart, purchase confirmation screen, and purchase completion, as shown in Fig. 2.

3.2   Experimental Methods

An experiment was conducted to clarify how the overall impression of the screen was affected by the addition of anthropomorphism to the interaction in the selected action

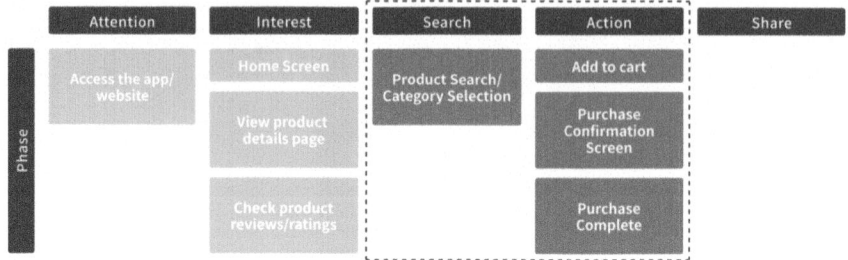

Fig. 2. Purchasing flow on an apparel e-commerce site.

phases. In this experiment, a sample created in the EC application was presented and tested, and impression evaluation experiments were conducted using the SD method for the four phases selected in preparation for the experiment. (product search, product selection, add to cart, and purchase procedure).

- **Experimental Objective:** To clarify how the impression of the UI is affected by adding anthropomorphism to the interaction.
- **Subjects:** 30 people
- **Devices used:** iPhone 15
- **Period:** September 22 to September 23, 2024
- **Experimental Methods:** Three samples were used in four phases (product search, product selection, add to cart, and purchase procedure), and the task of completing the purchase of a ribbed high-neck T from the product search was set for this experiment. In the prototype model used, the phases of accessing the app/website, displaying the home screen, viewing the product detail page, and reviewing/rating the product were partially omitted and a total of 10 phases of screen transitions were used to create an experience that falls under attention, interest, and sharing, which are less important for stimulating a Call to Action. An experience was created in which 10 phases of screen transitions were performed. We were concerned that if the prototype were to be embodied in a form that allowed actual information input, it would diverge from the purpose of clarifying whether Micro-interactions using emotions promote a positive impression of the overall UI. Thus, the prototype in this research was designed to reproduce a simulated experience by displaying dummy text through touch and confirming it. In the actual prototype (Fig. 3.), the subject performed 10 phases through Micro-interactions placed in similar locations (Fig. 4).

3.3 Experimental Results

1. Results of Mean Impression Rating

The profile analysis results showed that "Sample 1" tended to have lower mean scores than the other samples. In contrast, "Sample 3" tended to have higher mean scores than the other samples. "Sample 2" tended to have scores between those of the other samples and did not show extreme impression trends. The items for which changes in impressions

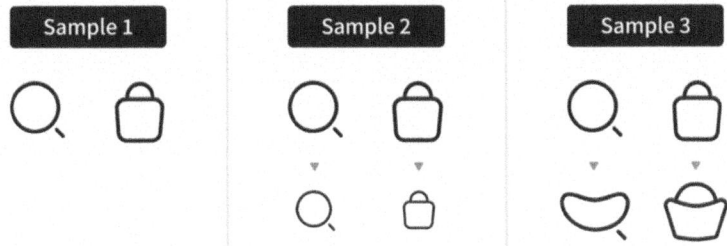

Fig. 3. Samples used in the experiment.

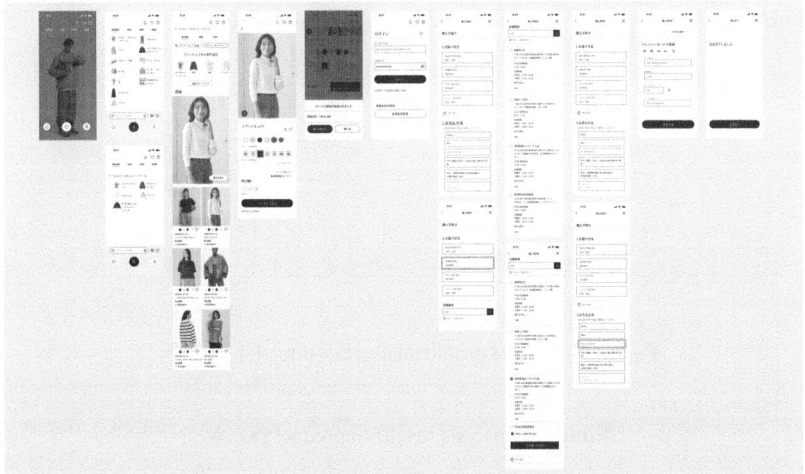

Fig. 4. Screen transition diagram of the UI prototype utilized in the experiment.

were obtained were "strong" and "weak", "new" and "old", "like" and "dislike", "fun" and "boring," and "friendly" and "unfriendly" (Fig. 5).

2. Results of one-way and two-way placement analysis by phase

Product Search. Significant differences were observed in the five items "kind", "powerful", "new", "fun," and "friendly." Table shows the distribution of scores for the five items for which significant differences were observed. No significant differences were found for "beautiful" and "likeable" according to the UI pattern. As the difference by gender was p > 0.05, there was no significant difference, indicating that "positive" feelings towards the UI did not interact with differences by gender or design experience during the product search phase (Table 1).

Product Selection. Significant differences were observed for the two items "new" and "fun." Table shows the distribution of the scores for the two items for which significant differences were observed. No significant differences were found for "beauty", "kindness", "strong", "likeable," and "friendly" for each UI pattern. The difference by gender was p > 0.05, indicating no significant difference, and the difference by major was p >

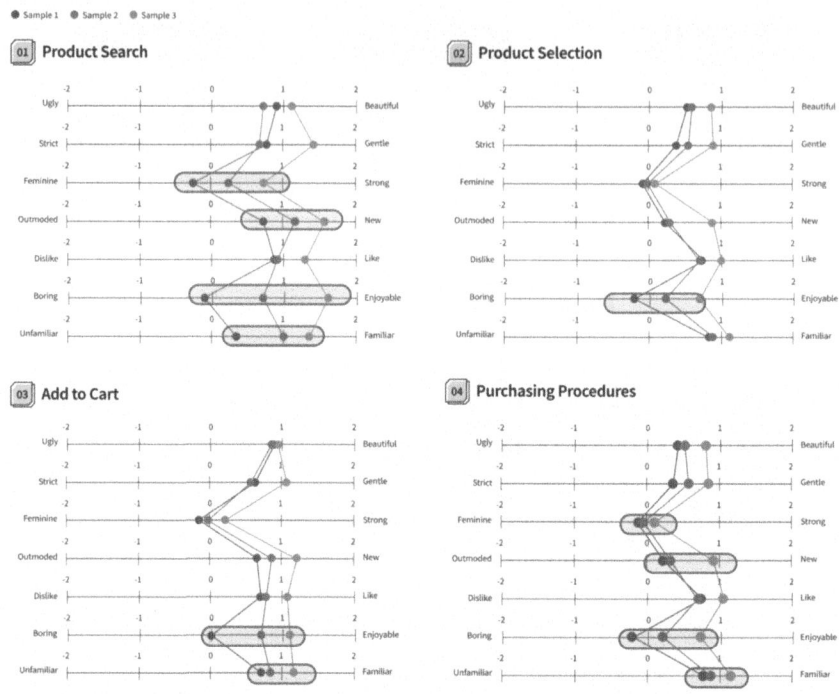

Fig. 5. Results of profile analysis of three UI samples

Table 1. Analysis results in product search.

Evaluation items	Magnitude relation of average	One-way ANOVA	Two-way ANOVA	
			Gender	Design experience or not
Strict - Gentle	②<①<③	$p < 0.05$	N.S	N.S
Feminine - Strong	②<①<③	$p < 0.05$	N.S	N.S
Outmoded - New	①<②<③	$p < 0.05$	N.S	$p < 0.05$
Boring - Enjoyable	①<②<③	$p < 0.05$	N.S	N.S
Unfamiliar - Familiar	①<②<③	$p < 0.05$	N.S	N.S

0.05, indicating no significant difference. We found no interaction between "positive" feelings towards UI in the product selection phase and differences by gender or design experience (Table 2).

Table 2. Analysis Results in Product Selection

Evaluation items	Magnitude relation of average	One-way ANOVA	Two-way ANOVA	
			Gender	Design experience or not
Outmoded - New	①<②<③	p < 0.05	N.S	N.S
Boring - Enjoyable	①<②<③	p < 0.05	N.S	N.S

Add to Cart. Significant differences were observed for the two items "new" and "fun." Table shows the distribution of the scores for the two items for which significant differences were found. No significant differences were observed for "beauty", "kindness", "strong", "likeable," and "friendly" for each UI pattern. The difference by gender was p > 0.05, indicating no significant difference, and the difference by major was also p > 0.05, indicating no significant difference. We found no interaction between "positive" feelings towards the UI in the carting phase and differences by gender or design experience (Table 3).

Table 3. Analysis Results in Add to Cart

Evaluation items	Magnitude relation of average	One-way ANOVA	Two-way ANOVA	
			Gender	Design experience or not
Outmoded - New	①<②<③	p < 0.05	N.S	N.S
Boring - Enjoyable	①<②<③	p < 0.05	N.S	N.S

Purchase Procedure. Significant differences were observed for the five items "powerful", "new", "likeable", "enjoyable," and "friendly." Table shows the distribution of the scores for the five items for which significant differences were found. No significant differences were observed for "beautiful" and "likeable" according to the UI pattern. As the difference by gender was p > 0.05, there was no significant difference, indicating that "positive" feelings towards the UI did not interact with differences by gender or design experience during the purchase procedure phase (Table 4).

3.4   Considerations

It was suggested that users may have negative impressions of "old", "boring," and "unfriendly" for Sample 1, which used the same design as existing apparel EC sites. In contrast, Sample 3 featured a design that utilizes facial expressions as an element to evoke positive emotions and was thought to provide users with positive impressions of "new", "fun," and "friendly." Furthermore, the results of one-way and two-way ANOVAs that were conducted for each of the four phases (product search, product selection, add

Table 4. Analysis Results in Purchase Procedures.

Evaluation items	Magnitude relation of average	One-way ANOVA	Two-way ANOVA	
			Gender	Design experience or not
Feminine - Strong	①<②=③	p < 0.05	N.S	N.S
Outmoded - New	①<②<③	p < 0.05	N.S	p < 0.05
Dislike - Like	①<②=③	p < 0.05	N.S	N.S
Boring - Enjoyable	①<②<③	p < 0.05	N.S	N.S
Unfamiliar - Familiar	①<②<③	p < 0.05	N.S	N.S

to cart, and purchase procedure) showed a statistically significant difference for Sample 3 in the impressions of "new" and "fun." This revealed that Sample 3 was more effective in promoting positive emotions. No interaction effects by gender or major were confirmed from the results of the one-way and two-way analyses, suggesting that the design of Sample 3 may have promoted positive impressions among a wide range of user groups. This suggests that the design of Sample 3 was effective in increasing the emotional affinity.

4   Sketching Experiments of Interactions Recalled from Emotions

A sketching experiment was conducted to identify the factors that influence users' pleasant emotions in EC applications. In this experiment, users were asked to sketch images of the emotions evoked by six words (pleasant, fulfilled, cheerful, joyful, pleasant, and motivated) for five icons.

4.1   Experimental Methods

- **Experimental Objective:** To identify anthropomorphic elements that promote specific positive emotions through icons.
- **Number of subjects:** 30 people
- **Duration:** October 18 to October 23, 2024
- **Experimental Method:** A survey was conducted in which the subjects were asked to sketch the anthropomorphic movements evoked by emotion-related language (pleasant, fulfilling, cheerful, joyful, pleasant-tempered, and motivated) for icons that were presented to them. In this manner, we limited the expressive elements available for the sketching survey to only "dots", "arrows," and "lines" to avoid difficulty in focusing on the essential elements of movement and shape [17].

4.2   Experimental Results

The results of the sketch survey were tabulated and categorized for each element of each icon. The degree to which the images were recalled by each subject was assessed for agreement, and characteristic patterns were identified. The results are as follows:

Cart. For the "pleasant", "fulfilling", "cheerful", "joyful", "pleasant," and "motivating" emotions, the icon was recalled in the form of a tilting motion. For the emotion "happy," the icon was recalled to bend similar to the corners of the mouth of a smiling face. In the emotion "contented," the motion of an object being added to the icon was recalled. In the "pleasant" emotion, the icon was associated with an elongated horizontal line (Fig. 6).

Fig. 6. Agreement of movement images held by subjects (Cart)

Basket. For the "happy" emotion, the movement of the icon was recalled as the corners of the mouth curving similar to the corners of a smile. For the emotion of "fulfilled," the icon was associated with the movement of an object being added. For the "fulfilled" and "motivated" emotions, the icon was associated with a bulge. For the emotion "pleasant," the icon was associated with a movement from left to right. (Fig. 7).

Bag. For the "pleasant", "cheerful," and "pleasant" emotions, the movement of the icon tilting was recalled. For the "pleasant", "cheerful," and "motivated" emotions, the icon evoked a movement in which the corners of the mouth curved similar to the corners of a smile. For the "fulfilled" emotion, the icon was associated with the movement of an object being added. For the "full" and "motivated" emotions, the icon was associated with small and large movements. For the "pleasant" emotion, the icon was associated with movements to the left and right (Fig. 8).

Clothes. This icon was associated with tilting movements for the "happy", "fulfilled", "cheerful", "pleasant", "pleasant-tempered," and "motivated" emotions. The icon was associated with small and large movements for the "fulfilled", "motivated," and "motivated" emotions. For the "happy", "cheerful," and "joyful" emotions, the icon was associated with movement of the sleeve part (Fig. 9).

Fig. 7. Agreement of movement images held by subjects (Basket)

Fig. 8. Agreement of movement images held by subjects (Bag)

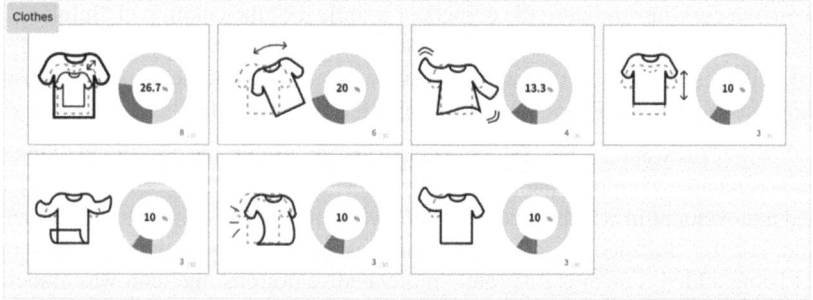

Fig. 9. Agreement of movement images held by subjects (Clothes)

Magnifying Glass. The icon was recalled to tilt for the "happy", "content", "cheerful", "pleasant," and "good-tempered" emotions. For the "pleasant" emotion, the icon was recalled to bend similar to the corners of the mouth of a smiling face. For the "happy" and "pleasant" emotions, the motion of adding facial expressions was recalled. The "full", "happy," and "motivated" emotions were associated with small and large movements of the icon. For the "pleasant" emotion, the icon was recalled to move left and right (Fig. 10).

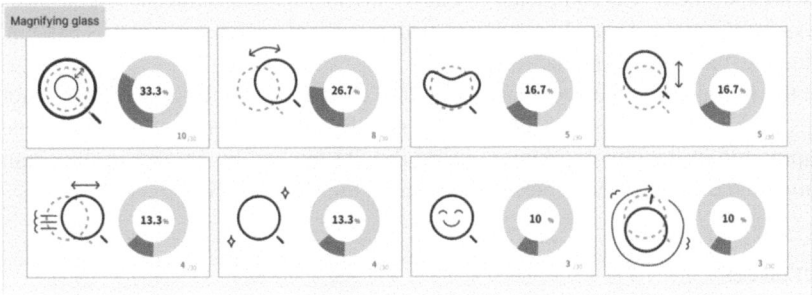

Fig. 10. Agreement of movement images held by subjects (Magnifying glass)

4.3 Consideration

It became clear that the "movement" of the icons themselves was an important factor in eliciting emotion and a sense of personification. In particular, it was suggested that the addition of movement to icons may express a natural and friendly anthropomorphism that cannot be conveyed by facial expressions alone. This suggests that movement is an important means of reinforcing emotional connections in icon design. In addition, there was a consistent pattern of movement in the expression of emotion through the icons. As a specific example, the movement of objects being added was recalled in relation to the "fulfilled" emotion. Therefore, it can be inferred that characteristic movements visually suggest certain emotions. These movements may function as visual metaphors between emotion and movement, potentially making emotion communication more effective. Furthermore, these findings have implications for icon design in practice. Incorporating elements of movement rather than simply a static facial expression design can better evoke action and provide a more user-friendly experience. In addition, further design optimization can be achieved by clarifying the relationship between emotions and movement.

5   Conclusion

In the previous research, we focused on dynamic Micro-interactions. As users feel dissatisfied when movements are unexpected, we investigated the elements that create dynamic Micro-interactions based on the characteristics of the movements of objects and people that are recalled from verbs, and the impact of these elements on the intuitive operation of the user [18].

However, this research focused on interactions that incorporate Emotional elements and examined their novelty and emotional impact. An experiment was conducted with the aim of clarifying how the overall impression of the screen is affected by the addition of anthropomorphism to the interaction, and it was found that the interaction can positively change the impression of the subject by increasing the anthropomorphism. In addition, a sketch experiment was conducted to clarify the factors that influence users' pleasant feelings in EC applications. It was found that consistent movement patterns exist in the emotional expression of interactions.

In the future, it will be necessary to explore the trends in anthropomorphic emotion images in the interactions compiled in the sketch survey. Therefore, we will conduct an impression evaluation experiment using the SD method by extracting the common emotion images among the subjects compiled in the sketch survey.

References

1. Yamazaki, K.: Propose to utilize KANSEI approach from user experience view point. User information and expression (2015)
2. Jeff, J., Musha, H., Musha, R.: Psychology of UI Design. IMPRESS Corporation, Japan (2015)
3. Rosenfeld, L., Morville, P., Arango, J.: Information Architecture: Easy to find and understand information design, 4th edn, O'reilly, Japan (2016)
4. Dan, S., Musha, H., Musha, R.: Micro Interaction UI/UX Design: Godsend Details, O'Reilly Japan (2014)
5. Orita, A., Mukaida, S., Kato, T.: Perceiving a momentary change in facial expression. Cognitive Psychology Research 2005, vol. 3–1, pp.1–11, Japan (2005)
6. Harada, H.: Textbook of UI Design. Shoei Corporation, Japan (2019)
7. Nakanoji, K.: Interaction design. Human Interface Research Group, Information Processing Society of Japan (IPSJ-SIG-HIL), vol. 2004, no. 115, pp. 1–3 (2004)
8. Oka, N.: The power of movement and interaction design. Measur. Control **48**(6), 463–469 (2009)
9. Muramatsu, K., et al.: Describing color and emotional states for sensory interaction. Information on the Second Research Group of the Society for Artificial Intelligence SIG-SWO-025-07, pp. 1–6 (2011)
10. Holbrook, M.B.: The experiential aspects of consumption: consumer fantasies, feelings, and fun. J. Cons. Res. **9**(2), 132–140 (1982)
11. de Vries, M., et al.: Fitting decisions: mood and intuitive versus deliberative decision strategies. Cogn. Emot. **22**(5), 931–943 (2008)
12. Inoue, K.: Design an attractive interface, Industrial Research Council, Japan (2008)
13. Norman, D.A.: Emotional Design - Why We Love (or hate) Everyday Things. Basics Books, Japan (2004)
14. Kurosu, M.: Fundamentals of Human-Centered Design. Modern Science Society, Japan (2013)
15. Kondo, F.: The modeling of AISAS marketing process. JSD **8**, 95–102 (2009)
16. Nakakoji, K., Yamamoto, Y., Aoki, A.: Interaction design as a collective creative process. In: Proceedings of Creativity and Cognition 2002, Loughborough, UK, pp. 103–110 (2002)
17. Owa, S., Yang, W.: On the use of verb for micro interactions in UI. AHFE **2024**, 198–204 (2024)

Research on the Role of Personalized Design of Digital Humans in Museums in Enhancing Users' Emotional Experience

Zihan Peng[✉]

Beijing City University, No. 269 Bei Si Huan Zhong Lu, Hai Dian District, Beijing, China
1739434876@qq.com

Abstract. This study focuses on the enhancing effect of personalized design of museum digital humans on users' emotional experience. In the current era of rapid technological development, the digital transformation of museums is accelerating, and digital humans have emerged as a new medium for display and interaction. However, the current design of museum digital humans mostly emphasizes functional realization, with insufficient consideration given to users' emotional experience. This study conducts research on personalized design in dimensions such as the image shaping, language expression, and interaction mode of digital humans, aiming to fill this gap and effectively enhance users' emotional experience, making museum digital humans into emotionally appealing cultural communication carriers and strengthening the cultural communication effectiveness of museums.

Keyword: Digital human in museums · Personalized design · User emotional experience

1 Introduction

1.1 Research Background

With the rapid development of information technology, the museum industry is actively promoting digital transformation. As an innovative product of the digital wave, museum digital humans, by leveraging computer graphics, artificial intelligence, and speech recognition technologies, simulate human appearance, movements, and language, providing visitors with novel interactive experiences and becoming an important means for museums to display cultural content and enhance audience engagement.

However, most current museum digital humans are mainly designed around information transmission and basic interaction functions, lacking in-depth consideration of the user's emotional level. This results in difficulty in establishing an emotional connection between digital humans and users, thus failing to fully leverage their cultural communication value.

M. Schrepp (Ed.): HCII 2025, LNCS 15794, pp. 185–199, 2025.
https://doi.org/10.1007/978-3-031-93221-2_13

1.2 Research Objectives

At present, the design of digital humans in museums focuses more on functionality than on emotional experience. This research aims to fill this gap by exploring personalized design methods in dimensions such as image, language, and interaction, to enhance the emotional connection between digital humans and users and improve the user's emotional experience. This will enable digital humans to better disseminate museum culture and enhance the effectiveness of museum cultural communication.

1.3 Research Significance

Theoretical significance: The application of emotional design in museum display has gradually received attention, which promotes its focus to the audience's emotional resonance, and can better improve the emotional experience of users. In the theory of emotional design, the application boundary is broadened to museum digital people, and the mechanism of emotional stimulation in cultural context is explored.

At the same time, it integrates multidisciplinary theories and methods, breaks disciplinary boundaries, promotes interdisciplinary integration and innovation, spawns new theoretical growth points, provides a comprehensive theoretical basis for the digital transformation of museums and the integration of culture and technology, and plays a leading and demonstration role in related fields.

Practical significance: Personalized virtual digital person is of great significance to the development of museums. It can improve the lack of interaction and personalization in traditional guided Tours and optimize the visiting experience. Digital person can provide customized guided Tours according to the characteristics of visitors, so that different groups can better enjoy culture. It can also enhance cultural communication, integrate elements with themes, and help popularize knowledge.

The virtual digital human guide system can reduce the working pressure of manual guide and improve the efficiency and accuracy of guide. The system can also provide museums with uninterrupted guided Tours, break the constraints of time and space, enable more people to benefit from the museum's cultural resources, facilitate digital transformation, and encourage museums to explore the use of new technologies, innovate in display and interaction, so that they can be more dynamic in the digital age and better meet the cultural needs of the public.

1.4 Research Features and Innovations

Features. In terms of personalized customization, the exhibition theme and audience of the museum are deeply analyzed, and the different needs from the digital human image to the interactive link are fully matched. According to the different characteristics of different museums, different costumes are designed for virtual digital people.

At the interactive level of emotional intelligence, advanced technologies are used to perceive user emotions, adjust language styles in real time, and enhance emotional resonance. In terms of cultural integration and innovation, it skillfully integrates ancient and modern cultural elements to present new forms while inheriting cultural essence. It combines traditional culture and modern popular elements into the design and explanation of digital people, which not only attracts young people's attention to museum culture, but also opens up new paths for cultural inheritance. The overall characteristics make the design unique charm and competitiveness in the field of museum digital people.

Innovative Points. Personalized Image Design of Virtual Digital Person: Design and build virtual digital person in line with museum characteristics, and create IP image of museum digital person, including realistic image and cartoon image imitating real person. Design personalized clothing that allows users to switch according to the characteristics of the cultural center.

Personalized Action Design of Virtual Figures: Design personalized actions of virtual figures according to the cultural characteristics of the museum. For example, for the science and technology Museum, when introducing space exploration, digital people can make the action of floating weightless in space. The body is slightly bent, in a semi-suspended state, the limbs are naturally extended, the fingers are gently wiggling, as if touching the surrounding stars, while the head is slowly rotating, the eyes are curious to observe around, creating an atmosphere of exploration in the vast universe, reflecting the mystery and infinite possibilities of science and technology.

Emotional Design Strategy: Explore how to give virtual digital people rich emotional expression ability, including facial expression, voice tone, body language and other aspects of design, so that they can establish emotional resonance with the audience.

Personalized Tour Mode: Study the method of personalized tour content recommendation and route planning through virtual digital person according to the age, interest, visit history and other factors of the audience. For example, for children under the age of 10, digital people use childlike, simple and easy to understand language, speaking at a moderate pace and lively tone. In the content of the tour, you can choose colorful, cute image, strong story exhibits. For example, in the art museum, the emphasis is on paintings with cartoon image elements, or art works with mythological stories, telling the story behind with vivid language, and stimulating children's imagination.

2 Literature Review

2.1 Current Situation of Museum Digitization Development

In recent years, the digital construction of museums has made remarkable progress on a global scale. Many well-known museums in the world, such as the British Museum and the Louvre Museum, have actively promoted the digitization of their collections and exhibitions, and achieved fruitful results. in their research on Virtual Humans in Museums and Cultural Heritage Sites, Stella Sylaiou and Christo systematically discussed the application of digital humans in the field of cultural heritage. The trends and characteristics of the use of virtual digital people in museums and cultural heritage sites are pointed out. Museum digitization is developing in a diversified direction, and digital people are gradually integrated into the museum exhibition system as a new form of display. For example, the digital people guide tour of the American Museum of Natural History provides visitors with a wealth of natural science knowledge.

Chinese museums have also achieved remarkable results in the digitization process, and many museums have launched featured digital human services. But overall, museum digital people are still in the development stage. Ye Yipei pointed out that as a pathfinder for the museum industry to enter the "meta-universe" world, the development mode, functional positioning and image characteristics of virtual digital people have been deeply analyzed. In addition, Gao Jingmin explored users' perceptions and attitudes toward virtual people in the museum through a questionnaire survey, and summarized the existing problems and the possibility of future development. For example, most digital people are unable to provide customized service content based on users' interests, preferences and visiting habits.

2.2   Research on Digital Human Design

Foreign research in the field of digital human design has long focused on technical realization. Professor Dinesh K. Pai of the University of British Columbia focuses on the research of data-driven digital human model, is committed to the development of realistic human body calculation model, through measurement, modeling, parameter estimation and data-driven simulation and other processes to create personalized digital avatars, applied to product design, virtual fitting and other fields. The results provide a technical reference for the personalization of digital human image building in museums.

However, the research on personalized design from the perspective of user emotional experience is relatively scarce. In his book "The Psychology of Design" and other works, Don Norman put forward the principle of human-centered design (HCD), emphasizing that the needs, behaviors and emotions of users should be fully considered in product design. However, in the field of digital human design, most studies only focus on the external expression form, and there is little discussion on how to make digital human understand and respond to emotional needs in interaction with users. In the review of existing research on digital human design, it is mentioned that although some digital humans can achieve basic voice interaction, there is a lack of effective algorithms and models for recognizing users' emotional states and giving corresponding emotional responses.

Domestic scholars are also actively exploring digital human design. For example, Professor Li Kun from Tianjin University has made remarkable achievements in the field of three-dimensional vision, especially in human-centered intelligent reconstruction and generation. He proposed Fourier occupancy field (FOF) and built a real-time single-color camera 3D human body reconstruction framework and neural rendering method to achieve high-quality 3D human body generation, which helps to improve the realism and expression of digital human images in museums. Guo Yudong, special associate researcher of the University of Science and Technology of China, has made achievements in efficient digital human modeling, and has been applied to the field of film and television media, providing a reference for the efficient modeling of digital human in museums. However, the research in China also has the problem of insufficient attention to user emotional experience, and fails to fully integrate user emotional needs into each design link in digital human design.

2.3 Research on User Emotional Experience

The application of emotional design in museum new media display has also received attention. Miao Ling, a Chinese scholar, wrote in his Research on the Application of Emotional Design in Museum New Media Display that emotional design can more accurately capture the inner needs and emotional changes of the audience, thus promoting the emotional communication between museum exhibitions and the audience. At the same time, the design concept of museum tour based on extended reality technology is proposed, emphasizing the importance of multi-modal interaction and immersive experience.

3 Research Methods

3.1 Literature Research Method

In the academic journey of exploring the personalized design of digital humans in museums and users' emotional experiences, the literature review method serves as the cornerstone, providing a solid theoretical framework for the entire research. During the retrieval stage, the powerful functions of authoritative academic databases such as Web of Science and CNKI are deeply explored. Besides using "museum digital humans", "personalized design", and "user emotional experience" as core search terms, Boolean logical operators are also employed to flexibly combine the search terms to obtain more precise and comprehensive literature. This ensures that the retrieval results closely revolve around the research topic.

In terms of time frame, the literature of the past ten years is the key research object, because at this stage, technology iteration is rapid, museum digital transformation is accelerated, digital human technology is constantly innovated, and relevant research results can reflect the latest academic dynamics and practical experience. At the same time, it retrospects the early classical literature, combs the historical evolution process from the sprout of museum digitization concept to the gradual application of digital human technology, and grasp the context and trend of academic development.

In the literature screening process, the retrieved literature is initially screened. In addition to browsing the title and abstract, attention is also paid to the journal level of publication of the literature, the academic background of the author and other information, and the literature with low quality and low relevance is excluded. Entering the detailed study stage, using the content analysis method, the research purpose, methods, results and conclusions of the literature are analyzed in detail. In the field of museum digitization, this paper analyzes the viewpoints of different literatures on digital transformation strategy and technology application bottleneck. In the digital human design principle, research from 3D modeling technology, motion capture technology to artificial intelligence-driven intelligent interaction technology application; In terms of influencing factors of user emotional experience, the paper discusses the mechanism of inspiring and influencing factors such as digital human image, language and interaction mode on user emotion. Through systematic review, the current research hotspots are identified, such as the application of multimodal interaction in museum digital people; Identify research gaps, such as differentiated research on users' emotional needs for digital people under specific cultural backgrounds, and anchor the direction for subsequent research.

3.2 Case Analysis

Case analysis method serves as a bridge for the deep integration of theory and practice, infusing research with rich practical wisdom. Selecting the digital human projects of renowned museums such as the Palace Museum and the National Museum of China as typical cases, these cases not only have extensive influence worldwide but also represent the practical achievements of digital humans under different cultural backgrounds, technological application levels, and design concepts (Fig. 1).

Each museum has a different way of taking a tour

Museum	Audio - Guided Tour	Mobile Application - Guided Tour	Virtual Tour
The Palace Museum, China	Audio - guided tour devices are available for rent. Visitors can input the exhibit number or scan the QR code to listen to the explanations.	There are official APPs and mini - programs, providing functions such as exhibition introductions, exhibit details, audio explanations, and tour route planning. There is also a "Panoramic Forbidden City" that allows visitors to enjoy the real Forbidden City online.	A digital sign - language guided tour project has been launched, with sign - language explanation videos. There are online sign - language tour maps and 50 explanation videos covering some buildings, spaces, and cultural relics in the museum. By scanning the code offline, visitors can watch the sign - language explanation videos. Digital treasure pavilions allow online viewing of cultural relics. The "Digital Forbidden City" mini - program has an AI exclusive tour guide "Little Lion", which provides tour suggestions for visitors through learning materials.
National Museum of China	Audio - guided tour devices are available. Visitors can obtain audio explanations by inputting the exhibit number.	There are official APPs and mini - programs, with functions such as exhibition recommendations, route planning, audio explanations of exhibits, and cloud exhibitions.	A virtual intelligent person "Ai Wenwen" has been created. "Ai Wenwen" has unlocked the function of voice explanation, but it can only be experienced online. It will also act as a tour guide in the digital twin cloud exhibition space of the "Cloud Exhibition of Chinese Civilization" to lead visitors to appreciate the exhibits.
National Art Museum of China	There is no clear mention of audio - guided tour devices, but there is a service of scanning the code to listen to sculpture introductions.	There are official APPs and mini - programs, providing functions such as exhibition information and exhibit introductions.	The "Ink Rhythm and Cultural Context Panoramic Virtual Exhibition Hall" restores the works in the original exhibition hall through 3D modeling and other technologies.
Capital Museum	Free audio - guided tour devices are provided. Visitors can handle the procedures at the consultation counter in the Etiquette Hall with their valid certificates. There are Chinese and English languages.	There are official APPs and mini - programs. The AI intelligent guided tour system is newly launched, integrating functions such as reservation, interaction with digital intelligent people, tour route recommendation, exhibit navigation, and audio explanation. New technologies such as check - in interaction and AR interaction can be experienced through mobile phones.	A virtual digital person "Jing Hui" has been launched. At the intelligent touch - screen terminal, visitors can ask voice questions. "Jing Hui" can chat with visitors like a real person and give accurate answers to visitors' needs such as exhibition consultation, exhibit navigation, tour route recommendation, and audio explanation.
China National Film Museum	Visitors can experience self - service audio - guided tour services by following the WeChat official account.	There is an official WeChat official account, and operations such as reservation can be carried out on the official account. There is no clear mention of APPs and mini - programs with rich functions.	There are multimedia display devices in the exhibition hall, which comprehensively introduce the development history of Chinese films, film - making technologies, etc. through pictures, models, and multimedia display means.

Fig. 1. Each museum has a different way of taking a tour.

From the above cases, it can be seen that virtual digital humans have been applied in museum tours and have presented different application models and functional characteristics. On the one hand, they have expanded the online tour services of museums, breaking through the limitations of time and space with digital technology; on the other hand, they have enhanced the visiting experience of audiences in physical venues through intelligent interaction, meeting diverse tour needs. With the continuous development of technology, virtual digital humans are expected to play a greater role in the field of museum tours, further promoting the digital transformation and service upgrade of museums.

In addition, an analysis was conducted on some museums that have implemented virtual digital humans, revealing differences in image shaping, language expression, and interaction patterns (Fig. 2).

Famous Museums Using Virtual Digital Humans

Museum	Virtual Digital Human	Application Scenarios	Guided - Tour Methods
National Museum of China	Ai Wenwen, Tong Gujin	Serving as volunteer docents to provide voice - over explanations for some exhibits, explaining the knowledge of the National Museum's fine cultural relics through special - effect videos, and leading people to visit the basic exhibition "Ancient China" in the virtual exhibition hall	Intelligent voice - over explanations, short videos, virtual exhibition hall guided tours, etc. Visitors can use the intelligent voice - over explanation function on the "National Museum" App and mini - program
Hunan Museum	The Digital Version of Xin Zhui	Telling modern people about the history and social customs of the Western Han Dynasty, helping people better understand the culture of the Mawangdui Han Tombs	Mainly through interactive communication, giving explanations and introductions according to visitors' questions. In the future, an AI intelligent agent may be launched for multi - round, long - cycle memory and conversational interaction
Dunhuang Academy	Jiayao	Spreading Dunhuang culture, appearing in some online activities and promotions, helping people better understand Dunhuang cultural art	Mainly through online means for display and promotion, interacting with the audience on some specific online platforms or activities
Shanghai Natural History Museum	Xiaoke	Providing guided - tour services for visitors in the exhibition, including answering various questions about the biological habits of natural exhibits, geological evolution, etc., and accurately recommending natural science knowledge according to visitors' interests	Visitors can interact with "Xiaoke" through handheld intelligent terminals to obtain explanation services
Beijing Arts and Crafts Museum	Li Jie	Creating an interactive explanation of collections with the model of "AI digital human + public service" offline, and promoting the collections through short videos on the new media matrix of Beijing Time online	Offline visitors can scan the QR code to watch the introduction of collections by "Li Jie"; online visitors can watch relevant short videos on the Beijing Time client

Fig. 2. Each museum has a different way of taking a tour

These museum cases indicate that the application of virtual digital humans in the museum field exhibits diverse characteristics. In terms of character design, there are those based on historical figures as well as original ones; application scenarios cover both online and offline; functions include explanations, interactive communication, knowledge recommendations, and promotional activities. Each museum explores suitable virtual digital human application models based on its own cultural themes and business needs to enhance cultural dissemination effects and visitor experience, thereby promoting innovation and development in museum services.

In terms of image creation, using image recognition technology and cultural semiotics theory, we can conduct quantitative analysis and cultural interpretation of the appearance features of digital humans. For example, for the digital humans of the Palace Museum, by analyzing elements such as clothing patterns, color combinations, and hairstyle accessories, we can assess their fidelity to and innovative expression of ancient court culture symbols. Additionally, by employing user profiling technology, we can analyze the preference differences of users of different ages, genders, and cultural backgrounds towards the digital.

In terms of language expression, using natural language processing technology, analyze the vocabulary richness, grammatical complexity, and semantic accuracy of the digital human's language to determine whether it accurately conveys the cultural connotation of the museum. At the same time, apply sentiment analysis algorithms to evaluate the emotional arousal effects of the digital human's language on different user groups.

For example, for the adolescent group, analyze the language's fun and inspirational qualities; for cultural researchers, analyze the language's professionalism and depth.

In the dimension of interactive mode, the research is carried out from two aspects: technical implementation and user experience. In terms of technical implementation, the integration and application of multimodal interaction technologies, such as gesture recognition, eye-tracking, and voice interaction, are studied, and their stability, accuracy, and response speed are analyzed. Regarding user experience, the effect of personalized guidance is evaluated through the analysis of user behavior data, such as interaction frequency, interaction duration, and interaction path, and the emotional changes of users during the interaction process, such as interest, participation, and satisfaction, are analyzed.

Through an in-depth analysis of these cases, we summarize successful experiences, such as the innovative expression methods of digital humans in cultural heritage at the Palace Museum, and the technical advantages of digital humans in multilingual interaction at the National Museum of China. At the same time, we analyze existing issues, such as delays in some digital human interactions and the balance between content depth and breadth, to extract key factors affecting user emotional experience, providing practical guidance for personalized design strategies.

3.3 User Research Method

User research is a key window for directly understanding user needs and emotional experiences, providing the most authentic and direct user feedback for research.

In the design of the questionnaire content, it comprehensively covers aspects such as user basic information, visiting habits, digital human cognition and usage experience, emotional needs, and expectations for personalized design. In the section on user basic information, in addition to conventional information such as age, gender, occupation, and educational level, it also collects information on users' cultural background and interests, to more deeply analyze the differences in user needs. Regarding visiting habits, it not only understands the frequency of visits, visiting purposes, and duration of stay, but also asks about the channels through which users obtain museum information and whether they have participated in the museum's educational activities, to comprehensively understand users' museum behavior patterns.

In the data collection stage, a combination of online and offline methods is fully utilized. Online, questionnaires are widely distributed through professional platforms such as Wenjuanxing and Tencent Wenjuan, and through channels such as social media, the museum's official website, and online communities, to expand the sample coverage; offline, questionnaires are randomly distributed to visitors at the museum entrance, exhibition halls, rest areas, etc., to ensure the randomness and representativeness of the samples.

In-depth interviews further reveal the inner thoughts of the audience. When asked about their overall impression of digital people, many users said that the current digital people function well, but lack uniqueness. When talking about the use of feelings, many users mentioned that they hope that digital people can give more targeted responses according to their own way of asking questions and emotional states. For example, when the audience shows a strong interest in an exhibit and repeatedly asks questions, the digital person should be able to detect this interest point and provide more rich and in-depth relevant knowledge, rather than the same fixed answer. In terms of expected improvement, users generally hope that digital people can have more personalized forms of interaction, such as being able to take the initiative to share interesting historical stories or behind-the-scenes anecdotes according to the progress of users' visits, increase the sense of companionship, and make the visit process more interesting and immersive.

According to the results of the survey, the audience expects that the virtual digital person of the museum will no longer be a uniform service model, but can provide personalized and differentiated services according to personal characteristics, visiting habits and real-time needs, so as to meet the diversified experience needs of different visitors in the process of museum visiting.

4 Dimensional Analysis of Museum Digital Personalization Design

4.1 Individuation of Image Building

Physical Features. Design the digital human appearance according to the theme and cultural characteristics of the museum. The figures in historical and cultural museums can learn from the shapes of ancient figures. For example, the figures in the Mausoleum Museum of the Emperor Qin Shihuang can wear the costumes of the Qin Dynasty and comb the hair of the Qin Dynasty to show the cultural features of the Qin Dynasty. The digital people of natural science museums can incorporate natural elements or science fiction styles, such as the digital people of science and technology museums are designed as futuristic creatures to enhance visual appeal. Advanced 3D modeling technology is used to finely depict the facial expressions, body movements and clothing details of digital people, making their images more vivid and realistic.

In the history museum, virtual digital people switch images and languages according to different exhibition halls, allowing visitors to feel the changes of history and the charm of culture more deeply. For example, in the ancient exhibition hall, the clothes and images of digital people can be ancient clothes wearing a robe with big sleeves, and the colors are mainly dark tones, such as black and vermilion, reflecting the solemn and elegant of ancient times. Fabric selection of silk texture, embroidered with delicate moire, dragon pattern and other traditional patterns, waist strap and hanging jade, highlighting status. In the language style, the use of quaint words and expressions, the tone is peaceful and full of charm. In the introduction of ancient cultural relics, the ancient text will be quoted; In the modern exhibition hall, the clothes and images of digital people will be changed into clothes with modern characteristics, and the language style is more easy to understand, but without losing the sense of history.

Through this design, virtual digital people can provide visitors with an immersive historical and cultural experience in different exhibition halls with images and languages that fit the background of The Times, helping them better understand the development of history.

Expression Management. Using expression recognition and generation technology, digital people can adjust their expressions in real time based on display content and user interaction. When introducing interesting historical stories, digital people show vivid expressions, such as surprise, joy, etc., to enhance emotional transmission; When the user asks a question, the digital person will slightly tilt his head forward, his eyes are focused on the user, his eyebrows are slightly raised, his face shows a look of serious thinking, and occasionally gently nod his head to give the user positive feedback, so that the user really feels concerned and valued, thereby enhancing the emotional resonance and narrowing the distance between the digital person and the user.

Individual Movements. In the personalized design of digital people in museums, individual action is an important dimension to enhance user experience and convey cultural connotation. The movement design of digital people should closely fit the theme of the museum, the characteristics of the exhibits, and the age level and interest preference of the users. In the natural science museum, when the digital man introduces the flight of birds, the digital man's arms are extended to simulate the flapping of wings, the movement is light and rhythmic, and the body is slightly undulating, as if flying freely in the air, so that visitors can better understand the ecological habits of animals.

For users of different ages, the movement design of digital people is also different. In the face of children, the actions of digital people are more exaggerated and childlike. When introducing fairy-tale related exhibits in the Children's Museum, digital people will imitate the classic movements of the characters in the story, such as imitating the movement of Snow White dancing with the dwarfs, the body rotates lightly, the arms are raised high, and the face is filled with a bright smile, and the imagination and participation of children are stimulated through vivid movements. For older users, digital people move slowly and kindly. When introducing the scenes of past life in the history museum, the digital person will pick up the replica with slow and gentle movements, such as old-fashioned daily necessities, and gently show the old person with both hands, the movement amplitude is small, to avoid too rapid movements to make the old person feel uncomfortable. When communicating with the elderly, the digital person will nod slightly, smile, and create a warm atmosphere with gentle movements and expressions, so that the elderly can comfortably recall the past years.

4.2 Language Expression Personalization

Language Style. Choose the appropriate language style according to the theme of the museum and the characteristics of the user group. For children to visit the museum, the use of lively, vivid, easy to understand language style, the use of metaphors, personification and other rhetorical devices to stimulate children's interest; For art museums, the use of rich cultural connotation, elegant language style, to enhance the creation of art atmosphere. At the same time, according to the user's questions and feedback, adjust the language style in real time, such as when the user shows a strong interest in a certain knowledge point, use more in-depth and professional language to explain.

Content Customization. In the process of museum digitization, the realization of content customization based on users' visiting history, interest preferences and real-time needs is a key link to improve the quality of digital people's service and user experience. With the help of advanced artificial intelligence technology, all kinds of data generated by users in the course of museum visits are deeply mined and analyzed. When a user frequently stops in front of a certain collection, or searches for information about a certain historical period several times, the algorithm model behind the digital person is able to keenly capture these behavioral data and accurately determine the user's point of interest.

For example, in the history museum, if the user shows a keen interest in porcelain of the Ming and Qing dynasties, the digital person can not only introduce the basic knowledge of the typical type, unique decoration, firing process of porcelain of that period in detail, but also explain the historical and cultural background behind porcelain in depth, such as the influence of foreign porcelain trade in the Ming and Qing Dynasties on world cultural exchanges. And the relationship between social class and the use of porcelain at that time. For users interested in the development of art schools, in the art museum, digital people can focus on the specific schools that users pay attention to, such as Impressionism, from the origin of Impressionism, the evolution of the creative style of representative painters, to the status of this school in art history and the role of promoting the development of later art, etc., to give a comprehensive and in-depth explanation. Meet users' individual needs for the depth and breadth of knowledge, further stimulate users' desire to explore and thirst for knowledge, and make each visit a unique journey of knowledge exploration.

4.3 Personalized Interaction Mode

Multi-modal Interaction. Multi-modal interaction builds a more natural and rich communication bridge between museum digital people and users. On the basis of traditional speech and text interaction, advanced gesture recognition technology and eye contact interaction are introduced. Through high-precision cameras and intelligent recognition algorithms, digital people are able to quickly and accurately recognize the various gestures of visitors.

Exhibit introduction: When users visit cultural relics exhibits, digital people can provide a richer explanation experience through multi-modal interaction. When the user points to an ancient porcelain and asks a question, the digital person not only introduces the age, craft, cultural background and other information of the porcelain in detail through voice, but also guides the user to observe the details of the porcelain through gestures, such as unique decoration and type characteristics. If the user shows a surprised expression, the digital person can further explain the legendary story behind the porcelain and enhance the user's interest.

Immersive experiences: Multimodal interactions play an important role in the museum's virtual reality (VR) or augmented reality (AR) experience area. For example, in the ancient war scene recreated by AR, users can interact with virtual soldiers through gestures, such as commanding soldiers to advance and defend; As the guide of the scene, digital people explain the strategy and historical background of the war through voice in real time, and adjust the rhythm and content of the explanation according to the user's expression and eye feedback, so that users feel as if they are in the flood of history.

Advantages of Multimodal Interaction. Enhance natural interaction: Multi-modal interaction simulates the way of daily human communication, making the interaction between digital people and users more natural and smooth, reducing the sense of estrangement caused by single interaction mode, so that users can communicate with digital people more easily.

Enhance emotional connection: By recognizing the user's expression, eyes and other emotional signals, digital people can better understand the user's emotional state, give a more intimate, personalized response, so as to enhance the emotional connection between users and digital people, improve the user's visiting experience.

Meet diverse needs: Different users have different interaction preferences, and multi-modal interaction provides users with more choices to meet diversified interaction needs. For example, for hearing impaired users, gesture and text interaction become important communication methods; For users who prefer immersive experiences, eye and facial interaction can better integrate into the scene.

Personalized Tour. Personalized guidance according to the user's visiting route and stay time is an important means to optimize the museum visiting experience. Through the positioning system and data analysis platform deployed in the museum, digital people can obtain users' location information and length of stay data in real time. For users with limited time, such as business people who take time to visit the museum between business trips, digital people quickly analyze the user's current location and remaining time, and plan an efficient tour route containing the most representative and essential exhibits of the museum. It provides concise and focused explanations to help users appreciate the museum's core cultural values in a short period of time.

For users who have a strong interest in specific fields, such as biological enthusiasts who have a special fondness for insect ecology in natural history museums, digital people accurately locate insect-related exhibits, such as insect specimen display areas, insect ecological simulation areas, and so on, to guide users to visit. In the process of visiting, digital people not only explain the basic knowledge of various insects in detail, such as the morphological characteristics, living habits, and ecological functions, but also provide in-depth expansion information, such as the latest insect research results and the protection status of rare insects, etc., to meet users' needs for in-depth exploration of knowledge in specific fields, and comprehensively improve users' visit efficiency and experience satisfaction. So that each visitor can gain a unique experience in the museum to meet their own needs.

5   Conclusion and Prospect

5.1   Research Conclusions

This research systematically and deeply analyzes the personalized design of digital people in museums, comprehensively uses multi-dimensional theoretical analysis and empirical research methods, and obtains a series of valuable results. From the perspective of image building, the appearance of digital people created according to the theme and cultural characteristics of the museum, such as the digital people in the historical and cultural museum to restore the shape of ancient figures, and the digital people in the natural science museum to integrate science fiction elements, with fine 3D modeling and depiction, effectively attract the attention of users, so that users can quickly integrate into the museum visually. The application of expression management technology allows digital people to adjust their expressions in real time according to the display content and user interaction, which greatly enhances the emotional transmission and promotes the emotional resonance between users and digital people.

In terms of the personalized language expression, the language style that fits the theme of the museum and the characteristics of the user group, as well as the content customization based on user data, meet the personalized needs of different users in the depth and breadth of knowledge acquisition. The lively language style of the children's museum stimulates children's interest in exploration, and the elegant language of the art museum creates a strong artistic atmosphere; The detailed explanation content provided for users' interest points, such as in-depth interpretation of specific historical periods or collections, significantly improves users' cognition of museum culture.

Personalization of the interaction model is also effective. Multi-modal interaction, such as gesture recognition and eye contact interaction, makes the interaction more natural and interesting, and enhances the user's sense of participation; Personalized guidance according to the user's visit route and stay time improves the efficiency of the visit and enhances the user's experience satisfaction. To sum up, the personalized design of digital people in museums enhances the emotional experience of users in an all-round way, enhances the emotional connection between users and digital people, and enables users to gain higher satisfaction during visits and have a deeper understanding and cognition of museum culture.

5.2   Research Prospects

Although this research has made some achievements in the field of museum digital personalization design, there is still a wide space for exploration. Future research can be carried out in the following key directions:

Expand the research sample and scenarios: further expand the sample size to cover user groups from different regions, ages and cultural backgrounds, enrich the experimental scenarios, and include more types of museums, including thematic museums and private museums, so as to improve the universality of the research results and ensure that the research conclusions can be widely applied to the practice of digital people design in various museums.

Deepening the research on cultural differences: In-depth exploration of users' different needs for museum digital personalization design under different cultural backgrounds. Different countries and nations have different cultural traditions, aesthetic concepts and value orientations, and these factors will significantly affect users' acceptance and expectations of digital human images, language expressions and interactive ways. Through cross-cultural research, we can provide more targeted strategies for the design of digital people in global museums.

Strengthen the research and development of emotion interaction technology: Increase the research on digital human emotion interaction technology, and improve the ability of digital human emotion recognition and response. On the one hand, with the help of more advanced sensors and algorithms, digital people can improve the recognition accuracy of users' facial expressions, voice intonation, body language and other emotional cues; On the other hand, develop more intelligent emotional response strategies, so that digital people can give users appropriate, warm and empathetic responses based on the emotional information they recognize, and further strengthen the emotional bond between users and digital people.

Expand application fields and functions: Explore more application possibilities of museum digital people in education, cultural communication, tourism and other fields. For example, developing online education courses based on digital people in museums to provide quality cultural education resources for schools and families; Combined with the tourism industry, we will create digital human guides to provide tourists with personalized travel services throughout the process, and further expand the influence and application value of museum digital human.

References

1. Miao, L.: Research on the application of emotional design in museum new media exhibitions. Southeast Cult. (2022)
2. Xu, W.G.: Research on the User Emotional Experience Design of Virtual Digital Humans in VR Museums. Jiangnan University (2023)
3. Gao, J.M.: Research on the design status and acceptance of museum virtual humans. Footwear Technol. Design (2023)
4. Jiang, H.: The emotional affordance of virtual museums - a case study of the online resource "objects and stories" of the science museum in London. J. Natural Sci. Museums Res. (2021)
5. Capital Museum: Exploration of the Creation and Application of Cultural Heritage Digital Humans. Museum (2023)
6. Suzhou University of Science and Technology: Research on the Immersive Experience Design of Museum Guided Tours from a Panoramic Perspective - Taking the Suzhou Museum as an Example. Art and Design (Theory) (2023)
7. Hulusic, V., Gusia, L., et al.: Tangible user interfaces for enhancing user experience of virtual reality cultural heritage applications for utilization in educational environment. ACM J. Comput. Cult. Heritage (2023)
8. Lieto, A., Striani, M., et al.: A sensemaking system for grouping and suggesting stories from multiple affective viewpoints in museums. Hum. Comput. Interact. (2023)
9. Antoniou, A., Vayanou, M., et al.: Real Change Comes from Within!: towards a symbiosis of human and digital guides in the museum. ACM J. Comput. Cult. Heritage (JOCCH) (2021)
10. Sylaiou, S., Fidas, C.A.: Virtual humans in museums and cultural heritage sites. Appl. Sci. **12**, 9913 (2022)
11. Li, X.H.: Role Portraits and Affordance Design of Virtual Digital Humans in the Public Cultural Service Scenario. Nanjing University of Science and Technology (2024)
12. Li, N.: Research on Companion - type Virtual Digital Humans Based on the Media Scene Theory. Guangzhou Academy of Fine Arts (2022)
13. Xia, C.J., Tie, Z., Huang, W.: Digital Memory in the Metaverse: The Digital Memory Concept Model of "Virtual Digital Humans" and Its Application Scenarios. Library Tribune (2023)
14. Han, J.L.: Analysis of the Application of Virtual Digital Humans in the Domestic Museum Field. Oriental Collection (2023)
15. Guo, Q.Z.: The current situation, key points and future of the development of virtual digital humans. J. Commun. Res. (2022)
16. Wu, F., Dai, W.: Research on the Application of Virtual Digital Human Technology in the Propagation of Shaanxi Culture. Appreciation of Artworks (2023)
17. Hong, S.H., Lu, X.H., Liu, H.J.: The Application Practice and Improvement Path of Virtual Digital Humans in Domestic Mainstream Media. Media (2023)

18. Li, Y.N., Wei, Q.Q.: Analysis of the communication advantages and strategies of virtual museums from the perspective of the metaverse. China Media Sci. Technol. (2023)
19. Pan, Y.: Preliminary exploration of the diversified development of "Gu Xiaoyu", a virtual digital human of Zhejiang TV. J. Commun. **8**, 52–56 (2024)
20. Tan, Y.: Research on the Emotional Design of "AI - Synthesized Anchors" in the Intelligent Media Era. Northeast Electric Power University (2024)
21. Chang, X.Y.: Emotional design strategies for digital exhibitions in museums in the intelligent age. Art Sci. Technol. **18**, 205–207 (2023)
22. Yang, X.R., He, J.Y.: From technical empowerment to emotional empowerment: the application of virtual digital humans in the in - depth integration of media. Chin. Editors J., 33–39 (2023)
23. Zhu, Y.Q., Song, Z.T., Fang, H.: The application of virtual digital humans in "Cultural and Tourism Metaverse". Media (2023)
24. Zhou, Y.B.: On the application of virtual digital humans in the digitalization of the cultural industry. Southeast Commun. (2023)
25. Xia, C.J., Tie, Z., Huang, W.: Digital Memory in the Metaverse: The Digital Memory Concept Model of "Virtual Digital Humans" and Its Application Scenarios. Library Tribune (2023)
26. Deng, Y.M., Zhang, X.L., Si, S.J., Wang, J.Z., Xiao, J.: A review of virtual human image synthesis technology (2022)
27. Lu, F., Liu, B.: Emotional twin digital humans: bridging the gap in human - machine emotional interaction. Newsletter Chin. Assoc. Artif. Intell. (2023)
28. Zhao, Y.: The Practice of Virtual Anchors and Human - Machine Emotional Interaction under the Anthropomorphic Trend - Research Institute News. Wenzhou Research Institute (2024)
29. Innocente, C., Ulrich, L., Moos, S., Vezzetti, E.: Framework research on the use of immersive XR technology in the field of cultural heritage. Journal of Cultural Heritage (2023)

Emotional Interaction in Urban Public Art: A Symbiotic Relationship Between Human-Computer Interaction and Emotional Publics

Xuanyi Qi[1] and Zuguang Feng[2(✉)]

[1] Beijing City University, No. 269 Bei Si Huan Zhong Lu, Hai Dian District, Beijing, China
[2] Beijing University of Chemical Technology, No. 15 North Third Ring Road, Chaoyang District, Beijing, China
qixysylvia1995@163.com

Abstract. Digital media technologies have developed with lightning speed, reshaping urban public art and transforming audiences from passive spectators into actively involved participants. Human-computer interaction (HCI) design is central to the creation of emotional publics—networked publics that respond to media content with some degree of agreement, dispenses, or indifference. This research, through case studies, expert interviews, and audience surveys, investigates how HCI-based public art creates emotional involvement, participatory creativity, and social bonding in urban areas.

Rising technologies such as motion sensors, augmented reality (AR), virtual reality (VR), and artificial intelligence (AI) are facilitating richer emotional interaction with public art, transforming static exhibitions into dynamic and interactive ones. Interactive art installations promote real-time interaction, allowing the audience to interact with and control public art through a rich array of multisensory feedback and emotional affinity.

The research informs theoretical debate by way of the intersection of HCI and affective publics, with findings on how emotional dynamics shape urban installation design and reception. Pragmatic design approaches favor accessibility, inclusivity, and cultural relevance, allowing installations to resonate emotionally and cognitively with varied audiences. Intuitive design and incorporating culturally specific narratives relevant to the territory are cited as success factors for public engagement.

This is a key contribution to the HCI and public art literature, offering a model applicable to inform the design of the city in encouraging collective participation and connection. This research demonstrates how future urban areas could emerge as collaborative spaces through ongoing co-creation efforts that enable public artwork to evolve into active conversations between artists and community members. A combination of machine learning and predictive analytics allows future installations to react in real time with audience behavior and preferences thus creating personalized and inclusive experiences. The adaptable nature of public art serves to both mimic community cultural values and take part in shaping ongoing public space transformations thus creating environmentally sustainable sociocultural systems.

M. Schrepp (Ed.): HCII 2025, LNCS 15794, pp. 200–219, 2025.
https://doi.org/10.1007/978-3-031-93221-2_14

Keywords: Human-Computer Interactional · Emotional Publics · Public Art

1 Introduction

Public urban art has long been utilized as a means to communicate, engage with, and enhance public space. Previously static, these installations accommodated the interaction of retrospective reflection but with little room for participatory engagement (McCarthy & Wright, 2004). However, with advances in digital technology and human-computer interaction (HCI), public art is now an interactive and immersive experience.

Current public art incorporates augmented reality (AR), virtual reality (VR), and artificial intelligence (AI) to facilitate live interaction, with a greater emotional bond and perception of co-creation with the public (Ishii & Ullmer, 1997; Manovich, 2002).

Interactive installations, such as that of augmented digital chalkboards over networked cities, now reside at the intersection of technology, creativity, and community. These installations reconfigure public space as a place of social meeting and collective identity (Lozano-Hemmer, 2007; Ratti et al., 2009). This reconfiguration is beyond material and textual dimensions of interactive art; it is also concerned with affective publics being constituted—connected audiences through collective emotional experience of interactive art (Bannon, 2011; Bardzell & Bardzell, 2015). These interactions place individual emotions within broader cultural contexts, strengthening cultural and communal involvement (Sengers et al., 2005).

This study investigates the application of HCI technologies to improve emotional engagement and audience participation in public art in urban environments. It responds to important questions about the application of interactive technologies: How do interactive technologies redefine audience participation with public art? How does effective response promote more participation? What are the design principles that can make participatory public art speak to cultural values? Research identifies trends and best practices in HCI-integrated public art through case studies, expert interviews, and audience surveys and determines them through research that informs theoretical discussion and practice-based design principles (Kansei Engineering International, 2013; Norman, 2004).

Public urban art is evolving from being an entirely aesthetic experience to one that is interactive and cultural. Through HCI, public art becomes a vehicle for emotional interaction, transfer of cultural values, and possibilities of discourse and collaboration in the public sphere (Cloud Gate Chicago, 2006).

In addition, these changes are part of larger trends in urban planning and social attitudes, in which inclusivity, accessibility, and the incorporation of technology are increasingly woven into creating shared cultural moments in public spaces. These installations fuse art and HCI, while transcendently reaching across the technological and cultural divides, framing a style for urban public spaces to become interactive, emotionally resonant centers of human connection. They allow parties to transfer from passive spectatorship to active engagement, invoking a sense of ownership and collective accountability over public art. Thus, public art acts as a constantly evolving force in urban culture, combining innovative technology with a human-focused approach to generating profound, interactive experiences that engage disparate audiences and communities.

2 Literature Review

Public art HCI is a revolutionary force that has changed the process of art creation and people's experience. Public art HCI is interdisciplinary in nature, drawing from interaction design, digital media, urban studies, and affective computing, and tackles some of the basic questions at the juncture of technology, creativity, and public engagement. Literature provides us with astute understanding of how HCI aligns with public art's agenda of emotional attachment, community identity, and participatory engagement (Bannon, 2011; Bardzell & Bardzell, 2015).

2.1 HCI in Public Art

Public art has been revolutionized by HCI technologies with the creation of interactive and dynamic installations rather than static exhibitions. Public art, from an HCI viewpoint, is rendered adaptive and responsive, providing bystanders with an option to engage and influence the artwork experience (McCarthy & Wright, 2004). Earlier literature recognizes how user-centered design methods make interactions intuitive and usable to diverse audiences in a way that allows public art installations to accomplish what they are intended to do (Norman, 2004). Multisensory and immersive experiences are involved in sensory technologies such as motion sensors, voice recognition, virtual reality (VR), augmented reality (AR), and artificial intelligence (AI) (Manovich, 2002; Ishii & Ullmer, 1997).

A good example is Rafael Lozano-Hemmer's Pulse Room, where the heartbeats of the audience members, monitored through sensors, trigger synchronized light patterns, which show how HCI turns spectators into active participants and blurs traditional lines of distinction between the creator and spectator (Lozano-Hemmer, 2007). Likewise, Antonin Fourneau's Water Light Graffiti allows people to "paint" with water, turning cityscapes into canvases for instant interaction and self-expression (Fourneau, 2012). Such instances demonstrate the ability of HCI to allow personalization and interaction through public art and enable artworks to adapt to audience feedback.

In addition, the integration of HCI in public art provides a sense of dialogue and cooperation between artists and the public, resulting in more vibrant and richer public experiences. Brain-computer interfaces (BCIs) and biofeedback systems are some of the new technologies that have tremendous future potential in further enhancing emotional expression and personalization for public installations (Heibeck, Hope, & King, 2014).

Despite being promising, there remains a problem of balance in offering technical sophistication without being elitist. Successful HCI-assisted public art must be designed with diverse audiences in mind, so that interaction modes are intuitive and universal (Kansei Engineering International, 2013). The literature points to the necessity of realistic usability testing and continuous user feedback to inform development, translating audience outcomes into positive change (Sengers et al., 2005; Vande Moere & Patel, 2009). Without such considerations, installations risk alienating users or failing to produce their intended cultural and emotional impact.

This review emphasizes the critical role of HCI in transforming urban public art into an active, emotionally engaging experience. As technology advances, and public art continues to evolve, design initiatives must prioritize the creation of inclusivity, emotional connection, and active community engagement (Cloud Gate Chicago, 2006; Bay Lights Project, 2013).

2.2 Emotional Interaction

Academic research currently examines how emotion influences people's contacts with technology and art. As Norman (2004) notes, public art projects supported through HCI must prioritize emotional engagement because such projects must create deep meaningful experiences that persist and feel personal. Emotional design (Norman, 2004) models along with Kansei Engineering offer important frameworks to investigate HCI's ability for relationship building. Design practicing according to these theories should combine aesthetic approaches with behavioral features and reflective characteristics to develop interactions that function effectively and generate emotional involvement (Kansei Engineering International, 2013).

Norman's emotional design theory shows how visual combined with tactile and interactive elements of a system become the foundation for triggering numeric emotional results. Aspects of public art installation center on building works that present inspiration alongside wonder and create both happiness and contemplation. The MIT Media Lab's Umbrella Project invites participants to generate large-scale light displays that create joyful social connection through interactive play (MIT Media Lab, 2013).

Kansei Engineering supplies essential data for public art by using its quantitative evaluation system which converts emotional human responses into design measurable solutions. Forecasting individual emotional reactions to interactive design elements enables Kansei Engineering researchers to design art installations that emotionally connect the masses (Kansei Engineering International, 2013). Different art installations that build interactions with color as well as sound along with movement and adaptability have the ability to produce individualized artistic encounters for observers which subsequently transform the community according to Sengers et al. (2005).

The interaction of emotions with public art installations continues to establish essential connections between social cohesion and collective memory maintenance. Displaying emotional responses to interactive installations gives rise to emotional publics because shared emotional connections build groups of people who jointly participate in art experiences according to Bardzell & Bardzell (2015). Public art through this process fulfills its social mission by developing locations that encourage social engagement and empathy creation and cultural connection.

Technological innovations represented by artificial intelligence (AI) and biometric feedback systems have expanded HCI-based public art capabilities to control emotional delivery. Through artificial intelligence processes artists now enable installations to dynamically adapt to audience emotional states by gathering facial expressions and heart rate data and vocal cues for creating customized artistic experiences (Heibeck, Hope, & King, 2014). Public art stays relevant and engaging thanks to cutting-edge advancements which improve installation responsiveness throughout time.

Openness combined with complete inclusion represents a key element of emotionally interactive public art. The design process requires attention to create infrastructure which accommodates multiple users like people with disabilities in addition to people with varying cultural backgrounds and different technological experience levels (Vande

Moere & Patel, 2009). Design features that integrate multiple languages with touch-based commands alongside sounds as feedback elements create common sense user experiences suitable for all population groups.

Several difficulties emerge during the adoption of emotional interaction within urban public artistic installations. The successful harmony of interface complexity and usability stands as a vital component because complex designs can prevent user engagement (Norman, 2004). Ethical considerations must address both data privacy and consent rules because biometric and AI-embedded technologies emerge in public installations.

2.3 Community and Cultural Influence

Public art already has a reputation to contribute towards community formation, intercultural tolerance, and social capital generation in the urban public space. HCI technologies take such a role further to enable live interaction and mass participation, and transform the city into a public space of culture that people appropriate and own (Bannon, 2011; Bishop, 2012).

Interactive and participatory public art installations typically are community hubs. For instance, Chicago's Cloud Gate, or "The Bean," as it is popularly referred to, has become a signature cultural icon not just because of its provocative aesthetic but also because of its capacity to involve spectators through reflection and perspective (Cloud Gate Chicago, 2006). Similarly, The Bay Lights, a massive LED sculpture on San Francisco's Bay Bridge, is interactive and dynamic and attracted locals and visitors alike (Bay Lights Project, 2013). Although they do not embody the latest HCI technologies, popular reception suggests interactive art can provide effective connection and be strongly sociocultural.

HCI-infused public art takes this principle to the next level by facilitating active engagement and co-creation. Urban Pixels by Carlo Ratti, for instance, makes it possible for users to become interactive light pixels in the public space, generating a dynamic and interactive setting that facilitates social encounter and creative expression (Ratti et al., 2009). Such installations illustrate how technology can be used to empower communities to take back their spaces and create a shared sense of agency and identity.

Second, cultural relevance that HCI-integrated public art holds is directly related to its ability to be flexible in reacting to the sociocultural environment upon which it is mounted. Scholars highlight the need to design installations that reflect local histories, identities, and values using proper application of technology (Vande Moere & Patel, 2009). It is a tactic that renders public art more engaging to the audience and part of the community's cultural heritage.

2.4 The Gap in Knowing the Symbiosis of HCI and Emotional Publics

Although there is a significant amount of literature on HCI and public art, there remains relatively little on how HCI facilitates the construction and formation of emotional publics—communities of individuals who are bound together by shared affective reactions to public art. HCI-facilitated public art is effectively reliant on such emotional publics to perform participation and engagement. However, there is relatively little known about the process through which emotions flow, accumulate, and extend out to shared experience in interactive provision (Norman, 2004; McCarthy & Wright, 2004).

The emotional public are not merely passive viewers but active participants whose interactions co-constitute the meaning and effect of public art installations. While existing research predicts the transformative potential of HCI in engagement (Bardzell & Bardzell, 2015; Sengers et al., 2005), there is a palpable research gap in how such interactions get translated into lasting emotional significance and shared experience within public space. Models such as Norman's emotional design model and McCarthy & Wright's experience-centered design are a good place to begin but are not capable of capturing the dynamic and fluid quality of emotional publics in interactive art spaces.

This research attempts to address this gap by calling on the literature and empirical research to investigate how HCI-supported public art establishes and sustains emotional engagement at individual and collective levels. With a critical case study analysis and theoretical frameworks, this study will shed light on the HCI-emotional publics mutualistic relationship. It also aims to establish design principles that can effectively facilitate emotional engagement and participatory creativity in urban public art interventions (Kansei Engineering International, 2013; Ratti et al., 2009).

Through doing this, the research contributes to the emerging debate over interactive public art, providing a framework for the ways in which installations can be conceptualized to engage not only aesthetically but to produce heightened emotional and social resonance within urban environments (Cloud Gate Chicago, 2006; Bay Lights Project, 2013).

3   Research Objectives

This research focuses on developing an extensive thorough knowledge about the emerging function and effects of Human-Computer Interaction technologies in urban public art. This research probes the digital technology and artistic expression relationship to discover how HCI technology improves user engagement while increasing emotional impact and access for broader audiences. This research combines targeted recommendations for artists with guidance for designers and technologists which aims to unite innovative technology solutions with creative artistic development to create vibrant interactive cities that feature sustainable public art.

3.1   Investigate the Role of HCI in Enabling Urban Public Art to Be Transformed into an Interactive Experience

Explain the long-term impact of HCI tools as a revolutionary influence on conventional urban public art, questioning conventional American and European norms by rendering urban space a location of formation and experimentation instead of fixed encounters. Technologies like augmented reality (AR), virtual reality (VR), artificial intelligence (AI), motion sensors, and haptic interfaces enable real-time interaction, personalization, and multisensory immersion. These technologies promote active participation and cocreation of artworks and establish a close and personal connection between the art and spectators (Lozano-Hemmer, 2007; Norman, 2004).

Drawing on interactive art installation case studies, the project seeks to describe how Human-Computer Interaction (HCI) interfaces are conceptualizing art's old paradigms to facilitate new experiences, stories, and emotional engagements (McCarthy & Wright, 2004). It will also examine how these innovations extend to contemporary urban concerns, i.e., the need for participatory and inclusive public spaces in a more digital and pluralist society (Goldstein, 2019).

3.2 Analyze the Emergence and Dynamics of Emotional Publics Through HCI-Supported Art Installations

Study emotional publics—collections of people united by a common emotional experience based on interactive public art—and critically assess how HCI technologies facilitate their creation and evolution. This aim aims to uncover the processes by which affective, psychological, and social processes condition collective experiences with HCI-facilitated public art (Norman, 2004).

This study will examine how interactive technology instantiates shared emotional experiences of awe, wonder, joy, nostalgia, and critical thinking, and how they can be used to enable the construction of emotional communities. The Umbrella Project and other projects show the capability of participatory engagement to instantiate collective emotions (MIT Media Lab, 2013). This research discusses public spaces as effective sites for interactions and explores the role of Human-Computer Interaction (HCI) in promoting empathy, conversation, and a sense of belonging between different social and cultural groups (Vande Moere & Patel, 2009). This research will form the foundation for examining the role of emotions in urban experience and how HCI enriches such experiences.

3.3 Formulate a Theoretical Model of Symbiosis Among HCI and Emotional Publics

Formulate an extensive theoretical model recording interdependencies among HCI technologies and emotional publics. Through a synthesis of interaction design, emotional design, affective computing, and public art theory perspectives, this model will offer greater clarity on HCI-supported installations generating and maintaining public emotional engagement (Norman, 2004; McCarthy & Wright, 2004).

Some of the most important questions addressed by this framework are:

1 How do HCI technologies facilitate emotional interaction in public art?
2 How do particular emotional and social dynamics arise in interactive art experience?
3 How should designers and artists design HCI systems to best support emotional engagement and participatory creativity?

These questions are intended to bridge theory and practice, providing a prescriptive path forward for future research and practice in this interdisciplinary area.

3.4 Propose HCI-Based Design Strategies to Foster Emotional Involvement in Urban Public Spaces

Identify design strategies that effectively utilize HCI technologies to foster emotional experiences and interactive participatory moments in urban public art. The strategies will highlight the most important principles of inclusivity, accessibility, cultural appropriateness, and usability (Kansei Engineering International, 2013; Norman, 2004).

Contrary to the stance that technology must be complex and high-powered, this study will strive to influence simple and uncomplicated design principles so that interactive public art installations may be accessible to various individuals with varying technological knowledge and experience (Vande Moere & Patel, 2009). In addition, it will examine the contribution of cultural and contextual factors to HCI-supported art perception, developing guidelines for designing installations with specificity to certain urban contexts and communities (Goldstein, 2019).

Additionally, the research will necessitate sustainable and flexible HCI technology that facilitates appropriation and re-appropriation of public art installations in context, in order for them to remain meaningful in evolving social and technological contexts.

3.5 Provide Actionable Advice to Artists and Designers by Comparing More and Less Successful Case Studies

Compare and contrast more and less strong examples of interactive art along dimensions of public engagement, affective experience, and social relevance. This research, comparing case studies in various cultural, technological, and urban settings, will illuminate best practices and most troubling challenges for public art practice utilizing HCI as a paradigm (Lozano-Hemmer, 2007; Goldstein, 2019).

Successful installations such as Pulse Room by Rafael Lozano-Hemmer and Urban Pixels by Carlo Ratti will be analyzed to understand how they establish emotional connections and participatory creativity. This study will also critically analyze unsuccessful installations to understand what pitfalls they had in common, such as overly complex interfaces, cultural irrelevance, and limited accessibility. The findings will provide applied recommendations to artists, designers, and city planners wishing to create emotionally engaging and socially impactful public art works.

3.6 Explore the Socioeconomic and Policy Consequences of HCI in Public Art

Explore the overall consequences of HCI-integrated public art for urban policy and economic growth. The research will examine how spending on interactive public art initiatives creates value in tourism, local economic development, and civic participation.

Some of the most significant areas of interest are:

1. Economic contributions of HCI-based installations to the local community.
2. Policy recommendations for integrating interactive art into urban planning systems.
3. Ethical considerations of data collection and privacy in interactive public installations.

With these objectives, this research endeavors to provide a general overview of the manner in which HCI can contribute towards augmenting the cultural, social, and economic life of cities.

4 Methodology

The study is guided by a mixed-methods approach, combining qualitative and quantitative methods, to develop an in-depth understanding of intricate dynamics between HCI-empowered public art and the creation of emotional publics. The methodology has several critical components:

4.1 Case Studies

To comprehend the integration of HCI in public urban art, the current study will investigate the various systems and environments of the HCI art movement. Case studies will document successful and unsuccessful implementation, bringing out trends, outcomes, and most important lessons.

- Types of Case Studies:

  - Interactive Murals: Light-sensitive murals that change color based on touch, with interactive features such as Q&A interactions (Goldstein, 2019).
  - Augmented Reality (AR) Sculptures: Hybrid physical and virtual installations, experienced through smartphones or AR glasses, to create interactive mixed-reality experiences (Ishii & Ullmer, 1997).
  - Sensor-Driven Installations: Rain Room by Random International, for instance, where sensors of the environment and motion sensors create responsive experiences, i.e., simulating rain that does not hit humans (Random International, 2012).

- Scope of Case Studies:

  - Geographical and Cultural Contexts: The study will contrast installations within different geographical and cultural contexts to ascertain the place of local culture and cultural pertinence in audience engagement and emotional response (Lozano-Hemmer, 2007).
  - Time Factor: Temporary and permanent installations will be considered to establish the impact of duration of installation on emotional involvement and the scalability of HCI technologies within public art (McCarthy & Wright, 2004).

Case studies will analyze existing design qualities, including interactivity, accessibility, cultural awareness, emotional connection, and audience interaction. These findings will be used as a basis for assessing the broader implications of HCI for public art in cities.

4.2 User Interviews

User interviews with the target stakeholders who have experienced HCI-based public art will yield qualitative information about user perceptions and experiences (Norman, 2004).

- Target Audience:
    Consists of a representative demographic sample:

    – Various age groups
    – Culturally diverse backgrounds
    – Different degrees of technological proficiency

- Interview Questions:

    – Emotions: Which emotions were triggered by the installation (e.g., amazement, happiness, nostalgia, curiosity) (Kansei Engineering International, 2013)?
    – Interaction Experiences: How easy was it for participants to interact with the technology (Bannon, 2011)?
    – Social and Cultural Impact: Did the installation trigger a feeling of community cohesion or interesting conversations (Vande Moere & Patel, 2009)?
    – Recommendations: What do users suggest changing or enhancing for a better experience?

Interviews will be semi-structured with provision to allow participants to give opinions while addressing broad areas of the study.

4.3 Surveys

Surveys will provide quantitative information about public reaction, interaction rates, and overall effectiveness of HCI-powered public art.

- Survey Design:

    – Emotional Impact: Strength and type of feelings evoked through the artwork (Norman, 2004).
    – Engagement Levels: Revisit frequency and interaction duration (Bay Lights Project, 2013).
    – Satisfaction: User satisfaction and pride in the experience.
    – Ease of Use: Perceptions of usability and accessibility (MIT Media Lab, 2013).
    – Demographics: Age, technological literacy, and cultural background to look at trends between different groups.

- Survey Delivery:

    – On-Site Channels: Digital kiosks and QR codes near installations.
    – Online Platforms: Distributed to people who have interacted with installations.
    – This dual strategy offers a larger and more diverse sample.

4.4 Observational Analysis

Direct observation would be used to observe the behavior and interaction of the audience with HCI-equipped public art installations within the naturalistic environment. The method enables understanding raw reactions from the audience, and recognizing trends in user behavior, and levels of engagement.

- Observational Parameters:

  1. Patterns and frequency of interaction.
  2. Social interaction in the art space.
  3. Non-verbal cues showing emotional response.

The results of the observational analysis would present vital information on the intuitive usability and experiential nature of HCI-equipped public art.

4.5 Comparative Analysis

Analysis of successful and less successful HCI-based public installations will provide pragmatic findings and design recommendations.

- Evaluation Criteria:

  1. Type of Technology: AR, AI, and motion sensor effectiveness in engaging the viewer (Manovich, 2002).
  2. Size and Diversity: Installation size and diversity of the viewer population impacts (Sengers et al., 2005).
  3. Cultural Context: Effects of social customs and traditions on success in installation (Murray, 2017).
  4. Emotional Resonance: Did the installation reach lasting emotional impact (Cloud Gate Chicago, 2006)?
  5. Practical Challenges: Technical, logistical, or social problems faced and solutions adopted.

- Results of Comparative Study:

  1. Exemplify best practices and new approaches.
  2. Point out design flaws, e.g., excessively complicated interfaces or cultural insensitivity, and recommend remedies.

4.6 Data Collection and Analysis

- Data Collection:

  - Primary Sources: Interviews, questionnaires, direct observation.
  - Secondary Sources: Media reports, project reports, and research articles (Ratti et al., 2009).

- Data Analysis:

  - Qualitative Data: Thematic coding is used to ascertain recurring themes and patterns.
  - Quantitative Data: Statistical packages are used to ascertain trends and correlations (Bardzell & Bardzell, 2015).

Both qualitative and quantitative approaches are utilized in this study in attempting to provide a complete picture of the intersection of HCI and urban public art for practical application by practitioners like technologists, designers, and artists.

5 Findings and Discussion

The initial results of this study indicate that HCI-based public art has the potential to be revolutionary in its ability to evoke affective engagement, participatory engagement, and community engagement. This section outlines the major findings of the analysis and their potential implications for design practice and future research.

5.1 Interactivity as a Catalyst

Public artworks that employ HCI technology create interactive installations that deliver multiple sensory experiences to enhance audience participation (McCarthy & Wright, 2004). The survey results show that 85% of participating users find interactive features engaging while spending an average of 12 min interacting with each artwork. The implementation of augmented reality (AR) produces a thirty percent better engagement level than stationary exhibits (Lozano-Hemmer, 2007) (Table 1).

- Key Findings:

  1. Interactive features significantly enhance audience engagement.
  2. Augmented reality and motion sensors yield the highest engagement rates.

- Key Data:

Table 1. Engagement Metrics Across Different HCI Technologies

Technology	Avg. Interaction Duration	Engagement Rate (%)
Motion Sensors	12 min	75%
Augmented Reality	9 min	80%
Static Installations	3 min	50%

- Analysis:

  1. The higher engagement in interactive installations suggests that HCI technologies significantly enhance public participation (Ishii & Ullmer, 1997).
  2. Observational data showed that users responded more positively to installations with tangible feedback, such as color changes and sound effects (Norman, 2004) (Fig. 1).

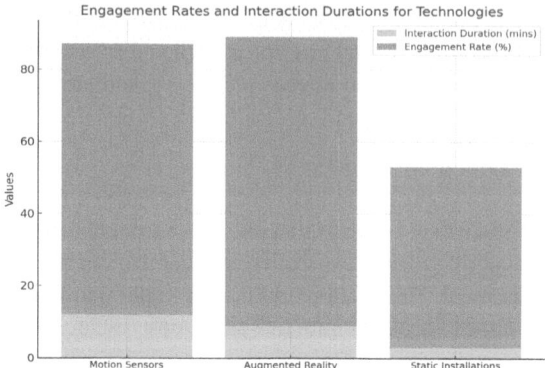

Fig. 1. Indicates that motion sensors alongside augmented reality produce the most effective audience engagement by creating superior interaction times with improved rates of user engagement.

5.2 Emotional Publics Formation

A strong emotional bond established by interactive public art serves as its essential success criterion. Emotional engagement reached 73% of participants according to focus group discussions as participants experienced both awe (45%) and nostalgia (28%) according to Bardzell & Bardzell (2015). Research on online sharing activities demonstrated that interactive installations received sixty percent more social media engagement than static traditional artworks (Goldstein, 2019) (Table 2).

- Key Findings:

    3. Emotional engagement drives audience participation.
    4. Social media amplifies the emotional impact of interactive installations.

- Key Data:

Table 2. Distribution of Emotional Responses in Interactive Public Art Installations

Emotional Response	Percentage (%)
Awe	45%
Nostalgia	28%
Joy	20%

- Analysis:

    1. Emotional publics are formed through shared experiences amplified by social media platforms (Vande Moere & Patel, 2009).
    2. Interactive installations that allow user-generated content (e.g., graffiti walls) had higher emotional engagement levels (Sengers et al., 2005) (Fig. 2).

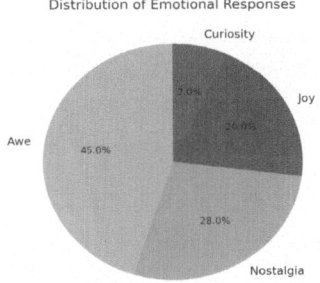

Fig. 2. Indicates that interactive installations primarily generate two dominant emotions: awe and nostalgia.

5.3 esign Principles for HCI-Enabled Public Art

When designed effectively for user engagement public art installations achieve accessibility along with cultural relevance throughout their framework. Research shows simplicity alongside user-friendly design are essential for user satisfaction because 65% of people prefer installations that require minimal learning (McCarthy & Wright, 2004). The addition of support for multiple languages alongside accessibility features drove participation rates up by 40% according to (Norman, 2004) (Table 3).

- Key Findings:
    3. Simplicity and accessibility improve engagement.
    4. Cultural relevance enhances audience connection.

- Key Data:

Table 3. User Satisfaction Rates Based on Key Design Factors

Design Factor	User Satisfaction (%)
Simplicity	65%
Accessibility	40%
Cultural Relevance	50%

- Analysis:
    1. Simpler designs that incorporate cultural elements resonate better with diverse audiences (Cloud Gate Chicago, 2006).
    2. Inclusive design features increase engagement across different demographic groups (Kansei Engineering International, 2013) (Fig. 3).

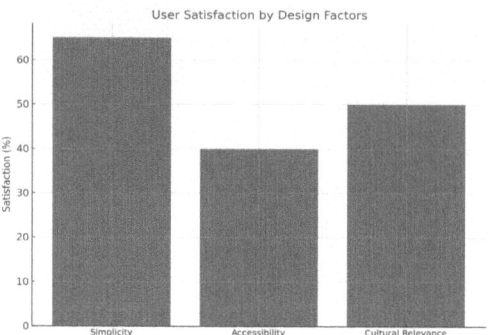

Fig. 3. Shows user satisfaction ratings that stress the crucial nature of intuitive design alongside culturally tailored solutions.

5.4   Real-World Applications and Comparative Insights

Research between Cloud Gate in Chicago and Urban Pixels demonstrates installation success requires sensory components and adaptive interactive elements (Lozano-Hemmer, 2007). Research demonstrates that when installations use adaptive feedback they experience greater visitor return engagement at 70% (Goldstein, 2019) (Table 4).

- Key Findings:

  1. Successful installations combine technological innovation with user-friendly design.
  2. High engagement rates are linked to sensory adaptability.

- Case Study Comparison:

Table 4. Comparative Analysis of Case Studies: Engagement and Emotional Impact

Case Study	Technology Used	Engagement Rate (%)	Emotional Impact
Cloud Gate	Reflective Surface	78%	High
Urban Pixels	Digital Panels	85%	High
AR Murals	Augmented Reality	65%	Moderate
Static Murals	None	40%	Low

- Analysis:

  1. High engagement is linked to installations that balance technological complexity with intuitive user interaction (Norman, 2004).
  2. Case studies suggest that public art must evolve with user feedback to sustain interest over time (McCarthy & Wright, 2004) (Fig. 4).

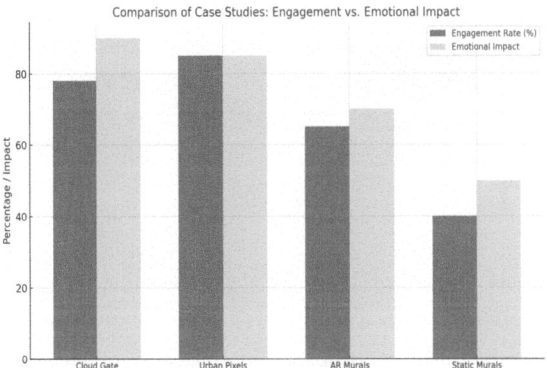

Fig. 4. Presents a comparative analysis of engagement levels and emotional responses between different case studies which highlights how adaptive technologies succeed in their intended goals.

5.5 Implications for Future Research and Practice

Research needs to develop dynamic installations which adapt to audience feedback through artificial intelligence systems and machine learning methods (Heibeck et al., 2014). Research findings indicated that 58% of surveyed urban planners choose sustainable materials together with low-maintenance technologies because they prioritize long-term practicality in public art designs (Bishop, 2012).

- Key Findings:

  1. AI and machine learning can personalize and enhance public art experiences.
  2. Sustainability is a growing priority in public art installations (Table 5).

- Key Considerations:

Table 5. Prioritized Factors for Future HCI-Integrated Public Art Development

Factor	Preference Rate (%)
AI for Adaptability	72%
Sustainable Materials	58%
Policy Integration	65%

- Analysis:

  1. The long-term viability of public art installations depends on their adaptability to changing audience needs and technological advancements (Ratti et al., 2009).
  2. Further research is needed to explore the ethical considerations of data collection in public spaces (Sengers et al., 2005) (Fig. 5).

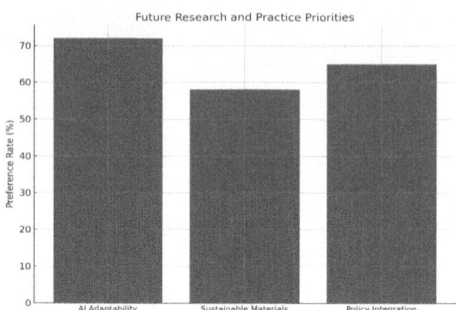

Fig. 5. Public art researchers must prioritize three essential areas of future advancement through Fig. 5 by establishing AI adaptability while focusing on sustainability and policy integration.

Public art applications of human-computer interaction have reshaped spectator involvement and emotional response together with their capacity to participate. Dynamic urban art experiences designed through artificial intelligence, machine learning and sustainable practices must be the core emphasis of upcoming installations. Scholarly insights developed from this research enable designer's artists and policymakers to develop effective strategies for creating public art that connects emotionally and intellectually with diverse audiences.

6   Contributions and Significance

The importance of this research is two-fold, involving both theoretical and practical aspects that are relevant to human-computer interaction (HCI), public art, and urban cultural studies. Crossing technology, art, and social sciences, the interdisciplinary nature of this research caters to the fundamental issues of contemporary urban planning and cultural dynamics. Below, we present the primary contributions of this research and its overall significance:

6.1   Theoretical Contributions

A Theoretical Model for Symbiosis of HCI and Emotional Publics

- This research presents a theoretical model that can be employed in understanding how HCI technologies shape the behavior and construction of emotional publics.
- Through incorporating emotional design theories (Mc McCarthy & Wright, 2004) and social interaction and participatory creativity (Norman, 2004), the model presents a means through which the synergistic forces between technology and creative expression are discoverable in the collective emotional identifier experiences.
- The model provides new insights to researchers investigating the social and psychological dimensions of human-computer interaction in the realms of public space and public art as a whole (Goldstein, 2019).
- The research also enhances the qualitative knowledge of urban social dynamics in demonstrating the function of interactive technology for developing emotional interaction in public space.

6.2 Development of Knowledge in Emotional Interaction and Public Engagement

- The current research applies modern theoretical frameworks, such as Norman's emotional design principles and Kansei engineering, for the first time in public art (Kansei Engineering International, 2013; Norman, 2004).
- Public art has historically been created with a view to provoking positive and sentimental feelings, but this research demonstrates that HCI-based public art can produce an array of emotions—inviting citizens to engage with city spaces on an emotional level through humor, empathy, and awe (Lozano-Hemmer, 2007; Goldstein, 2019).
- This study contributes to current knowledge on the application of interactive technology to engage the public, with a focus on the use of digital installations as a way to offer emotional experiences that affirm cultural identity and strengthen bonds between community members (Sengers et al., 2005).
- It contributes as well to the use of public art in affirming collective memory and common cultural heritage through technological-facilitated emotional experience.

6.3 Practical Contributions

Designing Emotionally Engaging HCI-Integrated Public Art Guidelines

- The study provides design suggestions and practical results that are grounded in user experience, accessibility, and culture to enable the maximum emotional impact of public art installations (Vande Moere & Patel, 2009).
- The guidelines will guide artists, designers, and urban planners in designing public art projects based on interactive technology to enable more audience involvement.
- The research highlights the relevance of sustainability in HCI-enabled public art by promoting the application of adaptive technologies that can change with community requirements.

6.4 Implications for Cultural Policy and Urban Development

- Findings from this research are capable of influencing urban development processes through the illustration of how HCI-infused public art has the potential to improve urban beauty, promote civic engagement, as well as drive place-making agendas (Cloud Gate Chicago, 2006).
- Policymakers and cultural institutions can use these findings to argue the case for additional investment in digital public art projects focused on inclusivity and emotional connection.
- The research offers strategic recommendations for incorporating HCI-art projects into current urban development policies to become relevant and effective in the long term.

7 Conclusion

HCI converts static public urban artwork into vibrant interactive experiences which serve their intended goals. Research explored HCI which creates deep connections between people and their environments by enabling individual involvement and group creative practice. HCI combined with effective public research demonstrates how interactive technologies transform cultural collaboration and emotional bonding through their design.

The current research produces applicable design principles designers can implement with artists and policymakers to produce successful public art using human-computer interaction systems. User-centered design practicalities together with accessibility principles and responsiveness design principles work to create installations that users can easily interact with. The research incorporates both cultural and emotional appropriateness standards to enable enhanced public art interactions with audiences and the public.

Because technology is advancing regularly urban public art requires HCI adaptations to these emerging digital concepts. New emerging technologies enabled by artificial intelligence (AI), machine learning and biometric sensing systems provide unique possibilities to develop customized artistic experiences adapting to specific situations. Future studies need to identify methods for integrating modern technologies which maintain all ethical standards along with achieving data privacy and complete inclusivity.

The social effects enabled by HCI-based public art transcend both artistic quality and audience engagement. HCI installations function as frameworks that enable participatory social exchanges through activism while also facilitating community assembly. Through its ability to involve citizens in artistic processes, HCI-based public art develops a deep connection between people and their urban space which produces a stronger cultural representation of city environments.

A deeper examination of how HCI integration with public art creates sustainable, scalable solutions should become a focus for future research. Through investments in low-cost construction materials and technological frameworks and through shared initiatives between public agencies and private entities institutions can reach lasting success in diverse urban environments.

Future inquiries should accept diverse perspectives to develop public art healing prospects and keep its significance active in today's digitized globalized urban environment. HCI-infused public artworks help improve mental well-being by creating healing situations through interactive connected and immersive engagements which may assist with stress management and emotional storytelling capabilities.

This research demonstrates the transformative ability of interactive technology applications in city art installations and shows pathways for future developments at the intersection of artistic expression and tech innovations with social science principles. The design of public space in complex effective cities operates beyond practical needs as it concentrates on the social and cultural aspects. The technological advancement of public art remains a fundamental option to foster experiential designs that succeed in creating emotionally absorbing and mutually beneficial connections. Cities will form their urban future through technological integration of public spaces that fosters inclusive communal settings along with emotional engagement across their metropolitan areas.

References

1. Bannon, L.J.: Reimagining HCI: toward a more human-centered perspective. Interactions 18(4), 50–57 (2011). https://scholar.google.com/citations?view_op=view_citation&hl=en&user=Un1nBHsAAAAJ&citation_for_view=Un1nBHsAAAAJ:K3LRdlH-MEoC
2. Bardzell, J., Bardzell, S.: Humanistic HCI. Synth. Lect. Hum.-Centered Inform. 8(4), 1–185 (2015). https://doi.org/10.2200/S00664ED1V01Y201508HCI031

3. Bishop, C.: Artificial hells: participatory art and the politics of spectatorship. Verso Books (2012). https://books.google.com.np/books?id=iX8nQrLrybUC&lpg=PP1&pg=PP1#v=one page&q&f=false
4. Cloud Gate Chicago. Anish Kapoor's Cloud Gate: Reflection and interaction in public art. J. Public Art Stud. **5**(2), 145–167 (2006). https://theconversation.com/anish-kapoors-cloud-gate-playing-with-light-and-returning-to-earth-our-finite-world-102272
5. Fourneau, A.: Water light graffiti (2012). https://www.waterlightgraffiti.com
6. Goldstein, B.: Interactive public art: a new perspective on community engagement. J. Urban Des. **24**(3), 347–365 (2019). https://doi.org/10.1080/13574809.2019.1584998
7. Heibeck, F., Hope, A., King, M.: Sensory fiction. ACM SIGGRAPH Emerging Technol. **1**(1), 1–1 (2014). https://doi.org/10.1145/2660579.2660585
8. Heibeck, F., Hope, A., & Legault, J.: Sensory fiction: a design fiction of emotional computation. In: ImmersiveMe@ MM, pp. 35–40 (2014)
9. Ishii, H., Ullmer, B.: Tangible bits: towards seamless interfaces between people, bits, and atoms. Proc. CHI '97, 234–241 (1997). https://doi.org/10.1145/258549.258715
10. Kansei Engineering International. Introduction to Kansei Engineering. Kansei Eng. Int. J. **1**(1), 1–10 (2013). https://doi.org/10.1504/IJBM.2008.018660
11. Lozano-Hemmer, R.: Relational architecture. Leonardo **40**(4), 362–363 (2007). https://www.lozano-hemmer.com/texts/bibliography/articles_panorama/31_ArchitecturalDesign.pdf
12. Manovich, L.: The Language of New Media. The MIT Press, Cambridge, MA (2002). https://dss-edit.com/plu/Manovich-Lev_The_Language_of_the_New_Media.pdf
13. McCarthy, J., Wright, P.: Technology as Experience. The MIT Press, Cambridge, MA (2004). https://www.researchgate.net/publication/224927635_Technology_as_Experience
14. MIT Media Lab. The umbrella project (2013). https://arts.mit.edu/pilobolus-dance-company-collaborates-with-mit-robotics/
15. Norman, D.A.: Emotional design: why we love (or hate) everyday things. Basic Books (2004). https://www.researchgate.net/publication/224927652_Emotional_Design_Why_We_Love_or_Hate_Everyday_Things
16. Ratti, C., et al.: Urban pixels: painting the city with light. ACM SIGGRAPH 2009 Emerging Technol. **1**(1), 1–1 (2009). https://doi.org/10.1145/1518701.1518829
17. Random International. Rain Room (2012). https://www.random-international.com/rain-room
18. Vande Moere, A., Patel, S.: The role of public visualization in engaging citizens. In: Proceedings of the 11th International Conference on Information Visualization, pp. 489–496 (2009). https://doi.org/10.1109/IV.2009.66
19. Sengers, P., Boehner, K., David, S., Kaye, J. J.: Reflective design. In: Proceedings of the 4th Decennial Conference on Critical Computing: Between Sense and Sensibility, pp. 49–58 (2005). https://doi.org/10.1145/1094562.1094569

Research on the Application of Emotional Interaction Design in Charity Posters

Na Xie, Feng He[(✉)], and MengXi Zhang

Guangxi Normal University, Guilin 541000, China
1337990798@qq.com

Abstract. This thesis aims to explore the application of emotional interaction design in public welfare posters, discussing how public welfare posters, as important tools for transmitting social values and changing behaviors, have always carried profound significance. With the rapid development of digital technology, traditional static public welfare posters have gradually transformed into more interactive forms, and emotional interaction design has shown great potential in this process, significantly enhancing public attention and participation. This study aims to explore the combination of interaction technology and emotional design to enhance the emotional expressiveness of public welfare posters, deepen the emotional resonance of the audience, and thereby improve their communication effectiveness. The research methods will include literature review, case analysis, experimental design, and user research to comprehensively analyze the practical application and value of emotional interaction design.

Keywords: Public welfare poster · Emotional design · Interaction design · Digital interaction design · Communication effect

1 The Overview and Development Trend of Public Welfare Posters

1.1 The Definition and Design Characteristics of Public Welfare Posters

The Definition of Public Welfare Posters. Public welfare posters, as a non-profit advertising media, serve the public interest, aiming to improve the public's awareness of social problems, influence their ideas and attitudes, and induce behavioral changes to promote the solution or mitigation of social problems. It belongs to the category of social welfare posters, is a kind of outdoor print advertising, posted in public places. As a key field of visual communication design, public welfare posters use diverse symbolic elements such as color, text and graphics to convey public welfare concepts to the public in a vivid and intuitive way, with a clear image and a wide range of popular characteristics [2].

Design Characteristics of Public Welfare Posters. The design features of public welfare posters contain profound connotations, and its core lies in the multi-dimensional integration of public welfare, popularity, and pertinence. First of all, as the soul of public welfare posters, the nature of public welfare goes beyond the scope of commercial interests. Public welfare is a government, no money, not a commercial behavior, reflecting a selfless commitment to social welfare and positive development. This commitment is not aimed at profit, but is aimed at arousing the public's deep concern about social issues, which in turn promotes the overall progress of society. Secondly, in terms of expression techniques, public welfare posters pursue an easy-to-understand realm, abandoning obscure professional terms and adopting intuitive and clear design language. Finally, public welfare posters also show a strong pertinence. It often focuses on a specific social problem or vulnerable groups, such as environmental protection, children's rights and interests protection and other key areas. Through accurate positioning and in-depth analysis, public welfare posters guide the public to have a deeper understanding and understanding of these social problems, so as to stimulate the public's sense of responsibility and action.

1.2   The Development Trend of Public Welfare Posters

As an important carrier for the dissemination of social welfare concepts and values, the development trend of public welfare posters is indeed changing from static to dynamic, from single media to diversified, and the technical content is also constantly improving. Here's a closer look at these trends:

The Transition from Static to Dynamic. Traditional public welfare posters are mainly static images, which convey social issues through visual and text, and arouse public concern and reflection, but their interaction is relatively weak. With the development of new media technology, dynamic public welfare posters are gradually emerging. These posters convey the core content more intuitively through dynamic elements such as animation and video, enhancing the audience's sense of participation and experience. Dynamic public welfare posters have better communication effects on social media and digital platforms, and are easier to share and spread by the audience, thus expanding their audience scope.

The Shift from Single Media to Diversity. In the early days, public welfare posters mainly relied on paper media, such as posters and leaflets, whose dissemination scope was limited and subject to time and space. However, with the popularity of digital media and the Internet, the media of public welfare posters have undergone revolutionary changes, expanding to digital media, social media, mobile applications and other channels. These diversified media not only have a broader audience base, but also significantly improve the efficiency of communication, so that the influence of public welfare posters has been greatly enhanced.

The Improvement of Technical Content. In the era of new media art, public welfare poster design has ushered in innovation. With the help of new media tools such as image processing software, animation and 3D modeling, designers have made their designs more flexible and diversified, creating works with stunning visual effects and rich details, which have greatly enhanced the artistic value and functionality of public welfare posters. More importantly, new media technology allows public welfare posters to go beyond the scope of traditional static images and incorporate interactive elements.

By scanning the QR code on the poster, the audience can experience the virtual reality scene on their mobile devices and deeply understand the value connotation of public welfare activities. This interactive way significantly enhances the sense of participation and experience. In addition, the data induction and integration ability of new media technology also brings new opportunities for public welfare poster design. Designers can connect to real-time data sources such as donation amount, number of participants, etc. through data interfaces (apis), and update this information in real time in the poster. This kind of public welfare poster with real-time data display function not only provides the audience with intuitive information about the progress of public welfare activities, but also further stimulates their enthusiasm to participate in the activities.

2   The Application of Interaction Design Technology in Public Welfare Posters

2.1   Interaction Design Features in Posters

The application of interactive design in posters has greatly enriched the presentation form of posters and the audience's participation experience. Its characteristics are mainly embodied in the interaction, participation and experience.

The characteristics of interactivity in public service posters are as follows: factual feedback and dynamic response, deep interaction and emotional resonance, personalized experience and information transmission.

Factual Feedback and Dynamic Response. The audience is allowed to interact with the poster in a certain way (such as touching the screen, scanning the QR code, etc.), and the poster can immediately respond to the audience's input and give corresponding feedback. The characteristics of real-time feedback and dynamic response enable public welfare posters to convey information more directly and effectively, and enhance the audience's sense of participation and experience [3].

Deep Interaction and Emotional Resonance. The interactive design not only realizes the basic operational interaction between the audience and the poster, but also further emphasizes the deep interaction and emotional resonance. Through the design of various interactive links, such as storytelling, game challenges, etc., the audience can have a deeper understanding of public welfare issues in the process of participation, so as to generate emotional resonance. This deep interaction and emotional resonance helps to enhance the communication effect and influence of public welfare posters.

Personalized Experience and Information Delivery. The characteristics of interactive design in public service posters can also dynamically adjust the interactive mode and content of posters according to the behavior pattern and preference of the audience, and provide personalized experience. For example, through data analysis to understand the audience's interest points, and then push public interest information or interactive links related to their interests. The characteristics of this personalized experience enable public welfare posters to more accurately reach the target audience and improve the pertinence and effectiveness of information transmission.

The Characteristics of Participation in Public Welfare Posters. First of all, participation puts users at the core of the design of public welfare posters. When designing public welfare posters, designers invite representatives of target user groups to participate in the design process to ensure that the posters can truly reflect their needs and expectations. This user centrality makes public welfare posters closer to the public and easier to arouse resonance and attention. Secondly, participatory design encourages designers to give full play to their creativity and provides diverse design ideas, which can be reflected in the integration of various creative elements in public welfare posters, such as hand-painting, minimalism and different artistic expression modes. Finally, a notable feature of participation in public service posters is their social inclusion. In charity poster design, this means that the design should take into account the needs and interests of different social groups to ensure that the poster can be widely disseminated and resonate with society. By involving users in the design process, designers can gather feedback and suggestions from diverse groups to create more inclusive posters.

The Characteristics of Experience in Public Welfare Posters. By telling the content of the poster, showing real cases or presenting shocking images, public welfare posters stimulate the emotional resonance of the audience and let the audience be touched in the soul. This kind of emotional resonance is the core of the reflective level of experience. As a designer, we should carefully select the elements that can strike a chord with the audience and ensure that the public welfare poster can leave a deep impression and memory point to the audience.

2.2 Interactive Technology in the Implementation of Public Welfare Posters

The application of interactive technology includes three aspects:

Visual and Tactile Design

Visual Touch Buttons: The designer sets up "buttons" in the poster with visual and tactile means to guide the user to touch and click. These "buttons" can be visually realistic, with three-dimensional effects or "press travel" buttons, or they can be more abstract, freehand touch guides. When users click the "button", the poster will give corresponding visual and tactile feedback, so that users know that their "touch" is perceived and recorded by the poster.

Dynamic Visual Feedback: After the user clicks the "button", the overall picture of the poster will respond, such as color changes, text information rolling, screen elements moving, etc., to convey the visual interactive feedback corresponding to the "button". This dynamic visual feedback not only enhances the interaction of public welfare posters, but also enables users to more deeply understand the public welfare information conveyed by public welfare posters. Figure 1 shows a design case combining vision and touch [6].

As shown in Fig. 1. Creative advertising I embedded card reader public welfare interactive poster. The interactive poster of embedded credit card swipe machine takes place in the square. The poster is an interactive machine named PlaCard-The SocialSwipe designed by Misereor, a German charity organization, according to the habit of paying by credit card up to 40% in Europe. The screen shows two random sets of photographs

Fig. 1. Creative advertising | embedded card reader public welfare interactive poster

representing the common hardships of life in poor areas - hunger and child incarceration. The design translates the action of swiping a card into the meaning of "cutting," cutting a rope that restricts freedom, as well as cutting bread, helping a hungry family, etc. 2 euros will also be deducted from your bank card to visually let you know how your donation will be used. The interactive poster uses a combination of sliding and cutting bread to enhance users' sense of participation and achievement. Interactive public welfare posters attract the attention of passers-by through dynamic effects and interactive ways combined with sliding bread cutting to promote their participation in public welfare activities.

Innovative Technology

Augmented Reality (AR): Using AR technology, designers can combine charity posters with users' real environments to create immersive and interactive experiences. For example, when the user scans the AR mark on the poster through the phone, a three-dimensional animation or virtual scene related to the content of the charity poster can be seen on the phone screen.

NFC (Near Field Communication) Technology: Embedding an NFC chip in a charity poster can automatically trigger some kind of interaction or information transfer when the user puts the phone close to the poster. For example, automatically redirect to a donation page for a cause or show more information about the project. Figure 2 shows a design case combining AR technology and NFC technology [8].

Fig. 2. Creative advertising | NFC interactive poster design

Figure 2 is a creative advertisement on the theme of famous paintings in the art exhibition. Four world famous paintings (Van Gogh Self-Portrait, Mona Lisa Smile, Girl with a Pearl Earring, Saint Mary) are taken as the creative core. Combined with Kivicube.AR technology, three-dimensional posters with AR space interaction function are designed. Through NFC sensing and image recognition, users can interact with the dynamic scenes and musical elements of famous paintings, achieving the perfect integration of traditional art and modern technology, adding unprecedented technological and artistic charm to the evening event.

Application of Multimedia and Animation Elements

SVG Animate: Using SVG (scalable vector graphics) technology, designers can create charity posters with dynamic effects. For example, by clicking or swiping, elements in a charity poster can automatically expand, expand, move, or change color to show more charity information or stories.

Audio and Video Embeddings: In some cases, designers can embed audio or video elements in a pro bono poster to enhance the message. For example, when a user clicks on an area on a poster, an audio or video presentation about a public good project can be played [9].

2.3   Interaction Design is a Common Scene in Public Service Posters

The application of interaction design in public welfare posters is not only limited to improving the attractiveness of posters, but also helps spread social public welfare information and enhance the public's sense of participation and action by providing participatory interactive experience. Through the integration of interactive technologies, public service posters have become a multi-dimensional medium that can communicate with the audience, inspiring a higher level of emotional resonance and social responsibility. Here are some practical scenarios of interaction design in public service posters:

Interactive Charity Posters in Public Spaces. In public Spaces, such as subway stations and shopping malls, interactive posters use modern technology to attract public attention. Through interactive projection technology, the content of the poster changes with the movement of the audience, displaying public welfare information. Touch screen posters let the audience click to learn more about the charity, or even directly participate in the donation or volunteer. AR technology allows the audience scanning the QR code to experience 3D virtual effects on the mobile screen, deepening their understanding of the theme of public welfare. These innovative designs have effectively improved the dissemination of public information and public participation.

Interactive Charity Posters in Digital Billboards. As a medium for interactive public service posters in high-traffic areas of cities, digital billboards stand out with real-time updated data, dynamic display content and gamified interactive design. Through instant feedback on fundraising and volunteer participation, information transparency and interaction are enhanced to attract pedestrian attention. Dynamic videos, animations and other rich content vividly show the progress of public welfare and stimulate public participation. Set up small games or tasks to allow the audience to contribute to the public welfare in the entertainment, enhance the experience and expand the influence. In short, interactive public welfare posters in digital billboards, with their real-time, dynamic and gamified characteristics, effectively enhance the dissemination efficiency of public welfare information and the enthusiasm of public participation.

Interactive Charity Posters at Exhibitions or Events. At the exhibition or event site, interactive public welfare posters are cleverly designed to form a strong interaction with the audience and enhance the sense of experience and immersion. By setting up interactive screens and touch panels, the audience can freely choose public welfare topics of interest, and have an in-depth understanding of the background, effectiveness and participation channels of the event. The application of voice recognition technology enables the audience to obtain details of public welfare projects through voice interaction and achieve instant information acquisition. In addition, the integration of VR/AR technology allows the audience to enter the virtual scene by scanning the poster, experience the situation of the public welfare project, and deeply feel its practical significance and extensive influence [1].

Social Media Interactive Charity Poster. As a key path for digital communication, social media platforms enable interactive public welfare posters to deeply interact with the public and effectively expand the influence of public welfare. Social media sharing function is embedded in the poster, and viewers can scan the QR code or click the link to share to Instagram, Facebook, Weibo and other social platforms, and attach a public welfare tag to accelerate the dissemination of information. At the same time, combined with social media challenges, such as public welfare action or green living challenges, users are encouraged to post relevant content and participate in online interactions to broaden the topic of public welfare. In addition, the poster also integrates interactive voting and questionnaire surveys, allowing the audience to participate in the decision-making of public welfare activities through social media platforms, enhancing the sense of participation and influence.

3   The Theoretical Basis of Emotional Design

3.1   Interaction Design Features in Posters

Emotional design is a design strategy that aims to promote specific behaviors by touching users' emotions. It focuses on the emotional communication between people and objects. The emotional design proposed by Norman is divided into three core levels: instinct level, behavior level and reflection level. The instinctive layer focuses on the intuitive physical characteristics of the product, such as appearance, material, color, etc., which directly affect the user's sensory experience and form the initial and direct physiological feelings. The behavioral layer focuses on product functionality, ease of use and user interaction, aiming to create a pleasant user experience through smooth operation and positive physical feedback. The highest level of reflection involves deep-level factors such as culture, educational background and personal experience, which requires designers to deeply understand the deep-level needs of users and accurately grasp their emotional resonance points, so as to form positive evaluation and identification when users conduct rational reflection after using products [4].

3.2 The Relationship Between Emotional Design and Interactive Experience

Interactive Experience of Instinctual Level and Public Welfare Poster. At the instinctive level, the interactive experience of public welfare posters is significantly affected by their intuitive feelings, especially the visual appeal and impact. This level corresponds to the initial perception stage of interactive experience. Through the use of rich color matching, unique composition and layout, and image elements with high visual impact, public welfare posters can instantly attract the attention of the public and encourage them to stop and watch. Attraction at this stage is not only a direct reflection of the instinctual level effect, but also a key prerequisite for stimulating further interactive behavior. In addition, instinctual level design is also good at evoking the emotional resonance of the public, especially those public welfare posters focusing on universal human emotions such as family, friendship or love, which can quickly penetrate the hearts of the people and stimulate the audience's strong emotional identification, thus enhancing the communication effect of public welfare information on a deep level [2].

Behavioral Level and Interactive Experience of Public Welfare Posters. The behavior level focuses on the optimization of the interaction between the public welfare poster and the audience, which corresponds to the in-depth participation stage of the interactive experience. At this stage, the public welfare poster encourages the audience to actively participate in the interactive process of the poster by cleverly setting up interactive devices, such as two-dimensional code scanning, touch screen and other media, so as to enhance their sense of participation and experience. This kind of interaction mechanism not only enables the audience to better understand and remember the information and ideas conveyed by the poster, but also deepens the connection between the audience and the public welfare information by providing practical operation and feedback. In addition, some public welfare posters also incorporate the element of skill learning, requiring the audience to master certain knowledge or skills in order to complete the interaction, such as solving puzzles, answering questions and other forms. This kind of design not only adds interest to the interactive process, but also effectively promotes the audience to learn new knowledge or skills in the interaction, and further improves the educational significance and communication effect of public welfare posters [6].

Reflection Level and Interactive Experience of Public Welfare Posters. The reflection level constitutes the core and peak of the emotional design of public welfare posters, and its importance is reflected in the deep thinking and perception of the audience after interaction, corresponding to the deep thinking stage of interactive experience. At this level, public welfare posters deeply touch the hearts of the audience through carefully constructed storytelling and emotional expression, and stimulate their emotional resonance and deep reflection. This emotional feedback mechanism prompts the audience to think deeply about social values and moral concepts, which may drive positive changes in their behavior and realize the ultimate goal of public interest information dissemination. In addition, the reflective level design also aims to leave a lasting imprint on the audience's mind, helping them to form a long-term memory of the content of the poster. When the audience encounters similar situations in the future, they can quickly recall the ideas and information conveyed by the poster, thus guiding them to make judgments and actions in line with the public welfare goals, further strengthening the social influence and educational value of the public welfare poster [4].

4   The Theoretical Basis of Emotional Design

4.1   Interactive Design of Public Welfare Posters at the Instinctive Level

The design of instinct level mainly focuses on the first impression and intuitive feeling of users, which involves visual, auditory, tactile and other sensory experiences. The following are the keys to the interaction design of charity posters at an instinctive level: First, it can be attractive through visual elements, such as: The use of color, the use of bright, strong contrast color combination, can quickly attract the attention of the audience, stimulate their curiosity and interest, at the same time, the choice of color should be based on the theme of public welfare and emotional expression, such as warm tones can convey hope and care.

Secondly, in the interactive design, public welfare posters create an emotional atmosphere through the stimulation of emotional resonance, the use of emotional expression, storytelling and other ways, and the combination of images, words and colors, so that the audience can feel the emotional value conveyed by public welfare posters. Designers need to deeply understand the emotional needs and psychological characteristics of the target audience, and choose the emotional elements that can touch their hearts [4].

Finally, through interactive experience, the public welfare poster uses sensory inter-action, call to action, feedback mechanism and other ways to interact with the audience by tactile, auditory and other sensory elements. The new VR/AR interactive experience can enhance the audience's sense of participation and memory of the public welfare poster.

4.2   Interactive Design of Public Welfare Posters at the Behavioral Level

The interactive design of public welfare posters is carried out at the behavioral level of emotional design, which mainly focuses on enhancing the user's sense of participation and the depth of experience, and arouses the audience's interest and attention to pub-lic welfare themes through interaction and action calls. The following are the keys to interactive design of public welfare posters at the behavioral level: First, public welfare posters can be equipped with interactive devices to enhance interactive experience, such as touch screen, AR (augmented reality) technology, so that the audience can touch, slide and other actions to interact with the poster.

Second, the public welfare poster on the clear call to action launched a brief and clear action instructions, so that the audience can quickly understand and take action, such as the use of "donate now", "join us" and other clear directive language. It can also provide convenient interactive participation methods on public welfare posters, such as providing convenient participation channels for the audience to donate online and share buttons on social media. Make sure the interaction in the poster is simple and easy to understand.

Finally, in the feedback and incentive mechanism, the instant feedback and incentive mechanism in the public welfare poster, when the participants interact or take actions, they should give timely feedback, such as confirmation messages, thank messages, etc. Instant feedback enhances audience engagement and satisfaction. In the incentive agency, it can stimulate the audience's participation consciousness and enthusiasm, and further promote the dissemination of public welfare activities.

4.3 Interactive Design of Public Welfare Posters at the Level of Reflection

In the design of public welfare posters, the reflective design can stimulate the audience to think deeply about the poster theme, so as to convey the public welfare concept and values more effectively. The following are the keys to the interactive design of public welfare posters at the reflective level:

First, in the design of public welfare posters, designers can skillfully integrate the scenes, emotions or values that the audience may experience into the poster, so as to arouse their resonance and memory, and build a visual language that can trigger the audience's association and reflection.

Secondly, the interactive design of public welfare posters can establish self-identity and sense of identity. Public welfare posters can present a positive value and lifestyle, so that the audience can establish self-identity and sense of identity while recognizing these values. Through the information or images in the posters, the audience can find experiences or emotions similar to their own, thereby increasing their sense of identity and belonging to the posters.

Finally, the interactive design of public welfare posters can promote reflection and action, and set some questions or prompts in public welfare posters that can trigger the audience to think, so that they can reflect on their own behavior and values. Through a clear call to action or suggestion, the audience is encouraged to take positive action in support of the good cause.

5   The Practice of Emotional Interaction Design in Public Welfare Posters

Figure 3 is a public interest interactive poster using Norman's emotional interaction design theory, which aims to arouse the public's deep concern for Marine conservation through carefully designed visual and tactile experiences. At the instinctive level, sand grains are isomorphic with Marine organisms, combined with the texture of plastic film, to intuitively show the severity of pollution, and stimulate the viewer's instinctive reaction and reflection. At the behavioral level, the innovative interactive design allows the viewer to "transform" the form of Marine organisms into plastic clumps when touching the poster. Through the haptic feedback mechanism, the viewer can personally experience the pollution hazards and deepen their understanding. Reflecting on the level, the red noise in the poster symbolizes the suffering of Marine animals, touching people's hearts, causing viewers to reflect deeply on the issue of Marine ecological protection, and resonating with the importance of protecting the balance of natural ecology. On the whole, through the double experience of vision and touch, as well as the elaborate design at the three levels of instinct, behavior and reflection, the work is not only an artistic expression, but also a powerful call for environmental protection, aiming to stimulate the public's concern and action on Marine pollution, and jointly protect our blue ocean home [7].

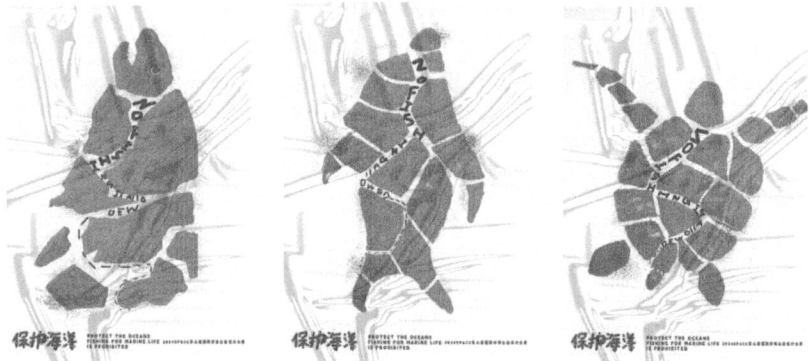

Fig. 3. Protect the ocean I interactive poster design

6   Conclusion

The application of emotional interaction design in public welfare posters has significantly improved its communication effect and influence. Traditional public welfare posters focus on the direct transmission of information, but often ignore the audience's emotional resonance and sense of participation. By incorporating interactive and emotional elements, the emotional interaction design transforms the public welfare poster into an interactive platform that inspires the audience's emotional resonance and promotes active participation. This design not only enhances the attractiveness of the poster, but also greatly improves the dissemination efficiency and influence of public welfare information, enabling the audience to deeply understand public welfare information in the interaction and actively participate in public welfare undertakings. Interactive technologies show great potential in stimulating public participation and improving communication efficiency. The use of touch screen, two-dimensional code, AR/VR and other technologies has made the public welfare poster more closely connected with the audience, enhanced the audience's sense of participation, and injected more impetus into the public welfare cause. Designers should have a deep understanding of the audience's emotional needs and psychological characteristics, choose the appropriate interaction technology and emotional elements, create both attractive and resonant public welfare posters, and pay attention to the ease of use and fun of interaction design.

Funding.   2024 Guangxi Higher Education Undergraduate Teaching Reform Key Project "Research on Teaching Innovation and Practice of Integrating AIGC into Product Design Major" (Project Number: 2024JGZ111).

References

1. Zhang, M., Yu, M.: Chinese public service advertising research. Contemp. Commun. (01), 68–70 (2004)
2. Zhou, J.: From viewing to participating. Nanjing University of the Arts (2021)
3. Hu, X.: Research on creation practice of interactive public service advertisement under new media. Yunnan Arts University (2020)
4. Norman, D.A.: Emotional design. Ind. Design (06), 32–33 (2017)
5. Xin, X.: Interaction Design: from physical logic to behavioral logic. Decoration (01), 58–62 (2015)
6. Xiao, L.: Creative design of situational interactive public service advertisement. Southeast Univ. (2018)
7. Ma, G., Fang, Q.: Research on emotion of interaction design elements. Design (09), 103–105 (2020)
8. Xu, S., Liu, Y.: Analysis on interaction design of new design platform based on behavioral logic. Ind. Design (09), 103–105 (2020)
9. Ni, Y.: How can enterprises consciously become the main body of public service advertising activities? – Try the definition of public service advertisement in China. China Advertising **12**, 68–69 (2020)

Children's Chess Robots Design Based on CAPS Theory and Kansei Engineering: Constructing Intelligent Educational Tools to Promote Children's Cognitive and Emotional Development

Jiaxin Yuan, Xin Liu, and Zhijuan Zhu[⊠]

School of Mechanical Science and Engineering, Huazhong University of Science and Technology, Wuhan, People's Republic of China
zhuzhijuan@hust.edu.cn

Abstract. In the era of deep integration between intelligent technologies and education, chess robots are playing an increasingly important role as tools for smart education. Children, as key participants in the information age, are no longer competing solely on the functional aspects of products; the competition now extends to multiple dimensions, including emotional design, cognitive engagement, and interactive experiences. The emotional and cognitive design elements for children play a critical role in enhancing user satisfaction and brand loyalty. However, the design theories for children's chess robots remain underdeveloped, lacking comprehensive coverage of these essential factors. Therefore, this paper aims to explore the application of integrating CAPS theory and Kansei Engineering in the design of children's chess teaching robots, building upon existing theoretical frameworks. By analyzing the dynamic structure and operational logic of the personality system within CAPS theory, combined with the established theoretical framework of Kansei Engineering, this study proposes a design framework that is more attuned to the needs of child users. This framework provides a scientific foundation for designing children's chess teaching products, helping to optimize these products in terms of functionality, emotional appeal, and interactivity. As a result, the design of children's chess robots will increasingly emphasize personalization and intelligence.

Keywords: CAPS theory · kansei engineering · cognitive and emotion · Children's Product Design · chess-playing robots

1 Introduction

1.1 Chess-Playing Robots: Empowering the Development of Children's Chess Education

Today, intelligent tech is integrating into education, and chess education's role in early - childhood development is more recognized [1]. Chess - playing robots (for various chess types) are key smart - education tools. In China, chess education during children's school years gets more attention. Parents and schools focus on kids' intellectual and overall skills. Courses like Xiangqi, Weiqi, and International Chess are becoming part of school curricula and extracurriculars. These chess games boost children's logical thinking, problem - solving, concentration, and patience, laying a learning foundation.

As chess education spreads, chess - playing robots will be crucial for its growth. They simulate games and offer interactive teaching, providing an intelligent and personalized learning experience. They solve issues like limited teaching resources and time, enabling kids to practice anytime, anywhere, especially helping remote areas. AI tech makes these robots more important in developing children's logical and strategic skills, serving as a great addition to modern chess education.

Now, chess education in China trends towards diversification and specialization, with online platforms offering more learning chances. In the future, with more social support for education, chess - playing robots will better promote children's intellectual and overall development of children.

1.2 Emotional and Cognitive Dimensions of Appearance Design for Children's Products in the Digital Age

In the digital age, children have become the primary users of digital products and services. In the face of a highly competitive market, emotional and cognitive design aspects play a crucial role in enhancing user satisfaction and brand loyalty. As active participants in the information age, children should not be overlooked in technological advancements. With the rise of consumer upgrading, parents and consumers are gradually shifting their focus from a singular emphasis on product functionality to a greater emphasis on the emotional experiences and multidimensional interactive value that products offer to children. The competition among children's products is no longer limited to functionality but extends to multiple dimensions, including emotion, cognition, and interactive experiences [2]. The appearance design of products also directly influences consumers' first impressions of children's products [3].

However, the existing design theories for chess-playing robots targeted at children are relatively underdeveloped. Exploring the design of chess and card game robots based on children's logical thinking can not only enhance the theoretical framework for children's robot design but also better meet the personalized needs of children, driving the development of more refined functional designs. Therefore, this paper aims to integrate the Cognitive-Affective Processing System (CAPS) theory with Kansei Engineering (KE), building on existing theoretical foundations. Using the design of a chess-teaching robot for children as a case study, the study seeks to thoroughly consider the practical needs of users throughout the design process, thereby proposing improved design guidelines for technologically innovative products.

1.3 Status of Existing Research

China has a profound historical and cultural heritage in traditional board games such as Go, Xiangqi (Chinese Chess), and Weiqi (Go). As a result, there has been significant attention and investment in the development of chess-playing robots. The Chinese AI teams in the field of Go have also made numerous important breakthroughs and achievements, such as the famous 2017 match between AlphaGo and Ke Jie, along with similar experiments and research. Additionally, many universities in China have implemented policies that lower admission scores for exceptional chess players, further promoting the development of chess education.

In the United States and Europe, significant progress has been made in the application of artificial intelligence to Go, chess, and other board games [4]. For example, computer programs such as AlphaGo and AlphaZero have achieved remarkable accomplishments in the field of Go. These programs utilize advanced technologies like deep learning and reinforcement learning, enabling them to secure victories against top human players [5].

2   Methods

This study aims to integrate the CAPS theory, proposed by psychologist Walter Mischel, with the KE research framework. Using the design of a chess-teaching robot for children as a case study, the research seeks to thoroughly consider the practical needs of users throughout the design process, thereby proposing improved design guidelines for technologically innovative products.

2.1   CAPS Theory: Cognitive-Affective Units

The CAPS theory, proposed by Walter Mischel in 1995 [6], integrates cognitive traits and affective factors into a unified framework for study. This theory places particular emphasis on emotional and affective elements, facilitating a deeper exploration of how various psychological mechanisms influence human behavior [7].

In the CAPS theoretical model, the personality system continuously engages in dynamic interactions with the external world. This interaction involves a bidirectional process: the behaviors generated by the personality system influence the social environment and shape the individual's selection of subsequent interpersonal situations. Conversely, these situations, in turn, impact the personal system. When an individual encounters specific situational features, certain cognitive and affective patterns are activated through the dynamic network structure of the personality system, while other units are constrained. This process ultimately activates plans, strategies, and potential behaviors that drive action. Within the personality network system, numerous possible connections exist among the units. A unit may be activated by specific situational features or by other units within the system, ultimately leading to overt behavior. This dynamic relationship is illustrated in Fig. 1 [8].

In the CAPS model, cognitive-affective units refer to all psychological representations, which are primarily composed of five types: encoding, expectations and beliefs, affects, goals and values, and competencies and self-regulating plans [7].

- **Encoding**: This refers to the cognitive processes through which individuals categorize and construct representations of external entities, including themselves, other people, events, or situations. These diverse encoding strategies subsequently influence how individuals perceive and respond to these stimuli, shaping their behavioral reactions.

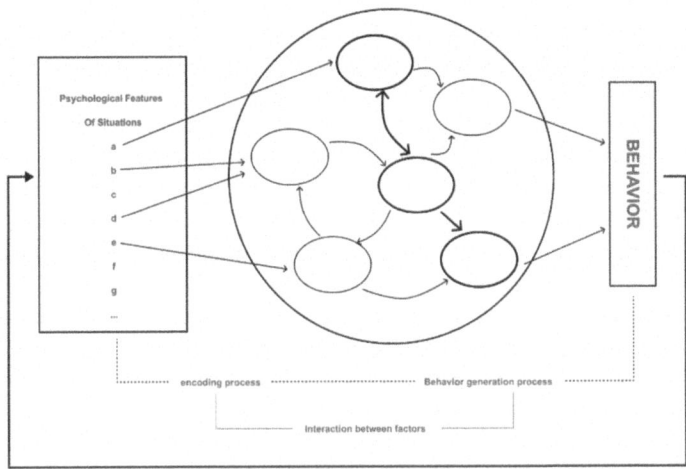

Fig. 1. Dynamic Structure of the CAPS Personality System.

- **Expectations and Beliefs**: These are rooted in human sociality and involve the prediction and evaluation of the outcomes of an individual's actions and their self-efficacy within social and specific situational contexts. They shape how individuals anticipate and interpret the consequences of their behavior, influencing their decision-making and adaptive responses.
- **Affects**: This component involves an individual's emotional responses, which also encompass physiological reactions. The emotions and feelings experienced by an individual significantly influence the processing of social information and the execution of behaviors, playing a crucial role in shaping interactions and decision-making.
- **Goals and Values**: Goals represent the anticipated outcomes of activities, guiding individuals' long-term actions and providing direction for their behavioral pursuits. They reflect an individual's motivations and priorities, shaping the choices they make and the efforts they undertake to achieve desired results.
- **Competencies and Self-Regulating Plans**: These influence an individual's behavior and internal states. They encompass the individual's potential behaviors and abilities, as well as the plans and strategies used to organize actions and affect personal behavior and internal states. This unit represents the internal mechanisms that shape behavior, enabling individuals to adapt and regulate their actions in response to situational demands.

2.2   Kansei Engineering

Kansei Engineering (KE) is an interdisciplinary approach that combines human sensibility with engineering principles. It is grounded in the emotional and perceptual needs of consumers and employs statistical methods to translate consumers' sensory perceptions of products into quantifiable engineering parameters. This process establishes a consumer-oriented product development system, which quantitatively or semi-quantitatively expresses consumers' emotional impressions of "objects" and maps these impressions to specific product design characteristics. The goal is to design products that align with users' sensory expectations and preferences, thereby creating products that resonate with human feelings and perceptions [9].

With the advent of the information and experience era, consumers' demands for product individuality have increasingly grown. Modern product design has gradually shifted from a function-oriented approach to one that emphasizes emotional and experiential engagement. Professor Mitsuo Nagamachi of Hiroshima University posits that Kansei Engineering is primarily "a customer-oriented product development technology, a technique that translates sensations or impressions into design elements." Specifically, it involves collecting users' emotional evaluations of products to establish a computer-based Kansei database and reasoning system. This framework aims to create products that align with users' sensory and psychological needs, thereby ensuring that the products better meet their emotional expectations [10].

2.3 Design Process for Children's Chess-Playing Robots Based on CAPS Theory and Kansei Engineering

Given the unique age group of children, the design of chess-playing robots for this demographic requires not only careful consideration of the robot's external features but also an in-depth understanding of children's psychological attributes. By adopting a child-centered psychological perspective and employing empathy, designers can better capture the multifaceted needs of children, which can then be applied to both the functionality and appearance of the robot. Therefore, this study integrates CAPS theory and Kansei Engineering to conduct a comprehensive, user-centered analysis, transforming abstract emotional needs into tangible design elements that guide the development process. Additionally, this research aims to innovate and deepen the theoretical framework for designing children's chess-playing robots, ensuring that the final products better meet the personalized needs of children.

This study primarily extracts the dynamic structure and operational logic of the personality system from CAPS theory to establish a highly feasible design process. Simultaneously, since KE has developed a relatively mature design framework over time, it can serve as a reliable guide for this research. By integrating these two approaches, the study aims to create a comprehensive and practical methodology for designing children's chess-playing robots, ensuring that both cognitive-affective dynamics and user-centered emotional needs are effectively addressed.

First, based on extensive preliminary research and comparisons of existing products, a multi-stage and multi-dimensional analysis is conducted according to CAPS theory. This process summarizes and refines the pain points and usage needs of children and their parents regarding chess-playing robots, leading to the proposal of relevant design strategies. Next, statistical methods are employed to translate consumers' emotional perceptions of the product into quantifiable engineering parameters, establishing a consumer-oriented product development system. Finally, the design elements of the chess-playing robot are extracted, and design outputs and solution validation are carried out in the later stages of the process. Additionally, a universal design framework applicable to such products is developed, as illustrated in Fig. 2.

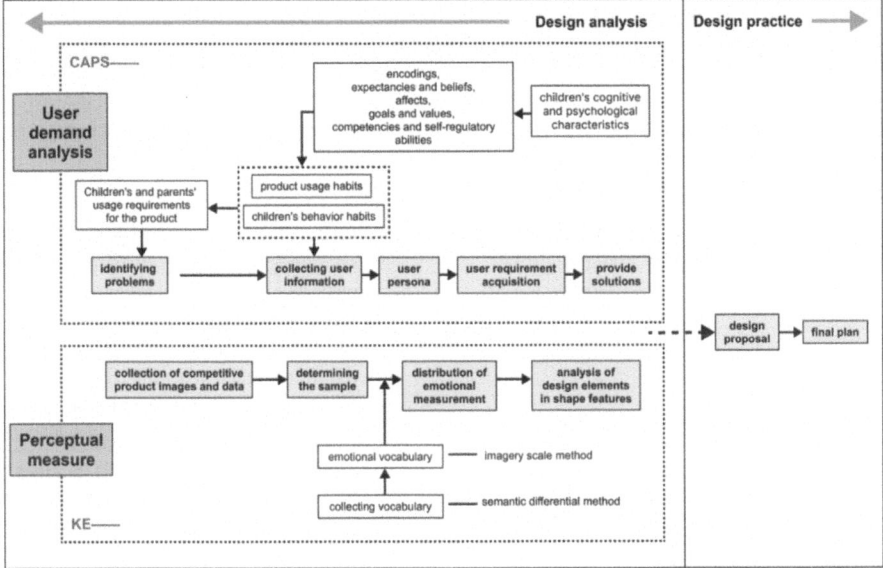

Fig. 2. Design Process of Children's Chess Robots Based on CAPS Theory and Kansei Engineering.

3   User Definition and Analysis

3.1   Scope of Product Users

According to the international Convention on the Rights of the Child, anyone under the age of 18 is considered a child [11]. Based on factors such as mental development and cognitive growth, children are generally divided into four categories: infants (0–3 years old), preschool children (3–6 years old), school-age children (6–12 years old), and adolescents (12–18 years old). This study primarily focuses on school-age children. During this stage, children's logical thinking and emotional management develop rapidly, and learning chess can effectively enhance their strategic thinking, concentration, and problem-solving abilities. Chess education during this period is particularly important as it not only promotes intellectual development but also fosters lasting learning interest and self-regulation skills.

3.2   User Pain Point Analysis

After conducting user interviews, questionnaire surveys, and online research, we identified three key stakeholders directly involved in children's chess education: parents, children, and teachers. Parents face challenges such as a lack of professional knowledge and insufficient time investment in chess education. Children, on the other hand, are easily influenced by fluctuations in learning interest and a sense of frustration. Teachers struggle to meet the differentiated teaching needs of each child and are constrained by limited resources. These pain points highlight areas within current chess education that urgently require optimization. Table 1 illustrates the pain point analysis of parents, children, and teachers regarding children's learning of chess.

Table 1. Pain Point Analysis of Parents, Children, and Teachers in Children's Chess Learning.

Stakeholder	Pain Point Summary	Pain Point Analysis Explanation
Parents	– Lack of professional knowledge – Difficulty managing time	1. Parents lack systematic chess knowledge, making it difficult to provide effective guidance to children 2. Busy work schedules result in insufficient time to accompany children in their learning, impacting the continuity and depth of learning
Children	– Fluctuations in learning interest – Low tolerance for frustration – Difficulty finding suitable practice partners	1. Children's motivation to learn is easily affected by frustration, leading to decreased enthusiasm and hindering continuous learning and skill mastery 3. Finding practice partners is difficult, as most chess games require at least two participants, and matching schedules is challenging. There is also a lack of practice partners who can match the child's skill level
Teachers	– Difficulty in differentiated teaching – Resource limitations	1. Teachers face difficulties addressing the differentiated needs of students with varying skill levels, making it challenging to provide personalized teaching support 4. Limited chess resources in schools restrict the ability to maximize teaching quality and learning outcomes

4 Design Guidance: CAPS Theory

In the CAPS theoretical model, the personality system constantly interacts dynamically with the external world [12]. The individual's cognitive - affective system consists of five types of cognitive - affective units that jointly influence human behavior, as shown in Fig. 2. External stimuli act on the cognitive - affective system, with the encoding unit most significantly affected. It serves as the cognitive foundation and impacts other units. The affective unit is also crucial, as emotions influence cognition and other units. The interaction within the system shapes behavior, which in turn affects external situation selection [13].

In the context of design, a product serves as an external stimulus. When users interact with the product, their cognitive-affective system processes the stimulus, leading to behavioral expressions aimed at achieving specific tasks. After completing these tasks, users decide whether to continue using the product or discontinue its use. When designing chess-playing robots for children, incorporating these cognitive-affective factors can create a more personalized and interactive learning experience. This approach not only enhances children's cognitive and emotional development but also ensures that the product aligns with their psychological and behavioral needs, fostering sustained engagement and satisfaction (Fig. 3).

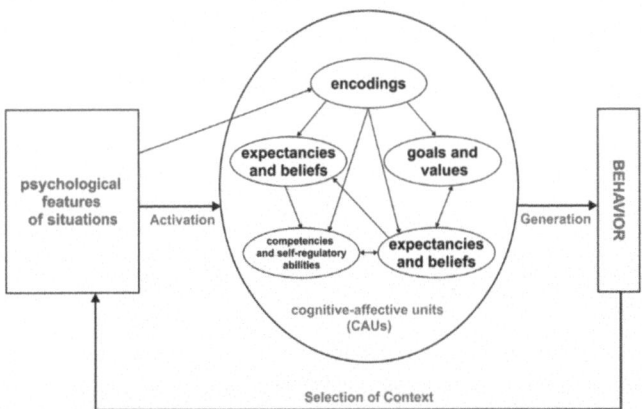

Fig. 3. Relationship Between Environment, Cognitive-Affective System, and Behavior.

Specifically, introducing the Cognitive-Affective Processing System (CAPS) theory from psychology into children's product design aims to systematically and accurately interpret users' behavioral patterns and cognitive responses, ensuring that the design aligns with users' psychological expectations. For the special user group of children, it is particularly important to understand the significant differences between them and adults in terms of cognitive development, psychological characteristics, and emotional expression. Children's cognitive processes are not yet fully mature, and their emotional regulation mechanisms differ from those of adults. Therefore, in design, it is essential to conduct in-depth research on children's cognitive development stages, information processing patterns, and emotional interaction needs to ensure that the design truly meets their psychological and emotional requirements, thereby fostering more enduring user loyalty (Table 2).

As the target users of this study are 6–12 - year - old school - age children, their cognitive and psychological traits are crucial for the design of chess - playing robots.

Through the above summary, these application frameworks are applied to the functional positioning and product appearance design of the product in the later stage.

Table 2. Application Framework of CAPS Theory in the Design of Chess-Playing Robots for Children.

Cognitive-Affective Units	Overview	Children's Chess Context	Design Strategy	Expected Outcome
Encoding	Learn chess rules & strategies	identifying piece positions, and judging opponents' strategies	1. Simple chess scenarios 5. Intuitive user interfaces 6. Diagram & animation demos 7. Step - by - step guidance	Establish basic chessboard cognition improve understanding and operation
Expectancies and Beliefs	Expect to win, have self - confidence	predicting game progress, receiving feedback	1. Instant feedback 2. Feedback & reward mechanisms 3. Clear learning goals	Enhance children's learning motivation and self-confidence
Affects	Emotional responses & regulation	Feelings of accomplishment, frustration, focus	1. Warm color tones 1. Encouraging feedback 2. Success sounds & visual feedback	Foster emotional connection and rapport with children
Goals and Values	Motivation & goal-setting	Aim for victory, intellectual development	1. Staged learning goals 3. Personalized challenges 4. Real - life examples	Strengthen learning value and practical significance
Competence and Self-Regulation	Strategies & reflection	Adjust tactics, respond to game changes	1. Dynamically adjust difficulty 2. Self - assessment and feedback tools 3. Incremental goals	Enhance self - regulation and adaptive learning

5 Design Research: Kansei Engineering

Based on the foundational principles of Kansei Engineering, the design process involves several key steps: collecting data on competing robot products, determining samples, selecting and defining Kansei vocabulary, conducting statistical analysis of sample evaluations, and extracting design elements. These steps ultimately lead to the completion of the design concept [14].

5.1 Selection of Representative Robot Samples

Selecting robot samples for analysis is the initial step in the Kansei Engineering - based research on children's chess - playing robot design. This step serves as the basis for subsequent Kansei vocabulary screening and analysis. We collected numerous child companion robots with various designs from the market and websites as product sample baselines. Samples were filtered from three aspects: child companion robots, child educational robots, and chess - playing robots. After evaluating key consumer - concerned factors like color, form, functionality, safety, materials, ergonomic dimensions, and performance, we finally selected nine most representative product samples.

5.2 Screening of Kansei Vocabulary and Kansei Evaluation of Robot Samples

By investigating websites, magazines, target users (school-age children aged 6–12 and their parents), books related to children, and promotional materials for children's products, emotional descriptive vocabulary related to child companion robots, child educational robots, and chess-playing robots was collected. From the aspects of color, form, and safety, 12 sets of the most representative Kansei words were selected:

- **Color**: colorful tones—gray tones, monochromatic—diverse color schemes, warm—cold, vibrant—calm.
- **Form**: minimalistic—complex, smooth—rigid, flexible—cumbersome, technological—traditional.
- **Safety**: durable—fragile, safe—vulnerable, efficient and user-friendly—inefficient and difficult to use, simple—complicated.

This study invited 15 children and parents, as well as individuals with and without design backgrounds, to participate in the evaluation. Using the Likert scale method, each robot sample and the 12 sets of Kansei words were scored. The evaluation scale was set to 7 levels, with scores ranging from "3" to "−3" indicating the degree of perception. For example, for the Kansei word pair "colorful tones—gray tones", 3 points represent extremely rich colors, 2 points represent relatively rich colors, 1 point represents colorful, 0 points represent neutral, −1 point represents light gray tones, −2 points represent medium gray tones, and −3 points represent dark gray tones. The specific questionnaire format is shown in Table 3, and the statistical scores yielded the average Kansei imagery, as shown in Table 4.

Table 3. Questionnaire Sample: Evaluation of Nine Samples by Users.

colorful tones	3	2	1	0	-1	-2	-3	gray tones
diverse color schemes	3	2	1	0	-1	-2	-3	monochromatic
warm	3	2	1	0	-1	-2	-3	cold
vibrant	3	2	1	0	-1	-2	-3	calm
minimalistic	3	2	1	0	-1	-2	-3	complex
smooth	3	2	1	0	-1	-2	-3	rigid
flexible	3	2	1	0	-1	-2	-3	cumbersome
technological	3	2	1	0	-1	-2	-3	traditional
durable	3	2	1	0	-1	-2	-3	fragile
safe	3	2	1	0	-1	-2	-3	vulnerable
simple	3	2	1	0	-1	-2	-3	complicated
efficient and user-friendly	3	2	1	0	-1	-2	-3	inefficient and difficult to use

Table 4. Sample perceptual metric statistics.

Kansei Vocabulary	Sample Cases								
	S1	S2	S3	S4	S5	S6	S7	S8	S9
colorful tones—gray tones	−0.58	−2	−0.33	0.83	1.5	0.5	−2.25	−2.42	0.83
diverse color schemes—monochromatic	−0.5	−1.92	−0.25	0.33	0.92	0.67	−2	−2.08	0.58
warm—cold	−0.58	−0.58	1.42	1.25	1.08	1.92	−1.75	−1.92	1.17
vibrant—calm	0.17	−1.58	1.25	2.17	1.42	1.08	−1.58	−1.67	0.33
minimalistic—Complex	0.67	0.83	−0.33	1.83	0.83	1.75	−1	−1.67	0.25
smooth—Rigid	1	0.58	1.33	2.42	0.92	1.92	0.33	−0.5	0.83
flexible—cumbersome	1.33	−0.92	1.67	2.25	−0.5	2	−1.25	−1.5	−0.33
technological—traditional	0.83	0.33	0.75	1.42	0.08	0.5	1.83	0.5	0.92
durable—fragile	0.92	1.42	0.42	1.5	1.58	1.25	0.92	0.67	0.92
safe—vulnerable	1.42	1.25	0.92	2.17	1.58	1.92	1	0.5	1.5
simple—complicated	1.33	0.92	1.08	2.08	1	1.25	−0.67	0	0.58
friendly—inefficient and difficult to use	0.75	1.33	1.58	2	0.75	1.5	1.08	0.33	0.75

5.3   Kansei Data Analysis and Design Element Extraction

The average values of the 15 Kansei evaluation results were calculated as the Kansei metric values for each sample, and a distribution map of the sample Kansei metrics was plotted. Specifically, each pair of Kansei vocabulary terms was assigned to the positive and negative axes of the coordinate system, with an adjacent pair of Kansei terms assigned to the positive and negative axes of the corresponding axis. For example, "colorful tones" was assigned to the positive x-axis, while "gray tones" was assigned to the negative x-axis, and "diverse color schemes" was assigned to the positive y-axis, while "monochromatic" was assigned to the negative y-axis. Thus, a Kansei metric value of (-0.58, -0.5) represents the coordinates of sample S1 in the "colorful tones—gray tones, diverse color schemes—monochromatic" coordinate system. The same method was applied to the other five coordinate systems. For the final selection of 9 samples (S1–S9) and 12 sets of Kansei vocabulary, six Kansei metric distribution maps were generated, categorized as follows (see Fig. 4): color (Figs. 4a–4b), form (Figs. 4c–4d), and safety (Figs. 4e–4f).

Color Dimension. From the data distribution, the samples exhibit a clear polarization trend in the color dimension. One group of samples leans toward the "colorful tones—diverse color schemes" and "warm—vibrant" end, while the other group tends toward the "gray tones—monochromatic" and "cold—calm" end. This polarization provides a clear directional reference for subsequent design.

Multicolored and diverse color schemes can evoke lively, warm, and energetic visual impressions, potentially attracting users who seek novelty and visual stimulation. On the other hand, gray and monotonous color combinations convey a sense of calm and composure, which may be more suitable for users who prefer minimalistic and understated styles. Designers can choose one color style as the primary design direction based on the preferences of the target user group and the product's positioning. For example, for children as the target user group, a multicolored and diverse color scheme may be more appealing to capture their attention. Alternatively, designers can innovate by blending both color styles to create a balanced scheme that combines vibrancy with stability, catering to a broader range of user needs.

Form Dimension. Data shows most samples are in the "minimalistic—smooth" quadrant, suggesting minimalistic styles prevail in form design. Also, the blend of technological and traditional elements is a key trend, with some samples balancing these features to varying degrees. Minimalistic forms have clean lines, regular shapes, and little decoration. They create a neat look, improve user understanding, and ease operation. Smooth edges make the product safer and more approachable, preventing harm from sharp edges. Technological elements give the product a modern, advanced look, fitting current aesthetics and tech trends. Traditional elements, on the other hand, add cultural depth and uniqueness. For chess - playing robots, linked to traditional activities, traditional elements can stir emotional resonance and cultural identity in users.

Safety Dimension. Data from Fig. 4e - f shows almost all samples are in the "durable - safe" and "simple - efficient & user - friendly" quadrants. This shows users prioritize safety, durability, and ease of use in product design.

Safety is crucial for children's products, meaning non - toxic materials, sturdy builds, and no sharp edges. Durability refers to long - lasting use and cost - effectiveness. Ease of use includes simple operation, a friendly interface, and clear functions for kids to learn fast, cut the learning curve, and lower safety risks.

By mapping user needs to Kansei vocabulary and categorizing design elements, key terms like safe, durable, simple, etc. were found. Picking related design elements for the robot's design formed a preliminary concept.

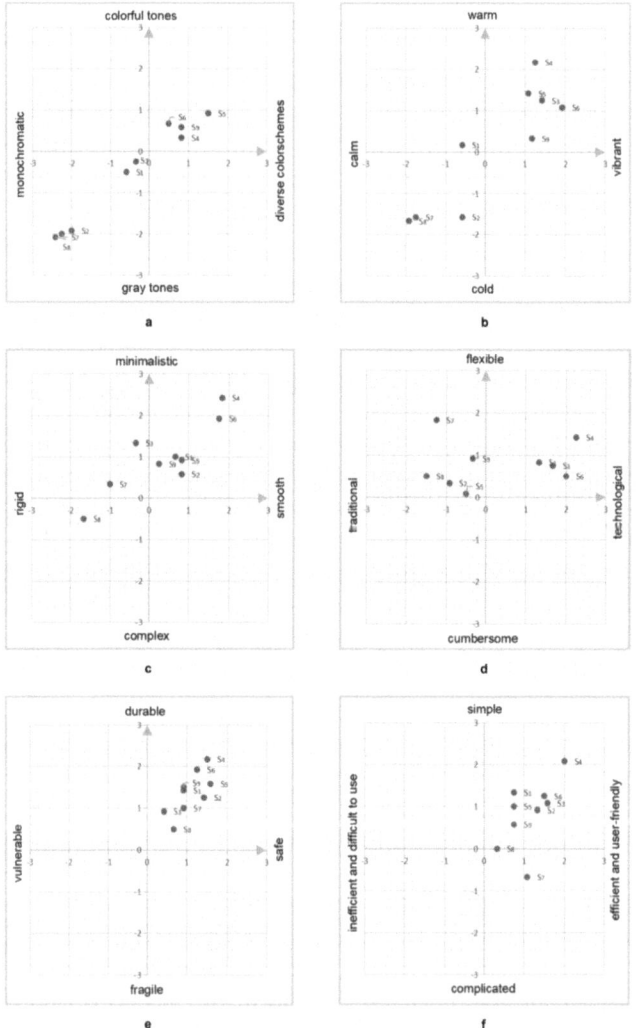

Fig. 4. Perceptual measurement profile of samples.

5.4 Points Analysis

This study has clarified the design elements of the product in terms of color, form, and safety, as shown in Table 5. Through a detailed analysis of these design elements, the research further reveals the relationship between each design element and the corresponding Kansei vocabulary [15], providing clear guidance for designers. During the design process, designers can use these design guidelines to direct specific aspects of product development, ensuring that the product not only meets users' functional needs but also effectively conveys the intended emotional experience [16] (Table 5).

Table 5. Extraction of design points.

Aspect	Trend	Characteristics	Design Focus
Color	Polarization (colorful vs. monochromatic)	Coexistence of vibrant diversity and subdued monotony	Choose one style or innovate by blending both
Form	Minimalism dominates	Integration of technology and tradition	Simplify forms, smooth edges, and blend technological and traditional elements
Safety	Safety, durability, ease of use	Emphasis on safety, durability, and user-friendliness	Ensure safety, enhance usability, and improve durability

6 Design Practice

6.1 Technical Support and References

Market research shows most current chess - playing robots have large boards, support only one chess type, and lack portability. This makes them less appealing and in low demand. To solve this, we propose an innovative design using medium - free projection virtual chessboard technology [10, 17]. It can support multiple chess types. Paired with customized chess pieces, we can scale the pieces proportionally, providing a multifunctional experience and reducing family purchase, storage, and organization burdens. This expands application scenarios.

We'll adjust piece sizes according to internal mechanical design for different games. Custom - made chess pieces will be available for purchase to boost market adaptability. This not only increases product flexibility but also creates a sustainable sales model for accessories, forming a stable commercial chain. The technologies we use are mature, like the medium - free holographic projection in our virtual chessboard, which has wide applications and high adaptability.

Our innovative design overcomes traditional robots' limitations, enhancing user experience and creating a flexible, sustainable business model, laying the groundwork for future product development.

6.2 Overview of Product Design Philosophy

The Q-MATE Chess Fun Robot aims to initiate and advance chess education through intelligent means, addressing the challenges faced by parents and children in this domain while achieving the objective of edutainment. This innovative approach allows children to enhance parent-child interaction while simultaneously improving their chess skills. The general operational framework of the product is illustrated in Fig. 5.

The product features learning and entertainment modes, paired with a parent - side app, to meet children's chess - learning needs. Inspired by anthropomorphic designs with chess elements, it uses medium - free projection and a virtual chessboard, supporting various chess types. Customizable pieces make it multifunctional, reducing family burdens and enhancing user experience. Functionally, the AI offers personalized learning plans. The interactive platform has curated exercises and step - by - step courses for children's skill progression. The immersive chess environment provides a unique learning experience for both kids and parents. We adopt an encouraging teaching method, considering children's psychology, with facial, behavioral, and voice interactions. Emotional support after losses boosts children's learning interest. The chess education system also promotes parent - child communication, improving family life quality.

After the product design was finished, the showcase drew much attention from children and parents, with most parents showing great interest in this intelligent chess - education product.

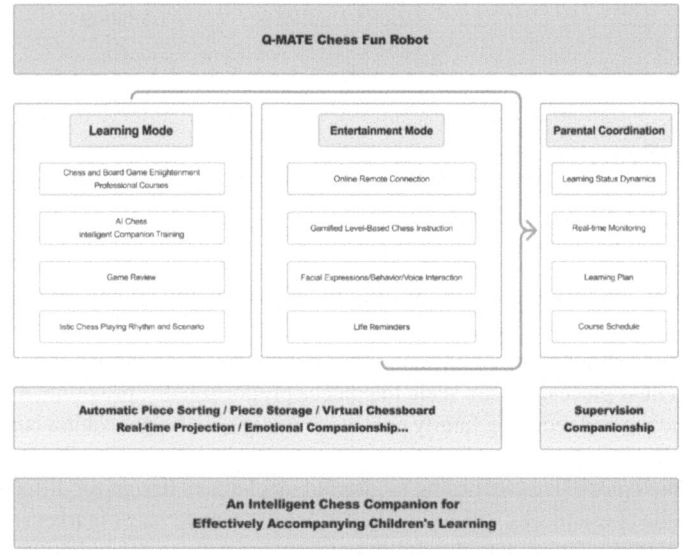

Fig. 5. Product Operational Framework.

6.3   Application of the Framework

This study developed a design framework integrating product design with user emotional needs, useful for product appearance and function creation. It helps select design tools and elements by required dimensions, better meeting functional and emotional demands. But it has limitations like a small sample library and less exploration of target users. Future research needs a more scientific theoretical base.

After product design, the demonstration drew much attention from children and parents. Most parents showed interest in this intelligent chess - educational product. A product showcase is in Fig. 6.

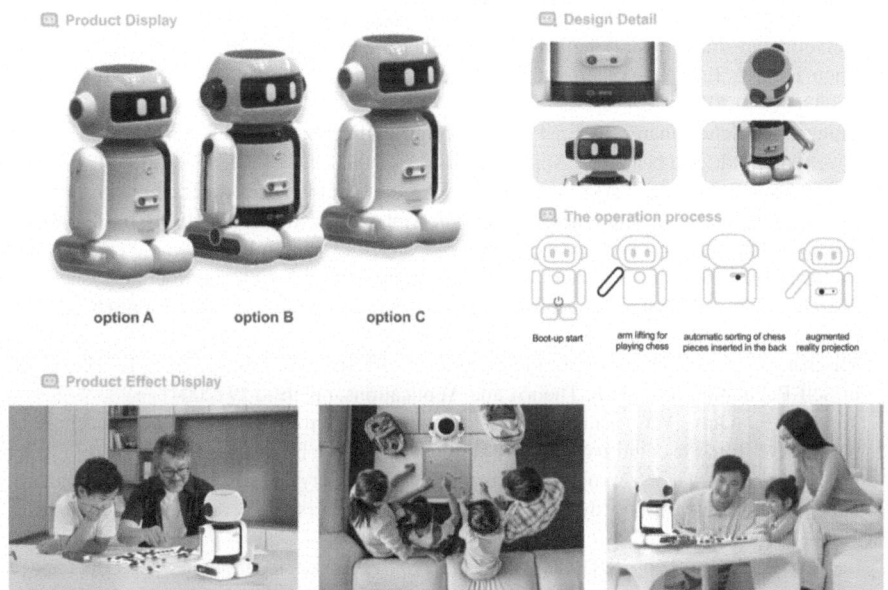

Fig. 6. Product Concept Demonstration.

7   Conclusion

This study focuses on improving the educational effectiveness of children's chess - playing robots through emotional and cognitive design. The aim is to develop products that suit children's psychological features and foster their intellectual growth. These robots act as teaching tools and external feedback sources, stimulating children's learning interest and promoting their intellectual and emotional development.

The design approach offers a systematic way to understand children's psychological and emotional needs, as well as robot functions. By meeting cognitive needs and enhancing emotional interaction, the product is optimized in function and appeal, increasing the depth and frequency of child - robot interactions. For designers, this framework provides a scientific basis for chess - playing robot design, emphasizing the importance of emotional and cognitive design in children's overall development.

In the future, with technological advancements and educational concept innovation, robot design will lean towards personalization and intelligence. Integrating AI and big data will help products adapt to individual differences, providing more customized learning experiences. Interdisciplinary cooperation will also bring more perspectives for the innovation of children's educational products.

References

1. McDonald, P.S.: The benefits of chess in education. ajedrez21.com (http://www.ajedrez21.com/circulares/descargas/BenefitsOfChessInEducation.pdf), (2000)
2. Zhou, F., Ji, Y., Jiao, R.J.: Emotional design. In: Handbook of Human Factors and Ergonomics, pp. 236–251 (2021)
3. Mugge, R., Schoormans, J.P.L.: Product design and apparent usability. The influence of novelty in product appearance. Appl. Ergon. **43**(6), 1081–1088 (2012)
4. Kołosowski, P., Wolniakowski, A., Miatliuk, K.: Collaborative robot system for playing chess. In: 2020 International Conference Mechatronic Systems and Materials (MSM), pp. 1–6. IEEE (2020)
5. Luqman, H.M., Zaffar, M.: Chess brain and autonomous chess playing robotic system. In: 2016 International Conference on Autonomous Robot Systems and Competitions (ICARSC), pp. 211–216. IEEE (2016)
6. Mischel, W., Ayduk, O.: Willpower in a cognitive-affective processing system. In: Handbook of Self-Regulation: Research, Theory, and Applications, pp. 99–129 (2004)
7. Yang, H.F., Guo, Y.Y.: Understanding personality from interpersonal relationships: a perspective from the cognitive-affective system theory. Psychol. Explor. **26**(1), 13–17 (2006)
8. Mischel, W., Shoda, Y.: A cognitive-affective system theory of personality: reconceptualizing situations, dispositions, dynamics, and invariance in personality structure. Psychol. Rev. **102**(2), 246 (1995)
9. Su, J.N., Wang, P., Zhang, S.T., et al.: Research progress on key technologies of product image modeling design. J. Mach. Design **30**(1), 4 (2013). https://doi.org/10.3969/j.issn.1001-2354.2013.01.023
10. Zhang, N., Huang, T., Zhang, X., et al.: 35.1: a novel in-situ interactive 3D floating autostereoscopic display system with aerial imaging plate. In: SID Symposium Digest of Technical Papers, vol. 52, pp. 244–247 (2021)
11. United Nations. Convention on the Rights of the Child [EB/OL]. (Sep. 2, 1990) [Apr. 30, 2018]. http://www.un.org/chinese/hr/issue/docs/24.PDF
12. Yu, S.M., Yang, L.Z.: A review of Mischel's cognitive-affective personality system theory. Adv. Psychol. Sci. **11**(2), 197–201 (2003)
13. Xiu, Q.Y., Gao, F.Q.: The integration of CAPS theory and personality psychology. J. Nanjing Normal Univ. (Soc. Sci. Ed.) (2), 89–93 (2005)
14. Gong, X., Guo, Z., Xie, Z.: Using kansei engineering for the design thinking framework: Bamboo pen holder product design. Sustainability **14**(17), 10556 (2022)
15. Ahmad, N.A.N., Lokman, A.M., Abdullah, M., et al.: Emotional kansei words for digital and pervasive product design. In: 2023 IEEE International Conference on Computing (ICOCO), pp. 386–390. IEEE (2023)
16. Mohd, L.A.: Design & Emotion: the kansei engineering methodology. Malays. J. Comput. (MJOC) **1**(1), 1–14 (2010)

17. Wei, H., Xu, J., Jiang, J., et al.: Holographic display in future automotive smart cockpit: application scenarios, interaction modals, and VACP analysis. In: Advanced Fiber Laser Conference (AFL2022), vol. 12595, pp. 200–209. SPIE (2023)

Competition, Cooperation, or Both? A Field Study on a Persuasive Smartwatch Fitness Application with Intergroup Competition for Promoting Physical Activity

Jiali Zhao[1] , Jie Yao[1]([⊠]) , Xinrui Guo[1] , and Tao Xiao[2]

[1] School of Humanities and Social Sciences, Harbin Institute of Technology (Shenzhen), Shenzhen, China
23s059008@stu.hit.edu.cn, yaojiejulie@hit.edu.cn
[2] College of Mathematics and Statistics, Shenzhen University, Shenzhen, China
taoxiao@szu.edu.cn

Abstract. Persuasive technology through interactive applications on wearable smartwatches holds great promise in the physical health domain. Its effectiveness for promoting physical activity might be further enhanced by social support strategies (such as competition and cooperation) from the Persuasive System Design (PSD) framework, particularly the combination of both elements in the form of intergroup competition. This study developed a smartwatch fitness application for the HarmonyOS platform with the core feature of intergroup competition, and evaluated its usability and effectiveness in the real-world setting through a two-week-long experiment on 16 smartwatch users. Under a within-subjects design, the field study assessed and compared daily exercise performance, attitudes, as well as user experiences with the application, based on the teammate relationship type (i.e., whether with a friend or a stranger). Results showed that intergroup competition effectively promoted the weekly total exercise time to an average of over 100 min regardless of teammate relationship type, while each type influenced exercise motivations and attitudes differently. The application also received positive user feedback, particularly from those new to smartwatches. This study provided empirical support for the use of smartwatch-based persuasive design to encourage healthier behaviors, and suggested the broader applicability of intergroup competition in digital interventions for increasing physical activity.

Keywords: Persuasive design · Physical activity · Smartwatch · Intergroup competition · Competition · Cooperation

1 Introduction

In recent years, as public awareness of health has increased, promoting physical activity as part of a healthy lifestyle has become a central goal in public health. However, many individuals still lack sufficient daily physical activity, mainly due to global shifts in living patterns and rising sedentary behaviors [1], the latter of which has been identified by the World Health Organization (WHO) as a leading cause of global mortality [2].

M. Schrepp (Ed.): HCII 2025, LNCS 15794, pp. 250–265, 2025.
https://doi.org/10.1007/978-3-031-93221-2_17

Fortunately, the field of behavior change research has helped address this concerning issue, with a focus on ways of modifying unhealthy habits and fostering healthy behaviors. One highly promising approach is to identify effective motivational technologies and systems to combat inertia in human nature and encourage regular physical activity [3], such as using persuasive technology to change user attitudes and behaviors [4]. At the same time, interaction design, which focuses on adjusting user behavior according to specific goals and contexts, provides ample opportunities for applying persuasive design in mobile health applications [5]. Specifically, the Persuasive System Design (PSD) framework [6], which includes socially oriented strategies like competition and cooperation, has become widely used in health interventions, as they leverage social influence to motivate behavior change [7]. However, pure competition or cooperation does not always yield positive outcomes. Almutari et al. [8] highlighted in their systematic review that while competition strategies in persuasive design for promoting physical activity generally yield positive effects, they may also lead to negative outcomes in certain cases, as do cooperation strategies. Chan et al. [9] also noted that wearable devices, especially smartwatches, are widely accepted for quantifying and visualizing physical activity data. These devices seamlessly integrate into users' daily lives, enabling the study of real-world activity patterns and enhancing persuasive technology impacts.

Therefore, future research should explore how to effectively leverage the significant interactive advantages of smartwatches, and utilize competition and cooperation strategies to motivate physical activity [10]. Given the existence of individual differences in response to persuasive techniques (e.g., competition that works for certain users may diminish the motivation for others) [11], this study will investigate the use of intergroup competition, a new strategy combining competition and cooperation, and evaluate its persuasive impact on physical activity through smartwatch technology.

2 Related Work

2.1 Persuasive Design

Persuasive design focuses on influencing and changing user behavior or attitudes through the application of persuasive technology. Rooted in the work of B.J. Fogg, persuasive design aims to leverage technology to address individual needs voluntarily and positively [12]. In the health domain, persuasive technologies have been found particularly valuable for smoking cessation [13], promoting physical activity [14], and encouraging healthy eating [13, 15]. Numerous studies and experiments have utilized these techniques to motivate healthier behaviors, aiming to prevent or reduce the risk of diseases [16, 17].

Key theoretical models related to persuasive design include the Fogg Behavior Model (FBM) [18], Fogg Behavior Grid (FBG) [19], and Oinas-Kukkonen's Persuasive System Design (PSD) [6]. The FBM, proposed by Fogg in 2009, serves as a theoretical foundation for persuasive design, while the FBG categorizes behavior change types, and the PSD model further elaborates on specific persuasive principles based on FBM. The PSD framework, developed for creating and evaluating persuasive technology, categorizes persuasive techniques into four components [6]: Primary Task Support, Dialogue Support, System Credibility Support, and Social Support. With 28 design guidelines, the PSD framework provides clear principles for software functionality and content presentation, in which competition and cooperation strategies are the focus of the present study.

2.2 Socially-Oriented Competition and Cooperation Strategies

Competition and cooperation are common and widespread social phenomena. They can be viewed as both external situational factors and stable personality traits, influencing individual social behaviors. In persuasive design, these socially-driven techniques have been extensively studied and applied. For instance, Malone and Lepper highlighted competition and cooperation as intrinsic motivators at the group level, emphasizing their potential role in persuasive technology [20].

In experimental social psychology, competition and cooperation orientations are classified as social orientations, i.e., stable personality tendencies reflecting preferences for outcome distribution between oneself and others. Deutsch [21] classified social orientation into cooperative, competitive, and individualistic, while Kelley and Stahelski's 'triangle hypothesis' posits that cooperation and competition lie on opposing poles of the same dimension, making simultaneous strong inclinations toward both unlikely [22]. Although competition and cooperation share benefits, such as increasing engagement and excitement, they also pose risks like stress and anxiety [23].

Fortunately, competition and cooperation are not inherently conflicting. Harackiewicz et al. [24] proposed an intergroup competition strategy, which integrated cooperative within-group efforts with between-group competition and leveraged the strengths of both strategies while minimizing their drawbacks. Specifically, intergroup competition had a more significant positive impact on exercise motivation than either pure competition or pure cooperation. This approach can enable participants to simultaneously experience the interpersonal warmth fostered by prosocial-oriented cooperation and the sense of competence challenge driven by proself-oriented competition [25]. As such, intergroup competition represents a promising persuasive strategy for future designs to encourage physical activity and overall well-being.

2.3 The Present Study

This study aimed to implement the intergroup competition strategy on the design of a smartwatch fitness application, and evaluate its usability and persuasiveness for promoting physical activity in the real-world setting. Compared with laboratory prototype testing, our research sought to track the daily exercise behaviors of users using the application, measure their user experiences in the field, and explore how different teammate relationship types (TRTs) during the intergroup competition might affect exercise attitudes and performance. Such findings on the synergistic effects of competition and cooperation will provide insights into enhancing the effectiveness of smartwatch-based persuasive applications.

3   Materials and Methods

To examine the impact of intergroup competition on physical exercise, it is essential to allow users to interact with and experience this strategy in a real system. Accordingly, we first developed a smartwatch fitness application for the HarmonyOS platform, based on the findings of an online survey experiment [26].

3.1   Intergroup Competition Interaction Design

Utilizing smartwatch technology (such as exercise data acquisition through sensors and data display), the fitness application integrates intergroup competition with visualized, precise activity tracking. Beyond basic fitness functions, intergroup competition allows the user to form a team with another user, compete against another team and track daily team performance and competition results. As shown in Figs. 1 and 2, the application features three main interfaces: the home page for activity tracking, a left-swipe for intergroup competition, and a right-swipe for weekly summaries and badge collections. The main interaction form of intergroup competition is represented by the outer ring on the smartwatch, as the dark-colored ring indicates the progress of user's team, while the light-colored ring represents the opponent team. A team wins when its ring surpasses the other team's.

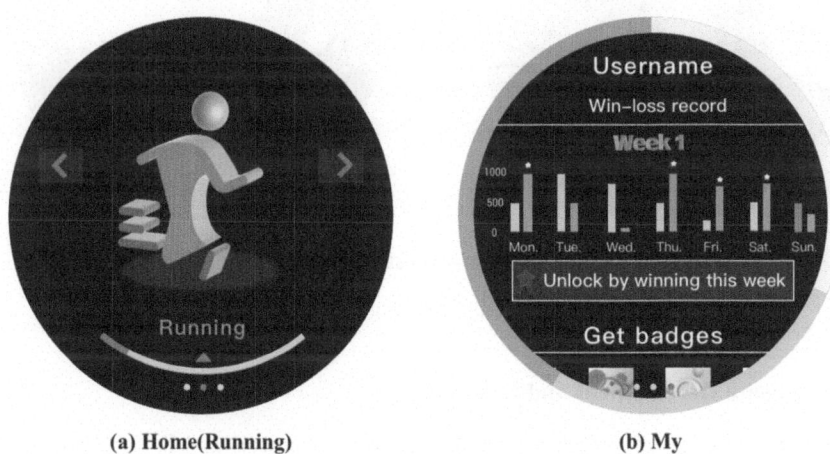

(a) Home(Running)   (b) My

Fig. 1. Fitness app main interfaces.

Figure 2 illustrates the interface of competition details, displaying either the current day's competition status (a) or the previous day's data (b). The left side shows the user's team activity (including names, exercise status, type, and duration), and the right side shows the opposing team's activity. The previous day's interface highlights the winning team with a special effect and rewards them with a badge. Additionally, users will receive a pop-up notification with the previous day's competition result the first time they open the application each day (c).

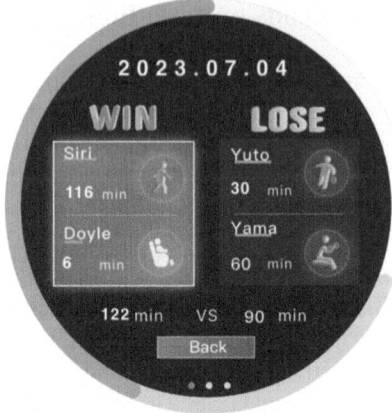

(a) Intergroup competition (Today)   (b) Intergroup competition (Yesterday)

(c) A pop-up notification each day

Fig. 2. Competition details interface.

3.2   Software Development and Design

With the front-end development utilizing a Vue-based framework and the back-end development using JavaScript and MongoDB databases, the software implemented functions such as acquiring all exercise data through sensors, data transmission, displaying user exercise data, earning badges, and changing teams, and so on.

3.3   Samples and Procedures

In order to assess the usability and effectiveness of this application, a field study combining quantitative and qualitative methods was conducted. First, a field experiment recruited users to form teams with either a friend or a stranger, and use the smartwatch application for intergroup competition in daily life for two weeks consecutively. The experiment employed a within-subjects design, since each participant was randomly assigned to a different team for each week. Following the experiment, one-on-one interviews were also conducted with all participants to further investigate user experience with the application, as well as attitudes towards its effects on exercise behaviors.

The experiment recruited college students regardless of gender and age. Participants were asked to bring a friend to participate in the experiment together, and a total of 16 participants were recruited, with the following conditions satisfied.

1. Each pair of friends had to be of the same gender.
2. Participants needed to have the capability to activate the eSIM function on the smartwatch (dual terminal).
3. Participants had to wear the smartwatch provided by the research team throughout the experiment.
4. Participants should not have any travel plans during the two weeks of the experiment.

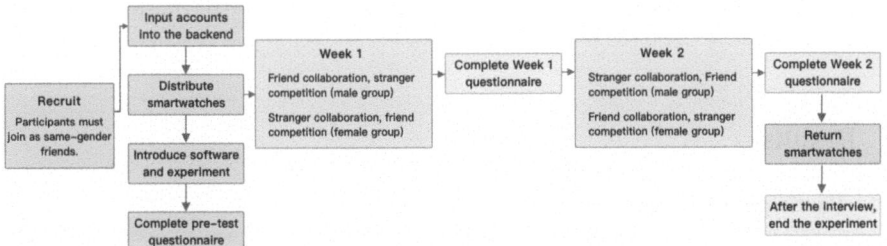

Fig. 3. Field study flowchart.

The study process shown in Fig. 3 required participants to wear and independently use a smartwatch for two weeks, with informed consent obtained to confirm their understanding and agreement. A printed user manual for the application, detailing its functions, was also distributed to each participant. The experiment alternated the TRT weekly in order to compare its influence on exercise performance and attitudes. Specifically, paired-participants competed against another team, with daily exercise time aggregated to determine winners at midnight. Weekly winners, based on the number of days winning, earned additional cash incentives. This study was approved by the Ethics Committee of Shenzhen University. All participant data were deidentified. Each participant was compensated with a cash incentive of 30 Chinese RMB (US $5).

3.4 Measures

In addition to objective exercise performance tracked by the smartwatch application, survey instruments were also used to collect data on exercise motivations and attitudes, as detailed below.

Exercise Performance. This variable was captured directly from the application's backend, which recorded real-time physical activity data and summarized the time of duration for each valid exercise session (in minutes).

Autonomous Motivation. This variable was assessed via the Behavioral Regulation in Exercise Questionnaire (BREQ) [27], which evaluates six motivation dimensions based on the Self-Determination Theory: external regulation, introjected regulation, identified regulation, integrated regulation, intrinsic motivation, and amotivation. Autonomous motivation is calculated as: Autonomous Motivation = 3 × Intrinsic Motivation + 2 × Integrated Regulation + Identified Regulation - Introjected Regulation - 2 × External Regulation - 3 × Amotivation.

Physical Activity Enjoyment. This variable was measured using the Physical Activity Enjoyment Scale (PACES) by Kendzierski and DeCarlo [28], known for high reliability and validity. For this study, "physical activity" was adapted to "this exercise mode" to gauge enjoyment under different teammate relationship conditions.

Goal Commitment. This variable was defined as the determination and willingness to pursue a goal over time, based on the Goal-Setting Theory. It was assessed using the Hollenbeck and Klein scale [29], which was validated across contexts (Cronbach's $\alpha >$ 0.798). The term "physical activity" was modified to "this exercise mode" for contextual alignment.

4   Results

4.1   Participant Characteristics

We first performed data cleaning and excluded one participant's data due to significant anomalies, identifying him as an outlier. All subsequent analyses were based on the cleaned dataset. Table 1 presents demographic statistics, including gender, age, and grade. Among the 15 participants, gender distribution was balanced, and all of them were master's students, with 54.4% of whom aged 22–23.

Table 1. Demographic statistics (n = 15).

Variable	Group	Sample Size	Proportion (%)
Gender	Male	7	46.6%
	Female	8	54.4%
Age	22–23 years	8	54.4%
	24–26 years	7	46.6%
Grade	1st-year graduate	7	46.6%
	2nd-year graduate	8	54.4%

Exercise Patterns. Exercise patterns include current exercise frequency, most frequently performed exercises, and liking for exercise, as shown in Table 2. Most participants exhibited regular exercise habits, with dual-player racquet sports being the most frequently performed activity (33.3%). The mean enjoyment level of exercise was 3.2 (measured on a 5-point scale), indicating a generally positive attitude toward physical activity.

Table 2. Exercise participation (n = 15).

Variable	Group	Sample Size	Proportion (%)
Current Exercise Frequency	2–3 times per month	2	13.3%
	1–2 times per week	9	60%
	3–5 times per week	3	20%
	Exercising almost every day	1	6.7%
	Running	3	20%
	Walking	2	13.3%
Most Common Exercise	Dual-Player Racquet Sports (e.g., table tennis, badminton, tennis, etc.)	5	33.3%
	Team-Based Ball Sports (e.g., basketball, soccer, volleyball, etc.)	1	6.7%
	Anaerobic fitness (e.g., weight training, bodyweight exercises)	2	13.3%
	Swimming / Hiking / Cycling / Jump rope	2	13.3%

Smartwatch Usage. Smartwatch usage includes prior experience with smartwatches/fitness bands and the specific models utilized, as summarized in Table 3. Among participants, 46.7% had never used a smartwatch or fitness band, indicating a nearly equal split between users and non-users. For those with prior experience, the Xiaomi Band was the most commonly used model, followed by the Huawei Band and Apple Watch.

Table 3. Smartwatch usage (n = 15).

Variable	Group	Sample Size	Proportion (%)
Ever Used a Smartwatch/Smart Band	Never Used	7	46.7%
	Huawei Band	2	13.3%
	Xiaomi Band	3	20%
	Apple Watch	2	13.3%
	OPPO Band	1	6.7%

4.2 Impact of TRT on Exercise Performance and Attitudes

Exercise Performance. Exercise performance was measured by the actual exercise time of duration recorded by smartwatches over two weeks. As shown in Table 4, the average weekly exercise time (in minutes) did not differ when the participants teamed either with a friend or a stranger in this field experiment.

Table 4. Overall weekly exercise time (n = 15).

Variable	Mean	Minimum	Maximum	SD
Weekly Exercise Time when teamed with a Friend	104.98	.00	534.22	158.31
Weekly Exercise Time when teamed with a Stranger	104.68	.00	406.25	143.18

Further analyses were conducted on the exercise data of each participant, by comparing his/her exercise performance on the basis of TRT, as illustrated in Table 5. Overall, exercise performance remained relatively consistent across the two types among the 15 participants, with 8 participants performing better with a friend and 7 better with a stranger. Also, the weekly exercise competition outcomes appeared to have little influence on performance, as the distribution was evenly balanced. However, an interesting gender difference was noted, as 6 out of the 7 male participants (i.e., 85.7%) achieved better exercise performance when teamed with a friend, while females showed the opposite trend.

Table 5. A comparison of exercise performance by TRT (n = 15).

Variable	Outcome	Gender		Total Sample Size
		Female	Male	
Better Performance with Friends	Won with Friends	2	2	8
	Won with Strangers	0	4	
Better Performance with Strangers	Won with Friends	2	1	7
	Won with Strangers	4	0	

In addition, we examined and compared the following three scenarios, i.e., participants whose exercise performance was similar between the two TRTs, those who performed better when paired with a friend, and those who performed better when paired with a stranger, with detailed exercise data from three typical users.

Similar Exercise Performance Between the Two Types. A female participant was paired with a stranger in the first week and a friend in the second week, winning in both weeks. As shown in Table 6, she exercised consistently for five days when paired with a stranger, stopping after securing the weekly win. During the second week, she exercised on only three days but with much higher daily totals in exercise time. Her total weekly exercise time was comparable between the two TRTs, suggesting that her performance was unaffected by her teammate or the outcome of team competition.

Table 6. Exercise performance of sample user 1.

Group	Day1	Day2	Day3	Day4	Day5	Day6	Day7	Total
Friends Week	117.62	99.52	0	175.98	0	0	0	393.12
Strangers Week	67.3	38.27	84.25	28.25	175.48	0	0	393.55

Better Exercise Performance with a Friend. A male participant exercised three times with a total of 49.22 min, when paired with a friend in the first week and achieved team victory. In contrast, he did not exercise at all during the second week when paired with a stranger, resulting in a loss (Table 7). The participant stated that he preferred exercising with friends due to the relaxing social interactions, while exercising with strangers was more taxing and less motivating.

Table 7. Exercise performance of sample user 2.

Group	Day1	Day2	Day3	Day4	Day5	Day6	Day7	Total
Friends Week	1.7	22.37	0	0	0	25.15	0	49.22
Strangers Week	0	0	0	0	0	0	0	0

Better Exercise Performance with a Stranger. A female participant teamed with a stranger in the first week, and completed two exercise sessions totaling 86.65 min, leading to a team victory. In the second week, when paired with a friend, she did not exercise and the team lost (Table 8). The participant preferred teaming with strangers, citing that the external pressure to behave appropriately encouraged consistent exercise. In contrast, familiarity with friends led to mutual slackness, reducing her motivation to exercise.

Overall, analysis of the above three typical users suggests that TRTs in intergroup competition may not significantly affect exercise behavior in smartwatch-based scenarios, although users could display different preferences towards the TRTs. This implies the broad applicability of the intergroup competition strategy for online applications, which allows for more flexible teammate options among users, such as providing virtual exercise partners.

Table 8. Exercise performance of sample user 3.

Group	Day1	Day2	Day3	Day4	Day5	Day6	Day7	Total
Friends Week	0	0	0	0	0	0	0	0
Strangers Week	0	0	0	46.93	39.72	0	0	86.65

Exercise Attitudes. Based on the questionnaires distributed at the end of each week, we collected data on participants' perceptions of different TRTs, goal commitment, task enjoyment, and autonomous motivation. As shown in Table 9, goal commitment was higher with a friend, while task enjoyment and autonomous motivation were greater with a stranger, indicating that TRT differentially affected exercise attitudes.

Table 9. Exercise attitudes by TRT (n = 15).

Variable	Mean	Minimum	Maximum	SD
Goal Commitment with Friends	4.48	1.00	7.00	1.523
Goal Commitment with Strangers	3.84	1.40	7.00	1.548
Task Enjoyment with Friends	4.12	2.25	7.00	1.285
Task Enjoyment with Strangers	5.07	2.25	7.00	1.403
Intrinsic Motivation with Friends	8.10	−4.25	19.17	7.411
Intrinsic Motivation with Strangers	9.82	−2.75	21.92	7.804

4.3   Insights from Post-experiment Interviews

We also conducted one-on-one interviews with all participants at the end of the field experiment, and the qualitative data were transcribed and coded, in order to gain deeper insights into participants' exercise behavior changes, attitudes toward exercise with different TRTs, and their experiences using the smartwatch application.

Participants' Views on TRTs. When asked about their preferred competition mode of TRTs, as shown in Table 10, most participants (n = 10) favored exercising with friends, as they noted that "*it is easier to communicate naturally with friends*," "*this mode exercise is more relaxing*," and "*doing something (i.e., exercise) together with friends is enjoyable*". On the other hand, a few participants (n = 4) preferred exercising with strangers, citing reasons such as "*making new friends*" and "*feeling motivated to exercise due to the inability to decline invitations from strangers*". In summary, those who preferred exercising with friends valued the social interaction as both relaxing and enjoyable, while those who preferred exercising with strangers were motivated by the opportunity to form new social connections.

Participants' Physical Behavior and Exercise Attitudes

Table 10. Preferred week of the competition (n = 15).

Variable	Group	Sample Size	Proportion (%)
Preferred Week of the Competition	Prefer Friends Week	10	66.7%
	Prefer Strangers Week	4	26.7%
	No Difference Between the Weeks	1	6.6%

Changes in Physical Activity. Among the participants, 68% (n = 11) reported changes in their physical behaviors during the two-week experiment, such as: increased exercise frequency and duration, with a generally more active approach (n = 6); exercising somewhat more despite lack of motivation, driven by the desire to win (n = 3); and exploring new forms of exercise, such as dancing with motion-sensing games. Additionally, some participants (n = 2) reported paying more attention to their heart rate changes.

Changes in Exercise Attitude. Participants reported several changes in exercise attitude during the experiment, including a more positive attitude towards exercise, no longer viewing it as difficult or exhausting, and feeling more motivated to compete with the goal of winning (n = 6). Some focused more on heart rate changes rather than strength or performance, aiming for overall fitness (n = 2). Others recognized the stress-relieving benefits of exercise and developed a consistent habit after a period of inactivity (n = 2), while one participant enjoyed the social aspect of exercising with friends.

Participants' Feedback on Smartwatch Usage. Participants' experiences with using the smartwatch for exercise were quite polarized. Some found that the sensor data provided by the smartwatch helped them clearly understand their exercise status and offered positive assistance, while others felt it interfered with their exercise status. This suggests that improving smartwatch data quality and display, as well as offering personalized solutions are needed and merit further research.

Overall, our results supported the effectiveness of the application for increasing physical activity among smartwatch users, considering the recommendation from the World Health Organization that adults should engage in at least 75 min of high-intensity exercises per week [30]. In addition, results from post-experiment interviews confirmed an overall positive attitude towards exercising, as over 70% of the participants noticed increases in both exercise frequency and intensity during the two weeks, primarily driven by the competitive environment in the smartwatch application. User experience with the application was also favorable, particularly for half of the participants who had not used a smartwatch before and appreciated the convenient functions and innovative design features.

5 Discussion

5.1 Theoretical Contributions

This study examined the benefits and limitations of stand-alone competitive and cooperative strategies, and contributed to a theoretical advancement of socially-oriented persuasive design for smartwatches. In the context of physical activity, it proposed the integration of intergroup competition—blending both competition and cooperation—into the Persuasive System Design (PSD) framework, thereby broadening the scope of social support in persuasive technologies. With a smartwatch-based persuasive fitness application designed and evaluated, this study focused on the role of intergroup competition in promoting physical exercise, as well as the influence of TRTs in online, non-face-to-face intergroup competition on exercise attitudes and behaviors.

Results from the two-week field study indicate that the application effectively enhanced participants' exercise performance and improved their attitudes toward exercise, with similar effects observed between the TRTs. Notably, the intergroup competition feature enabled participants to meet the World Health Organization's recommendation of at least 75 min of high-intensity exercise per week [30]. Meanwhile, both quantitative and qualitative data revealed that participants' exercise attitudes, measured across various dimensions, were influenced by TRTs. For example, task enjoyment was higher when exercising with friends compared to strangers. Regardless of the relationship type, however, the intergroup competition feature fostered positive changes in exercise attitudes, such as developing consistent exercise habits, enjoying physical activity, and adopting a more positive approach to exercise.

5.2 Practical Contributions

In persuasive design research, experimental materials were typically limited to prototype stages, with relatively simple methods for testing persuasive strategies. This study, however, went beyond prototyping by designing a fully functional fitness application centered around intergroup competition, developed with Huawei's HarmonyOS and implemented on Huawei smartwatches. The application incorporated visual interactive design to enhance the user experience and utilizes a Vue-based framework for front-end development, alongside JavaScript and MongoDB for back-end development. An experiment in the field for an extended period of time demonstrated the application's effectiveness in improving users' exercise performance, with strong evidence of its usability in helping users modify their exercise behavior and foster a more positive attitude toward physical activity.

5.3 Limitations

While the results of this study are promising, it is important to acknowledge some limitations. The sample size was relatively small, despite the detailed data collected during the two-week-long period. All the participants were graduate students aged 22–26, so the generalizability of the research findings may be limited and the effects on other age groups should be further examined. Nevertheless, this study marked an important beginning for more research on smartwatch-based persuasive design and evaluation in the wild instead of merely lab testing. Future studies can further explore the persuasive effects of intergroup competition in relation to different group sizes or usefulness of virtual teammates, implement persuasive designs on wearables with different functionalities, or validate the effectiveness of other persuasive strategies.

6 Conclusions

In contemporary society, physical activity is widely regarded as a fundamental component of a healthy lifestyle. Findings of this study provided empirical support for the power of persuasive technology applied on the smartwatch platform to encourage healthier behaviors. As a socially oriented persuasive strategy that takes advantage of both competition and cooperation, intergroup competition was effectively implemented on a smartwatch fitness application with good usability and user experience in the field. More important, it proved useful for motivating physical activity among daily users over an extended period of time, regardless of teammate relationship. This suggests the broader applicability of intergroup competition in online environments compared to offline settings, which offers more future opportunities for smartwatch-based persuasive design, contributing to the promotion of long-term health and well-being.

Acknowledgments. This study was funded by the Guangdong Philosophy and Social Science Fund (grant number GD22CJY05), the Guangdong Education Sciences Fund (grant number 2022GXJK425), and the Guangdong Adolescent Research Fund (grant number 2024WT007).

Disclosure of Interests. The authors have no competing interests to declare that are relevant to the content of this article.

References

1. Katzmarzyk, P.T., Powell, K.E., Jakicic, J.M., Troian, R.P., Piercy, K., Tennant, B., et al.: Sedentary behavior and health: update from the 2018 physical activity guidelines advisory committee. Med. Sci. Sport Exerc. **51**, 1227–1241 (2019)
2. Okely, A.D., Kontsevaya, A., Ng, J., Abdeta, C.: WHO guidelines on physical activity and sedentary behavior. Sports Med. Health Sci. **3**, 115–118 (2021)
3. Fritz, T., Huang, E.M., Murphy, G.C., Zimmermann, T.: Persuasive technology in the real world: a study of long-term use of activity sensing devices for fitness. In: Proceedings of the 32nd Annual ACM Conference on Human Factors in Computing Systems (CHI 2014), pp. 487–496. ACM, New York (2014)
4. Ndulue, C., Orji, R.: Exploring the impact of game framing on the motivational appeal of persuasive strategies and their effectiveness in behaviour change games. Behav. Inf. Technol., 1–18 (2024)
5. Némery, A., Brangier, E.: Set of guidelines for persuasive interfaces: organization and validation of the criteria. J. Usability Stud. **9**, 105–128 (2014)

6. Oinas-Kukkonen, H., Harjumaa, M.: A Systematic Framework for Designing and Evaluating Persuasive Systems. In: Oinas-Kukkonen, H., Hasle, P., Harjumaa, M., Segerståhl, K., Øhrstrøm, P. (eds.) PERSUASIVE 2008. LNCS, vol. 5033, pp. 164–176. Springer, Heidelberg (2008). https://doi.org/10.1007/978-3-540-68504-3_15

7. Orji, R., Oyibo, K., Lomotey, R.K., Orji, F.A.: Socially-driven persuasive health intervention design: competition, social comparison, and cooperation. Health Inform. J. **25**, 1451–1484 (2019)

8. Almutari, N., Orji, R.: How effective are social influence strategies in persuasive apps for promoting physical activity? A systematic review. In: Adjunct Publication of the 27th Conference on User Modeling, Adaptation and Personalization (ACM UMAP '19 Adjunct), pp. 167–172. ACM, New York (2019)

9. Chan, G., Nwagu, C., Odenigbo, I., Alslaity, A., Orji, R.: The shape of mobile health: a systematic review of health visualization on mobile devices. Int. J. Hum.-Comput. Interact., 1–19 (2023)

10. Longhini, J., Marzaro, C., Bargeri, S., Palese, A., Dell'Isola, A., Turolla, A., et al.: Wearable devices to improve physical activity and reduce sedentary behaviour: an umbrella review. Sports Med-Open **10**, 1–10 (2024)

11. Kaptein, M., Lacroix, J., Saini, P.: Individual differences in persuadability in the health promotion domain. In: Ploug, T., Hasle, P., Oinas-Kukkonen, H. (eds.) Persuasive Technology 2010. LNCS, vol. 6137, pp. 94–105. Springer, Berlin, Heidelberg (2010)

12. Fogg, B.J.: Persuasive Technology: Using Computers to Change What We Think and Do. Ubiquity 2002, Article 5 (2002)

13. Ndulue, C., Oyebode, O., Iyer, R., et al.: Personality-targeted persuasive gamified systems: exploring the impact of application domain on the effectiveness of behaviour change strategies. User Model. User-Adap. Inter. **32**, 165–214 (2022). https://doi.org/10.1007/s11257-022-09319-w

14. Oyebode, O., Ndulue, C., Alhasani, M., Orji, R.: Persuasive mobile apps for health and wellness: a comparative systematic review. In: Gram-Hansen, S., Jonasen, T., Midden, C. (eds.) Persuasive Technology: Designing for Future Change. PERSUASIVE 2020, LNCS, vol. 12064, pp. 163–181. Springer, Cham (2020)

15. Guan, V., Zhou, C., Wan, H., Zhou, R., Zhang, D., et al.: A novel mobile app for personalized dietary advice leveraging persuasive technology, computer vision, and cloud computing: development and usability study. JMIR Form. Res. **7**, e46839 (2023)

16. Taj, F., Klein, M.C.A., van Halteren, A.: Digital health behavior change technology: bibliometric and scoping review of two decades of research. JMIR mHealth uHealth **7**(12), e13311 (2019)

17. Aldenaini, N., Alqahtani, F., Orji, R., Sampalli, S.: Trends in persuasive technologies for physical activity and sedentary behavior: a systematic review. Front. Artif. Intell. **3**, 7 (2020)

18. Fogg, B.J.: A behavior model for persuasive design. In: Proceedings of the 4th International Conference on Persuasive Technology, p. 40. ACM, Claremont, California, USA (2009)

19. Fogg, B.J.: The behavior grid: 35 ways behavior can change. In: Proceedings of the 4th International Conference on Persuasive Technology, p. 42. ACM, Claremont, California, USA (2009)

20. Malone, T.W., Lepper, M.R.: Making learning fun: a taxonomy of intrinsic motivations for learning. In: Aptitude, Learning, and Instruction, pp. 223–254. Routledge (2021)

21. Deutsch, M.: Trust and suspicion. J. Confl. Resolut. **2**(4), 265–279 (1958)

22. Kelley, H.H., Staheliski, A.J.: Social interaction basis of cooperators' and competitors' beliefs about others. J. Pers. Soc. Psychol. **16**(1), 66 (1970)

23. Zhang, J., Jiang, Q.Q., Zhang, W.P., Kang, L.L., Lowry, P.B., Zhang, X.: Explaining the outcomes of social gamification: a longitudinal field experiment. J. Manag. Inf. Syst. **40**, 401–439 (2023)

24. Tauer, J.M., Harackiewicz, J.M.: The effects of cooperation and competition on intrinsic motivation and performance. J. Pers. Soc. Psychol. **86**(6), 849 (2004)
25. Ma, Z., Gao, Q., Tian, Y., Chen, Y., Yuan, Q.: Effectiveness of cooperative and competitive gamification in mobile fitness applications among occasional exercisers. Behav. Inf. Technol. **43**, 2401–2423 (2024)
26. Guo, X., Yao, J., Hou, S.: Smartwatch-based persuasive design with tailored competition and cooperation strategies for promoting physical activity. In: 14th International Conference on Applied Human Factors and Ergonomics (AHFE 2023). AHFE (2023)
27. Markland, D., Tobin, V.: A modification to the behavioural regulation in exercise questionnaire to include an assessment of amotivation. J. Sport Exerc. Psychol. Psychol. **26**, 191–196 (2004)
28. Kendzierski, D., DeCarlo, K.: Physical activity enjoyment scale: two validation studies. J. Sport Exerc. Psychol. **13**, 50–64 (1991)
29. Klein, H.J., Wesson, M.J., Hollenbeck, J.R., Wright, P.M., DeShon, R.P.: The assessment of goal commitment: a measurement model meta-analysis. Organ. Behav. Hum. Dec. **85**, 32–55 (2001)
30. World Health Organization. https://www.who.int/publications/i/item/9789240015128. Accessed 16 Jan 2025

AI-Enhanced Emotional Design: Transferring Biosignal Data to Music by Integrating Artificial Intelligence

Jing Zhao[1], Zhilu Cheng[2]($\boxtimes$), Chenxi Zhao[1], Mingyu Ye[1], Likai Chen[1], Xinran Zhang[1], and Yiming Ma[1]

[1] Beijing University of Technology, Beijing 100124, China
[2] Beijing Institute of Fashion Technology, Beijing 100124, China
zhilucheng_bift@163.com

Abstract. This paper explores an innovative approach to emotional design, that biological signal data is quantified and converted into music by integrating Artificial Intelligence (AI). Based on introduction of the theoretical foundations of emotion quantification and the techniques for biological signal collection, the design and implementation of fuzzy logic models is elaborated, capable of transforming physiological data into musical elements. Then the music is produced by using musical generative AI models. At the end, the application of the proposed route is validated through real-world cases and user evaluations. The results indicate that the design significantly alleviates stress, and improves emotional states. Finally, the potential applications and future research directions is discussed. This research provides a novel technological pathway for the field of emotional design and offers an innovative non-pharmacological intervention for mental health.

Keywords: Emotional Design · Biological Signal Data · Artificial Intelligence · Music Therapy · Emotion Quantification · Mental Health Intervention

1 Introduction

With rapid increase in the global population and the fast development of social diversification, there has been growing attention to mental health issues. According to the Mental Health Atlas report, an estimated 703,000 people worldwide died per year by suicide worldwide. It was estimated that 212.4 people per 100,000 population received mental health services for mental disorders [1]. Consequently, an increasing number of people are focusing on mental well-being and seeking solutions for emotional and psychological challenges.

In response to the rising demand for mental health care and a greater emphasis on emotional and psychological solutions, emotional design has emerged as a key area. This field addresses the growing awareness of mental health among users and provides support for improving user experiences. In addition to traditional emotional design theories, such as Donald A. Norman's hierarchical design approach [2], comprising the visceral,

M. Schrepp (Ed.): HCII 2025, LNCS 15794, pp. 266–285, 2025.
https://doi.org/10.1007/978-3-031-93221-2_18

behavioral, and reflective levels, new pathways of emotion-driven design methods are emerging in recent years.

Meanwhile, the rise of Artificial Intelligence (AI) has provided unprecedented tools and methods for the design field, elevating design practices to new levels. AI not only handles complex data analysis tasks but also simulates human cognitive processes through machine learning, even exhibiting a degree of creativity [3]. This technological advancement brings designers fresh perspectives and new possibilities, particularly personalization in emotional design. The core of emotional design lies in understanding and responding to users' emotional needs. Traditionally, this has required designers to possess sharp insight and a deep understanding of user experience. However, with social and technological development, user needs have become more diverse and personalized, making traditional design approaches insufficient for all user groups. The integration of AI offers a potential solution to this challenge. By collecting and analyzing vast amounts of user data, including behavioral patterns, preferences, and physiological and psychological responses, AI can reveal more nuanced user needs, guiding design decisions to better align with users' authentic emotional experiences [4].

This research focuses on how to integrate AI technology to enhance the quality of emotional design and explores a more personalized and responsive interaction approach. Traditional methods often rely on self-reports or predefined behavioral patterns, which may not accurately capture real-time or subtle emotional changes. In contrast, physiological data, such as heart rate and skin conductance, provide objective indicators that directly reflect an individual's emotional state [5]. This study aims to propose a design methodology that incorporates AI to collect and analyze users' physiological signals, understand emotional dynamics, and adjust design output behaviors or interface elements in real-time. By using AI to enhance emotional design quality, this research seeks to promote empathic communication between humans and machines, transforming emotional design products from mere functional tools into partners that can sense and respond to human emotions. This study not only strives to push the boundaries of technology but also aims to provide theoretical support and practical pathways for future emotional design practices, ultimately creating more human-centered, healing, and resonant products and services.

2   Related Work

With the rise of the emotional economy, the importance of emotionally-driven design is continually increasing. Currently, stress-relief and cathartic products aiming to alleviate stress through user interaction occupy the main market. As the era of smart technologies advances, emotional needs are being raised to new levels. While traditional theories of emotional design are well-established, methods for emotional design that support new intelligent interactive systems are still relatively scarce.

In recent years, there has been significant progress in research on emotional measurement and data-driven approaches in emotional design, leading to both theoretical and practical explorations. However, the integration of AI with emotional design remains underdeveloped, particularly in the areas of AI-assisted emotional visualization and auditory experiences. There is a notable gap in research regarding AI-supported emotional interaction design, which highlights an important direction for future studies.

2.1 Emotional Design

In recent years, considering consumers' emotional needs has become a key trend in product innovation, with emotional design emerging as a critical research focus. Theoretical studies on emotional design from semantic and qualitative perspectives are relatively mature, including Desmet's emotional measurement tools [6], Kansei Engineering theory [7], and Norman's "three-stage" viewpoint [2]. However, research on emotional interaction design from measurement and quantitative perspective remains in its early stages, particularly in leveraging emotional computing data to drive design.

The intelligent transformation of emotional design methods are supported by the measurement and interactive application of multimodal emotional signals. However, research on emotional interaction design is still limited. Significant progress has been made in emotional measurement, especially in collecting and analyzing multimodal signals like facial expressions, eye movements, speech, EEG, and behavioral data from multimedia platforms [8]. Multimodal emotional signals are applied mainly in product and service evaluation. For example, Lin et al. proposed a product shape perception engineering model based on eye tracking and EEG, predicting product shape imagery [9]. Liu and Wang analyzed users' emotional needs for car design by combining eye-tracking experiments with user comments [10]. Li and Qi developed an emotional interaction robot based on the "Perception-Cognition-Action" model [11], while Kim et al. introduced a shape-preserving multimodal sensing mask that collects pressure and humidity data to provide user feedback [12]. Rosello's HeartBit project enables human-computer emotional interaction through heart rate identification and color changes [13].

2.2 AI and Design

Currently, the integration of AI with the design field is deepening, revolutionizing traditional design concepts and giving rise to new tools and technologies. AI is widely applied in various aspects, from creative generation to personalized customization, significantly enhancing design efficiency and user experience. Researchers have leveraged AI for automated design, using big data analysis to quickly generate multiple design solutions [14]; at the same time, AI systems learn from vast amounts of case studies, providing designers with inspiration and innovative ideas. The dynamic iteration of solutions fosters the development of non-traditional thinking [15]. Furthermore, AI supports personalized services by customizing products according to user preferences, thereby increasing user satisfaction. AI also facilitates the integration with other cutting-edge technologies, such as advanced digital tools like AR and VR, and advanced ICT technologies like the Internet of Things (IoT) and cloud services [16], creating more interactive and immersive design experiences. Although research into the combination of AI and design has progressed rapidly, with significant achievements, achieving a comprehensive breakthrough still requires further exploration of practical applications and ethical considerations. AI is reshaping the design industry, bringing infinite possibilities to future design practices.

2.3 AI Design in Emotional Interaction

Research on AI applications in design is focusing on developing systems capable of accurately recognizing and responding to human emotions. These systems are utilizing machine learning, cross-modal art creation, and multimodal emotion recognition technologies, with a primary focus on emotional recognition and emotional design. In the field of emotional recognition, research is relatively mature; however, there is still considerable potential for development in the area of emotional therapy. Scholars such as Chan, K.Y. have explored the relationship between emotional customer needs and design elements by analyzing traditional survey data and big data from social media, identifying optimal settings for affective design elements [17]. Kaixin Han and others have attempted to create intelligent tools, such as a system for generating calligraphy fonts based on musical rhythm, which are designed to create according to the emotions conveyed, as well as models for emotion recognition using physiological signals [18]. These tools are capable of organically integrating quantitative emotional data with product design, offering new interactive experiences. Yue Lyu and colleagues have developed a tablet game combining AI and AR technologies, which enhances social-emotional learning in children with autism through personalized narratives and caregiver involvement. This game has shown significant effects in improving emotional recognition skills among children with autism [19]. Through these multi-faceted studies, it is evident that AI applications in emotional recognition and emotional design are becoming increasingly widespread and in-depth.

Emotional design has progressed in integrating emotional computing and data-driven methods. AI applications and research in design are growing rapidly. However, the integration of AI into quantified emotional design remains underexplored, which is essential for meeting emotional design needs. This paper uses AI tools to extract musical features from emotional data using fuzzy logic, converting them into inputs for music-generating AI. It then creates music based on emotional states, achieving emotional expression and therapeutic benefits.

3 Method and Framework

In order to establish the innovative emotional design method, a framework is set up as shown in Fig. 1. Five general parts are presented, including user research, AI music tools research, principles of Interactive Emotion-Musci generation, design practice and effect evaluation.

3.1 User Research

A variety of research methods have been employed to gain a deeper understanding of users' needs and emotional states. Through questionnaire surveys, we collected extensive data on users' basic needs and preferences. User interviews provided deeper insights, allowing us to hear directly from users about their needs and expectations. The emotion research section focuses on analyzing users' emotional experiences using both qualitative and quantitative methods, providing a more comprehensive understanding of their emotional responses. We used physiological sensors to collect users' physiological data, such as heart rate and skin conductance, which reflect their emotional states. Additionally, we conducted user interviews to gather their subjective descriptions of emotional experiences, offering a more holistic perspective for emotion.

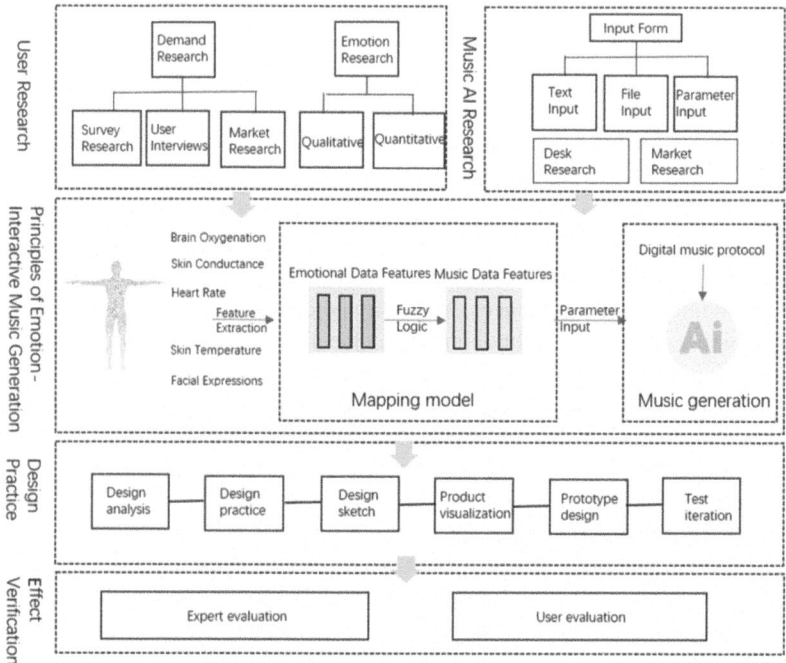

Fig. 1. Research Framework Diagram

3.2 Survey on Music AI

An in-depth survey of existing music AI systems was conducted. Music generation technologies are delved into to understand theoretical feasibility and practical principles. The characteristics and operational mechanisms of music AI are explored. Through this comprehensive survey, we aim to gain clearer insights into leveraging AI for unraveling the intricate connection between music and emotional responses.

3.3 Mapping Emotion Feature and Music Feature

The stage of emotion quantification and music generation involves converting the collected emotional data into music parameters. Key features are extracted from the emotional data. Essential patterns are identified. Then these features are mapped to music elements such as rhythm, melody, and harmony. Finally, leveraging AI technologies, music compositions that reflect the user's emotional state are generated.

3.4 Design

In the design module, our objective is to create a process that not only meets user needs but also embodies innovation. The design analysis phase includes design positioning, functional analysis, and innovation analysis, ensuring that our design direction aligns with both user demands and market trends. The design process begins with initial concept sketches, which gradually evolve into detailed product renderings, followed by process design and test iterations, culminating in functional demonstrations. This process involves interdisciplinary collaboration among psychologists, musicians, designers, and engineers to ensure that the final product meets high standards both technically and artistically.

3.5 Effect Verification

The effectiveness of the emotional design process for emotional healing is validated through user evaluation and expert evaluation. User evaluation is conducted by collecting feedback from users after they follow the process to produce their individual music, providing insights into the real-world effectiveness of the process. Expert evaluation involves inviting specialists from the fields of mental health and music therapy to ensure that our therapeutic approach is scientifically sound and reasonable.

4   Design Practice

The university student population aged 18 to 26 are of our concern, including both undergraduates and graduate students, for our design practice. This comprehensive project involves the development of an emotional healing music design process aimed at deeply understanding the emotional needs and life challenges faced by students in this age group. Using Artificial Intelligence (AI) technology, the personalized music could be generated tailored to students' physiological and emotional states.

Through this innovative design practice, we hope to offer university students a new, effective emotional healing tool that helps them achieve better balance across their academic, social, and personal growth.

4.1   User Research

To address the emotional needs and lifestyle characteristics of university students, data were collected through user interviews. 12 participants have been interviewed in this session. Open structure interview has been used in this session, to obtain the general emotional needs and lifestyles of the young group. It was found that up to 95% of the participants are experiencing different levels of anxiety, disorders or even depression. They are in urge of an effective tool that could heal the emotion and quite available to use in common.

4.2 Define Target Music AI

The application of music artificial intelligence (AI) in the emotional therapy of college students is focused in this part. To ensure that AI systems can understand and create music that resonates with the aesthetic preferences and emotional needs of college students, we conducted a survey of multiple AI music generation models. Based on the type of input data, the current mainstream AI music generation models can be broadly categorized into four types: text, symbolic, audio, and multimodal input. Details are shown in Table 1.

Table 1. Classification of AI Music Models

	Input data type	Input content	AI model
1	Text or semantics	Language text, keywords, emotional tags, or theme tags that describe music styles or emotions	Mubert、MusicGen (Meta)、Amper Music
2	Music symbol data	MIDI files, note sequences, beat information, and other music symbol data	MuseNet、Music Transformer、Magenta Studio、MusicVAE
3	Audio clip	Original audio wave form、spectrum diagram or other time-domain signals	WaveNet、Jukebox、Stable Audio、NSynth Super
4	Multimodal input	Text description Note sequenceImages, videos Action data EEG waves Multimodal data such as heart rate	MusicLM、AIVA、AI Duet、Flow Machines、Endlesss

After considering various factors such as the research objectives, data collection methods, the needs and interests of college students, and their habits, we decided to use the second category of AI models—those based on musical symbolic data—as our primary focus. Subsequently, we conducted an in-depth analysis and comparison of the strengths and weaknesses of several mainstream models within this category. Details are shown in Table 2.

Both Music Transformer and Music VAE require high musicality in the input audio (i.e., the input audio needs to be close to real musical fragments) and are not well-suited for processing audio directly generated from physiological data. MuseNet can generate diverse styles of audio but is overly time-consuming. After a comprehensive evaluation, Magenta Studio achieves the best balance between functional requirements and the feasibility of current resource conditions. Therefore, we ultimately selected it as the final music generation tool.

Table 2. Comparison of Music AI Models in 2nd Category

Model	Unique Features	Strengths	Weaknesses
MuseNet	Multi style and multi track music generation	Diverse styles and rich melodies	Lack of emotional control, time-consuming generation
Music Transformer	Single track long-term dependency capture	Strong melodic coherence and excellent structural sense	Single track only, does not support multiple instruments
Magenta Studio	Plug in music generation tool	Easy to use, suitable for non professional users	The generated results are limited by the functionality of the plugin
MusicVAE	Music interpolation and fragment deformation	Highly innovative and suitable for exploratory creation	Fragment based, weak control ability

4.3   Emotion Data Collection

In this part, we used facial expressions to collect emotional data. Facial expression measurement typically involves encoding facial behaviors. Facial expression data was collected from the participants using the Affectiva platform and its API through a PC program. Data collection can be conducted in offline video analysis, static photo sequences, or real-time online analysis by using the PC's webcam. During the online recording, the camera should be positioned directly in front of the participant's face, with a distance of approximately 40 cm, to ensure accurate capture of subtle facial expression changes. The system used Affectiva's default collection rate of 30Hz to calculate the emotion confidence score. For each frame, the system estimated the confidence level of different emotions based on facial feature extraction algorithms, classifying emotional expressions accordingly. Once the experiment begins, the Affectiva API would continuously record facial expression characteristics under various emotional states, automatically recognizing and analyzing emotions along with their corresponding confidence values.

The six basic emotions model proposed by Paul Ekman was exploited. It includes happiness, sadness, anger, fear, disgust, and surprise, which will be used to extract emotion data features corresponding to each emotional state [20].The emotional data collection process is exhibited in Fig. 2.

4.4   Extraction of Emotional Data Features

The features of emotional data are primarily used to quantify and analyze an individual's emotional responses, aiming to gain a deeper understanding of the patterns and intensity of different emotions. When Affectiva recorded the six basic emotions, it captured8 corresponding timestamps, providing real-time facial expression analysis results for each

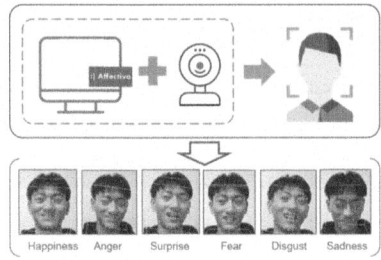

Fig. 2. Emotional Data Collection Flowchart

emotional state. From the output, multiple data points can be derived, including emotion recognition confidence, the time an emotion occurred, and its duration, which can then be transformed into graphical representations to express key features like emotional intensity fluctuations.

These features not only help accurately identify emotional types but also reveal the patterns of emotional changes. The process of extracting emotional data features is shown in Fig. 3. For example, the fluctuations of the six emotion confidence curves in the waveform indicate the variations in emotional intensity. The higher the peak, the stronger the emotion; the trough indicates that the emotional intensity is weaker or that the emotion is not present. The time when the peak occurs in the waveform curve of each emotion can also reflect the process of emotional transition and switching.

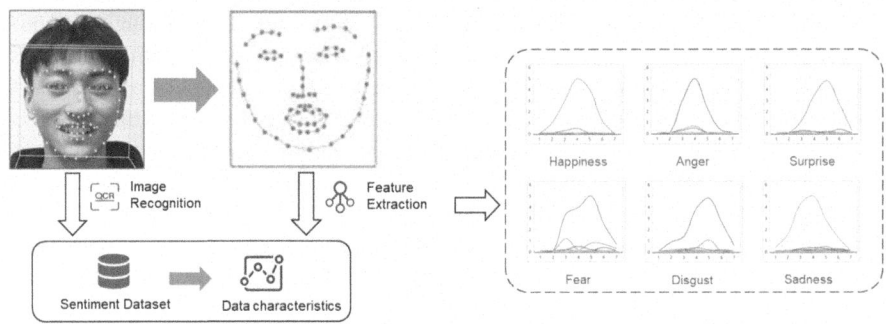

Fig. 3. Emotional Data Feature Extraction Flowchart

Periods with higher values in the waveform represent the duration of the emotion, which shows the length of time the emotion persists and its sustained pattern. If there were significant fluctuations during this period, it indicates that the individual's emotional variability was high. Some subjects were recruited from university students. The wave form of a subject's emotion is shown as an example in Fig. 4, which are happiness and sadness respectively. These data are crucial for extracting an individual's emotional traits, providing sufficient data features for subsequent feature mapping.

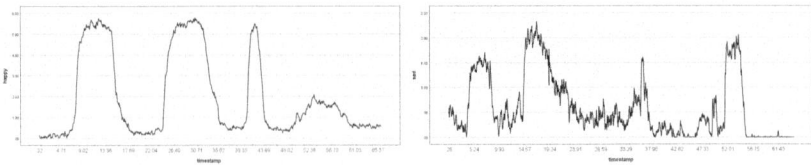

Fig. 4. Example of curve for happiness and sadness emotion

4.5 Mapping Model

A fuzzy processing approach was exploited, aiming at quantifying the complex relationship between an individual's physiological data and music parameters. This process began with defining fuzzy sets. There were three key fuzzy sets. Fuzzy set A was defined by three key physiological data features: the peak of emotional intensity, the onset time of emotion, and the duration of emotion. Fuzzy set B was for music parameters, we selected the three primary elements of sound: pitch, loudness, and timbre. These two fuzzy sets, after designing specific membership functions and creating fuzzy rules, would generate a mapped music parameter fuzzy set C, allowing changes in physiological states, such as increased heart rate, to be linked to music parameters through the fuzzy rules.

Following the fuzzy logic mapping was the defuzzification stage. It was a critical step in converting the parameters from the music parameter fuzzy set C into actionable information. In this process, the parameters in fuzzy set C would be transformed into concrete information that can be recognized by the MIDI (Musical Instrument Digital Interface) system, such as key musical elements as pitch, loudness, and timbre. Specifically, pitch, which is a crucial factor in the melody, is represented by 128 different numbers in the MIDI standard, where 60 corresponds to middle C (Do), the reference note for instruments like the piano. Loudness, or volume, ranges from 0 to 127, with higher numbers indicating louder sounds. Timbre is controlled by 128 MIDI controllers, with each controller adjusting different aspects of sound characteristics to achieve rich tonal variations.

The defuzzification process required precise calculations to ensure that the transformed parameters both faithfully reflect the original fuzzy logic results and achieve the best musical performance. The complete technical roadmap is shown in Fig. 4.

4.5.1 User Emotion and Physiological Data

Based on the facial expression data obtained from the volunteers listening to different styles of music in the previous section, three indicators were selected as inputs—the peak of emotional intensity, the duration of emotion, and the fluctuation of emotional intensity.

4.5.2 Data Collection

Based on the previous emotional data, further data preprocessing was carried out: the peak of the participants' pleasure emotion intensity was 5.77. There were three time segments during which the pleasure emotion intensity remained at a relatively high level

(>5), with a total duration of 12.583 s. The changes in emotion intensity are shown in Fig. 5. The peak of the participants' sadness emotion intensity was 2.23. There were three time segments during which the sadness emotion intensity remained at a relatively high level (>2), with a total duration of 1.691 s.

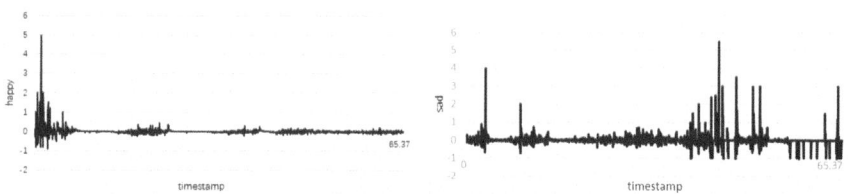

Fig. 5. The Fluctuation of Pleasure and Sadness Emotion Intensity

4.5.3   Design of Fuzzy Sets and Membership Functions

Based on the pre-processed data, two fuzzy sets were defined:

Fuzzy Set A (Emotion Data): This set included three characteristics—the peak of emotional intensity, the duration of emotion, and the fluctuation of emotional intensity. Fuzzy Set B (Musical Parameters): This set included three musical parameters—pitch, loudness, and tempo. The mapping relationship between emotion data and musical data is shown in Fig. 6.

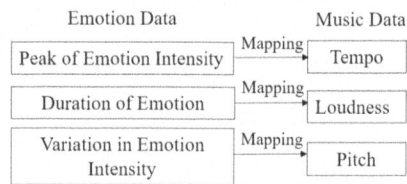

Fig. 6. Mapping Relationship between Emotional Data and Musical Data

We designed membership functions for each physiological data feature. The membership functions are illustrated in Fig. 7.

4.5.4   Design of Fuzzy Rules

The fuzzy rules were designed as following: If the peak of emotional intensity is High, then the tempo is Fast. If the duration of the emotion is Short, then the loudness is Low. If the fluctuation of emotional intensity is Long, then the pitch is Bright.

4.5.5   Input of Actual Data and Calculation

Based on the actual physiological data of our participants, we calculated the membership values for each feature according to the membership functions. The membership value of

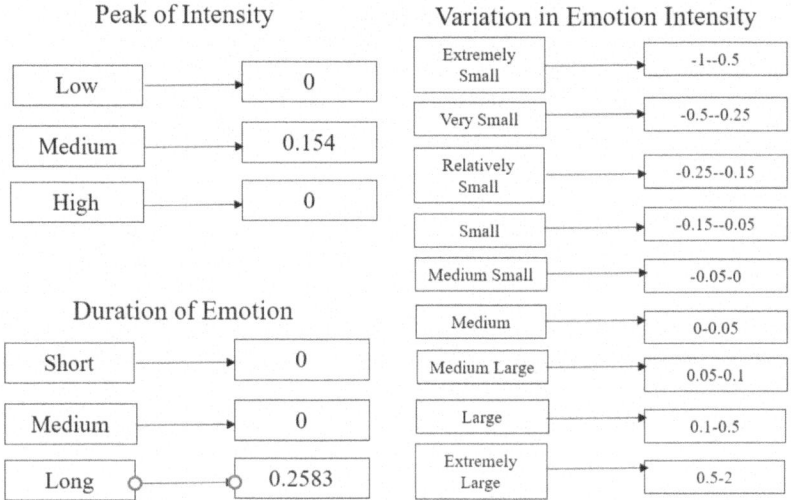

Fig. 7. Membership Functions for Peak Intensity of Emotion, Duration of Emotion, and Variation in Intensity

the fluctuation of emotional intensity was computed based on the membership function and varied over time. This process is illustrated in Fig. 8.

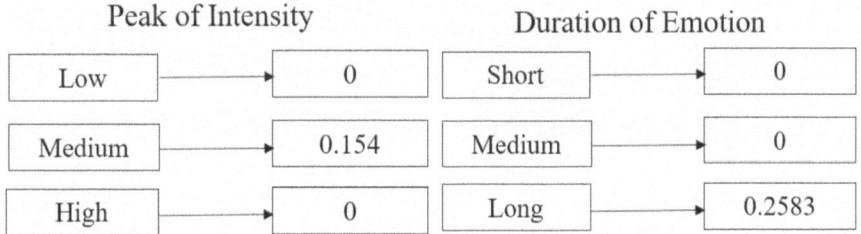

Fig. 8. Membership Degrees of Peak Intensity of Emotion and Duration of Emotion

4.5.6 Application of Fuzzy Rules and Defuzzification

For each physiological data feature, the its membership in the relevant fuzzy sets was calculated firstly. Then, the fuzzy rules were applied to map these features to musical parameters. Subsequently, Center of Gravity (COG) method for defuzzification was used to convert the fuzzy sets into specific numerical values.

After feature mapping, defuzzification was performed to obtain specific musical parameter values. Defuzzification is the process of converting a fuzzy set into a crisp decision or numerical value, which is crucial for applying fuzzy logic to actual music composition. Common defuzzification methods include the Center of Gravity (COG) and the Max Membership (MM) method etc. The COG method was adopted in our research. The formula for the COG method was:

$$COG = \frac{\sum (\text{ value } \times \text{ membership })}{\sum \text{ membership}} \tag{1}$$

where *value* is the value in the fuzzy set, and *membership* is the corresponding membership value.

After the peak was calculated, a triangular membership function was used to define the "Medium" fuzzy set for musical parameters, with parameters (80, 90, 100). The starting point a = 80, where the membership began to increase. The peak point b = 90, where the membership reaches its maximum value of 1. The ending point c = 100, where the membership began to decrease. Similarly, when calculating the duration, a triangular membership function was used to define the fuzzy set. The specific MIDI numerical values after conversion are shown in Fig. 9.

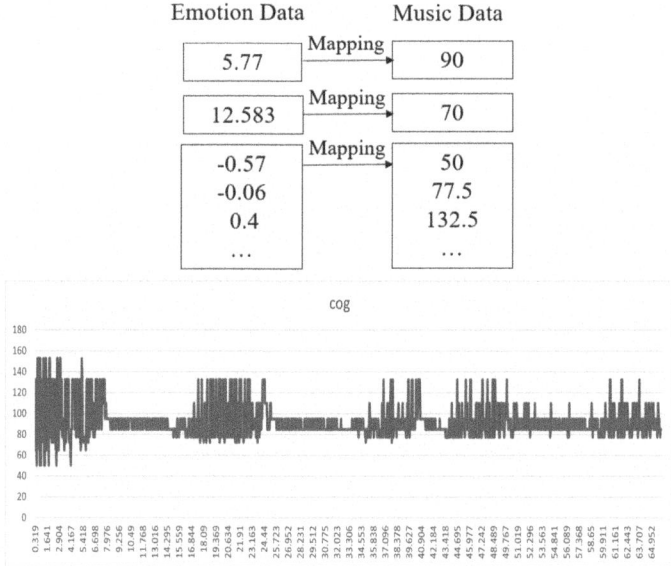

Fig. 9. Specific Numerical Values of the Mapping between Emotional Data and Musical Data(left), Curve of Pitch Data(right)

Based on these parameters, a piece of music that reflects the emotional state of the participant was generated according to the fuzzy mapping logic described above. The data operation process from collection to the final music was shown in Fig. 10. By employing fuzzy logic, emotional data could be effectively transformed into musical parameters, establishing a clear mapping relationship between the generated music and the user's emotional state.

4.6 Music Generation

The Musical Instrument Digital Interface (MIDI) plays a crucial role in the automation and intelligent design of music creation and production, serving as a foundational

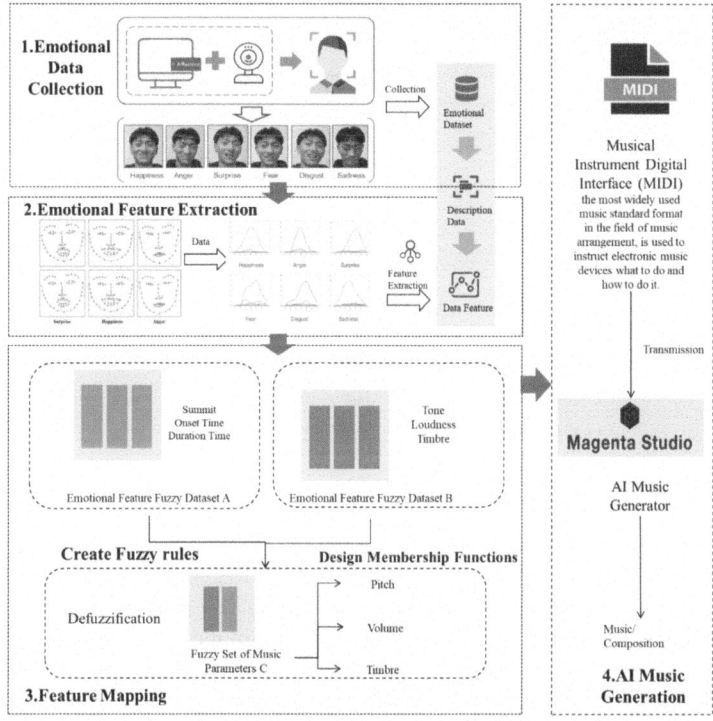

Fig. 10. AI Music Composition Technical Roadmap

technology for digital music. MIDI signal technology allows for the precise transmission of musical elements such as notes, rhythm, and dynamics, which are key factors in assessing the quality of music production. Therefore, in this study, we chose to input the deblurred data information—specifically, the notes that have been mapped through a blurring process—into the MIDI system. This step enabled the initial conversion of physiological data into musical information. The specific mappings are shown in Table 3.

Since MIDI-formatted audio only achieved the conversion from physiological data to pitch levels, the resulting music may not fully possess the aesthetic appeal of musicality. To further optimize the intelligence of music creation and the quality of the output, a Music AI tool named Magenta Studio was employed. This is an intelligent music plugin suite built on the Magenta open-source tools and models. It can recognize musical information in MIDI files and perform high-quality secondary creation rapidly.

Magenta Studio primarily used MIDI files as both input and output formats, leveraging their digital nature for easy parsing and manipulation of musical data. Magenta Studio includes five core plugins officially released: Continue, Generate, Interpolate, Groove, and Drumify. The basic logic used by the plugin is to input a segment of audio, and the plugin will use large models such as RNN and VAE for translation and prediction, and finally output a processed audio segment. Different plugins have different functions and can process audio differently. For example, Continue can extend the continuation of music segments, Generate can fuse and connect two pieces of music, Interpole can

Table 3. Correspondence between Deblurred Data and Pitch under Happy Emotion

	Data	Pitch	Pitch
1	50	B3	B2
2	65	C4	C3
3	72.5	D4	D3
4	77.5	E4	E3
5	85	F4	F3
6	95	G4	G3
7	110	A4	A3
8	132.5	B4	B3
9	152.5	C5	C4
10	167.5	--	D4

extract the features of two audio and superimpose them to generate a new audio, Groove can add a suitable rhythm melody to the main melody you provide, and Drumify can convert the main melody you provide to it into a rhythm melody (Figs. 11, 12, 13, 14, 15 and 16).

To make the generated melody more rich, the Interpolate plugin was firstly used to superimpose two MIDI files, which were obtained from two sets of physiological data of the same subject in both happy and sad moods.

Then the main melody (Interpolate Melody) was generated by the overlay into the Groove plugin to obtain the rhythm melody (Groove Drums) that was most compatible with Melody.

Finally, Melody and Drums were merge to obtain the final melody. Whether it's overlaying melodies or generating rhythm melodies that match the main melody, the above operations can produce multiple results at once. Users could choose based on their personal preferences and feelings.

4.7 User Experience Evaluation

To evaluate the effectiveness of the emotional design method and verify its ability to meet the daily emotional healing needs of young users, an evaluation was conducted by combining actual user experience with questionnaire surveys, referring the design principles and user requirements of emotional healing design. The evaluation process was as following:

(1) 30 users(14 male, 16 female) aged between 18–26 were invited randomly to participate in the usage experiment. Before the trial, the process was introduced to the users, followed by hands-on operation.
(2) During the trial, users were asked to report their usage experiences, emotional state changes, and feelings, and complete an evaluation questionnaire.

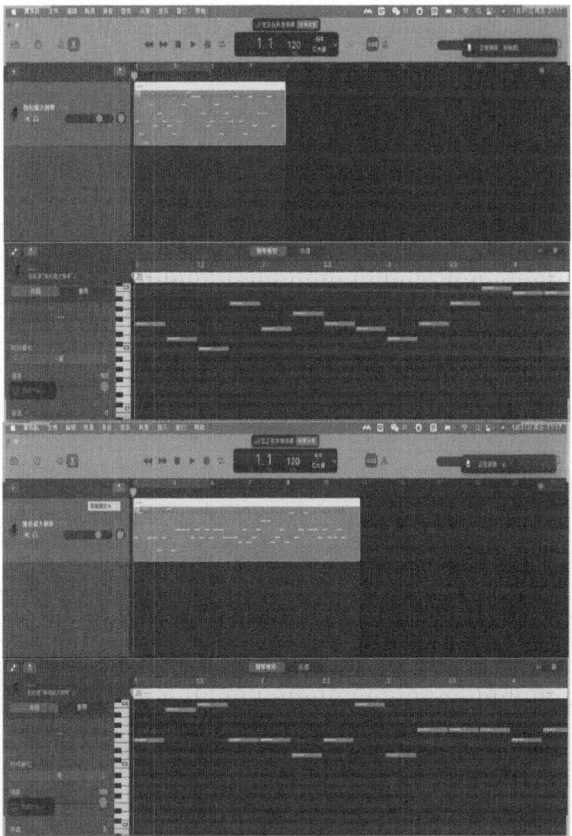

Fig. 11. Generation of MIDI files from deblurred emotion data(happiness, sadness)

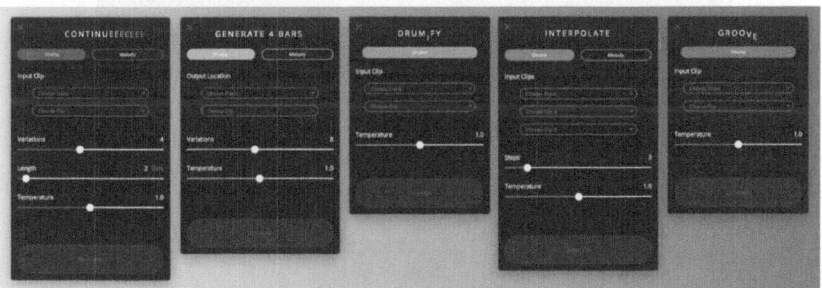

Fig. 12. User interface display of five basic plugins

(3) The questionnaire used a 5-point Likert scale, where 1 indicated strong disagreement with the statement, and 5 indicated strong agreement, with varying degrees in between. The questionnaire included the following questions: 1) Correlation: The produced music correlate closely with my present emotional state. 2) Control: I am

Fig. 13. Overlay two audio segments using the *Interpolate* plugin for the main melody file

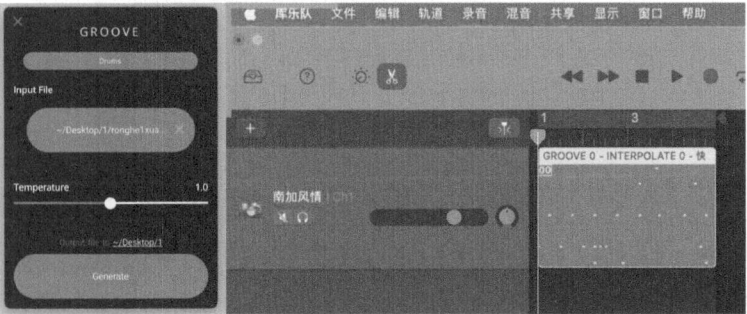

Fig. 14. Drum melody file obtained from the main melody file using the *Groove* plugin

Fig. 15. Final music piece

controlling or influencing the music by myself. 3) Enjoyment: It provides me with a pleasant experience. 4) Comfort: Using this emotional transforming process makes me feel comfortable. 5) Stress relief: Using this system helps reduce my stress. 6)

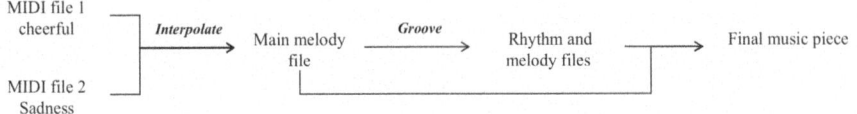

Fig. 16. Magenta Studio uses partial technology roadmap

Healing effect: Using this system when feeling down helps restore my mood. The questionnaire results are shown in Table 4.

(4) Analysis of the scoring results revealed that users generally think that the porcess performs excellently in relieving stress, maintaining emotional stability, and restoring a positive state of mind, proving that the design largely met the target users' expectations for an emotional healing deal.

Table 4. Product evaluation questionnaire score results

Evaluation Levels	Usability Level		Experience Level		Emotional Level	
Questions	Correlation	Control	Enjoyment	Comfort	Stress relief	Healing effect
Average Score	3.33	3.20	3.13	3.50	4.00	4.13

5   Discussion

5.1   Research Significance and Innovations

1) Integration of emotional design and AI was explored, particularly how physiological signals were used to generate personalized music for emotional therapy. Emotional design traditional qualitative methods was transformed to data-driven quantitative approaches.

2) Interdisciplinary collaboration was emphasized. The synergistic roles of psychology, musicology, computer science, and design were discussed, in this study, highlighting the importance of interdisciplinary collaboration in addressing complex emotional design challenges.

3) New pathways for non-pharmacological interventions was explored. This AI-based emotional design method offers a novel non-pharmacological approach for mental health interventions, especially its potential applications in addressing contemporary mental health crises.

5.2   Research Limitations

There are two major limitations in this research. Firstly, the physiological signals discussed in this study is facial expressions. In future additional types of physiological signals (e.g., heart rate, skin conductance) could be considered to enhance the accuracy of emotion quantification. Secondly, influencing factors are limited in the current study, such as the diversity of generated music, depth of emotional expression, and adaptability to users from different cultural backgrounds.

6 Conclusion

This study has explored the innovative integration of Artificial Intelligence (AI) in emotional interaction design, specifically focusing on transforming physiological signals into therapeutic music. By developing a novel method that quantifies emotional states through biosignal data and generates personalized music using AI, this research has demonstrated the potential of AI-driven emotional design in enhancing mental well-being and alleviating stress. The proposed framework and methodology have shown significant promise in achieving emotional healing through music. The process of emotion quantification, mapping emotional features to musical elements, and generating music using AI tools such as Magenta Studio have been validated through user evaluations. The results indicate that the system effectively correlates with users' emotional states, providing a sense of control, enjoyment, and comfort. Importantly, the design has proven effective in stress relief and emotional restoration, with users reporting positive experiences in terms of both usability and emotional impact.

However, there are several directions for future research and development. The integration of multi-biosignals and the exploration of advanced AI models could further improve the precision and depth of emotional quantification. Additionally, the ethical and privacy concerns associated with the collection and processing of physiological data must be carefully addressed to ensure user trust and data security. In conclusion, this research provides a foundation for the development of AI-driven emotional design methods, offering a novel approach to mental health intervention through the creative use of technology and design.

Acknowledgments. This paper was supported by Research Project on Ideological And Political Work in Beijing Universities (BJSZ2024YB47); The General Project of the Beijing Higher Education Society (MS2024165).

References

1. World Health Organization. Mental health atlas 2020. World Health Organization (2021). https://iris.who.int/handle/10665/345946
2. Norman, D.: Emotional design: why we love (or hate) everyday things. Basic Books (2007)
3. Xu, Y., Zhou, Q., Deng, J., Zhang, Y., Fu, X.: Application and development of artificial intelligence in design industry. Packaging Eng. **45**(08), 1–10 (2024).https://doi.org/10.19554/j.cnki.1001-3563.2024.08.001
4. Yan, H., Liu, J., Qin, J.: Emotional interaction design in artificial intelligence context. Packaging Eng. **41**(06), 13–19 (2020). https://doi.org/10.19554/j.cnki.1001-3563.2020.06.003

5. Wang, S., Xu, Z., Li, Y., Mather, M., Bayrak, R.G., Chang, C.: Reconstructing physiological signals from fMRI across the adult lifespan. arXiv preprint arXiv:2408.14453 (2024)

6. Desmet, P.: Measuring emotion: development and application of an instrument to measure emotional responses to products. In: Blythe, M., Monk, A. (eds) Funology 2: From Usability to Enjoyment, 391–404 (2018). https://doi.org/10.1007/978-3-319-68213-6_25

7. Mohd Lokman, A.: Design & Emotion: the kansei engineering methodology. Malays. J. Comput. (MJOC) 1(1), 1–14 (2010)

8. Yao, H.X., et al.: An overview of research development of affective computing and understanding. J. Image Graph. 27(06), 2008–2035 (2022). https://doi.org/10.11834/jig.220085

9. Lin, L., Yin, X., Guo, Z., Deng, Y., Yang, P.: KE model of product form based on eye-tracking weighting and image cognition by EEG. Packaging Eng. 43(14), 37–44 (2022)

10. Liu, C., Wang, Z.Q.: A method for obtaining emotional design requirements of automotive styling based on Kansei engineering and online reviews: A case study of the design of automotive front fascia. J. Anhui Univ. Technol. (01), 62–70 (2022)

11. Jia, L., Na, Q.: Research on design of robots accompanying empty nesters based onemotional computation. Ind. Design 11, 26–28 (2021)

12. Kim, J.H., et al.: A conformable sensory face mask for decoding biological and environmental signals. Nature Electron. 5(11), 794–807 (2022)

13. Zhao, J., Cheng, Z., Liu, X., Li, J.: An emotion driven intelligent product design method from a quantitative perspective. In: Marcus, A., Rosenzweig, E., Soares, M.M. (eds) International Conference on Human-Computer Interaction, pp. 641–660. Springer Nature Switzerland, Cham (2023)

14. Wang, S.S.: Application and development strategies of AIGC technology in fashion design [J/OL]. Textile Dyeing and Finishing J. SSN 1005–9350,CN 32–1420/TQ .http://kns.cnki.net/kcms/detail/32.1420.TQ.20241213.1414.002.html

15. Zou, Z., Chen, S.: Research on furniture design based on AI image generation technology. China Forest Products Ind. 61(11), 62–67 (2024). https://doi.org/10.19531/j.issn1001-5299.202411011

16. Wang, Z., Liang, X., Li, M., Li, S., Liu, J., Zheng, L.: Towards cognitive intelligence-enabled product design: the evolution, state-of-the-art, and future of AI-enabled product design. J. Ind. Inf. Integr., 100759 (2024)

17. Chan, K.Y., et al.: Affective design using machine learning: a survey and its prospect of conjoining big data. Int. J. Comput. Integr. Manuf. 33(7), 645–669 (2020)

18. Han, K., You, W., Zuo, H., Li, M., Sun, L.: Glancing back at your hearing: generating emotional calligraphy typography from musical rhythm. Displays 80, 102529 (2023)

19. Lyu, Y., et al.: EMooly: supporting autistic children in collaborative social-emotional learning with caregiver participation through interactive AI-infused and AR activities. Proc. ACM Interact. Mobile, Wearable Ubiquitous Technol. 8(4), 1–36 (2024)

20. Ekman, P., Friesen, W.V.: Unmasking the face: a guide to recognizing emotions from facial clues. Ishk (2003)

21. Shi, D.: The automatic conversion of electronic music melody by MIDISignals based on deep learning. (11), 20–23+28 (2024).https://doi.org/10.14016/j.cnki.1001-9227.2024.11.020

22. Zou, R.: Application of artificial intelligence accompaniment generationtechnology in mixed electronic music "LiuYinMingZheng". Wuhan Conservatory Music (2023).https://doi.org/10.27385/d.cnki.gwyyc.2023.000022

Designing Emotional Interaction in Smart Homes: Actor-Network Theory for Enhanced User Experience

JiaHui Zhou(ID) and YuLin Zhao(✉)(ID)

Faculty of Innovation and Design, City University of Macao, Macao 999078, China
U23091110051@cityu.edu.mo

Abstract. With the rapid development of the Internet of Things technology, the application of smart home systems in modern families is becoming increasingly popular, which has greatly changed people's lifestyle. However, while smart home systems have made significant progress in automation and functionality, existing systems still have many shortcomings in emotional interaction design. Users not only expect the smart home to have basic operating functions, but also expect the system to provide a more personalized interactive experience with emotional resonance through emotional recognition and emotional feedback. The theory of actor network provides an important analytical framework for this study. Through user interviews, questionnaires and behavior analysis, this study constructed an actor network model of emotional interaction in smart homes and identified the "forced crossing point". The crossing point is a key node in emotional interaction design, covering the accurate capture of users' emotional needs, seamless collaboration between devices, and the accuracy of AI emotion recognition. Based on the analysis of point, the research proposes an emotional interaction design strategy from the instinct level, the behavior level and the reflection level to optimize the sensory experience, interaction logic and continuous iteration. Future research can further refine the emotion interaction design strategy, and combine advanced technologies such as artificial intelligence and big data to achieve more accurate and personalized emotion recognition and feedback. At the same time, it is necessary to pay attention to the protection of user privacy and ensure that technological development does not harm the rights and interests of users.

Keywords: Actor Network Theory · Smart Home · Emotional Interaction Design · Emotional Experience · Emotion Recognition and Equipment Collaboration

1 Research Background

1.1 Smart Home Development Trend

With the concept of the Internet of Things and the corresponding technological development, people have also put forward higher requirements for future life. Smart home, as a sub-industry in the development of the Internet of Things, has become an inevitable

M. Schrepp (Ed.): HCII 2025, LNCS 15794, pp. 286–307, 2025.
https://doi.org/10.1007/978-3-031-93221-2_19

development trend to improve people's quality of life [1]. Compared with traditional home products, smart home is a residential management system that integrates products related to home life [2]. As the scene carrier of smart home realization, the home is the main place to realize interactive behavior between users and products, which carries not only the daily behavior of users, but also the emotional elements of users [3]. In the future, any smart home may be able to proactively understand the needs of users, so as to provide users with personalized smart home services [4].

1.2 Smart Home Existing Problems

In most application scenarios, smart homes still play the role of servants, and their services still rely on the user's "instructions" to a certain extent and obey the user's requirements. How to cultivate products to establish emotional relationships with people has not been fully concerned [5]. The logic of mechanical, submissive behavior is not the norm of human existence. This lack not only limits the further improvement of the user experience of smart home products, but also leads to insufficient mining of market demand, and it is difficult to stimulate the broad interest and sustained enthusiasm of consumers, which explains to a certain extent why the smart home market has not yet shown an explosive growth trend, but is in a relatively stable and lukewarm state of development.

1.3 The Importance of Emotional Interaction in Smart Home

At present, there is little research on the emotional interaction mode between smart home assistants and users. The improvement of the degree of emotional interaction will improve the user's satisfaction to some extent [6]. This status quo reflects that although smart homes have made significant progress in functionality and can perform a variety of complex tasks to meet the practical needs of users, there is still a huge development space and challenge in building a more delicate and humane emotional connection with users.

2 Literature Review

2.1 Smart Home

In recent years, many technology giants, such as Apple HomeKit, Ali Alink, Huawei HiLink, etc., have launched smart home development platforms, and gradually expanded the smart home ecosystem with AI as the core [7].

As shown in Fig. 1, at present, the common smart home products on the market are:

a) Instrumental products, such as widely used smart door locks [8].
b) Sensing human-like physical products, such as chatbots that can communicate with people, such as smart speakers [9].
c) Connect interpersonal products, such as smart refrigerators that negotiate purchases with external retail stores on behalf of users [10].

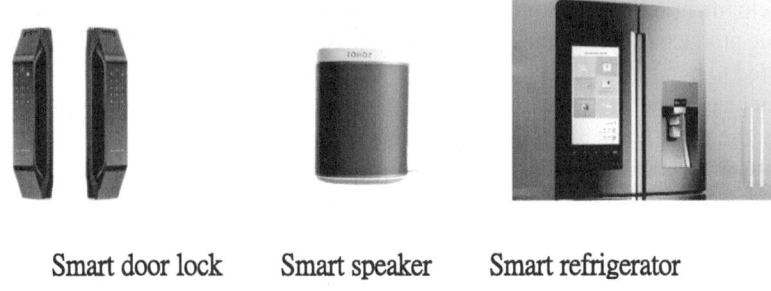

Smart door lock   Smart speaker   Smart refrigerator

Fig. 1. Smart home product diagram.

This study will focus on the chatbot category of sentient human-like materiality products in the smart home, whose market size is expanding rapidly, from $250 million in 2017 to more than $1.34 billion in 2024.Chatbots are text-based virtual service robots that interact with users to provide services [11]. They are based on natural language processing to simulate human-to-human communication, potentially replacing real-life or computer-mediated contact with human service providers [12]. Since chatbots can not only handle service requests 24/7, but also have real-time and personalized interactions, they can mimic real-life human interactions [13, 14]. In particular, the additional social-emotional and relational layers of user interaction with chatbots are in contrast to interactions with traditional self-service technologies, which are only functional. Chatbot, as a kind of computer program capable of dialogue and interaction with human beings, can be subdivided into three main types according to its core functions and design intention: information retrieval type, dialogue understanding type and task execution type [15]. Specifically, information retrieval chatbots mainly focus on providing users with required information and knowledge query services, they have been widely used in online customer service systems, intelligent assistant platforms and various question-and-answer services, aiming to provide users with instant and accurate information support, for example, our common FAQ (frequently asked questions) chatbots belong to this category. Conversational understanding chatbots can not only answer users' questions, but also deeply understand and generate natural language content, and at the same time, show a keen perception and deep understanding of context in the dialogue process, Microsoft's Xiaoice and Apple's Siri are outstanding representatives of this type. Task-performing chatbots, on the other hand, focus on completing specific tasks. They usually have rich domain knowledge and business logic, and collect necessary information through effective dialogue with users to ensure the smooth completion of tasks. For example, the chatbot we use when booking tickets online is a typical application of such robots.

In addition, in terms of the depth and nature of interaction with human users, chatbots can be further divided into three categories: companion, intelligent assistant and task-oriented. Among them, virtual companion robots can carry out in-depth dialogue and communication with users, which often touch on the emotional level to provide users with emotional comfort and companionship. Intelligent assistant and task-oriented robots are more focused on specific areas, aiming to quickly meet the actual needs of users through the most concise and efficient means of communication. Although the two have their own features, they both reflect the ultimate pursuit of efficient service and user satisfaction.

This paper focuses on chatbots in humanoid products in the field of smart home research, and focuses more on companion robots in chatbots. Liu Hailong gave this kind of intelligent chatbot a unique title - "new ordinary people", which means that although they have a wide range of knowledge, they maintain an ordinary state in the cognitive level [16]. These bots follow the behavior patterns of "ordinary individuals" and aim to optimize the accuracy of replies and the flow of conversations, seeking to eliminate ambiguity and misunderstanding and ensure smooth communication. Although this design strategy is excellent in terms of security and rationality, it has been criticized for its lack of innovation and personality characteristics, which has caused a lot of criticism. The current research on smart home can be divided into two parts, smart home products and smart home systems. The research theme can be divided into two directions. First, from the product, product safety, technological innovation, product innovation and other content research. Second, from the perspective of user use, the user needs, user interaction experience and other contents are studied [17].

2.2 Emotional Interaction

Beginning in the 1950s, design was primarily concerned with function, utilitarian ethics, and aesthetics. In the face of the challenges posed by the growing interest in emotion in the above research, the modernist "form follows function" can no longer meet people's needs for emotion. They found the functional design too boring. This dissatisfaction with consumer social products led designers to try a new approach in the 1990s.Cooper (1999) is the first professional designer to study emotion and design. He believes that most existing technological devices (such as video recorders, car immobilizers, apps, etc.) will leave users feeling dissatisfied and frustrated. After Cooper, more and more design scholars began to explore the emotional factors in design. Overbeeke and Hekkert (1999) first proposed the concept of "design and emotion".

"Emotional design" refers to a design designed to capture the user's attention and elicit an emotional response in order to increase the likelihood that the user will perform a particular action [18]. Through carefully planned "stimuli", emotional design aims to touch the inner world of users and clarify the "purpose" of design - to solve users' "pain points", that is, the actual needs and emotional loss that bother users in daily life (Fig. 2). Emotional design not only focuses on the functionality of the product, but also depends on whether it can touch people's hearts, stimulate the resonance of users, and lay the emotional tone for the subsequent design. Interaction design is more like a bridge, connecting the communication and interaction between products and users. Put the user at the center and understand their habits, expectations and potential needs. By optimizing the interface layout, simplifying the operation process, and providing intuitive "instructions" and instant "feedback", interaction design aims to create a smooth, natural and full of human interaction experience. Emotional interaction refers to the interaction between human and machine through the simulation of human emotions, so that the machine can understand, perceive and express emotions like humans, so as to achieve a more natural and humane communication experience. "Emotional interaction design" aims to skillfully integrate the emotional dimension into the conception and creation of products. Enhance the humanization and affinity of the product, trigger the emotional resonance of users, and meet the deep psychological needs. Emotional interaction design not only focuses on the surface interaction behavior, but also on the deep emotional communication and resonance.

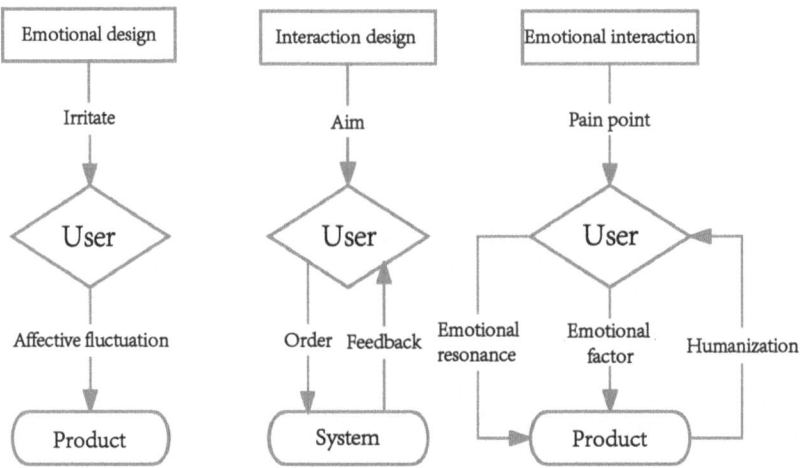

Fig. 2. Emotion, Interaction, Emotion interaction diagram.

The book Emotional Design by American psychologist Donald A. Hamilton divides emotional interaction into three levels: emotional interaction at the instinctive level, emotional interaction at the behavioral level and emotional interaction at the reflective level (Fig. 3).Instinctive level of smart home product design, in the environment, products, materials, colors and other different levels, the use of the feeling of the character to arouse human residential resonance, mobilize their emotions, in order to obtain a positive emotional response, and then improve the user's desire to use smart home products [19]. The behavior layer is a high level of emotional effect, and the direction of smart product home is mainly reflected in the function of home products in the process of user use. Designers need to deeply understand the hidden needs of users, transform them into product functions, and integrate emotional needs into the design. In this way, the product not only meets the practical needs, but also promotes the emotional communication between users and products. Reflective level design focuses on deep symbolic meaning and social value, outputs cultural connotation and aesthetic concept to consumers, and encourages consumers to have a deeper understanding [20]. Build organic emotional interaction between users' daily behaviors and product functions, enhance the humanization and fun of the interaction between the two, use user emotions to achieve product goals and enhance product attractiveness.

From the perspective of design, the core elements of emotional interaction in smart homes include personalization features [6], Emotion recognition and understanding [21], Personalized service, interaction mode and mode.

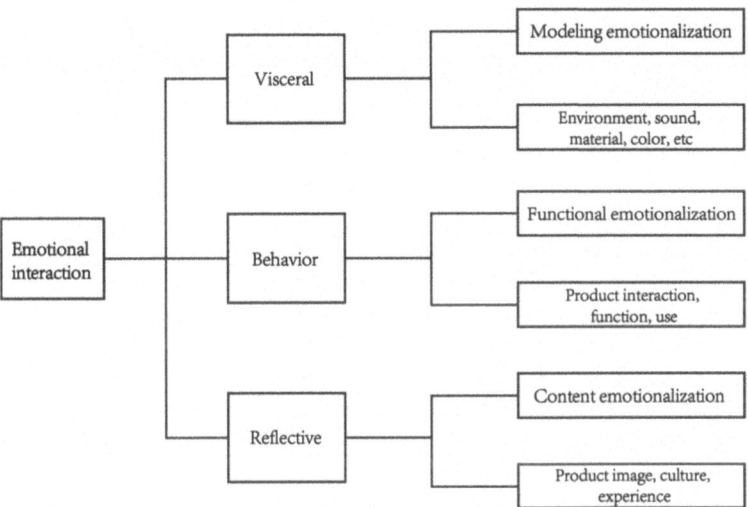

Fig. 3. Smart home product diagram.

Numerous surveys dating back decades prove it [22, 23], Married people live longer and are generally healthier emotionally and physically than unmarried people. The protective/supportive hypothesis suggests that unmarried people are more prone to physical and emotional illness than married people because they lack the constant companionship of their spouse, are unable to get emotional satisfaction, and are unable to resist the changes of daily life. Empirical support going back to the 19th century shows that suicide rates are highest among people who have never been married, the lowest is for married people [24].

In view of extensive historical and contemporary research, it has been found that unmarried people have unique needs for emotional support. Compared with married people, unmarried individuals often lack stable partner companionship and emotional support, which may exacerbate their loneliness and affect their physical and mental health. In this context, the companion chatbot, as an innovative emotional interaction tool, is particularly important in the smart home environment. They can not only provide continuous emotional comfort and sustenance for unmarried people, but also act as their interactive partners in daily life, effectively alleviating the emotional vacancy caused by the lack of partner relationship, so as to play an indispensable role in emotional support.

2.3 Actor Network Theory

Follizzi and Disalvo proposed that robotics in the home is social, so domestic robots have social social connotations [25]. For example, cleaning robots may influence the social dynamics so that all members of the family care about cleaning [26]. In terms of emotional interaction of smart home, it is necessary to deeply understand the needs of users, improve the user experience, promote the harmony of interpersonal relations, enhance the social adaptability of the system, and promote the sustainable development of smart home technology. While current research on emotion focuses on individual inner experiences, sociology excels at revealing how these experiences are interwoven in social interactions and structures. In view of the possible lack of interactivity and relevance in emotion research, this study attempts to introduce a sociological perspective to understand the social nature and dynamics of emotion more comprehensively. Three theories related to interaction in sociology are explored: the theory of symbolic interaction, the theory of interactive ritual chain and the theory of actor network. The theory of symbolic interaction originates from pragmatism and is a microsociological framework summarized and developed by H. Blumer [27]. The core point of the theory is that human beings create and use symbols [28]. In the interactive ritual chain theory, the interactive ritual was first proposed by Goffman, and later, the sociologist Collins (1967) put forward its theoretical model and analytical framework. The key elements of the theory are: physical co-existence, alien barriers, mutual attention, common emotions, and collective bubbles [29]. However, it is found that symbolic interaction theory and interactive ritual chain theory mainly discuss the interaction between people in sociology, and cannot be applied to human-computer interaction.

There are three core concepts of the activist network: agency, mediator, and network. Latour sees the Internet as a series of actions. This network is not a purely technical network like the Internet, but a way to describe the connection, which emphasizes the process of work, interaction, flow, and change, so it should be worknet, not network [30].

Anything that changes the state of things by making a difference can be called an actor, both human and non-human. In addition, Latour treats human actors and non-human actors symmetrically, and the two have equal status in the analysis [31]. This is because they move away from the functionalist role of intermediary and become active "translators," meaning that any information changes through the node of the actor, even if the change is small [32].

In the process of emotional interaction research, it is necessary to pay attention to how both human and machine participate in the interactive network. Based on the framework of actor network theory, this study adopts a systematic and detailed methodology to promote the analysis of emotional interaction in smart homes. First, it is necessary to identify each actor in the emotional interaction scenario of the smart home, which includes both humans as users and diverse technical elements such as smart devices, software applications, and network connectivity. Based on this, we scientifically categorize these actors in order to clearly delineate the roles and functions of the different components of the smart home ecosystem. The intricate network of relationships among these actors is then dissected in depth. This includes not only the intuitive interaction between humans and smart devices, but also the collaborative work between devices, data processing and decision support for software applications, and the key role of network connectivity in information transfer. Through this step, we are able to fully understand the dynamic and complex nature of emotional interactions in smart homes.

3   Research Method

3.1   Research Object and Sample

According to data from the 2024 Smart Home Research report, Chinese smart home consumers show significant distribution characteristics in terms of gender and age. In terms of gender, according to Fig. 2, there are slightly more female consumers than male consumers, accounting for 57.9%, while male consumers account for 42.1%. According to Fig. 3, in terms of age distribution, consumers aged 25–30 account for the highest proportion, reaching 28.8%, followed by consumers aged 31–35, accounting for 33.7%. Together, these two age groups account for more than 60% of the smart home market, demonstrating the strong interest and acceptance of smart home technology among young consumers. In general, in 2024, China's smart home consumers will be 25–35 years old, second - and third-tier consumers, and high-income white-collar workers as the main group, with males accounting for 42.1% and females accounting for 57.9%, with little gender deviation, all driven by demand; In terms of age, the core group of 36–40 years old is the potential consumer of smart home.

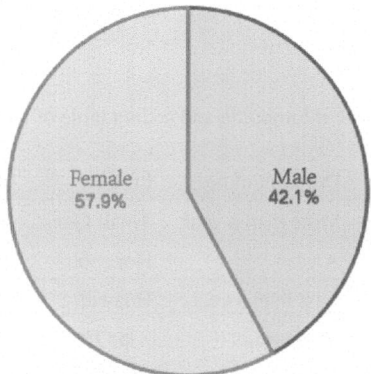

Fig. 4. Gender ratio of smart home consumers in China in 2024.

Therefore, a total of 12 participants, aged between 25 and 55, were selected for this study and were all unmarried. All participants had certain experience in using smart homes, and semi-structured interviews and questionnaires were conducted.

3.2   Research Method

In this paper, based on the premise that the emotional interaction of smart home is related to user privacy, we decide to conduct research on the in-depth users of intelligent chatbots by semi-structured interview method. In terms of the selection of interview subjects, this paper goes deep into Huawei, Tmall, Apple and other stores, and selects qualified interview subjects through communication with sales staff, observation of consumers and introduction by friends. The screening criteria were set to use for more than one month and maintain one or more conversations per day. In addition, subjects between the

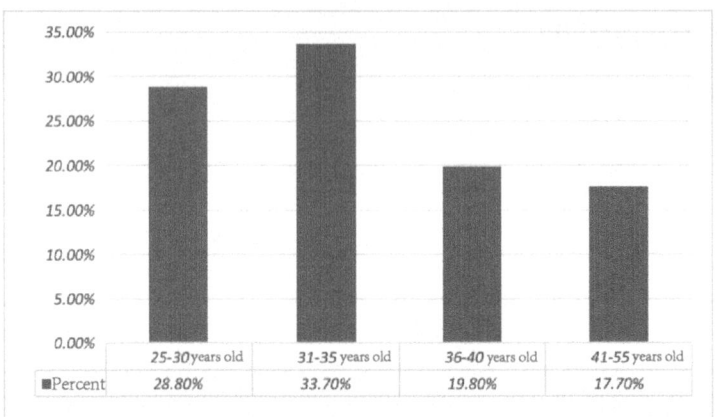

Fig. 5. Age ratio of Chinese smart home consumers in 2024.

ages of 25 and 55, with unmarried marital status, but without any restriction on gender and occupation, were selected for interview.

The following table describes the basic information and encoding of the object (Table 1).

Table 1. Basic information and coding table of interviewees.

Encoding	Sex	Age	Duration of use	Product	Interview method/Length
F1	Female	45	More than a year	Tmall Genie	Voice /30 min
F2	Female	30	A year	Honepod	Voice /20 min
F3	Female	32	Less than a year	Huawei	Voice /30 min
F4	Female	54	Many years	Xiao Du	Voice /30 min
F5	Female	29	Many years	Xiao Du	Voice /30 min
F6	Female	25	Four years	Xiao Ai	Voice /30 min
M1	Male	27	A year	Xiao Ai	Voice /20 min
M2	Male	36	Half a year	Tmall Genie	Voice /30 min
M3	Male	29	More than a yea	Maika	Voice /30 min
M4	Male	43	Six years	Honepod	Voice /30 min
M5	Male	34	Three years	Maika	Voice /30 min
M6	Male	26	A year	Xiao Ai	Voice /20 min

Then this study conducted a questionnaire survey, the composition of the questionnaire covers the introduction of the questionnaire, demographic characteristics data and evaluation scale three parts. The introduction part of the questionnaire elaborates the core functions and application scenarios of intelligent chatbots in improving user experience, providing a clear research background for respondents. In the process of demographic data collection, the age level, gender information and educational background of the respondents were obtained. For descriptive statistics of the sample, see Table 2. The gender distribution of the research samples is basically balanced, and the sample group is younger as a whole, mainly concentrated in the 25–30 years old and 31–35 years old.

Table 2. Description of the respondent's basic information.

		Frequency	Percent
Gender	Female	209	55.4
	Male	168	44.6
Age group	25 ~ 30	97	25.7
	31 ~ 35	146	38.7
	36 ~ 40	72	19.1
	41 ~ 45	28	7.4
	46 ~ 50	16	4.2
	51 ~ 55	18	4.8

The main part of the questionnaire draws on the measurement indicators in the existing intelligent technology user adoption research, and makes corresponding adjustments and optimization according to the specific situation of this study. We used a five-point Likert scale as an assessment tool, with 1 being "strongly disagree" and 5 being "strongly agree".

In order to delve deeper into the satisfaction of the user experience of intelligent chatbots, this study identified four key measurement variables. In the dimension of personification characteristics, the scale of Mishra A (2021) and Fernandes T (2021) is used to evaluate perceived humaneness, the scale of Mishra A (2021) is used to measure perceived entertainment, and the evaluation criteria of perceived relationality is set by referring to the questions of Fernandes T (2021). Enter the interaction mode and mode stage, and conduct word frequency analysis on the interview content, as shown in Table 3. The words with high weight, such as emotion, intelligence, interaction, understanding, response, support and other directions with high user attention, are used to judge the user experience of the existing interaction mode. In the personalized service phase, Lu's (2019) scale was used to assess perceived service quality, combined with perceived usage cost, and Dogan Gursoy's (2019) and Lu's (2019) scales were used to measure users' willingness to adopt behaviors. Then, at the level of emotion recognition, it pays more attention to the accuracy of emotion recognition and the achievement performance of task goals that users pay more attention to during the interview. In terms of behavioral outcomes, we refer to Fernandes T (2021) and Dogan Gursoy (2019) scales to measure users' behavioral intentions, including adoption and rejection intentions.

Table 3. Word frequency analysis of user questionnaire interview.

Single word	Length	count	Weighted percentage (%)
emotional	9	229	2.95
intelligent	11	162	2.09
interaction	11	123	1.59
understand	10	105	1.35
response	8	75	0.97
support	7	48	0.62
accurately	10	46	0.59
solve	5	41	0.53
enough	6	40	0.52
information	11	38	0.49

3.3 Affective Behavior Analysis

Based on the summary of interviews with intelligent chatbot users, the process of emotional interaction between users and them is as follows: emotional link - emotional involvement - emotional dimension - emotional withdrawal.

1. Emotional connection
   In the early stages of relationship development, users are mainly attracted to the chatbot's tool "clues". In the Theory of Interactive Media Effects (TIME), Sundar pointed out that the function and use of artificial intelligence products are direct factors in shaping their presentation and technical image. This presentation in turn involves "cues" in the user's product selection process [33]. In other words, the user's choice of a particular chatbot product is not random, but contains a clear purpose that runs through the core of the entire interactive experience - that is, the unique charm of the chatbot to attract users.

2. Emotional involvement
   In the process of human-computer interaction, users tend to transfer their emotional patterns cultivated in the real social environment to the interaction with the machine, projecting their emotions onto the machine. Even when users are well aware of the non-human nature of the machine, the barriers of the virtual chat environment often lead users to be unconsciously misled into believing that the chatbot is a communication partner no different from the real person.

3. Emotional dimension
   "Scene" constitutes the key cornerstone of human-machine relationship construction. From the dimension of "field" analysis, chatbot, as a tool, builds an interactive space for users that can fully demonstrate personalized characteristics. In this space, users can freely choose chat topics according to their personal interests, and the chatbot can respond to these choices in real time, so as to achieve instant interaction between the two sides. This real-time interaction between human and machine creates

a strong "presence experience" for the user. As for the "landscape" level, the accompanying atmosphere and immersion created by chatbots deepen users' cognition of "landscape" and give them a sense of integration as if they are in a real scene.

4. Emotional withdrawal

In the past human-computer interaction process, due to the lack of social clues, users tend to over-beautify chatbots, so as to ignore their technical shortcomings. However, this phenomenon of "selective neglect" gradually diminishes as the depth of the interaction increases. As users explore most of the features of chatbots and the novelty of this new technology wears off, the appeal of chatbots diminishes significantly. In the end, it may be just because of some "flaws" that did not appear to be serious problems in the past, which will cause the user to break the relationship with the chatbot.

3.4 Data Processing

This study mainly used the SPSS (Statistical Package for the Social Sciences) data analysis software to conduct in-depth analysis of the questionnaire data (Table 4).

Table 4. Reliability statistics.

Scale	Cronbach's Alpha	Cronbach's Alpha Based on Standardized Items
Personality traits	0.825	0.829
Interaction Style and Mode	0.766	0.772
Personalisation	0.864	0.867
Emotion Recognition and Understanding	0.875	0.877
Purchase intention	0.859	0.868
total	0.934	0.937

1. Reliability test

A total of 400 questionnaires were collected, 23 invalid questionnaires were excluded, and 377 valid questionnaires were tested on 5 dimensions and 21 questions in the scale. Klonbach Alpha value is 0.937, indicating that the questionnaire questions have a high reliability coefficient, so the survey data are considered to be relatively reliable.

2. Validity test (Table 5)

Table 5. KMO and Bartlett's Test.

Kaiser-Meyer-Olkin Measure of Sampling Adequacy		0.890
Bartlett's Test of Sphericity	Approx. Chi-Square	13006.928
	df	1485
	Sig.	0.000

If the KMO value is greater than 0.7, the significance of Bartlett sphericity test is 0.000 < 0.01, and the validity of the data is considered good.
3. Description and analysis (Table 6)

Table 6. Descriptive Statistics.

	Mean	Std. Deviation	N
Purchase intention	3.5199	0.92699	377
Perceptual anthropomorphism	3.4711	0.82206	377
Perceived relationality	3.6189	0.90576	377
Sensory Entertainment	3.4058	0.78230	377
Personality traits	3.4986	0.56691	377
Service Stability	3.7630	0.86662	377
Style richness	2.8656	1.16346	377
Response Speed/Smoothness	2.9602	1.17746	377
Speech Recognition Accuracy	3.2511	1.08095	377
Interaction Style and Mode	3.0256	0.70536	377
Richness in style	3.5889	1.03306	377
Comprehensiveness of user information	3.7763	0.86964	377
Sensing the quality of service	3.6170	0.87405	377
Perceived cost of use	2.3015	0.92262	377
Personalisation	3.6626	0.63435	377
Accuracy of Emotional Feedback	3.4682	0.66067	377
Task Target Achievement Performance	3.6322	0.82924	377
Using Emotional Change	3.8064	0.78980	377
Emotion Recognition and Understanding	3.6356	0.59056	377

In descriptive statistical analysis, the average value and standard deviation are generally used to measure the index level of each variable. The higher the average value is, the higher the average level of the sample for this index. The discrete trend is used to describe the degree of dispersion of the data in the data distribution. For example, the standard deviation represents the difference of different samples on the same index. The higher the score, the higher the degree of agreement.

As can be seen from the above table, the scores of most aspects are higher, indicating that the subjects are more approved of this.

4. Correlation analysis (Table 7)

Table 7. Correlation analysis.

	Purchase intention
Purchase intention	0.471**
Perceptual anthropomorphism	0.471**
Perceived relationality	0.368**
Sensory Entertainment	0.647**
Personality traits	0.315**
Service Stability	0.303**
Response Speed	0.295**
Response Smoothness	0.319**
Speech Recognition Accuracy	0.494**
Interaction Style and Mode	0.352**
Richness in style	0.389**
Comprehensiveness of user information	0.317**
Sensing the quality of service	−0.339**
Perceived cost of use	0.499**
Personalisation	0.330**
Accuracy of Emotional Feedback	0.536**
Task Target Achievement Performanc	0.367**
Using Emotional Change	0.537**

**Correlation is significant at the 0.01 level (2-tailed).
*Correlation is significant at the 0.05 level (2-tailed)

Correlation analysis refers to the process of describing and analyzing the nature and degree of correlation between two or more variables. Mark * in the upper right corner of the correlation coefficient to indicate that there is a relationship; The reverse does not matter. When the correlation coefficient is greater than 0, it indicates that there is a positive correlation between the two variables; when it is less than 0, it indicates that there is a negative correlation between the two variables.

Purchase intention and Perceptual anthropomorphism, Perceived relationality, Sensory Entertainment, Personality traits, Service Stability, Response Speed, Response Smoothness, Speech Recognition Accuracy, Interaction Style and ModeRichness in speech style, Comprehensiveness of user information, Sensing the quality of service, Personalisation, Accuracy of Emotional There is a significant correlation between Feedback, Task Target Achievement performance, Using Emotional Change, Emotion Recognition and Understanding. The correlation coefficient of each variable is greater than 0, indicating a significant positive correlation.

There is a significant negative correlation between Purchase intention and Perceived cost of use.

5. Regression analysis (Tables 8, 9 and 10)

Table 8. Model Summary.

Model	R	R Square	Adjusted R Square	Std. Error of the Estimate
1	0.730a	0.533	0.527	0.63721

a. Predictors: (Constant), Emotion Recognition and Understanding, Personality traits, Interaction Style and Mode, Personalisation

Table 9. ANOVAa.

Model		Sum of Squares	df	Mean Square	F	Sig.
1	Regression	172.057	4	43.014	105.938	0.000b
	Residual	151.044	372	0.406		
	Total	323.101	376			

a. Dependent Variable: Purchase intention
b. Predictors: (Constant), Emotion Recognition and Understanding, Personality traits, Interaction Style and Mode, Personalisation

It can be seen through the fit test that the R square is 0.533, indicating that 53.3% of the dependent variable can be explained by the regression equation, and the significance of the F test is less than 0.05, which reaches the significance level, indicating that the established regression model is effective. VIF is less than 5, indicating that the collinearity is weak and the model effect is good.

The significance of Personality traits (beta = 0.467, P < 0.05) was less than 0.05, and the regression coefficient was greater than 0, indicating a significant positive effect on Purchase intention.

The Interaction Style and Mode (beta = 0.142, P < 0.05) was less than 0.05, and the regression coefficient was greater than 0, indicating a significant positive impact on Purchase intention.

The significance of Personalisation (beta = 0.143, P < 0.05) was less than 0.05, and the regression coefficient was greater than 0, indicating a significant positive impact on Purchase intention.

Table 10. Coefficients[a].

Model		Unstandardized Coefficients		Standardized Coefficients	t	Sig.	Collinearity Statistics	
		B	Std. Error	Beta			Tolerance	VIF
1	(Constant)	−1.423	0.249		−5.713	0.000		
	Personality traits	0.764	0.066	0.467	11.620	0.000	0.777	1.288
	Interaction Style and Mode	0.186	0.059	0.142	3.129	0.002	0.614	1.629
	Personalisation	0.210	0.071	0.143	2.972	0.003	0.539	1.854
	Emotion Recognition and Understanding	0.258	0.083	0.164	3.116	0.002	0.452	2.213

a. Dependent Variable: Purchase intention

The significance of Emotion Recognition and Understanding (beta = 0.164, $P <$ 0.05) was less than 0.05, and the regression coefficient was greater than 0, indicating a significant positive impact on Purchase intention.

As can be seen from the beta influence coefficient, the beta value of Personality traits is large, indicating a high degree of influence.

4 Intelligent Home Emotional Interaction Analysis

4.1 Actor Extraction

In the emotional interaction of smart home, there are human actors and non-human actors. Human actors play a crucial role, not only as users of smart home systems, but also as their creators and maintainers. The human actors are: users, developers, designers, and marketing departments. Non-human actors are the Internet, speakers, microphones, chips, and so on. Through the analysis of the text extracted from the interview (see Table 11), three non-human actors are extracted: smart home, speaker and video platform.

In the long-term use of smart home systems, it usually involves the interaction of multiple users, including the interaction of family members and users outside the family [34]. The Marketing Department needs to have a deep understanding of consumer needs, and through effective market research and analysis, provide strong support for product development and marketing strategies to overcome these challenges and seize market opportunities [35]. In smart home products, developers play the role of designing, creating and optimizing systems to meet user needs and drive smart home technology development. In the design of smart home products, designers need to deeply investigate user needs, accurately match and customize functions, and integrate and optimize to improve user experience. Based on the perspective of emotionalization, the behavioral level design of smart home is not simply limited to space, environment and products, but more importantly, it is necessary to improve the user's behavioral experience through smart home products [19]. The Internet plays a key role in connecting devices in smart homes, realizing remote control and data exchange, and improving the intelligent level of home life. The main functions include remote access control, data sharing between devices, forming an intelligent ecosystem, and improving the convenience of life. Speakers play the role of audio output and interaction in smart homes, not only as a key component of voice interaction, to achieve smooth dialogue between users and home devices, but also play the role of entertainment center, providing music playback and diversified entertainment experience. The microphone is the core component of voice capture and conversion in the smart home, it is not only a key component to achieve voice interaction, capable of capturing the user's voice commands and converting them into executable digital signals, but also equipped with advanced speech recognition algorithms to accurately understand and respond to these commands. Smart chip is the key component of processor and intelligent function realization in smart home, and its functions are diverse and significant. The mobile phone plays the role of the core control and interaction platform in the smart home. As a control center, it realizes the remote control of smart devices in the home through wireless network technology, provides real-time monitoring and security protection, supports personalized Settings and automatic scene creation, and realizes natural interaction with voice control technology. Wi-Fi plays an important role in the gateway layer of the smart home system architecture of the Internet of Things, and is a bridge connecting each terminal device and the server. The gateway communicates with the terminal device through the Zigbee interface or serial port to obtain data, and forwards the data to the server via Ethernet or Wi-Fi or GPRS interface [36].

Table 11. Actor extraction.

Serial number	Content analysis	Actor extraction
1	I hope that Xiaoai students and those smart devices at home are connected together, so that I can control the lights, air conditioning, TV and curtains, and feel that the home suddenly becomes good smart	Intelligent furniture
2	I have bought it for five or six years, I use it every day, and I am satisfied with it, but it is generally used as a stereo	sound
3	The TV series recommended is also very old, not a comedy, is completely wrong to answer the question	Video platform

4.2 Analysis of Key Actors

From the perspective of smart home emotional interaction network, only designers can play the role of key actors. First, the designer is the direct executor of the emotional interaction design of smart home. They are not only responsible for conceiving and designing the look, function, and user experience of products, but also for turning these ideas into practical products. In the process of emotional interaction design, designers need to deeply understand the needs and expectations of users, and integrate emotional elements into products through smart design, so as to create smart home products that can have emotional resonance with users. Second, the designer is the decisive factor to make the design work play the social function, but also the important driving force to promote the development of human society [37]. Designers need to master the latest technology trends, understand the operating principles of smart home systems, and be able to apply these technologies in the design of products. In addition, designers also need to have innovative thinking and constantly explore new design concepts and interaction ways to promote the continuous upgrading and optimization of smart home products. Third, designers are the bridge between user feedback and product iteration. In the process of using smart home products, users will put forward valuable opinions and suggestions according to their own experience. Designers/need to actively collect and analyze this feedback, understand users' needs and pain points, and iterate and optimize the product based on this information. Through continuous feedback and improvement, designers are able to continuously enhance the emotional interaction experience of the product and meet the expectations and needs of users.

4.3 Analyze Forced Crossing Points

A detailed questionnaire survey was conducted on the influencing factors of consumers' purchase of intelligent chatbots, and then a regression analysis was conducted on the collected data. This analysis process aims to reveal which factors play a more critical role in the consumer decision making process. According to the results of regression analysis on the questionnaire, the regression coefficient value of personified features is the largest among the four dimensions, indicating that personified features have the greatest impact on consumers' purchase of intelligent chatbots. This data strongly suggests that personalization features play the most critical role in consumers' decision to purchase an intelligent chatbot. It is not only an important factor in influencing consumer preferences, but also becomes a "forced crossing point" between consumer demand and the supply of intelligent chatbot market.

4.4 Classification and Function of Each Actor

Given the large number of actors, subsequent analysis will be difficult, so it is necessary to scientifically categorize all actors into several main categories: users, developers, designers, marketing departments, and technical components. In this classification, technical components refer specifically to all non-human actor entities. When discussing the multi-level framework of emotional interaction design, this paper makes an in-depth analysis of the actors corresponding to each level and their core roles in solving existing emotional interaction problems according to Fig. 4. The following is a detailed explanation of the framework (Fig. 5):

First, the instinctive layer: the basic construction of sensory experience.

At the instinctive level, sensory factors such as environment, sounds, materials and colors directly trigger basic emotional responses in humans. Therefore, the problem solving of emotional interaction at this level mainly depends on the designer. Designers, as the core actors of emotional interaction design, need sensory experience that can stimulate users' positive emotions. For example, in the design, the designer should pay attention to the detail design while ensuring that the size and proportion of the robot's appearance are coordinated and in line with the ergonomic principle, so as to make it more vivid, natural and friendly.

In addition to designers, technical components will also play a role in the natural past, such as speakers. Speakers enable a smooth dialogue between users and home devices, and also act as an entertainment hub, providing music playback and diverse entertainment experiences. The special voice intonation and character voice during the conversation can better make the intelligent chatbot more personal.

Second, the behavior layer: the optimization and implementation of interactive experience.

At the behavioral level, designers and developers share the responsibility of optimizing the interactive experience of the product. Designers are responsible for creating intuitive, easy-to-use interface designs that make it easy for users to understand and operate the product; Developers are responsible for translating these designs into actual code and functionality to achieve stable operation of the product. In addition, technology component providers also play a key role at this level, providing the necessary hardware and software support to ensure that products can meet the diverse needs of users. Through the efforts of the behavioral layer, we can create products that both meet the needs of users and are easy to operate, thus further enhancing the emotional experience of users.

Third, reflection layer: continuous iteration and optimization of emotional interaction.

At the reflection level, designers, developers, and marketing departments work together to rethink and adjust the product. Designers constantly optimize the appearance and interface design of products based on user feedback and market demand; Developers continue to improve the functionality and performance of the product to meet the diverse needs of users; The Marketing Department collects and analyzes market data to develop more effective marketing strategies and enhance the market competitiveness of products. Through the efforts of the reflection layer, we can continuously meet the needs and expectations of users and improve the overall emotional experience of products, so as to achieve continuous iteration and optimization of emotional interaction design (Fig. 6).

5   Intelligent Home Emotional Interaction Design Strategy

In the emotional interaction design of smart home, we can base on the three-level theory of emotion, starting from the instinct level, the behavior level and the reflection level, formulate the corresponding solution strategy for each level, and clarify the corresponding action that should be taken by the actor. At the instinctive level, designers need to use the principles of color psychology and morphological aesthetics to design a beautiful and practical appearance of smart home devices, while choosing comfortable, environmentally friendly and safe materials to create a warm and friendly family atmosphere.

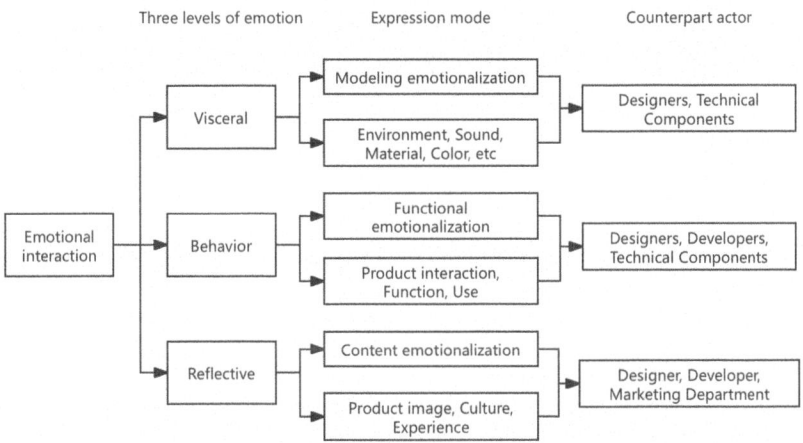

Fig. 6. Three levels of emotion correspond to actors

In addition, user research experts should conduct in-depth research on user interaction habits and needs, and guide the design of intuitive and easy-to-use interactive interfaces to enhance the initial emotional connection between users and devices. At the behavioral level, software engineers need to optimize the interaction logic and response speed of smart home devices to ensure that users can smoothly complete various operations; Interaction designers need to design practical and emotional features based on user needs and market demands. The product manager needs to collect user feedback and market data on a regular basis, and iterate and upgrade the product to improve its market competitiveness. On the reflection level, brand planners need to dig deeply into brand story and brand value, and stimulate users' emotional resonance through emotional marketing means; Marketing needs to use a variety of marketing channels and strategies to enhance the awareness and influence of smart home brands; User experience experts need to deeply investigate the user experience, find and solve existing problems in a timely manner, and pay attention to the integration of emotional elements to enhance the emotional connection between users and devices. Through the implementation of this series of strategies, we aim to improve the emotional interaction ability of smart home products, and promote the development of smart home industry to a more humane and intelligent direction.

Italian scholar Sucameli Irene once pointed out that in effective human-machine communication, the machine should have "three.Quotient ", i.e. "IQ", "EQ", "trustworthiness quotient" [38]. Aside from the "emotional intelligence" point of view, today, the "IQ" of the agent has been fully developed, and in some levels, it has even surpassed humans, and has become a tool for robot developers to promote. In addition, the most critical point of "trust quotient" is to ensure the transparency of human-computer communication and maintain the correctness of ethics, such as basic respect for users, protection of privacy, and rejection of discrimination. There is still much room for improvement in the "trusted quotient" of machines in this regard. As Penland pointed out, the improvement of machine "emotional intelligence" and "trust quotient" depends very much on the understanding of various elements of human-computer communication, especially the context of dialogue, emotional expression, and experience sharing [39].

References

1. Yang, F.: Interactive design of smart home software based on user emotional experience. Master dissertation, Xi'an Polytechnic University (2018)
2. Ma, X.: The smart home, intelligent life. TV Technol. (S1), 58+54–66 (2014). https://doi.org/10.16280/j.videoe.2014.S1.005
3. Luo, Y.: Design trend of smart home products under the development of Internet of Things technology. Footwear Technol. Des. (24), 139–141 (2023). (in Chinese) CNKI:SUN:ZWXE.0.2023-24-046
4. Zhang, X.D.: Research on China Smart home industry. Future Dev. **12**, 14–19 (2021). CNKI:SUN:WLYF.0.2021-12-003
5. Xie, Q., Lu, D.B.: Research on design of social emotion expression for intelligent home robots. Furniture Interior Décor. **04**, 80–84 (2024). https://doi.org/10.16771/j.cn43-1247/ts.2024.04.012
6. Liao, Q.L., Wang, M., Feng, Z.: Voice interaction design of smart home products based on emotional interaction. Packag. Eng. (16), 37–42+66 (2019). https://doi.org/10.19554/j.cnki.1001-3563.2019.16.006
7. Xu, X .P., Lin, Y.: AI+ smart home technology and its trend. Digit. Commun. World (01), 65 (2019). CNKI:SUN:SZTJ.0.2019-01-041
8. Hoffman, D.L., Novak, T.P.: Consumer and object experience in the internet of things: an assemblage theory approach. J. Consum. Res. **44**(6), 1178–1204 (2018)
9. Luo, X., Tong, S., Fang, Z., Qu, Z.: Frontiers: machines vs. humans: the impact of artificial intelligence chatbot disclosure on customer purchases. Market. Sci. **38**(6), 937–947 (2019)
10. Verhoef, P.C., et al.: Consumer connectivity in a complex, technology-enabled, and mobile-oriented world with smart products. J. Interact. Mark. **40**(1), 1–8 (2017)
11. Wirtz, J., et al.: Brave new world: service robots in the frontline. J. Serv. Manag. **29**(5), 907–931 (2018)
12. Schuetzler, R.M., Grimes, G.M., Giboney, J.S., Nunamaker Jr., J.F.: The influence of conversational agents on socially desirable responding. In: Proceedings of the 51st Hawaii International Conference on System Sciences, p. 283 (2018)
13. Go, E., Sundar, S.S.: Humanizing chatbots: the effects of visual, identity and conversational cues on humanness perceptions. Comput. Hum. Behav. **97**, 304–316 (2019)
14. Shevat, A.: Designing Bots: Creating Conversational Experiences. O'Reilly Media, Inc. (2017)
15. Cao, B., Luo, L.: Development characteristics and mechanism effects of companion chatbots. Young Journal. (02), 19–22 (2023). https://doi.org/10.15997/j.carolcarrollnkiQNJZ.2023.02.008
16. Liu, H., Lian, X.: The coming of the new ordinary people's rule: ChatGPT and communication research. Journalists (06), 11–20 (2023). https://doi.org/10.16057/j.carolcarrollnki/g2.2023.06.00831-1171
17. Huang, L., He, Y., Ma, Z., Mi, H., Yao, Y.: Research trends of smart home from the perspective of human-computer interaction. J. Comput.-Aided Des. Graph. (02), 165–184 (2023)
18. Chen, G.: Internet + Smart home. Inf. Secur. Commun. Secur. **11** (2015)
19. Huang, M.: The application of emotional design in smart home design. J. Heihe Univ. (07),137–139+148 (2023). CNKI:SUN:HHXY.0.2023-07-041

20. Song, R., Gu, Z.-H.: Design practice of three-level theory of emotional design in Qiuci Mural cultural and creative textile products. Dyeing Finish. Technol. (09), 109–111 (2024). CNKI:SUN:RZJS.0.2024-09-029
21. Reisinger, M.R., Prost, S., Schrammel, J., Fröhlich, P.: User requirements for the design of smart homes: dimensions and goals. J. Ambient. Intell. Humaniz. Comput. **14**(12), 15761–15780 (2023)
22. Dayton, N.A.: Marriage and mental disease. N. Engl. J. Med. **215**(4), 153–155 (1936)
23. Ødegaard, H.: Crossed Renal Ectopta. Acta Radiol. **27**(5), 543–551 (1946)
24. Dublin, L.I., Bunzel, B.: To be or not to be: a study of suicide (1933)
25. Forlizzi, J., DiSalvo, C.: Service robots in the domestic environment: a study of the roomba vacuum in the home. In: Proceedings of the 1st ACM SIGCHI/SIGART Conference on Human-Robot Interaction, pp. 258–265 (2006)
26. Forlizzi, J., Zimmerman, J., Mancuso, V., Kwak, S.: How interface agents affect interaction between humans and computers. In: Proceedings of the 2007 Conference on Designing Pleasurable Products and Interfaces, pp. 209–221 (2007)
27. Wei, X.-N., Lin, L.: Intergenerational digital interaction design from the perspective of symbolic interaction theory. Design (09), 132–136 (2024). https://doi.org/10.20055/j.cnki.1003-0069.001741
28. Chen, Y.-Y., Xu, J.-C.: Research on optimization of art classroom interaction from the perspective of symbolic interaction theory – a case study of junior high school art appreciation class. Art Educ. Res. (12), 174–176 (2023). CNKI:SUN:MSJY.0.2023-12-057
29. Joo, D., Cho, H., Woosnam, K.M., Suess, C.: Re-theorizing social emotions in tourism: applying the theory of interaction ritual in tourism research. In: Theoretical Advancement in Social Impacts Assessment of Tourism Research, pp. 138–153. Routledge (2023)
30. Wu, Y., Lu, Y., Chen, J., Wang, Y.: Reorganizing society with actors: reading Latour's reorganizing society: a theory of actor networks. Sociol. Res. (2), 218–234 (2008)
31. Yao, Z.-Y., Lu, G.: An analysis on the Internet actions of social media robots under the actor network theory. News Forum (05), 18–21 (2023). https://doi.org/10.19425/j.cnki.cn15-1019/g2.2023.05.018
32. Yang, D.-X., Yang, F.: Research on AIGC film production framework from the perspective of actor network. Film Lit. (01), 93–98 (2024). CNKI:SUN:DYLX.0.2024-01-013
33. Sundar, S.S., Jia, H., Waddell, T.F., Huang, Y.: Toward a theory of interactive media effects (TIME) four models for explaining how interface features affect user psychology. In: The Handbook of the Psychology of Communication Technology, pp. 47–86 (2015)
34. Pan, M.J.: A multi-user intelligent household scenarios human-machine collaborative interaction design research. A Master's degree thesis, Jiangnan University (2024). https://kns.cnki.net/KCMS/detail/detail.aspx?dbname=CMFDTEMP&filename=1024697384.nh
35. LuXin, Z., Yang, C.: Under the background of the Internet of things smart home market development prospects, based on the analysis of consumer behavior survey. Natl. Circul. Econ. (07), 6–8 (2021). https://doi.org/10.16834/j.carolcarrollnkiissn1009-5292.2021.07.002
36. Shen, B., Zhang, G.Q., Wang, M., Li, C.: Design and implementation of smart home based on Internet of Things. Autom. Instrum. **28**(2), 6–10 (2013)
37. Li, X., Zhang, Y.: The important role of designers in contemporary design. Popular Arts (06), 77 (2014)
38. Sucameli, I.: Improving the level of trust in human-machine conversation. Adv. Robot. **35**(9), 553– (2021)
39. Jiang, L.: Intelligent communication, the future has come: an overview of eight people's views on "inspiring AIGC" digital communication. Media Observ. (03), 48–54 (2023)

Interactive Systems and User Behavior

Honesty or Harmony? How Friendships Shape Frustration Reporting in Usability Tests

Lucy Cui[1,2(✉)] (iD) and Austin Wuthrich[2]

[1] State University of New York at New Paltz, New Paltz, NY 12561, USA
lucy.cui.phd@gmail.com
[2] University of California, Los Angeles, Los Angeles, CA 90095, USA

Abstract. In order to keep the development of a new product secret from competitors, convenience sampling within a company may be unavoidable. Convenience sampling, such as recruiting friends or coworkers, can introduce biases into the data collection process. These participants could be distinctly different from the rest of the population and the relationships between the interviewee and the interviewer could skew what kinds of feedback can be collected. In our study, we recruited friends of six interviewers to participate in a usability test on a high-fidelity prototype that was designed to be frustrating in different ways. The goal was to investigate what features of friendships and of the interviewee determine how likely one is to report frustration in an "objectively" frustrating prototype. The interviewees reported their ease and frustration with requested tasks, comfort in being honest and how much they adjusted their ratings from the truth. We collected friendship details from both the interviewer and the interviewee and categorized those friendships to be mutual or lopsided/one-sided (friendship type) based on how much their responses agreed with one another. We identified certain qualities of friendships rated by the interviewee (*companionship, transcending problems*) and by the interviewer (*aid*), or combining both (*reflected appraisal*) that predicted the interviewee's frustration ratings, but did not find any differences in friendship type, gender dynamics or big five personality traits. We discuss implications for selecting participants.

Keywords: user experience · usability testing · convenience sampling · friends

1 Introduction

1.1 Background

Usability testing is often recommended for product development as part of an iterative design process. Some companies may need to depend on convenience sampling for usability testing. These participants may end up being the coworkers or friends of the interviewer. With long-term social relationships, such as with friends or coworkers, we may be socially incentivized to leave out negative feedback in order to protect our egos or theirs [1–4]. These dynamics may often depend on the relationship between the interviewee and the interviewer. Employees show that power dynamics can influence

© The Author(s), under exclusive license to Springer Nature Switzerland AG 2025
M. Schrepp (Ed.): HCII 2025, LNCS 15794, pp. 311–328, 2025.
https://doi.org/10.1007/978-3-031-93221-2_20

willingness to provide constructive feedback [5]. Some coworkers could be our friends, but not always. Even within friends, friendships could look and feel very different within a person's social circle. Those that we ask to voluntarily participate in our usability testing may be distinctly different from the rest of the population. For example, we most likely will not ask the coworker who does not like us or the one that says no to every request. Just as we may ask some friends for help and not others.

To study the potential of differential qualities of social relationships on the feedback we can get from usability testing, we recruited friends of our researchers. Friends are different from coworkers in many ways, such as where we met them, whether there is a social hierarchy, how the members got recruited, and how the members interact with each other. However, there are some similarities in the functions the relationships can serve. There are four coworker relationship functions: (1) mentorship, (2) information exchange, (3) power, control and influence, such as concertive control, or a socially constructed norms made by and monitored by the employees, and (4) social support, such as instrumental, informational or emotional support [6]. Some of these functions could exist in friendships, especially those that exist during college years.

Friendships can exist between two people of the same sex or two people of opposite sexes. There are some complexities within opposite-sex friendships that may be less of a concern in a workplace setting with rules and consequences. While workplace rules against dating coworkers and the fear of sexual harassment claims promote self-monitoring and help enforce boundaries, opposite-sex friends may need to rely on other pressures to maintain their platonic friendships. Messman et al. [7] identified six reasons for keeping opposite-sex friendships platonic: no attraction (may not be mutual), network disapproval, third party (friend, sibling) disapproval, time out from dating, safeguarding the friendship, and risk aversion. Maintaining these platonic friendships requires reassuring behaviors and minimal flirtatious behaviors [7]. Men and women have different reasons for initiating and dissolving opposite-sex friendships, with men listing sexual attraction as a primary reason and women listing physical protection [8].

Another possibility within opposite-sex friends, that are not exclusive to opposite-sex friendships, is the possibility for inequity, i.e., the friendship is lopsided and not mutually beneficial. Reciprocity, as in equitable friendships, is important for friendship quality and satisfaction [9, 10], inequity could change what ends up being communicated. In inequitable opposite-sex friendships, the overbenefited friend has a tendency to engage in avoidance behaviors (e.g., avoiding them, acting badly, lying to them) to maintain the platonic friendship [7]. Other opposite-sex social interactions could also introduce bias or lying tendencies. When looking at people's tendency to lie in opposite-sex dating contexts, we see that people tend to lie to physically attractive people in order to be considered more similar to the attractive target on things like personality traits, income, past relationship outcomes, career skills and intelligence [11].

Lying could be more common from a gender or more common towards a gender. People are more likely to tell white lies covering up poor performance when the individual is a woman [12]. Men are more likely to lie when it benefits them (black lie) and when it benefits others (white lie) [13]. In a study that paired people into same- or opposite-gender partners to have 10-min conversations and informed them of 0 additional or 3 additional meetings with their partner, females lied more when they expected future interaction than when they thought they'd never see them again [14]. Other gender effects may also be relevant. People tend to prefer the female style of communication (e.g., expressing empathy and concern, sharing similar experiences, asking further questions), regardless of their own gender [15]. Gender may play a role in administering sensitive interview questions [16]. This literature suggests that we should consider not only the gender of the interviewee and the interviewer but also the gender-pairing—whether the gender matches or mismatches, and who is the male and female in the pairing.

Our study seeks to understand whether friendship dynamics play a role in reporting frustration with a frustrating user interface. Lies told to friends are more likely to be altruistic than self-serving [17], which could result in more honest feedback but not necessarily. Personality can play a factor in the feedback received from a usability test [18]. We consider the friendship characteristics between the interviewer and interviewee. If there is an imbalance within a friendship, a friend could be differentially inclined to be honest with the interviewer.

1.2   Our Study

In this study, we investigated cognitive (digital fluency and working memory issues) and social (friendship qualities, friendship reciprocity, personality traits) factors that may influence ease and frustration ratings, comfort being honest and tendency to adjust ratings so as not to offend the interviewer and design team. Friends of the interviewers were recruited to be participants of a usability test of a purposely frustrating high-fidelity chat app prototype. During the usability testing, they were asked to think out loud as they completed six tasks with the prototype. After each task, they were asked to rate on a scale of 1 to 10 how easy and frustrating the task was to complete, and whether there was learning from a previous task that helped them complete the current task (yes/no). After the usability testing, they completed questionnaires about their friendship, personality traits, digital fluency and working memory.

For the cognitive factors, we investigated whether digital fluency and working memory (issues) relate to frustration ratings and could vary between friendship types (one-sided vs. mutual/reciprocal) – opposites may attract. Digital fluency is an important consideration when designing complex interfaces [19], which our app was meant to be. Considering working memory constraints is also important for designing mobile app user interfaces for accessibility [20].

For the social factors, we investigated whether friendship qualities, friendship type (one-sided vs. mutual/reciprocal), and gender of the interviewee and the interviewee-interviewer pair would predict frustration ratings, comfort with being honest, and tendency to adjust ratings as to not offend the interviewer or design team.

1.3   Purpose and Hypotheses

The purpose of this study was to identify the cognitive and social factors that encourage truthful frustration reporting in usability testing of unintuitive app designs within convenience samples. Cognitive factors we considered included working memory issues and digital fluency, both self-reported. We anticipated potential interviewer effects on digital fluency and working memory (issues), such that each interviewer's friends may be systematically different on these measures. Social factors we considered included individual differences of the interviewee (participant) and the friendship factors of the dyads (interviewee (participant) and interviewer). We will refer to interviewee as participant from now, so it is easily distinguishable from interviewer.

We were concerned that friendship qualities, friendship alignment, researcher, and gender would influence reporting of frustration, as well as whether the participant adjusted their ratings (from the truth) to protect the interviewer and how comfortable they felt being honest with the interviewer.

We anticipated that friendship qualities between the participant and interviewer may predict the participant to report more frustration. Our predictions come down to the motivations for lying or underreporting (e.g., saving face, reducing conflict) and motivations for reporting truthfully (e.g., helping the interviewer with their project). As such, we expected protection and conflict to be negatively correlated to frustration ratings, i.e., they serve as barriers to the truth. On the other hand, we expected reliable alliance and reflected appraisal to be positively correlated with frustration ratings, serving as motivations for truthful reporting of frustration.

We believed that the friendship dynamic, that is whether the friends (participant and interviewer) are on the same page about the friendship, i.e., mutual friendship, or different pages, i.e., either the interviewer or the participant is more invested in the friendship, to be a determining factor for whether the participant feels more comfortable being honest and therefore is more honest. If the friendship is lopsided, such that the participant knows the interviewer better, then the participant may have an easier time with perspective taking. This could reduce the cognitive load from perspective taking and free up cognitive load for problem solving of the prototype, leading to more successful task completion and lower frustration ratings. On the other hand, if the participant rates the positive friendship qualities as being higher than the interviewer (i.e., they are the overbenefited), they may have a tendency to lie and rate their frustration lower. This could be more pronounced in the opposite-sex friendships.

The literature on gender effects and opposite-gender effects would support different predictions. We may expect the men to give lower frustration ratings, as they tend to lie more often. We may expect people to give lower frustration ratings when the interviewer is a woman, as a white lie, or higher frustration ratings because they are more comfortable sharing their experience on "sensitive" questions, or because they prefer female communication styles. Female friends may give lower frustration ratings because they anticipate future interaction with this interviewer friend. A mismatch in gender between the participant and interviewer could result in higher frustration ratings if the friendship is lopsided as an avoidance behavior, or lower frustration ratings if the men are trying to appear more attractive.

2 Methods

2.1 Participants

The study was approved by the Institutional Review Board of the University of California, Los Angeles. Informed consent was obtained from the participants. Six (three female, three male) interviewers recruited 48 friends to participate in our study, one of which (from interviewer F3) did not complete the friendship survey and was excluded. These friends volunteered their time, much like the coworkers or friends at a company would. One of the interviewers recruited two siblings.

The 47 participants had an average age of 20.62 years (SD = 1.64). The group was predominantly female, with 61.7% identifying as female and 38.3% as male. On average, participants reported knowing each other for 3.72 years (SD = 4.68), with relationships ranging from 4 months to 22 years. The mean ratings of how well participants knew and how close they felt to the researcher conducting their experiment were 4.51 and 4.71, respectively, on a 5-point scale.

The predominant source of meeting their researchers according to participants was through clubs (40.4%), followed by other activities (25.5%), and classes (19.1%). Roommates (10.6%) and family members or relatives (4.3%) comprised smaller proportions of the group. Regarding the time frame in which participants met their researcher, the majority (78.7%) met during college, 14.9% during high school, and smaller proportions met in preschool or kindergarten (4.3%) or elementary school (2.1%).

2.2 Materials

Prototype. The prototype was designed to be frustrating (see link), including click pathways and buttons that are unintuitive and/or hidden in unusual places. Each of the six tasks were designed to not overlap in click pathways with each other to reduce the amount of learning that can happen from task to task.

Subjective Rating Survey. This survey was filled out by the interviewer during the usability test. The survey included each of the six scenarios and tasks for the participants to complete. After each task, interviewers recorded the participants' ratings on the ease of the task (on a scale of 1 to 10), frustration of the task (on a scale of 1 to 10), task completion (yes/no) and whether the participant saw any of the solution pathway from a previous task (yes/no).

Individual Differences Survey. This survey was completed by the participants after the usability test and included questions about their overall app experience. In their own privacy, participants rated their app experience overall on a scale of 1 (very bad) to 10 (very good), whether they would use the app again (yes/no), their comfort with sharing honest thoughts and ratings (on scale 1 to 7), how much they adjusted (higher or lower) their ratings as not to offend the research or the design team (scale 1 to 7), their issues with working memory [21, see Appendix], their digital fluency [22, see Appendix], their shortened Big 5 Personality Inventory [23], and provided their gender and age.

Friendship Survey. The Friendship survey started with a disclaimer that we will not share any of the ratings with the respective friends (interviewer to participant and participant to interviewer) and that the interviewer will be left out of the data analysis process. The friends were asked to leave their initials so that we can pair their data back with their interviewer friend, but would be otherwise, anonymized in data analyses. The interviewers were not informed whether they are M1, M2, M3, F1, F2, or F3 in this paper.

The survey asked the respondent to answer questions about their friendship with the participant or interviewer. This survey was later used to categorize friendships into mutual or lopsided friendship types. Respondents answered questions about how they consider their friend (best friend, close friend, causal friend, acquaintance), how close they are to the friend (1: not very close to 7: very close), how well they know the friend (1: barely to 7: very well), how long in years they have known this friend, where they met this friend (e.g., elementary school, classes, club, etc.), frequency of hanging out (yearly, seasonally, monthly, weekly, daily basis), and completed a Friendship Qualities questionnaire [24], which has subscales of companionship, conflict, closeness, aid, protection, reliable alliance, transcending problems, affective bond and reflected appraisal (see Table 1 for questions).

2.3 Procedure

Participants read a study information sheet and consented to participation in the study before the start of the usability test. The interviewers started with small talk questions and then warm-up questions about the domain-of-interest (chat apps). The interviewers then read through a script of instructions for the upcoming tasks. They were reminded and asked to repeat the instruction back to the interviewer, specifically checking that they mention thinking out loud while completing the tasks. Participants talked through [25] and completed six tasks that had no overlap in click pathways. After each task, the interviewers verbally asked the subjective rating questions (ease rated 1–10, frustration: 1–10) and the participants verbally answered. Afterwards, participants rated and summarized their overall experience and completed questionnaires for working memory [21], digital fluency [22], and shortened Big 5 Personality Inventory [23]. On a separate day and in the absence of their friend, the interviewers and their friends completed a survey that included questions about their friendships. Prior to starting this survey, interviewers and participants were informed that their responses to the friendship survey would not be shared with their friends.

2.4 Data Processing

To assess the dynamics of friendships, we calculated difference scores (or "pair-deltas") by subtracting the participant's score from the researcher's score for each subscale (e.g., Big Five traits, Friendship Qualities, self-reported closeness, and familiarity). We took the Friendship Qualities difference scores and standardized them (z-scores) within subscales in order to compare across different scales. A friendship was categorized as interviewer-lopsided if at least one subscale's z-score exceeded 1.5 (researcher's score is higher than participant's score) or participant-lopsided if the z-score was below −1.5 (researcher's score is lower than participant's score). Friendships were considered mutual/reciprocal if the z-scores across all subscales indicated agreement (z-score between −1.5 and 1.5).

One exception to these categorization rules involved a sibling pair, which was classified as mutual despite extreme z-scores on two subscales: 2.25 for the conflict subscale and −1.69 for the reliable alliance subscale. This manual override follows from the unique relational context of sibling dynamics, where deviations in individual perceptions may not signify true friendship asymmetry.

Additionally, pair-deltas were used to quantify measurable differences within each pair. These scores were derived from survey data submitted by both researchers and participants, capturing disparities in self-reported familiarity, closeness, and other psychological constructs. Large positive or negative pair-delta values highlighted areas of significant disagreement between pairs, offering insight into the degree of symmetry within the relationship. These deltas were subsequently analyzed for statistical significance to identify patterns and trends across the dataset.

2.5 Dependent Variables

We assessed several dependent variables derived from survey responses of researchers and participants, aimed at capturing the quality and dynamics of their relationships, individual traits, and task-related experiences. These variables are categorized into measures of friendship characteristics, psychological traits, and task-related perceptions.

The Friendship Qualities Questionnaire was used to evaluate friendship dynamics across eight subscales, each comprising multiple items rated for truthfulness on a 5-point scale (1 = "not at all", 5 = "really true"). Scores for each subscale were computed by summing the responses to its associated questions. Higher scores indicated greater agreement with the scale's construct (see FQ qualities in Table 1). Other dependent variables that came from administered surveys are listed in Table 1.

3 Results

We first assessed whether there was an interviewer effect. Analyses revealed no reliable evidence that interviewer assignment systematically influenced participant responses about subjective experiences. Interviewer assignment had no significant impact on rating adjustments, $F(5,41) = 2.05$, $p = .09$, with $BF_{10} = 0.89$ indicating inconclusive evidence. Further, neither Ease mean nor Frustration Mean varied significantly by interviewer, $p = .17$ and $p = .55$ respectively, with Bayes Factors $BF_{10} = 0.47$ and $BF_{10} = 0.22$ providing moderate-to-strong evidence in favor of the null hypothesis. We later discuss variations in recruited friends and closeness ratings (see Table 2). Despite these variations, we did not find an interviewer effect, suggesting that their unique interviewing styles and personal characteristics did not meaningfully influence task-related perceptions.

Participants generally reported high comfort levels with being honest with their responses (M = 6.72, SD = 0.58 on a 7-point scale), suggesting that they did not feel pressured or uncomfortable when providing ratings. Additionally, most participants reported minimal adjustments to their ratings throughout the experiment (M = 1.66, SD = 1.27), with the majority indicating no or very minor changes (median = 1). These findings suggest that participants consciously believed they provided honest responses and did not systematically alter their ratings, even when their friend was administering the experiment. Further analyses will explore whether implicit factors, such as friendship dynamics, influenced response patterns despite participants' reported honesty.

Table 1. Dependent variables used for our analyses. Listed is the full variable name, number of survey items it is associated with (more than 1 was computed as a composite score) and description or example questions. FQ = Friendship Qualities Questionnaire and BFI = Big Five Inventory.

Variable	# of items	Description/Question
Closeness	1	"How close do you feel to your friend?"
Wellness	1	"How well do you feel you know your friend?"
FQ Companionship (+)	4	Captures shared activities (e.g., "My friend and I spend all our free time together.")
FQ Conflict (-)	4	Measures disagreements (e.g., "My friend can bug me or annoy me even though I ask him/her not to.")
FQ Aid (+)	3	Reflects willingness to assist each other (e.g., "My friend helps me when I am having trouble with something.")
FQ Protection (+)	2	Assesses emotional and social support (e.g., "My friend would stick up for me if another kid was causing me trouble.")
FQ Reliable Alliance (+)	2	Reflects trust and dependability (e.g., "If there is something bothering me, I can tell my friend about it.")
FQ Transcending Problems (+)	3	Examines conflict resolution (e.g., "If my friend or I do something that bothers the other one of us, we can make up easily.")
FQ Affective Bond (+)	3	Captures emotional connection (e.g., "I feel happy when I am with my friend.")
FQ Reflected Appraisal (+)	2	Reflects affirmation and validation (e.g., "When I do a good job at something, my friend is happy for me.")
BFI Openness to experience	2	"I see myself as someone who has an active imagination."
BFI Conscientiousness	2	"I see myself as someone who does a thorough job."
BFI Extraversion	2	"I see myself as someone who has few artistic interests"
BFI Agreeableness	2	"I see myself as someone who is generally trusting."

(continued)

Table 1. (*continued*)

Variable	# of items	Description/Question
BFI Neuroticism	2	"I see myself as someone who gets nervous easily."
Working Memory Issues (see Appendix)	5	"When you are carrying out an activity, if you realize that you are making a mistake, do you find it difficult to change strategy?"
Digital Fluency (rest in Appendix)	8	"I can know how to solve the problems I will encounter in the digital environment."

3.1 Friendship Qualities

Given that we had 47 participants total and that each of the six interviewers had only 4–13 participants (see Table 2, one of F3's participants was excluded), we decided to run Spearman's correlations instead of multiple linear regression. We discuss the significant and marginally significant results by interviewer, participant and delta (interviewer minus participant), but all correlations can be found in Table 3. We frame these results in terms that relate to higher frustration reporting.

From the perspective of the interviewer, recruiting participants based on their *aid* and *reflected appraisal* seems to be important for frustration reporting. When the interviewer receives less help (*aid*) from their friend, then their friend rates the prototype as more frustrating, $r(46) = -0.31$, $p = .03$. Perhaps giving your friend better ratings, even if not truthful, is seen by the participant as a helpful behavior. When interviewers rated getting positive feedback (*reflected appraisal*) in their friendships higher, their friends reported more frustration with the frustrating prototype, but this correlation was only marginally significant, $r(46) = 0.25$, $p = 0.09$. This suggests that the participant may feel more comfortable giving negative feedback (reporting frustration) when the participant has given the interviewer positive feedback in the past. In other words, recruiting friends who are low aid but high in appraisal may be beneficial in receiving negative feedback.

From the perspective of the participant, the most important qualities seem to be *companionship* and *transcending problems*, in other words, we want participants who are low in companionship with the interviewer and low on needing conflict resolution. When participants perceived their friendships as being lower in companionship (e.g., shared activities), they rated the prototype more frustrating, but this correlation was significant, $r(46) = -0.29$, $p = .05$. This negative correlation can be interpreted in two ways: those high in companionship may want to preserve the friendship by underreporting frustration and those lower in companionship may either feel safe to report the frustration (i.e., nothing to lose) or be transferring their frustration of low companionship to the task.

When participants rated their conflict resolution abilities (*transcending problems*) in their friendships lower, they reported more frustration, and this correlation was significant, $r(46) = -0.29$, $p = .04$. It is important to note that this subscale measures the likeliness of resolving conflict when conflict arises and does not measure the amount of conflict that already exists. It is possible that someone with low conflict resolution abilities with their friend also has low conflict with their friend. Nonetheless, this result suggests that low conflict resolution is not preventing frustration reporting. Another interpretation could be that those who see more yet resolve less conflict in their friendships could also see more pain points in prototypes.

The predictors: conflict, aid, protection and affective bond are only marginally significant. When participants perceived less *conflict* in their friendships, they rated the prototype more frustrating, but this correlation was marginally significant, $r(46) = -0.26$, $p = 0.07$. Fewer pre-existing conflicts may make the participant feel more comfortable to report frustration, just as more pre-existing conflicts may make the participant want to avoid conflict.

When participants received less help (*aid*) from their friend, they reported more frustration, but this correlation was only marginally significant, $r(46) = -0.25$, $p = .09$.

If the participants received less help from their friend in the past, they may not be as inclined to help their friend by giving them better ratings, or lower frustration ratings. Conversely, the higher frustration ratings could again be seen as transference of frustration about not getting more help in other aspects of the friendship onto the task.

When the participants receive less emotional and social support (*protection*) from their friend, they report more frustration, but this correlation was marginally significant, $r(46) = -0.24$, $p = .09$. Participants who do not get much emotional or social support from their friends may not feel the need to be reciprocal in giving emotional support on the interviewer's project or product design. When the participants feel less of an *affective bond* (e.g., interviewer is happy to see them) from their friend, they report more frustration, but this correlation was marginally significant, $r(46) = -0.26$, $p = 0.07$. This again could reflect something about the friendship more than the task itself. It also suggests that the energy the interviewer brings to the interview could also influence the emotions, including frustration, and the sharing of the emotions of the participant. If the interviewer is more positive, maybe the participant would be inclined to be more positive about the prototype as well.

Finally, we found a significant correlation between the difference in *reflected appraisal* between interviewer and participant and frustration reporting. The more the interviewer has given positive feedback to the participant in the past, the more likely they are to give higher frustration ratings. This could reflect both a perceived safety to report the negative feedback to the friend (the friend will take it well) and a safety from being perceived negatively (the friend will not think poorly of me and my skills).

3.2 Friendship Lopsidedness

We sought to determine whether the six interviewers recruited systematically different types of friends and whether friendship lopsidedness (the degree of asymmetry in friendship perception) was associated with differences in task performance and cognitive responses. To test this, we used friendship lopsidedness as an independent variable to predict differences in frustration levels, working memory, and digital fluency. Separate one-way ANOVAs were conducted for each dependent variable to assess whether significant differences existed across mutual, interviewer-lopsided, and participant-lopsided

Table 2. Correlations between the eight qualities from the Friendship Qualities Questionnaire (rated by the interviewer, participant and the delta or difference between the two) and average frustration ratings across our six tasks

Friendship Quality	Interviewer	Participant	Delta (Interviewer - Participant)
companionship	−0.15	**−0.29***	0.21
conflict	−0.16	−0.26+	−0.03
Aid	**−0.31***	−0.25+	0.09
protection	−0.13	−0.24+	0.09
reliable alliance	−0.22	−0.199	−0.03
transcending problems	−0.15	**−0.29***	0.13
affective bond	−0.14	−0.26+	0.17
reflected appraisal	0.25+	−0.19	**0.36***

+ p < .10, * p < .05 ** p < .01, *** p < .001

friendships. We computed Bayes Factors (BFs) to quantify the strength of evidence against an effect of friendship lopsidedness.

Across all analyses, friendship lopsidedness did not significantly predict any dependent variable, p's > .10. A one-way ANOVA revealed no significant effect of friendship lopsidedness on frustration mean, $F(2,44) = 1.18$, $p = .32$, working memory difficulties, $F(2,44) = 0.17$, $p = .85$, or digital fluency, $F(2,44) = 0.16$, $p = .85$. To further examine the strength of these null results, Bayes Factors were computed, with $BF_{10} = 0.36$ for frustration mean and $BF_{10} = 0.18$ for both working memory and digital fluency. These values suggest that friendship lopsidedness does not meaningfully impact cognitive performance, frustration, or digital fluency in this experimental context.

An ANOVA of friendship lopsidedness on pair delta closeness was also conducted. The ANOVA showed a marginal effect on pair delta closeness, $F(2,44) = 2.76$, $p = .075$, with a Bayes Factor ($BF_{10} = 1.04$) indicating weak evidence for an effect. On average, participant-lopsided friendships had the largest discrepancy ($M = −0.73$, $SD = 1.39$), while mutual friendships showed a smaller difference ($M = −0.33$, $SD = 1.33$), and interviewer-lopsided friendships exhibited a positive closeness delta ($M = 0.43$, $SD = 1.34$), which is a trend consistent with the construction of the lopsidedness groupings. While inconclusive, this result raises the question of whether individual interviewers systematically influenced the closeness ratings reported by participants.

The potential presence of such effects will be explored in the next section.

3.3 Interviewer Effect

We examined whether researcher effects influenced participant responses, in terms of friendship lopsidedness, rating adjustments, and task-related experiences.

Since the assumptions of a regular Chi-square test were not met (80% of expected frequencies not above 5), we performed a Fisher's Exact Test, using Monte Carlo simulation on our 6 interviewer × 3 friendship type contingency table in Table 2. Using

Table 3. Characteristics of the friends recruited for the usability test per interviewer. M denotes male interviewer and F denotes female interviewer.

Interviewer	M1	M2	M3	F1	F2	F3
# of Participants	10	7	13	6	7	4
% Male Participants	20	57.14	46.15	50	28.57	25
% Female Participants	80	42.86	53.85	50	71.43	75
# Mutual Friendships	5	1	5	2	2	3
# Participant-Lopsided Friendships	2	6	2	2	2	1
# Interviewer-Lopsided Friendships	3	0	6	2	3	0
Mean Close Delta	−0.7	−0.14	0.85	−1.17	−0.43	−1
SD Close Delta	1.16	0.69	1.52	1.60	1.13	0.82
Mean Well Delta	−0.9	0.14	0.62	−0.33	0.71	−1.25
SD Well Delta	1.10	1.07	1.04	1.03	1.98	0.96

a log-likelihood chi-square approximation, we get a marginally significant relationship between interviewer and friendship lopsidedness (participant-lopsided, mutual, or interviewer-lopsided), $2(10) = 17.28$, $p = .07$, the Bayes Factor ($BF_{10} > 100$) suggests strong evidence in favour χ of an effect. This result could be because the distribution of friendship lopsidedness across interviewers was uneven. M2 possessed the highest portion of participant-lopsided friendships while M3 possessed the highest portion of interviewer-lopsided friendships. Although this pattern raises the possibility that some researchers systematically recruited or interacted with different types of friends, the evidence remains inconclusive.

3.4 Gender

Our results did not reveal any significant effects of gender on frustration reporting, rating behavior, or overall task experience, which we will discuss further later. However, an interesting but non-significant trend emerged: men tended to report lower Ease mean scores compared to women, though their variance in responses was comparable. This pattern suggests that men and women may use different implicit baselines when rating task experiences, with men systematically assigning lower numerical scores while maintaining similar response variability. The following subsections examine these findings in greater detail, considering both individual gender effects and gender dynamics within pairs.

Gender Pairings. We examined whether the gender composition of interviewer-participant pairs (M-M, M-F, F-M, F-F) influenced consistency in perceived closeness (close delta) or task-related experiences (ease and frustration means). No significant effects were observed across any of these measures. Close delta was not significantly influenced by gender pairing, $F(3,43) = 1.85$, $p = .15$, with $BF_{10} = 0.63$, suggesting moderate evidence in favor of the null hypothesis. Similarly, gender pairing did not affect the Ease mean, $F(3,43) = 0.84$, $p = .48$, or Frustration mean, $F(3,43) = 0.07$, $p = .98$, with Bayes Factors of $BF_{10} = 0.26$ and $BF_{10} = 0.13$, respectively, providing strong evidence that gender composition did not systematically influence perceived ease or frustration during the experiment. These results indicate that the specific gender pairing of interviewer and participant did not meaningfully shape perceptions of interpersonal closeness or task experience.

We also tested whether being in a same-gender (M-M, F-F) or different-gender (F-M, M-F) pairing influenced task-related experiences and rating adjustments, but found no significant effects across any measures. The Ease mean, $F(1, 45) = 0.23$, $p = .64$, Frustration mean, $F(1, 45) = 0.15$, $p = .70$, and app experience, $F(1, 45) = 0.04$, $p = .85$, all yielded Bayes Factors ($BF_{10} < 0.32$), providing moderate evidence in favor of the null hypothesis. Similarly, tendency to adjust ratings, $F(1, 45) = 2.05$, $p = .16$, showed no significant difference by gender pairing, with $BF_{10} = 0.66$, indicating inconclusive evidence for an effect. These findings indicate that whether the interviewer and participant were of the same or different gender did not systematically influence their responses or task-related experiences.

There was also no effects of gender pairing (match vs. mismatch), friendship type (mutual or lopsided) or its interaction on frustration ratings, $F(1, 104.3) = <0.99$, p's > 0.33.

Participant's Gender. Analyses examining the effect of participant gender on task-related perceptions and rating behavior revealed no statistically significant findings. Frustration mean, $F(1, 45) = 0.02$, $p = .88$, tendency to adjust rating, $F(1, 45) = 0.25$, $p = .62$, and comfort being honest, $F(1, 45) = 1.10$, $p = .30$, all produced Bayes Factors ($BF_{10} < 0.47$), indicating moderate evidence in favor of the null hypothesis.

There was an interesting trend observed when examining Ease mean ($F(1, 45) = 2.63$, $p = .11$, $BF_{10} = 0.85$) and app experience ($F(1, 45) = 2.40$, $p = .13$, $BF_{10} = 0.77$), where men tended to provide lower scores (Ease: $M = 5.67$, $SD = 1.18$; App Experience: $M = 5.44$, $SD = 2.12$) than women (Ease: $M = 6.29$, $SD = 1.33$; App Experience: $M = 6.49$, $SD = 2.18$). An ANOVA on Ease mean standard deviation revealed no difference in variance between men and women, suggesting that while men may have rated experiences using a consistently lower numerical range, the overall spread of their responses was comparable to women's. This pattern may suggest men and women rely on different implicit baselines when using rating scales, with men systematically anchoring their responses lower on the scale while maintaining a similar degree of variability. This gender difference was not explained by a difference in agreeableness, $t(45) = 1.20$, $p = 0.24$.

4 Discussion

In our study, we were interested in understanding the social/relational dynamics that may influence frustration reporting when recruiting friends to participate in an usability testing and whether recruiting in this way would produce systematic differences (i.e., a person's friends may be systematically different than another person's friends). We had six researchers (three female, three male) recruit their friends to complete tasks within a purposefully frustrating digital prototype. Both parties then filled out a Friendship Qualities Questionnaire [15] and other details about their friendships so we can identify mutual/reciprocal friendships and lopsided ones.

We anticipated interviewer effects on working memory issues and digital fluency but we did not find this difference. All interviewers recruited participants with similar levels of working memory and digital fluency, which may be due to recruiting from the same age group. While friends tend to be within the same age group, coworkers may be from different age groups.

We expected friendship qualities of protection and conflict (rated by participant) to be negatively correlated with frustration ratings, serving as barriers to the truth, and did in fact find marginally significant negative correlations. On the other hand, we expected reliable alliance and reflected appraisal (rated by the participant, as motivation to be truthful) to be positively correlated with frustration ratings, but did not find a reliable correlation. However, we did find that reflected appraisal (rated by the interviewer and in combination with the participant) was positively correlated with frustration ratings. Other qualities that were significant were *aid* received by the interviewer, *companionship* rated by participant, and *transcending problems* (resolving conflicts) rated by the participant. Friendships that are low on each of these were predictive of more frustration reporting, which could reflect a lack of desire to *help* make the friend look good or a transference of friendship dissatisfaction to the frustrating task. Other marginal correlations with other friendship qualities suggest a similar narrative. Currently, our design is unable to distinguish between these two interpretations.

We also anticipated that friendship lopsidedness would play a role in frustration reporting, with lower frustration ratings from interviewer-lopsided friendships due to easier perspective taking and participant-lopsided due to a tendency to lie in these friendships. However, we did not find that friendship lopsidedness predicted ease or frustration ratings, comfort being honest or adjustment of ratings to protect feelings.

We did find, however, a marginally significant effect of the interviewer on the friendship lopsidedness, with some interviewers recruiting more lopsided (and in one direction lopsided) friends than others. This could reflect natural friendship tendencies of the interviewers or a self-selection effect of who the interviewers asked and which participants agreed to participate in the study. Another consideration is our definition of these three friendship categories (mutual, interviewer-lopsided, participant-lopsided), which used -1.5 and 1.5 z-scores as benchmarks and nicely divided our friendship pairs into relatively equivalent groups. A different definition of these friendships may have changed the result of our analyses.

Finally, we anticipated some gender effects: men giving lower frustration ratings as white lies, women giving lower frustration ratings to avoid conflict in future interactions, the female interviewers getting lower frustration ratings from white lies or higher frustration ratings from participants being more comfortable, and gender-pairings influencing frustration ratings. None of these were found. However, we did find that men gave significantly lower ease ratings than the women, perhaps reflecting a greater comfort with using the lower end of the scale. Women, on the other hand, may feel uncomfortable giving a lower ease rating and give inflated ease ratings as a white lie. This correlation was not explained by differences in agreeableness. We also anticipated an interaction between gender pairing and friendship type (mutual vs. lopsided) that we also did not observe.

While friends are different from coworkers in many ways, such as not having a named leader, they are still long-term relationships with people that we know better than strangers. There are still similar qualities of social exchange, social support, perspective taking, and opposite-sex dynamics. Some of the friendship qualities we assessed are relevant for coworkers too, such as conflict, transcending problems, aid, etc. While our study does not necessarily directly generalize to coworkers, and a sample using coworkers is more desirable, our study reveals concerns with convenience sampling that could still be concerns with sampling from coworkers. The correlations we found could be the complete opposite with coworkers; only a sample with coworkers would tell. Of course, there are other considerations to make, such as whether the coworker is the same-level on the employment hierarchy as the interviewer, whether they are working on the same team, have very different roles, etc.

Some limitations in our study are the friends that could be recruited. Each interviewer had pre-existing friends and these naturally occurring friendships could be different for each person. We did not carefully pick our interviewers to meet certain criteria of the Big Five Inventory, have a certain number of friends, or a certain number of lopsided friendships, but we certainly could have in order to keep these characteristics more balanced. We ended up with interviewers who had opposite profiles of lopsided friendships (M2, M3), more female friends than male friends (M1, F2, F3) and roughly even-split (M2, M3, F2). Our female interviewers also had fewer friends in their sample than the male interviewers. One of the female interviewers had a friend not fill out their friendship survey, resulting in 4 instead of the 5 intended participants. We did balance the genders and ethnicities of the interviewers (3 male: 2 East Asians, 1 Pacific Islander; 3 female: 2 East Asians, 1 South Asian). Directly manipulating the interview style (or training for particular interview style) would be an interesting dimension to explore in the future.

Our measures for honesty may not have captured any unconscious biases. Our participants reported high honesty with a favorable mean and restricted range in reporting their comfort being honest ($M = 6.72$, $SD = 0.58$ on a 7-point scale) or the adjustments of ratings ($M = 1.66$, $SD = 1.27$ on a 7-point scale, median = 1). These scores could be taken at face value but could also be a result of demand characteristics. Future research should look for subtler ways to measure this.

Finally, we made the assumption that the participant and interviewer reports of friendship qualities could be trusted equivalently. However, the participants could have trusted the disclaimer that their ratings would not be shared with their friends less than the interviewers. For fear of potential consequences of not rating their friends highly and them seeing the scores (during data analysis), the participants may have slightly inflated the scores on the Friendship Qualities Questionnaire [15].

Our study has implications for recruiting participants when convenience sampling cannot be avoided. If the goal is to detect frustration when frustration exists, then the characteristics the interviewer should be looking for in their friend recruits are low on the dimensions of aid, companionship, and conflict resolution tendencies, and those that the interviewer has given positive feedback in the past. If one wants to avoid participants who would rate favorably to keep good relations or keep the peace, then one should avoid recruiting fruits high on these dimensions. One could also consider whether to use ease ratings or frustration ratings depending on their goal. If one wants to avoid gender differences, one could use frustration ratings. To get more truthful responses, ease ratings may be better, but more indicative from male participants. In a work setting, where there are no other conflicts of interest, one can use our results as general guidelines for selecting amongst friends who are not directly related to one's own team or project.

Acknowledgments. We would like to thank Brandon Day, Khoa Le, Jonathan Keung, Maleeha Zaman, Ashley Wang, and Sharon Zhao for serving as interviewers and their friends for participating in the study. We would also like to thank Brandon Day and Sharon Zhao for creating the Figma prototype and Maleeha Zaman for her feedback on this paper. There is an overlap in samples with [26] and [27].

Disclosure of Interests.   The authors have no competing interests to declare that are relevant to the content of this article.

Appendix

Selected items from Digital Fluency [22].
Rated on scale 1 (totally disagree) to 5 (totally agree)

1. I have the necessary motivation to develop my digital competencies.
2. I can use digital tools without any problems.
3. I can know how to solve the problems I will encounter in the digital environment.
4. I can adapt to new technologies.
5. I can use different digital devices.
6. I can benefit from expert guidance on new technologies.
7. I am concerned about acquiring digital skills.
8. I feel lazy about improving my digital skills.

Selected items from Working Memory Questionnaire [21].
Rate on scale 0 (not at all) to 4 (extremely)

1. If somebody speaks quickly to you, do you find it difficult to remember what you were told or asked? (storage domain)
2. Do you have difficulty remembering what you have read? (storage domain)
3. When you are interrupted during an activity by a loud noise (door slam, car horn) do you have difficulty in getting back to the activity? (attention domain)
4. When you are carrying out an activity, if you realise that you are making a mistake, do you find it difficult to change strategy? (executive domain)
5. Are you particularly disturbed if an unexpected event interrupts your day or what you are in the process of doing? (executive domain)

References

1. Turner, R.E., Edgley, C., Olmstead, G.: Information control in conversations: honesty is not always the best policy. Kansas J. Sociol. **11**(1), 69–89 (1975)
2. Tosone, C.: Living everyday lies: the experience of self. Clin. Soc. Work J. **34**(3), 335–348 (2006)
3. Cupach, W.R., Metts, S.: Facework. Sage, Thousand Oaks (1994)
4. Goffman, E.: Interaction Ritual: Essays in Face-to-Face Behavior. Adrine, Chicago (1967)
5. Smith, A.F.R., Fortunato, V.J.: Factors influencing employee intentions to provide honest upward feedback ratings. J. Bus. Psychol. **22**, 191–207 (2008)
6. Sias, P.M.: Peer coworker relationships. In: Peer Coworker Relationships, pp. 57–88. SAGE Publications, Inc. (2009). https://doi.org/10.4135/9781452204031
7. Messman, S.J., Canarym, D.J., Hause, K.S.: Motives to remain platonic, equity, and the use of maintenance strategies in opposite-sex friendships. J. Soc. Pers. Relat. **17**(1), 67–94 (2000)
8. Bleske-Rechek, A.L., Buss, D.M.: Opposite-sex friendship: sex differences and similarities in initiation, selection, and dissolution. Pers. Soc. Psychol. Bull. **27**(10), 1310–1323 (2001). https://doi.org/10.1177/01461672012710007
9. Badhwar, N.K.: Thirty-three friends as ends in themselves. Sex Love Friendsh. (1992). https://doi.org/10.1163/9789004495050_039
10. Kitts, J.A., Leal, D.F.: What is(n't) a friend? Dimensions of the friendship concept among adolescents. Soc. Netw. **66**, 161–170 (2021)
11. Rowatt, W.C., Cunningham, M., Druen, P.: Lying to get a date: the effect of facial physical attractiveness on the willingness to deceive prospective dating partners. J. Soc. Pers. Relat. **16**(2), 209–223 (1999)
12. Jampol, L., Zayas, V.: Gendered white lies: women are given inflated performance feedback compared with men. Pers. Soc. Psychol. Bull. **47**(1), 57–69 (2021). https://doi.org/10.1177/0146167220916622
13. Capraro, V.: Gender differences in lying in sender-receiver games: a meta-analysis. Judgm. Decis. Mak. **13**(4), 345–355 (2018). https://doi.org/10.1017/S1930297500009220
14. Tyler, J.M., Feldman, R.S.: Truth, lies and self-presentation: how gender and anticipated future interaction relate to deceptive behavior. J. Appl. Soc. Psychol. **34**(12), 2602–2615 (2004)
15. Wright, R.R.: The effects of gender communication patterns on opposite gender attraction. Undergraduate Honors Capstone Projects. 701 (2006)
16. Huddy, L., Billig, J., Bracciodieta, J., Hoeffler, L., Moynihan, P.J., Pugliani, P.: The effect of interviewer gender on the survey response. Polit. Behav. **19**(3), 197–220 (1997). http://www.jstor.org/stable/586516
17. DePaulo, B.M., Kashy, D.A.: Everyday lies in close and casual relationships. J. Pers. Soc. Psychol. **74**(1), 63–79 (1998). https://doi.org/10.1037/0022-3514.74.1.63
18. Vassar, A.: The effect of personality in sample selection for usability testing. Master's thesis, The University of New South Wales (2011)
19. Xu, J., Liu, S., Fu, X.: Applying working memory theory to redesign a mobile application user interface: take a handicraft self-learning page as an example. In: Marcus, A., Wang, W. (eds.) DUXU 2017. LNCS, vol. 10289, pp. 324–332. Springer, Cham (2017). https://doi.org/10.1007/978-3-319-58637-3_26
20. Nouri, S.S., Avila-Garcia, P., Cemballi, A.G., Sarkar, U., Aguilera, A., Lyles, C.R.: Assessing mobile phone digital literacy and engagement in user-centered design in a diverse, safety-net population: mixed methods study. JMIR Mhealth Uhealth **7**(8), e14250 (2019). https://doi.org/10.2196/14250
21. Vallat-Azouvi, C., Pradat-Diehl, P., Azouvi, P.: The working memory questionnaire: a scale to assess everyday life problems related to deficits of working memory in brain injured patients. Neuropsychol. Rehabil. **22**(4), 634–649 (2012)

22. Demir, K., Odabasi, H.F.: Development of digital fluency scale: validity and reliability study. Themes eLearning **15**, 1–20 (2022)
23. Rammstedt, B., John, O.P.: Measuring personality in one minute or less: a 10 item short version of the Big Five Inventory in English and German. J. Res. Pers. **41**, 203–212 (2007)
24. Bukowski, W.M., Hoza, B., Boivin, M.: Measuring friendship quality during pre- and early adolescence: the development and psychometric properties of the friendship qualities scale. J. Soc. Pers. Relat. **11**, 471–484 (1994)
25. McDonald, S., Cockton, G., Irons, A.: The impact of thinking-aloud on usability inspection. Proc. ACM Hum.-Comput. Interact. **4**(88), 1–22 (2020). https://doi.org/10.1145/3397876
26. Cui, L., Cross, M., Day, B., Wan, C.: Speaking fast, speaking more: how personality and social context affect user interview dynamics - a transcript text analysis. In: Human-Computer Interaction International 2025 Proceedings, Gothenburg, Sweden, 22–27 June 2025. Springer, Cham (2025)
27. Cui, L., Zaman, M.: Knowing the interviewer: friend or foe? Differences in ease, frustration and quit rates between friends and strangers in usability testing. In: Human-Computer Interaction International 2025 Proceedings, Gothenburg, Sweden, 22–27 June 2025. Springer, Cham (2025)

Speaking Fast, Speaking More: How Personality and Social Context Affect User Interview Dynamics - A Transcript Text Analysis

Lucy Cui[1,2(✉)] [iD], Matthew Cross[2], Brandon Day[2], and Chelsea Wan[2]

[1] State University of New York at New Paltz, New Paltz, NY 12561, USA
lucy.cui.phd@gmail.com
[2] University of California, Los Angeles, Los Angeles, CA 90095, USA

Abstract. Typical usability tests may use task performance and subjective ratings as the main forms of feedback on the prototype. We take a step further and analyze the transcripts of usability tests for the quality and quantity of feedback, assessed through interview duration, speech rate, unique adjective use, and negativity percentage. We had six interviewers (three female, three male) recruit strangers and friends to complete a usability test of an intentionally frustrating prototype. We had them rate their experienced ease and frustration with the tasks and complete questionnaires about their personality traits and the perceived personality traits of the interviewer. We then transcribed their interviews and compared these objective metrics to their subjective ratings, considering their relationship with the interviewer, their gender and the personality traits of the interviewee and interviewer. We found significant correlations between our objective metrics (e.g., adjectives and negativity, speech rate and adjectives), differences between groups (friends spoke faster and more), and influences of personality on objective metrics (e.g., extraversion on adjectives and negativity) and perceptions of the interviewer (e.g., conscientiousness sees conscientiousness). The correlations we found between speech rate and extraversion were loosely consistent with previous literature. We discuss the implications of our findings for recruiting participants for and analyzing the data of usability tests.

Keywords: usability testing · user experience · interviews · text analysis · personality

1 Introduction

Usability testing can often be a part of iterative design and product development. When it is part of the process, there are considerations on participant selection. Not every company can afford (e.g., proprietary, financial) to use crowdsourced participants, so convenience sampling within the company for usability testing is common. However, the issues this introduces to usability testing outcomes, like the validity and reliability of the feedback collected, are understudied. People we know, such as friends or coworkers, may have social incentives to leave out negative feedback and/or protect our egos [1–4].

© The Author(s), under exclusive license to Springer Nature Switzerland AG 2025
M. Schrepp (Ed.): HCII 2025, LNCS 15794, pp. 329–344, 2025.
https://doi.org/10.1007/978-3-031-93221-2_21

Not all frustration is consciously reported in usability testing - other measures, like eye tracking and mouse tracking, could be better indicators [5]. That considered, interviews with users are still the quickest way to get feedback and do not require fancy software or hardware and specialized researchers. Literature on how to craft the ideal environment for truth-finding of a product's usability from user interviews is lacking.

Usability testing could be broken down into logistical components: who are the participants, who are the researchers, what is the task and what are the questions being asked. The former two (interviewee and interviewer characteristics) get assigned more automatically. Beyond general eligibility criteria for the interviewees (e.g., age, gender, background) and qualifications of the interviewer (e.g., design, research or product management background), other social aspects are not readily considered when choosing the interviewee, interviewer, and the pair of them.

Little to no literature exists on these methodological considerations for user interviews. Only one study investigated the impact of personality on user feedback - extraversion predicted more talking and more detailed feedback [6]. That study was a master's thesis. There is, however, research from other domains and contexts, such as job interviews, ethnographic interviews, and first impressions between strangers, that we can draw on to predict the influence of personality, interviewer (characteristics), interviewee (characteristics) on the type of feedback (e.g., speech rate, subjective ratings) user could provide during a user interview. We discuss the literature from these other domains and then how social dynamics (e.g., coworker or friend versus stranger) may play a role in honest frustration reporting.

1.1 Personality Traits

One of the most researched personality tests is the Big Five Inventory. The Big Five Inventory [7] measures personality on five dimensions: Openness to Experience, Consciousness, Extraversion, Agreeableness and Neuroticism and has been found to correlate with job performance [8] to academic performance [9]. Openness to experience reflects traits like curiosity, imagination and creativity. Conscientiousness captures qualities like being organized, responsible, and goal-oriented. Extraversion reflects how sociable one is with others. Agreeableness describes being compassionate and harmonious with others. Neuroticism represents one tendency towards negative emotions, such as stress, anxiety and mood swings.

These Big Five personality dimensions have been considered in workplace dynamics and interpersonal contexts. Aspects of extraversion have been thought to positively impact leadership, such as being a role model, inspirational, optimistic, coaching and guiding others [10]. Personality traits also seem to determine how people approach conflicts [11]. For example, having a compromising style (or integrating style) in conflict resolution is positively associated with agreeableness, extraversion, openness to experience, and conscientiousness [11]. Extraverted people tend to have more dominating styles and agreeable people tend to have less dominating styles [18]. Agreeable people tend to have obliging styles instead [11]. Neurotic people are less likely to have an integrating style [11].

Given the tendency for Big Five personality dimensions to predict approaches to job functions, we wanted to consider the Big Five dimensions of the interviewees and the interviewers. Both aspects may be relevant for revealing the true experience of the user during a usability test. For example, the more agreeable someone is, the more likely they may suppress the expression of their own needs and sharing of opinions to reduce conflict.

1.2 Interviewer Effects

Previous literature has suggested the relevance of Big Five personality dimensions in interviewers' performance and style. Interviewers who are higher on conscientiousness are more likely to read questions verbatim from an interview script [12]. The interviewers' personality may also play a role in the variability of interview outcomes [13]. The authors were concerned that interviewers high on agreeableness, openness, and extraversion would adopt a 'chatty' and informal approach to interviewing, giving rise to more variable responses. However, they found no such relationship.

Other qualities of interviewers are important to consider. For example, the interviewer seemed to make a difference in interview outcomes depending on the amount of interviewing experience and whether one is in a supervisory role [37, 38].

Demographic variables, such as gender, age, and ethnicity have been found to predict these interviewer differences [14], but whether a difference is found depends greatly on the question type and survey topic. O'Muircheartaigh and Campanelli found an interviewer effect of age and gender for the British Household Panel but not in other surveys [15]. Others found interviewer effects among older interviewers and ethnic minority groups for many but not all items [16].

The question type could also influence what the interviewers get as responses. Sensitive questions, non-factual questions and open questions had systematically larger interviewer effects than other types of interview questions [17]. Gender may play a role in these sensitive questions too. Some researchers found a gender-of-interviewer effect on questions related to women's rights, with less educated and younger participants being more susceptible [18].

In our case, these "sensitive" questions could be asking the participants to disclose their true frustrations with the prototype and whether they would want to use the app again. Interviewers with certain personality traits may make the interviewee more comfortable to answer these questions.

1.3 Interviewee Effects

Interviewer effects may also depend on the interviewee. Besides the aforementioned relationship between extraversion and the quantity and quality of user feedback [6], the most common relationship discussed regarding interviewee effects is matching interviewee with the interviewer. An *interviewer matching effect*, where the interviewer matches some quality of the interviewee, has been found [19]. Race-of-the-interviewer seems to affect the reported attitudes of out-group races from the interviewee. Blacks would express more warmth of closeness towards whites when interviewed by whites than when interviewed by blacks (Anderson). This could be a way to reduce potential conflicts and to appear to be more open-minded and less prejudiced than one is. Regardless, this example shows that social pressures could influence attitude reporting.

Gender Effects on Lying. Previous literature has shown that gender may influence the type and rate of lying and for what purpose. People are more likely to tell white lies related to (under)performance to women, giving more positive comments on the same quality of work [20]. Men are more likely than females to tell black lies (benefiting themselves at the cost of others) and white lies (benefiting others at the cost of themselves), and no reliable difference in Pareto white lies (benefiting both parties) [21]. Thus, we expect that the gender of the interviewer and the interviewee may influence the reporting of frustration and other usability issues, how comfortable they are to report honestly and how much they adjusted their ratings to protect feelings.

1.4 Perceived Credibility in Speech

People tend to make assumptions about speakers and their messages based on different acoustic features of their speech. When it comes to trustworthiness of information, people tend to judge speakers with higher-pitched voices and slower speech rate as being less truthful [22]. More specifically, higher-pitched voices signal nervousness, and slower speech rate signal a lack of fluency and passivity [22]. On the other hand, people find faster speakers to be more credible, more persuasive, more competent, and more confident [22–24]. Normal, or average, speech rate was perceived as most benevolent [24]. Faster speech rates could be perceived as more persuasive because people may not get the chance to carefully evaluate the message [23]. In fact, people had a harder time cognitively elaborating a quickly spoken message than a slower-spoken one [24, 25]. We use this literature as a basis for inferring credibility of the interviewee and their reporting of frustration through the analysis of speech rate in our interview transcripts.

1.5 Social relationships: Coworkers and Friends

There is to some degree self-selection concerns when using those who are coworkers or friends with each other as participants. Coworkers may have similar cognitive preferences (e.g., they chose the same company, industry, or occupation), similar backgrounds (e.g., locals in the area, educational status, specialization), similar values (e.g., salary, work-life balance, location), etc. Friends may have similar cognitive preferences (e.g., conversational topics), similar backgrounds (e.g., same school, same town), similar interests (e.g., hobbies, clubs, social events), etc. This self-selection into a "group" may produce systematic differences between the people in the group and those who are not part of the group.

Even though coworkers (some of whom may be friends) are often the targets of convenience sampling within companies, we used a sample that was convenient to us, the friends of the interviewers in our study. This sample introduces the familiarity and long-term social consequence aspects that we would get with coworkers but is in no way an equivalent group. We discuss the potential differences and similarities between coworkers and friends in our use of the literature and later on, in our discussion of our results.

Coworkers, as a group, and friends, as a group, form differently and have different dynamics in play. One's attainment of group membership may be distinctly different, such that coworkers went through an interviewing and hiring process that may have involved a few coworkers, whereas new friends can join friend groups through just one mutual friend. The leader of a workgroup may select for particular characteristics in their subordinates or select to form a well-balanced team, whereas friend groups typically do not have this conscious selection process unless the friend group stemmed from a student organization or club that uses such protocols. Thus, the group boundaries may be more or less firm between coworkers and between friends.

The dynamics of people within these two groups may also be distinctively different. In a workplace, the leader may contribute to the culture of the group but the employees may create this culture too, through concertive control (socially constructed norms) [26] or through employee-organization relationships (performing beyond their job functions to align with organizational values) [27]. Employees may also hide their true negative feelings from their managers and use their coworkers as an outlet. Displaced aggression theory postulates that employees who cannot show aggression towards their managers may displace their aggression to their coworkers [28]. While there may be hierarchies within friendships, the above behaviors may be less frequent or pronounced.

Certainly, coworkers could be friends or have friendly or mutually beneficial relationships with their coworkers. There are four types of peer-coworker relationship functions: (1) mentorship that could be influenced by in-group dynamics, e.g., sex, race), (2) information exchange, (3) power, control, and influence, such as coworker talk, concertive control (socially constructed norms reinforced by employees), and bullying, and (4) social support, which could be instrumental, informational, or emotional (Sias, 2009). Some of these functions may overlap with friendships as well, such as social support, information exchange or mentorship.

Some similarities may exist between coworkers and friendships. In both, there is a high possibility of shared experiences. There may also be shared group identities. The self-categorization theory says that people define themselves as members of a social group and this category could influence group behavior [29]. Self-categorization could influence the perceptions and behaviors of coworkers - shared group identity promotes feelings of inclusion whereas rigid groups may alienate others [30]. The social exchange theory, commonly talked about with friendships can also be applied to coworkers, where the quality of the relationship depends on time, trust developed and mutual benefits received [30, 31].

Finally, both coworkers and friends may regularly participate in perspective-taking. Perspective-taking happens in friendships for social support and communication [32]. At work, perspective-taking fosters positive social relationships and is helpful for idea exploration, harmonization, and coworker support [33]. This tendency may also influence the nature of feedback, as coworkers might focus on maintaining harmonious relationships rather than providing honest critiques. Perspective-taking is specific to the dyad or pair of people and could have differential implications depending on who is doing the perspective-taking and getting their perspective taken [33]. Friends may engage in more emotion- and experience-related perspective-taking while coworkers may engage in more domain- and work-related perspective-taking to complete job functions.

In general, perspective-taking is an effortful cognitive process [33]. Perspective-taking may be easier to do with someone we are familiar with than with someone we are unfamiliar with. Therefore, the friends may have more cognitive resources available to complete the frustrating tasks in our study than the strangers.

2 Our Study

In our study, we have strangers and friends complete a usability test of an intentionally frustrating prototype. They verbally respond to questions about their experience completing the tasks (reported ease and frustration) and with the prototype in general. We transcribe these user interviews and analyze their interview duration, word count, speech rate, and (negative) adjective use. We then explore the relationships of these dependent measures to social relationships (stranger or friend), gender, and personality traits of the interviewees (participants) and interviewers. We will refer to interviewees as participants from now on to improve readability.

2.1 Hypotheses

We divide the hypotheses into general results, group differences, participant-level effects, and interviewer-level effects. The influence of gender will be discussed in both the participant- and interviewer-level effects.

General Results. We expect speech rate to be positively related to ease and negatively related to frustration, mostly from a cognitive load perspective. If a task is easy to complete, we would expect that the participant would be able to (remember to) talk out loud and be more descriptive about what they are doing and thinking. Alternatively, if a task is frustrating, we would expect that most of the participant's cognitive resources are dedicated to trying to figure out the task and less to talking out loud.

Group Differences. We anticipated that friends would talk faster and talk more. This could occur for a couple of reasons: (1) friends, as participants, are more familiar with the interviewer and more comfortable talking, (2) potential differences in digital fluency between the friends and the strangers. Since the interviewers were all interested in pursuing a career in user experience, they may have friends who have similar interests or have heard the interviewers talk about their career interests. The friends could have higher digital fluency as a result.

Depending on whether the friends were more motivated to be helpful or more motivated to save face, they could have used more or less, respectively, negative adjectives during their user interview.

Interviewee (Participant) Effects. We anticipate a relationship between gender and frustration ratings based on tendencies to lie. Based on previous research [21], we anticipate that the male participants may give less harsh frustration ratings, i.e., more likely to give a white lie of their experienced frustration. Additionally, we anticipate participants giving female interviewers less harsh frustration ratings, based on a previous study finding more positive feedback to women who underperformed [20]. Given that speech rate has been related to credibility and confidence, we may see some of this hiding of one's true frustration level in speech rate. In other words, we anticipate gender differences in comfort with being honest, adjustment of ratings, and speech rate.

Personality-wise, we expect extraverted participants to have longer user interviews, talk more, and talk faster. They may also use more adjectives or more unique adjectives. Participants high in agreeableness may have lower rates of negative adjective use while those high in neuroticism may have higher rates of negative adjective use.

Speech rate may be related to self-esteem (those who are more confident, may speak faster), working memory issues (working memory issues may make talking out loud during task completion more difficult, reducing the amount of words spoken), and digital fluency (those with higher digital fluency may have more cognitive resources available to talk out loud during task completion).

Interviewer Effects. Following up on previous concerns about personality traits that could influence an interviewer's tendency to fall off script [13], we anticipated that interviewers higher in openness to experience, extraversion and agreeableness could have higher word counts for their part of the interview. Alternatively, we expected conscientiousness of the interviewer to be negatively correlated with the interviewer's word count.

We may anticipate gender and personality traits to be predictive of more informative usability feedback (e.g., higher frustration ratings, more variable frustration ratings). As there seem to be common interviewer effects for sensitive questions [17] (e.g., reporting frustration in our case), interviewers with qualities that make the participant feel more comfortable, such as being female, being extraverted, open to experience and agreeable, may be correlated with higher frustration ratings and more variable frustration ratings (across our 6 tasks). We could also see a higher speech rate as a sign of comfort.

3   Methods

3.1   Participants

The study was approved by the Institutional Review Board of the University of California, Los Angeles. A total of 159 people participated in this study. 111 undergraduates from the University of California, Los Angeles were recruited from the subject pool and participated for partial course credit. 48 friends were recruited from 6 (3 female, 3 male) interviewers' friend groups. Interviewers were cognitive science majors, interested in pursuing a career in user experience.

3.2   Prototype

We intentionally designed the prototype to be frustrating (see link). We did this by creating unintuitive click pathways and buttons, like hiding the solution in unusual places. We made sure that the six tasks did not overlap in click pathways to reduce learning from task to task.

3.3   Survey

The interviewers recorded participant's responses to subjective ratings (ease and frustration) of the tasks and their overall experience with the app (on a scale of 1 (very bad) to 10 (very good)) and whether they would use the app again (yes or no). In the participants' own privacy, they completed a survey. The survey asked the participants to rate themselves and the researchers (perceived personality) on the abbreviated Big Five Inventory [34] (dimensions of extraversion, openness to experience, agreeableness, conscientiousness, and neuroticism). Then, they answered questions on a scale of 1 (strongly disagree) to 7 (strongly agree) about whether they were motivated during the study, felt comfortable sharing honest thoughts and ratings, and adjusted (higher or lower) their ratings so as not to offend the research or the design team. Finally, they answered demographic questions: age, gender and ethnicity.

3.4 Procedure

Informed consent was obtained from participants. The usability interview started with small talk questions and warm-up questions (e.g., experience with chat apps). The interviewer then read through a script of the instructions of the usability testing and asked the participant for their permission to screen- and audio-record the session using Zoom. Participants talked through their tasks while they were completing them, using the thinking aloud protocol [7]. After each task, the participants rated the task on ease (out of 10) and frustration (out of 10) and elaborated on their ratings. At the end of the interview, participants rated their overall experience and summarized their experience. The interviews were transcribed using screenapp.io. After the interview, participants completed the survey described above in their own privacy.

3.5 Identifying Common Usability Problems

Common usability issues in the prototype were identified through a thorough review of user recordings, focusing on common themes and recurring comments about specific features of the user interface that contributed to user frustration or prompted suggestions for improvement. Attention was focused on interface aspects of the interface that users found confusing or difficult to navigate. Observations were cross-checked and confirmed amongst interviewers and designers of the prototype. A coding framework was then developed to systematically track and categorize the identified usability issues, allowing for a more structured and objective analysis of the prototype's user experience. This process ensured that the most critical usability problems were effectively captured and categorized for further analysis. The full set of usability problems documented for each participant can be found in Table 1.

3.6 Interview Transcription Cleaning

To transcribe each interview, we uploaded each interview's audio file into screenapp.io, an AI-based transcription software. We then went through each transcript and cleaned them for clarity and accuracy. Edits that were made included removing erroneously repeated words, and correcting speaker labeling. The AI-based transcription software would sometimes mislabel the speakers (i.e., participant and interviewer swapped). Research assistants went through the transcripts to correct the speaker labeling and to double-check for the accuracy of the words transcribed.

Table 1. Common usability problems that we coded for each participant. They were coded as binary (0: participant did not mention vs. 1: participant mentioned).

Problem	Description
Search	Expected to be able to search members for contacts through chat
Contact List	Noted names on the contact list didn't have a specific order
Empty Chat	Asked if emptying the chat history would be the same thing as leaving the chat
Profile	Called it unusual for the profile page to be the first page on the app
Swipe	Never discovered or interacted with swipe on chat feature
Start Group Chat	Never noticed clipboard and/or text was clickable

3.7 Dependent Measures

The primary dependent measures we calculated from the transcripts included speech rate (words per second), negativity percentage (percentage of words spoken that were negative), and adjective usage rate (percentage of words that were adjectives). All our dependent measures can be found under Table 2.

Table 2. Dependent variables and their operational definitions, including formulas where appropriate.

Term	Definition/Formula
Total duration	Total interview duration
Interviewer speaking duration	Total amount of time in which the interviewer is speaking
Participant speaking duration	Total amount of time in which the participant is speaking
Interviewer speech rate	Interviewer's speech rate in words per second (wps)
Participant speech rate	Participant's speech rate in words per second (wps)
Negativity percentage	Percentage of words spoken by the participant that are negative (match one of the following: frustrated/ing, confused/ing, hate/ed, dislike(d), annoyed/ing)
Unique words	Number of unique words spoken by the participant
Adjective percentage	Total number of adjectives spoken by the participant/total number of words spoken
Adjective vocabulary dominance	Unique adjectives spoken by the participant/total unique words spoken by the participant
Speech rate SD	Standard deviation of words spoken by the participant in each of 10 equal length segments across the course of the interview

We calculated various dependent measures to reflect aspects of participant behavior. The transcripts and metadata were parsed into a pandas dataframe using regex. We first calculated speech rate as words per second by taking the total number of words spoken and dividing it by the total duration of speaking time (s) for the interviewer and participant individually.

Negativity was calculated by generating a dictionary of commonly used words that indicate negativity, including: frustrated/ing, confused/ing, hate/ed, dislike(d), annoyed/ing. These were counted as a single total, then divided by the total participant word count to determine what percent of words fit this negative dictionary, or a negativity percentage.

Next, we processed the transcripts through an NLP model using the spaCy package (we used en_core_web_md - medium sized English language model). This allowed us to tag words with a part of speech which we used to determine *adjective usage*, along with the number of *unique words* each participant utilized. From here, we calculated an *adjective vocabulary dominance* score by dividing the number of unique adjectives by the number of unique words, along with an *adjective usage* score, the total number of adjectives divided by the total number of words. These metrics reflect participant speech patterns and can indicate the relative richness or descriptiveness of one's vocabulary and the interview as a whole.

We also created a custom script to inspect the trends in speech rate throughout the interview. This was accomplished by breaking each transcript into 10 segments, then determining the word count in each segment. We then looked into the standard deviation across segments to indicate how consistent each participant's speech rate was throughout the interview.

4   Results

Our analyses will primarily focus on the relationship between characteristics of the participant's usability test responses (i.e., their transcript) (considered more objective) and their reported ratings of ease, frustration, app experience and honesty, taking into consideration individual differences in demographics and perception of the researcher. We first discuss the relationships amongst our dependent measures of the participant's transcript and then discuss the relationship of these dependent measures with individual differences in demographics and perception of the researcher.

4.1   Dependent Measures

We began by validating the most obvious correlations to ensure that our data was reliable and could be used for more nuanced analyses. We found that, as expected, total duration correlated significantly with both participant word count ($r(157) = 0.53$, $p = <0.001$) and interviewer word count ($r(157) = 0.58$, $p = <0.001$) along with their respective speaking durations ($r(157) = 0.48$, $p = <0.001$; $r(157) = 0.60$, $p = <0.001$). Longer interviews also naturally exhibited a higher unique word count, $r(157) = 0.53$, $p = <0.001$.

Additionally, faster interviewer speech rate resulted in shorter interview total duration, $r(157) = -0.28$, $p = <0.001$. This interviewer speech rate was also significantly correlated with task completion rate (out of the 6 tasks), $r(157) = 0.27$, $p = <0.001$. This correlation could either mean that confused participants required more clear, thoughtful instruction from the interviewer or that interviewers subconsciously sped through more successful interviews.

After verifying that our data passed sanity checks, we explored more nuanced connections. Longer interviews tended to produce more varied participant speech patterns with a greater number of total adjectives, $r(157) = 0.51$, $p = <0.001$, and unique words, $r(157) = 0.53$, $p = <0.001$, along with a higher speech rate standard deviation, $r(157) = 0.45$, $p = <0.001$. Participants with higher speech rate tended to use more total negative words, $r(157) = 0.37$, $p = <0.001$, and express a greater adjective vocabulary dominance, $r(157) = 0.36$, $p = <0.001$. Additionally, adjective percentage and negativity percentage were highly linked, $r(157) = 0.32$, $p = <0.001$, suggesting that these participants were more descriptive and potentially more honest about their experience.

Participant speech rate did not predict task ease, $r(157) = 0.03$, $p = 0.71$, or frustration, $r(157) = -0.07$, $p = 0.39$, suggesting that task difficulty did not play a significant role in speech rate. There was also no significant correlation between participant speech rate and self-esteem, $r(157) = 0.03$, $p = 0.70$, working memory, $r(157) = 0.01$, $p = 0.88$, or digital fluency, $r(157) = 0.13$, $p = 0.09$.

We found a significant correlation between negativity percentage and frustration, $r(157) = 0.19$, $p = 0.02$, and a slightly significant correlation between negativity percentage and app experience ($r(157) = -0.06$, $p = 0.42$), or task completion, $r(157) = -0.06$, $p = 0.43$. Furthermore, the number of identified usability problems (see Table 1) was not correlated with word count, duration, speech rate, and personality traits (of the participant and the interviewer), all p's > 0.06.

4.2 Strangers vs. Friends

Friends talked faster (M = 1.65 words per second, SD = 0.53) than strangers (M = 1.42 words per second, SD = 0.51), $t(157) = 2.68$, $p = 0.008$, which could reflect more comfort with the interviewer, who is their friend. Interestingly though, the reverse was not true. Interviewers did not reliably speak faster with their friends (M = 2.32 wps, SD = 0.66) than strangers (M = 2.15, SD = 0.61), $t(157) = 1.49$, $p = 0.14$. This is a sign of good interview technique and that whether the participant is a friend or stranger did not bias the interviewer. Friends (participants) showed a significantly higher *word count* (M = 1086, SD = 689) than strangers (M = 796, SD = 387), $t(157) = 3.38$, $p = <0.001$.

We found that friends (M = 0.42%, SD = 0.28%) did not reliably use a smaller *percentage of negative words* than strangers (M = 0.46%, SD = 0.38%), $t(157) = 0.81$, $p = 0.42$. Friends (M = 7.02, SD = 3.74) also did not exhibit a significantly different *working memory score* than strangers (M = 8.33, SD = 4.22), $t(157) = 1.87$, $p = 0.06$. Friends and strangers also showed no significant difference in *digital fluency* (M = 21.88 vs 21.15, SD = 3.23 vs. 3.04), $t(157) = 1.35$, $p = 0.18$.

4.3 Personality

Perceived Interviewer Personality. *Interviewer duration* (r(157) = 0.26, p = 0.001) and *interviewer speech rate* (r(157) = −0.22, p = 0.006) were both predicted by *perceived interviewer agreeableness,* but not other interviewer big 5 personality traits (openness, conscientiousness, extraversion, and neuroticism; p's > 0.56 for duration and p > 0.62 for speech rate).

Interviewer conscientiousness, r(157) = 0.18, p = 0.02, and *extraversion* (r(157) = 0.18, p = 0.02, significantly predicted *participant speech rate,* while conscientiousness was a reliable predictor of several measures of experience. Participants who perceived their interviewer as more *conscientious* reported *easier tasks* (r(157) = 0.22, p = 0.004), less *frustration* (r(157) = −0.22, p = 0.005), lower *frustration standard deviation* (r(157) = −0.21, p = 0.008), and better *app experience* (r(157) = 0.34, p = <0.001) along with more *motivation* (r(157) = 0.34, p = <0.001).

We found that *extraversion* along predicted *adjective usage,* r(157) = 0.17, p = 0.03, while *agreeableness* predicted *negativity,* r(157) = 0.18, p = 0.02. No other big 5 traits predicted either *negativity,* p's > 0.14 for negativity, or *adjective usage,* p's > 0.35 for adjective usage.

We found no significant correlation between any *perceived researcher personality trait* and *interviewer word count* (all p's > 0.16), suggesting that unlike the concern of previous researchers [13], agreeable, open and extraverted interviewers were not more 'chatty' in their approach to interviewing.

Interviewee (Participant) Personality. We explored the connections between participant's Big 5 personality traits and participant characteristics as well. We found a minor significant connection between *neuroticism* and *participant word count,* r(157) = 0.16, p = 0.04, along with participant duration, r(157) = 0.18, p = 0.03. Participants who were more neurotic also tended to achieve a higher *working memory issues score* (r(157) = 0.39, p = <0.001. We found no significant correlations between any Big 5 traits and participant speech rate, p's > 0.19) and no additional correlations with participant word count, p's > 0.19, or participant duration, p's > 0.12. Interestingly, those that were more *conscientious* also tended to perceive their interviewers as more *conscientious,* r(157) = 0.19, p = 0.02, suggesting a social projection effect.

4.4 Gender

We also looked into the impact of participant and interviewer gender on interview metrics. We found no difference between female (M = 3.74, SD = 1.62) and male (M = 3.77, SD = 1.34) participants in terms of mean frustration, t(157) = 0.10, p = 0.92, or frustration standard deviation (female M = 2.51, SD = 1.06, male M = 2.65, SD = 1.06), t(157) = 0.66, p = 0.51. Participant gender also did not have a significant impact on comfortability being honest (female M = 6.68, SD = 0.91, male M = 6.67, SD = 0.68), t(157) = 0.10, p = 0.92, or participant rating adjustment (female M = 1.68, SD = 1.26, male M = 1.89, SD = 1.41), t(157) = 0.84, p = 0.40. We did find a significant gender difference for participant speech rate, with females speaking slower (M = 1.43, SD = 0.52) than males (M = 1.65, SD = 0.51), t(157) = 2.18, p = 0.03, but not with interviewer speech rate, (female M = 2.16, SD = 0.61, male M = 2.33, SD = 0.67), t(157) = 1.47, p = 0.14.

We found only one significant interviewer gender difference in their speech rate, with the female interviewers talking slower (M = 2.07, SD = 0.53) than male interviewers (M = 2.30, SD = 0.69), t(157) = 2.36, p = 0.02. Mean frustration, frustration standard deviation, comfortability being honest, participant rating adjustment, and participant speech rate were all no different based on interviewer gender, p's > 0.51).

5 Discussion

The purpose of this study was to investigate whether the relationship between participant and interviewer (stranger vs. friend) would influence the interview process and dynamic (duration, speech rate), the valence of verbal feedback (negativity), and subjective ratings (ease and frustration). We further investigated whether the personality traits of the participant and interviewer (perceived) would change the dynamic during the interview in terms of the quality and quantity of speech. We also checked for gender differences for good measure.

Generally, we expected speech rate to predict ease and frustration ratings, such that a more difficult and frustrating task would take cognitive resources away from talking through one's thought processes, but we did not find such a correlation. We did, however, find that the percentage of negative words used by the participant was correlated with reported frustration, but the effect size was small r = 0.19, suggesting that self-reported frustration may not capture all of the experienced frustration.

Next, we expected friends to talk more and faster than strangers with the interviewer and we did find this significant difference. Next, we expected gender differences in speech rate, based on the idea that telling a white lie would take extra effort. While we did not find gender differences in subjective ratings, we did find that female participants spoke significantly slower than male participants. This difference cannot be explained by self-esteem differences either.

Next, we investigated the role of personality traits. We expected extraverted participants to talk more and faster, agreeable participants to use fewer negative words and neurotic participants to use more negative words. Instead of extroverted participants, we found that neurotic participants talked more and longer. The longer interview duration could be explained by reporting more working memory issues. The neurotic participants may have needed more time to complete the task or for the task instructions to be repeated. The extraversion that predicted word count and speech rate of the participant is that of the interviewer. Participants spent more time in an interview and talked slower when they perceived the interviewer to be more agreeable.

On the other hand, agreeable interviewers (perceived) tended to speak slower. In terms of getting negative feedback, participants who were more extraverted and agreeable tended to use more negative words during their interview. The correlation with extraversion is consistent with a previous study [6]. The correlation with agreeableness may be surprising, as we may think an agreeable person would want to avoid conflict by pointing out negative things about a design. It is possible that these agreeable individuals were cooperative in their efforts to improve the design and saw the negative comments as helpful behavior. Additionally, while agreeable individuals may avoid interpersonal conflict, they may not feel as strong a need when discussing an inanimate object - the prototype.

Limitations of our study include the overlapping demographics of the friends and strangers recruited for this study and the variety of our interviewers. Many of the friends of the interviewers were also students from UCLA, just like the strangers. While we intentionally picked an equal number of male and female interviewers and were mindful of having similar ethnic variability within them (male: 2 East Asian, 1 Pacific Islander, female: 2 East Asian, 1 South Asian), we did not select for the Big Five personality traits. To have a wider range of interviewer styles and Big Five personality traits represented, we would need to select interviewers based on these characteristics. Instead of using perceived personality traits of the interviewers, we could use their actual (self-reported) personality traits. Future studies could also include more interviewers to cover a wider range of possibilities.

Our study has implications for choosing participants for usability testing. The only difference we identified between friends and strangers is their word count and speech rate during the usability tests. All other objective and subjective measures were not reliably different between friends and strangers, suggesting no major concerns about using friends as participants. While friends are not coworkers, they serve similar functions, such as social and information exchange, social support, and mentorship. They share the qualities of being long-term relationships where conflicts may arise. While we did not find concerns with using friends instead of strangers for the quality of usability testing feedback, this may not be the case with coworkers. There are more complexities in the workplace that do not exist within friendships, so generalizing to coworkers should be done cautiously.

Our study also resulted in a few general recommendations for usability testing: recruit extraverted and agreeable participants and have extraverted and agreeable interviewers interview them. In our study, this combination resulted in longer interviews and more negative feedback (with a frustrating app). We also showed a positive correlation between negative words used during the usability test and frustration reporting, though lower than expected, $r = 0.19$. Checking the percentage of negative words used may be one way to measure frustration when participants are against openly admitting their frustration. Future research can investigate other qualities of the interview setup that would encourage honest reporting of frustration and also other objective measures of frustration.

Acknowledgments. We would like to thank the interviewers: Brandon Day, Khoa Le, Jonathan Keung, Maleeha Zaman, Ashley Wang, and Sharon Zhao and the designers of the prototype: Brandon Day and Sharon Zhao. We would also like to thank Brandon Day, Maleeha Zaman, Khoa Le, Harmony Trinh, Alice Huang, Chelsea Wan for helping clean the AI-transcribed interview videos. Special thanks to Maleeha Zaman for helping to develop the coding scheme for the usability problems. There is an overlap in samples with [35] and [36].

Disclosure of Interests.   The authors have no competing interests to declare that are relevant to the content of this article.

References

1. Turner, R.E., Edgley, C., Olmstead, G.: Information control in conversations: honesty is not always the best policy. Kansas J. Sociol. **11**(1), 69–89 (1975)
2. Tosone, C.: Living everyday lies: the experience of self. Clin. Soc. Work J. **34**(3), 335–348 (2006)
3. Cupach, W.R., Metts, S.: Facework. Sage, Thousand Oaks, CA (1994)
4. Goffman, E.: Interaction Ritual: Essays in Face-to-Face Behavior. Adrine, Chicago (1967)
5. Stone, S.A., Chapman, C.S.: Unconscious frustration: dynamically assessing user experience using eye and mouse tracking. Proc. ACM Hum.-Comput. Interact. **7**(168), 1–17 (2023). https://doi.org/10.1145/3591137
6. Vassar, A.: The effect of personality in sample selection for usability testing. Master's thesis, The University of New South Wales (2011)
7. McCrae, R.R., Costa Jr., P.T.: The five-factor theory of personality. In: John, O.P., Robins, R.W., Pervin, L.A. (eds.) Handbook of Personality: Theory and Research, 3rd edn. pp. 159–181. The Guilford Press (2008)
8. Barrick, M.R., Mount, M.K.: The big five personality dimensions and job performance: a meta-analysis. Person. Psychol. Study People Work **44**(1), 1–26 (1991)
9. Mammadov, S.: Big five personality traits and academic performance: a meta-analysis. Personality **90**(2), 222–225 (2021)
10. Do, M.H., Minbashian, A.: A meta-analytic examination of the effects of the agentic and affiliative aspects of extraversion on leadership outcomes. Leadersh. Q. **25**(5), 1040–1053 (2014)
11. Terrain, H.D., Yamini, S.: Personality traits and conflict resolution styles: a meta-analysis. Person. Individ. Differ. **157**, 109794 (2020)
12. Goldberg, L.: An alternative "description of personality": The Big-Five factor structure. J. Pers. Soc. Psychol. **59**, 1216–1229 (1990)
13. Turner, M., Sturgis, P., Martin, D., Skinner, C.: Can interviewer personality, attitudes and experience explain the design effect in face-to-face surveys? In: Engel, U., Jann, B., Lynn, P., Scherpenzeel, A., Sturgis, P. (eds.) Improving Survey Methods: Lessons from Recent Research. Routledge, Abingdon (2014)
14. Hox, J.J.: Hierarchical regression models for interviewer and respondent effects. Sociol. Methods Res. **22**, 300–318 (1994)
15. O'Muircheartaigh, C., Campanelli, P.: The relative impact of interviewer effects and sample design effects on survey precision. J. Roy. Stat. Soc. **161**, 63–77 (1998)
16. Davis, P., Scott, A.: The effect of interviewer variance on domain comparisons. Surv. Methodol. **21**, 99–106 (1995)
17. Schnell, R., Kreuter, F.: Separating interviewer and sampling point effects. J. Off. Stat. **21**, 389–410 (2005)
18. Huddy, L., Billig, J., Bracciodieta, J., Hoeffler, L., Moynihan, P.J., Pugliani, P.: The effect of interviewer gender on the survey response. Polit. Behav. **19**(3), 197–220 (1997). http://www.jstor.org/stable/586516
19. Anderson, B.A., SIlver, B.D., Abramson, P.R.: The effects of the race of the interviews on race-related attitudes of black respondents in SRC/CPS national election studies. Publ. Opin. Q. **52**(3), 289–324 (1988)
20. Jampol, L., Zayas, V.: Gendered white lies: women are given inflated performance feedback compared with men. Pers. Soc. Psychol. Bull. **47**(1), 57–69 (2021). https://doi.org/10.1177/0146167220916622
21. Capraro, V.: Gender differences in lying in sender-receiver games: a meta-analysis. Judgm. Decis. Mak. **13**(4), 345–355 (2018). https://doi.org/10.1017/S1930297500009220

22. Apple, W., Streeter, L.A., Krauss, R.M.: Effects of pitch and speech rate on personal attributions. J. Person. Soc. Psychol. **37**(5), 715–727 (1979). https://doi.org/10.1037/0022-3514.37.5.715

23. Guyer, J., Fabrigar, L.R., Vaughan-Johnston, T.: Speech rate, intonation, and pitch: investigating the bias and cue effects of vocal confidence on persuasion. Person. Soc. Psychol. 1–17 (2018)

24. Smith, S.M., Shaffer, D.R.: Speed of speech and persuasion: evidence for multiple effects. Pers. Soc. Psychol. Bull. **21**, 1051–1060 (1995)

25. Smith, S.M., Shaffer, D.R.: Celerity and cajolery: rapid speech may promote or inhibit persuasion through its impact on message elaboration. Pers. Soc. Psychol. Bull. **17**, 663–669 (1991)

26. Sias, P.M.: Peer coworker relationships. In: Peer Coworker Relationships, pp. 57–88. SAGE Publications, Inc. (2009). https://doi.org/10.4135/9781452204031

27. Wang, T., Long, L., Zhang, Y., He, W.: A social exchange perspective of employee-organization relationships and employee unethical pro-organizational behaviour: the moderating role of individual moral identity. J. Bus. Ethics **159**, 473–489 (2019). https://doi.org/10.1007/s10551-018-3782-9

28. Mackey, J.D., Brees, J.R., McAllister, C.P., Zorn, M.L., Martinko, M.J., Harvey, P.: Victim and culprit? The effects of entitlement and felt accountability on perceptions of abusive supervision and perpetration of workplace bullying. J. Bus. Ethics **153**, 659–673 (2018). https://doi.org/10.1007/s10551-016-3348-7

29. Friedkin, N.E., Johnsen, E.C.: Social Influence Network Theory: A Sociological Examination of Small Group Dynamics. Cambridge University Press (2011). https://doi.org/10.1017/CBO9780511976735

30. Oyefusi, F.: Team and group dynamics in organizations: effect on productivity and performance. J. Hum. Resour. Sustain. Stud. **10**, 111–122 (2022)

31. Laursen, B., Hartup, W.W.: The origins of reciprocity and social exchange in friendships. New Direct. Child Adolescent Dev. **95** (2002)

32. Bryant, B.K.: Mental health, temperament, family, and friends: perspectives on children's empathy and social perspective taking. In: Eisenberg, N., Strayer, J. (eds.) Empathy and Its Development, pp. 245–270. Cambridge University Press, Cambridge (1987)

33. Fasbender, U., Rivkin, W., Gerpott, F.H.: Good for you, bad for me? The daily dynamics of perspective taking and well-being in coworker dyads. J. Occup. Health Psychol. **29**(1), 1–13 (2024)

34. Rammstedt, B., John, O.P.: Measuring personality in one minute or less: a 10-item short version of the Big Five Inventory in English and German. J. Res. Pers. **41**, 203–212 (2007)

35. Cui, L., Wuthrich, A.: Honesty or harmony? How friendships shape frustration reporting in usability tests. IN: Human-Computer Interaction International 2025 Proceedings, Gothenburg, Sweden, 22–27 June 2025. Springer, Cham (2025)

36. Cui, L., Zaman, M.: Knowing the interviewer: friend or foe? Differences in ease, frustration and quit rates between friends and strangers in usability testing. In: Human-Computer Interaction International 2025 Proceedings, Gothenburg, Sweden, 22–27 June 2025. Springer, Cham (2025)

37. Hughes, A., Chromy, J., Giacoletti, K. and Odom, D.: Impact of interviewer experience on respondent reports of substance use. In: Redesigning an Ongoing National Household Survey: Methodological Issues, Substance Abuse and Mental Health Services Administration (eds J. Gfroerer, J. Eyerman and J. Chromy), pp. 161–184 (2002). Rockville: Office of Applied Studies

38. van Tilburg, T.: Interviewer effects in the measurement of personal network size: a nonexperimental study. Soc. Methods Res. **26**, 300–328 (1998)

Interactive Behavior and Experience in Social Activities Within Virtual Spaces: An Exploratory Study

Gao Erdong[✉]

School of Animation and Digital Arts, Communication University of China, Beijing 100024, China
gaoerdong@cuc.edu.cn

Abstract. Immersive virtual spaces, defined by computer-generated environments embedded with three-dimensional data, represent a new paradigm in the digital world and internet models. While experiments exploring social activities in virtual worlds are still in their early stages, there remains a lack of systematic analysis regarding the reconstruction of social interaction spaces and the narrative of experiential behaviors. This paper reviews and synthesizes cases and data related to immersive, gamified social interactions, ceremonial rituals, and other social activities within virtual spaces. We argue that virtual space activities rely on flexible, cross-temporal interactions that facilitate gamification and experiential narratives. These activities are shaped by three key forces: participant behaviors, the combined influence of network infrastructure (including bandwidth, hardware, game engines, and intelligent computing power), and the guiding role of rule-makers. The interactive mechanisms inherent in virtual environments push the boundaries of user behavior, dissolve the limitations imposed by traditional physical spaces, and transcend the spatial constraints of real-world venues. Ultimately, this study aims to reconstruct human-centered experiences that emphasize the intrinsic value of participation and shared social interaction in virtual settings. Returning to the intrinsic experiential and spiritual value of humans as co-participants.

Keywords: Virtual space · Social interaction · Interactive experience · Behavioral dynamics

1 Introduction

Since Michael Benedikt introduced the concept of "virtual space" in 1991, scholars from diverse disciplines—spanning architecture, sociology, physics and philosophy—have sought to establish a theoretical understanding of "virtual cyberspace." Advances in virtual reality, spatial computing, and spatial intelligence technologies, supported by computer networking, computer vision, and spatial intelligence systems, are gradually shaping open, public, gamified digital spaces and three-dimensional virtual worlds. This paper, focusing on these emerging mediated environments, examines collective social activities as its central research topic and explores the design logic for creating shared virtual experiences that encourage free and inclusive participation.

© The Author(s), under exclusive license to Springer Nature Switzerland AG 2025
M. Schrepp (Ed.): HCII 2025, LNCS 15794, pp. 345–353, 2025.
https://doi.org/10.1007/978-3-031-93221-2_22

Social activities are defined as purposeful actions undertaken by individuals or groups, aimed at engaging others to achieve specific objectives. With the maturation of computer technologies and digital arts, immersive and gamified social activities within virtual spaces have evolved into critical arenas for both social engagement and inter-action. These activities integrate the foundational attributes of physical spaces with the functional characteristics of virtual environments, including gaming scenarios and mechanisms.

Activities within gamified virtual spaces can be characterized as purpose-driven, systematically organized, creative, and inherently enjoyable social interactions occurring within three-dimensional virtual environments. Their core attributes include:

- Immersive 3D Virtual Environments

    These activities take place within three-dimensional virtual spaces constructed through advanced computer network technologies. Such environments are character-ized by their immersive, participatory, gamified, interactive, mobile, and immediate qualities, offering users a compelling sense of engagement and presence.
- Organized and Structured Events

    The activities are purposefully planned, systematically organized, and carried out in a step-by-step manner following established rules and guidelines by specialized personnel. They involve a defined number of participants, underscoring the collective and structured nature of these events.
- Hybrid User Identities

    Participants engage in these activities not as natural individuals but through fic-tionalized, context-specific, and self-defined user identities. These virtual personas possess a dual nature, incorporating the attributes of natural individuals and the customized, virtualized characteristics of their digital representations

In Behavior in Public Places, Erving Goffman observes and analyzes the order of human interactions, keenly identifying how gatherings and organized activities embed themselves into social life as expressions of its dynamic fabric. Individuals navigate these activities by adhering to situational rules and dynamically adjusting their behavior. Despite the constraints of habits, discourse frameworks, and atmospheres, they strive to maintain a shared definition of the situation, ensuring cooperative interactions under contextual pressures.

The emergence of new media environments and the construction of gamified scenar-ios challenge traditional relational paradigms. Computer simulations have transitioned activities from physical spaces to online virtual domains, reshaping these engagements and providing novel experiences through digital and virtual modalities.

In virtual spaces, users adopt new identities, enabling emotional expression or cathar-sis within appropriately defined spatial proximities. These interactions often culminate in joyful, celebratory, and meaningful collective behaviors, enriching the cultural and spir-itual domains of human life. For instance, recent online events have showcased unprece-dented diversity and engagement. The Communication University of China hosted virtual red carpet ceremonies in Minecraft and graduation ceremonies in VRChat and Peace-keeper Elite. In June 2022, VRChat-based graduation season activities amassed 2.8 million clicks, with nearly 10,000 messages exchanged in a single interactive session.

Through virtual avatars, participants generated vibrant interactions, breaking the formality of traditional ceremonies and creating dynamic, gamified social spaces. Compared to traditional offline ceremonies, these events saw significantly higher levels of student autonomy in planning and decision-making, fostering a heightened sense of agency and laying the groundwork for collective intelligence and co-creation (Fig. 1).

Fig. 1. An online virtual space hosting a graduation ceremony.

Similarly, gamified virtual concerts have demonstrated immense participatory potential. The 2020 Travis Scott concert in Fortnite attracted over 10 million participants, while the 2024 "Remix: The Finale" music festival on the same platform drew a record-breaking 14 million simultaneous attendees, even in a post-pandemic era of restored offline activity. Virtual technologies have redefined artistic performance spaces, breaking away from traditional narrative structures and the "spectator-performer" dichotomy. Instead, they create platforms centered on gamified participation and virtual interaction. Platforms such as Roblox and Rec Room, where users co-create virtual scenarios and personalize behaviors, are increasingly recognized as critical venues for activities and immersive gaming experiences.

These emerging activity scenarios stem from both the objective needs of reality and the subjective emotional demands of individuals. Rooted in everyday life and enhanced by the imaginative possibilities of digital environments, they combine structured frameworks with opportunities for individual self-expression. By transcending the rigid patterns of traditional, formulaic activities, these gamified spaces provide users with creative freedom, fostering active participation, emergent behaviors, and innovative reproductions of social engagement.

2 Establishing Gamified Social Activities in Virtual Spaces

2.1 Reconstructing Social Spaces Through Virtual Media

"Media can cultivate new perceptual habits," and virtual spaces achieve the "production of space," fundamentally reshaping how and where social activities occur. Through virtual media, users can participate in events across time and space without leaving their homes. This practice reimagines and alters the objective world while externalizing and extending reality via gamified virtual worlds. The result is a balanced integration of external experiences and internal sensations.

During such activities, users engage collectively in "public spaces" or immerse themselves in personal "private spaces," with actions represented by multiple avatars replacing their physical presence. This shift transforms participation from mere "viewing and sharing" to "active experiencing." The coexistence of virtual and real selves introduces disparities in behavior, identity, and value. Over time, users increasingly accept their idealized virtual avatars, with evolving media environments in heterogeneous scenarios fostering shifts in self-recognition. This transformation in identity redefines the relationships between individuals and society, as well as those among individuals themselves.

2.2 Limitations of Traditional Activity Design

In terms of behavioral motivations, traditional activity arrangements are typically guided by a single objective, with the entire process meticulously designed to serve a predetermined goal. The core premise of such activities—functional exclusivity—assumes that spaces must be "filled" with predefined purposes in a top-down manner. This rigid structure disregards flexibility, spontaneity, fun, and diversity, stifling improvisation and deviation from rules. Consequently, these activities fail to achieve their fundamental goals of fostering "expressive enjoyment" and enabling "free communication."

In contrast, gamified and intelligent approaches offer a transformative path. On the technological front, they provide users with convenient, creative tools. Meanwhile, emotionally secure and inclusive environments evoke feelings of safety, belonging, and relaxation. These factors collectively encourage proactive and spontaneous personal expression and communication. By liberating spatial flexibility and openness, these approaches unlock the latent potential for social interactions, activate the dynamics of social engagement, and, through creative gamified behaviors and activities, facilitate diverse experiences, enhanced social exchanges, and the seamless connection of cultural symbols.

2.3 The Power of Emergent Dynamics

Additionally, emergent dynamics, fueled by interactions among participants, unleash greater energy and complexity in activities. Emergence refers to the intricate interplay among components, generating complexity that far surpasses the sum of individual behaviors. Within such activities, the spontaneous actions of each participant coalesce into a cohesive, complex, yet orderly system of collective behavior.

Compared to traditional activity designs, new frameworks supported by intelligent data systems demonstrate greater tolerance for spontaneous and unplanned behaviors. This adaptability accommodates the unique characteristics of individual actions, dynamically coordinating them within the system. Such openness increases the likelihood of generating outcomes that exceed expectations, fostering engagement and creating unforeseen positive impacts. These emergent dynamics pave the way for new value and innovation, amplifying the potential of social and cultural interactions.

3 The Value Expression and Design Thinking of Gamified Virtual Social Activities

Luhmann's theory of social differentiation posits that societies evolve from relatively simple and closed structures to complex, open, and multidimensional systems. In social spaces, this complexity is indirectly reflected in the diverse and dynamic equilibrium of multiple relationships. Against the backdrop of highly differentiated and complex modern social systems, at the micro-level, specific spatial systems foster spatial narratives where individuals engage in intricate tasks and self-production while enabling self-expression (Fig. 2).

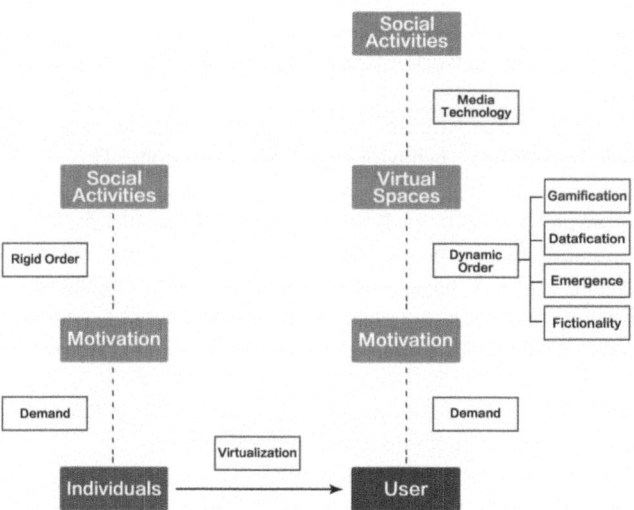

Fig. 2. Foundational logical framework for the transition from traditional activity models to virtual immersive activity models.

When users participate in social activities within virtual spaces, their physical presence remains anchored in the real world, while their interactions involve virtual entities within cyberspace. During these activities, the user's location, the information they share and disseminate, and the content of their interactions with others all form part of the broader process of social activity engagement and communication. In virtual spaces, users exhibit variability, anonymity, and subjectivity, resulting in a separation between their real-world identity and the virtual consciousness shaped by their self-awareness. The essence of virtual worlds transcends the confines of screens, shifting from screen-based interactions to a seamless integration of virtual and real experiences. This transformation aims to create immersive environments where users no longer perceive screens as barriers.

From the perspective of digital identities in virtual spaces, participants' avatars are designed to align with the thematic style of the event, forming a cohesive and user-selectable set of virtual representations. These avatars must adhere to the overarching aesthetic tone of the event, balancing user autonomy with the constraints of cultural norms and established conventions. Visually, they exhibit uniformity in color and style, in accordance with the event's guidelines—similar to the strict dress codes of traditional formal occasions. While the technical conditions allow for easy customization, the authority to define and control avatar options remains firmly with the event organizers. At the same time, offering users sufficient diversity in choice is vital to satisfy their natural desire for personal expression. A balance is thereby maintained, enabling users to select or adjust their avatars within predefined limits.

Identity verification is an indispensable component of virtual participation, utilizing technologies such as facial recognition and biometric data to ensure the legitimacy of participants' identities. This process establishes baseline control over participants, predetermines legal responsibilities, and provides essential safeguards for user security and privacy. The virtual world is not a realm of boundless freedom; it is an extension of the ethical, legal, and moral frameworks of the physical world, operating under fundamental, inviolable rules.

In virtual activities, the progression of events and dissemination of information points are driven by gamified, behavior-triggered interactions. This approach diverges from traditional event designs, which are typically structured around rigorous, linear processes. In conventional settings, hosts play a dominant role, regulating participant behavior and dictating the rhythm of events. By contrast, virtual environments embed all spatial elements and key stages within a sophisticated computational framework. Algorithms drive event progression, evaluate participant actions, and activate triggers, ensuring precise control over the pace and direction of activities. Behind this framework lies the implicit intentions of decision-makers, subtly influencing and guiding participants through soft interventions, ultimately fostering a well-orchestrated and positive interactive mechanism throughout the entire activity process.

Virtual spaces fundamentally differ from physical venues by eliminating constraints like physical capacity and hardware costs, offering participants significantly more freedom in choosing and interacting with the environment. The adaptability of virtual spaces allows for greater flexibility in design, style, scale, and configuration of the activity areas. However, virtual spaces are not infinite; their scale is primarily defined by the relationship between participants and the degree of behavioral freedom allowed during activities.

In traditional events, seating arrangements form the structural framework for organizing behaviors and guiding the event's flow. By contrast, in immersive virtual environments, the significance of seating diminishes, replaced by dynamic mechanisms that organize activities based on participant interactions. This shift enables spatial layouts to adjust flexibly, allowing for dynamic clustering and dispersion that better accommodate the fluid nature of virtual engagements.

The distinction between frontstage and backstage in virtual spaces has evolved into a completely new paradigm. The rigid physical boundaries that traditionally separate onstage and offstage areas are dissolved, replaced by programmatic and data-driven mechanisms that ensure the orderly flow of activities. Conventional constraints, such as rigid action limitations and "air wall" spatial divisions, are supplanted by game mechanics that use flexible instructions, inducements, and reward systems to guide and shape participant behavior.

Through the lens of users' virtual identities and perspectives, the system effectively organizes the participant hierarchy and structure. Algorithms are instrumental in predefining triggers for events and responses to user actions, ensuring a seamless progression of activities. This approach maintains a dynamic equilibrium between behavioral freedom and structured order, fostering an engaging and fluid virtual experience.

The core value of virtual activities lies in balancing respect for the autonomous will of participants with the high-quality achievement of the anticipated outcomes outlined in the activity design and planning. To accomplish this, it is essential to incorporate pre-established behavioral and reward mechanisms. In gamified virtual spaces, the flexibility of social activities is grounded in user-initiated actions, with the degree of flexibility determined by the interaction tools and gameplay settings. The platform offers users instructions, actions, and personal creative tools, with the value of the activity being realized through the creative behaviors that emerge during its execution.

Currently, virtual open-world platforms that support user-generated content are flourishing. On platforms such as Roblox, millions of user-created games, scenes, and characters are uploaded daily, with the total number of user-generated items exceeding 20 million. Similarly, on Minecraft, about 30% of users participate in content creation to varying degrees, including building structures and developing plugins.

Gamified social activities significantly enhance participants' desire for expression, relaxation, and creativity. These environments highlight dynamic aesthetics, the creation of unique contextual settings, and the interpretation of cross-regional and cross-temporal interactions. By adopting "gamified thinking" as the foundational logic for the atmosphere and progression of activities, these spaces fuse individual ingenuity with collective collaboration, enabling a "spiritual" expression. This, in turn, unleashes the enthusiasm and potential for user participation and active creation. Future virtual activity planning will inevitably shift from individual decision-making to multi-party coordination and collective co-creation.

Beyond intentional virtual space design, with the advancement and maturation of spatial intelligence and world-modeling technologies, artificial intelligence will increasingly understand and influence human behavior and social dynamics within virtual societies. A world model, serving as a tool to rapidly generate virtual scenes, establish or predefine new game rules, and anticipate environmental changes, provides core value through abstract representations within AI systems, facilitating the management and coordination of complex decisions and actions.

Through internal representations and predictive mechanisms powered by machine learning, AI systems transcend direct sensory inputs, enabling deep reasoning and planning in complex action environments, such as game strategies or competitive scenarios. These models demonstrate the integration of intelligent computational power into user-driven creative expression, motivating users to collaboratively expand and regenerate action content while updating the dynamic systems for social activity design and interaction. Consequently, machines will profoundly shape the trajectory of virtual activities through tangible, impactful actions.

Based on these models, virtual characters can, to some extent, participate autonomously in social behaviors, establish relationships, and form emotional connections, independent of human control. This autonomy enables the creation of intrinsic social bonds, interactive virtual personas, and "interesting" event nodes, thereby generating new social needs and enriching the virtual experience.

Overall, the design of virtual activities can originate from the physical world or emerge natively within the virtual realm. The success of such activities hinges on cultivating consensus and fostering connections among participants. This requires a distinctive social ecosystem that channels collective aspirations and emotional resonance into actionable motivations, translating them into gamified actions. Traditionally, established celebrations and commemorative holidays have arisen from shared spiritual consensus, forming unified systems of values (Fig. 3).

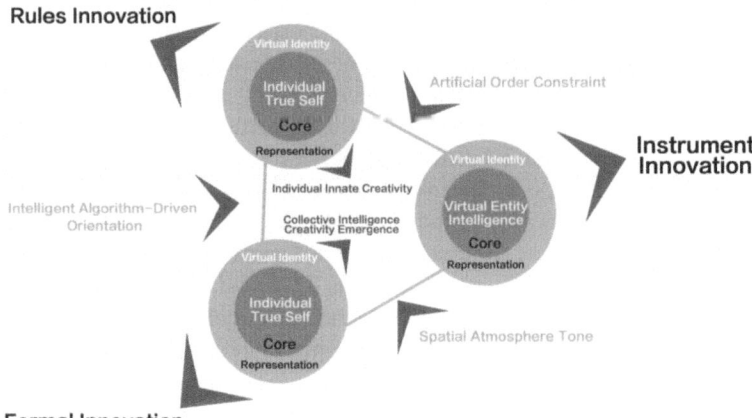

Fig. 3. User roles in virtual activities: identity, status, relationships, and the structural mechanism for content regeneration.

For virtual activity experiences, emotional expression extends beyond a mere transplantation of real-world emotions into virtual spaces. Under the influence of external order and algorithmic guidance, it stems from intrinsic human aspirations and expectations, giving rise to novel social relationships, emotions, and needs. On a cultural and spiritual level, it uncovers the intersections and connections between the virtual and physical worlds, generating broader shared visions and fostering collective value identities that are both connected to and independent from reality. By combining intelligent algorithms with emergent individual behaviors, human-machine symbiosis and collaborative synergy are achieved, allowing for the co-creation of collective intelligence and shared memories within the virtual world.

Social activities in virtual spaces replicate the immersive experience of reality, restoring the sense of order found in the real world while simultaneously reconstructing irrational behaviors within a fantasy world. These behaviors are rationalized as self-constructed, action-driven pathways. True activities must focus on expressions of human vitality and emotional tension. Engaging activities are not simply entertainment; however, if an activity is reduced to rigid processes and monotonous procedures, it confines creativity and suppresses individual expression.

Successful activities ultimately rely on an open and flexible spatial atmosphere, accessible creative tools, and an inclusive interpersonal environment. The true purpose and value of new technologies lie in amplifying the role of "humans" as active participants in society, broadening the scope and impact of their actions. This leads to the definition of a future-oriented model for social activities that is multidimensional, creative, and transcends both time and space.

References

1. Putnam, R.: Virtual communities: bowling alone, online together. Am. Prospect. 12 (2000)
2. Pannese, L.: The design of virtual spaces for collaborative learning. Int. J. Eng. Educ. (2009)
3. van Brakel, V., Barreda-Ángeles, M., Hartmann, T.: Feelings of presence and perceived social support in social virtual reality platforms. Comput. Hum. Behav. (2023)
4. Han, E., Bailenson, J.N.: Social Interaction in VR, Published online (2024). https://doi.org/10.1093/acrefore/9780190228613.013.1489
5. Windecker, G.: Virtual Space and the Rise of the Public Sphere: Social Media in the Sultanate of Oman (2019)
6. Berger, V.: Phenomenology of Online Spaces: Interpreting Late Modern Spatialities (2019)

Promoting Healthy Hydration Among College Students: A Behavior Design Approach Integrating the Fogg Behavior Model for Sustainable Development Goals

Mingzhen Li[(⊠)] and Zhen Liu

School of Design, South China University of Technology, Guangzhou 510006, People's Republic of China
sdmingzhenli@mail.scut.edu.cn

Abstract. Access to adequate hydration is essential to public health and well-being, which is a key component in achieving Sustainable Development Goals (SDGs) and promoting global public health. In Chinese universities, students often exhibit suboptimal hydration behavior, and there is an urgent need to promote proactive hydration through proper behavioral guidance. This research explores the solution to promote healthy drinking among college students from the perspective of behavior design. Through literature review and user research, the study gained insights into the pain points of college students in their daily life. Healthy hydration product design strategies were constructed based on the Fogg Behavior Model, and ultimately proposes a smart hydration product system consisting of a smart coaster and an APP. The product system supports students to develop healthy hydration habits, and ultimately contributes to the attainment of the Sustainable Development Goals.

Keywords: Fogg Behavior Model · Healthy Hydration · Behavior Design · Smart Product System · Health Promotion

1 Introduction

In recent years, the emphasis on healthy lifestyles has increased significantly, of which adequate hydration constitutes a vital aspect. However, college students' long periods of sedentary activity, coupled with the widespread consumption of sugar-sweetened beverages, results in unsatisfactory hydration practices. Therefore, promoting healthy hydration behaviors among college students is critically important.

The current research lacks a theoretical framework that focuses on the theme of healthy hydration and behavior design, which in turn makes it difficult to guide product practices at the application level. Therefore, this study aims to explore a healthy hydration solution for college students based on the Fogg behavior model. The study will be guided by the following three research questions (RQ):

1. What is the current state of research on healthy hydration and behavior design?

M. Schrepp (Ed.): HCII 2025, LNCS 15794, pp. 354–368, 2025.
https://doi.org/10.1007/978-3-031-93221-2_23

2. How to output design strategies that address the hydration needs of Chinese college students?
3. How to apply theoretical models of behavior design to the practical application?

2 Method

The research is divided into three stages, each corresponding to a specific research question. First, a literature review was conducted to determine the interconnected framework between healthy hydration and behavior design (RQ1). Secondly, the current situation of hydration among college students was analyzed through field research, questionnaires and interviews. The results were combined with the Fogg Behavior Model to output user portraits, user journey maps, and to construct the healthy hydration product design strategies (RQ2). Finally, based on the design strategies, a smart hydration product system consisting of a smart coaster and an application was constructed to enhance the healthy hydration behavior of college students (RQ3).

2.1 Literature Review

Qualitative Analysis. This research selected the Web of Science Core Collection (WoSCC) as the core data retrieval platform, and conducted a keyword search around the research themes of "healthy hydration" and "behavior design" and their synonyms. A total of 171 articles were retrieved as of January 18, 2025.

The collected literature data was imported into VOS viewer (1.6.20) to construct a network visualization chart. The keywords extracted from the literature form the labels and nodes in the chart, where the size of the node represents the weight of the label in the network. The distance between nodes and the number of connections represents the strength of the association between keywords. As shown in Fig. 1, the topics related to healthy hydration and behavior design research are divided into five clusters according to color, focusing on behavior change and design strategies (purple cluster), comprehensive health risks linked to adolescent beverage intake (red cluster), hydration interventions and health promotion (green cluster), the availability of safe and sustainable drinking water (yellow cluster), and finally, access to water, along with economic and technological assistance in developing countries (blue cluster).

The overlay visualization attempts to analyze the hotspots in the field of healthy hydration and behavior design. The color of the circles corresponding to the keyword transitions from dark blue (furthest year) to light yellow (closest year) with each year, as shown in Fig. 2. Since 2018, the research topic has gradually shifted from the macroscopic level of drinking water resource access and disease safety management to the microscopic level of individual healthy hydration behavior research. Keywords such as "hydration", "water intake", "sugar-sweetened beverages", "mobile health" and "adolescent" have the lightest colors, which shows that behavior research related to daily water intake and sugary beverages has become an emerging hotspot in recent years, and is trending towards younger users.

The results of Fig. 1 and Fig. 2 reveals that "developing countries" and "young people" are important research focuses in the field of healthy hydration. Furthermore, the closely-related keywords "mobile health" and "behavior design" highlight the recent

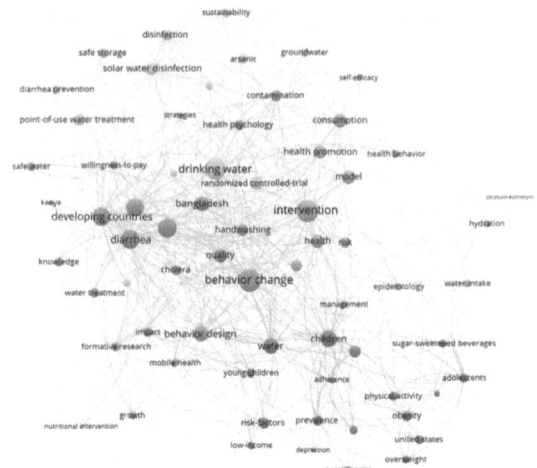

Fig. 1. Keyword co-occurrence network visualization.

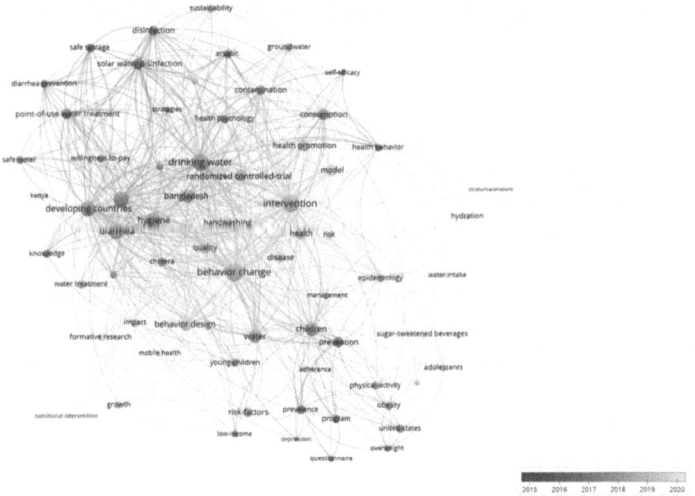

Fig. 2. Keyword co-occurrence overlay visualization.

surge in digital technology applications. Developing countries face particular challenges in terms of healthy hydration, especially among adolescents and children [1]. To address these challenges, the application of smart digital technology to the field of health has become a promising solution. Mobile health applications, through real-time monitoring and scientific behavioral guidance, offer a promising approach to fostering healthy habits in young populations [2].

Healthy Hydration Practices and Challenges. Water is an essential element of the human body and plays an important role in regulating physiological functions and maintaining metabolic balance [3]. Healthy hydration significantly reduces the risk of chronic diseases, while inappropriate hydration negatively affects cognitive performance and physical activity, thereby affecting the quality of daily life [4].

Considering regional, climatic, cultural and individual differences, healthy hydration research requires tailored norms and recommendations for target populations. Dietary Guidelines for Chinese Residents (2022) emphasizes adequate, frequent hydration with daily plain water intakes of 1700ml for men and 1500ml for women, which provides relatively clear guidance for scientific water intake for the Chinese population [5].

However, inadequate hydration remains prevalent in China, particularly among university students. A survey of 15 universities in China revealed that 17.2% of university students consumed less than 1,000 mL of water daily [6]. Further studies indicated that only one-quarter of male university students maintained good hydration status [7], with their hydration levels being particularly concerning during the summer and autumn months [8].

The poor hydration among college students is often caused by their characteristic lifestyle. On the one hand, the intense focus on academics often takes priority over adequate hydration, and the sedentary lifestyles also increase the risk of dehydration, which in turn impairs visual tracking, short-term memory and attention [9]. On the other hand, students often prefer sugary beverage over plain water, and the widespread availability of sugary beverage on campus further increases the risk of metabolic diseases such as overweight [10]. Ensuring healthy hydration for university students in China is therefore a multifaceted challenge.

Enhancing Hydration Through Behavior Design and The Fogg Behavior Model. Behavior Design is an academic discipline that integrates behavioral science, design, and psychology. It aims to persuade people to perform specific behaviors through conscious design activities, guide the development of new behaviors, and optimize the user experience [11]. Effective UX design requires user-centered research, and behavior design provides the theoretical basis for understanding user needs, motivations and decisions.

The Fogg Behavior Model is an influential framework in the field of behavior design [12]. As shown in Fig. 3, the model emphasizes the three key elements required for individual behavior to occur and their interactions: Motivation, Ability, and Prompts (also known as triggers). Behavior will only occur when there is a strong enough intention to act, the individual has the ability to perform the behavior, and the proper prompt exists.

The Fogg Behavior Model provides a new theoretical framework for designing effective solutions. By understanding college students' behavior, the model helps promote healthy hydration habits and ultimately make healthy hydration a sustainable lifestyle.

Healthy Hydration and the Sustainable Development Goals. The United Nations 2030 Agenda for Sustainable Development sets out 17 Sustainable Development Goals (SDGs) with tangible implementation targets for sustainable development in the context of globalization [13]. Healthy hydration is not only important for personal health, but is also significant for achieving SDG 3: "Ensure healthy lives and promote well-being for all at all ages" [14].

358   M. Li and Z. Liu

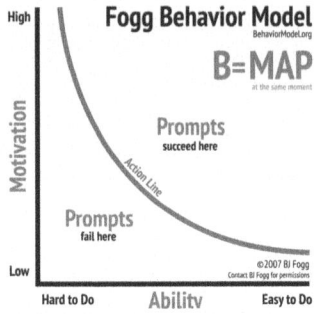

Fig. 3. Fogg Behavior Model (Source: behaviormodel.org)

In addition, promoting the use of tap water instead of bottled water also contributes to environmental sustainability [15]. From a circular economy perspective, this reduces the frequent use and disposal of plastic products, as well as the environmental impact of bottled water production and transportation [16], which contributes to achieving Sustainable Development Goal 12: Responsible Consumption and Production [17].

Healthy hydration is also closely linked to Sustainable Development Goal 6: Clean Water and Sanitation. The premise for promoting healthy hydration is to ensure that people have access to safe, sufficient and affordable sources of clean water [18]. This requires greater efforts to cope with water shortages and pollution, especially in developing countries [19].

The results of the literature review provide support for this study to conduct behavior design research targeting Chinese college students. This young population has an urgent need for healthy hydration, and it is important to promote the development of healthy hydration habits through behavior design. Therefore, targeted behavior design strategies need to be developed, and the use of mobile health technology should be encouraged to help college students achieve healthier hydration behaviors, thereby improving the overall health and well-being.

2.2   Field Research

This research selected South China University of Technology as a reference case for field research. As shown in Fig. 4, Chinese universities provide students with a relatively good drinking water environment. Teaching buildings and dormitories are usually equipped with direct drinking water dispenser to provide a safe, clean and inexpensive drinking water resource, which provides strong external environmental support for promoting healthy hydration. Apart from using the direct drinking water dispenser, vending machines, supermarkets and shops in the school area also provide students with sufficient bottled water and beverages.

Fig. 4. Campus hydration facilities in field research.

2.3   User Research

Questionnaire. A questionnaire was distributed to students at South China University of Technology to investigate their healthy hydration habits. A total of 32 valid questionnaires were returned. As shown in Fig. 5, 75% of students drink less than 1500ml of water per day, which is generally lower than the recommended standard of Dietary Guidelines for Chinese Residents (2022). 87.5% of people only drink water when they are thirsty. Other drinking scenarios include meals, exercise and breaks, but only 12.5% of people drink water at regular times. Nearly 60% (56.25%) of the respondents were dissatisfied with their current hydration habits, with busyness, forgetfulness and a lack of supervision being the main reasons for their poor hydration habits. This shows that the current state of hydration among college students is not optimistic. People often passively hydrate rather than actively doing so, making it difficult to form a scientific and regular habit of hydration.

Fortunately, students generally have a positive attitude towards hydration. 84.38% are willing to accept hydration knowledge and improve hydration behavior. Although most students have not used healthy hydration products, they have expressed a willingness to obtain effective healthy hydration services through new healthy hydration products, especially in terms of more accurate hydration tracking, intuitive and simple operation, customized reminders and interactive incentives.

User Interview. Four students with typical characteristics were further invited for interviews to understand in detail their experiences and attitudes towards healthy hydration behaviors in combination with the three elements of the Fogg Behavior Model, so as to provide inspiration for healthy hydration product design strategies (Fig. 6).

Regarding motivation, all interviewers understand the importance of healthy hydration, but their previous lifestyles have accustomed them to inadequate hydration. Furthermore, they lack an intuitive perception of their daily hydration quality and the associated health risks, which makes it difficult to increase their willingness to improve their

No.	Question	Options	Count	Percentage
1	What is your gender?	a. Male	18	56.25%
		b. Female	14	43.75%
2	What is your academic year?	a. Freshman	3	9.38%
		b. Sophomore	2	6.25%
		c. Junior	1	3.13%
		d. Senior	8	25.00%
		e. Graduate Year 1	7	21.88%
		f. Graduate Year 2	7	21.88%
		g. Graduate Year 3	4	12.50%
3	How much water do you usually drink per day?	a. Less than 500 ml	6	18.75%
		b. 500-1000 ml	12	37.50%
		c. 1000-1500 ml	6	18.75%
		d. 1500-2000 ml	5	15.63%
		e. More than 2000 ml	3	9.38%
4	Under what circumstances do you usually hydrate?	a. When I feel thirsty	28	87.50%
		b. During meals	12	37.50%
		c. After exercise	16	50.00%
		d. During study/work	4	12.50%
		e. During breaks	20	62.50%
		f. At fixed times	4	12.50%
		g. Other	2	6.25%
5	What is your main source of daily water intake?	a. School direct drinking machine	24	75.00%
		b. Bottled water	5	15.63%
		c. Beverages (sugary drinks, alcoholic drinks, etc.)	2	6.25%
		d. Other	1	3.13%
6	How satisfied are you with your current drinking habits?	a. Very satisfied	4	12.50%
		b. Somewhat satisfied	3	9.38%
		c. Neutral	7	21.88%
		d. Somewhat dissatisfied	12	37.50%
		e. Very dissatisfied	6	18.75%
7	Which of the following factors do you think contribute to your suboptimal drinking habits?	a. Busy schedule	22	68.75%
		b. Forgetfulness	26	81.25%
		c. Lack of supervision	17	53.13%
		d. Inconvenient access to water	6	18.75%
		e. Dislike for drinking water	5	15.63%
		f. Lack of awareness of drinking importance	1	3.13%
		g. Other	4	12.50%
8	Are you willing to improve your drinking habits?	a. Very willing	16	50.00%
		b. Somewhat willing	11	34.38%
		c. Neutral	3	9.38%
		d. Somewhat unwilling	2	6.25%
		e. Very unwilling	0	0.00%
9	Have you ever used smart drinking products ?	a. Yes, and I use them frequently	3	9.38%
		b. Yes, but I rarely use them	4	12.50%
		c. Never used them	25	78.13%
10	What aspects of current drinking products could be improved in your opinion?	a. Reminders are not timely/smart enough	16	50.00%
		b. Features are not practical enough	7	21.88%
		c. Interface is not user-friendly/intuitive	10	31.25%
		d. Product price is too high	3	9.38%
		e. Lack of continuous incentives	21	65.63%
		f. Cumbersome usage process	19	59.38%
		g. Other	2	6.25%
11	What are your needs for future smart drinking products?	a. More precise water intake tracking	24	75.00%
		b. Personalized healthy drinking recommendations	22	68.75%
		c. Timed supervision for drinking	20	62.50%
		d. Social features	10	31.25%
		e. Fun and engaging interaction	19	59.38%
		f. Simple and intuitive operation	25	78.13%
		g. Sustained incentive mechanisms	17	53.13%
		h. Other	1	3.13%
12	Are you willing to try new healthy drinking products?	a. Very willing	16	50.00%
		b. Willing	11	34.38%
		c. Neutral	4	12.50%
		d. Unwilling	1	3.13%
		e. Completely unwilling	0	0.00%

Fig. 5. Questionnaire content and results.

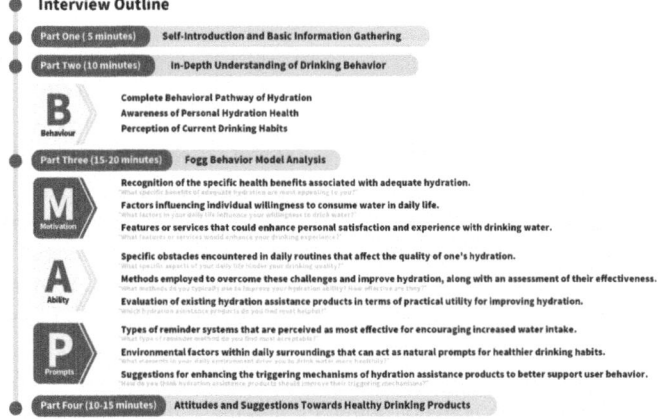

Fig. 6. Interview outline.

hydration behavior. By contrast, providing specific health data feedback can increase their motivation to maintain healthy hydration habits.

Regarding ability, busy lifestyles prevent students from creating opportunities for regular hydration. Conscious hydration is often stressful, leading to procrastination as the norm. Students also struggle to resist the temptation of sugary beverages, which further reduces their drinking water intake. Some students have tried alarming themselves to encourage hydration, but these approaches often require multiple steps, increasing the barrier to entry for the user, making conscious adherence difficult. External support is needed to improve people's ability to hydrate healthily.

Regarding Prompts, due to a lack of sustained motivation, students generally have high enthusiasm in the early stages of planning healthy hydration, but gradually lose motivation over time. They highlighted the effectiveness of gamification incentives and social interactions in promoting behavior change, claiming the product experience of shared progress particularly inspiring. In addition, students prefer non-intrusive hydration reminders, and expressed the desire to customize the timing and frequency of reminders to better suit their personal rhythms.

The interview also explored the complete path of how college students form hydration habits and identified the following five stages:

- Stage 1. Unconscious: Students lack the perception of the importance of healthy hydration. They are satisfied with their current hydration status and have not considered the possible negative effects of insufficient hydration.
- Stage2. Contemplation: Students gradually experience the consequences of inadequate hydration, such as frequent dry mouth and mental fatigue, and begin to reflect on their hydration habits. They weigh up the benefits and potential inconveniences of making a change, and consider whether it is necessary.
- Stage 3. Preparation: Students are determined to improve their drinking habits. They begin to formulate a rough plan and look for resources that can support them in their efforts to healthy hydration.
- Stage 4. Action: Students begin to take action, actively increasing their daily hydration as planned, and reinforce healthy behaviors through self-monitoring and support from the external environment.
- Stage 5. Maintenance: After a period of time following the healthy hydration pattern, the behavior is gradually internalized as a natural habit. However, regular monitoring and adjustment of behavior is still required during this stage to prevent relapse.

Based on the research results, the common characteristics of the user group promoting healthy hydration were extracted, and the user portrait was constructed (Fig. 7), listing the pain points and goals of the core and secondary user.

Fig. 7. Core and secondary user portrait.

Subsequently, combining the five stages of the above analysis to create the user journey map (Fig. 8) to analyze the behaviors and feelings of college students and transform them into chance points.

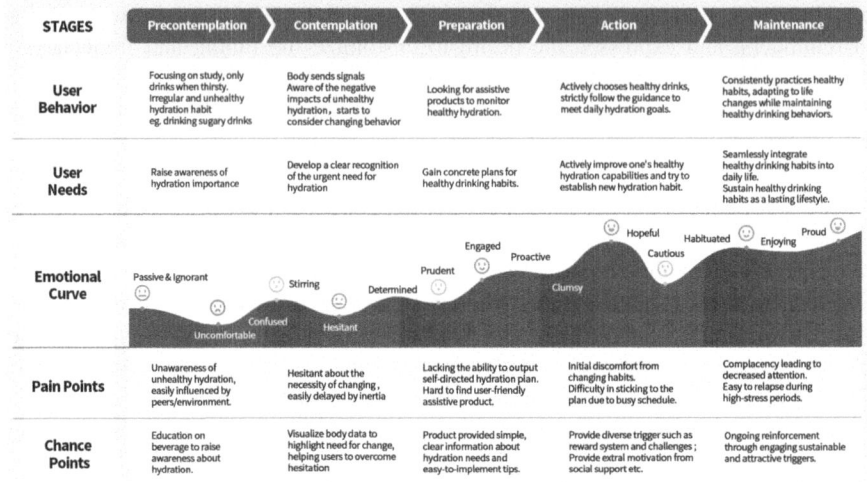

Fig. 8. User journey map.

3 Result

3.1 Healthy Hydration Product Design Strategies

The final theoretical output is a design strategy for healthy hydration products for the Chinese college students, which maps the Fogg Behavior Model, user demand and product function to each other, and outputs a healthy hydration product design architecture, as shown in the Fig. 9.

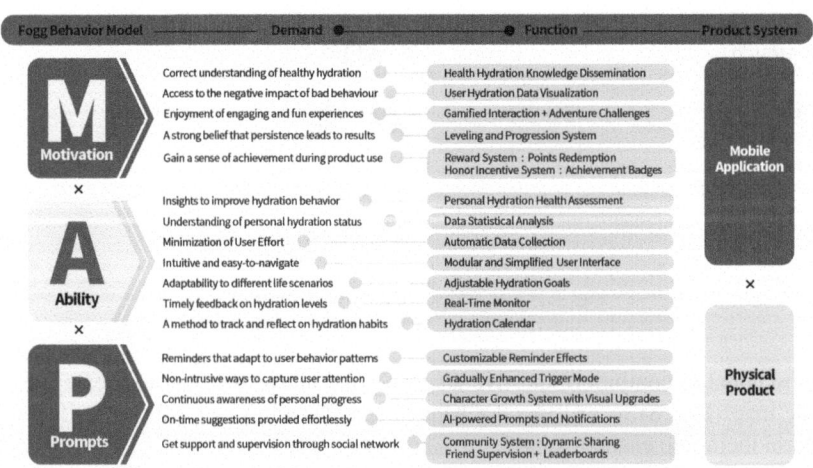

Fig. 9. Healthy hydration product design architecture architecture.

Internal and External Incentives Strengthen the Motivation. Increasing motivation is crucial for transitioning students from the unconscious stage to the contemplation stage, laying the foundation for subsequent behavior change.

Recognizing that healthy hydration significantly impacts academic performance and quality of life, healthy hydration products should initially educate users on the positive effects of scientific hydration, while highlighting dehydration risks.

When students begin to implement hydration actions, the product interaction should provide sufficient health feedback, such as visualizing daily hydration statistics, so that users can visually see their hydration patterns and their impact on health. When students visually perceive their own progress, their sense of self-efficacy will also promote the continued growth of intrinsic motivation.

External incentives are also an effective means of consolidating healthy hydration behaviors, especially in the maintenance stage. A balanced combination of rewards and penalties is effective. The healthy hydration product implements a level growth system, converting the points students earn by achieving their daily hydration goals into redeemable rewards, so that students can intuitively feel the lasting benefits of healthy hydration. Correspondingly, inappropriate hydration will result in point and level reductions, encouraging consistent adherence to healthy habits.

User-Friendly Product Interactions Enhance Implementation Ability. The human-centered design concept emphasizes optimizing the user experience, in which the ease of use and usefulness of healthy hydration products are crucial.

In the preparation stage, students are already in a restricted state of incorrect hydration, and they are looking for solutions that match their abilities to improve their hydration habits. An interactive design that is easy to access will enhance the competitiveness of healthy hydration products, avoid frustrating users with complex operations, and ultimately abandon the hydration plan. Entering the action stage, digital health products should provide an easy-to-understand user interface to reduce additional cognitive load. By applying smart technology, the product can further simplify the operation process and reduce the difficulty of implementing healthy hydration behaviors by automatically recording hydration instead of manual input.

In practical terms, the product should also enhance the user's ability to drink healthily. This includes providing real-time data feedbacks, hydration reminders and the ability to identify abnormal hydration patterns to enhance the user's awareness of healthy hydration habits. On the other hand, the product needs to allow users to flexibly adjust their daily hydration plan according to their personal health conditions or daily schedules, and improve the practicality of the product through personalized support, ultimately focusing on improving students' self-management ability to drink water actively.

Smart-Technology-Driven Prompts for Sustainable Hydration. A persuasive, adaptable and diverse prompt strategy can help college students gradually develop regular healthy hydration habits which is sustainable.

Effective hydration prompts should promptly alert users to negative behaviors, interrupt unhealthy habits, and refocus them on their hydration needs. The prompt format should adapt to college students' lifestyles, using gentle visual and auditory cues to gradually deliver the message of healthy hydration, thereby avoiding intrusiveness or being ignored and preventing a defensive mindset. In addition, allowing students to customize the prompt mode can enhance the adaptability of the product to different individuals.

In the maintenance stage, the prompt design must also consider sustainability. As the usage time increases, the prompt content needs to be constantly innovated to prevent users from becoming numb or even actively ignoring the prompts due to repetition. Integrating gamification, such as character development and achievement unlocks, provides challenging prompts to motivating students to maintain healthy hydration. Social network support also significantly promotes healthy hydration by fostering a sense of honor and social belonging through mutual sharing, supervision and competition, promoting collective behavior change towards healthy hydration.

The product system is driven by smart technology to support the coordinated prompting of mobile application and product hardware. The hardware tracks hydration data, provides indicator feedback, and uses IoT to transmit data to the app for simultaneous prompting. The prompting signal is enhanced by combining multi-sensory feedback from sight, sound and touch, which increases the dimension of the prompt to elevates user attention towards healthy hydration.

3.2 Design Practice

Combining the proposed healthy hydration product design strategies, this research ultimately designed a smart product system called "OASIS" which includes a healthy hydration APP and smart coaster.

Application Design. The online platform's core feature is "OASIS", a virtual character that evolves through gamified progression based on real-time hydration data, guiding users towards healthy hydration habits.

When first used, the APP provides a short quiz to collect basic health data from the user and tailors a personalized daily hydration plan for the user through AI algorithms. After user confirmation, the APP provides prompts to ensure that users maintain adequate hydration at the recommended times and in the recommended amounts according to Dietary Guidelines for Chinese Residents (2022).

The design strategy is reflected in the APP information architecture (Fig. 10), which includes five main sections:

1. "Home page": this section displays real-time levels and status of "OASIS", presenting dynamic visual to encourage sustained participation.
2. "Adventure": this section displays daily hydration goals and progress, the function of timed supervision of hydration is presented with a gamified effect of adventure and challenge.
3. "Community": this section fosters social interaction through community sharing, peer monitoring, leaderboards and health tutorial, creating a supportive online community for healthy hydration.
4. "Growth Record": This section presents users' health data, including hydration calendars and personal achievements, to increase user awareness and sustain their motivation to hydrate.

5. "Mine": This section provides personalized settings, personal information and device management for the smart coaster. It also supports direct data sync from campus direct drinking water dispenser through QR code scanning.

The high-fidelity prototype of the APP is shown in Fig. 11.

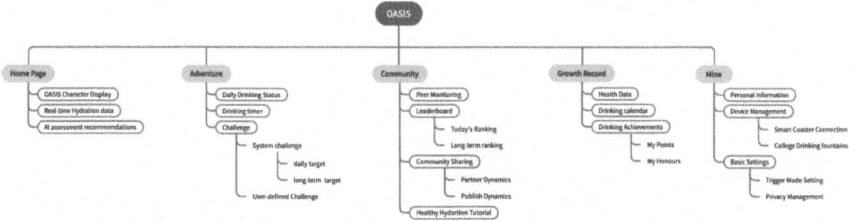

Fig. 10. APP Information architecture.

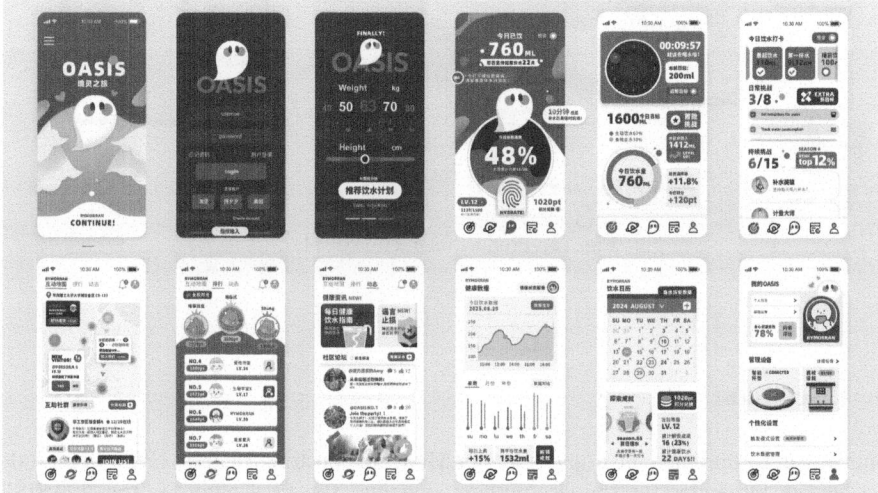

Fig. 11. APP high-fidelity prototype.

Product Design. The smart coaster of the product system is shown in Fig. 12. Considering the individual needs of different students, the overall size of the smart coaster is moderate enough to adapt to a variety of containers used by college students for daily hydration, and can also adapt to various desktop environments.

The coaster is equipped with a gravity sensor that detects small changes in weight when the container is placed on or removed from the coaster, thus capturing the user's daily drinking actions and recording the corresponding amount of water consumed.

One of the core features of the smart coaster is the soft visual prompt mode. This is mainly achieved through the product's equipped LED system, which visually reflects the user's current hydration status via the color and blinking frequency of a breathing light. When the product system detects that the user has not been drinking properly, the smart coaster provides gradually increasing reminders, which symbolizes the dying of the virtual character in the application, giving students an appropriate sense of tension to promote behavioral adjustment.

Another feature of the smart coaster lies in its data transmission capability. It can synchronize the user's hydration data with the APP in real time via Bluetooth, automating the process and eliminating the need for manual recording.

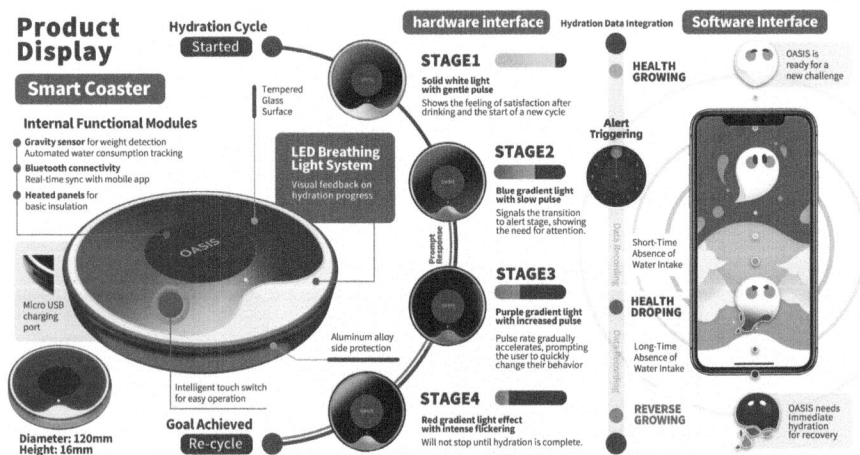

Fig. 12. Product interaction display.

4   Discussion

This research combined the Fogg Behavior Model to construct Healthy Hydration Product Design Strategies for Chinese college students. The final output is the "OASIS" healthy hydration product system which comprises a smart coaster and an APP. The system promotes the frequency and quality of hydration through a game-based interactive experience that combines rewards and punishments, helping students develop healthy hydration habits that they can maintain in the long term.

This research also has certain limitations that can be further optimized in future research:

1. The data collection for this study was conducted at a specific school, which may limit its applicability. In particular, it was found in the literature review that there are differences in the environmental resources for healthy hydration around the world. Therefore, future research needs to expand the sample size to include different universities and regions, and continuously improve the product system to reflect responsibility for global wellbeing.

2. This research focuses on exploring the topic of healthy hydration from the perspective of behavior design and the Fogg Behavior Model. Future research should integrate interdisciplinary theories and methods for more comprehensive intervention strategies to promote healthy hydration.
3. While the current mobile APP solution is cost-effective, emerging technologies like AR and digital twins offer new opportunities to enhance user experience. Future research can integrate these emerging technologies to iterate the product system and improve the overall usability.
4. Considering the variety of drinking water equipment provided by Chinese universities which has not yet been standardized, follow-up designs should focus on creating an integrated product system in collaboration with manufacturers to enhance the user experience, and further support students to actively use campus water dispenser for hydration.

5 Conclusion

This study focuses on healthy hydration among Chinese university students from the perspective of behavior design. A literature review was conducted to establish the relationship between behavior design and healthy hydration, highlighting the significance of healthy hydration in achieving the Sustainable Development Goals. The study employed field research, questionnaires and interviews to gain insights into the pain points and needs of college students when it comes to hydration, and created user portraits and user journey maps to identify opportunities for healthy hydration design.

Based on the Fogg Behavior Model, the study constructs a design strategy for healthy hydration product. Ultimately, the study proposes a healthy hydration product system including a smart coaster and an application. The product system rationally plans the different stages of the user's healthy hydration, stimulates intrinsic motivation through gamification mechanisms, enhances the user's ability to engage in healthy hydration, and provides multiple prompts for sustained behavior.

As the result, the healthy drinking behavior design strategy enriches existing research theories and provides effective practical guidance for health product design, and the proposed product system is effective in promoting the willingness and sustainability of healthy hydration behaviors among the college students. The product solution can also be extended to all groups in society, promoting broader public health and well-being. With the popularization of smart technologies, it is expected that subsequent healthy hydration product systems will be further iterated to better enhance people's hydration experience, improve users' overall health and support the Sustainable Development Goals.

Acknowledgments. The authors would like to express their sincere gratitude to all people who provided invaluable guidance and support throughout this research.

Disclosure of Interests. The authors have no competing interests to declare that are relevant to the content of this article.

References

1. Pereira, C.T., Sorlini, S., Sátiro, J., Albuquerque, A.: Water, Sanitation, and Hygiene (WASH) in schools: a catalyst for upholding human rights to water and sanitation in Anápolis, Brazil. Sustainability **16**(13), 5361 (2024)
2. AlSlaity, A., Suruliraj, B., Oyebode, O., Fowles, J., Steeves, D., Orji, R.: Mobile applications for health and wellness: a systematic review. Proc. ACM Hum.-Comput. Interact. **6**(EICS), 1–29 (2022)
3. Hakam, N., et al.: Outcomes in randomized clinical trials testing changes in daily water intake: a systematic review. JAMA Netw. Open **7**(11), e2447621 (2024)
4. Cheuvront, S.N., Carter, R., III., Sawka, M.N.: Fluid balance and endurance exercise performance. Curr. Sports Med. Rep. **2**(4), 202–208 (2003)
5. Cao, Q., Wang, W., Zhang, L., Zhou, W., Wang, Y.: The practice of balanced diet model for Chinese residents: interpretation of dietary guidelines for Chinese residents (2022). Food Mach. **38**(6), 19–26 (2022)
6. Song, J., et al.: Present situation of dietary behaviors among college students. Chin. J. Sch. Health **33**(6), 661–662 (2012)
7. Zhang, N., Du, S.M., Zhang, J.F., Ma, G.S.: Effects of dehydration and rehydration on cognitive performance and mood among male college students in Changzhou, China: a self-controlled trial. Int. J. Environ. Res. Publ. Health **16**(11), 1891 (2019)
8. Lin, Y., Zhang, N., Zhang, J., Lu, J., Ma, G.: Comparison of hydration status of male and female college students in four seasons in Hebei Province. In: Abstract Book of the 14th Asian Congress of Nutrition–Public Nutrition and Health, p. 361. Asian Federation of Nutrition Societies, Chinese Nutrition Society (2023)
9. Maughan, R.J.: Impact of mild dehydration on wellness and on exercise performance. Eur. J. Clin. Nutr. **57**(2), S19–S23 (2003)
10. Scharf, R.J., DeBoer, M.D.: Sugar-sweetened beverages and children's health. Annu. Rev. Publ. Health **37**(1), 273–293 (2016)
11. Li, B., Wang, Q., Lu, G., Zheng, G.: Application research of product design based on behavior design theory. Packag. Eng. **44**(10), 54–59 (2023)
12. Fogg, B.J.: A behavior model for persuasive design. In: Proceedings of the 4th International Conference on Persuasive Technology, pp. 1–7 (2009)
13. Hák, T., Janoušková, S., Moldan, B.: Sustainable development goals: a need for relevant indicators. Ecol. Ind. **60**, 565–573 (2016)
14. Omone, O.M., Kozlovszky, M., Ferenci, T., Inalegwu, I.G.: Hydration assessment among foreign university students. In: 2019 IEEE 19th International Symposium on Computational Intelligence and Informatics and 7th IEEE International Conference on Recent Achievements in Mechatronics, Automation, Computer Sciences and Robotics (CINTI-MACRo), pp. 000161–000168. IEEE (2019)
15. Etale, A., Jobin, M., Siegrist, M.: Tap versus bottled water consumption: the influence of social norms, affect and image on consumer choice. Appetite **121**, 138–146 (2018)
16. Mbavarira, T.M., Grimm, C.: A systemic view on circular economy in the water industry: learnings from a Belgian and Dutch case. Sustainability **13**(6), 3313 (2021)
17. Borusiak, B., Szymkowiak, A., Pierański, B., Szalonka, K.: The impact of environmental concern on intention to reduce consumption of single-use bottled water. Energies **14**(7), 1985 (2021)
18. Hutton, G., Chase, C.: The knowledge base for achieving the sustainable development goal targets on water supply, sanitation and hygiene. Int. J. Environ. Res. Publ. Health **13**(6), 536 (2016)
19. Montgomery, M.A., Elimelech, M.: Water and sanitation in developing countries: including health in the equation. Environ. Sci. Technol. **41**(1), 17–24 (2007)

Wearable Product Design for Pain Management and Behavioral Support in Bipolar Disorder

Xiangqin Shi[1] , Bingjian Liu[1](✉) , Xu Sun[1,2] , Loic Faulon[1], and Jiang Wu[1]

[1] University of Nottingham Ningbo China, Ningbo, China
Bingjian.Liu@nottingham.edu.cn

[2] Nottingham Ningbo China Beacons of Excellence Research and Innovation Institute, Ningbo, China

Abstract. This study proposes a wearable device for young women suffering from bipolar disorder (BD), with the objective of managing stress and alleviating musculoskeletal pain associated with psychological distress. Utilizing a user-centered design (UCD) approach, the research team conducted a comprehensive review of the existing literature, administered questionnaires, and conducted observational studies, with the aim of identifying the user needs. The proposed neckband product design, in conjunction with a mobile application, employs heart rate variability (HRV) monitoring to assess stress levels and electromyography (EMG) to detect pain, providing users with relaxation reminders and medication management. Ergonomically and aesthetically designed, the device aims to address stigma and enhance treatment adherence, with preliminary user feedback indicating levels of comfort and appeal. Further testing is recommended to refine its usability.

Keywords: Wearable Technology · Bipolar Disorder · Stress Monitoring · Pain Management · User-Centered Design

1 Introduction

Bipolar disorder (BD) is a severe and chronic mental health condition characterized by extreme mood swings between mania and depression, often leading to significant impairment in emotional regulation, social functioning, and daily activities [1]. Patients with BD are also at an elevated risk of experiencing musculoskeletal pain, particularly in the spine, triggered by psychological distress [2]. The management of these symptoms is challenging, as traditional treatment methods—primarily pharmacological interventions—tend to focus on controlling mood fluctuations without addressing the physical discomfort or stress associated with the disorder [3]. Consequently, there is a critical need for non-pharmacological interventions that can support BD patients in managing both their mental and physical health in a comprehensive manner.

The primary problem addressed by this study is the lack of effective tools for continuous, real-time monitoring of both the psychological and physical symptoms of BD.

M. Schrepp (Ed.): HCII 2025, LNCS 15794, pp. 369–385, 2025.
https://doi.org/10.1007/978-3-031-93221-2_24

While some wearable devices focus on heart rate and activity tracking, they fail to provide comprehensive support for emotional regulation and pain management specific to BD patients. Furthermore, many BD patients experience stigma, which deters them from using medical devices that may draw attention to their condition [4]. These factors highlight the need for a wearable device that is discreet, easy to use, and tailored to the unique needs of BD patients, especially in reducing stress and managing pain.

To address these challenges, this study proposes a wearable neck device—referred to as "WIND & WAVE"—designed specifically for BD patients. The device integrates heart rate variability (HRV) and electromyography (EMG) sensors to monitor stress and pain levels in real time. It also provides real-time feedback and relaxation prompts, including breathing exercises and meditation guides, which have been shown to alleviate stress-induced pain and improve emotional regulation [5, 6]. By focusing on user-centered design, the device aims to minimize the stigma associated with medical wearables by offering a discreet, fashion-forward design that aligns with the aesthetic preferences of young female BD patients, who often favor decorative, non-medical-looking products [5].

The design process followed an iterative approach, starting with an exploration of user needs through questionnaires and observational studies, which revealed that young female BD patients prefer devices that are aesthetically pleasing and non-intrusive. Based on these insights, the design method included mood board creation, 3D CAD modelling, and multiple prototype iterations to refine the device's ergonomic design, sensor placement, and functionality. The result is a wearable device that combines real-time stress and pain monitoring with user-friendly features such as wireless charging, a mobile app for data visualization, and customizable modes for daily use, sleep, and meditation.

2   Context Research

2.1 Bipolar Disorder

Bipolar disorder (BD) is a severe mood disorder that significantly affects emotional stability and daily activities. Classified by the World Health Organization (WHO) as the second most significant illness impacting activities of daily living (ADLs) [6], BD is characterized by alternating episodes of mania and depression (as shown in Fig. 1), often impairing basic daily functioning. This study focuses on bipolar II disorder, which involves more frequent depressive episodes and higher rates of psychiatric comorbidities [1]. In addition to emotional challenges, BD is often accompanied by physical pain and discomfort, complicating treatment.

Among the various types of discomfort exhibited by individuals diagnosed with bipolar disorder, pain is a prevalent problem for those with BD, with 83% experiencing it, a prevalence comparable to that in homeless populations [2]. This pain is often misunderstood as emotional in origin, though it frequently has physiological causes. Musculoskeletal discomfort, especially in the back, head, lumbar region, and shoulders, is exacerbated by physical activity and emotional stress [2]. Despite the significant impact of pain on quality of life, many BD patients do not receive adequate pain management, which not only diminishes their quality of life but also increases the risk of suicidal ideation [2, 3]. Non-pharmacological treatments, such as mindfulness, physio-therapy, and acupuncture, have shown promise in alleviating pain, yet barriers to effective management remain [7].

2.2 Treatment of Bipolar Disorder

In addition to addressing physical pain, treatment for BD often involves psychological approaches. Pharmacological treatments can stabilize mood swings but may exacerbate depressive symptoms and come with high costs and side effects [8, 9]. Cognitive Behav-ioral Therapy (CBT), a widely used psychological intervention, has shown positive post-treatment effects for BD patients [10]. CBT is structured in four phases: assessment, psy-choeducation, intervention, and relapse prevention [10], aiming to help patients develop structured routines, engage in rewarding activities, and alleviate depressive symptoms.

Additionally, CBT can be explained from a biopsychosocial perspective, address-ing the interconnected domains of environment, cognition, emotion, physiology, and behavior [11]. Based on these theories, it is shown that CBT emphasizes documenting daily behaviors, emotional fluctuations, and cognitive thoughts, which provides valu-able insights for both patients and healthcare professionals, fostering tailored therapeu-tic feedback. Through structured goal setting, cognitive restructuring, mindfulness, and behavioral activation, CBT helps patients recognize triggers, develop healthier coping mechanisms, and build emotional resilience over time [12].

Despite the numerous advantages associated with CBT, individuals diagnosed with BD frequently encounter challenges in adhering to the prescribed protocol for data col-lection. This includes the inability to consistently record physiological changes and emotional state. Moreover, they demonstrate a heightened vulnerability to the collection of objective data. This can impede effective communication and hinder the efficacy of treatment. In addition to this, non-adherence to treatment remains a significant barrier for BD patients, as the recurrent nature of mood episodes leads to inconsistent participa-tion in long-term treatments [13]. To improve adherence, patient-centered approaches, including innovative monitoring and reminder systems, are needed. Recovery from BD requires a holistic approach that integrates environmental and psychological factors to support personalized, balanced recovery strategies [14, 15]. Integrating digital monitor-ing platforms into CBT can improve adherence and provide real-time feedback, further optimizing the therapeutic process [12].

3 User and Technology Research

This study aims to design a wearable device for individuals with bipolar disorder (BD), focusing on managing stress and pain. The design process integrates both user-centered research and technology aspects to address BD patients' needs.

3.1 Challenges of Bipolar Disorder (BD)

Bipolar Disorder (BD) is a severe mood disorder characterized by extreme mood fluctu-ations, including episodes of mania and depression, which disrupt daily functioning and

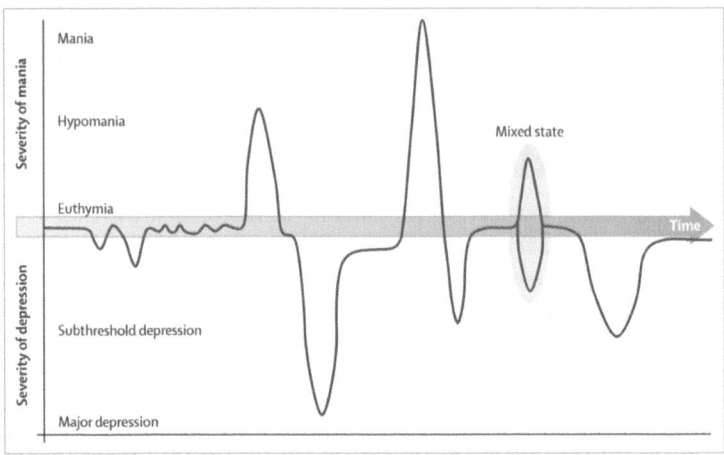

Fig. 1. Life chart showing progression of bipolar disorder [1].

emotional stability. This condition often leads to significant physical discomfort, making treatment more challenging. Bipolar II disorder, in particular, is marked by more frequent depressive episodes and a higher prevalence of psychiatric comorbidities, further complicating management [1]. Among the most concerning aspects of BD are the emotional and physical distress experienced by patients, with chronic pain and stress frequently interacting and exacerbating each other.

Pain and stress in BD patients are interrelated, with stress often triggering or intensifying physical pain, especially musculoskeletal discomfort, commonly affecting areas like the back and shoulders. Chronic stress can disrupt physiological balance, increasing emotional distress and further aggravating pain. Moreover, this pain can lead to a negative cognitive-emotional phenomenon called "pain catastrophizing," where patients' negative thoughts about their pain amplify their stress, leading to a vicious cycle. This connection between pain and stress is particularly problematic for individuals with bipolar disorder, as they may experience both simultaneously, worsening their emotional tension and complicating the management of their condition. Current treatments have yet to fully address the chronic pain that many BD patients suffer from, leaving a significant gap in comprehensive care [2].

3.2 Technology Possibilities

Real-time monitoring through wearable devices offers a promising solution to the complex interplay of pain and stress in bipolar disorder (BD) patients. Wearable sensors, including ECG, EEG, and EMG, can track key physiological markers in real-time, enabling patients to monitor their stress and pain levels more effectively. For instance, heart rate variability (HRV), measured through electrocardiogram (ECG) and photoplethysmography (PPG) sensors, serves as an essential indicator of stress levels, as it reflects autonomic nervous system (ANS) activity, which is heavily influenced by stress [16]. By continuously assessing HRV, wearable devices can provide valuable insights into the physiological state of BD patients, helping them better understand and manage their stress responses.

The integration of photoelectric sensors, such as those utilizing green LEDs, allows for even more accurate detection of HRV through skin changes. This technology enhances the ability to monitor stress levels by capturing subtle variations in blood flow and pulse frequency, providing deeper insights into the patient's emotional and physiological state. This continuous data collection can empower patients and clinicians to take timely and informed actions, improving stress management and reducing the impact of stress on BD symptoms. By offering real-time, actionable data, wearable devices could significantly enhance personalized treatment strategies for BD patients, ultimately improving their quality of life.

Wearable devices also provide a transformative opportunity for the continuous monitoring of BD symptoms, particularly stress and pain management. Devices like smartwatches or clothing with embedded sensors offer seamless tracking of physiological markers such as heart rate variability (HRV) and electromyographic (EMG) signals, which are key indicators of stress and pain in BD patients [17]. The integration of advanced sensor technologies into these devices allows for more precise data collection on emotional fluctuations, enabling clinicians to tailor interventions with greater accuracy. With the potential to monitor symptoms in real time, these wearable devices could lead to more individualized and effective treatment plans, enhancing both the physical and emotional well-being of BD patients [18].

3.3 User Interaction (UI) Design Principles

Designing user interfaces for individuals with bipolar disorder (BD) requires a deep understanding of their unique challenges, such as cognitive impairments and the stigma they often face. BD patients frequently encounter societal exclusion and discomfort due to widespread misconceptions about their condition [4]. To mitigate these effects, wearable devices should feature discreet, aesthetically pleasing designs that minimize the visibility of medical functions, thus promoting privacy and reducing stigma [19].

Additionally, the UI needs to accommodate cognitive impairments, such as attention deficits and memory difficulties, which are common among BD patients. For example, self-tracking features should prioritize emotional stabilization over performance metrics, helping users maintain emotional equilibrium [20]. This approach encourages long-term engagement, which is essential to overcoming the frequent issue of non-adherence in mental health applications [21].

Effective wearable solutions for BD patients must be both user-centered and empathetic. Key design considerations include:

- **Simplified Visualizations:** Intuitive graphs and charts to track emotional trends and detect early warning signs [22].
- **Routine Adherence Tools:** Features such as medication and sleep reminders to support consistency and behavioral stability [22].
- **Enhanced Communication Features:** Secure channels for patient-therapist interaction, fostering stronger engagement and therapeutic relationships [23].

4   Market Research

4.1   Competitor Products

This product concept is designed to address the needs of individuals with bipolar disorder and anxiety symptoms by offering real-time data collection and pain relief. While there are a few directly comparable products on the market, a review of existing competitors highlights gaps in both the market and research. To fill these gaps, the proposed design integrates strengths from current offerings while focusing on emotional regulation and pain management.

Heart Rate Monitoring Devices such as the Apple Watch, Fitbit Charge 6, and Oura Ring are popular for tracking metrics like heart rate and activity levels. However, these devices lack specialized features for emotional regulation and mental health support, leaving a significant opportunity for targeted improvements in the context of bipolar disorder.

Similarly, Relaxation Tools and PMR (Progressive Muscle Relaxation) Assistance, including products like Headspace, Spire Stone, and massage tools, focus on general stress relief through guided exercises, mindfulness, and PMR techniques. While these products are effective for stress management, they do not address the specific challenges posed by bipolar disorder, particularly in managing emotional fluctuations and anxiety symptoms.

4.2   Target Market

The product comparison identifies market gaps, focusing on individuals with bipolar disorder as the target audience. Most wearables emphasize advanced technology, while healthcare products rely primarily on apps with minimal physical interaction. This highlights the need for simplified technology to improve user engagement and address the specific requirements of emotional regulation and pain management.

4.3   Proposed Persona

The target user is Chen Ling, a 27-year-old professional woman from Shanghai, China, managing bipolar disorder for three years. She values discreet, fashionable wearables that support mental health management while ensuring privacy and reducing stigma. Her key challenges include maintaining stable sleep patterns and managing emotional regulation. Chen Ling prefers user-friendly, accessory-like devices with intelligent tracking features to aid in her self-management journey.

5   Methodology

This section applies user-centered design principles to identify the needs of individuals with BD. Empirical data, gathered through questionnaire surveys and video-based observations, informed the design direction and enabled thoughtful and well-informed solutions.

5.1 Questionnaire Study

A structured questionnaire (as shown in Table 1) collected data on demographics, stress-related pain, and preferences for pain relief and wearable devices [24]. Responses (as shown in Fig. 2) from 166 participants, predominantly young women, revealed stress-induced pain in the back (83.56%), head (77.40%), and shoulders (52.74%). Preferred pain relief methods included deep breathing (69.3%) and muscle relaxation (56.3%), with a preference for discreet wearable designs like rings and necklaces.

Table 1. Questionnaire on Stress-Induced Muscle Pain and Wearable Solutions.

No.	Question Type	Content
1	Single Choice	What is your gender?
2	Single Choice	What is your age group?
3	Open Ended	Which city in China are you from?
4	Single Choice	Do you experience pain in your muscles and joints (e.g. in the shoulders or back) because of everyday stress?
5	Multiple Choice	Where do your aches and pains usually appear?
6	Scale Question	Does stress-induced muscle pain have a significant impact on your life (1–6)?
7	Single Choice	Do you deliberately choose methods to relieve pain?
8	Multiple Choice	Do you know of or have tried any other ways to relieve this type of stress-induced pain?
9	Scale Question	Can you clearly perceive your level of relaxation (1–6)?
10	Single Choice	Do you need a reminder to relax?
11	Single Choice	When you are a beginner, do you need aids to help you better relieve pain caused by stress?
12	Multiple Choice	Which type of wearable device would you prefer as an auxiliary reminder?

5.2 Video-Observational Study

Due to privacy constraints, video-based observation was employed to study BD patients' behaviours [25]. Observations based on the YouTube video 'Living With Bipolar Disorder' [26] highlighted the importance of structured routines, symptom tracking, and physical activity in managing BD (as shown in Table 2).

The video features two patients, one male and one female, with different types of bipolar disorder. It highlights their management strategies, including regular medication, symptom monitoring, and physical activity. The study also explores their daily routines, frustrations, and coping mechanisms, providing insights into their unique needs and perspectives.

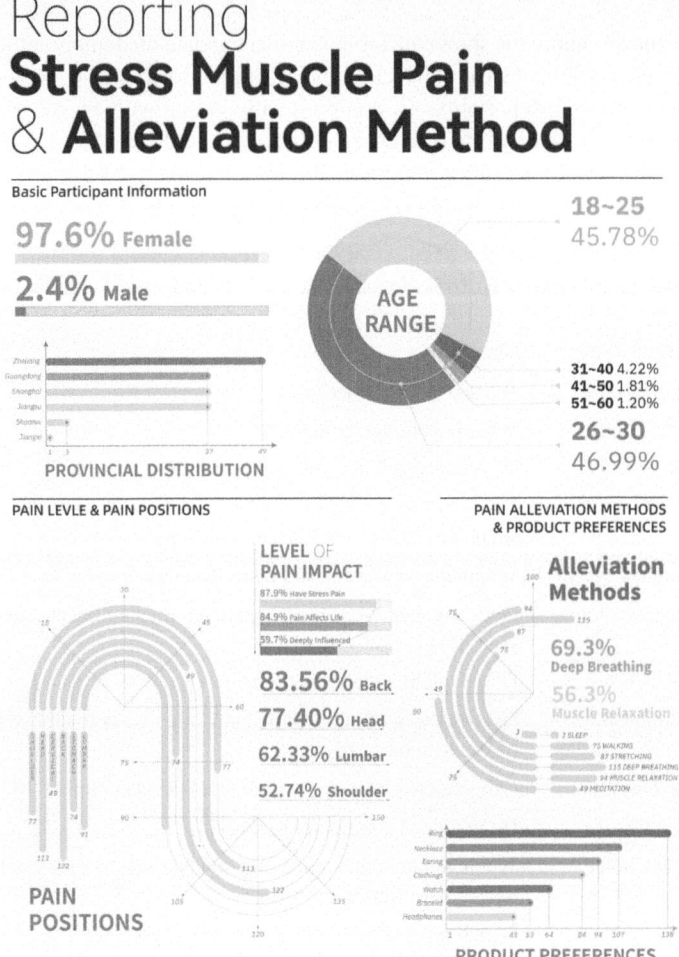

Fig. 2. Questionnaire results on pain and alleviation methods.

5.3 Ethics Considerations

This study adhered to strict ethical principles to protect participants and ensure research integrity.

At the outset, participants were fully informed about the study's purpose and procedures through a warning statement provided before the questionnaire. This statement highlighted the voluntary nature of participation and assured confidentiality. During the user testing phase, participants further reviewed the '*Participant Information Sheet*' and signed the '*Participant Consent Form*,' ensuring a clear understanding of their involvement.

Table 2. Observees and Key Findings: *Living with Bipolar Disorder* [26].

Perspectives	Observee A	Observee B
Name	ALLISTER MCGUIRE	ANDREA GARCIA
Gender	Male	Female
BD Type	Bipolar II disorder	Bipolar I disorder
Daily Routines	• Takes daily medication including Effexor, anti-psychotic, mood stabilizer, and vitamin D • Follows strict medication schedule	• Managed heavy workload with classes, athletics, and campus involvement • Relied on planners to stay organized and manage racing thoughts
Behaviors	• Rapidly cycles between highs and lows • Withdraws during depressive episodes	• Experienced manic episodes with risky behaviors • Balanced mania and depression, often experiencing a crash after mania
Frustrations (Quotes)	*"Logic brain is telling me this will end soon, you'll get out of this, it's just a cycle; and then the emotional side of my brain is like nothing's ever goanna be okay again, you are goanna be stuck like this forever this is the rest of your life."*	*"If you don't know my situation you might think, oh hey, this girl is really fun, she's really great. When in reality, I'm going down more of a destructive path."*
Management	• Open communication and support • Coping with tough times together • Recognizing and managing manic episodes • Finding constructive outlets for emotions	• Manages bipolar with running • Finds peace in running • Enjoys Track Club and sports with dad
Attitudes to BD	He sees bipolar disorder as an important part of who he is and wouldn't change it, even though it brings challenges	She sees bipolar disorder as part of who she is and prefers living with it, as it has shaped who she is

In addition, participants were made aware of their right to withdraw from the study at any time, without the need for explanation. This voluntary participation approach emphasized their autonomy, allowing them to retract consent or data at any point without any negative consequences.

To ensure privacy, all collected data was anonymized and securely stored, with access restricted to authorized personnel only. After the defined retention period, the data will be securely disposed of to maintain confidentiality.

Overall, transparency, respect for participant autonomy, and rigorous data management were fundamental to this study, ensuring that sensitive information was handled with care and that research integrity was upheld throughout.

6 Proposed Design Solution

6.1 Design Process

This section outlines the design process, beginning with the creation of mood boards and progressing through 3D modelling and iterative prototype refinement.

Firstly, the mood board was created with young women as the target demographic, focusing on aesthetics and portability. The design emphasizes slim, minimalistic forms in black, white, and grey tones, with subtle low-saturation color accents to add visual interest. These design choices aim to make the wearable feel like an everyday accessory rather than a medical device, reflecting a balance between fashion and functionality. The mood board also considers the fluidity of form, evoking a sense of calm to support emotional regulation and pain relief.

Secondly, the CAD modelling process defined the product's configuration, structural framework, and individual parts. As shown in Fig. 3, CAD modeling processes involved creating detailed 3D models to visualize the product's form, assembly, and components. The process allowed for precise adjustments to the design, ensuring that all aspects, from ergonomics to functionality, were accounted for. The following stages from the draft report describe these steps in more detail:

- **Basic Dimensions**: In the first stage, the basic dimensions of the product were defined according to human data.
- **Surface Loft**: In the second stage, the main body of the neckband was created using surface-loft and mirror functions.
- **Induction Zone**: In the third stage, the shape and position of the induction zone for sensors were defined.
- **Charging Zone**: In the fourth stage, the shape and position of the charging zone were defined.
- **Charging Dock Component**: In the final stage, the shape of the charging dock component was defined.

These detailed 3D modelling steps helped define every aspect of the product, from its form to the individual components, ensuring the feasibility and quality of the design.

Finally, the initial neckband prototypes focused on three key aspects: ergonomics, dimensions, and resilience. These prototypes were developed to ensure the product would be comfortable, lightweight, and flexible for wearability. As shown in Fig. 4, the second phase of prototyping refined these aspects:

- **Ergonomics**: The second phase of prototypes focused on improving the fit of the neckband for enhanced comfort. The shape was optimized to better align with the natural contours of the neck, improving overall wearability.
- **Product Strength**: Thickness was added to the neckband to enhance its strength and durability without compromising comfort.

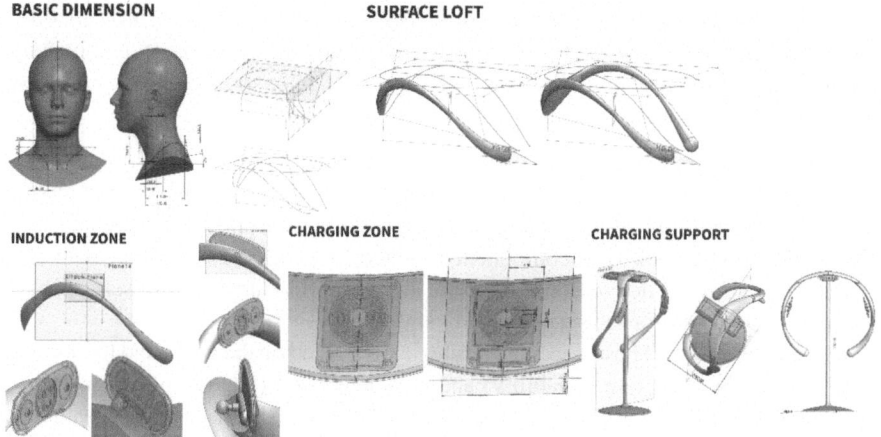

Fig. 3. CAD Modelling Process.

- **Product Functionality**: Flat induction zones were integrated into the design to better accommodate the sensors, improving their functionality for stress and pain monitoring.
- **Surface Finish**: To improve the aesthetic appeal and comfort of the product, a smoother resin finish was achieved through 3D printing.

Fig. 4. Second phase of prototyping.

6.2 Wearable Devices Features

This wearable neck device, specifically designed for young female patients with bipolar disorder, is a multifunctional tool for real-time monitoring of heart rate and stress levels. It provides relaxation prompts based on these physiological metrics, supporting users in managing their emotional and physical well-being. In addition to stress monitoring, the device facilitates guided activities, including meditation and breathing exercises, to help reduce stress and muscle tension.

The neck band consists of four main components (as shown in Fig. 5): an ergonomic body, neck ring, dual sensor zones, and a charging/alert area. These components work together to monitor users' stress levels, provide relaxation prompts, and offer functionality for pain management.

- **Ergonomic Body**: Designed to fit comfortably around the neck, ensuring it can be worn for extended periods without causing discomfort. The ergonomic shape supports long-term wearability while aligning with the natural contours of the neck.
- **Neck Ring**: The neck ring component is made of soft, biocompatible materials, ensuring comfort while providing structure and support to the device. It serves as the primary framework for the sensors and charging area.
- **Dual Sensor Zones**: These zones are strategically placed on the neckband to measure both stress (via heart rate variability) and muscle tension (via electromyography or EMG). The sensors detect pressure and muscle status in real-time, providing valuable data for managing emotional fluctuations and physical discomfort.
- **Charging/Alert Area**: This component is located at the back of the neckband and serves multiple functions. It supports **wireless charging**, allowing the device to be easily recharged without the need for cables. It also acts as an **alert zone** for providing **relaxation prompts**, **medication reminders**, and **guided breathing exercises** through gentle vibrations, ensuring the user stays on track with their mental health management.

The charging dock provides wireless recharging and convenient storage for the wearable device (as shown in Fig. 6). It is designed to be placed on a bedside table, where it also serves as a sleep monitor. While the device is charging, the dock monitors the user's sleep status, collecting valuable data about the user's sleep patterns to offer insights into their overall health. This feature helps users better understand how their sleep affects stress and pain levels, supporting more informed decisions about their well-being.

- **Wireless Charging**: The dock uses a set of wireless charging coils to replenish the device's battery, ensuring that the wearable is ready to use at all times without the need for cumbersome cords.
- **Sleep Monitoring**: By placing the device on the bedside table, the dock tracks the user's sleep status, collecting data on sleep quality and duration. This information is integrated into the wearable mobile app, providing users with detailed feedback about their sleep patterns and offering recommendations for improving rest.

6.3 Mobile Application of "WIND & WAVE"

A mobile application (as shown in Fig. 7) features account registration, fingerprint-secured privacy, medication tracking, and real-time stress and muscle monitoring. Designed with BD patients in mind, it aligns with UI principles to enhance usability and efficiency.

Following user-centred design (UCD) principles, "WIND & WAVE" focuses on usability and accessibility. The navigation bar employs simplified icons and intuitive data visualization, such as bar charts for stress detection, making the app easy to use. Personalization features include three modes—Daily, Sleep, and Meditation—paired with emotional design elements to support users' mental well-being. To address cognitive impairments often seen in BD, the app minimizes memory burden through clear medication reminders and passive real-time data collection.

The wearable device's aesthetic mirrors traditional decorative items, reducing stigma associated with medical devices. Privacy is prioritized with fingerprint-secured access to protect user data. The app empowers BD patients to monitor their emotional and physical health independently, fostering a participatory and supportive experience.

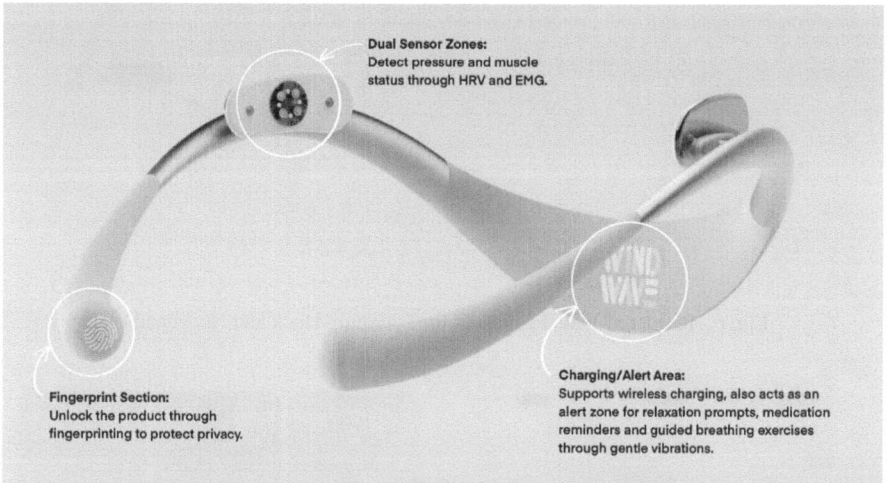

Fig. 5. Rendered Visualization of the Neckband Product.

6.4 Utilization Logic

The three functional modes (as shown in Fig. 8)—Daily, Sleep, and Meditation—are designed to integrate seamlessly into users' daily routines. From putting on the neckband to engaging with the application for stress tracking and relaxation activities, the product supports users in managing stress and emotional regulation throughout the day. This integration into everyday life enhances its practicality and provides meaningful support for managing the mental health challenges faced by individuals with BD.

7 Limitations and Future Considerations

7.1 User Feedback

Testing with two users across six prototypes (as shown in Fig. 9) provided initial insights into size, comfort, and sensor placement. Although the feedback was positive, the limited sample size restricts generalizability. Broader testing is recommended to refine ergonomics and functionality. Here is feedback from two participants:

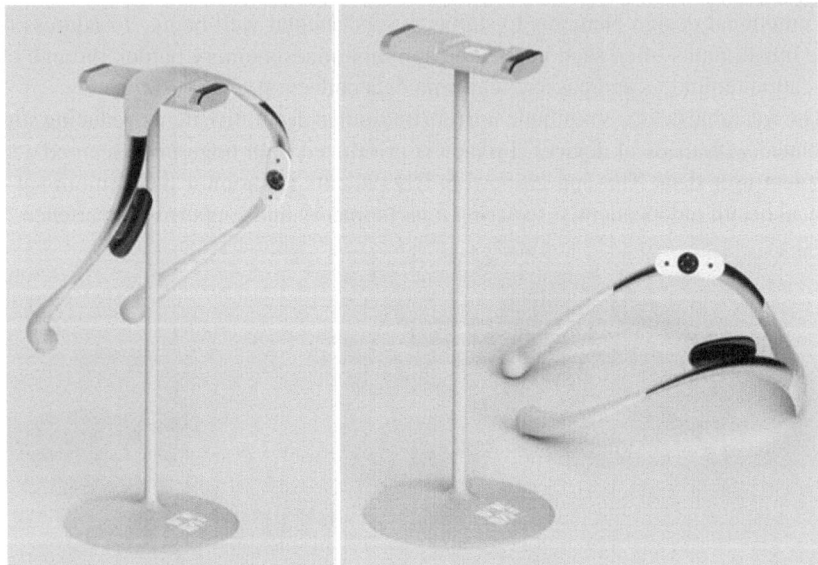

Fig. 6. Rendered Visualization of the Charging Dock and Neckband.

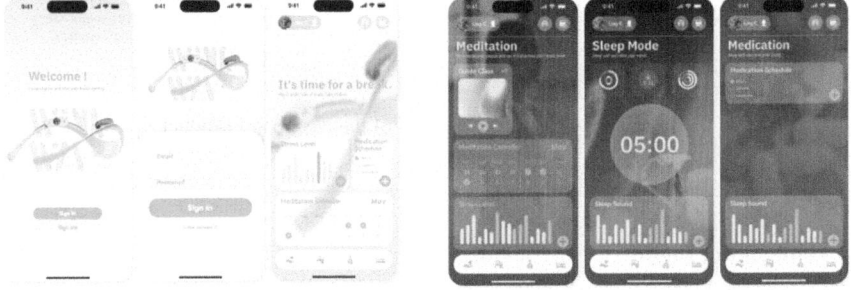

Fig. 7. Mobile App: WIND Design Overview.   **Fig. 8.** Mobile App: WAVE Design Overview.

- **User A**: "The product is beautifully shaped with well-positioned sensors, aesthetically pleasing, and comfortable."
- **User B**: "It's easy to wear, stylish, and promotes health with its fashionable design."

7.2 Limitations

- **Ergonomics Testing.** Testing with only two participants limits applicability. Future studies should involve diverse participants and real-world evaluations.
- **Product Design.** The design meets basic user needs but requires further iterations to integrate electronic components and enhance functionality for a broader audience.
- **Research Scope.** The study focuses on initial prototyping, lacking comprehensive validation of long-term effectiveness in real-world settings.

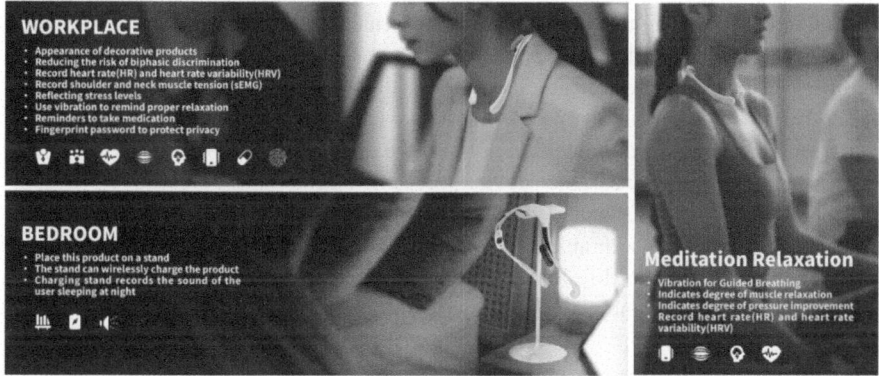

Fig. 9. Three Functional Modes: Daily, Sleep, and Meditation.

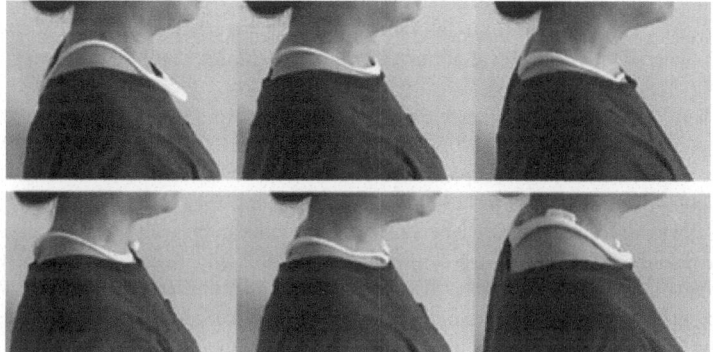

Fig. 10. Ergonomic Testing of Neckband Prototype for Wearability and Comfort.

8   Conclusion

This study has developed the wearable neck device "WIND & WAVE," designed to monitor stress and pain in individuals with bipolar disorder (BD) through the use of heart rate variability (HRV) and electromyography (EMG) sensors. With its ergonomic design and emphasis on user comfort and stigma reduction, the device supports symptom self-management by providing real-time data for emotional and physical health monitoring. Through user-centered design, the device aims to reduce the emotional burden of BD and improve the overall quality of life for users by offering personalized prompts for relaxation and pain management.

However, the study acknowledges several limitations, including the small sample size and the early-stage design of the model. As the device is not yet fully integrated with programming and circuit systems, the full functionality of the device remains untested in real-world contexts. These constraints highlight the need for further research to assess the device's effectiveness and refine its design.

Future research should aim to expand user testing to a more diverse population to assess the device's performance across various demographics and contexts. Longitudinal studies would provide valuable insights into the real-world effectiveness and long-term benefits of the device. Additionally, enhancing sensor integration and collaborating with healthcare professionals will ensure the device's therapeutic potential is fully validated. These efforts will be crucial in optimizing the device's functionality and supporting the integration of wearable health technology into the management of bipolar disorder.

In conclusion, the wearable device presents significant potential as a non-pharmacological tool for managing BD symptoms, particularly stress and pain. With further advancements in wearable health technology, this device could play a key role in improving the quality of life for individuals with bipolar disorder and other chronic conditions requiring continuous management.

References

1. Grande, I., Berk, M., Birmaher, B., Vieta, E.: Bipolar disorder. Lancet **387**, 1561–1572 (2016). https://doi.org/10.1016/s0140-6736(15)00241-x
2. Rosa, A.C.F., Leão, E.R.: Pain in the bipolar disorder: prevalence, characteristics and relationship with suicide risk. Rev. Latino-Am. Enfermagem. **29**, e3463 (2021). https://doi.org/10.1590/1518-8345.4737.3463
3. Onwumere, J., et al.: Pain management in people with severe mental illness: an agenda for progress. Pain **163**, 1653–1660 (2022). https://doi.org/10.1097/j.pain.0000000000002633
4. Brooten-Brooks, M.C.: Why Bipolar Disorder Stigma Exists. https://www.verywellhealth.com/bipolar-disorder-stigma-5211304. Accessed 16 Apr 2024
5. Tran, T., Nathan-Roberts, D.: Design considerations in wearable technology for patients with bipolar disorder. In: Proceedings of the Human Factors and Ergonomics Society Annual Meeting, vol. 62, pp. 1187–1191 (2018). https://doi.org/10.1177/1541931218621273
6. Alonso, J., et al.: Days out of role due to common physical and mental conditions: results from the WHO world mental health surveys. Mol. Psychiatry **16**, 1234–1246 (2011). https://doi.org/10.1038/mp.2010.101
7. Osser, MD, D.N.: Addressing Pain in Patients with Bipolar Disorder. https://www.psychiatrictimes.com/view/addressing-pain-patients-bipolar-disorder. Accessed 16 Apr 2024
8. Baldessarini, R.J., Tondo, L., Vázquez, G.H.: Pharmacological treatment of adult bipolar disorder. Mol. Psychiatry **24**, 198–217 (2018). https://doi.org/10.1038/s41380-018-0044-2
9. Geddes, J.R., Miklowitz, D.J.: Treatment of bipolar disorder. Lancet **381**, 1672–1682 (2013). https://doi.org/10.1016/S0140-6736(13)60857-0
10. Szentagotai, A., David, D.: The efficacy of cognitive-behavioral therapy in bipolar disorder: a quantitative meta-analysis. J. Clin. Psychiatry **71**, 66–72 (2010). https://doi.org/10.4088/JCP.08r04559yel
11. .Özdel, K., Kart, A., Türkçapar, M.H.: Cognitive behavioral therapy in treatment of bipolar disorder. Arch. Neuropsychiatry (2021). https://doi.org/10.29399/npa.27419
12. Ramirez Basco, A.J.R.: Cognitive-behavioral Therapy for Bipolar Disorder - 336 pages.pdf. The Guilford Press (2005)
13. Chakrabarti, S.: Treatment-adherence in bipolar disorder: a patient-centred approach. World J Psychiatry **6**, 399–409 (2016). https://doi.org/10.5498/wjp.v6.i4.399
14. Jagfeld, G., Lobban, F., Marshall, P., Jones, S.H.: Personal recovery in bipolar disorder: systematic review and "best fit" framework synthesis of qualitative evidence – a POETIC adaptation of CHIME. J. Affect. Disord. **292**, 375–385 (2021). https://doi.org/10.1016/j.jad.2021.05.051

15. Dodd, A.L., Mezes, B., Lobban, F., Jones, S.H.: Psychological mechanisms and the ups and downs of personal recovery in bipolar disorder. Br. J. Clin. Psychol. **56**, 310–328 (2017). https://doi.org/10.1111/bjc.12140
16. Chen, J., Abbod, M., Shieh, J.-S.: Pain and stress detection using wearable sensors and devices—a review. Sensors. **21**, 1030 (2021). https://doi.org/10.3390/s21041030
17. Liu, F., et al.: Research and application progress of intelligent wearable devices. Chin. J. Anal. Chem. **49**, 159–171 (2021). https://doi.org/10.1016/s1872-2040(20)60076-7
18. Sheikh, M., Qassem, M., Kyriacou, P.A.: Wearable, environmental, and smartphone-based passive sensing for mental health monitoring. Front. Digit. Health **3** (2021). https://doi.org/10.3389/fdgth.2021.662811
19. O'Donnell, L., et al.: Social aspects of the workplace among individuals with bipolar disorder. J. Soc. Soc. Work Res. **8**, 379–398 (2017). https://doi.org/10.1086/693163
20. Patoz, M.-C., et al.: Patients' adherence to smartphone apps in the management of bipolar disorder: a systematic review. Int. J. Bipolar. Disord. **9**, 19 (2021). https://doi.org/10.1186/s40345-021-00224-6
21. Dodd, A.L., Mallinson, S., Griffiths, M., Morriss, R., Jones, S.H., Lobban, F.: Users' experiences of an online intervention for bipolar disorder: Important lessons for design and evaluation. Evid. Based Mental Health **20**, 133–139 (2017). https://doi.org/10.1136/eb-2017-102754
22. Heydarian, S., Shakiba, A., Rostam Niakan Kalhori, S.: The minimum feature set for designing mobile apps to support bipolar disorder-affected patients: proposal of essential functions and requirements. J. Healthc. Inform. Res. **7**, 254–276 (2023). https://doi.org/10.1007/s41666-023-00134-5
23. Majid, S., et al.: The extent of user involvement in the design of self-tracking technology for bipolar disorder: literature review. JMIR Mental Health **8**, e27991 (2021). https://doi.org/10.2196/27991
24. Taherdoost, H.: Designing a questionnaire for a research paper: a comprehensive guide to design and develop an effective questionnaire. AJMS **11**, 8–16 (2022). https://doi.org/10.51983/ajms-2022.11.1.3087
25. George, T.: What Is an Observational Study? I Guide & Examples. https://www.scribbr.com/methodology/observational-study/. Accessed 15 Apr 2024
26. Living with Bipolar Disorder I My Life With (2020)

User Interaction Behavior Analysis for Cognitive Load Detection in Online Learning Processes

Mira Suryani[1,2] , Harry Budi Santoso[1(✉)] , Rizal Fathoni Aji[1] ,
Setiawan Hadi[2] , and Martin Schrepp[3]

[1] Universitas Indonesia, Depok 16424, Indonesia
harrybs@cs.ui.ac.id
[2] Universitas Padjadjaran, Sumedang 45363, Indonesia
[3] SAP SE, 69190 Walldorf, Germany

Abstract. The widespread use of online learning platforms has highlighted the challenge of managing student engagement and cognitive load. Poor interface design, complex layouts, dense contents, and redundant elements can increase cognitive strain, hindering learning effectiveness. To address this, adaptive interfaces based on user models are essential for optimizing cognitive load management in online learning environments. This study employs a mixed-method approach, focusing on user interaction behaviors as cognitive load indicators. Quantitative data were collected from 33 computer science students at a public university in Indonesia using the Hotjar service on an LMS. Participants engaged in a 150-min asynchronous learning session involving reading learning materials, watching instructional videos, participating in discussions, and taking quizzes. Learners' cognitive load was assessed using the NASA-TLX questionnaire. Findings reveal that key interaction metrics—access duration, text input, clicks, and U-turns—correlate with cognitive load levels. Over 80% of respondents reported high cognitive load, with the most engaged learners experiencing the highest strain. K-means clustering identified four learner profiles, showing that intense interaction does not always lead to efficient learning. Feature importance analysis confirmed text input and access duration as the strongest predictors of cognitive load. This study highlights the need for adaptive learning systems that dynamically adjust user interface, content, and complexity based on real-time behavioral indicators. Future research should explore real-time adaptation, physiological data integration, and personalized learning pathways to enhance cognitive efficiency in online education.

Keywords: Adaptive Learning System · Behavior Analysis · Cognitive Load · NASA-Task Load Index · Online Learning · User Interaction

1 Introduction

The widespread use of online learning platforms has made managing student engagement and cognitive load a major challenge in educational technology. From a user interface perspective, several design aspects such as: interactive learning media, immersion,

M. Schrepp (Ed.): HCII 2025, LNCS 15794, pp. 386–403, 2025.
https://doi.org/10.1007/978-3-031-93221-2_25

disfluency, realism, and redundant elements can increase cognitive load if not managed properly in an LMS [1]. This is also reinforced by research [2] which states that poor interface design can add unnecessary cognitive load and hinder students' learning process. Furthermore, the complexity of the LMS interface also increases the user's cognitive load [3]. Therefore, it is important for system developers to design adaptive interfaces based on user models to help manage students' cognitive load [4] in addition to implementing cognitive strategies in online learning environments [5].

Cognitive load itself is defined as the total amount of mental load required to process information in working memory when completing a task [6]. This cognitive load is closely related to the theory of information processing which physically describes how information is received by the five senses, processed in the prefrontal cortex of the brain, and stored in long-term memory [7]. When processing information, humans have limitations in terms of their working memory capacity, so Sweller specifically put forward cognitive load theory with the aim of providing a better understanding of how cognitive load affects human learning, especially in the context of instruction and learning design. Cognitive load theory states that information overload inhibits learners' ability to process and remember content, thereby affecting outcomes [8].

Therefore, to prevent cognitive overload, we need to know the status of cognitive load when someone obtains information by detecting or measuring it. Chen suggests that there are 4 basic approaches that can be taken to detect or measure cognitive load, namely: subjective, behavioral, task performance, and physiological.

Several researchers have used subjective self-reports using questionnaires [1, 9, 10] to measure cognitive load. Another approach in the form of task performance has also been carried out by several researchers [11, 12]. A different approach to measuring cognitive load is physiological. Some researchers who use this approach use several different data modalities that characterize physiological signals such as electro-oculography (EOG) signals [13], electro-encephalogram (EEG) [14], heart rate and pupillometry [15] to measure cognitive load. Although the task performance and physiological approaches are quite objective methods, in the context of learning, especially online learning, these methods tend to be intrusive and can increase cognitive load.

In online learning, detecting students' cognitive load through user interaction behavior, which is a behavioral measurement approach, can help optimize the learning process [16].. However, in the context of online learning, it is necessary to investigate what modalities can describe these behavioral patterns. Therefore, this study explores how user interaction behavior, combined with cognitive load validation, can enhance online learning. To address the challenges posed by varying cognitive load levels in online learning environments, it is crucial to understand how user interaction behaviors can reveal valuable insights. This study intends to address the following research questions:

- how can user interaction behaviors in online learning processes be used to detect cognitive load?
- what are the key indicators of cognitive load in online learning environments based on user interaction behaviors? and
- how can adaptive online learning systems be designed to respond to detected cognitive load in real-time?

By analyzing metrics like clicks, navigation, text input, and access duration, the overarching goal of this research are to:

- discover how behavior can be used to automatically detect cognitive load;
- identify key factors or behavioral metrics that indicate cognitive load; and
- create mechanisms that enable learning systems to automatically adjust interface, content, tasks, or assistance when cognitive load exceeds optimal limits.

This research provides a crucial contribution to online learning by identifies key behavioral metrics that indicate cognitive load, enabling the design of more efficient learning systems. The findings not only advance our understanding of cognitive load in digital education but also lay the groundwork for future research in artificial intelligence and adaptive learning technologies, ultimately fostering innovative approaches to online education.

2 Related Work

2.1 Cognitive Load, Cognitive Load Theory and Measurement

According to Sweller et al. [17], cognitive load is the amount of cognitive resources used in processing information when someone is learning. This concept relates to how information is presented and processed by an individual's cognitive system. Sweller argued that working memory has a limited capacity, so cognitive load must be managed so that learning or task completion can be optimal. Therefore, he developed a theoretical framework called Cognitive Load Theory (CLT) [18].

CLT was developed to understand how human working memory capacity processes information during learning or complex tasks. This theory divides cognitive load into three types: Intrinsic Cognitive Load (ICL), Extraneous Cognitive Load (ECL), and Germane Cognitive Load (GCL). ICL is the load inherent in the complexity of the material/task itself (e.g., learning calculus vs. basic arithmetic). ECL is the load resulting from the way information is presented or designed (e.g., unclear instructions or poor interface design). Then, GCL is the load associated with the effort of forming mental schemas (deep understanding) to process new information [19].

In order for the CLT concept to be implemented optimally, a person's cognitive load status needs to be known first. According to Chen et al. [20], there are at least four approaches in detecting or measuring a person's cognitive load: subjective, behavioral, task performance, and physiological. Chen et al., also conveyed the possibility of using a fusion method called Multimodal Cognitive Load Measurement (MCLM).

Subjective approaches to measuring cognitive load are quite widely used by researchers. There are several subjective questionnaires and scales for this purpose such as the use of NASA-TLX [21], 9-points Paas Scale [22], and 7-points Klepsch Scale [23]. However, there are several weaknesses in this subjective approach such as limited self-reflection and mood abilities [24], and reliance on memory because the test is conducted at the end of the session [25].

Researchers employ frequently task performance-based approaches to measure cognitive load. Modanwal et al. [12] compared gesture-based input methods (Dactylology vs. Braille) for visually impaired users, linking performance metrics (response time, error rates) to cognitive load. Moser et al. [26] explored VR motion tracking as a non-invasive cognitive load indicator in immersive learning. Meanwhile, Sguerra et al. [27] developed the AUHWM framework to estimate users' working memory capacity in real time, particularly for individuals with dementia. These studies underscore the importance of cognitive load assessment in designing adaptive interfaces responsive to diverse user needs.However, this approach also has disadvantages since the quality of the measurement results depends on how well the task is designed to evaluate cognitive load [24]. Another weakness of task performance is that it is not only influenced by cognitive load but also by other factors, such as individual skills, previous experience, motivation, and emotional state [20].

The physiological approach in measuring cognitive load is also widely used by researchers. This is possible due to the rapid is the rapid technological advances in detecting physiological signals. Ahmadi et al. [28] investigate physiological cognitive load measurement in VR during physical activity, addressing movement-induced sensor inaccuracies. Caldiroli et al. [29] compares cognitive load in online tasks (comprehension/information-seeking) across mobile and PC devices. Both studies advance adaptive technology by analyzing context-specific cognitive demands. However, in the context of online learning, this physiological approach is difficult to implement because of the need for supervision in the use of tools that record physiological signals and can cause distractions that may increase cognitive load.

Behavioral approaches complement subjective and task-based methods in cognitive load measurement. Abbad et al. [30] introduced a fine-grained eye-tracking method to pinpoint mentally demanding code sections in software development, addressing limitations of coarse-grained assessments. Arjun et al. [31] designed a VR dashboard leveraging eye-tracking to automate pilots' cognitive load estimation in flight simulators, replacing manual evaluations. Similarly, Pradhan et al. [32] developed the Oculo-Cognitive Addition Test (OCAT), using eye movements to rapidly assess cognitive impairment. These studies demonstrate eye-tracking's versatility in capturing cognitive load across domains, from programming to aviation and healthcare. Behavioral cognitive load measurement faces limitations: indirect indicators (e.g., eye movements) risk conflating cognitive load with external factors [33], lack of standardized metrics hampers cross-task validity [24], context-dependency limits generalizability (e.g., programming vs. aviation) [30, 31], and isolating cognitive load types (intrinsic/extraneous) remains challenging [19].

Judging from the current trend, more and more research in the field of online learning is measuring cognitive load using user interaction behavior. This approach is becoming popular because it is non-invasive and utilizes data that is already naturally available during the learning process. Several similar studies include Hutt et al. [34] who developed a machine learning model to predict cognitive load based on click patterns and response times. In addition, there is Zhou et al. [35] who observed that interactions with videos and quizzes in MOOCs correlated significantly with cognitive load levels. Opportunities for research on this topic are still quite open, the use of user interaction behavior such as response time and click patterns can be supplemented with text input and U-turn patterns as proposed in this study. In addition, in this study, learning activities are not only watching videos and quizzes but also reading, discussing, and doing assignments.

2.2 User Interaction Behavior

User interaction behavior refers to the pattern of actions, responses, and habits of users when interacting with a system or technology, encompassing cognitive, emotional, and physical aspects [36]. This theory is rooted in the field of Human-Computer Interaction (HCI), where effective interface design must take into account users' cognitive limitations, such as working memory load [18], as well as their motivation and ability to complete tasks [37]. One key model that explains the interaction process is the Action Cycle by Norman [38], which divides interaction into seven stages: from goal formation to outcome evaluation. This model emphasizes the importance of intuitive design to minimize the gap between user goals and interpretation of action outcomes.

User interaction behavior is influenced by personal and contextual factors. Personal aspects include user experience formed from perceptions of usability and enjoyment [39], while contextual factors include task complexity and usage environment. For example, interfaces with excessive menus can increase extraneous cognitive load and reduce user efficiency [40]. Therefore, design principles such as simplicity, consistency, and clear feedback are key to guiding effective interaction behavior [41].

2.3 Adaptive Learning Systems

Adaptive learning systems have garnered significant attention in recent years due to their potential to personalize educational experiences. One notable approach is the use of Intelligent Tutoring Systems (ITS), which provide customized feedback based on learners' individual needs and progress [42]. Additionally, research by Brusilovsky and Millán highlights the importance of user modeling in adaptive learning, emphasizing how effective learner profiles can enhance personalization and engagement [43]. Another critical aspect is the integration of learning analytics, as discussed by Siemens, which enables real-time monitoring of student performance and facilitates timely interventions [44]. Furthermore, the incorporation of machine learning algorithms has shown promise in predicting student behavior and adapting learning paths accordingly [45]. These studies collectively illustrate the evolving landscape of adaptive learning systems and their reliance on advanced technologies to create more effective educational environments.

3 Methodology

This study employs a mixed-method approach. Quantitative methods are used in collecting user interaction behavior data via the Hotjar service on an online learning platform. Hotjar is a platform that provides tools for website and user behavior analysis. It offers features such as heatmaps, session recordings, surveys, and feedback forms. Thirty-three computer science students from one of the large public universities in West Java, Indonesia, participated as respondents. The respondents had an average age of 21 years, with 25 males and 8 females. They engaged in asynchronous learning sessions with a 150-min scenario involving reading materials, watching videos, accessing web pages, discussions, and multiple-choice quizzes. After the session, respondents completed the NASA-TLX questionnaire [46] to assess their cognitive load (CL). Figure 1 illustrates the research methodology to determine their cognitive load (CL) status.

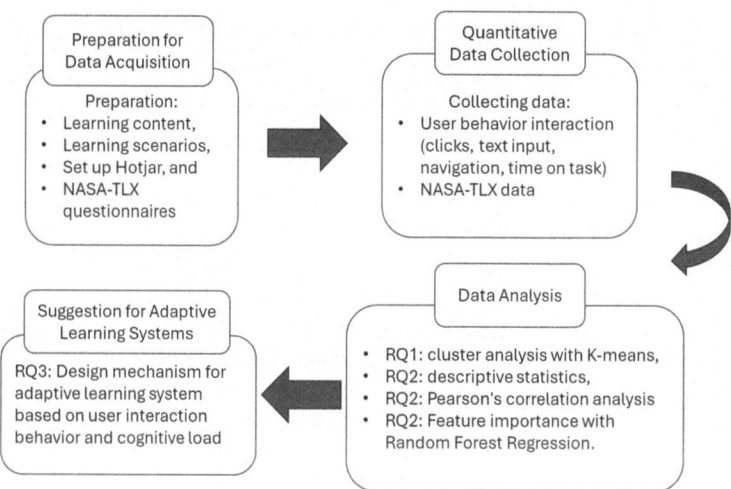

Fig. 1. Research methodology.

The data was then processed and analyzed using methods suited to the research questions. To answer the first research question, user interaction behavior data obtained from hotjar recordings were preprocessed and their features were extracted. The user interaction behavior features generated from the Hotjar service are click data, text input, navigation sequence (U-turn), and task duration. In addition, the results of filling out the NASA-TLX questionnaire were processed to obtain the cognitive load status of each respondent. From the combination of the two data based on the respondent's ID, a complete dataset of user interaction behavior and cognitive load status was obtained. Then, descriptive analysis is carried out to determine the distribution of data.

Furthermore, cluster analysis using the k-means method was carried out to obtain groups of respondents based on their interaction behavior patterns and seeing if there is a relationship with cognitive load levels. K-Means is a clustering algorithm that attempts to partition data into k groups (clusters) based on minimizing variance within the group. The basic formula is to minimize the sum of the squares of the differences between the data and the cluster centroid [47]. The objective function of k-means clustering can be seen in Eq. 1.

$$ J = \sum_{i=1}^{k} \sum_{x \in C_i} \|x - \mu_i\|^2 \tag{1} $$

where, k: number of clusters, C_i: cluster i, x: data point within cluster C_i, μ_i: Centroid (mean) of cluster C_i, $\|x - \mu_i\|^2$: Euclidean distance between data point x and centroid μ_i. The k value of k-means clustering is determined using the elbow method, with a k value of 4.

Then to answer the second research question regarding key factors or behavioral metrics that indicate cognitive load, a correlation analysis was carried out to determine which features generated from Hotjar were positively correlated in determining cognitive load. The correlation analysis used was Pearson Correlation [48] with the following Eq. 2.

$$r = \frac{\sum (x_i - \bar{x})(y_i - \bar{y})}{\sqrt{\sum (x_i - \bar{x})^2 \sum (y_i - \bar{y})^2}} \tag{2}$$

where, r (Pearson correlation coefficient): the correlation value between two variables x and y. x_i and y_i: the individual values of variables x and y at data point i. $\bar{x}$ and $\bar{y}$: the mean (average) of variables x and y. The result of this correlation calculation is to find out which features of user interaction behavior have the strongest to the weakest correlation.

In addition to determining the correlation between features, to answer the second research question it is also necessary to calculate the correlation of each feature with its cognitive load status. To determine this, feature importance analysis needs to be performed to assess how different features contribute to predicting the target variable, in this case, cognitive load status using Random Forest Regression [49].

Random Forest Regression is an ensemble learning method that uses many decision trees to predict continuous values. This model works by building a large number of decision trees and taking the average of the predictions from all the trees to get the final result. The final prediction ($\hat{y}$) in Random Forest Regression is given by (see Eq. 3):

$$\hat{y} = \frac{1}{T} \sum_{t=1}^{T} f_t(x) \tag{3}$$

where, $\hat{y}$: the final predicted value for input x, T: the number of decision trees in the random forest, $f_t(x)$: the prediction made by the t-th decision tree for the given input x, and x: the input feature vector.

The next stage carried out to answer the third research question is to make inferences from the answers to the first and second research questions which are strengthened by qualitative studies. Qualitative methods are used when validating and providing recommendations for design mechanisms related to adaptive learning systems by comparing them with other relevant literature.

4 Results and Discussion

4.1 Addressing RQ1: How Can User Interaction Behaviors in Online Learning Processes Be Used to Detect Cognitive Load?

This question is answered by collecting, preprocessing and extracting data from user interaction behavior. A total of 33 respondents successfully participated in the data collection activities until completion. User behavior data obtained from Hotjar consists of access duration, clicks, text input, and U-turns.

Access duration is the time duration calculated from the beginning of participant login to logout from the system. Clicks are the number of clicks made by respondents on all system pages. Text input is the intensity of respondents in inputting text in columns that require text input such as username and password columns, search bars, and discussion forums. U-turns are the number of navigations back to the previous page made by participants when using the platform, either the back button on the system page or the back button on the browser. The summary of user behavior data can be seen in the following Table 1.

Table 1. Summary of user interaction behaviors data.

Metric	Mean	Std-Dev	Min	Max
Access Duration (min)	70.64	66.47	1.12	240.93
Clicks	52.06	31.26	5	103
Text Input	14.67	15.11	0	65
U-turns	3.18	3.40	0	15

The statistics in Table 1 reveals important insights into student engagement with the learning materials. On average, students spend approximately 70.64 min accessing the content, indicating a significant investment of time in their learning experience. However, the high standard deviation suggests considerable variability in engagement duration among different students. Regarding interaction, students recorded an average of 52 clicks, with a range from 5 to 103 clicks, highlighting diverse levels of interaction with the learning platform. Interestingly, the mean text input was relatively low at around 14.67, suggesting that not all students are deeply engaging with text-based activities. Additionally, students averaged about 3.18 U-turns, indicating a tendency to navigate back to previous content, which may reflect confusion or a need to revisit information for better understanding. However, one participant exhibited an unusually short access duration (1.12 min) with only five recorded clicks. This may indicate early termination, technical issues, or non-serious engagement. However, we retained this data for completeness and future reference. Overall, these findings illustrate the varied interaction patterns and engagement levels of students within the online learning environment.

The results of the NASA-TLX measurements obtained the distribution of respondents' CL when carrying out learning activities, which can be seen in the Fig. 2. Based on Fig. 2, the data reveals a critical trend—over 80% of respondents (High + Very High) experienced significant cognitive strain. This overwhelming trend toward increased mental workload signals potential systemic inefficiencies or stressors in the context being evaluated (e.g., task, interface, or workflow). The near absence of "Low" responses underscores the urgent need to investigate contributing factors (e.g., task complexity, design flaws, or environmental stress) and implement targeted interventions to reduce cognitive strain. Based on these data, efforts are needed to prioritize usability improvements, resource adjustments, or training programs to enhance user experience and productivity.

Furthermore, the dataset from the extraction of user interaction behavior was then used as input for clustering analysis using K-means (k = 4 using the Elbow method), four groups were found with different characteristics in their interaction behavior during the learning session. Table 2 is the cluster characteristics summary of the k-means clustering results.

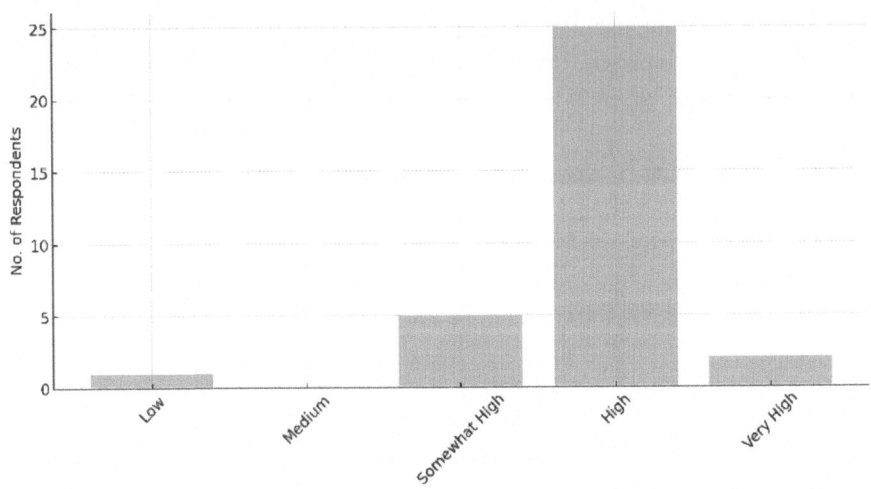

Fig. 2. Cognitive load status distribution during the learning process

Table 2. Cluster characteristics summary of user interaction behaviors data.

Cluster	Avg Access Duration (m)	Avg Clicks	Avg Text Input	Avg U-turn	Avg CL Status
0	15.62	38.20	8.07	2.00	3.87
1	120.68	39.80	10.40	1.90	3.80
2	247.38	97.00	62.00	15.00	4.00
3	91.80	92.86	28.14	5.86	3.71

Figure 3 presents the clustering results of user interaction data related to cognitive load. The clustering analysis reveals distinct patterns of user interaction, engagement, and cognitive load across four clusters. Cluster 0 is characterized by the lowest average access duration, suggesting limited engagement with the content. Despite moderate clicks, which imply minimal interaction, the cluster exhibits moderate frustration and engagement levels, pointing to a potentially satisfactory experience but with opportunities for improvement. On the other hand, Cluster 1 demonstrates moderate access duration, reflecting reasonable engagement with the materials. With click patterns similar to Cluster 0 and the lowest frustration level among all clusters, this group seems to have a positive and stable experience, as indicated by their manageable cognitive load. Cluster 2 stands out for its highest access duration, accompanied by the highest number of clicks and text input, signaling an intense level of interaction and effort. However, this group also shows the highest frustration and engagement levels, indicating struggles with the material and potentially overwhelming cognitive load. Finally, Cluster 3 shares similarities with Cluster 1 in terms of moderate access duration but shows higher clicks, indicative of active engagement. While this group experiences moderate frustration levels, their cognitive load remains manageable, suggesting they face some challenges yet maintain an effective learning process.

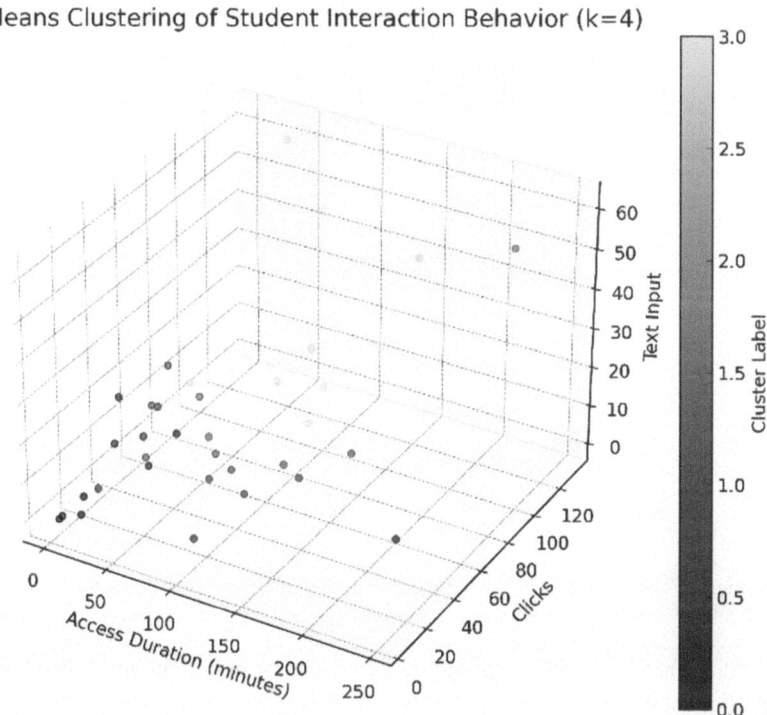

Fig. 3. Visualization of clustering results of user interaction behavior features against cognitive load status.

The results of this clustering provide insight to identify user profiles in the online learning process. Then these results can be used to design more effective interventions or strategies, especially those related to the design of system interfaces or methods of delivering materials that can reduce cognitive load and improve learning outcomes.

4.2 Addressing RQ2: What are the Key Indicators of Cognitive Load in Online Learning Environments Based on User Interaction Behaviors?

After knowing the characteristics of each cluster based on the results of k-means clustering, the next step is to investigate how the correlation between features relates to cognitive load. This is intended to find out whether there is a positive or negative correlation between one feature and another in the online learning process. Then it is also investigated what the correlation is between each user interaction behavior feature and its cognitive load status. The results of the correlation analysis of the four user interaction behavior features using Pearson Correlation can be seen in Fig. 4.

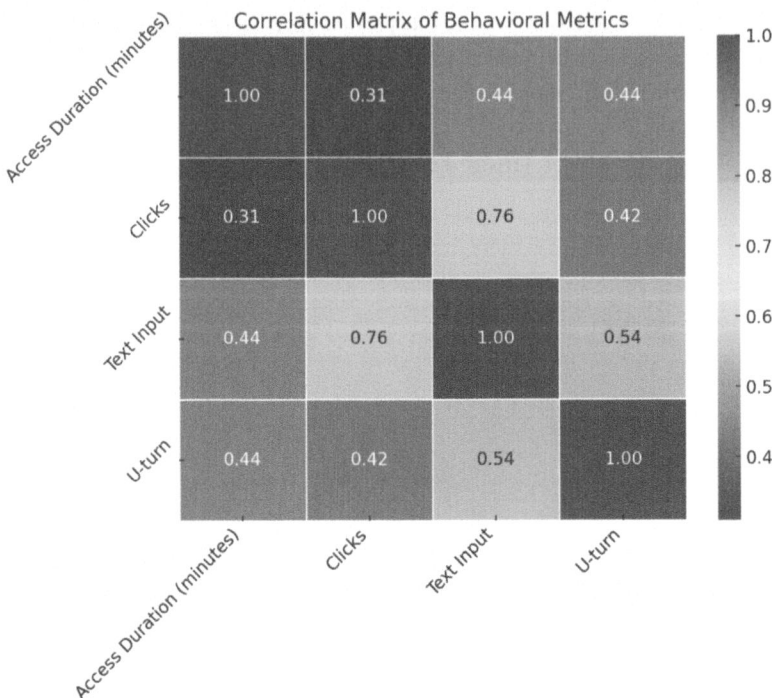

Fig. 4. The heatmap visualizing the correlation matrix of the behavioral metrics.

The data analysis in Fig. 4. Reveals key correlations in student interactions. A strong positive correlation between text input and clicks (0.759) indicates increased engagement with more text input. Moderate correlations include access duration with text input (0.444) and U-turns with access duration (0.442), showing that more time spent leads to more text input and revisiting content. Additionally, the clicks and U-turns correlation (0.420) suggests frequent clicking is associated with content revisits.

In addition to the correlation between features, the answer to the second research question is also strengthened by the results of Random Forest Regression which investigates the correlation of each feature of user interaction behavior to cognitive load status. The data in Fig. 5 indicates that text input holds the highest importance, strongly influencing cognitive load status. Access duration also plays a significant role, showing that the time spent on materials affects cognitive load. Clicks have a moderate impact, contributing to cognitive load but less so than text input and access duration. Finally, u-turns have the lowest importance, suggesting that navigating back to previous content has the least effect on cognitive load.

4.3   Addressing RQ3: How Can Adaptive Online Learning Systems Be Designed to Respond to Detected Cognitive Load in Real-Time?

Based on the clustering results, correlation matrix for behavioral metrics, and the frustration and engagement levels, here are design mechanisms that could enable a learning

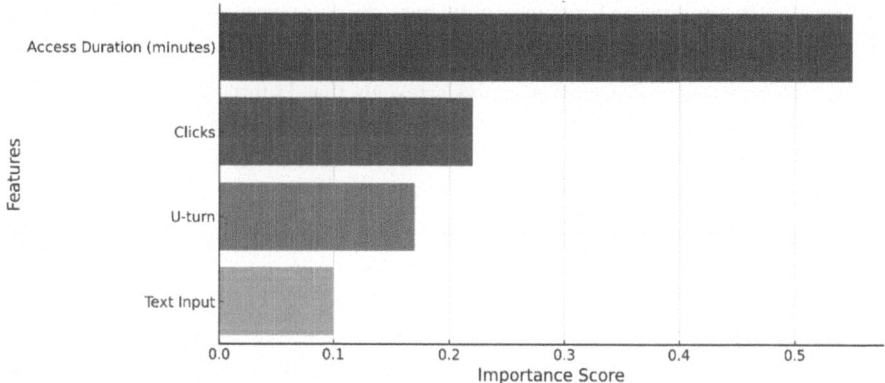

Fig. 5. Feature importance in predicting cognitive load status.

system to automatically adjust its content, task complexity, assistance when a student's cognitive load exceeds optimal limits, and interface adaptation.

Adaptive Content Presentation. In online learning, an adaptive system has the capability to recognize behavioral indicators that reflect cognitive load and dynamically adjust content presentation. This approach aims to enhance user engagement and understanding.

Behavioral Indicators. Text input and access duration are identified as strong cognitive load indicators through clustering analysis. For instance, a combination of high text input and increased frustration indicates cognitive overload.

Adaptive Mechanism. The system addresses these indicators with tailored interventions:

- **Micro-learning**: When prolonged access duration and excessive U-turns are detected, the system divides lessons into smaller, easier-to-digest segments. This is in line with research conducted by Bo Zhu [50] that adaptive microlearning systems dynamically adjust learning content based on the learner's cognitive load, ensuring information is presented in manageable segments to improve comprehension and retention.

Example: A lengthy tutorial is transformed into three concise modules, each focusing on a core concept.

- **Progressive Disclosure**: Content is revealed incrementally, adapting complexity based on the user's performance. This approach simplifies the user interface, making applications easier to learn and reducing the likelihood of errors [51].

Example: As the user successfully completes tasks, advanced topics are gradually introduced, maintaining an optimal challenge level.

Real-time Task Complexity Adjustment. In adaptive learning systems, the ability to adjust task complexity in real-time is crucial for maintaining student engagement and performance. By monitoring behavioral indicators, the system can identify when learners are struggling and adapt accordingly.

Behavioral Indicators. Correlation analysis reveals that U-turns are associated with access duration and text input, which may indicate confusion or difficulty. Additionally, clusters characterized by high cognitive load and frustration suggest that students might be struggling with task complexity.

Adaptive Mechanism. The system responds to these indicators by dynamically adjusting task difficulty:

- **Simplify Tasks:** When U-turns and frustration levels increase, the system simplifies tasks by offering hints, breaking down questions into sub-tasks, or providing scaffolding. By providing hints and breaking tasks into sub-tasks, educators can address increased frustration and help students navigate complex problems more effectively [52].

Example: If a student repeatedly navigates back on a math problem, the system might offer a hint or divide the problem into smaller, manageable parts, such as asking for the first step in isolation.

- **Provide Alternative Formats:** If a student struggles with text-heavy tasks, the system offers the same task in multimedia formats (e.g., video explanations or visual aids). According to Çeken and Taşkın [53], presenting information in a variety of formats can meet a variety of learning preferences and can reduce the difficulties associated with text-heavy material.

Example: Instead of a lengthy textual explanation of a scientific concept, the system could provide a short video or an infographic that summarizes the information visually.

Intelligent Assistance and Feedback. In adaptive learning systems, providing intelligent assistance and timely feedback is essential for supporting student learning and mitigating frustration. By analyzing behavioral indicators, the system can offer targeted help to enhance the learning experience.

Behavioral Indicators. The correlation matrix indicates that text input and clicks are strongly correlated. When a student inputs large amounts of text but is marked as frustrated (high frustration, low engagement), the system can detect cognitive overload.

Adaptive Mechanism. The system responds to these indicators with intelligent assistance and feedback:

- **Just-in-time Assistance:** Provide real-time contextual help when high text input and frustration levels are detected. This is in line with Liu et al.'s [54] research that real-time feedback plays an important role in changing negative emotions and maintaining student engagement.

Example: If a student is typing a long response in an essay and shows signs of frustration, a pop-up tip might appear suggesting, "Try summarizing your main point in a few sentences.".

- **Smart Hints:** Offer personalized hints or feedback tailored to the specific area of difficulty. This is also in line with Parakh [55] which offers personalized hints and feedback tailored to individual learners' areas of difficulty.

Example: If a student struggles with a particular concept in programming (indicated by high frustration and low engagement), the system might provide a hint like, "Review the previous section on algorithm to clarify your understanding.

Interface Adaptation. In adaptive learning systems, interface adaptation is crucial for enhancing user experience and minimizing cognitive load. By monitoring behavioral indicators, the system can make real-time adjustments to help students navigate and comprehend the interface more effectively.

Behavioral Indicators. High clicks and U-turns, along with elevated frustration levels, may indicate that a student is struggling to navigate or understand the current interface.

Adaptive Mechanism. The system responds to these indicators by adapting the interface in real-time to reduce cognitive load:

- **Simplified Navigation:** When frequent U-turns and clicks are detected, the system reduces the complexity of the user interface by simplifying menus, providing direct links, or enabling a more linear navigation path. The study from Romero [56] found that by adapting the interface based on user behavior, such as frequent backtracking, the system could simplify navigation paths and improve overall usability.

Example: If a student repeatedly returns to the main menu while trying to access a lesson, the system might simplify the menu structure by highlighting the most relevant links and minimizing unnecessary options.

- **Dynamic Focus Mode:** Implement a "focus mode" that reduces on-screen elements and distractions, simplifying the interface and guiding the student through key tasks step-by-step. This is in line with research by Pérez-Juárez et al. [57] which shows that focus mode can minimize distractions on the screen, thereby increasing focus and learning outcomes.

Example: When a student shows signs of confusion, the system could activate focus mode, hiding non-essential elements and providing a streamlined view that emphasizes the task at hand, such as completing a quiz.

5 Conclusion and Future Works

This study investigated the relationship between user interaction behaviors and cognitive load in online learning environments. The findings suggest that key interaction metrics— such as access duration, clicks, text input, and U-turns—serve as indicators of cognitive load levels. The results of NASA-TLX measurements revealed that more than 80% of respondents experienced high or very high cognitive load, highlighting significant cognitive strain during the learning process.

Through k-means clustering analysis, four distinct learner interaction profiles were identified, each exhibiting different engagement and cognitive load characteristics. Cluster 2, which showed the highest engagement levels (longest access duration, highest number of clicks and text input), also experienced the highest cognitive load, indicating that intense interaction does not always lead to efficient learning but may instead contribute to cognitive strain. Additionally, correlation and feature importance analyses confirmed that text input and access duration are the strongest predictors of cognitive load, while clicks and U-turns had moderate and minimal effects, respectively.

The study further explored design implications for adaptive learning systems, proposing mechanisms such as adaptive content presentation, adaptive user interface, real-time task complexity adjustment, and intelligent assistance. These strategies leverage real-time behavioral indicators to dynamically modify learning content and tasks, helping to optimize cognitive load and enhance learning effectiveness.

Future research should explore several key areas to enhance adaptive learning systems. Real-time implementation of adaptive mechanisms needs to be tested through dynamic content adjustments based on cognitive load. Longitudinal studies can provide deeper insights into cognitive load variations over time. Integrating physiological data, such as eye-tracking or EEG, with behavioral metrics may improve detection accuracy. Personalized learning pathways should be explored using machine learning to tailor optimal learning experiences. Additionally, cross-cultural and multi-domain validations can ensure adaptability across different educational contexts.

Acknowledgments. This research was supported by the Direktorat Riset dan Pengembangan (Risbang) Universitas Indonesia through Hibah Publikasi Terindeks Internasional (PUTI) Q1 TA 2023-2024 under Grant NKB 294/UN2.RST/HKP.05.00/2023. The work of Mira Suryani was supported by the Beasiswa Riset Disertasi Doktor Universitas Padjadjaran under Grant 1549/UN6.3.1/PT.00/2023.

Disclosure of Interests.   The authors have no competing interests to declare that are relevant to the content of this article.

References

1. Skulmowski, A., Xu, K.M.: Understanding cognitive load in digital and online learning: a new perspective on extraneous cognitive load. Educ. Psychol. Rev. **34**, 171–196 (2022). https://doi.org/10.1007/s10648-021-09624-7
2. Zhao, Y.: The impact of cognitive load theory on online learning outcomes for adolescent students. J. Educ. Human. Soc. Sci. **18**, 50–55 (2023). https://doi.org/10.54097/ehss.v18i.10946
3. Masyura Ahmad Faudzi, Z., Che Cob, Z., Sharudin, S.A., Omar, R., Ghazali, M.: The effects of user interface design for mobile learning application on learner's extraneous cognitive load: a conceptual framework. In: Proceedings of the Asian HCI Symposium 2023 (Asian CHI '23), pp. 51–57. Association for Computing Machinery, New York, NY, USA (2023). https://doi.org/10.1145/3604571.3604579

4. Suryani, M., Sensuse, D.I., Santoso, H.B., et al.: An initial user model design for adaptive interface development in learning management system based on cognitive load. Cogn. Technol. Work **26**, 653–672 (2024). https://doi.org/10.1007/s10111-024-00772-8, LNCS Homepage, http://www.springer.com/lncs. Accessed 25 Oct 2023

5. Costley, J.: Using cognitive strategies overcomes cognitive load in online learning environments. Interact. Technol. Smart Educ. **17**(1), 1–15 (2020). https://doi.org/10.1108/ITSE-09-2019-0053

6. Sweller, J., Van Merriënboer, J.J.G., Paas, F.: Cognitive architecture and instructional design. Educ. Psychol. **54**(1), 9–28 (2019). https://doi.org/10.1080/00461520.2018.1440954

7. Anderson, J.R.: Cognitive Psychology and Its Implications, 7th edn. Worth Publishers, New York (2009)

8. Sweller, J., Ayres, P., Kalyuga, S.: Cognitive Load Theory, pp. 1–274. Springer, New York (2011). https://doi.org/10.1007/978-1-4419-8126-4

9. Dönmez, O., Akbulut, Y., Telli, E., et al.: In search of a measure to address different sources of cognitive load in computer-based learning environments. Educ. Inf. Technol. **27**, 10013–10034 (2022). https://doi.org/10.1007/s10639-022-11035-2

10. Chen, Y., Zhang, L., Mao, C.: Investigating Chinese college students' cognitive load in a gamified foreign language class: a pilot study. In: Proceedings of the 5th International Conference on Big Data and Education (ICBDE '22), pp. 217–221. ACM, New York (2022). https://doi.org/10.1145/3524383.3524447

11. Koć-Januchta, M.M., Schönborn, K.J., Roehrig, C., et al.: "Connecting concepts helps put main ideas together": cognitive load and usability in learning biology with an AI-enriched textbook. Int. J. Educ. Technol. High. Educ. **19**, 11 (2022). https://doi.org/10.1186/s41239-021-00317-3

12. Modanwal, G., Rai, S.B., Jaiswal, A., Singh, T., Sarawadekar, K.: Can visually impaired use gestures to interact with computers? A cognitive load perspective. IEEE Trans. Hum.-Mach. Syst. **52**, 267–275 (2022). https://doi.org/10.1109/THMS.2022.3144002

13. Belkhiria, C., Peysakhovich, V.: EOG Metrics for cognitive workload detection. In: Proceedings of Procedia Computer Science, vol. 192, pp. 1875–1884. Elsevier (2021). https://doi.org/10.1016/j.procs.2021.08.193

14. Liang, Y., Liang, W., Qu, J., Yang, J.: Experimental study on EEG with different cognitive load. In: 2018 IEEE International Conference on Systems, Man, and Cybernetics (SMC), pp. 4351–4356. IEEE, Xi'an, China (2018). https://doi.org/10.1109/SMC.2018.00735

15. Urrestilla, N., St-Onge, D.: Measuring cognitive load: heart-rate variability and pupillometry assessment. In: 2020 International Conference on Multimodal Interaction (ICMI), pp. 405–410. ACM, Montréal, PQ, Canada (2020). https://doi.org/10.1145/3395035.3425203

16. von Janczewski, N., Kraus, J., Engeln, A., Baumann, M.: A subjective one-item measure based on NASA-TLX to assess cognitive workload in driver-vehicle interaction. Transp. Res. Part F Traffic Psychol. Behav. **86**, 210–225 (2022). https://doi.org/10.1016/j.trf.2022.02.012

17. Sweller, J., van Merriënboer, J.J.G., Paas, F.G.W.C.: Cognitive architecture and instructional design. Educ. Psychol. Rev. **10**(3), 251–296 (1998)

18. Sweller, J.: Cognitive load during problem solving: effects on learning. Cogn. Sci. **12**(2), 257–285 (1988). https://doi.org/10.1207/s15516709cog1202_4

19. Sweller, J., van Merriënboer, J.J.G., Paas, F.: Cognitive architecture and instructional design: 20 years later. Educ. Psychol. Rev. **31**(2), 261–292 (2019). https://doi.org/10.1007/s10648-019-09465-5

20. Chen, F., et al.: Robust Multimodal Cognitive Load Measurement, pp. 1–254. Springer, Cham (2016). https://doi.org/10.1007/978-3-319-31700-7

21. Herbert, B., Wigley, G., Ens, B., Billinghurst, M.: Cognitive load considerations for augmented reality in network security training. Comput. Graph. **102**, 566–591 (2022). https://doi.org/10.1016/j.cag.2021.09.001

22. Kelleher, C., Hnin, W.: Predicting cognitive load in future code puzzles. In: Proceedings of the CHI Conference on Human Factors in Computing Systems (CHI 2019), pp. 1–12 (2019). https://doi.org/10.1145/3290605.3300487

23. Albus, P., Vogt, A., Seufert, T.: Signaling in virtual reality influences learning outcome and cognitive load. Comput. Educ. **166**, 104154 (2021). https://doi.org/10.1016/j.compedu.2021.104154

24. Paas, F., Tuovinen, J.E., Tabbers, H., Van Gerven, P.W.M.: Cognitive load measurement as a means to advance cognitive load theory. Educ. Psychol. **38**(1), 63–71 (2003). https://doi.org/10.1207/S15326985EP3801_8

25. Sweller, J.: Cognitive load theory. In: Mestre, J.P., Ross, B.H. (eds.) Psychology of Learning and Motivation, vol. 55, pp. 37–76. Academic Press, San Diego (2011). https://doi.org/10.1016/B978-0-12-387691-1.00002-8

26. Moser, I., Comsa, I.-S., Parsaeifard, B., Bergamin, P.: Work-in-progress-motion tracking data as a proxy for cognitive load in immersive learning. In: Proceedings of the 8th International Conference on Immersive Learning Research Network (iLRN 2022), pp. 1–3 (2022). https://doi.org/10.23919/iLRN55037.2022.9815894

27. Massoni Sguerra, B., Jouvelot, P.: 'An unscented hound for working memory' and the cognitive adaptation of user interfaces. In: Proceedings of the 27th ACM Conference on User Modeling, Adaptation and Personalization (UMAP 2019), pp. 78–85 (2019). https://doi.org/10.1145/3320435.3320443

28. Ahmadi, M., et al.: Cognitive load measurement with physiological sensors in virtual reality during physical activity. In: Proceedings of 29th ACM Symposium on Virtual Reality Software and Technology, Oct. 2023, pp. 1–11 (2023). https://doi.org/10.1145/3611659.3615704

29. Caldiroli, C.L., et al.: Comparing online cognitive load on mobile versus PC-based devices. Pers. Ubiquitous Comput. **27**(2), 495–505 (2023). https://doi.org/10.1007/s00779-022-01707-8

30. Abbad-Andaloussi, A., Sorg, T., Weber, B.: Estimating developers' cognitive load at a fine-grained level using eye-tracking measures. In: Proceedings of the IEEE/ACM 30th International Conference on Program Comprehension (ICPC), May 2022, pp. 111–121 (2022). https://doi.org/10.1145/3524610.3527890

31. Arjun, S., Hebbar, A., Sanjana, Biswas, P.: VR cognitive load dashboard for flight simulator. In: Proceedings of Symposium on Eye Tracking Research and Applications, pp. 1–4 (2022). https://doi.org/10.1145/3517031.3529777

32. Pradhan, G.N., Hagen, K.M., Cevette, M.J., Stepanek, J.: Oculocognitive addition test: quantifying cognitive performance during variable cognitive workload through eye movement features. In: Proceedings of the IEEE 10th International Conference on Healthcare Informatics, May 2022, pp. 422–430 (2022). https://doi.org/10.1109/ICHI54592.2022.00064

33. Brunken, R., Plass, J.L., Leutner, D.: Direct measurement of cognitive load in multimedia learning. Educ. Psychol. **38**(1), 53–61 (2003). https://doi.org/10.1207/S15326985EP3801_7

34. Hutt, S., et al.: Modeling cognitive load in online learning environments using interaction logs. In: Proceedings of ACM Conference on Learning Analytics and Knowledge (LAK), pp. 1–12 (2022). https://doi.org/10.1145/3491140.3528324

35. Zhou, M., et al.: Cognitive load assessment in MOOCs via behavioral engagement patterns. Comput. Educ. **187**, 104803 (2023). https://doi.org/10.1016/j.compedu.2023.104803

36. Norman, D.A.: The Design of Everyday Things: Revised and Expanded Edition. Basic Books (2013)

37. Fogg, B.J.: A behavior model for persuasive design. In: Proceedings of 4th International Conference on Persuasive Technology (2009). https://doi.org/10.1145/1541948.1541999

38. Norman, D.A.: The Psychology of Everyday Things. Basic Books (1988)

39. Hassenzahl, M., Tractinsky, N.: User experience - a research agenda. Behav. Inf. Technol. **25**(2), 91–97 (2006). https://doi.org/10.1080/01449290500330331

40. Paas, F., van Merriënboer, J.J.G.: Cognitive-load theory: methods to manage working memory load in the learning of complex tasks. Curr. Dir. Psychol. Sci. **29**(4), 394–398 (2020). https://doi.org/10.1177/0963721420922183
41. Shneiderman, B., Plaisant, C., Cohen, M., Jacobs, S., Elmqvist, N., Diakopoulos, N.: Designing the User Interface: Strategies for Effective Human-Computer Interaction, 6th edn. Pearson (2016)
42. Woolf, B.P.: Building Intelligent Interactive Tutors: Student-Centered Strategies for Revolutionizing e-Learning. Morgan Kaufmann (2010)
43. Brusilovsky, P., Millán, E.: User modeling for adaptive hypermedia and adaptive educational systems. In: The Adaptive Learning Systems, pp. 3–20 (2015)
44. Siemens, G.: Learning analytics: the emergence of a new discipline. Int. Rev. Res. Open Distrib. Learn. **14**(4), 1–3 (2013)
45. Zawacki-Richter, O., Marín, V.I., Bond, M., Gouverneur, F.: Systematic review of research on artificial intelligence in higher education: the future of education. Int. J. Educ. Technol. High. Educ. **16**(1), 1–27 (2019)
46. Hart, S.G.: NASA-Task Load Index (NASA-TLX); 20 years later. In: Proceedings of the Human Factors and Ergonomics Society 50th Annual Meeting, pp. 904–908. SAGE Journals (2006)
47. Bishop, C.M.: Pattern Recognition and Machine Learning. Springer, New York (2006)
48. Hinkle, D.E., Wiersma, W., Jurs, S.G.: Applied Statistics for the Behavioral Sciences, 5th edn. Houghton Mifflin, Boston (2003)
49. Rokach, L.: Decision forest: twenty years of research. Inf. Fusion **27**, 111–125 (2016). https://doi.org/10.1016/j.inffus.2015.06.005
50. Zhu, B., Chau, K.T., Mokmin, N.A.M.: Optimizing cognitive load and learning adaptability with adaptive microlearning for in-service personnel. Sci. Rep. **14**, 25960 (2024). https://doi.org/10.1038/s41598-024-77122-1
51. Nielsen Norman Group: Progressive disclosure. https://www.nngroup.com/articles/progressive-disclosure/. Accessed 22 Jan 2025
52. Van de Pol, J., Mercer, N., Volman, M.: Scaffolding student understanding in small-group work: students' uptake of teacher support in subsequent small-group interaction. J. Learn. Sci. **28**, 206–239 (2019). https://doi.org/10.1080/10508406.2018.1522258
53. Çeken, B., Taşkın, N.: Multimedia learning principles in different learning environments: a systematic review. Smart Learn. Environ. **9**(1), 19 (2022). https://doi.org/10.1186/s40561-022-00200-2
54. Liu, H.L., Wang, T.H., Lin, H.K., Lai, C.F., Huang, Y.M.: The influence of affective feedback adaptive learning system on learning engagement and self-directed learning. Front. Psychol. **13**, 858411 (2022). https://doi.org/10.3389/fpsyg.2022.858411
55. Parakh, D., Lodha, P., Subalalitha, C.N.: Adaptive personalized learning system with generative AI. Front. Health Inform. **13**(8), 2612–2637 (2024)
56. Romero, O.J., Haig, A., Kirabo, L., Yang, Q., Zimmerman, J., Tomasic, A., Steinfeld, A.: A long-term evaluation of adaptive interface design for mobile transit information. In: 22nd International Conference on Human-Computer Interaction with Mobile Devices and Services (MobileHCI '20), pp. 1–11. ACM, Oldenburg, Germany (2020). https://doi.org/10.1145/3379503.3403536
57. Pérez-Juárez, M.Á., González-Ortega, D., Aguiar-Pérez, J.M.: Digital distractions from the point of view of higher education students. Sustainability **15**(7), 6044 (2023). https://doi.org/10.3390/su15076044

An Empirical Study of Video Duration on Users' Discontinuous Sage Intention: Based on the TAM Model

Wu Wei[1], Wenjia Zhang[1], and Chen Wang[2](✉)

[1] School of Film Television and Communication, Xiamen University of Technology, Xiamen, Fujian, China
[2] School of Art and Design, Fuzhou University of International Studies and Trade, Fuzhou, Fujian, China
`wangchen@fzfu.edu.cn`

Abstract. Nowadays, new media applications are accompanying people's daily life. With the continuous development of media technology, meanwhile, the problems like information overload and social fatigue in social media have gradually appeared. Accordingly, the habits and preferences of new media users have also shifted. Public statistics show that short video platforms, including tiktok, have experienced a crisis of user loss, while the number of users on video platforms such as Netflix has continued to increase. Whether users' psychological perceptions during watching are affected by the information content and whether their behavioural intentions are influenced by the duration of the video, then, becomes the concern of this study.

Based on the classical technology acceptance model, this study explored the correlation between perceived usefulness and ease of use on cognitive load and perceived fatigue. Meanwhile, two dimensions of information overload and information ambiguity were added to extend the model. And video duration was introduced to explore its effect on the behavioural intention to discontinue use. After building up the theoretical framework, this study carried out a quantitative approach by collecting data through online questionnaires. Through data analysis, this study found that information overload and ambiguity can positively affect video users' cognitive load and perceived fatigue, while perceived usefulness and ease of use can have a negative effect; cognitive load and perceived fatigue can positively affect users' intention of discontinuous behaviours; and users' discontinuous usage intentions will decrease with the increase of video duration. Finally, based on the findings, this study provided some suggestions for the development of video platforms/applications.

Keywords: Technology Acceptance Model · Discontinuous Usage Intention · Video Duration Information · Overload Information Ambiguity

1 Introduction

Nowadays, 'watching videos online' has been integrated into people's daily life. With the rapid development of network infrastructure and communication technologies, online streaming media content on various platforms and applications (Apps) has become a

M. Schrepp (Ed.): HCII 2025, LNCS 15794, pp. 404–422, 2025.
https://doi.org/10.1007/978-3-031-93221-2_26

popular way of relaxation, information and social interaction for the general public [1]. According to a survey by Statista, as of November 2024, Tik Tok had more than 4.92 billion downloads and more than 15.82 billion monthly active users worldwide; YouTube had more than 2 billion active users worldwide; Netflix's global subscribers grew from 33 million in 2013 to more than 220 million in 2024 [2]. These figures show that the use of Internet video platforms for online streaming content plays an important role in our daily lives.

However, according to relevant studies, the users are facing a dilemma when watching online videos: on the one hand, technology advancement enables them to obtain valuable new messages more easily; on the other hand, the explosion of information poses a serious challenge to users' processing capability. The overload of information not only triggers heavy psychological pressure on users, but also leads to the 'information diseases', which in turn gives rise to a series of negative effects such as unhealthy internet usage behaviour. Fu *et al.* believed that users will gradually stop using social media when they feel overloaded with system features, information and social interactions. According to the work of Swar *et al.*, overload of health information may lead to psychological discomfort, and affect the online search behavior of users, making them stop searching for health information.

In contrast to the shrinking trend in the size of short-video users in recent years, the number of users on medium- and long-video platforms/Apps has shown a steady and significant increase. A survey shows that most users on the short video platform rarely posted any videos and showed a declined interest in short videos [5]. In comparison, on medium and long video platforms, the number of users had a year-on-year of 14.4% in 2024 [6]. This suggests a subtle and profound change in the watching preferences of users. Users start to prefer longer videos with richer and more in-depth content. By exploring the characteristics of short- and long-videos on YouTube, Seidel found that users' preference for knowledge-based video content is changing - they are more likely to invest time in watching long videos that provide value, entertainment and meaningful content [7]. This significant shift in users' interests will have a profound impact on the market landscape, which has been dominated by short videos in the past. It is very likely to lead to a brand new video consumption trend, injecting new hope into the entire video industry and further boosting its development. For example, in a study of the drivers of user rewarding behaviour on online video sharing platforms, Cao *et al.* found that longer and engaging video content increased users' satisfaction and reward frequency [8].

Therefore, whether the video's duration has an impact on users' watching experience and behaviours becomes the concern of this study. Based on the theoretical framework of technology acceptance model (TAM), this study will investigate the effect of video duration on users' discontinuous behaviours during watching by measuring their psychological perceptions and behavioural intentions.

2 Theoretical Background and Hypothesis Building

2.1 TAM

Based on the theory of reasoned action, Davis proposed TAM in 1986, which aimed to verify the influence of system external factors on individuals' willingness to use information in an organisational context [9]. In TAM, two key variables - perceived usefulness and perceived ease of use - were identified by Davis as affecting users' acceptance. Perceived usefulness refers to the user's perception of whether the technology is useful, while perceived ease of use represents the ease an individual feel when using a particular information technology.

In order to improve the explainability of the model, past studies have introduced different variables to extend the TAM. For example, content satisfaction, as an independent variable [10], and perceived entertainment, as an indirect variable, have been shown to influence users' intention to use [11]. Fussell *et al.* developed an extended TAM to explore the application of virtual reality in a dynamic learning environment [12]. Chen *et al.* discussed the role of flow experience in TAM in the context of mobile shopping [13]. Chen added variables such as trust and perceived enjoyment, and expanded TAM to explore the determinants of users' use of self-driving shuttle services [14].

Current TAM studies can be divided into two types. The first type focused on the application of the model in a particular field. For example, in the field of e-commerce, Fayad *et al.* proposed to add four predictive variables (process satisfaction, outcome satisfaction, expectations and e-commerce use) to the original TAM to better understand the user behavior in the e-commerce environment [15]. In the field of health care, Zhang *et al.* expanded TAM using factors such as initial trust, perceived security risk and perceived privacy risk, so as to improve the explanatory power of the model [16]. Mustafa *et al.* reviewed the intention to continuously use TAM in online learning applications, helped educational institutions to formulate online education policies, and provided empirical references [17]. The second type of study focused on the general developmental overview of the model itself. For example, Gaddi *et al.* provided new perspectives for understanding the future development of TAM by overviewing its origins and development [18]. In addition, TAM was used in the studies of video watching. For example, Zhang *et al.* explored the influencing factors on users' intention of continuous use on short video platform with health-related short videos as example [19]. Based on TAM, Xie *et al.* constructed a model investigating the influencing factors on mobile short video use among rural elderly [20]. Zhao *et al.* explored the impact of consumption attribute cognition, perceived accuracy and other attributes of short video platform advertisements on users' willingness to participate [21].

However, there are not many studies related to video duration in the past TAM studies. As an explicit external factor in the video viewing process, video duration may not only affect the user's viewing experience, but may also be associated with the density and complexity of video information. Therefore, based on expanded TAM, this study added video duration as an influencing factor.

2.2 Dimension Construction

Discontinuous Usage Intention. The concept of discontinuous usage intention was initially proposed by Rogers in the theory of innovation diffusion. Rogers defined discontinuous usage intention as a negative use behavior after adoption. This specifically refers to that the users refuse to continue the use or discontinue the use of an innovation after making an adoption decision and starting to use it [22]. Ravindran *et al.* made a more detailed classification of such behaviors, which can be divided into three levels: controlled use, short breaks and suspended use [23]. Among them, controlled use represents the users' initiative to control and adjust the time and frequency of using high-tech products. Short breaks refer to a temporary pause in the use of a product by a user, but not completely stopping using the product. Suspended use reflects a relatively serious intermittent interruption behavior, which means that users temporarily stop using a certain technology or product, but this suspension is not a permanent or long-term decision.

Studies have shown that users' discontinuance behaviour on social media platforms or Apps arises from two main sources: personal factors and external factors. In terms of personal factors, users may experience emotions such as jealousy, anxiety, or discomfort during use, thereby reducing the frequency of use [24]. For example, fans no longer relied on social media to follow their idols [25]. External factors include a poor social situation, too much hostility, quarrels, [26] and so on. For example, trivial messages and unsubstantiated statements on some platforms can interfere users' obtainment and judgement of information [27].

Cognitive Load. The cognitive load theory was proposed by Sweller in 1988. Sweller believed that cognitive processing activities that occur during learning or problem-solving require the consumption of cognitive resources [28]. According to the resource limitation theory, the human brain has limited capacity for cognitive resources and can only store 5–9 pieces of basic information or information blocks at a time. Therefore, when there is too much information that needs to be processed, people will experience cognitive load, and the efficiency of learning or problem-solving will decrease [29]. There are various types of information on social media. Most short video recommendation on social media is based on artificial intelligence algorithms. These algorithms push short videos accurately according to the user's usage path, viewing habits and preferences. But the user's needs are changing in real time, and intelligent recommendation may lead to users watching similar videos repeatedly. As a result, the users will receive a lot of unnecessary information, which will generate cognitive load. Accordingly, the following hypothesis is proposed in this study:

H1: Cognitive load can positively influence users' discontinuous usage intention.

Perceived Fatigue. Nowadays, people carry out various activities, such as information acquisition, social interaction, entertainment and leisure, through the intelligent terminals. People spend a lot of time on these social platforms, and continuous use of these platforms will make the users overloaded with information, which in turn leads to perceived fatigue. Perceived fatigue on social media is accompanied by the rise of social networks and social media. Based on the stressor-strain-outcome model, Zhang *et al.* found that users' burnout has a significant positive impact on their discontinuous use of social media [30]. According to the work of Maier *et al.*, when an individual feels tired due to something, his or her behavior will change accordingly. When users feel tired, it is easy to lead to the intermittent use of social media by them [31]. Luqman *et al.* found that burnout had a significant impact on users, causing them to stop or reduce the use of Facebook [32]. Based on these, this study proposed the following hypothesis:

H2: Perceived fatigue can positively influence users' discontinuous usage intention.

Information Overload. Information overload refers to excessive amount of information irrelevant or beyond the personal processing capacity, resulting in a decline in the quality of information and a negative impact [33]. When people receive excessive information, they often face difficulties in effectively integrating, absorbing and rationally using this information, which will affect their work efficiency, quality of life and social activities. Dhir *et al.* found that when people spend a lot of time online, it will increase their boredom with social media. If overloaded information, users may suffer from loss of analytical ability, anxiety and insomnia, as well as self-doubt and perceived fatigue [34]. Wurman believed that people will have information anxiety when they face a large amount of information beyond their information processing ability, mainly manifested as mental and psychological fatigue, tension and helplessness [35].

The Internet is an important and efficient channel for the public to obtain information. However, there is massive information on the Internet, which is updated in a fast speed, thus making it difficult for users to filter out accurate and reliable information that truly meets their needs, whether in the process of active search or passive acceptance of information. Facing such massive information, the public often feel powerless, and it is difficult for them to quickly understand and digest a large amount of knowledge and content in a short time, resulting in an increase in individual cognitive load and negative emotions. Dai *et al.* found that the phenomenon of information overload directly led to the negative emotions such as fatigue, frustration and dissatisfaction felt by WeChat users [36]. Guo *et al.* found that information overload and information irrelevance can induce social media users' fatigue and lead to information avoidance behavior [37]. The following hypotheses were proposed by this study:

H3: Information overload can positively influence users' cognitive load.

H4: Information overload can positively influence users' perceived fatigue.

Information Ambiguity. Information ambiguity refers to the information with low quality and unclear expression. The content of the fuzzy information is obscure and difficult to understand, and such information can be interpreted in many ways. The source and data of information are not accurate, the language expression is not clear, and the misunderstanding in the process of transmission is the cause of information ambiguity. Starcevic *et al.* pointed out that the uncertainty of information could exacerbate the users' cyberchondria, causing them to search for health-related information on the Internet excessively or repeatedly [38]. Based on the analysis of pressure theory, Maier *et al.* found that Facebook users were stressed on Facebook due to various factors, such as complexity, uncertainty, privacy risks, and information overload, which eventually prompted users to intermittently deactivate Facebook and explore other social platforms [39]. The following hypotheses were formulated in this study:

H5: Information ambiguity can positively influence users' cognitive load.

H6: Information ambiguity can positively influence users' perceived fatigue.

Perceived Usefulness and Perceived Ease of Use. Perceived usefulness refers to the user's subjective belief that the use of a technology or system can improve their work or learning efficiency. In other words, when users choose a particular product or service, this choice is largely driven by the unique value that the product or service can provide. Oviatt found that the complex functions of the interface of educational product interfered with the users' thinking and problem solving processes. Therefore, irrelevant and unnecessary functions should be reduced to avoid cognitive load [40]. The findings of Khan *et al.* show that the most important driver of social media continuance intention is perceived usefulness [41]. Therefore, in the context of this study, social media users' perception of the service and value of video platforms or Apps will weaken the negative impact of social media burnout. Combined with TAM, it is inferred that perceived usefulness will reduce the fatigue caused by users' use of social media.

Perceived ease of use refers to the ease with which users feel using an information system. When users obtain information through video platforms/Apps, if they feel it is easy to use these platforms/Apps, their sense of self-control and self-confidence will increase, and their attitude towards using these information systems will become more optimistic. Ayyagari found that too many functions of the learning system would enhance complexity of the system, increase the learning stress, lead to operational errors, and thus reduce the user's willingness for continuous use [42].

Meanwhile, in TAM studies, it is generally accepted that perceived ease of use positively influences perceived usefulness [43], and indirectly influences willingness to use through perceived usefulness [44]. With reference to previous TAM studies, the following hypotheses were developed in this study:

H7: Perceived usefulness can negatively influence users' cognitive load.

H8: Perceived usefulness can negatively influence users' perceived fatigue.

H9: Perceived ease of use can negatively influence users' cognitive load.

H10: Perceived ease of use can negatively influence users' perceived fatigue.

H11: Perceived ease of use can positively influence users' perceived usefulness.

Video Duration. According to published data, most users on short video platforms/Apps hardly post content anymore. In other words, users' interest in short videos has waned. In contrast, the number of users on medium- and long-video platforms/Apps was growing gradually. Such a change was particularly seen in video platforms/Apps that mainly provide information. For example, Martínez-Martínez *et al.* found that well-conceived videos can increase watching time after analyzing how the duration and content of videos affect students' learning behavior and effectiveness [45]. Manasrah *et al.* evaluated the impact of the ideal duration of online learning videos on the learning effect [46]. Based on previous study, this study contended that the longer duration of videos provided by video platforms/Apps may help to mitigate the negative effects caused by social media use fatigue and cognitive load. Therefore, the hypothesis of this study was developed:

H12: When users browse videos through video platforms/Apps, the duration of the video can negatively influence users' discontinuous usage intention.

The theoretical framework constructed in this study is shown in Fig. 1.

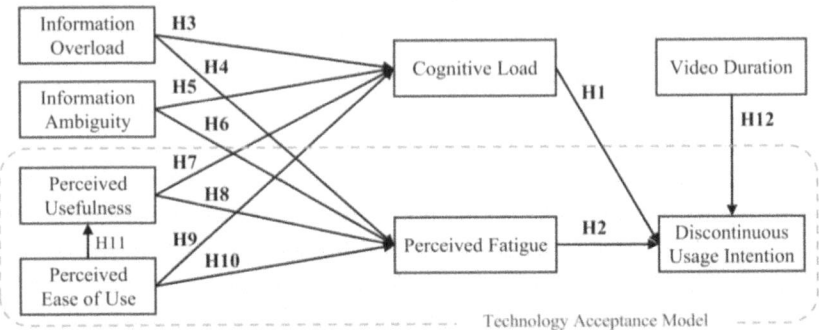

Fig. 1. Theoretical framework of this study.

3   Methodology

3.1   Sample and Data Collection

Data for this study were collected through an online questionnaire, 400 questionnaires were distributed, and 350 valid questionnaires (87.5%) were returned. Overall, the sample group was characterised by youthfulness and a concentration of short video watching behaviours (see Table 1).

3.2   Measurement Development

The questionnaire used in this study was developed from previous studies (see Table 2). Specifically, the cognitive load scale was adapted from a study by Hu, Hu & Fang [47]. The scale used to measure perceived fatigue was referenced from a survey by Michielsen, Vries & van Heck [48]. The items for information overload were taken from the Fu *et al.* [49] and the items for information ambiguity were from Rizzo, House and Lirtzman's study [50]. Perceived usefulness and perceived ease of use were measured by scales developed by Bhattacherjee [51] and Davis [52]. The question items for discontinuous usage intention were taken from the investigation of Maier *et al.* [53]. All items in this study were measured on a 5-point Likert scale ranging from 1 (strongly disagree) to 5 (strongly agree).

Table 1. Demographic Characteristics of the Sample.

Category		Frequency	%
Gender	Male	174	49.7
	Female	176	50.3
Age	Under 20 years old	53	15.1
	21–30 years old	198	56.6
	31–40 years old	29	8.3
	41–50 years old	37	10.6
	Over 51 years old	33	9.4
Place of Residence	City	180	51.4
	Rural Area	170	48.6
Education	Under Bachelor	113	32.3
	Bachelor	137	39.1
	Master	69	19.7
	Ph.D	31	8.9
Preferred Video Duration	Less than 15 s	16	4.6
	15 s–60 s	146	41.7
	1 min–3 min	35	10.0
	3 min–10 min	13	3.7
	10 min–30 min	79	22.6
	30 min–90 min	35	10.0

3.3 Measurement Analysis

In order to test the reliability and validity of the variables, this study constructed a structural equation model by using AMOS 26.0, and conducted a confirmatory factor analysis and model fit indices. Cronbach's alpha (CA), factor loadings (FLs), composite reliability (CR), and average variance extracted (AVE) were used to test the reliability and validity of each dimension. The results indicated that all the values were within the acceptable range [54], indicating that the model of this study has good reliability and validity (see Table 3). Meanwhile, the results of the model fit indices were within widely accepted ranges (RMSEA = 0.061, CFI = 0.956, NFI = 0.925, IFI = 0.956, RFI = 0.915, and NNFI = 0.950), which is in line with the recommended values [55].

Table 2. Measurement of the Constructs.

Construct	Items	Ref.
Cognitive Load (CL)	CL1: I needed a lot of thinking when deciding how to navigate from a current page towards the target page/content on the short video platform	Hu, Hu & Fang [47]
	CL2: I often considered which of the hyperlinks in the current interface to choose to locate the target content	
	CL3: Locating targeted content using short-form video platforms is very demanding on my cognitive skills	
Perceived Fatigue (PF)	PF1: I am bothered by fatigue	Michielsen, Vries & van Heck [48]
	FP2: I get tired very quickly	
	FP3: I have enough energy for everyday life	
	FP4: Physically, I feel exhausted	
	FP5: I have problems starting things	
	FP6: I have problems thinking clearly	
	FP7: I feel no desire to do anything	
	FP8: Mentally, I feel exhausted	
Information Overload (IO)	IO1: I am often distracted by an excessive amount of information available to me on short video platforms	Fu *et al.* [49]
	IO2: I find that I am overwhelmed by the amount of information I have to process on short video platforms every day	
	IO3: There is too much information on short video platforms that is relevant to my immediate surroundings and I find it overwhelming to process	
	IO4: I find that only a small part of the information on short video platforms is relevant to my needs	

(*continued*)

Table 2. (*continued*)

Construct	Items	Ref.
Information Ambiguity (IA)	IA1: I am confident in my ability to use short video platforms	Rizzo, House & Lirtzman [50]
	IA2: I watch short videos with clear, planned goals and objectives	
	IA3: I am able to carry out the actions I want to, no matter which short video platform I am on	
	IA4: I know what my purpose is when watching short videos	
Perceived Usefulness (PU)	PU1: Watching short videos broadens my knowledge	Bhattacherjee [51]
	PU2: Watching short videos improves my learning	
	PU3: I find short video platforms very useful for accessing information	
Perceived Ease of Use (PE)	PE1: Learning to operate the short video platform is easy for me	Davis [52]
	PE2: I find the short video platform easy for me to get videos that I want to watch	
	PE3: It is easy for me to become skillful at using the short video platform	
	PE4: I find the short video platform easy to use	
Discontinuous Usage Intention (DU)	DU1: I will be cancelling my account on the short video platform	Maier *et al.* [53]
	DU2: In the future, I will use other platforms for other types of media	
	DU3: In the future, I will use short video platforms even less than I do now	

Table 3. Results of the Confirmatory Factor Analysis.

Construct		Loadings	Cronbach's Alpha	AVE	CR
Perceived Fatigue (PF)	PF1	0.907	0.947	0.695	0.948
	PF2	0.921			
	PF3	0.813			
	PF4	0.725			
	PF5	0.807			
	PF6	0.863			
	PF7	0.842			
	PF8	0.773			
Information Overload (IO)	IO4	0.852	0.942	0.807	0.944
	IO3	0.915			
	IO2	0.916			
	IO1	0.908			
Cognitive Load (CL)	CL1	0.728	0.85	0.656	0.851
	CL2	0.862			
	CL3	0.834			
Discontinuous Usage Intention (DU)	DU1	0.885	0.922	0.801	0.923
	DU2	0.89			
	DU3	0.909			
Information Ambiguity (IA)	IA1	0.916	0.946	0.816	0.947
	IA2	0.915			
	IA3	0.872			
	IA4	0.91			
Perceived Ease of Use (PE)	PE1	0.909	0.94	0.799	0.941
	PE2	0.93			
	PE3	0.895			
	PE4	0.839			

(*continued*)

Table 3. (*continued*)

Construct		Loadings	Cronbach's Alpha	AVE	CR
Perceived Usefulness (PU)	PU1	0.929	0.935	0.829	0.936
	PU2	0.878			
	PU3	0.924			

Correlation analysis indicated the relationship between the dimensions (see Table 4). The results indicated that cognitive load, information overload and ambiguity, would enhance user-perceived fatigue. However, the higher of the users' perceived usefulness and ease of use, the lower of the fatigue. In contrast, when perceived usefulness and ease of use were higher, users' intention to continue using was stronger.

Table 4. Results of the Correlation Analysis.

	Mean	SD	IO	IA	PF	CL	PU	PE	DU
IO	2.8381	1.23354	1						
IA	3.0214	1.09566	.640	1					
PF	2.6189	1.18495	.583	.662	1				
CL	3.2562	0.8008	.472	.501	.412	1			
PU	3.04	1.40552	−.558	−.722	−.743	−.539	1		
PE	3.2443	1.33177	−.536	−.614	−.776	−.517	.748	1	
DU	2.7248	1.28226	.507	.695	.729	.451	−.761	−.738	1

IO, Information Overload; IA, information ambiguity; PF, perceived fatigue; CL, cognitive load; PU, perceived usefulness; PE, perceived ease of use; DU, discontinuous usage intention.

3.4 Hypothesis Testing

In this study, a regression path model was constructed in order to test the proposed hypothesis (see Fig. 2) and the results were presented in Table 5.

The results of the analysis indicated that, firstly, perceived ease of use has a significantly positive effect on perceived usefulness ($\beta = 0.7$, $p < 0.001$, **H11** was supported). Both information overload and ambiguity have a significant positive effect on perceived fatigue ($\beta = 0.118$, $p < 0.001$; $\beta = 0.122$, $p < 0.001$, respectively, **H4** and **H6** were supported), and also a positive effect on cognitive load ($\beta = 0.233$, $p < 0.001$; $\beta = 0.175$, $p < 0.01$, respectively, **H3** and **H5** were supported). However, perceived usefulness and perceived ease of use have a significantly negative influence on perceived fatigue of usage ($\beta = -0.294$, $p < 0.001$; $\beta = -0.558$, $p < 0.001$, respectively, **H8** and **H10** were supported), and the corresponding negative effect on cognitive load ($\beta = -0.249$, $p < 0.01$; $\beta = -0.223$. $p < 0.05$, respectively, **H7** and **H9** were supported). In addition, the

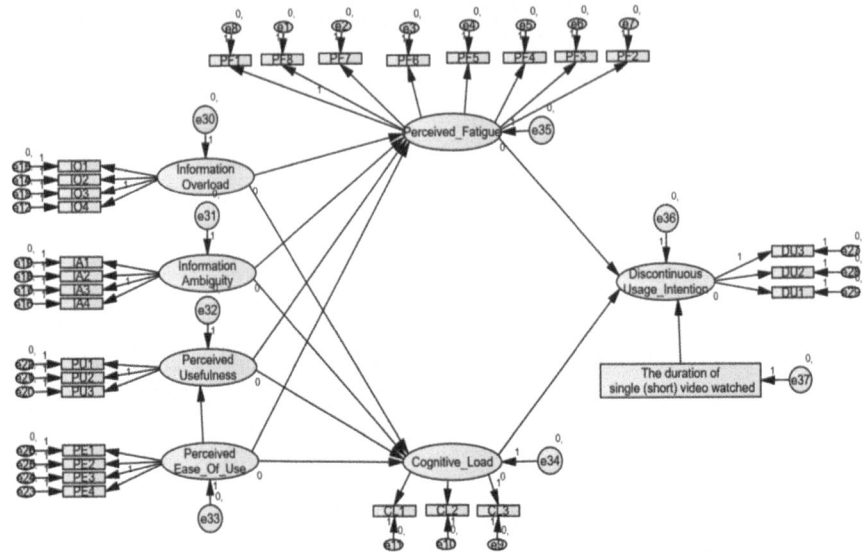

Fig. 2. Regression path model based on the theoretical framework.

Table 5. Results of the Hypothesis Testing.

Regression Path			Estimate	S.E	Standard Estimate	C.R	p
PU	←	PE	0.98	0.060	0.790	16.246	***
PF	←	IO	0.114	0.034	0.118	3.391	***
PF	←	IA	0.118	0.034	0.122	3.525	***
PF	←	PU	−0.221	0.047	−0.294	−4.703	***
PF	←	PE	−0.519	0.062	−0.558	−8.435	***
CL	←	IO	0.144	0.034	0.233	4.275	***
CL	←	IA	0.109	0.033	0.175	3.265	**
CL	←	PU	−0.12	0.046	−0.249	−2.613	**
CL	←	PE	−0.133	0.057	−0.223	−2.34	*
DU	←	PF	0.461	0.047	0.468	9.847	***
DU	←	CL	0.255	0.073	0.166	3.475	***
DU	←	the duration of the video	−0.324	0.024	−0.566	−13.753	***

*** $p < 0.001$; ** $p < 0.01$; * $p < 0.05$

usage fatigue and cognitive load perceived by users lead to a significant positive effect on their intention to discontinue behaviour ($\beta = 0.468$, $p < 0.001$; $\beta = 0.166$, $p < 0.001$, respectively, **H2** and **H1** were supported). Finally, the duration of the video significantly and negatively affects users' intention to stop watching behaviour ($\beta = -0.566$, p < 0.001, **H12** was supported).

4 Discussion

Through the results of the data analysis, all of the hypotheses proposed in this study were supported. Firstly, the results of this study were consistent with the findings of previous extended studies based on TAM, [11, 12, 56]. The suitability of TAM to the current research context was indicated. Secondly, this study found that cognitive load and perceived fatigue influence users' discontinuance usage intention, which was consistent with the findings of previous studies [13, 57, 58]. And, this study verified that information overload, information ambiguity, perceived usefulness and perceived ease of use in previous studies affect video users' psychological perception and behavioural intention [59–62]. In addition, this study also found that video duration can influence users' intention to continue usage when using a video platform/App, which was similar to the results of previous studies about online learning.

Through empirical research, this study can provide some practical suggestions for the products and services of video platforms/Apps. In terms of information overload and ambiguity, too much uncertain information increases the cognitive load of the user during the browsing process, which results in negative emotions such as stress and fatigue. This indicates that users need to spend more time and energy to acquire, screen and understand information when processing and digesting excessive information. Therefore, we suggest that the video creators and platforms/Apps should reduce information overload and ambiguity felt by users and lower their cognitive load and fatigue, thus ultimately reducing their discontinuous usage intention. Specifically, a customized operational interface can be created according to the users' personal experience of information acquisition, social interaction and service. In other words, the service or function of online videos should be integrated into the concept of use center at the time of design, so as to create user-friendly products from the perspective of user experience. User-oriented design strategies and highly personalized services can not only help to reduce users' perceived stress and fatigue, but also enhance users' loyalty and dependence on the products / platforms.

In terms of perceived usefulness and ease of use, it has been verified in previous studies that they would positively affect users' intention to continue using [42, 63–65]. The present study suggests that video creators, providers and operators need to focus on the relationship between perceived usefulness and perceived ease of use with cognitive load and perceived fatigue. More specifically, at the early stage of platform/App development, algorithms should be written according to the principles of 'usefulness first' and 'ease of use first'. For example, clear titles, keywords or charts should be used to present complex information in an intuitive and concise way to reduce cognitive load. In addition, intelligent recommendations and personalised settings can be provided according to the user's habits and needs, and chapter navigation can be set up in the video so that viewers can easily find the content they are interested in, thus improving the cognitive efficiency of users. Also can provide detailed, easy-to-understand help documents and tutorials in the process of software use to help users quickly get started with the platform/App. In short, by optimizing the interface design and functions, refining the content, and providing user guidance and support, users' perceived usefulness and perceived ease of use for videos can be improved, thereby reducing cognitive load and perceived fatigue.

Furthermore, this study suggests that platforms/Apps can encourage creators to extend the duration of their videos to enhance the comprehensiveness of information. When users are browsing videos, more duration will allow video creators to elaborate the topic and content in more detail, making the information expression clearer and more logically coherent, which reduces comprehension pressure due to information fragmentation. At the same time, by enhancing the depth and breadth of the information and weakening the ambiguity and ambiguity of the information, it reduces cognitive pressure and perceptive fatigue. With the advent of the information age, the interest of the user community is gradually shifting from short, fast-consumption content to more in-depth, detailed, and prolonged experiences. This trend also suggests that users are beginning to prefer accessing information that is more effective and better tailored to their individual needs. It's important to note that extending doesn't mean simply increasing the duration. Creators and platforms/Apps must recognize that extending the video duration should be based on ensuring the quality of the content, enhancing the watching experience, and meeting the needs of the user. Creators and platforms/Apps should carefully curate video content to avoid duplication and repetition in order to provide users with a sustainable and enjoyable experience.

Finally, the limitations of this study and the inspiration for the future are, firstly, the age distribution of the sample in this study was mainly focused on the 21–30 year olds. Age also has the potential to influence video users' psychological perceptions and behavioural intentions. However, there are not many studies on video use behaviour across age groups. Therefore, future studies can further include people with different demographic characteristics, such as students, middle-aged and elderly, to enrich the diversity of the sample. Secondly, the data of this study came from a cross-sectional survey, which could not further illustrate the long-term effects of video duration on users' perceptions and intentions. Finally, this study only adopted the dimensions of information overload and ambiguity.While other dimensions that may affect watching behaviour, such as self-efficacy [66] perceived risk [67] and confidence [68], have been proposed in previous studies. Therefore, in the future, more dimensions can be considered to increase the explainability of TAM.

Funding. This Study Was Supported by the Social Science Foundation of the Fujian Province, China (Grant No. FJ2024C060).

References

1. Zheng, C.: Research on the flow experience and social influences of users of short online videos. A case study of DouYin. Sci. Rep. **13**, 3312 (2023)
2. Statista: U.S. time per day on Netflix, TikTok, YouTube (2024). https://www.statista.com/topics/1137/online-video/. Accessed 19 Nov 2024
3. Fu, S., Li, H., Liu, Y., Pirkkalainen, H., Salo, M.: Social media overload, exhaustion, and use discontinuance: examining the effects of information overload, system feature overload, and social overload. Inf. Process. Manag. **57**(6), 102307 (2020)

4. Swar, B., Hameed, T., Reychav, I.: Information overload, psychological ill-being, and behavioral intention to continue online healthcare information search. Comput. Hum. Behav. **70**, 416–425 (2017)
5. Statista: TikTok content engagementrate (2024). https://www.socialinsider.io/blog/tiktok-benchmarks/. Accessed 19 Aug 2024
6. Netflix Subscribers Statistics (Q32024) — New Growth Data. https://recreationrush.com/netflix-subscribers-statistics/. Accessed 24 Nov 2024
7. Seidel, N.: Dataset: Short, Long, and Segmented Learning Videos: From YouTube Practice to Enhanced Video Players. OSF, 2 Web (2024)
8. Cao, W., Liu, Y., Li, S., Pu, Z.: What drives users to tip? The impact of contributor experience, content length, and content type on online video sharing platforms. Inf. Manag. **61**(8), 104054 (2024)
9. Davis, F., Bagozzi, R., Warshaw, P.: User acceptance of computer technology: a comparison of two theoretical models. Manag. Sci. **35**(8), 982–1003 (1989)
10. Zheng, W.: Influence of short evaluation video on users' consumption behavior under TAM model. Heilongjiang Sci. **15**(03), 156–158 (2024)
11. Liu, H., Yan, M.: Influence of mobile short-form video on tourist behavioral intentions. Tour. Tribune **36**(10), 62–73 (2021)
12. Fussell, S.G., Truong, D.: Using virtual reality for dynamic learning: an extended technology acceptance model. Virtual Real. **26**, 249–267 (2022)
13. Chen, Y., Hsu, T., Lu, Y.J.: Impact of flow on mobile shopping intention. J. Retail. Consum. Serv. **41**, 281–287 (2017)
14. Chen, C.F.: Factors affecting the decision to use autonomous shuttle services: evidence from a scooter-dominant urban context. Transp. Res. Part F: Traff. Psychol. Behav. **67**, 195–204 (2019)
15. Fayad, R., Paper, D.: The technology acceptance model e-commerce extension: a conceptual framework. Int. J. Bus. Manag. Study - IJBMS **3**(1)
16. Zhang, T., Tao, D., Qu, X., Zhang, X., Lin, R., Zhang, W.: The roles of initial trust and perceived risk in public's acceptance of automated vehicles. Transp. Res. **98**(JAN), 207–220 (2019)
17. Mustafa, A.S., Garcia, M.B.: Theories Integrated With Technology Acceptance Model (TAM) in Online Learning Acceptance and Continuance Intention: A Systematic Review, Alcalá de Henares, Spain, pp. 68–72 (2021)
18. Gaddi, A., Prashantha, C.: A review of technology acceptance model (TAM) - origin, development & future directions. Int. J. Res. Eng. Appl. Manag. (IJREAM) **06**(12) (2021)
19. Zhang, B., Cui, H., Shan, S., Wang, W.: Research on the influential factors of users' continuance intention towards short video platforms: taking health short videos as an example. Libr. Res. **53**(02), 97–109 (2023)
20. Xie, J., Xue, P.: The influence mechanism of rural elderly mobile short video use-an exploratory study based on grounded theory. New Media Res. **8**(01), 27–32 (2022)
21. Zhao, X.: Research on the influencing factors of short video platform advertising users' willingness to participate. China Market **12**, 27–30 (2022). (in Chinese)
22. Beal, G.M., Rogers, E.M.: The communication process in the purchase of new products: an application of reference group theory. Publ. Opin. Q. **22**(2), 186–187 (1958)
23. Ravindran, T., Kuan, A.C.Y., Lian, D.G.H.: Antecedents and effects of social network fatigue. J. Am. Soc. Inf. Sci. **65**(11), 2306–2320 (2014)
24. Gan, C., Lin, J., Xiao, C.: An exploratory study on WeChat users' discontinuance behavior from the perspective of grounded theory. J. Inf. Resour. Manag. **11**(05), 96–102+113 (2021). (in Chinese)
25. Li, S., Lei, T., Cui, Z.: Mechanism and model of dropout behavior in weak-ties social media based on the 'I&Me'. TheoryMod. Intell. **41**(03), 52–59 (2021)

26. Gan, C., Lin, J., Xiao, C.: Factors affecting user intermittent discontinuance behavior of social networking sites. Intell. Theory Pract. **44**(01), 118–123 (2021)
27. Zhang, M., Xue, Y., Luo, M., Zhang, Y.: Research on the formation mechanism of users' intermittent discontinuance behavior of mobile social network under the framework of stress analysis. J. Mod. Inf. Mod. Intell. **39**(07), 44–55+85 (2019). (in Chinese)
28. Sweller, J.: Cognitive load during problem solving: effects on learning. Cogn. Sci. **12**(2), 257–285 (1988)
29. Zhang, J., Hu, X., Wu, D., Yan, H.: Exploring the influence mechanism of Chinese young researchers' academic information avoidance behavior. J. Acad. Librariansh. (2023). (in Chinese)
30. Zhang, S., Zhao, L., Lu, Y., Yang, J.: Do you get tired of socializing? An empirical explanation of discontinuous usage behaviour in social network services. Inf. Manag. **7**, 904–914 (2016)
31. Maier, C., Laumer, S., Eckhardt, A.: Giving too much social support: social overload on social networking sites. Eur. J. Inf. Syst. **24**(5), 447–464 (2015)
32. Luqman, A., Cao, X., Ali, A., Masood, A., Yu, L.: Empirical investigation of Facebook discontinues usage intentions based on SOR paradigm. Comput. Hum. Behav. **70**, 544–555 (2017)
33. Klapp, O.E.: Overload and boredom: essays on the quality of life in the information society. Soc. Forces **66**(4), 1125–1126 (1987)
34. Ravindran, T., Kuan, A.C.Y., Lian, D.G.H.: Antecedents and effects of social network fatigue. J. Am. Soc. Inf. Sci. **11**(65), 2306–2320 (2014)
35. Wurman, R.S.: Information Anxiety. Doubleday, 20, Exploring Information Avoidance Intention of Social Media Users: A Cognition–Affect–Conation Perspective (1989)
36. Dai, B., Ali, A., Wang, H.: Exploring information avoidance intention of social media users: a cognition–affect–conation perspective. Internet Res. **30**(5), 1455–1478 (2020)
37. Guo, Y., Lu, Z., Kuang, H., Wang, C.: Information avoidance behavior on social network sites: information irrelevance, overload, and the moderating role of time pressure. Int. J. Inf. Manag. **52**, 102067 (2020). (in Chinese)
38. Starcevic, V., Berle, D.: Cyberchondria: towards a better understanding of excessive health-related Internet use. Expert Rev. Neurotherapeutics **13**(2), 205–213 (2013)
39. Maier, C., Laumer, S., Weinert, C., Weitzel, T.: The effects of technostress and switching stress on discontinued use of social networking services: a study of Facebook use. Inf. Syst. J. **25**(3), 275–308 (2015)
40. Oviatt, S.: Human-centered design meets cognitive load theory: designing interfaces that help people think. In: Proceedings of the 14th ACM International Conference on Multimedia. ACM, Santa Barbara (2006)
41. Mi, K., Ma, S.: Facebook users' satisfaction and intention to continue using it: applying the expectation confirmation model. Soc. Sci. Comput. Rev. **41**(3), 983–1000 (2023)
42. Ayyagari, R.: Impact of information overload and task - technology fit on technostress. In: SAIS 2012 Proceedings Atlanta: Association for Information Systems, pp. 17–22 (2012)
43. Heijden, H.: Factors influencing the usage of websites: the case of a generic portal in the Netherlands. Inf. Manag. **6**, 541–549 (2003)
44. Chan, M.M., Hoyos, C.A., Hernández, R., Plata, R.B., Medina, J.A., De, M.: Analysis of behavioral intention to use cloud-based tools in a MOOC: a technology acceptance model approach. J. UCS **24**(8), 1072–1089 (2018)
45. Martínez-Martínez, A., Montoliu, R., RemolarI.: which videos are better for the studentsanalyzing the student behavior and video metadata. Heliyon **10**(21) (2024)
46. Manasrah, A., Masoud, M., Jaradat, Y.: Short videos, or long videos? A study on the ideal video length in online learning. In: International Conference on Information Technology (ICIT), Amman, Jordan, pp. 366–370 (2021)

47. Hu, P.J., Hu, H., Fang, X.: Examining the mediating roles of cognitive load and performance outcomes in user satisfaction with a website: a field quasi-experiment. MIS Q. **41**(3), 975–987 (2017)
48. Michielsen, H.J., Vries, J.D., Heck, G.L.V.: Psychometric qualities of a brief self-rated fatigue measure: the fatigue assessment scale. J. Psychosom. Res. **54**(4), 345–352 (2003)
49. Fu, S., Li, H., Liu, Y., Pirkkalainen, H., Salo, M.: Social media overload, exhaustion, and use discontinuance: examining the effects of information overload, system feature overload, and social overload. Inf. Process. Manag. **57**(6), 102307 (2020). (in Chinese)
50. Rizzo, J.R., House, R.J., Lirtzman, S.I.: Role conflict and ambiguity in complex organizations. Adm. Sci. Q. **15**(2), 150–163 (1970)
51. Bhattacherjee, A.: Understanding information systems continuance: an expectation-confirmation model. MIS Q. **25**(3), 351–370 (2001)
52. Davis, F.D.: Perceived usefulness, perceived ease of use, and user acceptance of information technology. MIS Q. **13**(3), 319–340 (1989)
53. Maier, C., Laumer, S., Eckhardt, A., Weitzel, T.: Giving too much social support: social overload on social networking sites. Eur. J. Inf. Syst. 1–18 (2014)
54. Hair, J.F., Gabriel, M.L.D.S., Patel, V.K.: AMOS covariance-based structural equation modeling (CB-SEM): guidelines on its application as a marketing research tool. Revista Brasileira de Marketing, Edição Especial **13**(2) (2014)
55. Arpaci, I., Baloglu, M.: The impact of cultural collectivism on knowledge sharing among information technology majoring undergraduates. Comput. Hum. Behav. **56**, 65–71 (2016)
56. Li, X., Liu, L.C., Zhang, B.Q.: An empirical study on social media users' fatigue and negative behavior from the perspective of cognitive load theory: taking WeChat for example. Libr. Forum **11**, 94–106 (2018). (in Chinese)
57. Zhang, M., Xue, Y., Luo, M., Zhang, Y.: Research on the formation mechanism of users' intermittent discontinuance behavior of mobile social network under the framework of stress analysis. J. Mod. Inf. Mod. Intell. **39**(07), 44–55+85 (2019). (in Chinese)
58. Guo, J., Cao, F., Yang, X.: Research on users' discontinuous usage intention in SNS from fatigue perspective. Inf. Sci. (2018). (in Chinese)
59. Lin, S., Lin, J., Luo, X., Liu, S.: Juxtaposed effect of social media overload on discontinuous usage intention: the perspective of stress coping strategies. Inf. Process. Manag. **58**(1), 102419 (2021)
60. Starcevic, V., Berle, D.: Cyberchondria: towards a better understanding of excessive health-related Internet use. Expert Rev. Neurother. **13**(2), 205–213 (2013)
61. Ayyagari, R.: Impact of information overload and task-technology fit on technostress. In: SAIS 2012 Proceedings Atlanta: Association for Information Systems, pp. 17–22 (2012)
62. Li, C.: Perceived value, social network embeddedness and eco-tourism consumption intention-multi-group analysis based on extended TAM. Bus. Econ. Res. **24**, 86–89 (2021). (in Chinese)
63. Li, J., Guan, Z., Xie, F.: TAM-based smart medical APP user sticky model construction and technology research. J. Northwest Univ. (Nat. Sci. Ed.) **51**(01), 24–32 (2021). (in Chinese)
64. Ma, J., Mao, C.: Research on the influencing factors of ChatGPT user acceptance and usage intention: based on the integrated perspective of TAM and TTF. Technol. Commun. **16**(17), 118–124 (2024). (in Chinese)
65. Feng, Z., Zhou, W.: Research on the influencing factors of tourists' VR tourism willingness based on TAM model. China Bus. Rev. **20**, 086–090 (2024). (in Chinese)
66. Al-Adwan, A.S., Li, N., Al-Adwan, A., Abbasi, G.A., Albelb, N.A., Habibi, A.: Extending the technology acceptance model (TAM) to predict university students' intentions to use metaverse-based learning platforms. Educ. Inf. Technol. **28**, 15381–15413 (2023)
67. Luo, C., Zhu, X.: Empirical study on factors influencing customers' intention of Yu Ebao based on TAM/TPB with perceived risk. J. Mod. Inf. (2015). (in Chinese)

68. Wang, Y., Yu, J., Zhang, Z.: Older people's willingness to utilize medical escort service and its influencing factors: based on the extended model of TPB/TAM. Aging Sci. Res. **12**(01), 49–64 (2024). (in Chinese)

Author Index

M. Schrepp (Ed.): HCII 2025, LNCS 15794, pp. 423–424, 2025.
https://doi.org/10.1007/978-3-031-93221-2

The manufacturer's authorised representative in the EU is Springer
Nature Customer Service Centre GmbH, Europaplatz 3, 69115 Heidelberg,
Germany. If you have any concerns regarding our products, please
contact ProductSafety@springernature.com

Printed and bound by CPI Group (UK) Ltd, Croydon, CR0 4YY
29/04/2026
02099511-0006